Oracle Database 11g PL/SQL Programming

Oracle Press™

Oracle Database 11g PL/SQL Programming

Michael McLaughlin

New York   Chicago   San Francisco
Lisbon   London   Madrid   Mexico City   Milan
New Delhi   San Juan   Seoul   Singapore   Sydney   Toronto

The McGraw·Hill Companies

Cataloging-in-Publication Data is on file with the Library of Congress

McGraw-Hill books are available at special quantity discounts to use as premiums and sales promotions, or for use in corporate training programs. To contact a special sales representative, please visit the Contact Us page at www.mhprofessional.com.

Oracle Database 11*g* PL/SQL Programming

1234567890 DOC DOC 0198

ISBN 978-0-07-149445-8
MHID   0-07-149445-6

Sponsoring Editor	**Indexer**
Lisa McClain	Claire Splan
Editorial Supervisor	**Production Supervisor**
Jody McKenzie	Jean Bodeaux
Project Editor	**Composition**
Carolyn Welch	Apollo Publishing Services
Acquisitions Coordinator	**Illustration**
Mandy Canales	Lyssa Wald
Technical Editor	**Art Director, Cover**
A. Scott Mikolaitis	Jeff Weeks
Copy Editor	**Cover Designer**
Bob Campbell	Pattie Lee
Proofreader	
Carolyn Welch	

To Lisa, my eternal companion, inspiration, wife, and best friend; and to Sarah, Joseph, Elise, Ian, Ariel, Callie, Nathan, Spencer, and Christianne— our terrific heaven-sent children. Thank you for your constant support, patience, and sacrifice that made writing *yet* another book possible.

About the Author

Michael McLaughlin is a professor at BYU—Idaho in the Computer Information Technology Department of the Business and Communication College. He is also the founder of Techtinker.com.

Michael worked at Oracle Corporation for over eight years in consulting, development, and support. He is the inventor of the ATOMS transaction architecture (U.S. Patents #7,206,805 and #7,290,056). The patents are assigned to Oracle Corporation.

Prior to his tenure at Oracle Corporation, Michael worked as an Oracle developer, systems and business analyst, and DBA beginning with Oracle 6. He is the author of *Oracle Database 10g Express Edition PHP Web Programming*. He is also the co-author of *Oracle Database AJAX & PHP Web Application Development*, *Oracle Database 10g PL/SQL Programming*, and *Expert Oracle PL/SQL*.

About the Technical Editor

A. Scott Mikolaitis is an Applications Architect at Oracle Corporation and has worked at Oracle for over ten years. He works on prototyping and standards development for the SOA technology in Oracle Fusion.

Scott also enjoys working with web services in Java as well as Jabber for human and system interaction patterns. He spends his spare time on DIY home improvement and gas-fueled RC cars.

Contents at a Glance

PART IV

Appendixes

Contents

PART I
PL/SQL Fundamentals

PART II
PL/SQL Programming

PART III

PL/SQL Advanced Programming

Acknowledgments

any thanks go to Lisa McClain and Mandy Canales at McGraw-Hill for their tireless work on this project; Carolyn Welch who heroically moved the text through copyedit and production; Robert Campbell for his thoroughness and attention to detail; and A. Scott Mikolaitis for his patience and good humor working through drafts and redrafts, concepts, and ideas.

Special thanks go to Ian McLaughlin, who proofread for me. Thanks to Joseph McLaughlin for experimenting with presentation ideas and coding samples. Acknowledgment and thanks for ideas from Michael Farmer, an Oracle DBA, Developer, Data Warehouse Designer, and friend.

Thanks to the Computer Information Technology Department faculty at BYU, especially R. Kent Jackson for reading and commenting on the text; Lee Barney for brainstorming ideas and concepts notwithstanding his MySQL bias; Art Ericson for reading segments as a nonprogrammer; and Rex Barzee for helping me talk through concepts and presentation ideas about illustrating functions and procedures. Grateful thanks to the students who wanted to read and extend their knowledge as manuscript proceeded to book: Craig Hokanson, Brittany Mullen, Gallus Runyeta, Christina Robinson, and Sergey Zasukha.

Finally, no acknowledgment would be complete without thanking the production department for their conscientious attention to detail and hard work in putting all the pieces together.

Introduction

his book is designed to be read from beginning to end by those new to PL/SQL. Part I covers PL/SQL fundamentals. Part II covers the backbone of the programming language, which consists of functions, procedures, packages, triggers, and large objects. Part III dives into some advanced topics that should help you immediately with your development projects.

The appendixes in Part IV provide primers on Oracle DBA tasks, SQL programming, PHP scripting, Java development, regular expressions, and wrapping PL/SQL. Introductory primers are provided to help you learn about the PL/SQL Hierarchical Profiler and PL/Scope. There is also an appendix that reviews reserved words and built-in functions that support your programming tasks.

Part I: PL/SQL Fundamentals

Part I introduces you to recent Oracle Database 10*g* Release 2 features and Oracle Database 11*g* new features. It provides a quick start guide to the language and coverage of language semantics, types, control structures, and error management.

- *Chapter 1: PL/SQL Overview* explains the basis of PL/SQL. It also covers Oracle 10*g* Release 2 features and Oracle 11*g* new features.

- *Chapter 2: PL/SQL Basics* provides a quick tour of writing PL/SQL. It is designed as a jump-start introduction to the language.

- *Chapter 3: Language Fundamentals* teaches you about PL/SQL language semantics. This chapter covers lexical units, block structures, variable types, and variable scope.

- *Chapter 4: Control Structures* explains the conditional and iterative structures of PL/SQL. It also covers cursors (including system reference cursors) and bulk operations in the language.

- *Chapter 5: Error Management* explains how error management works in PL/SQL. It teaches you how to handle exceptions, define your custom exceptions, and manage error stacks.

Part II: PL/SQL Programming

Part II introduces you to functions, procedures, packages, and triggers. It also covers Oracle LOBs. These are tools to build robust database applications.

- *Chapter 6: Functions and Procedures* explains how to create functions and procedures. It provides examples for pass-by-value and pass-by-reference models, and shows you how to build deterministic, parallel enabled, pipelined, and result cache functions. It also covers call semantics, such as positional, named, and mixed notation, as well as autonomous program units.

- *Chapter 7: Collections* explains VARRAYs, nested tables, and associative arrays (known previously as PL/SQL tables). It also covers the collection API and collection set operators. Examples in this chapter include working with numeric and string indexes for associative arrays.

- *Chapter 8: Large Objects* explains large objects and demonstrates how to work with them. Examples show you how to read them from the file system and write them to the database. You also learn how to read and write them in your PL/SQL or web-enabled applications, and upload them through web pages and PHP scripts.

- *Chapter 9: Packages* teaches you how to create libraries of related functions and procedures. You learn how to leverage serially a non-serially reusable package, and how to implement definer and invoker rights models. There is also a section in this chapter that shows you how to find, validate, and describe packages in the data catalog. You learn how to check dependencies and compare and contrast timestamp versus signature validation methods.

- *Chapter 10: Triggers* explains how you implement database triggers. Examples include DDL triggers, DML triggers, compound triggers (*new* in Oracle Database 11*g*), instead-of triggers, and system or database event triggers. This chapter also contains a complete set of examples for using the event attribute functions that support database triggers.

Part III: PL/SQL Advanced Programming

Part III introduces you to dynamic SQL, intersession communications, external procedures, object types, Java libraries, and web application development.

- *Chapter 11: Dynamic SQL* explains how to use Native Dynamic SQL (NDS) and the older DBMS_SQL package. Examples in this chapter illustrate calling programs with dynamically built statements, vetted by the new DBMS_ASSERT package. You will also see examples using placeholders or bind variables, including an example of creating a dynamic list of placeholders.

- *Chapter 12: Intersession Communication* shows you how to use DBMS_ALERT and DBMS_PIPE to communicate between two concurrent sessions.

- *Chapter 13: External Procedures* explains how to use external procedures, and shows you how to build them in external C and Java libraries. This chapter also covers the Oracle Heterogeneous Server and how to configure the listener.ora file to support external procedures.

- *Chapter 14: Object Types* explains how you define and use transient object types, which is an alternative approach to using packages. You will learn how to create object types and implement object bodies, as well as how to build subtypes. This chapter also shows you how to query and access object type columns in your database tables.

- *Chapter 15: Java Libraries* shows you how to create and deploy Java libraries inside the database. It explains why and how PL/SQL wrappers work as an interface to your Java class methods. You will also learn the new method for communicating with the database in Oracle 11*g*.

- *Chapter 16: Web Application Development* teaches you how to write web-enabled PL/SQL procedures and PL/SQL Server Pages (PSPs). This chapter covers how to configure and deploy these PL/SQL only web solutions using the standalone Oracle HTTP Server and Oracle XML Database.

Part IV: Appendixes

Part IV contains a series of primers to help jump-start those new to Oracle or related technologies, including Oracle DBA tasks, SQL programming, PHP scripting, Java development, regular expressions, and wrapping PL/SQL. It also covers PL/SQL Hierarchical Profiler, PL/Scope, reserved words, and a series of key built-in functions.

- *Appendix A: Oracle Database Administration Primer* explains how to use the SQL*Plus interface, start up and shut down the database, and start up or shut down the Oracle listener.

- *Appendix B: Oracle Database SQL Primer* begins by covering Oracle's implementation of SQL, starting with Oracle SQL*Plus datatypes, and then covers the SQL language commands needed to build database applications: Data Definition Language (DDL), Data Manipulation Language (DML), Data Query Language (DQL), and Data Control Language (DCL).

- *Appendix C: PHP Primer* covers the fundamentals of PHP, the implementation of Zend Core for Oracle, and how to write PHP web pages against the Oracle 11*g* database.

- *Appendix D: Oracle Database Java Primer* covers the fundamentals of the Java programming language, and discusses the Oracle JDBC connection for Oracle 11*g*. It also demonstrates how to build standalone Java applications that work with the database, including LOBs.

- *Appendix E: Regular Expression Primer* explains the implementation and use of regular expressions in the Oracle 11*g* database.

- *Appendix F: Wrapping PL/SQL Code Primer* explains how you can wrap PL/SQL stored programs to protect their logic from prying eyes.

- *Appendix G: PL/SQL Hierarchical Profiler Primer* explains how the hierarchical profiler works and provides a demonstration of how to use it.

- *Appendix H: PL/Scope* explains how it works and provides a quick concept analysis.

- *Appendix I: PL/SQL Reserved Words and Keywords* explains reserved words and keywords and shows you how to find them in the data catalog.

- *Appendix J: PL/SQL Built-in Functions* covers a large number of the most useful built-in functions. It provides key examples to use these functions, which are also referenced by other chapters in the book.

Video Store Example

Most of the examples in this book use or leverage the Video Store model, which you can download from the publisher's web site. You can create the `plsql` user referenced in the book by running the `create_user.sql` script. You build the model with the `create_store.sql` script. The latter script also seeds the model with basic data to support examples in the book.

The following illustration provides an ERD of the model.

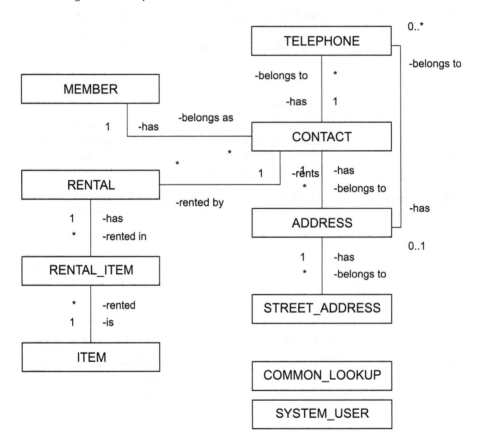

PART
I

PL/SQL Fundamentals

CHAPTER
1

Oracle PL/SQL Overview

his chapter introduces you to the Procedure Language/Structured Query Language (PL/SQL). It explains the history, architecture, and block structure of PL/SQL, reviews Oracle 10*g* new features, and discusses Oracle 11*g* new features. The chapter is divided into the following sections:

- History and background

- Architecture

- Basic block structures

- Oracle 10*g* new features

- Oracle 11*g* new features

History and Background

The PL/SQL was developed by Oracle in the late 1980s. Originally, PL/SQL had limited capabilities, but that changed in the early 1990s. PL/SQL provides the Oracle database with a built-in *interpreted* and operating system–independent programming environment. SQL statements are natively integrated in the PL/SQL language. You can also call PL/SQL directly from the command-line SQL*Plus interface. Similar direct calls can be made in your external programming language calls to the database, as illustrated in Appendices C and D.

The Oracle 8 Database introduced object types into the database. It moved the Oracle database from a purely relational model into an object-relational (or extended relational) model. These types were of limited value as collections of scalar variables until they became instantiable in Oracle 9*i*, Release 2. The ability to instantiate SQL object types made internal Oracle objects compatible with C++, Java, or C# object types. SQL object types are implemented in PL/SQL and are covered in Chapter 15.

PL/SQL evolved with the advent of full object-oriented programming capabilities delivered in Oracle 9*i*, Release 2. PL/SQL is no longer a purely procedural language. It is now both a procedural and object-oriented programming language.

The Oracle 11*g* Database also evolved PL/SQL from an interpreted language to a natively compiled language. You may ask: "Doesn't that eliminate the benefit of an operating system–independent language?" The answer to that question is not at all. Now you can write PL/SQL once in an operating system–independent form. Then, you can deploy it and let Oracle manage its native compilation. Oracle 11*g* automates the process for you on supported platforms.

PL/SQL Versions
Initial PL/SQL versions were not sequenced with the version of the database. For example, PL/SQL 1.0 shipped with the Oracle 6 Database. PL/SQL 2.*x* shipped with the Oracle 7.*x* Databases. Beginning with Oracle 8, PL/SQL versions correspond to the database release numbers, like PL/SQL 11.1 in the Oracle 11*g* Release 1 Database.

As well as being callable from external programs, PL/SQL is also the primary gateway to external libraries. The external library label is deceiving, since Java libraries can also be stored inside the database. Oracle calls external libraries external procedures through PL/SQL regardless of where they are stored. PL/SQL programs serve as wrappers to external libraries. Wrappers are interfaces that mask type conversion between the database and external programs.

You can extend the functionality of the Oracle 11*g* Database when you build stored functions and procedures in PL/SQL, C, C++, or Java. Java programs can be directly stored inside the Oracle 11*g* Database in all releases except the Oracle Express Edition. Chapter 12 demonstrates how to build and run external procedures. Chapter 14 covers how you build and deploy Java libraries inside the database.

PL/SQL continues to evolve and become more robust. This is great for those skilled in PL/SQL, just as the evolution between Java releases is great for skilled Java programmers. PL/SQL programming presents challenges to those new to the language because it serves so many masters in the Oracle database. As *you* develop skills in the language, you will learn how to use PL/SQL to solve ever more complex problems.

Is PL/SQL Programming a Black Art?

Early on PL/SQL 1.0 was little more than a reporting tool. Now the `CASE` statement in SQL delivers most of that original functionality. In the mid-nineties, developers described PL/SQL 2.*x* programming as a Black Art. This label was appropriate then. There was little written about the language, and the availability of code samples on the web was limited because the web didn't really exist as you know it today.

Today, there are still some who see PL/SQL as a Black Art. They also are passionate about writing database-neutral code in Java or other languages. This is *politically correct speak for avoiding PL/SQL solutions* notwithstanding their advantages. Why is Oracle PL/SQL still a Black Art to many, when there are so many PL/SQL books published today?

You might say that it's the cursors, but the cursors exist in any programs connecting through the Oracle Call Interface (OCI) or Java Database Connectivity (JDBC). If not cursors, you might venture it's the syntax, user-defined types, or nuances of functions and procedures. Are those really that much different than in other programming languages? If you answer no to this question, you've been initiated into the world of PL/SQL. If you answer yes to this or think there's some other magic to the language, you haven't been initiated.

How do you become initiated? The cute answer is to read this book. The real answer is to disambiguate the Oracle jargon that shrouds the PL/SQL language. For example, a variable is always a variable of some type, and a function or procedure is always a subroutine that manages formal parameters by reference or value that may or may not return a result as a right operand. These types of simple rules hold true for every component in the language.

Architecture

The PL/SQL language is a robust tool with many options. PL/SQL lets you write code once and deploy it in the database nearest the data. PL/SQL can simplify application development, optimize execution, and improve resource utilization in the database.

The language is a case-insensitive programming language, like SQL. This has led to numerous formatting best practice directions. Rather than repeat those arguments for one style or another, it seems best to recommend you find a style consistent with your organization's standards and consistently apply it. *The PL/SQL code in this book uses uppercase for command words and lowercase for variables, column names, and stored program calls.*

PL/SQL was developed by modeling concepts of structured programming, static data typing, modularity, exception management, and parallel (concurrent) processing found in the Ada programming language. The Ada programming language, developed for the United States Department of Defense, was designed to support military real-time and safety-critical embedded systems, such as those in airplanes and missiles. The Ada programming language borrowed significant syntax from the Pascal programming language, including the assignment and comparison operators and the single-quote delimiters.

These choices also enabled the direct inclusion of SQL statements in PL/SQL code blocks. They were important because SQL adopted the same Pascal operators, string delimiters, and declarative scalar datatypes. Both Pascal and Ada have declarative scalar datatypes. Declarative datatypes do not change at run time and are known as strong datatypes. Strong datatypes are critical to tightly integrating the Oracle SQL and PL/SQL languages. PL/SQL supports dynamic datatypes by mapping them at run time against types defined in the Oracle 11*g* Database catalog. Matching operators and string delimiters means simplified parsing because SQL statements are natively embedded in PL/SQL programming units.

NOTE
Primitives in the Java programming language describe scalar variables, which hold only one thing at a time.

The original PL/SQL development team made these choices carefully. The Oracle database has been rewarded over the years because of those choices. One choice that stands out as an awesome decision is letting you link PL/SQL variables to the database catalog. This is a form of run-time type inheritance. You use the %TYPE and %ROWTYPE pseudotypes to inherit from the strongly typed variables defined in the database catalog (covered in Chapters 3 and 9).

Anchoring PL/SQL variables to database catalog objects is an effective form of structural coupling. It can minimize the number of changes you need to make to your PL/SQL programs. At least, it limits how often you recode as a result of changes between base types, like changing a VARCHAR2 to DATE. It also eliminates the need to redefine variable sizes. For example, you don't need to modify your code when a table changes the size of a variable-length string column.

Oracle also made another strategic decision when it limited the number of SQL base types and began subtyping them in the database catalog. Subtyping the base types let Oracle develop a multiple-hierarchy object tree, which continues to grow and mature. The object-oriented approach to design contributed and continues to contribute to how Oracle evolves the relational model into an object-relational model (also known as the extended-relational model). PL/SQL takes full advantage of the subtyping SQL variable types.

The PL/SQL run-time engine exists as a resource inside the SQL*Plus environment. The SQL*Plus environment is both interactive and callable. Every time you connect to the Oracle 11*g* Database, the database creates a new session. In that session, you can run SQL or PL/SQL statements from the SQL*Plus environment. PL/SQL program units can then run SQL statements or external procedures as shown in Figure 1-1. SQL statements may also call PL/SQL stored functions or procedures. SQL statements interact directly with the actual data.

Calls directly to PL/SQL can be made through the Oracle Call Interface (OCI) or Java Database Connectivity (JDBC). This lets you leverage PL/SQL directly in your database applications. This is important because it lets you manage transaction scope in your stored PL/SQL program units. This tremendously simplifies the myriad tasks often placed in the data abstraction layer of applications.

PL/SQL also supports building SQL statements at run time. Run-time SQL statements are dynamic SQL. You can use two approaches for dynamic SQL: one is Native Dynamic SQL (NDS) and the other is the DBMS_SQL package. The Oracle 11*g* Database delivers new NDS features and improves execution speed. With this release, you only need to use the DBMS_SQL package when you don't know the number of columns that your dynamic SQL call requires. Chapter 11 demonstrates dynamic SQL and covers both NDS and the DBMS_SQL package.

You now have a high-level view of the PL/SQL language. The next section will provide a brief overview of PL/SQL block structures.

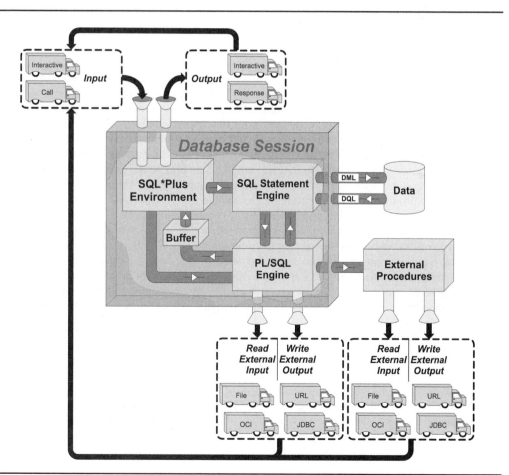

FIGURE 1-1   *Database processing architecture*

Basic Block Structures

PL/SQL is a blocked programming language. Program units can be named or unnamed blocks. Unnamed blocks are known as anonymous blocks and are labeled so throughout the book. The PL/SQL coding style differs from that of the C, C++, and Java programming languages. For example, curly braces do not delimit blocks in PL/SQL.

Anonymous-block programs are effective in some situations. You typically use anonymous blocks when building scripts to seed data or perform one-time processing activities. They are also effective when you want to nest activity in another PL/SQL block's execution section. The basic anonymous-block structure must contain an execution section. You can also put optional declaration and exception sections in anonymous blocks. The following illustrates an anonymous-block prototype:

```
[DECLARE]
   declaration_statements
BEGIN
   execution_statements
[EXCEPTION]
   exception_handling_statements
END;
/
```

The declaration block lets you define datatypes, structures, and variables. Defining a variable means that you give it a name and a datatype. You can also declare a variable by giving it a name, a datatype, and a value. You both define and assign a value when declaring a variable.

Some object types cannot be defined as locally scoped variables but must be defined as types in the database catalog, as discussed in Chapter 14. Structures are compound variables, like collections, record structures, or system reference cursors. Structures can also be locally named functions, procedures, or cursors. Cursors act like little functions. Cursors have names, signatures and a return type—the output columns from a query or SELECT statement. The DECLARE reserved word begins the declaration block, and the BEGIN reserved word ends it.

The execution block lets you process data. The execution block can contain variable assignments, comparisons, conditional operations, and iterations. Also, the execution block is where you access cursors and other named program units. Functions, procedures, and some object types are named program units. You can also nest anonymous-block programs inside the execution block. The BEGIN reserved word starts the exception block, and the optional EXCEPTION or required END reserved word ends it. You must have at least one statement inside an execution block. The following minimum anonymous-block statement includes a NULL statement:

```
BEGIN
   NULL;
END;
/
```

This does nothing except let the compilation phase complete without an error. Compilation in any language includes a syntax parsing. The lack of a statement in the block raises a parsing error as covered in Chapter 5.

The exception handling block lets you manage exceptions. You can both catch and manage them there. The exception block allows for alternative processing; in many ways it acts like combination of a *catch* and *finally* block in the Java programming language (see Appendix D for more information on Java). The EXCEPTION reserved word starts the section, and the END reserved word ends it.

TIP
You have the same rule requiring a minimum of one statement for any blocks in a conditional statement block (like an IF statement), and loops.

Named-block programs have a slightly different block structure because they are stored in the database. They also have a declaration section, which is known as a header. The name, list of formal parameters, and any return type of named PL/SQL blocks are defined by the header. The name and list of formal parameters are known as the signature of a subroutine. The area between the header and execution blocks acts as the declaration block for a named block. This same rule holds true for object type bodies covered in Chapter 14.

The following illustrates a named-block function prototype:

```
FUNCTION function_name
[( parameter1    [IN][OUT] [NOCOPY] sql_data_type | plsql_data_type
,  parameter2    [IN][OUT] [NOCOPY] sql_data_type | plsql_data_type
,  parameter(n+1) [IN][OUT] [NOCOPY] sql_data_type | plsql_data_type )]

RETURN [ sql_data_type | plsql_data_type ]
[ AUTHID {DEFINER | CURRENT_USER}]
[ DETERMINISTIC | PARALLEL_ENABLED ]
[ PIPELINED ]
[ RESULT_CACHE [RELIES ON table_name]] IS
 declaration_statements
BEGIN
 execution_statements
[EXCEPTION]
 exception_handling_statements
END;
/
```

Chapter 6 discusses the rules governing functions. Functions can behave as pass-by-value or pass-by-reference subroutines. Pass-by-value subroutines define formal parameters using an IN mode only. This means that the variable passed in cannot change during execution of the subroutine. Pass-by-reference subroutines define formal parameters using IN and OUT, or OUT-only modes.

Oracle 11*g* continues passing copies of variables instead of references to variables, unless you designate a NOCOPY hint. Oracle implements pass-by-reference behaviors this way to guarantee the integrity of IN OUT mode variables. This model guarantees variables are unchanged unless a subprogram call completes successfully. You can override this *default* behavior by using a NOCOPY hint. Oracle recommends against using the NOCOPY hint because using it can result in partial changes to your actual parameter values. Ultimately, the database chooses whether to act on a hint and send a reference.

Functions can query data using `SELECT` statements but cannot perform DML statements, such as `INSERT`, `UPDATE`, or `DELETE`. All other rules apply to stored functions the same as those that apply to anonymous blocks. Functions that define formal parameters or return types that use PL/SQL datatypes cannot be called from the SQL command line. However, you can call functions that use SQL datatypes from the SQL command line.

The `AUTHID` default value is `DEFINER`, which is known as definer rights. Definer rights means that any one with privileges to execute the stored program runs it with the same privileges as the user account that defined it. The `CURRENT_USER` alternative lets those with execute privileges call the stored program and run it against only their user/schema data. This is known as invoker rights, and it describes the process of calling a common source program against individual accounts and data.

You should avoid using the `DETERMINISTIC` clause when functions depend on the states of session-level variables. `DETERMINISTIC` clauses are best suited to function-based indexes and materialized views.

The `PARALLEL_ENABLE` clause should be enabled for functions that you plan to call from SQL statements that may use parallel query capabilities. You should look closely at this clause for data warehousing uses.

The `PIPELINED` clause provides improved performance when functions return collections, like nested tables or `VARRAY`s. You'll also note performance improvements when returning system reference cursors by using the `PIPELINED` clause.

The `RESULT_CACHE` clause indicates a function is cached only once in the SGA and available across sessions. It is new in the Oracle 11*g* Database. Cross-session functions only work with `IN` mode formal parameters.

Chapter 6 contains the implementation details about these clauses. It also provides examples that demonstrate how to use them.

The following illustrates a named-block procedure prototype:

```
PROCEDURE procedure_name
( parameter1      [IN][OUT] [NOCOPY] sql_data_type | plsql_data_type
, parameter2      [IN][OUT] [NOCOPY] sql_data_type | plsql_data_type
, parameter(n+1) [IN][OUT] [NOCOPY] sql_data_type | plsql_data_type )
[ AUTHID {DEFINER | CURRENT_USER}]
  declaration_statements
BEGIN
  execution_statements
[EXCEPTION]
  exception_handling_statements
END;
/
```

Chapter 6 discusses the rules governing procedures. They act like functions in many ways but cannot return a datatype. This means that you can't use them as right operands. Unlike functions, procedures must be called by PL/SQL blocks. *Procedures can both query the data and manipulate the data.* Procedures are also the foundation subroutines for passing values from and to external languages such as C, C++, Java, and PHP.

This section has presented and discussed the basics structure of PL/SQL program units. The next sections will review recent features in the Oracle 10*g* Database, and new features in the Oracle 11*g* Database.

Oracle 10*g* New Features

Several changes were introduced in the Oracle 10*g* Database. Not all were available when the preceding edition was written because they didn't ship until the second release of the database.

New PL/SQL features introduced in Oracle 11*g* include

- Built-in packages

- Compile-time warnings

- Conditional compilation

- Number datatype behaviors

- An optimized PL/SQL compiler

- Regular expressions

- Quoting alternatives

- Set operators

- Stack tracing errors

- Wrapping PL/SQL stored programs

The subsections cover recent features introduced in Oracle 10*g*. They also cross-reference Oracle 11*g* Database–related features, which are covered later in this chapter.

Built-in Packages

Beginning with Oracle 10*g* Release 2, you can gain access to several new or improved built-in packages. Three that merit mention here are

- DBMS_SCHEDULER Replaces the DBMS_JOB built in and provides new functionality to schedule and execute batch jobs.

- DBMS_CRYPTO Now includes the ability to encrypt and decrypt large objects, and to support globalization across multiple character sets.

- DBMS_MONITOR Delivers an API supporting tracing and statistic gathering by sessions.

Compile-Time Warnings

Beginning with Oracle 10*g* Release 1, you can gain insight into the performance of your PL/SQL programs by enabling the PLSQL_WARNINGS parameter in your development instances. You can set this for a session or the database. The former is the recommended practices because of the overhead imposed on the database. You set this parameter by using the following command:

```
ALTER SESSION SET plsql_warnings = 'enable:all';
```

Conditional Compilation

Beginning with Oracle 10*g* Release 2, you can use conditional compilation. Conditional compilation lets you include debugging logic or special-purpose logic that runs only when session-level variables are set. The following command sets a PL/SQL compile-time variable DEBUG equal to 1:

```
ALTER SESSION SET PLSQL_CCFLAGS = 'debug:1';
```

This command sets a PL/SQL compile-time variable DEBUG equal to 1. You should note that the compile-time flag is case insensitive. You can also set compile-time variables to *true* or *false* so that they act like Boolean variables. When you want to set more than one conditional compilation flag, you need to use the following syntax:

```
ALTER SESSION SET PLSQL_CCFLAGS = 'name1:value1 [, name(n+1):value(n+1) ]';
```

The conditional compilation parameters are stored as name and value pairs in the PLSQL_CCFLAG database parameter. The following program uses the $IF, $THEN, $ELSE, $ELSIF, $ERROR, and $END directives that create a conditional compilation code block:

```
BEGIN
  $IF $$DEBUG = 1 $THEN
    dbms_output.put_line('Debug Level 1 Enabled.');
  $END
END;
/
```

Conditional code blocks differ from normal if-then-else code blocks. Most notably, the $END directive closes the block instead of an END IF and semicolon as covered in Chapter 4. You should also note that the $$ symbol denotes a PL/SQL conditional compilation-time variable.

The rules governing conditional compilation are set by the SQL parser. You cannot use conditional compilation in SQL object types. This limitation also applies to nested tables and VARRAYs (scalar tables). Conditional compilation differs in functions and procedures. The behavior changes whether the function or procedure has a formal parameter list. You can use conditional compilation after the opening parenthesis of a formal parameter list, like

```
CREATE OR REPLACE FUNCTION conditional_type
( magic_number $IF $$DEBUG = 1 $THEN SIMPLE_NUMBER $ELSE NUMBER $END )
RETURN NUMBER IS
BEGIN
  RETURN magic_number;
END;
/
```

Alternatively, you can use them after the AS or IS keyword in parameterless functions or procedures. They can also be used both inside the formal parameter list and after the AS or IS in parameter functions or procedures.

Conditional compilation can only occur after the BEGIN keyword in triggers and anonymous-block program units. Please note that *you cannot encapsulate a placeholder or a bind variable inside a conditional compilation block.*

Chapter 4 contains examples using conditional compilation techniques.

Number Datatype Behavior

Beginning with Oracle 10*g* Release 1, the database now uses machine arithmetic for BINARY_
INTEGER, INTEGER, INT, NATURAL, NATURALN, PLS_INTEGER, POSTIVE, POSITIVEN, and
SIGNTYPE. This means that they now use the same resolution as the BINARY_INTEGER datatype.
In prior versions of the database these worked like the NUMBER datatype, and they used the same
C math library as the NUMBER datatype. The new versions of these datatypes can be compared
against infinity or NaN (not a number).

A downside of this change is that they now use numeric precision, not decimal precision.
Financial applications should continue to use the NUMBER datatype for that reason.

A single-precision BINARY_FLOAT and a double-precision BINARY_DOUBLE are also provided
in the Oracle 10*g* Database. They are ideal for mathematical or scientific computations.

Optimized PL/SQL Compiler

Beginning with Oracle 10*g* Release 1, the database now optimizes your PL/SQL compilation.
This is set by default and applies to both interpreted p-code and natively compiled PL/SQL code.
You unset or modify the optimizer's aggressiveness by resetting the PLSQL_OPTIMIZE_LEVEL
parameter. Table 1-1 qualifies the three possible values for the parameter.

You can disable session optimization by using

```
ALTER SESSION SET plsql_optimize_level = 0;
```

You can also set the level of optimization for a procedure. The prototype is

```
ALTER PROCEDURE some_procedure COMPILE plsql_optimize_level = 1;
```

After you've set the optimization level, you can use the REUSE SETTINGS clause to reuse
the prior setting, like

```
ALTER PROCEDURE some_procedure COMPILE REUSE SETTINGS;
```

While this is informative, you should generally leave it at the default. Optimized code always
runs faster than non-optimized code.

> **NOTE**
> *The* PLSQL_OPTIMIZE_LEVEL *must be set at 2 or higher for
> automatic subprogram inlining to occur in the Oracle 10g or 11g
> Database.*

Optimization Level	Optimization Meaning
0	No optimization.
1	Moderate optimization, may eliminate unused code or exceptions.
2 (default)	Aggressive optimization, may rearrange source code flow.

TABLE 1-1 *Available PLSQL_OPTIMIZE_LEVEL Values*

Regular Expressions

Beginning with Oracle 10*g* Release 1, the database now supports a set of regular expression functions. You can access them equally in SQL statements or PL/SQL program units. They are

- `REGEXP_LIKE`   This searches a string for a regular expression pattern match.

- `REGEXP_INSTR`   This searches for the beginning position of a regular expression pattern match.

- `REGEXP_SUBSTR`   This searches for a substring using a regular expression pattern match.

- `REGEXP_REPLACE`   This replaces a substring using a regular expression pattern match.

These are powerful functions. Appendix E discusses, reviews, and demonstrates regular expressions using the Oracle 11*g* Database regular expression functions.

Quoting Alternative

Beginning with Oracle 10*g* Release 1, the database now lets you replace the familiar single quote with another quoting symbol. This is helpful when you've got a bunch of apostrophes in a string that would individually require back-quoting with another single quote. The old way would be like the following:

```
SELECT 'It''s a bird, no plane, no it can''t be ice cream!' AS phrase
FROM    dual;
```

The new way is

```
SELECT q'(It's a bird, no plane, no it can't be ice cream!)' AS phrase
FROM    dual;
```

Both of these produce the following output:

```
PHRASE
--------------------------------------------------
It's a bird, no plane, no it can't be ice cream!
```

There are opportunities to use the newer syntax and save time, but the old way also continues to work. The old way is more widely understood and portable.

Set Operators

Beginning with Oracle 10*g*, Release 1, the database now supports set operators for nested tables. These include the `MULTISET EXCEPT`, `MULTISET INTERSECT`, `MULTISET UNION`, and `MULTISET UNION DISTINCT` operators. `MULTISET UNION` performs like the familiar `UNION ALL` operator. It returns two copies of everything in the intersection between two sets and one copy of the relative complements. `MULTISET UNION DISTINCT` works like the `UNION` operator. It returns one copy of everything by performing an incremental sort operation. Chapter 7 covers these operators as it discusses collections.

Stack Tracing Errors

Beginning with Oracle 10*g* Release 1, you can finally format stack traces. Stack traces produce a list of errors from the initial call to the place where the error is thrown. You use the `DBMS_UTILITY.FORMAT_ERROR_BACKTRACE` function to produce a stack trace. You can also call the FORMAT_CALL_STACK or FORMAT_ERROR_STACK from the same package to work with thrown exceptions.

The following is a simple example:

```
DECLARE
  local_exception EXCEPTION;
  FUNCTION nested_local_function
  RETURN BOOLEAN IS
    retval BOOLEAN := FALSE;
  BEGIN
    RAISE local_exception;
    RETURN retval;
  END;
BEGIN
  IF nested_local_function THEN
    dbms_output.put_line('No raised exception');
  END IF;
EXCEPTION
  WHEN others THEN
    dbms_output.put_line('DBMS_UTILITY.FORMAT_CALL_STACK');
    dbms_output.put_line('------------------------------');
    dbms_output.put_line(dbms_utility.format_call_stack);
    dbms_output.put_line('DBMS_UTILITY.FORMAT_ERROR_BACKTRACE');
    dbms_output.put_line('-----------------------------------');
    dbms_output.put_line(dbms_utility.format_error_backtrace);
    dbms_output.put_line('DBMS_UTILITY.FORMAT_ERROR_STACK');
    dbms_output.put_line('-------------------------------');
    dbms_output.put_line(dbms_utility.format_error_stack);
END;
/
```

This script produces the following output:

```
DBMS_UTILITY.FORMAT_CALL_STACK
------------------------------
----- PL/SQL Call Stack -----
  object       line  object
  handle     number
name
20909240         18  anonymous block

DBMS_UTILITY.FORMAT_ERROR_BACKTRACE
-----------------------------------
ORA-06512: at line 7
ORA-06512: at line 11

DBMS_UTILITY.FORMAT_ERROR_STACK
-------------------------------
ORA-06510: PL/SQL: unhandled user-defined exception
```

You will likely find the FORMAT_ERROR_BACKTRACE the most helpful. It captures the line where the first error occurs at the top, and then moves backward through calls until it arrives at the initial call. Line numbers and program names are displayed together when named blocks are involved in an event stack. Chapter 5 contains more on error management.

Wrapping PL/SQL Stored Programs

Beginning with Oracle 10*g* Release 2, the database now supports the ability to wrap, or obfuscate, your PL/SQL stored programs. This is done by using the DBMS_DDL package CREATE_WRAPPED procedure. You use it as follows:

```
BEGIN
  dbms_ddl.create_wrapped(
    'CREATE OR REPLACE FUNCTION hello_world RETURN STRING AS '
    ||'BEGIN '
    ||'  RETURN ''Hello World!''; '
    ||'END;');
END;
/
```

After creating the function, you can query it by using the following SQL*Plus column formatting and query:

```
SQL> COLUMN message FORMAT A20 HEADING "Message"
SQL> SELECT hello_world AS message FROM dual;

Message
--------------------
Hello World!
```

You can describe the function to inspect its signature and return type:

```
SQL> DESCRIBE hello_world
FUNCTION hello_world RETURNS VARCHAR2
```

Any attempt to inspect its detailed operations will yield an obfuscated result. You can test this by querying stored function implementation in the TEXT column of the USER_SOURCE table, like the following:

```
SQL> COLUMN text FORMAT A80 HEADING "Source Text"
SQL> SET PAGESIZE 49999
SQL> SELECT text FROM user_source WHERE name = 'HELLO_WORLD';
```

The following output is returned:

```
FUNCTION hello_world wrapped
a000000
369
abcd
. . . et cetera . . .
```

This is a very useful utility to hide the implementation details from prying eyes. We will revisit this in Appendix F.

Oracle 11*g* New Features

New PL/SQL features introduced in Oracle 11*g* include

- Automatic subprogram inlining
- A continue statement
- A cross-session PL/SQL function result cache
- Dynamic SQL enhancements
- Mixed, named, and positional notation SQL calls
- A multiprocess connection pool
- A PL/SQL Hierarchical Profiler
- That the PL/SQL Native Compiler now generates native code
- PL/Scope
- Regular expression enhancements
- A SIMPLE_INTEGER datatype
- Direct sequence calls in SQL statements

These enhancements are briefly reviewed in the following subsections. Chapter 3 covers the SIMPLE_INTEGER datatype. Chapter 4 covers the continue statement. Chapter 6 demonstrates the cross-session PL/SQL function result cache, and both mixed, named, and positional notation calls. Automatic subprogram inlining and the PL/SQL Native Compiler are covered in Chapter 9. Chapter 16 covers web application development and the multiprocess connection pool. You will also find more information about the Regular Expression, PL/SQL Hierarchical Profiler, and PL/Scope in Appendixes E, G, and H, respectively.

Automatic Subprogram Inlining

Inlining a subprogram replaces the call to the external subprogram with a copy of the subprogram. This almost always improves program performance. You could instruct the compiler to inline subprograms by using the PRAGMA INLINE compiler directive in PL/SQL starting with the Oracle 11*g* Database. You must set the PRAGMA when you have the PLSQL_OPTIMIZE_LEVEL parameter set to 2.

Let's say you have an ADD_NUMBERS stored function in a schema; you can then instruct a PL/SQL program unit to inline the call to the ADD_NUMBERS function. This would be very useful when you call the ADD_NUMBERS function in a loop, as in this example:

```
CREATE OR REPLACE PROCEDURE inline_demo
  ( a NUMBER
  , b NUMBER ) IS
  PRAGMA INLINE(add_numbers,'YES');
BEGIN
  FOR i IN 1..10000 LOOP
```

```
      dbms_output.put_line(add_function(8,3));
   END LOOP;
END;
/
```

The database automates inlining choices when you set the `PLSQL_OPTIMIZE_LEVEL` parameter to 3. This generally frees you from identifying when it is appropriate to inline function calls. However, these are only recommendations to the compiler. It is recommended that you let the engine optimize your code during compilation.

Continue Statement

The `CONTINUE` statement has finally been added to the PL/SQL language. Some may have mixed emotions. There are opinions that the continue statement leads to less-than-optimal programming, but generally it simplifies loop structures.

The `CONTINUE` statement signals an immediate end to a loop iteration and returns to the first statement in the loop. The following anonymous block illustrates using a continue statement when the loop index is an even number:

```
BEGIN
   FOR i IN 1..5 LOOP
     dbms_output.put_line('First statement, index is ['||i||'].');
     IF MOD(i,2) = 0 THEN
       CONTINUE;
     END IF;
     dbms_output.put_line('Second statement, index is ['||i||'].');
   END LOOP;
END;
/
```

The `MOD` function returns a zero when dividing any even number, so the second line is never printed, because the `CONTINUE` statement aborts the rest of the loop. More on using this command is in Chapter 4. Appendix J covers the `MOD` function.

Cross-Session PL/SQL Function Result Cache

The cross-session PL/SQL function result cache is a mechanism to share frequently accessed functions in the SGA between sessions. Prior to the Oracle 11*g* Database, each call to a function with the same actual parameters, or run-time values, was cached once per session. The only work-around to that functionality required you to code the access methods.

You designate either of the following to cache results:

```
RESULT_CACHE clause
```

or

```
RESULT_CACHE RELIES_ON(table_name)
```

The `RELIES_ON` clause places a limitation on the cached result. Any change to the referenced table invalidates the function, as well as any functions, procedures, or views that depend on the function.

The overhead when calling the function for the first time is no different than that from calling a non-cached result. Likewise, the cache will age out of the SGA when it is no longer actively called by sessions.

Dynamic SQL Enhancements

Dynamic SQL still has two varieties in the Oracle 11*g* Database. You have Native Dynamic SQL, also known as NDS, and the `DBMS_SQL` built-in package. Both have been improved in this release.

Native Dynamic SQL

In Oracle 11*g*, native dynamic SQL now supports dynamic statements larger than 32KB by accepting `CLOB`. You access it them in lieu of a SQL statement by using the following syntax:

```
OPEN cursor_name FOR dynamic_string;
```

The dynamic string can be a `CHAR`, `VARCHAR2`, or `CLOB`. It cannot be a Unicode `NCHAR` or `NVARCHAR2`. This removes the prior restriction that limited the size of dynamically built strings.

The DBMS_SQL Built-in Package

Several changes have improved the utility of the `DBMS_SQL` package. Starting with Oracle 11*g*, you can now use all NDS-supported datatypes. Also, you can now use the `PARSE` procedure to work with statements larger than 32KB. This is done by using a `CLOB` datatype. The `CLOB` replaces the prior work-around that used a table of `VARCHAR2` datatypes (typically `VARCHAR2A` or `VARCHAR2S`). Fortunately, the `DBMS_SQL` package continues to support the work-around, but you should consider moving forward to the better solution.

`DBMS_SQL` has added two new functions: the `TO_REFCURSOR` and `TO_CURSOR_NUMBER` functions. They let you transfer reference cursors to cursors and vice versa. There naturally are some words of wisdom on using these. You must open either the cursor or system reference cursor before using them, and after running them you cannot access their old structures. Basically, the code reassigns the interactive reference from the cursor to system reference cursor or from the system reference cursor to the cursor.

Last but certainly not least, you can now perform bulk binding operations against user-defined collection types. Collection types can be scalar arrays. You were previously restricted to the types defined by the `DBMS_SQL` package specification.

Mixed Name and Position Notation Calls

The Oracle 11*g* Database brings changes in how name and positional notation work in both SQL and PL/SQL. They actually now work the same way in both SQL and PL/SQL. This fixes a long-standing quirk in the Oracle database.

PL/SQL Calls

Previously, you had two choices. You could list all the parameters in their positional order or address some to all parameters by named reference. You can now use positional reference, named reference, or a mix of both.

The following function will let you experiment with the different approaches. The function accepts three optional parameters and returns the sum of three numbers.

```
CREATE OR REPLACE FUNCTION add_three_numbers
  ( a NUMBER := 0, b NUMBER := 0, c NUMBER := 0 ) RETURN NUMBER IS
BEGIN
  RETURN a + b + c;
END;
/
```

The first three subsections show how you call using positional, named, and mixed notation. In these you provide actual parameters for each of the formal parameters defined by the function signature.

You can also exclude one or more values because all formal parameters are defined as optional, which means they have default values. This is done in the subsection "Exclusionary Notation."

Positional Notation

You call the function using positional notation by

```
BEGIN
   dbms_output.put_line(add_three_numbers(3,4,5));
END;
/
```

Named Notation

You call the function using named notation by

```
BEGIN
   dbms_output.put_line(add_three_numbers(c => 4,b => 5,c => 3));
END;
/
```

Mixed Notation

You call the function using a mix of both positional and named notation by

```
BEGIN
   dbms_output.put_line(add_three_numbers(3,c => 4,b => 5));
END;
/
```

There is a restriction on mixed notation. All positional notation actual parameters must occur first and in the same order as they are defined by the function signature. You cannot provide a position value after a named value.

Exclusionary Notation

As mentioned, you can also exclude one or more of the actual parameters when the formal parameters are defined as optional. All parameters in the ADD_THREE_NUMBERS function are optional. The following example passes a value to the first parameter by positional reference, and the third parameter by named reference:

```
BEGIN
   dbms_output.put_line(add_three_numbers(3,c => 4));
END;
/
```

When you opt to not provide an actual parameter, it acts as if you're passing a null value. This is known as exclusionary notation. This has been the recommendation for years to list the optional variables last in function and procedure signatures. Now, you can exclude one or a couple but not all optional parameters. This is a great improvement, but be careful how you exploit it.

SQL Call Notation

Previously, you had only one choice. You had to list all the parameters in their positional order because you couldn't use named reference in SQL. This is fixed in Oracle 11*g; now you can call them just as you do from a PL/SQL block.* The following demonstrates mixed notation in a SQL call:

```
SELECT add_three_numbers(3,c => 4,b => 5) FROM dual;
```

As in earlier releases you can only call functions that have `IN` mode–only variables from SQL statements. You cannot call a function from SQL when any of its formal parameters are defined as `IN OUT` or `OUT` mode–only variables. This is because you must pass a variable reference when a parameter has an `OUT` mode. Functions return a reference to `OUT` mode variables passed as actual parameters.

Multiprocess Connection Pool

Enterprise JavaBeans (EJBs) just got better with the release of multiprocess connection pooling in the Oracle 11*g* Database. It is officially Database Resident Connection Pooling (DRCP). This feature lets you manage a more scalable server-side connection pool. Prior to this release you would leverage shared server processes or a multithreaded Java Servlet.

The multiprocess connection pool significantly reduces the memory footprint on the database tier, and it boosts the scalability of both the middle and database tiers. A standard database connection requires 4.4MB of real memory; 4MB is allotted for the physical connection and 400KB for the user session. Therefore, 500 dedicated concurrent connections would require approximately 2.2GB of real memory. A shared-server model is more scalable and requires only 600MB of real memory for the same number of concurrent users. Eighty percent of that memory would be managed in Oracle's Shared Global Area (SGA). Database Resident Connection Pooling scales better and would require only 400MB of real memory. Clearly for web-based applications DRCP is the preferred solution, especially when using OCI8 persistent connections.

The behaviors of these models dictate their respective scalability. Figure 1-2 graphically depicts memory use for the three models from 500 to 2,000 concurrent users.

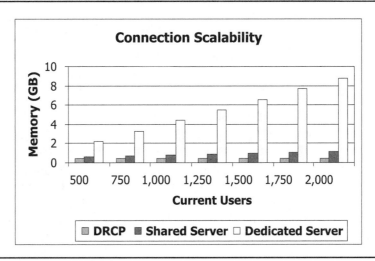

FIGURE 1-2   *Connection scalability*

The new feature is delivered by the new DBMS_CONNECTION_POOL built-in package. This package lets you start, stop, and configure connection pooling parameters such as size and time limit. You start the connection pool as the SYS user by using the following command:

```
SQL> EXECUTE DBMS_CONNECTION_POOL.START_POOL();
```

You must enable your tnsnames.ora file to support the connection to the shared pool. The following enables a shared pool connect descriptor, provided you substitute a correct hostname, domain, and Oracle listener port number:

```
ORCLCP =
  (DESCRIPTION =
    (ADDRESS = (PROTOCOL = TCP)
               (HOST = hostname.domain)
               (PORT = port_number)
    )
    (CONNECT_DATA = (SERVER = POOLED)
                    (SERVICE_NAME = orcl)
    )
  )
```

The SERVER key in the connect descriptor directs connections to the connection pooling service. You can only use the connection pool when you have a supported Oracle 11*g* Database or Oracle 11*g* Client, though this feature could be subsequently backported. The following error is raised when attempting to connect with an older release client or server library:

```
ERROR:
ORA-56606: DRCP: Client version does not support the feature
```

The message is signaled from the server when it fails to create an appropriate socket; it indicates that it is dropping the remote connection pool request.

Table 1-2 lists the data dictionary views for auditing connection pools. You can use these to monitor connections or performance characteristics.

You stop the connection pool as the SYS user by using the following command:

```
SQL> EXECUTE DBMS_CONNECTION_POOL.STOP_POOL();
```

View	Description
DBA_CPOOL_INFO	The status, maximum and minimum connections, and idle timeouts are available in this view for each connection pool.
V$CPOOL_STAT	The number of session requests, the number of times a session that matches a request is found in the pool, and the total wait time per session request are available in this view.
V$CPOOL_CC_STATS	The connection class level statistics for each instance of the connection pool.

TABLE 1-2 *Connection Pooling Data Dictionary Views*

It appears that the initial release will only support a single connection pool. The connection pool name is `SYS_DEFAULT_CONNECTION_POOL`. You also have three other procedures in the `DBMS_CONNECTION_POOL` package to manage the connection pool: the `ALTER_PARAM()`, `CONFIGURE_POOL()`, and `RESTORE_DEFAULTS()` procedures. You change a single connection pool parameter with the `ALTER_PARAM()` procedure. When you want to change more than one to all parameters, you use the `CONFIGURE_POOL()` procedure. The `RESTORE_DEFAULTS()` procedure resets all connection pool parameters to their defaults.

This new Oracle 11*g* Database feature certainly improves the scalability of web applications. It is a critical feature that empowers the persistent connection feature introduced in the OCI8 libraries in the Oracle 10*g* Release 2 database.

PL/SQL Hierarchical Profiler

The hierarchical profiler delivered in the Oracle 11*g* Database lets you see how all components in an application perform. This differs from a non-hierarchical (flat) profiler that simply records the time spent in each module. Hierarchical profilers follow the execution cycle from the containing program down to the lowest subprogram.

The PL/SQL Hierarchical Profiler does the following:

- It reports the dynamic execution profile of your PL/SQL program, which is organized by subprogram calls.

- It divides SQL and PL/SQL execution times and reports them separately.

- It requires no special source or compile-time preparation, like the `PRAGMA` required for recommending inlining.

- It stores results in a set of database tables, which you can use to develop reporting tools or alternatively use the `plshprof` command-line tool to generate simple HTML reports.

The subprogram-level summary includes information about the number of subprogram calls, time spent in subprograms or their subtrees, and detailed information between modules. Appendix G covers how to read and use the PL/SQL Hierarchical Profiler.

PL/SQL Native Compiler Generates Native Code

PL/SQL Native compilation changes in the Oracle 11*g* Database. Unlike prior versions where the PL/SQL was translated first into C code and then compiled, you can now compile directly. Execution speed of the final code in some cases is twice as fast or an order of magnitude greater.

Oracle recommends that you run all PL/SQL in either `NATIVE` or `INTERPRETED` mode. `INTERPRETED` mode is the database default, and PL/SQL modules are stored as clear text or wrapped text. You can view stored programs by querying the `ALL_SOURCE`, `DBA_SOURCE`, or `USER_SOURCE` data dictionary tables. `NATIVE`-mode code is compiled into an intermediate form before being reduced to machine-specific code. A copy of the code is also stored in the data dictionary, while the library is positioned in an external directory. You map the physical directory to the virtual directory defined by the `PLSQL_NATIVE_LIBRARY_DIR` database parameter.

Natively compiled code is advantageous when the PL/SQL code run time is slow. This can happen with compute-intensive code, but generally performance delays are caused by SQL statement processing. You should use the new PL/SQL Hierarchical Profiler to determine if there is a significant advantage to support your conversion effort.

PL/Scope

The PL/Scope is a compiler-driven tool that lets you examine identifiers and their respective behaviors in the Oracle 11*g* Database. It is disabled by default. You can enable it for the database or session. You should consider enabling it for the session, not the database. You enable it by using the following command:

```
ALTER SESSION SET PLSCOPE_SETTINGS = 'IDENTIFIERS:ALL';
```

The PL/Scope utility does not collect statistics until you enable it. The statistics let you examine how your programs use identifiers. It should be added to your arsenal of tuning tools. Appendix H gives you a brief introduction to this new feature.

Regular Expression Enhancement

Oracle 11*g* Release 1 enhances the functionality of the `REGEXP_LIKE` and `REGEXP_INSTR` functions and introduces the `REGEXP_COUNT` function. Appendix E discusses, reviews, and demonstrates regular expressions using the Oracle 11*g* Database regular expression functions.

SIMPLE_INTEGER Datatype

The Oracle 11*g* Database introduces the `SIMPLE_INTEGER`. It is a derived subtype of `BINARY_INTEGER`, and it has the same range of values. Unlike `BINARY_INTEGER`, `SIMPLE_INTEGER` excludes the null value and overflow is truncated. Also, the truncation from overflow does not raise an error. You should use the `SIMPLE_INTEGER` type if you opt to natively compile your code because it provides significant performance improvements in compiled code.

This section has reviewed the Oracle 11*g* Database new features, or it has referred you to other areas of the book for more information. Clearly, the new features make upgrading very appealing.

Direct Sequence Calls in SQL Statements

Oracle 11*g* finally lets you call a sequence with the `.nextval` or `.currval` inside SQL commands, which means you can dispense with this:

```
SELECT some_sequence.nextval
INTO   some_local_variable
FROM   dual;
```

This book uses the old and new style. The new style is simpler and easier to use.

Summary

This chapter has reviewed the history, utility, coding basics, and recent features added to the PL/SQL programming language. It has also explained the importance of PL/SQL, and how it can leverage your investment in the Oracle 11*g* database. You should now see that a combination of SQL and PL/SQL can simplify your external application development projects in languages like Java and PHP.

CHAPTER
2

PL/SQL Basics

common beginning place is a summary of language components. This chapter tours PL/SQL features. Subsequent chapters develop details that explain why the PL/SQL language is a robust tool with many options.

As an introduction to PL/SQL basics, this chapter introduces and briefly discusses

■ Oracle PL/SQL block structure

■ Variables, assignments, and operators

■ Control structures

■ Conditional structures

■ Iterative structures

■ Stored functions, procedures, and packages

■ Transaction scope

■ Database triggers

PL/SQL is a case-insensitive programming language, like SQL. While the language is case insensitive, there are many conventions applied to how people write their code. Most choose combinations of uppercase, lowercase, title case, or mixed case. Among these opinions there is no standard approach to follow.

PL/SQL Standard Usage for This Book
The PL/SQL code in this book uses uppercase for command words and lowercase for variables, column names, and stored program calls.

Oracle PL/SQL Block Structure

PL/SQL was developed by modeling concepts of structured programming, static data typing, modularity, and exception management. It extends the ADA programming language. ADA extended the Pascal programming language, including the assignment and comparison operators and single-quote string delimiters.

PL/SQL supports two types of programs: one is an anonymous-block program, and the other is a named-block program. Both types of programs have *declaration, execution,* and *exception* handling sections or blocks. Anonymous blocks support batch scripting, and named blocks deliver stored programming units.

The basic prototype for an anonymous-block PL/SQL programs is

```
[DECLARE]
    declaration_statements
BEGIN
    execution_statements
[EXCEPTION]
    exception_handling_statements
END;
/
```

As shown in the prototype, PL/SQL requires only the execution section for an anonymous-block program. The execution section starts with a `BEGIN` statement and stops at the beginning of the optional `EXCEPTION` block or the `END` statement of the program. *A semicolon ends the anonymous PL/SQL block, and the forward slash executes the block.*

Declaration sections can contain variable definitions and declarations, user-defined PL/SQL type definitions, cursor definitions, reference cursor definitions, and local function or procedure definitions. *Execution* sections can contain variable assignments, object initializations, conditional structures, iterative structures, nested anonymous PL/SQL blocks, or calls to local or stored named PL/SQL blocks. *Exception* sections can contain error handling phrases that can use all of the same items as the execution section.

The simplest PL/SQL block does nothing. You must have a minimum of one statement inside any execution block, even if it's a `NULL` statement. The forward slash executes an anonymous PL/SQL block. The following illustrates the most basic anonymous-block program:

```
BEGIN
    NULL;
END;
/
```

You must enable the SQL*Plus `SERVEROUTPUT` variable to print content to the console. The `hello_world.sql` print a message to the console:

```
-- This is found in hello_world.sql on the publisher's web site.
SET SERVEROUTPUT ON SIZE 1000000
BEGIN
  dbms_output.put_line('Hello World.');
END;
/
```

The SQL*Plus `SERVEROUTPUT` environment variable opens an output buffer, and the `DBMS_OUTPUT.PUT_LINE()` function prints a line of output. All declarations, statements, and blocks are terminated by a semicolon.

NOTE
Every PL/SQL block must contain something, at least a NULL; statement, or it will fail run-time compilation, also known as parsing.

SQL*Plus supports the use of substitution variables in the interactive console, which are prefaced by an ampersand, `&`. Substitution variables are variable-length strings or numbers. You should never assign dynamic values in the declaration block, like substitution variables.

The following program defines a variable and assigns it a value:

```
-- This is found in substitution.sql on the publisher's web site.
DECLARE
  my_var VARCHAR2(30);
BEGIN
  my_var := '&input';
  dbms_output.put_line('Hello '|| my_var );
END;
/
```

The assignment operator in PL/SQL is a colon plus an equal sign (`:=`). PL/SQL string literals are delimited by single quotes. Date, numeric, and string literals are covered in Chapter 3.

You run anonymous blocks by calling them from Oracle SQL*Plus. The @ symbol in Oracle SQL*Plus loads and executes a script file. The default file extension is `.sql`, but you can override it with another extension. This means you can call a filename without its `.sql` extension.

The following demonstrates calling the `substitution.sql` file:

```
SQL> @substitution.sql
Enter value for input: Henry Wadsworth Longfellow
old   3:   my_var VARCHAR2(30) := '&input';
new   3:   my_var VARCHAR2(30) := 'Henry Wadsworth Longfellow';
Hello Henry Wadsworth Longfellow
PL/SQL procedure successfully completed.
```

The line starting with `old` designates where your program accepts a substitution, and `new` designates the run-time substitution. Assigning a string literal that is too large for the variable fires an exception. Exception blocks manage raised errors. A generic exception handler manages any raised error. You use a `WHEN` block to catch every raised exception with the generic error handler—`OTHERS`.

TIP
You can suppress echoing the substitution by setting SQL*Plus VERIFY off.

The following `exception.sql` program demonstrates how an exception block manages an error when the string is too long for the variable:

```
-- This is found in exception.sql on the publisher's web site.
DECLARE
  my_var VARCHAR2(10);
BEGIN
  my_var := '&input';
  dbms_output.put_line('Hello '|| my_var );
EXCEPTION
  WHEN others THEN
    dbms_output.put_line(SQLERRM);
END;
/
```

The anonymous block changed the definition of the string from 30 characters to 10 characters. The poet's name is now too long to fit in the target variable. Assigning the variable raises an exception. The console output shows the handled and raised exception:

```
SQL> @exception.sql
Enter value for input: Henry Wadsworth Longfellow
old   4:   my_var := '&input';
new   4:   my_var := 'Henry Wadsworth Longfellow';
ORA-06502: PL/SQL: numeric or value error: character string buffer too small
PL/SQL procedure successfully completed.
```

You can also have: (a) nested anonymous-block programs in the *execution* section of an anonymous block; (b) named-block programs in the *declaration* section that can in turn contain the same type of nested programs; and (c) calls to stored named-block programs.

The outermost programming block controls the total program flow, while nested programming blocks control their subordinate programming flow. Each anonymous- or named-block programming unit can contain an *exception* section. When a local exception handler fails to manage an exception, it throws the exception to a containing block until it reaches the SQL*Plus environment.

Error stack management is the same whether errors are thrown from called local or named PL/SQL blocks. Error are raised and put in a *first-in, last-out* queue, which is also known as a stack.

You have explored the basic structure of PL/SQL block programs and error stack management. The block structure is foundational knowledge to work in PL/SQL.

Variables, Assignments, and Operators

Datatypes in PL/SQL include all SQL datatypes and subtypes qualified in Table B-2 of Appendix B. Chapter 3 covers PL/SQL-specific datatypes. PL/SQL also supports scalar and composite variables. Scalar variables hold only one thing, while composite variables hold more than one thing. The preceding programs have demonstrated how you declare and assign values to scalar variables.

Variable names begin with letters and can contain alphabetical characters, ordinal numbers (0 to 9), the $, _, and # symbols. Variables have local scope only. This means they're available only in the scope of a given PL/SQL block. The exceptions to that rule are nested anonymous blocks. Nested anonymous blocks operate inside the defining block. They can thereby access variables from the containing block. That is, unless you've declared the same variable name as something else inside the nested anonymous block.

A declaration of a number variable without an explicit assignment makes its initial value null. The prototype shows that you can assign a value later in the execution block:

```
DECLARE
  variable_name NUMBER;
BEGIN
  variable_name := 1;
END;
/
```

An explicit assignment declares a variable with a not-null value. You can use the default value or assign a new value in the execution block. Both are demonstrated next. You can use an assignment operator or the DEFAULT reserved word interchangeably to assign initial values. The following shows a prototype:

```
DECLARE
  variable_name NUMBER [:= | DEFAULT ] 1;
BEGIN
  variable_name := 1;
END;
/
```

The Assignment Model and Language

All programming languages assign values to variables. They typically assign a value to a variable on the left.

The prototype for generic assignment in any programming language is

```
left_operand assignment_operator right_operand statement_terminator
```

This assigns the right operand to the left operand, as shown here:

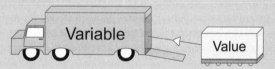

You implement it in PL/SQL as follows:

```
left_operand := right_operand;
```

The left operand must always be a variable. The right operand can be a value, variable, or function. Functions must return a value when they're right operands. This is convenient in PL/SQL because all functions return values. Functions in this context are also known as expressions.

The trick is that only functions returning a SQL datatype can be called in SQL statements. Functions returning a PL/SQL datatype only work inside PL/SQL blocks.

Oracle 11*g* performs many implicit casting operations. They fail to follow the common rule of programming: *implicitly cast when there is no loss of precision.* This means you can assign a complex number like 4.67 to an integer and lose the 0.67 portion of the number. Likewise, there are a series of functions to let you *explicitly* cast when there is greater risk of losing precision. You should choose carefully when you *explicitly* downcast variables. Appendix J covers explicit casting functions.

There are also several product-specific datatypes. They support various component products in Oracle 11*g*. You can find these datatypes in the *Oracle Database PL/SQL Packages and Type Reference.*

The assignment operator is not the lone operator in the PL/SQL programming language. Chapter 3 covers all the comparison, concatenation, logical, and mathematical operators. In short, you use

- The equal (=) symbol to check matching values

- The standard greater or less than with or without an equal component (>, >=, <, or <=) as comparison operators to check for inequalities

- The negation (<>, !=, ~= or ^=) comparison operators to check for non-matching values

You define CURSOR statements in the declaration section. CURSOR statements let you bring data from tables and views into your PL/SQL programs. A CURSOR statement can have zero or many formal parameters. CURSOR parameters are *pass-by-value,* or IN mode–only variables. Chapter 4 covers CURSOR statements.

You have now reviewed variables, assignments, and operators. You have also been exposed to PL/SQL-specific user-defined types.

Control Structures

Control structures do two things. They check a logical condition and branch program execution, or they iterate over a condition until it is met or they are instructed to exit. The conditional structures section covers *if, elsif, else,* and *case* statements. The later section "Iterative Structures" covers looping with for and while structures.

Conditional Structures

Conditional statements check whether a value meets a condition before taking action. There are two types of conditional structures in PL/SQL. One is the IF statement, and the other is the CASE statement. The IF statement that has two subtypes, *if-then-else* and *if-then-elsif-then-else.* **The *elsif* is not a typo** but the correct reserved word in PL/SQL. This is another legacy from Pascal and ADA.

IF Statement

All IF statements are blocks in PL/SQL and end with the END IF phrase. CASE statements are also blocks that end with END CASE phrase. Semicolons follow the ending phrases and terminate all blocks in PL/SQL. The following is the basic prototype for an if-then-else PL/SQL block:

```
IF [NOT] left_operand1 = right_operand1 [[AND|OR]
    [NOT] left_operand2 = right_operand2 [[AND|OR]
    [NOT] boolean_operand ]] THEN
  NULL;
ELSE
  NULL;
END IF;
```

The foregoing if-then-else block prototype uses an equality comparison, but you can substitute any of the comparison operators for the equal symbol. You can also evaluate one or more conditions by using AND or OR to join statements. Boolean outcomes then apply to the combination of expressions. You can negate single or combined outcomes with the NOT operator.

Logical operators support conjoining and including operations. A conjoining operator, AND, means that *both statements must evaluate as true or false.* An include operator, OR, means that *one or the other must be true.* Include operators stop processing when one statement evaluates as true. Conjoining operators check that all statements evaluate as true.

BOOLEAN variables are comparisons in and of themselves. Other operands can be any valid datatype that works with the appropriate comparison operator, but remember variables must be initialized. Problems occur when you fail to initialize or handle non-initialized variables in statements.

TIP
You can check if a BOOLEAN *value is true by using a comparison operator and constant (like* some_boolean = TRUE*), but it isn't the best way to use a Boolean variable in a comparison operation.*

For example, when you use an IF statement to evaluate a non-initialized BOOLEAN as *true,* it fails and processes the ELSE block; however, when you use an IF NOT statement to evaluate a non-initialized BOOLEAN as *false,* it also fails and processes the ELSE block. This happens because a non-initialized BOOLEAN variable isn't *true* or *false.*

The solution to this problem is to use the SQL `NVL()` function. It lets you substitute a value for any *null* value variables. The `NVL()` function takes two parameters: the first is a variable, and the second is a literal, which can be a numeric, string, or constant value. The two parameters must share the same datatype. *You can access all the standard SQL functions natively in your PL/SQL programs.* The following program demonstrates how you use the `NVL()` against a non-initialized `BOOLEAN` variable:

```
-- This is found in if_then.sql on the publisher's web site.
DECLARE
  -- Define a Boolean variable.
  my_var BOOLEAN;
BEGIN
  -- Use an NVL function to substitute a value for evaluation.
  IF NOT NVL(my_var,FALSE) THEN
    dbms_output.put_line('This should happen!');
  ELSE
    dbms_output.put_line('This can''t happen!');
  END IF;
END;
/
```

The `IF NOT` statement would return *false* when the `BOOLEAN` variable isn't initialized. The preceding program finds the `NVL()` function value to be *false,* or `NOT` *true,* and it prints the following message:

```
This should happen!
```

NOTE
The `ELSE` *block contains a backquoted string. The single quote mark is a reserved character for delimiting strings. You backquote an apostrophe by using another apostrophe, or a single quote, inside a delimited string. You can also substitute another backquoting character, as covered in the Oracle 10g recent features section.*

The if-then-*elsif*-then-else statement works like the if-then-else statement but lets you perform multiple conditional evaluations in the same `IF` statement. The following is the basic prototype for an if-then-*elsif*-then-else PL/SQL block:

```
IF     [NOT] left_operand1 > right_operand2 [AND|OR]
  NULL;
ELSIF [NOT] left_operand1 = right_operand1 [[AND|OR]
      [NOT] left_operand2 = right_operand2 [[AND|OR]
      [NOT] boolean_operand ]] THEN
  NULL;
ELSE
  NULL;
END IF;
```

CASE Statement

The other conditional statement is a `CASE` statement. A `CASE` statement works like the if-then-*elsif*-then-else process. There are two types of `CASE` statements: one is a *simple* `CASE`, and the other is a *searched* CASE. A simple CASE statement takes a scalar variable as an expression and then evaluates it against a list of like scalar results. A searched CASE statement takes a BOOLEAN variable as an expression and then compares the Boolean state of the WHEN clause *results as an expression.*

The following is the generic prototype of the CASE statement:

```
CASE [ TRUE | [selector_variable]]
  WHEN [criterion1 | expression1] THEN
    criterion1_statements;
  WHEN [criterion2 | expression2] THEN
    criterion2_statements;
  WHEN [criterion(n+1) | expression(n+1)] THEN
    criterion(n+1)_statements;
  ELSE
    block_statements;
END CASE;
```

The next program demonstrates a searched CASE statement:

```
BEGIN
  CASE TRUE
  WHEN (1 > 3) THEN
    dbms_output.put_line('One is greater than three.');
  WHEN (3 < 5) THEN
    dbms_output.put_line('Three is less than five.');
  WHEN (1 = 2) THEN
    dbms_output.put_line('One equals two.');
  ELSE
    dbms_output.put_line('Nothing worked.');
  END CASE;
END;
/
```

TIP
You can leave TRUE out (because it is the default selector), but don't. Putting it in adds clarity.

The program evaluates WHEN clause results as expressions, finding that 3 is less than 5. It then prints

```
Three is less than five.
```

You can find out more about CASE statements in Chapter 4. This subsection has demonstrated the conditional expressions available to you in PL/SQL. It has also suggested an alternative to non-initialized variables.

Iterative Structures

PL/SQL supports FOR, SIMPLE, and WHILE loops. There's no syntax for a *repeat until* loop block, but you can still perform one. Loops typically work in conjunction with cursors but can work to solve other problems, like searching or managing Oracle collections.

FOR Loops

PL/SQL supports *numeric* and *cursor* FOR loops. The *numeric* FOR loop iterates across a defined range, while the *cursor* FOR loop iterates across rows returned by a SELECT statement cursor. FOR loops manage how they begin and end implicitly. You can override the *implicit* END LOOP phrase by using an explicit CONTINUE or EXIT statement to respectively skip an iteration or force a premature exit from the loop.

Numeric FOR loops take two implicit actions. They automatically declare and manager their own loop index, and they create and manage their exit from the loop. A *numeric* FOR loop has the following prototype:

```
FOR i IN starting_number..ending_number LOOP
   statement;
END LOOP;
```

The *starting_number* and *ending_number* must be integers. The *loop index* is the i variable, and the loop index scope is limited to the FOR loop. The index variable is a PLS_INTEGER datatype number. When you have previously defined or declared a variable i, the numeric loop will ignore the externally scoped variable and create a new locally scoped variable.

The following sample program prints index values from 1 to 10:

```
BEGIN
   FOR i IN 1..10 LOOP
     dbms_output.put_line('The index value is ['||i||']');
   END LOOP;
END;
/
```

The *cursor* FOR loop requires a locally defined CURSOR. You cannot use a *cursor* FOR loop to iterate across a reference cursor (REF CURSOR) because *reference cursors can only be traversed by using explicit loop structures, like simple and while loops.* The cursor FOR loop can also use a SELECT statement in lieu of a locally defined CURSOR, and has the following prototype:

```
FOR i IN {cursor_name[(parameter1,parameter(n+1))] | (sql_statement)} LOOP
   statement;
END LOOP;
```

The *cursor_name* can have an optional parameter list, which is enclosed in parentheses. A *cursor_name* without optional parameters does not require parentheses. You are using an *explicit* cursor when you call a *cursor_name* and an *implicit* cursor when you provide a SELECT statement.

The following demonstrates how you write an explicit cursor in a FOR loop and use the data seeded by the downloadable scripts:

```
DECLARE
   CURSOR c IS SELECT item_title FROM item;
BEGIN
   FOR i IN c LOOP
     dbms_output.put_line('The title is ['||i.item_title||']');
   END LOOP;
END;
/
```

The following demonstrates how you write an implicit cursor in a FOR loop and use the data seeded by the downloadable scripts:

```
BEGIN
  FOR i IN (SELECT item_title FROM item) LOOP
    dbms_output.put_line('The title is ['||i.item_title||']');
  END LOOP;
END;
/
```

The index variable is not a `PLS_INTEGER` number in a cursor `FOR` loop. It is a reference to the record structure returned by the cursor. You combine the cursor index variable and column name with a dot, also known as the component selector. In this case, the cursor index is the component. The component selector lets you select a column from the row returned by the cursor.

The *statement* must be a valid `SELECT` statement, but you can dynamically reference locally scoped variable names without any special syntax in all clauses except the `FROM` clause. Unless you override the exit criteria, the *cursor* `FOR` loop will run through all rows returned by the *cursor* or *statement*.

Simple Loops

Simple loops are explicit structures. They require that you manage both loop index and exit criteria. Typically, simple loops are used in conjunction with locally defined cursor statements and reference cursors (`REF CURSOR`).

Oracle provides six cursor attributes that help you manage activities in loops. The four cursor attributes are: `%FOUND`, `%NOTFOUND`, `%ISOPEN`, and `%ROWCOUNT`. Two others support bulk operations. They are all covered in Chapter 4.

The simple loops have a variety of uses. The following is the prototype for a simple loop, using an explicit `CURSOR`:

```
OPEN cursor_name [(parameter1,parameter(n+1))];
LOOP
  FETCH cursor_name
  INTO  row_structure_variable | column_variable1 [,column_variable(n+1)];
    EXIT WHEN cursor_name%NOTFOUND;
    statement;
END LOOP;
CLOSE cursor_name;
```

The prototype demonstrates that you `OPEN` a `CURSOR` before starting the simple loop, and then you `FETCH` a row. While rows are returned you process them, but when a `FETCH` fails to return a row, you exit the loop. Place the `EXIT WHEN` statement as the last statement in the loop when you want the behavior of a repeat until loop. Repeat until loops typically process statements in a loop at least once regardless of whether the `CURSOR` returns records.

The following mimics the cursor `FOR` loop against the `ITEM` table:

```
DECLARE
    title item.item_title%TYPE;
    CURSOR c IS SELECT item_title FROM item;
BEGIN
  OPEN c;
  LOOP
    FETCH c INTO title;
    EXIT WHEN c%NOTFOUND;
    dbms_output.put_line('The title is ['||title||']');
```

```
      END LOOP;
      CLOSE c;
END;
/
```

WHILE Loops

The WHILE loop differs from the simple loop because it guards entry to the loop, not exit. It sets the entry guard as a precondition expression. The loop is only entered when the guard condition is met. The basic syntax is

```
OPEN cursor_name [(parameter1,parameter(n+1))];
WHILE condition LOOP
   FETCH cursor_name
   INTO   row_structure_variable | column_variable1 [,column_variable(n+1)];
     EXIT WHEN cursor_name%NOTFOUND;
     statement;
END LOOP;
CLOSE cursor_name;
```

When the condition checks for an opened CURSOR, then the WHILE *condition* would be *cursor_name*%ISOPEN. There are many other possible condition values that you can use in WHILE loops. The following code demonstrates how you can use a cursor %ISOPEN attribute as the guard on entry condition:

```
DECLARE
   title item.item_title%TYPE;
   CURSOR c IS SELECT item_title FROM item;
BEGIN
   OPEN c;
   WHILE c%ISOPEN LOOP
     FETCH c INTO title;
     IF c%NOTFOUND THEN
       CLOSE c;
     END IF;
     dbms_output.put_line('The title is ['||title||']');
   END LOOP;
END;
/
```

The WHILE condition is true only until the IF statement closes the cursor inside the loop. You should note that repeating instructions come after the IF statement.

This section has demonstrated how you can use implicit and explicit looping structures. It has also introduced you to the management of the CURSOR statement in the execution section of PL/SQL programs. Chapter 4 covers the CONTINUE and GOTO statements.

Stored Functions, Procedures, and Packages

PL/SQL stored programming units are typically functions, procedures, packages, and triggers. You can also store object types, but that discussion is in Chapter 14.

Oracle maintains a unique list of stored object names for tables, views, sequences, stored programs, and types. This list is known as a namespace. Functions, procedures, packages, and objects are in this namespace. Another namespace stores triggers.

Stored functions, procedures, and packages provide a way to hide implementation details in a program unit. They also let you wrap the implementation from prying eyes on the server tier.

Stored Functions

Stored functions are convenient structures because you can call them directly from SQL statements or PL/SQL programs. All stored functions must return a value. You can also use them as right operands because they return a value. Functions are defined in local declaration blocks or the database. You frequently implement them inside stored packages.

The prototype for a stored *function* is

```
FUNCTION function_name
[( parameter1     [IN][OUT] [NOCOPY] sql_datatype | plsql_datatype
[, parameter2     [IN][OUT] [NOCOPY] sql_datatype | plsql_datatype
[, parameter(n+1) [IN][OUT] [NOCOPY] sql_datatype | plsql_datatype )]]]
RETURN [ sql_data_type | plsql_data_type ]
[ AUTHID [ DEFINER | CURRENT_USER ]]
[ DETERMINISTIC | PARALLEL_ENABLED ]
[ PIPELINED ]
[ RESULT_CACHE [ RELIES ON table_name ]] IS
  declaration_statements
BEGIN
  execution_statements
  RETURN variable;
[EXCEPTION]
  exception_handling_statements
END [function_name];
/
```

Functions can be used as right operands in PL/SQL assignments. You can also call them directly from SQL statements, provided they return a SQL datatype. Procedures cannot be right operands. Nor can you call them from SQL statements.

You can query a function that returns a SQL datatype by using the following prototype from the pseudotable DUAL:

```
SELECT  some_function[(actual_parameter1, actual_parameter2)]
FROM    dual;
```

You are *no longer limited to passing actual parameters by positional order* in SQL statements. This means that you can used PL/SQL named notation in SQL. Chapter 6 covers how named, positional, and mixed notation work.

The following is a *named notation* prototype for the same query of a PL/SQL function from the pseudotable DUAL:

```
SELECT  some_function[(formal_parameter => actual_parameter2)]
FROM    dual;
```

Named positional calls work best when default values exist for other parameters. There isn't much purpose in calling only some of the parameters when the call would fail. Formal parameters are optional parameters. Named positional calls work best with functions or procedures that have optional parameters.

You can also use the `CALL` statement to capture a return value from a function into a bind variable. The prototype for the `CALL` statement follows:

```
CALL some_function[(actual_parameter1, actual_parameter2)]
INTO some_session_bind_variable;
```

The following is a small sample case that concatenates two strings into one:

```
-- This is found in join_strings.sql on the publisher's web site.
CREATE OR REPLACE FUNCTION join_strings
( string1 VARCHAR2
, string2 VARCHAR2 ) RETURN VARCHAR2 IS
BEGIN
  RETURN string1 ||' '|| string2||'.';
END;
/
```

You can now query the function from SQL:

```
SELECT join_strings('Hello','World') FROM dual;
```

Likewise, you can define a session-level bind variable and then use the `CALL` statement to put a variable into a session-level bind variable:

```
VARIABLE session_var VARCHAR2(30)
CALL join_strings('Hello','World') INTO :session_var;
```

The `CALL` statement uses an `INTO` clause when working with stored functions. You dispense with the `INTO` clause when working with stored procedures.

Selecting the bind variable from the pseudo–`DUAL` table, like this

```
SELECT :session_var FROM dual;
```

you'll see

```
Hello World.
```

Functions offer a great deal of power to database developers. They are callable in both SQL statements and PL/SQL blocks.

Procedures

Procedures cannot be right operands. Nor can you use them in SQL statements. You move data into and out of PL/SQL stored procedures through their formal parameter list. As with stored functions, you can also define local named-block programs in the declaration section of procedures.

The prototype for a stored *procedure* is

```
PROCEDURE procedure_name
[( parameter1     [IN][OUT] [NOCOPY] sql_datatype | plsql_datatype
[, parameter2     [IN][OUT] [NOCOPY] sql_datatype | plsql_datatype
```

```
[, parameter(n+1) [IN][OUT] [NOCOPY] sql_datatype | plsql_datatype )]]]
[ AUTHID DEFINER | CURRENT_USER ] IS
  declaration_statements
BEGIN
  execution_statements
[EXCEPTION]
  exception_handling_statements
END [procedure_name];
/
```

You can define procedures with or without formal parameters. Formal parameters in procedures can be either *pass-by-value* or *pass-by-reference* variables in stored procedures. *Pass-by-reference* variables have both and IN and OUT modes. As in the case of functions, when you don't provide a parameter mode, the procedure creation assumes you want the mode to be a *pass-by-value*.

Procedures can't be used as right operands in PL/SQL assignments, nor called directly from SQL statements. The following implements a stored procedure that uses a *pass-by-reference* semantic to enclose a string in square brackets:

```
-- This is found in format_string.sql on the publisher's web site.
CREATE OR REPLACE PROCEDURE format_string
( string_in IN OUT VARCHAR2 ) IS
BEGIN
  string_in := '['||string_in||']';
END;
/
```

You can also use the CALL statement to call and pass variables into and out of a procedure. Like the earlier function example, this example uses the CALL statement and bind variable:

```
VARIABLE session_var VARCHAR2(30)
CALL join_strings('Hello','World') INTO :session_var;
CALL format_string(:session_var);
```

The first CALL statement calls the previously introduced function and populates the :session_var variable. You should note that the second CALL statement does not use an INTO clause when passing a variable into and out of a stored procedure. This differs from how it works with stored functions.

You also can use the EXECUTE statement with stored procedures. The following works exactly like the CALL statement:

```
EXECUTE format_string(:session_var);
```

When you select the bind variable from the pseudo–DUAL table,

```
SELECT :session_var FROM dual;
```

you'll see

```
[Hello World.]
```

unless you ran both examples, which means you'll see double brackets:

```
[[Hello World.]]
```

Procedures offer you the ability to use pass-by-value or pass-by-reference formal parameters. As you'll see in Chapters 6 and 16, stored procedures let you exchange values with external applications.

Packages

Packages are the backbone of stored programs in Oracle 11*g*. They act like libraries and are composed of functions and procedures. Unlike standalone functions and procedures, packages let you create overloaded functions and procedures. Chapter 9 covers these features of packages.

Packages have a published specification. The specification avoids single parser limitations because all functions and procedures are published. Publishing acts like forward referencing for local functions and procedures. Package bodies contain the hidden details of the functions and procedures rather than their defined signature.

Package bodies must mirror the function and procedure signatures provided in the package specifications. Package bodies may also contain locally defined types, functions, and procedures. These structures are only available inside the package body. They mimic the concept of private access variables in other modern programming languages, like C++ and Java.

Transaction Scope

Transaction scope is a thread of execution—a process. You establish a session when you connect to the Oracle 11*g* database. The session lets you set environment variables, like SERVEROUTPUT, which lets you print from your PL/SQL programs. What you do during your session is visible only to you until you commit the work. After you commit the changes, other sessions can see the changes you've made.

During a session, you can run one or more PL/SQL programs. They execute serially, or in sequence. The first program can alter the data or environment before the second runs, and so on. This is true because your session is the main transaction. All activities potentially depend on all the prior activities. You can commit work, making all changes permanent, or roll back to reject work, repudiating all or some changes.

The power to control the session rests with three commands. They were once called transaction control language (TCL) commands. Some documentation now speaks of them as data control language (DCL) commands. The book uses DCL to represent these three commands. The problem is trying to disambiguate this group of commands from Berkeley's Tcl. The commands are

- **The COMMIT statement**   Commits all DML changes made from the beginning of the session or since the last ROLLBACK statement.

- **The SAVEPOINT statement**   Divides two epochs. An epoch is defined by the transactions between two relative points of time. A SAVEPOINT delimits two epochs.

- **The ROLLBACK statement**   Undoes all changes from now to an epoch or named SAVEPOINT, or now to the beginning of a SQL*Plus session.

These commands let you control what happens in your session and program routines. The beginning of a session is both the beginning of an epoch and an implicit SAVEPOINT statement. Likewise, the ending of a session is the ending of an epoch and implicit COMMIT statement.

How you manage transaction scope differs between a single transaction scope and multiple transaction scopes. You create multiple transaction scopes when a function or procedure is designated as an autonomous stored program unit.

Single Transaction Scope

A common business problem involves guaranteeing the sequential behavior of two or more DML statements. The idea is that they all must either succeed or fail. Partial success is not an option. DCL commands let you guarantee the behavior of sequential activities in a single transaction scope.

The following program uses DCL commands to guarantee both INSERT statements succeed or fail:

```
-- This is found in transaction_scope.sql on the publisher's web site.
BEGIN
   -- Set savepoint.
   SAVEPOINT new_member;
   -- First insert.
   INSERT INTO member VALUES
   ( member_s1.nextval, 1005,'D921-71998','4444-3333-3333-4444', 1006
   , 2, SYSDATE, 2, SYSDATE);

   -- Second insert.
   INSERT INTO contact VALUES
   ( contact_s1.nextval, member_s1.currval + 1, 1003
   ,'Bodwin','Jordan',''
   , 2, SYSDATE, 2, SYSDATE);
   -- Print success message and commit records.
   dbms_output.put_line('Both succeeded.');
   COMMIT;
EXCEPTION
   WHEN others THEN
      -- Roll back to savepoint, and raise exception message.
      ROLLBACK TO new_member;
      dbms_output.put_line(SQLERRM);
END;
/
```

The second INSERT statement fails because the foreign key constraint on member_id in the member table isn't met. The failure triggers an Oracle exception and shifts control to the exception block. The first thing the exception block does is roll back to the initial SAVEPOINT statement set by the anonymous-block program.

Multiple Transaction Scopes

Some business problems require that programs work independently. Independent programs run in discrete transaction scopes. When you call an autonomous program unit, it runs in another transaction scope.

You can build autonomous programs with the AUTONOMOUS_TRANSACTION precompiler instruction. A precompiler instruction is a PRAGMA and sets a specific behavior, like independent transaction scope. Only the following types of programs can be designated as autonomous routines:

- Top-level (not nested) anonymous blocks
- Local, standalone, package subroutines—functions and procedures
- Methods of the SQL object type
- Database triggers

The beginning transaction scope is known as the main routine. It calls an autonomous routine, which then spawns its own transaction scope. A failure in the main routine after calling an autonomous program can only roll back changes made in the main transaction scope. The autonomous transaction scope can succeed or fail independently of the main routine. However, the main routine can also fail when an exception is raised in an autonomous transaction.

Chapter 5 includes an example of this type of parallel activity. The primary INSERT statement fails because of activities in an autonomous database trigger. When the event fires the autonomous trigger, it writes the attempt to an error table, commits the write, and then raises an exception. The trigger exception causes the original INSERT statement to fail.

Multiple transaction scope programs are complex. You should be sure the benefits outweigh the risk when using multiple transaction scope solutions.

Database Triggers

Database *triggers* are specialized stored programs that are triggered by events in the database. They run between when you issue a command and when you perform the database management system action. Because they come in between, you cannot use SQL Data Control Language in triggers: SAVEPOINT, ROLLBACK, or COMMIT. You can define five types of triggers in the Oracle Database 11*g* family of products:

- *Data Definition Language (DDL) triggers*   These triggers fire when you *create, alter, rename,* or *drop* objects in a database schema. They are useful to monitor poor programming practices, such as when programs *create* and *drop* temporary tables rather than use Oracle collections effectively in memory. Temporary tables can fragment disk space and over time degrade the database performance.

- *Data Manipulation Language (DML) or row-level triggers*   These triggers fire when you *insert, update,* or *delete* data from a table. You can use these types of triggers to audit, check, save, and replace values before they are changed. Automatic numbering of pseudonumeric *primary keys* is frequently done by using a DML trigger.

- *Compound triggers*   These triggers act as both statement- and row-level triggers when you *insert, update,* or *delete* data from a table. These triggers let you capture information at four timing points: (a) before the firing statement; (b) before each row change from the firing statement; (c) after each row change from the firing statement; and (d) after the firing statement. You can use these types of triggers to audit, check, save, and replace values before they are changed when you need to take action at both the statement and row event levels.

- *Instead of triggers*   These triggers enable you to stop performance of a DML statement and redirect the DML statement. INSTEAD OF triggers are often used to manage how you write to views that disable a direct write because they're not updatable views. The INSTEAD OF triggers apply business rules and directly *insert, update,* or *delete* rows in appropriate tables related to these updatable views.

■   *System or database event triggers*   These triggers fire when a system activity occurs in the database, like the logon and logoff event triggers used in Chapter 13. These triggers enable you to track system events and map them to users.

We will cover all five trigger types in Chapter 10.

Summary

This chapter has reviewed the Procedural Language/Structured Query Language (PL/SQL) basics and explained how to jump-start your PL/SQL skills. The coverage should serve to whet your appetite for more.

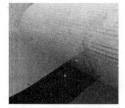

CHAPTER
3

Language Fundamentals

his chapter builds on the discussion of PL/SQL architecture in Chapter 1. It explains the building blocks of the language, and how you define and declare variables. It describes how you assign values to variables and demonstrates datatype concepts. The chapter is divided into the following sections:

- Character and lexical units
- Block structures
- Variable types
    - Scalar datatypes
    - Large objects
    - Composite datatypes
    - System reference cursors
- Variable scope

Character and Lexical Units

Lexical units are the basic building blocks in programming languages. They build PL/SQL programs. You develop lexical units by combining valid characters and symbols. Lexical units can be delimiters, identifiers, literals, or comments. Identifiers include reserved words and keywords as well as both subroutine and variable names.

Delimiters

Lexical delimiters are symbols or symbol sets. They can act as delimiters or provide other functions in programming languages. Other functions provided by lexical delimiters are assignment, association, concatenation, comparison, math, and statement controls.

The most common example of a delimiter is the character string delimiter. In PL/SQL, you delimit string literals by using a set of apostrophes or single quotes. Table 3-1 covers the full set of delimiters and it provides some examples of how to use delimiters in the language. The examples include coding techniques and concepts explained in more detail later in this book.

Symbol	Type	Description
:=	Assignment	The assignment operator is a colon immediately followed by an equal symbol. It is the *only* assignment operator in the language. You assign a right operand to a left operand, like `a := b + c;` This adds the numbers in variables b and c, and then assigns the result to variable a. The addition occurs before the assignment due to operator precedence, which is covered later in this chapter.

TABLE 3-1 *PL/SQL Delimiters*

Symbol	Type	Description

:	Association	The host variable indicator precedes a valid identifier name, and designates that identifier as a session-level variable. Session-level variables *are also known as bind variables.* You use SQL*Plus to define a session-level variable. Only the CHAR, CLOB, NCHAR, NCLOB, NUMBER, NVARCHAR2, REFCURSOR, and VARCHAR2 datatypes are available for session variables. You can define a session variable by using a prototype like:
		VARIABLE *variable_name datatype_name*
		This implements the prototype by creating a session-level variable-length string:
		SQL> VARIABLE my_string VARCHAR2(30)
		Then, you can assign a value using an anonymous-block PL/SQL program, like
		BEGIN
		 :my_string := 'A string literal.';
		END;
		/
		You can then query the result from the DUAL pseudotable:
		SELECT :my_string FROM dual;
		Alternatively, you can reuse the variable in another PL/SQL block program because the variable enjoys a session-level scope. A subsequent anonymous-block program in a script could then print the value in the session variable:
		BEGIN
		 dbms_output.put_line(:my_string);
		END;
		/
		This is a flexible way to exchange variables between multiple statements and PL/SQL blocks in a single script file. You also use the host variable indicator as a placeholder in dynamic SQL statements. Chapter 11 contains full details on how you use placeholders.

&	Association	The substitution indicator lets you pass actual parameters into anonymous-block PL/SQL programs. You should never assign substitution variables inside declaration blocks because assignment errors don't raise an error that you can catch in your exception block. You should make substitution variable assignments in the execution block. The following demonstrates the assignment of a string substitution variable to a local variable in an execution block: a := '&string_in';
%	Association	The attribute indicator lets you link a database catalog column, row, or cursor attribute. You are anchoring a variable datatype when you link a variable to a catalog object, like a table or column. The section "Variable Types" later in the chapter examines how to anchor variables to database catalog items with this operator. Chapter 4 shows how to leverage cursor attributes. Chapter 9 covers the use of %TYPE and %ROWTYPE attributes.
=>	Association	The association operator is a combination of an equal sign and a greater-than symbol. It is used in name notation function and procedure calls. Chapter 6 covers how you use the association operator.

TABLE 3-1 *PL/SQL Delimiters* (continued)

Symbol	Type	Description

.	Association	The component selector is a period, and it glues references together, for example, a schema and a table, a package and a function, or an object and a member method. Component selectors are also used to link cursors and cursor attributes (columns). The following are some prototype examples:
		`schema_name.table_name`
		`package_name.function_name`
		`object_name.member_method_name`
		`cursor_name.cursor_attribute`
		`object_name.nested_object_name.object_attribute`
		These are referenced in subsequent chapters throughout this book.

@	Association	The remote access indicator lets you access a remote database through database links.
||	Concatenation	The concatenation operator is formed by combining two perpendicular vertical lines. You use it to glue strings together, as shown: `a := 'Glued'||' '||'together. ';`
=	Comparison	The equal symbol is the comparison operator. It tests for equality of value and implicitly does type conversion where possible. (A chart showing implicit conversions is shown in the section "Variable Types" later in this chapter.) There is no identity comparison operator because PL/SQL is a strongly typed language. PL/SQL comparison operations are equivalent to identity comparisons because you can only compare like typed values.
−	Comparison	The negation operator symbol is a minus sign. It changes a number from its positive to negative value and vice versa.
<> != ^=	Comparison	There are three not-equal comparison operators. They all perform exactly the same behaviors. You can use whichever suits your organizational needs.
>	Comparison	The greater-than operator is an inequality comparison operator. It compares whether the left operand is greater than the right operand.
<	Comparison	The less-than operator is an inequality comparison operator. It compares whether the left operand is smaller than the right operand.
>=	Comparison	The greater-than or equal comparison operator is an inequality comparison operator. It compares whether the left operand is greater than or equal to the right operand.
<=	Comparison	The less-than or equal comparison operator is an inequality comparison operator. It compares whether the left operand is greater than or equal to the right operand.

TABLE 3-1   *PL/SQL Delimiters* (continued)

Symbol	Type	Description
'	Delimiter	The character string delimiter is a single quote. It lets you define a string literal value. You can assign a string literal to a variable by `a := 'A string literal.';` This creates a string literal from the set of characters between the character string delimiters and assigns it to the variable a.
(	Delimiter	The opening expression or list delimiter is an opening parenthesis symbol. You can place a list of comma-delimited numeric or string literals, or identifiers, inside a set of parentheses. You use parentheses to enclose formal and actual parameters to subroutines or to produce lists for comparative evaluations. You can also override order of precedence by enclosing operations in parentheses. Enclosing operations in parentheses lets you override the natural order of precedence in the language.
)	Delimiter	The closing expression or list delimiter is a closing parenthesis symbol. See the opening expression or list delimiter entry for more information.
,	Delimiter	The item separator is a comma and delimits items in lists.
<<	Delimiter	The opening guillemet (a French word pronounced *gee^uh mey*) is the opening delimiter for labels in PL/SQL. Labels are any valid identifiers in the programming language. Perl and PHP programmers should know these don't work as HERE document tags. Chapter 4 discusses labels.
>>	Delimiter	The closing guillemet (a French word pronounced *gee^uh mey*) is the closing delimiter for labels in PL/SQL. Labels are any valid identifiers in the programming language. Perl and PHP programmers should know these don't work as HERE document tags. Chapter 4 discusses labels.
--	Delimiter	Two adjoining dashes are a single comment operator. Everything to the right of the single comment operator is treated as text and not parsed as part of a PL/SQL program. An example of a single-line comment is: `-- This is a single line comment.`

/*	Delimiter	This is the opening multiple-line comment delimiter. It instructs the parser to ignore everything until the closing multiple-line comment delimiter as text. An example of a multiple-line comment is:
		`/* This is line one.`
		`  This is line two. */`
		There are many suggestions on how to use multiple-line comments. You should pick one way of doing it that suits your organization's purposes and stick with it.

*/	Delimiter	This is the closing multiple-line comment delimiter. It instructs the parser that the text comment is complete, and everything after it should be parsed as part of the program unit. See the opening multiple-line comment entry for more information.

TABLE 3-1   *PL/SQL Delimiters* (continued)

Symbol	Type	Description

"	Delimiter	The quoted identifier delimiter is a double quote. It lets you access tables created in case-sensitive fashion from the database catalog. This is required when you have created database catalog objects in case-sensitive fashion. You can do this from Oracle 10*g* forward.
		For example, you create a case-sensitive table or column by using quoted identifier delimiters:
		`CREATE TABLE "Demo"`
		`("Demo_ID" NUMBER`
		`, demo_value VARCHAR2(10));`
		You insert a row by using the following quote-delimited syntax:
		`INSERT INTO "Demo1" VALUES`
		`(1,'One Line ONLY.');`
		Like the SQL syntax, PL/SQL requires you to use the quoted identifier delimiter to find the database catalog object, like
		`BEGIN`
		` FOR i IN (SELECT "Demo_ID", demo_value`
		` FROM "Demo") LOOP`
		` dbms_output.put_line(i."Demo_ID");`
		` dbms_output.put_line(i.demo_value);`
		` END LOOP;`
		`END;`
		`/`
		Beyond the quoted identifier in embedded SQL statements, you must refer to any column names by using quote-delimited syntax. This is done in the first output line, where the loop index (`i`) is followed by the component selector (`.`) and then a quote-delimited identifier (`"Demo_ID"`). You should note that no quotes are required to access the case-insensitive column. If you forget to enclose a case-sensitive column name (identifier), your program returns a `PLS-00302` error that says the identifier is not declared.
		You can also use the quoted identifier delimiter to build identifiers that include reserved symbols, like an `"X+Y"` identifier.

+	Math	The addition operator lets you add left and right operands and returns a result.
/	Math	The division operator lets you divide a left operand by a right operand and returns a result.

TABLE 3-1   *PL/SQL Delimiters (continued)*

Symbol	Type	Description

**	Math	The exponential operator raises a left operand to the power designated by a right operand. The operator enjoys the highest precedence for math operators in the language. As a result of that, a fractional exponent must be enclosed in parentheses (also known as expression or list delimiters) to designate order of operation. Without parentheses, the left operand is raised to the power of the numerator and the result divided by the denominator of a fractional exponent.
		
		You raise 3 to the third power and assign the result of 27 to variable a by using the following syntax:
		
		`a := 3**3;`
		
		You raise 8 to the fractional power of 1/3 and assign the result of 2 to variable a by using the following syntax:
		
		`a := 8**(1/3);`
		
		The parentheses ensures that the division operation occurs first. Exponential operations take precedence on other mathematical operations without parenthetical grouping.

*	Math	The multiplication operator lets you multiply a left operand by a right operand and returns a result.
−	Math	The subtraction operator lets you subtract the right operand from the left operand and returns a result.
;	Statement	The statement terminator is a semicolon. You must close any statement or block unit with a statement terminator.

TABLE 3-1   *PL/SQL Delimiters* (continued)

Identifiers

Identifiers are words. They can be reserved words, predefined identifiers, quoted identifiers, user-defined variables, subroutines, or user-defined types. You can find reserved and key words in Appendix I, and built-in functions in Appendix J.

Reserved Words and Keywords

Both reserved words and keywords are lexical units that provide basic tools for building programs. For example, you use the NOT reserved word as a negation in comparison operations, and the NULL to represent a null value or statement. You cannot use these words when defining your own programs and datatypes.

Predefined Identifiers

Oracle 11*g* provides a `STANDARD` package, and it globally grants access to the package through a public grant. The `STANDARD` package defines the built-in functions found in Appendix J. It also contains the definitions for standard datatypes and errors.

You should be careful to not override any predefined identifiers by creating user-defined identifiers with the same names. This happens any time you define a variable that duplicates a component from the `STANDARD` package, just as you can define a variable in a nested PL/SQL block that overrides the containing block variable name.

Quoted Identifiers

Oracle 11*g* provides you the ability to use *quoted identifier* delimiters to build identifiers that would otherwise be disallowed because of symbol reuse. Quoted identifiers can include any printable characters, including spaces. However, you cannot embed double quotes inside identifiers. The maximum size of a quoted identifier is 30 characters.

You can also use quoted identifiers to leverage reserved words and keywords. This is allowed but strongly discouraged by Oracle. For example, the following program creates a quoted identifier "End," which is a case-insensitive reserved word:

```
DECLARE
  "End" NUMBER := 1;
BEGIN
  dbms_output.put_line('A quoted identifier End ['||"End"||']');
END;
/
```

Again, while this is possible, you should avoid it.

User-Defined Variables, Subroutines, and Datatypes

You create identifiers when you define program components. User-defined datatypes can be defined in SQL as schema-level datatypes, or in PL/SQL blocks. User-defined identifiers must be less than 30 characters and start with a letter; they can include a $, # or _. They cannot contain punctuation, spaces, or hyphens.

Anonymous-block identifiers are only accessible inside a block or nested block. When you define identifiers in functions and procedures, they are likewise only accessible inside named blocks. Package specifications let you define package-level datatypes that are available in your schema. They are also available in other schemas when you grant execute privilege on them to other scheme. You reference them by using the component selector to connect the package and datatype names. Chapter 9 discusses PL/SQL packages.

Literals

A *literal* is an explicit character, string, number or Boolean value. Literal values are not represented by identifiers. String literals can also represent date or time literals.

Character Literals

Character literals are defined by enclosing any character in a set of apostrophes or single quotes. The literal values are case sensitive, while the programming language is case insensitive. This mirrors the behavior of SQL and data stored in the database as character or string data (the `VARCHAR2` datatype is the most commonly used type).

You assign a character literal to a variable using the following syntax:

```
a := 'a';
```

String Literals

String literals are defined like character literals, using single quotes. String literals can contain any number of characters up to the maximum value for the datatype. You typically use the VARCHAR2 datatype, or one of its subtypes.

You assign a string literal to a variable using the following syntax:

```
a := 'some string';
```

You can also assign a string literal with double quotes inside it by using the following syntax:

```
a := 'some "quoted" string';
```

The double quotes are treated as normal characters *when embedded in single quotes.*

NOTE
Behavior of a VARCHAR2 *datatype differs between SQL and PL/SQL. The maximum size of a* VARCHAR2 *column in a table is 4,000 bytes. The maximum size in PL/SQL is 32,767 bytes. This does not guarantee 32,767 characters because some Unicode character sets use multibyte character sets. You may only be able to store half or a third as many characters using a multibyte character set.*

Numeric Literals

Numeric literals are defined like numbers in most programming languages. The generic numeric literal assignment is done by using the following syntax:

```
a := 2525;
```

You have the ability to assign a large number with the following exponent syntax:

```
n := 2525E8; -- This assigns 252,500,000,000 to the variable.
```

You may attempt to assign a number beyond the range of a datatype. The numeric overflow or underflow exception is raised when the number is outside the datatype's range.

You also can assign a float or a double by using the respective syntax:

```
d := 2.0d; -- This assigns a double of 2.
f := 2.0f; -- This assigns a float of 2
```

These assignments only work with their respective type. A d works with a BINARY_DOUBLE, while an f works with a BINARY_FLOAT.

Boolean Literals

Boolean Literals can be TRUE, FALSE, or NULL. This three-valued state of Boolean variables makes it possible that your program can incorrectly handle a *not true* or *not false* condition any time the variable is NULL. Chapter 4 covers how to manage conditional statements to secure expected results.

You can make any of the following assignments to a previously declared BOOLEAN variable:

```
b := TRUE;   -- This assigns a true state.
b := FALSE;  -- This assigns a false state.
b := NULL;   -- This assigns a null or default state.
```

TIP
It is a good practice to assign an initial value of TRUE *or* FALSE *to all Boolean variables, which means always explicitly define their initial state. You should also consider declaring Boolean columns as not null constrained.*

Date and Time Literals

Date literals have an implicit conversion from a string literal that maps to the default format mask. *The default format masks for dates are* DD-MON-RR or DD-MON-YYYY. The DD represents a two-digit day, the MON represents a three-character month, the RR represents a two-digit relative year, and the YYYY represents a four-digit absolute year. Relative years are calculated by counting 50 years forward or backward from the current system clock. You assign a relative or absolute date as follows to previously declared DATE datatype variables:

```
relative_date := '01-JUN-07';   -- This assigns 01-JUN-2007.
absolute_date := '01-JUN-1907'; -- This assigns 01-JUN-1907.
```

Implicit assignment fails when you attempt other format masks, like MON-DD-YYYY. You can explicitly assign date literals by using the TO_DATE() or CAST() functions. Only the Oracle proprietary TO_DATE() function lets you use apply a format mask other than the default. The syntax variations for the TO_DATE() function are

```
date_1 := TO_DATE('01-JUN-07');            -- Default format mask.
date_2 := TO_DATE('JUN-01-07','MON-DD-YY'); -- Override format mask.
```

The CAST() function can use either of the default format masks discussed earlier, as shown:

```
date_1 := CAST('01-JUN-07' AS DATE);   -- Relative format mask.
date_2 := CAST('01-JUN-2007' AS DATE); -- Absolute format mask.
```

You can use the TO_CHAR(date_variable, 'MON-DD-YYYY') function to view the fully qualified date. These behaviors in PL/SQL mirror the behaviors in Oracle SQL.

Comments

You can enter single- or multiple-line comments in PL/SQL. You use two dashes to enter a single-line comment, and the /* and */ delimiters to enter a multiple-line comment. A single-line comment is

```
-- This is a single-line comment.
```

A multiple-line comment is

```
/* This is a multiple-line comment.
   Style and indentation should follow your company standards. */
```

Planned comments are straightforward, but you can introduce errors when you comment out code to test or debug your programs. The biggest problem occurs when you comment out all executable statements from a code block. This will raise various parsing errors because every coding block must have at a minimum one statement, as discussed in the next section, "Block Structures." The other problem frequently introduced with single-line comments arises from placing them before either a statement terminator (a semicolon) or an ending block keyword. This also raises a parsing error when you try to run or compile the program unit.

NOTE
Compilation in PL/SQL programs can mean attempting to run an anonymous-block program or creating a stored program unit. In both cases, you are parsing the program into PL/SQL p-code. PL/SQL runs the p-code.

This section has presented the valid characters and symbols in the language. It has also explained that delimiters, identifiers, literals, or comments are lexical units.

Block Structures

PL/SQL is a blocked programming language. Program units can be named or unnamed blocks. Unnamed blocks are known as anonymous blocks and are so labeled throughout the book. The PL/SQL coding style differs from the C, C++, and Java programming languages. For example, curly braces do not delimit blocks in PL/SQL.

Anonymous-block programs are effective in some situations. You typically use anonymous blocks when building scripts to seed data or perform one-time processing activities. They are also effective when you want to nest activity in another PL/SQL block's execution section. The basic anonymous-block structure must contain an execution section. You can also put *optional* declaration and exception sections in anonymous blocks. Figure 3-1 illustrates both anonymous- and named-block prototypes.

The declaration block lets you declare datatypes, structures, and variables. Declaring a variable means that you give it a name and a datatype. You can also define a variable by giving it a name, a datatype, and a value. You both declare and assign a value when defining a variable. Figure 3-2 demonstrates the concept of assigning a single value to a variable. Scalar variables hold only one thing at a time.

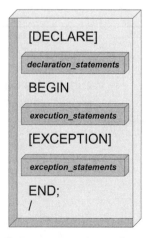 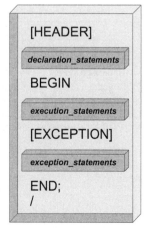

FIGURE 3-1 *PL/SQL block structure*

FIGURE 3-2 *Scalar variable assignment*

You define a variable by declaring the variable (providing a variable name and a datatype) and initializing it by assigning a value, like a date, string, or numeric literal. The general definition prototype is

```
variable_name datatype_name := literal_value;
```

Some object types cannot be declared as locally scoped variables and must be declared as types in the database catalog, as discussed in Chapter 14. Structures are compound variables, like collections, record structures, or system reference cursors. Structures can also be locally named functions, procedures, or cursors.

Cursors act like little functions. Cursors have names, signatures, and a return type. The signature is the list of formal parameters accepted by the cursor. The output columns from a query or SELECT statement create a cursor structure as the return type.

Composite variables, like scalar variables, follow similar definition rules. The difference is that you're assigning multiple values to one variable. Figure 3-3 illustrates the idea of populating an array of values by loading a set of similar values. Composite assignments are a bit more complex than the generic prototype for scalar variables, which are described in the section "Composite Datatypes" later in this chapter.

Some composite variables are structures that contain different things, like the element of an address book. A structure is like a row in a database table. Figure 3-4 illustrates the idea of populating a structure—a set of different variables.

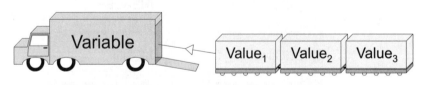

FIGURE 3-3 *Composite variable assignment: collections*

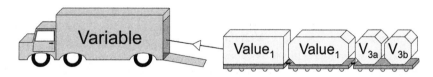

FIGURE 3-4 *Composite variable assignment: structures*

You use the DECLARE reserved word to begin a declaration block and the BEGIN reserved word to end an anonymous block. The header of named blocks begins the declaration block for stored programming units. Like anonymous-block programs, the BEGIN reserved word ends the declaration section for named blocks. The declaration block is where you declare and initialize variables; it can include local named blocks.

The execution block lets you process data. The execution block can contain variable assignments, comparisons, conditional operations, and iterations. Also, the execution block is where you access cursors and other named program units. Functions, procedures, and some object types are named program units. You can also nest anonymous-block programs inside the execution block. The BEGIN reserved word starts the exception block, and the optional EXCEPTION or required END reserved word ends it. *The semicolon ends the block.*

TIP
You must have at least one statement inside an execution block or it fails compilation.

The following minimum anonymous-block statement includes a NULL statement:

```
BEGIN
  NULL;
END;
/
```

Scalar and Compound Variables
Scalar variables hold only one thing at a time and are frequently labeled as primitives; these include numbers, strings, and timestamps. Oracle timestamps are dates precise to one thousandth of a second. You can also define compound variables that are alternatively labeled as composite variables. There's not much difference in the words, but Oracle 11*g* documentation uses composite variables. So, *this book uses composite variables to describe arrays, structures, and objects.* Composite variables are variables built from primitives in a programming language.

This does nothing except let the compilation phase complete without an error. Compilation in any language includes a syntax parsing. The lack of a statement in the block raises a parsing error as covered in Chapter 5. *You should note the forward slash (/),* which dispatches the PL/SQL program for execution.

The exception handling block lets you manage exceptions. You can both catch and manage them there. The exception block allows for alternative processing and in many ways acts like combination of a *catch* block and a *finally* block in the Java programming language (see Appendix D for more information on Java). The EXCEPTION reserved word starts the section, and the END reserved word ends it.

TIP
You have the same rule requiring a minimum of one statement for any blocks in a conditional statement block (like an IF *statement) and for loops.*

Named-block programs have a slightly different block structure because they are stored in the database. They also have a declaration section, which is known as the header. The name, the signature, and any return type of named PL/SQL blocks are defined by the header. The area between the header and execution blocks acts as the declaration block for a named block. This same rule holds true for object type bodies covered in Chapter 14.

The following illustrates a named-block function prototype:

```
FUNCTION function_name
[( parameter1      [IN][OUT] [NOCOPY] sql_data_type | plsql_data_type
 , parameter2      [IN][OUT] [NOCOPY] sql_data_type | plsql_data_type
 , parameter(n+1) [IN][OUT] [NOCOPY] sql_data_type | plsql_data_type )]

RETURN [ sql_data_type | plsql_data_type ]
  [ AUTHID {DEFINER | CURRENT_USER}]
  [ DETERMINISTIC | PARALLEL_ENABLED ]
  [ PIPELINED ]
  [ RESULT_CACHE [RELIES ON table_name]] IS
  declaration_statements
BEGIN
  execution_statements
[EXCEPTION]
  exception_handling_statements
END;
/
```

Chapter 6 discusses the rules governing functions. Functions can behave as pass-by-value or pass-by-reference subroutines. Pass-by-value subroutines define formal parameters using an IN mode only. This means that the variable passed in cannot change during execution of the subroutine. Pass-by-reference subroutines define formal parameters using IN and OUT, or OUT-only modes.

Oracle 11*g* continues passing copies of variables instead of references to variables, unless you designate a NOCOPY hint. Oracle implements pass-by-reference behaviors this way to guarantee the integrity of IN OUT mode variables. This model guarantees variables are unchanged unless a subprogram call completes successfully. You can override this *default* behavior by using a NOCOPY hint. Oracle recommends against using the NOCOPY hint because using it can result in partial changes to your actual parameter values. Ultimately, *the database reserves the right to act on or ignore your* NOCOPY hint.

Functions can query data using SELECT statements and can perform DML statements, such as INSERT, UPDATE, or DELETE. All other rules apply to stored functions the same as those that apply to anonymous blocks. Functions that define formal parameters or return types that use PL/SQL datatypes cannot be called from the SQL command line. However, you can call functions that use SQL datatypes from the SQL command line.

The AUTHID default value is DEFINER, which provides what are known as definer rights. Definer rights means that any one with privileges to execute the stored program runs it with the same privileges as the user account that defined it. The CURRENT_USER alternative lets those with execute privileges call the stored program and run it against only their user/schema data. This is known as invoker rights, and it describes the process of calling a common source program against individual accounts and data.

You should avoid using the DETERMINISTIC clause when functions depend on the states of session-level variables. DETERMINISTIC clauses are best suited to function-based indexes and materialized views.

The PARALLEL_ENABLE clause should be enabled for functions that you plan to call from SQL statements that may use parallel query capabilities. You should look closely at this clause for data warehousing uses.

The PIPELINED clause provides improved performance when functions return collections, like nested tables or VARRAYs. You'll also note performance improvements when returning system reference cursors by using the PIPELINED clause.

The RESULT_CACHE clause indicates a function is cached only once in the SGA and available across sessions. It is new in the Oracle 11*g* Database. Cross-session functions only work with IN mode formal parameters.

The following illustrates a named-block procedure prototype:

```
PROCEDURE procedure_name
[( parameter1     [IN][OUT]  [NOCOPY] sql_datatype | plsql_datatype
 , parameter2     [IN][OUT]  [NOCOPY] sql_datatype | plsql_datatype
 , parameter(n+1) [IN][OUT]  [NOCOPY] sql_datatype | plsql_datatype )]
[ AUTHID {DEFINER | CURRENT_USER}] IS
  declaration_statements
BEGIN
  execution_statements
[EXCEPTION]
  exception_handling_statements
END;
/
```

Chapter 6 discusses the rules governing procedures. They act like functions in many ways but cannot return a datatype. This means that you can't use them as right operands. Unlike functions, procedures must be called by PL/SQL blocks. *Procedures can both query the data and manipulate the data.* Procedures are also the foundation subroutines for passing values from and to external languages like C, C++, Java, PHP, and so on.

This section has presented and discussed the basics structure of PL/SQL program units. The next section discusses how you can define and use variables.

Variable Types

PL/SQL supports two principal variable datatypes: scalar and composite variables. Scalar variables contain only one thing, like a character, date, or number. There's not much difference in the words, but *this book uses composite variables to describe arrays, structures, and objects.* Composite variables are variables built from primitives or base types in a programming language. Composite variables in Oracle are records (structures), arrays, reference cursors, and object types.

PL/SQL uses all Oracle SQL datatypes. PL/SQL also introduces a Boolean datatype and several subtypes derived from the SQL datatypes. Subtypes inherit the behavior of a datatype but also typically have constrained behaviors. An unconstrained subtype doesn't change a base type's behavior. Unconstrained types are also called as aliases. You can also call any base datatype a supertype because it is the model for subtypes. Unconstrained subtypes are interchangeable with their base types, while only qualified values can be assigned to constrained subtypes from base types. You can extend these types by building your own subtypes as discussed and demonstrated in several sections later in this chapter.

Like other programming languages, PL/SQL lets you both define types and declare variables. You label a datatype and designate how to manage the datatype in memory when you define a type. You define a variable by both declaring the variable and assigning it a value. A variable name is mapped to a known datatype and then added to the program's namespace as an identifier when you declare a variable. In some programming languages no value is assigned to a declared variable. PL/SQL *automatically* assigns most declared variables a null value. This means that variables are generally defined in the language.

You declare variables by *assigning them a type* or *anchoring their type to a database catalog column.* The prototypes for both declarations are

```
variable_name variable_type;    -- An explicit datatype.
variable_name column_name%TYPE; -- An anchored datatype.
```

Anchoring a variable using the %TYPE means that your program automatically adjusts as the column datatype changes. This is true when only the size changes but not *necessarily* true when the base type changes. For example, some logic, assignments, and comparisons may fail when the base type began as a string but mutated to a date, because implicit conversions may not meet all logical conditions.

TIP
Altering the column datatype does not raise an error but invalidates any stored procedures that misuse the new variable type.

Implicit conversions are determined by the PL/SQL engine. Unlike some programming languages, PL/SQL allows implicit conversions that result in *loss of precision* (or details). If you assign a BINARY_FLOAT variable to a BINARY_INTEGER, any digits to the right of the decimal place are discarded implicitly. Explicit conversions require you to convert the data, like calling the TO_CHAR() built-in function to display the timestamp of a DATE variable. A list of implicit conversions is shown in the following chart.

FROM \ TO	BINARY_DOUBLE	BINARY_FLOAT	BINARY_INTEGER	BLOB	CHAR	CLOB	DATE	LONG	NCHAR	NCLOB	NUMBER	NVARCHAR2	PLS_INTEGER	RAW	UROWID	VARCHAR2
BINARY_DOUBLE		X	X		X				X	X		X	X	X		X
BINARY_FLOAT	X		X		X				X			X	X	X		X
BINARY_INTEGER	X	X			X				X			X	X	X		X
BLOB														X		
CHAR	X	X	X			X	X	X	X	X		X	X	X	X	X
CLOB					X				X			X				X
DATE					X			X	X			X				X
LONG					X		X		X			X		X		X
NCHAR	X	X	X		X	X	X	X		X	X	X	X	X	X	X
NCLOB					X	X		X	X			X				X
NUMBER	X	X	X		X			X	X			X	X			X
NVARCHAR2	X	X	X		X	X		X		X						X
PLS_INTEGER	X	X	X		X			X	X	X	X	X				X
RAW				X	X			X	X							X
UROWID					X				X	X		X				X
VARCHAR2	X	X	X		X	X	X	X	X	X	X	X	X	X	X	

There is one pseudo-exception to the variable declaration rule. Weakly typed system reference cursors are not defined until run time. A weakly typed system reference cursor takes an assigned cursor number and adopts the record structure of a row assigned to the cursor. Record structures can only be assigned to composite variables. You can also anchor a strongly typed system reference cursor to a catalog table or view. This works much like how you anchor variables to columns. The prototypes for declaring composite variables are

```
composite_variable_name record_type;              -- An explicit datatype.
composite_variable_name catalog_object%ROWTYPE; -- An anchored datatype.
```

You anchor a composite variable by using the %ROWTYPE attribute. It updates your program to reflect any changes in the row definition of the catalog object. This type of anchoring ensures that you know the datatype always matches the catalog object. You should also anchor any other dependent variable datatypes too.

Variable datatypes can be defined in SQL or PL/SQL. You can use SQL datatypes in both SQL statements and PL/SQL statements. You can only use PL/SQL datatypes inside your PL/SQL program units.

The PL/SQL Buffer and Outputting to the Console

As shown in earlier Figure 1-1, there is an output buffer between the SQL*Plus and PL/SQL engines. You can open the buffer in SQL*Plus by enabling the SERVEROUTPUT environment variable, like

```
SQL> SET SERVEROUTPUT ON SIZE 1000000
```

Once you enable this SQL*Plus environment variable, the output generated by the PUT(), PUT_LINE(), and NEW_LINE() procedures of the DBMS_OUTPUT package will be displayed in your SQL*Plus environment. It is possible that you may get more output than you expect the first time you run a program after enabling the environment variable. This can happen when you run a program in PL/SQL that enables the buffer from PL/SQL without enabling the environment variable first.

You enable the buffer in PL/SQL by using the following command:

```
dbms_output.enable(1000000);
```

The first write to the buffer after enabling the environment variable will flush all contents to the SQL*Plus environment. You clear the prior contents by disabling any open buffer before enabling it using the following two procedures sequentially:

```
dbms_output.disable;
dbms_output.enable(1000000);
```

The DISABLE procedure is recommended to ensure that you don't capture some undesired prior output when running your program. You output to the console using either the PUT() or PUT_LINE() procedure. The PUT() procedure outputs a string to the buffer without a line return, while the PUT_LINE() procedure outputs a string and newline character to the buffer. You use the NEW_LINE() procedure after one or more PUT() procedure calls to write a line return.

The following demonstrates how to output information from your PL/SQL program to the SQL*Plus environment:

```
BEGIN
  dbms_output.put('Line ');
  dbms_output.put('one.');
  dbms_output.new_line;
  dbms_output.put_line('Line two.');
END;
/
```

This anonymous-block program outputs

```
Line one.
Line two.
```

This is the technique that you'll use to get output to the console for debugging or to file for reporting. You can also combine the SQL*Plus SPOOL command to split standard output to both the console and a file (like the Unix tee command). This technique lets you generate text files for reporting.

TIP
*SQL*Plus environment variable settings are lost when you change
schemas. Don't forget to reset the* SERVEROUTPUT *variable if you
change schemas, because the output buffer is effectively closed the
minute you change schemas.*

The first subsection covers scalar datatypes, the second large objects, the third composite
datatypes, and fourth reference types. Items are organized for reference and flow. The scalar
datatypes are the primitives of the language and therefore the building blocks for the composite
datatypes. The next section covers these primitive building blocks.

Scalar Datatypes

The primitives are grouped into alphabetical sections. Each section describes the datatype,
demonstrates how to define and/or declare the type or variables of the type, and shows how
to assign it values. Figure 3-5 qualifies the four major types of scalar variables and their
implementation base types and subtypes.

Scalar datatypes use the following prototype inside the declaration block of your programs:

```
variable_name  datatype [NOT NULL] [:= literal_value];
```

Some datatypes require that you provide a precision when defining a variable. The precision
defines the maximum size in bytes or characters for a datatype. You also have the scale for
NUMBER datatypes. The scale defines the number of decimal places to the right of the decimal
point. These mirror the conventions found in SQL for these datatypes.

Boolean

The BOOLEAN datatype has three possible values: TRUE, FALSE, and NULL. This three-valued
state of Boolean variables makes it possible that your program can incorrectly handle a *not true*
or *not false* condition any time the variable is NULL. Chapter 4 covers how to manage conditional
statements to secure expected results.

The following is the prototype for declaring a BOOLEAN datatype:

```
BOOLEAN [NOT NULL]
```

You can define Boolean variables by implicit null assignment or by explicit assignment of a
TRUE or FALSE value. The following syntax belongs in the declaration block:

```
var1  BOOLEAN;                      -- Implicitly assigned a null value.
var2  BOOLEAN NOT NULL := TRUE;  -- Explicitly assigned a TRUE value.
var3  BOOLEAN NOT NULL := FALSE; -- Explicitly assigned a FALSE value.
```

You should always initialize Boolean variables explicitly in your program units. This practice
avoids unexpected behaviors in programs. Using the NOT NULL clause during declaration
guarantees Boolean variables are never null.

There is little need to subtype a BOOLEAN datatype, but you can do it. The subtyping syntax is

```
SUBTYPE booked IS BOOLEAN;
```

This creates a subtype BOOKED that is an unconstrained BOOLEAN datatype. You may find this
useful when you need a second name for a BOOLEAN datatype, but generally subtyping a Boolean
is not very useful.

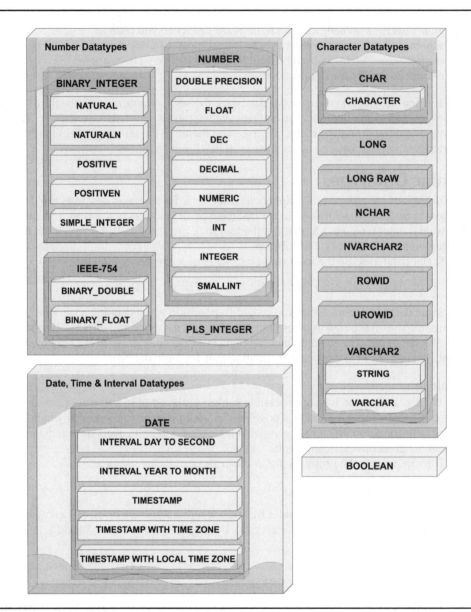

FIGURE 3-5 *Scalar types*

As shown in the earlier subsection "Boolean Literals," you assign a Boolean variable a literal value inside the execution block by using the following syntax:

```
var1 := TRUE;
```

Unlike strings, the TRUE, FALSE, or NULL values are not delimited by single quotes. All three words are PL/SQL reserved words.

Characters and Strings

Characters and strings work more like the *String* class in the Java programming language. Strings are known as single-dimensional character arrays in the C and C++ programming languages. Character datatypes store a fixed-length string. You size the string by stating the number of bytes or characters allowed inside the string. Any attempt to store more than the maximum number of bytes or characters throws an exception.

The following program illustrates the memory allocation differences between the CHAR and VARCHAR2 datatypes:

```
DECLARE
    c CHAR(32767)      := ' ';
    v VARCHAR2(32767) := ' ';
BEGIN
    dbms_output.put_line('c is ['||LENGTH(c)||']');
    dbms_output.put_line('v is ['||LENGTH(v)||']');
    v := v || ' ';
    dbms_output.put_line('v is ['||LENGTH(v)||']');   END;
/
```

The program defines two variables, prints their length (see the PL/SQL Built-in Functions in Appendix J), and then concatenates another whitespace value to VARCHAR2 to demonstrate memory allocation. Provided you have enabled the SQL*Plus buffer (setting SERVEROUTPUT on), this will output the following to the console:

```
c is [32767]
v is [1]
v is [2]
```

The output shows that a CHAR variable sets the allocated memory size when defined. The allocated memory can exceed what is required to manage the value in the variable. The output also shows that the VARCHAR2 variable dynamically allocates only the required memory to host its value.

CHAR and CHARACTER Datatypes The CHAR datatype is a base datatype for *fixed*-length strings. You can size a CHAR datatype up to 32,767 bytes in length, but its default length is 1 byte. Unfortunately, a PL/SQL CHAR is larger than the 4,000-byte maximum allowed in a SQL CHAR column. You can store character strings larger than 4,000 bytes in CLOB or LONG columns. Oracle recommends you use the CLOB datatype because the LONG and LONG RAW datatypes are only supported for backward compatibility purposes.

The following is the prototype for defining a CHAR datatype:

```
CHAR[(maximum_size [BYTE | CHAR])] [NOT NULL]
```

The four ways to declare a variable using the CHAR datatype and a default null value are

```
var1 CHAR;           -- Implicitly sized at 1 byte.
var2 CHAR(1);        -- Explicitly sized at 1 byte.
var3 CHAR(1 BYTE);   -- Explicitly sized at 1 byte.
var4 CHAR(1 CHAR);   -- Explicitly sized at 1 character.
```

When you use character space allocation, the maximum size changes, depending on the character set of your database. Some character sets use 2 or 3 bytes to store characters. You divide 32,767 by the number of bytes required per character, which means the maximum for a CHAR is 16,383 for a 2-byte character set and 10,922 for a 3-byte character set.

You can use the NOT NULL clause to ensure a value is assigned to a CHAR variable. The general practice is to not restrict CHAR variables without other compelling business rationale.

The CHARACTER datatype is a subtype of the CHAR datatype. The CHARACTER datatype has the same value range as its base type. It is effectively an alias datatype and was formally known as an unconstrained subtype. Assignment between variables of CHAR and CHARACTER datatypes are implicitly converted, provided the variables have the same size.

The size for characters has two factors: the number of units allotted and the type of units allotted. A string of three characters (derived from the character set) cannot fit in a string of three bytes, and more naturally a string of three characters cannot fit in a string of two characters. Any attempt to make that type of assignment raises an ORA-06502, which means a character string buffer is too small to hold a value.

You can declare a CHAR subtype by using the following prototype:

```
SUBTYPE subtype_name IS base_type[(maximum_size [BYTE | CHAR])] [NOT NULL];
```

The following example creates and uses a constrained subtype CODE:

```
DECLARE
    SUBTYPE code IS CHAR(1 CHAR);
    c CHAR(1 CHAR) := 'A';
    d CODE;
BEGIN
    d := c;
END;
/
```

Characters and strings cannot specify character ranges. They can only set the maximum size. This differs from the subtyping behaviors of numbers because they can restrict ranges.

Globalization raises a host of issues with how you use variable-length strings. You should consider using NCHAR datatypes when managing multiple character sets or Unicode.

LONG and LONG RAW Datatypes The LONG and LONG RAW datatypes *are only provided for backward compatibility*. You should use the CLOB or NCLOB where you would use a LONG and the BLOB or BFILE instead of a LONG RAW. The LONG datatype stores character streams, and the LONG RAW stores binary strings.

The LONG and LONG RAW datatypes stores variable-length character strings up to 32,760 bytes in your PL/SQL programs. This limitation is much smaller than the 2 gigabytes that you can store in LONG or LONG RAW database columns. The LONG and LONG RAW datatype maximum size is actually smaller than the maximum for the CHAR, NCHAR, VARCHAR2, and NVARCHAR2 datatypes, and it is dwarfed by the 8 to 128 terabytes of the LOB datatypes.

The following are the prototypes for declaring the LONG and LONG RAW datatypes:

```
LONG [NOT NULL]
LONG RAW [NOT NULL]
```

You can use the NOT NULL clause to ensure a value is assigned to LONG and LONG RAW variables. The general *practice* is to not restrict these datatypes without some other compelling business rationale.

The LONG and LONG RAW datatypes can be declared with a default null value by

```
var1 LONG;          -- Implicitly sized at 0 byte.
var2 LONG RAW;      -- Implicitly sized at 0 byte.
```

You can define variables of these types and assign values by using the following syntax:

```
var1 LONG := 'CAR';
var2 LONG RAW := HEXTORAW('43'||'41'||'52'); -- CAR assigned in Hexadecimal.
```

While the LONG datatype is easy to use, it is tiny by comparison to the CLOB and NCLOB datatypes. The CHAR or VARCHAR2 datatypes also store seven bytes more character data than the LONG datatype.

TIP
You should consider using variable datatypes that map to your column datatypes because over time it is simpler (cheaper) for maintenance programmers to support. It is advisable that you migrate LONG column datatypes to LOBs.

You should note that the HEXTORAW() function is required to convert hexadecimal streams into raw streams before assignment to LONG RAW datatypes. An attempt to assign an unconverted character stream raises an ORA-06502 as a hexadecimal-to-raw conversion error. Also, you should note that the LONG RAW data stream is not interpreted by PL/SQL.

ROWID and UROWID Datatypes   The ROWID datatype maps to the pseudocolumn ROWID in any Oracle database table. You can convert it from a ROWID to an 18-character string by using the ROWIDTOCHAR() function, or back from a character string using the CHARTOROWID() function. Appendix J covers these two built-in functions. An invalid conversion between a string and a ROWID raises a SYS_INVALID_ROWID error.

NOTE
The ROWID datatype is now only provided for backward compatibility, and it is recommended that you use the universal rowid (UROWID) data type.

The UROWID datatype is the *universal rowid*. It works with logical ROWID identifiers stored by an indexed-organized table, whereas the ROWID datatype doesn't. You should use the UROWID value for all Oracle ROWID management in PL/SQL programs, and when you are working with non-Oracle ROWID values.

The following are the prototypes for declaring the ROWID and UROWID datatypes:

```
ROWID
UROWID
```

Implicit conversion works well for both ROWID and UROWID types. There is seldom any need to use either the ROWIDTOCHAR() or CHARTOROWID() function.

VARCHAR2 Datatype   The VARCHAR2 datatype is a base datatype for *variable*-length strings. You can size a VARCHAR2 datatype up to 32,767 bytes in length. Unfortunately, a PL/SQL VARCHAR2 datatype can be larger than the 4,000-byte maximum stored in a SQL VARCHAR2 column. You can store character strings larger than 4,000 bytes in CLOB or LONG columns. Oracle recommends you use the CLOB datatype because the LONG datatype is only supported for backward compatibility purposes.

The following is the prototype for declaring a VARCHAR2 datatype:

```
VARCHAR2(maximum_size [BYTE | CHAR]) [NOT NULL]
```

You can use the NOT NULL clause to ensure a value is assigned to a VARCHAR2 variable. The general practice is to not restrict variable-length strings without some other compelling business rationale. You should consider creating a subtype that enforces the constraint.

You may notice that the physical size is required for VARCHAR2 datatypes, whereas it is optional for the CHAR datatype and its subtypes. Physical size is required because the database needs to know how much space to allocate for a variable using this datatype. When you size a VARCHAR2 variable with 2,000 or more bytes of space, the PL/SQL engine only allocates enough space to manage the physical data value. This typically optimizes your program run time.

TIP
Oracle 11g allocates 1,999 bytes when you declare a VARCHAR2 variable of 1,999 bytes regardless of the physical size of your data. Large variable-length strings should always be defined to be 2,000 bytes or greater.

There are three ways to define a VARCHAR2 variable with a default null value:

```
var1 VARCHAR2(100);      -- Explicitly sized at 100 byte.
var2 VARCHAR2(100 BYTE); -- Explicitly sized at 100 byte.
var3 VARCHAR2(100 CHAR); -- Explicitly sized at 100 character.
```

When you use character space allocation, the maximum size changes, depending on the character set of your database. Some character sets use two or three bytes to store characters. You divide 32,767 by the number of bytes required per character, which means the maximum for a VARCHAR2 is 16,383 for a two-byte character set and 10,922 for a three-byte character set.

The STRING and VARCHAR datatypes are subtypes of the VARCHAR2 datatype. They both have the same value range as the VARCHAR2 base type. They are effectively aliases and formally known as unconstrained subtypes. Assignments between variables of these subtypes are implicitly converted, provided the variables have the same size.

The size for strings has two factors: the number of units allotted and the type of units allotted. A string of three characters (derived from the character set) cannot fit in a string of three bytes, and more naturally a string of three characters cannot fit in a string of two characters. Any attempt to make that type of assignment raises an ORA-06502, which means a character string buffer is too small to hold a value.

You can declare a VARCHAR2 subtype by using the following prototype:

```
SUBTYPE subtype_name IS base_type(maximum_size [BYTE | CHAR]) [NOT NULL];
```

The following example creates a constrained subtype DB_STRING:

```
DECLARE
  SUBTYPE db_string IS VARCHAR2(4000 BYTE);
  c VARCHAR2(1 CHAR) := 'A';
  d DB_STRING;
BEGIN
  d := c;
END;
/
```

The example creates a subtype that cannot exceed the physical limit for a VARCHAR2 column. It works uniformly regardless of the database character set. This can be useful when you want to ensure compliance to physical database limits in PL/SQL code blocks.

Strings cannot specify character ranges the way that number subtypes can specify number ranges. They can only set the maximum size, which can be overridden by declaring the subtype with a new maximum size less than or equal to 32,767 bytes.

Globalization raises a host of issues with how you use variable-length strings. You should consider using NVARCHAR2 datatypes when managing multiple character sets or Unicode.

Dates, Times, and Intervals

The DATE datatype is the base type for dates, times, and intervals. There are two subtypes to manage intervals and three to manage timestamps. The next three subsections cover date, intervals, and timestamps.

DATE Datatype   The DATE datatype in Oracle contains an actual timestamp of activity. The valid range is any date from January 1, 4712 BCE (Before Common Era) to December 31, 9999 CE (Common Era). The most common way to capture a timestamp is to assign the SYSDATE or SYSTIMESTAMP built-in function. They both return fully qualified dates and contain all field elements of a DATE variable or column. The field index for a DATE datatype are in Table 3-2.

Field Name	Valid Range	Valid Internal Values
YEAR	–4712 to 9999 (excluding year 0)	Any nonzero integer
MONTH	01 to 12	0 to 11
DAY	01 to 31 (limited by calendar rules)	Any nonzero integer
HOUR	00 to 23	0 to 23
MINUTE	00 to 59	0 to 59
SECOND	00 to 59	0 to 59.9 (where tenths are the fractional interval second)
TIMEZONE_HOUR	–12 to 14 (range adjusts for daylight saving time changes)	Not applicable
TIMEZONE_MINUTE	00 to 59	Not applicable
TIMEZONE_REGION	Value in V$TIMEZONE_NAMES	Not applicable
TIMEZONE_ABBR	Value in V$TIMEZONE_NAMES	Not applicable

TABLE 3-2   *DATE Datatype Field Index*

The following is the prototype for declaring a DATE datatype:

```
DATE [NOT NULL]
```

You can use the NOT NULL clause to ensure a value is assigned to a DATE variable. There are many cases where you will want to restrict DATE variables. If you don't restrict them, then you'll need to wrap them in NVL() built-in functions to support logical comparisons.

You can define a DATE variable with a default null or initialized value, as shown:

```
var1 DATE;                 -- Implicitly assigns a null value.
var2 DATE := SYSDATE;      -- Explicitly assigns current server timestamp.
var3 DATE := SYSDATE + 1;  -- Explicitly assigns tomorrow server timestamp.
var4 DATE := '29-FEB-08';  -- Explicitly assigns leap year day for 2008.
```

The TO_DATE() function can also convert non-conforming date formats into valid DATE values. Alternatively, the CAST() function also works with the default format mask. *The default format masks for dates are* DD-MON-RR or DD-MON-YYYY.

Use the TRUNC(*date_variable*) when you want to extract a date from a timestamp. This is useful when you want to find all transactions that occurred on a particular day. By default the TRUNC() built-in function shaves off the time, making a date with 00 hours, 00 minutes, and 00 seconds. The following program demonstrates the concept:

```
DECLARE
  d DATE := SYSDATE;
BEGIN
  dbms_output.put_line(TO_CHAR(TRUNC(d),'DD-MON-YY HH24:MI:SS'));
END;
/
```

Running this script produces this:

```
31-JUL-07 00:00:00
```

The EXTRACT() built-in function also lets you capture the numeric month, year, or day from a DATE value. Appendix J lists other functions that let you manipulate DATE datatypes.

You can declare a DATE subtype by using the following prototype:

```
SUBTYPE subtype_name IS base_type [NOT NULL];
```

You should note that as when using the character subtypes, you cannot set a date range. Creating a DATE subtype that requires a value is possible. Using DATEN for a null required DATE follows the convention used by the NATURALN and POSITVEN subtypes.

Interval Subtypes   You have two DATE subtypes that let you manage intervals: INTERVAL DAY TO SECOND and INTERVAL YEAR TO MONTH. Their prototypes are

```
INTERVAL DAY[(leading_precision)] TO SECOND[(fractional_second_precision)]
INTERVAL YEAR[(precision)] TO MONTH
```

The default value for the day's leading precision is 2, and the second's fractional second precision is 6. The default value for the year's precision is 2.

You can define an INTERVAL DATE TO SECOND variable with a default null or initialized value, as shown:

```
var1 INTERVAL DAY TO SECOND;        -- Implicitly accept default precisions.
var2 INTERVAL DAY(3) TO SECOND;     -- Explicitly set day precision.
var3 INTERVAL DAY(3) TO SECOND(9); -- Explicitly set day and second precision.
```

You assign a variable value by using the following prototype for an INTERVAL DAY TO SECOND datatype, where D stands for day and HH:MI:SS stands for hours, minutes, and seconds respectively:

```
variable_name := 'D HH:MI:SS';
```

An actual assignment to the same type would look like

```
var1 := '5 08:21:20';  -- Implicit conversion from the string.
```

You can declare an INTERVAL YEAR TO MONTH variable with a default null or initialized value, as shown:

```
var1 INTERVAL YEAR TO MONTH;        -- Implicitly accept default precisions.
var2 INTERVAL YEAR(3) TO MONTH;     -- Explicitly set year precision.
```

There are four assignments methods. The following program demonstrates an assignment to var2:

```
DECLARE
  var2 INTERVAL YEAR(3) TO MONTH;
BEGIN
  -- Shorthand for a 101 year and 3 month interval.
  var2 := '101-3';
  var2 := INTERVAL '101-3' YEAR TO MONTH;
  var2 := INTERVAL '101' YEAR;
  var2 := INTERVAL '3' MONTH;
END;
/
```

This would output the following values, respectively:

```
+101-03
+101-03
+101-00
+000-03
```

Arithmetic operations between the DATE datatype and interval subtypes follow the rules in Table 3-3. The classic operation is an interval calculation, like subtracting one timestamp from another to get the number of days between dates.

The intervals simplify advanced comparisons but do require a bit of work to master. More information on this SQL and PL/SQL datatype is in the *Oracle Database SQL Language Reference* and the *Oracle Database Advanced Application Developer's Guide.*

Operand 1 Type	Operator	Operand 2 Type	Result Type
Timestamp	+	Interval	Timestamp
Timestamp	-	Interval	Timestamp
Interval	+	Timestamp	Timestamp
Timestamp	-	Interval	Interval
Interval	+	Interval	Interval
Interval	-	Interval	Interval
Interval	*	Numeric	Interval
Numeric	*	Interval	Interval
Interval	/	Numeric	Interval

TABLE 3-3   *Timestamp and Interval Arithmetic*

TIMESTAMP Subtypes   The TIMESTAMP subtype extends the DATE base type by providing a more precise time. You'll get the same results if the TIMESTAMP variable is populated by calling the SYSDATE built in. The SYSTIMESTAMP provides a more precise time dependent on platform.

The following is the prototype for declaring a TIMESTAMP datatype:

```
TIMESTAMP[(precision)] [NOT NULL]
```

You can use the NOT NULL clause to ensure a value is assigned to a TIMESTAMP variable. There are many cases where you will want to restrict TIMESTAMP variables. If you don't restrict them, then you'll need to wrap them in NVL() built-in functions to support logical comparisons.

You can define a TIMESTAMP variable with a default null or initialized value, as shown:

```
var1 TIMESTAMP;                     -- Implicitly assigns a null value.
var2 TIMESTAMP := SYSTIMESTAMP;     -- Explicitly assigns a value.
var3 TIMESTAMP(3);                  -- Explicitly sets precision for null value.
var4 TIMESTAMP(3) := SYSTIMESTAMP;  -- Explicitly sets precision and value.
```

The following program demonstrates the difference between the DATE and TIMESTAMP datatypes:

```
DECLARE
  d DATE := SYSTIMESTAMP;
  t TIMESTAMP(3) := SYSTIMESTAMP;
BEGIN
  dbms_output.put_line('DATE      ['||d||']');
  dbms_output.put_line('TO_CHAR   ['||TO_CHAR(d,'DD-MON-YY HH24:MI:SS')||']');
  dbms_output.put_line('TIMESTAMP ['||t||']');
END;
/
```

The anonymous block returns

```
DATE      [31-JUL-07]
TO_CHAR   [31-JUL-07 21:27:36]
TIMESTAMP [31-JUL-07 09.27.36.004 PM]
```

The other two timestamp subtypes demonstrate similar behaviors. Their prototypes are

```
TIMESTAMP[(precision)] WITH TIME ZONE
TIMESTAMP[(precision)] WITH LOCAL TIME ZONE
```

You can declare a TIMESTAMP WITH TIME ZONE variable with a default null or initialized value, as shown:

```
var1 TIMESTAMP WITH LOCAL TIME ZONE;
var2 TIMESTAMP WITH LOCAL TIME ZONE := SYSTIMESTAMP;
var3 TIMESTAMP(3) WITH LOCAL TIME ZONE;
var4 TIMESTAMP(3) WITH LOCAL TIME ZONE := SYSTIMESTAMP;
```

The difference between these timestamps is that those with time zones append the time zone to the timestamp. The time zone qualifier returns the standard time and an indicator whether the time zone is using daylight saving time. The local time zone qualifier returns the difference between the local time and Greenwich Mean Time (GMT).

Unicode Characters and Strings

Unicode characters and strings exist to support globalization. Globalization is accomplished by using character encoding that supports multiple character sets. AL16UTF16 or UTF8 encoding are provided by the Oracle database. AL16UTF16 encoding stores all characters in two physical bytes, while UTF8 encoding stores all characters in three physical bytes.

The NCHAR datatype is a Unicode equivalent to the CHAR datatype, and the NVARCHAR2 datatype is a Unicode equivalent to the VARCHAR2 datatype. You should use these datatypes when building applications that will support multiple character sets in the same database.

NCHAR Datatype   The NCHAR datatype is a base datatype for *variable* Unicode strings. The NCHAR datatype shares the 32,767 bytes maximum length for other character and string datatypes. You can store a maximum length of 16,383 (32,767 divided by 2) characters using AL16UTF16 encoding or 10,922 (32,767 divided by 3) characters using UTF8 encoding.

Like the CHAR datatype, the NCHAR datatype is also a *fixed*-length string datatype. A fixed-length string sets the physical size of the variable in memory notwithstanding the actual size of the value inside the variable.

The PL/SQL NCHAR datatype can be larger than the 4,000-byte maximum stored in a SQL NCHAR column. You should store Unicode character strings larger than 4,000 bytes in NCLOB columns.

The following is the prototype for declaring a NCHAR datatype:

```
NCHAR[(maximum_size)] [NOT NULL]
```

You may notice that the physical size for NCHAR datatype differs from that of the CHAR and VARCHAR2 datatypes. There is no option to specify bytes or characters when declaring the space allocation for NCHAR variables. Unicode space is always allocated in characters by a numeric literal.

You can use the NOT NULL clause to ensure a value is assigned to a NCHAR variable. The general practice is to not restrict string variables without some other compelling business rationale.

There is only one way to define a NCHAR variable with a default null value:

```
var1 NCHAR;           -- Implicitly sized at 1 character.

var1 NCHAR(100);      -- Explicitly sized at 100 character.
```

You can declare a NCHAR subtype by using the following prototype:

```
SUBTYPE subtype_name IS base_type(maximum_size) [NOT NULL];
```

The maximum size changes are dependent on the Unicode character encoding. As mentioned, the maximum is 16,383 characters using AL16UTF16 encoding or 10,922 characters using UTF8 encoding. Any attempt to specify a maximum size with a BYTE keyword raises an error disallowing the byte semantic, which is a PLS-00639 error code.

Globalization is best suited to NCHAR or NVARCHAR2 datatypes. You should use these types when the database supports Unicode or may support it in the future.

NVARCHAR2 Datatype   The NVARCHAR2 datatype is a base datatype for *variable* Unicode strings. NVARCHAR2 datatypes share the 32,767 bytes maximum length for other character and string datatypes. You can store a maximum length of 16,383 (32,767 divided by 2) characters using AL16UTF16 encoding or 10,922 (32,767 divided by 3) characters using UTF8 encoding.

Like other character types, the PL/SQL NVARCHAR2 datatype can be larger than the 4,000-byte maximum stored in a SQL NVARCHAR2 column. You should store Unicode character strings larger than 4,000 bytes in NCLOB columns.

The following is the prototype for declaring a NVARCHAR2 datatype:

```
NVARCHAR2(maximum_size) [NOT NULL]
```

You may notice that the physical size for NVARCHAR2 datatype differs from that of the CHAR and VARCHAR2 datatypes. There is no option to specify bytes or characters when declaring the space allocation for NVARCHAR2 variables. Unicode space is always allocated in characters by a numeric literal.

You can use the NOT NULL clause to ensure a value is assigned to a NVARCHAR2 variable. The general practice is to not restrict string variables without some other compelling business rationale. You should consider creating a subtype that enforces the constraint.

There is only one way to define a NVARCHAR2 variable with a default null value:

```
var1 NVARCHAR2(100); -- Explicitly sized at 100 character.
```

You can define a NVARCHAR2 subtype by using the following prototype:

```
SUBTYPE subtype_name IS base_type(maximum_size) [NOT NULL];
```

The maximum size changes are dependent on the Unicode character encoding. As mentioned, the maximum is 16,383 characters using AL16UTF16 encoding or 10,922 characters using UTF8 encoding. Any attempt to specify a maximum size with a BYTE keyword raises an error disallowing the byte semantic, which is a PLS-00639 error code.

Globalization is best suited to NCHAR or NVARCHAR2 datatypes. You should use these types when the database supports Unicode or may support it in the future.

Numbers

There are four principal number datatypes. The datatypes are the BINARY_INTEGER, IEEE 754-format (BINARY_DOUBLE and BINARY_FLOAT), NUMBER, and PLS_INTEGER. The BINARY_INTEGER and PLS_INTEGER datatypes are identical, and they both use the native operating system math libraries. Oracle uses PLS_INTEGER to describe both BINARY_INTEGER and PLS_INTEGER as interchangeable, and so does this book.

IEEE 754–format numbers both provide single- and double-precision numbers to support scientific computing. The NUMBER datatype uses a custom library provided as part of the Oracle 11*g* Database. It can store very large fixed-point or floating-point numbers.

BINARY_INTEGER Datatype The BINARY_INTEGER datatype is identical to PLS_INTEGER and stores integer numbers from –2,147,483,648 to 2,147,483,647 as 32 bits or 4 bytes. Like the PLS_INTEGER type, it computes more efficiently within its number range and takes much less space than a NUMBER datatype in memory. Math operations using two BINARY_INTEGER variables that yield a result outside of the datatype range will raise an ORA-01426 numeric overflow error.

The following is the prototype for declaring a BINARY_INTEGER datatype:

```
BINARY_INTEGER
```

You can define a BINARY_INTEGER variable with null value or initialized during declaration. The syntax for both follows:

```
var1 BINARY_INTEGER;
var2 BINARY_INTEGER := 21;
```

The BINARY_INTEGER uses native math libraries, and as such the declaration statement does not allocate memory to store the variable until a value is assigned.

You can define a BINARY_INTEGER subtype by using the following prototype:

```
SUBTYPE subtype_name IS base_type [RANGE low_number..high_number] [NOT NULL];
```

There are several predefined subtypes of the BINARY_INTEGER type. The NATURAL and POSITIVE subtypes restrict their use to only positive integer values. The NATURALN and POSITIVEN subtypes restrict null assignments. A PLS-00218 error is raised when you attempt to declare a NATURALN or POSITIVEN without initializing the value. They both enforce a not-null constraint on the datatype.

The newest subtype is the SIMPLE_INTEGER datatype introduced in Oracle 11*g*. It truncates overflow and suppresses the raising of any error related to overflow. The performance of the SIMPLE_INTEGER type is dependent on the value of the plsql_code_type database parameter. The performance is superior when plsql_code_type is set to NATIVE because arithmetic operations are performed with the operating system libraries and both overflow and null value checking are disabled. Performance is slower when the plsql_code_type is set to INTERPRETED because it prevents overload and performs null value checking.

NOTE
Overloading behavior of base types and subtypes in PL/SQL packages is typically disallowed, but the same name or positional formal parameter can be overloaded by using PLS_INTEGER *or* BINARY_INTEGER *in one signature and* SIMPLE_INTEGER *in another.*

You should also know that a casting operation from a `PLS_INTEGER` or `BINARY_INTEGER` to a `SIMPLE_INTEGER` does no conversion unless the value is null. A run-time error is thrown when casting a null value to a `SIMPLE_INTEGER` variable.

IEEE 754–Format Datatype   IEEE 754–format single-precision and double-precision numbers are provided to support scientific computing. They bring with them traditional overflow and infinities problems as part of their definition and implementation.

Both the SQL and PL/SQL environments define the `BINARY_FLOAT_NAN` and `BINARY_FLOAT_INFINITY` constants. The PL/SQL environment also defines four other constants. All six are found with their values in Table 3-4.

NOTE
Oracle 11g Database documentation does not list these constants in the reserved word or keyword lists. They can be found by printing them from a PL/SQL program or querying the `V$RESERVED_WORDS` *table.*

The following is the prototype for declaring IEE-754 datatypes:

```
BINARY_DOUBLE
BINARY_FLOAT
```

You can define variables of these types with null values or initialize them during declaration. The syntax for both follows:

```
var1 BINARY_DOUBLE;
var2 BINARY_DOUBLE := 21d;
var3 BINARY_FLOAT;
var4 BINARY_FLOAT := 21f;
```

Constant Name	Environment	Value
BINARY_FLOAT_NAN	SQL & PL/SQL	It contains Nan, but comparison operations treat it as a case-insensitive string. NaN in scientific notation means *Not a Number*.
BINARY_FLOAT_INFINITY	SQL & PL/SQL	It contains Inf, but comparison operations treat it as a case-insensitive string.
BINARY_FLOAT_MIN_NORMAL	PL/SQL	It contains 1.17549435E-038.
BINARY_FLOAT_MAX_NORMAL	PL/SQL	It contains 3.40282347E+038.
BINARY_FLOAT_MIN_SUBNORMAL	PL/SQL	It contains 1.40129846E-045.
BINARY_FLOAT_MAX_SUBNORMAL	PL/SQL	It contains 1.17549421E-038.

TABLE 3-4   *IEEE-754 Constants*

You must always use a d for numeric literals assigned to a BINARY_DOUBLE and an f for numeric literals assigned to a BINARY_FLOAT. The Oracle 11g Database overloads subroutines that leverage the processing speed of these IEEE-754 datatypes.

You can also define a BINARY_DOUBLE or BINARY_FLOAT subtype by using the following prototype:

```
SUBTYPE subtype_name IS base_type [NOT NULL];
```

You should note that unlike other number datatypes, these cannot be range constrained. The only constraint that you can impose is that the subtypes disallow null value assignments.

NUMBER Datatype   The NUMBER datatype uses a custom library provided as part of the Oracle 11g Database. It can store numbers in the range of 1.0E-130 (1 times 10 raised to the negative 130th power) to 1.0E126 (1 times 10 raised to the 126th power). Oracle recommends using the NUMBER datatype only when the use or computation result falls in the range of possible values. The NUMBER datatype does not raise a NaN (not a number) or infinity error when a literal or computational value is outside the datatype range. These exceptions have the following outcomes:

- A literal value below the minimum range value stores a zero in a NUMBER variable.

- A literal value above the maximum range value raises a compilation error.

- A computational outcome above the maximum range value raises a compilation error.

The NUMBER datatype supports fixed-point and floating-point numbers. Fixed-point numbers are defined by specifying the number of digits (known as the precision) and the number of digits to the right of the decimal point (known as the scale). The decimal point is not physically stored in the variable because it is calculated by the relationship between the precision and the scale.

The following is the prototype for declaring a fixed-point NUMBER datatype:

```
NUMBER[(precision, [scale])] [NOT NULL]
```

Both precision and scale are optional values when you declare a NUMBER variable. The NUMBER datatype default size, number of digits, or precision is 38. You can declare a NUMBER variable with only the precision, but you must specify the precision to define the scale.

You can declare fixed-point NUMBER variables with null values or define them during declaration. The syntax for NUMBER datatype declarations with null values is

```
var1 NUMBER;              -- A null number with 38 digits.
var2 NUMBER(15);          -- A null number with 15 digits.
var3 NUMBER(15,2);        -- A null number with 15 digits and 2 decimals.
```

The syntax for NUMBER datatype declarations with initialized values is

```
var1 NUMBER := 15;           -- A number with 38 digits.
var2 NUMBER(15) := 15;       -- A number with 15 digits.
var3 NUMBER(15,2) := 15.22;  -- A number with 15 digits and 2 decimals.
```

You can also declare fixed-point numbers by using the DEC, DECIMAL, and NUMERIC subtypes. Alternatively, you can declare integers using the INTEGER, INT, and SMALLINT subtypes. They all have the same maximum precision of 38.

The following are prototypes for declaring a floating-point NUMBER datatype, known as DOUBLE PRECISION or FLOAT subtypes:

```
DOUBLE PRECISION[(precision)]
FLOAT[(precision)]
```

Defining the precision of DOUBLE PRECISION or FLOAT variables is optional. You risk losing the natural precision of a floating-point number when you constrain the precision. Both of these variables have a default size, number of digits, or precision of 126. You can define the precision of a FLOAT variable, but not the scale. Any attempt to define the scale of either of these subtypes raises a PLS-00510 error because they cannot have a fixed number of digits to the right of the decimal point.

The syntax for DOUBLE PRECISION or FLOAT declarations with null values is

```
var1 DOUBLE PRECISION;        -- A null number with 126 digits.
var2 FLOAT;                   -- A null number with 15 digits.
var3 DOUBLE PRECISION;        -- A null number with 126 digits.
var4 FLOAT(15);               -- A null number with 15 digits.
```

The syntax for DOUBLE PRECISION or FLOAT declarations with initialized values is

```
var1 DOUBLE PRECISION := 15;     -- A number with 126 digits.
var2 FLOAT := 15;                -- A number with 126 digits.
var3 DOUBLE PRECISION(15) := 15; -- A number with 15 digits.
var4 FLOAT(15) := 15;            -- A number with 15 digits.
```

You also have the REAL subtype of NUMBER that stores floating-point numbers but only uses a precision of 63 digits. The REAL subtype provides 18-digit precision to the right of the decimal point.

PLS_INTEGER Datatype   The PLS_INTEGER and BINARY_INTEGER datatypes are identical and use operating system–specific arithmetic for calculations. They can store integer numbers from –2,147,483,648 to 2,147,483,647 as 32 bits or 4 bytes. The PLS_INTEGER takes much less space than a NUMBER datatype to store in memory. It also computes more efficiently, provided the numbers and result of the math operation are within its number range. You should note that any math operation that yields a result outside of the range will raise an ORA-01426 numeric overflow error. The error is raised even when you assign the result of the mathematical operation to a NUMBER datatype.

The following is the prototype for defining a NVARCHAR2 datatype:

```
PLS_INTEGER
```

You can declare a PLS_INTEGER variable with a null value or initialized during declaration. The syntax for both follows:

```
var1 PLS_INTEGER;      -- A null value requires no space.
var2 PLS_INTEGER := 11; -- An integer requires space for each character.
```

The PLS_INTEGER uses native math libraries, and as such, the declaration statement doesn't allocate memory to store the variable until a value is assigned. You can test this by using the LENGTH() built-in function.

The LENGTH() Built-in Function

This behavior is consistent with what you'll see writing C or C++ programs. When a value is assigned, the `LENGTH()` built-in function returns the number of characters, not the number of bytes required for storage. This means that a `PLS_INTEGER` with five or six numbers would appear to have a character length of 5 or 6 respectively but actually only takes four bytes of space in both cases. This result appears linked to how the `NUMBER` datatype works, where `NUMBER` column values are stored as C single-dimensional character arrays. The `LENGTH()` function appears to count the positions in all number datatypes.

You can declare a `PLS_INTEGER` subtype by using the following prototype:

```
SUBTYPE subtype_name IS base_type [RANGE low_number..high_number] [NOT NULL];
```

NOTE
Don't confuse a `PLS_INTEGER` with an `INTEGER`. The former uses operating system mathematics libraries, while the latter is a subtype of the `NUMBER` base type.

Large Objects (LOBs)

Large objects (LOBs) provide you with four datatypes – `BFILE`, `BLOB`, `CLOB`, and `NCLOB`. The `BFILE` is a datatype that points to an external file, which limits its maximum size to 4 gigabytes. The `BLOB`, `CLOB` and `NCLOB` are internally managed types, and their maximum size is 8 to 128 terabytes, depending on the `db_block_size` parameter value.

LOB columns contain a locator that points to where the actual data is stored. You must access a LOB value in the scope of a transaction. You essentially use the locator as a route to read data from or write data to the LOB column. Chapter 8 provides details of how you access LOB columns and work with LOB datatypes, including the `DBMS_LOB` built-in package.

BFILE Datatype

The `BFILE` datatype is a read-only datatype *except for setting the virtual directory and file name for the external file.* You use the built-in `BFILENAME()` function to set locator information for a `BFILE` column. Before you use the `BFILENAME()` function, there are several setup steps. You must create a physical directory on the server, store the file in the directory, create a virtual directory that points to the physical directory, and grant read permissions on the directory to the schema that owns the table or the stored program that accesses the `BFILE` column.

You retrieve the descriptor (the column name), alias (a virtual directory to the physical directory location), and filename by using the `FILEGETNAME()` procedure from the `DBMS_LOB` package. The database `session_max_open_files` parameter sets the maximum number of open `BFILE` columns. Chapter 8 assembles how these pieces fit together and provides you with some stored program units to simplify the process.

The following is the prototype for declaring a `BFILE` datatype:

```
BFILE
```

There is one way to define a `BFILE` variable, and it always contains a null reference by default:

```
var1 BFILE;        -- Declare a null reference to a BFILE.
```

A BFILE cannot be defined with a reference unless you write a wrapper to the DBMS_LOB. FILEGETNAME() procedure. Chapter 8 provides a wrapper function and explanation of the limitations that require the wrapper function.

BLOB Datatype

The BLOB column is a read-write binary large datatype. BLOB datatypes participate in transactions and are recoverable. You can only read and write between BLOB variables and database columns in a transaction scope. BLOB datatypes are objects and treated differently than scalar variables. They have three possible states: null, empty and populated (not empty). They require initialization by the empty_blob() function to move from a null reference to an empty state, or a direct hexadecimal assignment to become populated.

BLOBs can store binary files between 8 and 32 terabytes. Unfortunately, you can only access BLOB columns by using the DBMS_LOB package to read and write values after the initial assignment of a value.

PL/SQL lets you declare local BLOB variables in your anonymous and named blocks. However, you must establish an active link between your program and the stored BLOB column to insert, append, or read the column value. Generally, you'll want to only read or store chunks of large BLOB values, or you may exhaust your system resources.

The following is the prototype for declaring a BLOB datatype:

```
BLOB
```

There is one way to declare a BLOB variable with a default null reference:

```
var1 BLOB;                        -- Declare a null reference to a BLOB.
```

There are two ways to define an empty and populated BLOB variable:

```
var1 BLOB := empty_blob();        -- Declare an empty BLOB.
var2 BLOB := '43'||'41'||'52';    -- Declare a hexadecimal BLOB for CAR.
```

BLOB datatypes are especially useful when you want to store large image files, movies, or other binary files. Their utility depends a great deal on how well you write the interface. Chapter 8 discusses ways to handle interactions between BLOB columns and PL/SQL variables.

CLOB Datatype

The CLOB column is a read-write character large datatype. CLOB datatypes participate in transactions and are recoverable. You can only read and write between CLOB variables and database columns in a transaction scope. CLOB datatypes are objects like the BLOB and are treated differently than scalar variables. They also have three possible states: they can be null, empty, or populated (not empty). CLOBs require initialization by the empty_clob() function to move from a null reference to an empty state, or from a direct character assignment to becoming populated.

CLOBs can store character files between 8 and 32 terabytes. CLOBs also suffer from the same limitation as non-Unicode variable types. Space allocation is in bytes, while the Unicode encoding is done in characters defined by 2 or 3 bytes each. As with BLOBs, you can only access CLOB columns by using the DBMS_LOB package to read and write values after the initial assignment of a value.

PL/SQL lets you declare local CLOB variables in your anonymous and named blocks. As with BLOBs, you must establish an active link between your program and the stored CLOB column to insert, append, or read the column value. Generally, you'll want to only read or store chunks of large CLOB values, or you may exhaust your system resources.

The following is the prototype for declaring a CLOB datatype:

```
CLOB
```

There is one way to define a CLOB variable with a default null reference:

```
var1 CLOB;                  -- Declare a null reference to a CLOB.
```

There are two ways to define an empty CLOB variable and a populated one:

```
var1 CLOB := empty_clob();  -- Declare an empty CLOB.
var2 CLOB := 'CAR';         -- Declare a CLOB for CAR.
```

CLOB datatypes are especially useful when you want to store large text files. Examples of large text files are customer notes that support transactions, refunds, or other activities. Large text elements are suited to reading and writing only small chunks at a time. Otherwise, you'll exhaust your system resources. Chapter 8 discusses ways to handle interactions between CLOB columns and PL/SQL variables.

NCLOB Datatype

The NCLOB column is a read-write Unicode character large datatype. NCLOB datatypes participate in transactions and are recoverable. You can only read and write between NCLOB variables and database columns in a transaction scope. NCLOB datatypes are objects like the BLOB and CLOB and are treated differently than scalar variables. They also have three possible states. They can be null, empty, or populated (not empty). NCLOBs require initialization by the same empty_clob() function used to initialize a CLOB variable or column. The empty_clob() function changes the null reference to an empty state. Alternatively, you can make a direct character string assignment to populate the variable.

NCLOBs can store Unicode character files between 8 and 32 terabytes. Unicode character string limitations set the maximum size relative to the database character set. Some character sets use 2 or 3 bytes to store characters. You divide the maximum size (8 to 32 gigabytes) by the number of bytes required per character, which means the maximum for a NCLOB is 4 to 16 gigabyte for a 2-byte character set (AL16UTF16), and 2.67 to 8.66 gigabyte for a 3-byte character set (UTF8). As with BLOBs and CLOBs, you can only access NCLOB columns by using the DBMS_LOB package to read and write values after the initial assignment of a value.

PL/SQL lets you declare local NCLOB variables in your anonymous and named blocks. As with BLOBs and CLOBs, you must establish an active link between your program and the stored NCLOB column to insert, append, or read the column value. Generally, you'll want to only read or store chunks of large NCLOB values, or you may exhaust your system resources.

The following is the prototype for declaring a NCLOB datatype:

```
NCLOB
```

There is one way to define a NCLOB variable with a default null reference:

```
var1 NCLOB;                 -- Declare a null reference to a NCLOB.
```

There are two ways to define an empty and populated NCLOB variable:

```
var1 NCLOB := empty_clob(); -- Declare an empty NCLOB.
var2 NCLOB := 'CAR';        -- Declare a NCLOB for CAR.
```

NCLOB datatypes are especially useful when you want to store large text files. Examples of large text files are customer notes that support transactions, refunds, or other activities. Large text elements are suited to reading and writing only small chunks at a time. Otherwise, you'll exhaust your system resources. Chapter 8 discusses ways to interact between NCLOB columns and PL/SQL variables.

Composite Datatypes

There are two composite generalized datatypes: records and collections. A record, also known as a structure, typically contains a collection of related elements like a normalized database table. Collections are sets of like things. The things can be scalar variables, large objects, user-defined objects (see Chapter 8), or records.

The next two subsections describe the declaration of records and collections. The book implements records throughout the book. While records are not primitives, they are essential structures in the language. Chapter 7 covers collections in detail.

Records

A record datatype is a structure. A structure is a composite variable that contains a list of variables that typically have names and different datatypes. You define a record datatype either implicitly or explicitly. There are restrictions on the use of implicitly built records. You cannot use an implicitly built record in an array. The %ROWTYPE enables you to define an implicitly anchored record type. When you want to build a record and use it in another record or array, you must build the record explicitly.

The following is the prototype for explicitly defining a record datatype:

```
TYPE type_name IS RECORD
( element1     sql_datatype | plsql_datatype [NOT NULL][[DEFAULT | :=] literal]
, element2     sql_datatype | plsql_datatype [NOT NULL][[DEFAULT | :=] literal]
, element(n+1) sql_datatype | plsql_datatype [NOT NULL][[DEFAULT | :=] literal]
);
```

The sql_datatype of an element in the explicitly defined record type can use an implicitly anchored column. You anchor the column using %TYPE attribute. The plsql_datatype of an element in the explicitly defined record type can use an implicitly anchored record type (using the %ROWTYPE). After you define the record type, it is available as a local datatype. You can declare a variable using the record datatype in both anonymous- and named-block programs.

The following demonstrates declaration of an initialized structure:

```
DECLARE
  TYPE demo_record_type IS RECORD
  ( id      NUMBER        DEFAULT  1
  , value   VARCHAR2(10)  :=       'One');
  demo DEMO_RECORD_TYPE;
BEGIN
  dbms_output.put_line('['||demo.id||']['||demo.value||']');
END;
/
```

The execution block prints the contents of the record by using dot notation. The dot is the component selector from earlier Table 3-1. The component selector separates the variable and element names. This is also called attribute chaining in some Oracle documentation.

It is also possible to nest records. You access the names of the nested records by using another component selector, or period, as shown:

```
DECLARE
  TYPE full_name IS RECORD
  ( first    VARCHAR2(10 CHAR) := 'John'
  , last     VARCHAR2(10 CHAR) := 'Taylor');
  TYPE demo_record_type IS RECORD
  ( id          NUMBER       DEFAULT  1
  , contact   FULL_NAME);
  demo DEMO_RECORD_TYPE;
BEGIN
  dbms_output.put_line('['||demo.id||']');
  dbms_output.put_line('['||demo.contact.first||']['||demo.contact.last||']'
END;
/
```

Records are extremely useful when working with cursors and collections. Chapter 4 covers cursors because you need to understand iterative control structures to work with them. The next section, "Collections," shows how to build collections of records.

Records are exclusively available inside your PL/SQL execution scope. You can define a stored function to returning a record type, but that limits how you can use the function. *SQL can only access stored functions when they return SQL datatypes.* The alternative to returning a record type is a SQL object type. Chapter 14 covers object types, but you should note they are not available in Oracle 11*g* Express Edition. You can also return a record type by using a pipelined function that converts it into a single row aggregate table. Chapter 6 demonstrates how to implement pipelined functions.

Collections

Collections are arrays and lists. Arrays differ from lists in that they use a sequentially numbered index, while lists use a non-sequential numeric or unique string index. Arrays are densely populated lists because they have sequentially numbered indexes. While lists can have densely populated numeric indexes, they can also be sparsely populated. Sparsely populated means there are gaps in a sequence or they are not sequential.

Oracle supports three types of collections. Two are both SQL and PL/SQL datatypes, depending on how you define them: VARRAY and nested table. The third collection type is a PL/SQL-only datatype, called an associative array. The associative array is also known as a PL/SQL table or an index-by table. The subsections demonstrate how to declare collections of VARRAY, nested table, and associative array types. Chapter 7 covers collections in detail.

VARRAY Datatype   The VARRAY datatype is the most like a traditional array. Elements are of the same type and use a sequential numeric index. This means the index of VARRAY variables is densely populated. You opt to use a VARRAY when you know the number of items that will go in the collection before declaring the variable. Like arrays in other programming languages, the VARRAY cannot grow in size after it is declared. You should use a nested table or associative array when you aren't sure whether you know the maximum number values in advance.

There are two prototypes for a VARRAY because you can define it in SQL or PL/SQL. Also, you should note that the datatype is defined, not declared. This difference occurs because the VARRAY is an object type. Objects require explicit construction. Chapter 14 on object types explains more about how you construct objects.

A VARRAY has three states: defined, initialized, or allocated. You define a VARRAY by assigning it a name and a type. You initialize a VARRAY by calling a constructor, which is always the same name as the defined VARRAY datatype. You allocate space implicitly or by calling the EXTEND() method found in the collection API found in Chapter 7.

The following is the SQL prototype to define a VARRAY of scalar variables:

```
CREATE OR REPLACE TYPE varray_name AS VARRAY(maximum_size)
  OF sql_datatype [NOT NULL];
/
```

The following prototype defines a VARRAY of any datatype in a PL/SQL block:

```
TYPE varray_name IS VARRAY(maximum_size) OF [sql_datatype | plsql_datatype]
  [NOT NULL];
```

Both type definitions specify a fixed size. The maximum size limits the number of elements that you can store in a VARRAY. You can also define VARRAY variables that use SQL user-defined objects or PL/SQL record types. Chapter 14 shows you how to build VARRAY variables with user-defined object types. Chapter 7 shows you how to leverage PL/SQL record types in VARRAY variables.

There is one prototype for declaring a VARRAY collection, and there are two prototypes for defining a VARRAY collection. You can define a VARRAY collection as an initialized collection without allocating any memory, or as an initialized collection with allocated memory. You allocate memory by using a constructor that puts data into the collection.

The following are the aforementioned prototypes that you would use in a PL/SQL block:

```
var1 varray_name;
var2 varray_name := varray_name();
var3 varray_name := varray_name(value1, value2, .. ., value9, value10);
```

Calling the variable name of the VARRAY type without any arguments creates an empty but initialized variable. A like call of the variable name with arguments creates and allocates values to the VARRAY. Unless you have specified the not-null constraint, you can allocate space by assigning null values.

The following code demonstrates declaring a VARRAY of scalar variable:

```
DECLARE
  TYPE number_varray IS VARRAY(10) OF NUMBER;
  list   NUMBER_VARRAY := number_varray(1,2,3,4,5,6,7,8,NULL,NULL);
BEGIN
  FOR i IN 1..list.LIMIT LOOP
    dbms_output.put('['||list(i)||']');
  END LOOP;
  dbms_output.new_line;
END;
/
```

The program prints the following to the console:

```
[1][2][3][4][5][6][7][8][][]
```

It initializes the first eight elements with values and last two with nulls. The declaration allocates space for ten elements by setting all elements to a value, which can include a null. The LIMIT()

method returns the maximum size; it is part of the Oracle Collection API and only applies to VARRAY variables. You cannot use the DELETE method to remove an element after it is defined. VARRAY indexes are always densely populated.

Nested Table Datatype   The nested table datatype is the more like a numerically indexed list or Java class. As in the VARRAY, elements are of the same type and use a sequential numeric index. This means the index of nested table variables is densely populated. You should use a nested table when you don't know the number of items that will go in the collection before declaring the variable. Like lists in other programming languages, the nested table can grow in size after it is declared.

There are two prototypes for a nested table because you can define it in SQL or PL/SQL. Also, you should note that the datatype is defined, not declared. This difference occurs because the nested table is an object type. Objects require an explicit construction. Chapter 14 on object types explains more about object construction.

A nested table has three states: defined, initialized, or allocated. You define a nested table by assigning it a name and a type. You initialize a nested table by calling a constructor, which always has the same name as the defined nested table datatype. You allocate space implicitly or by calling the EXTEND method found in the collection API described in Chapter 7.

The following is the SQL prototype to define a nested table of scalar variables:

```
CREATE OR REPLACE TYPE table_name AS TABLE
  OF sql_datatype [NOT NULL];
/
```

The following prototype defines a nested table of any defined datatype in a PL/SQL block:

```
TYPE table_name IS TABLE OF [sql_datatype | plsql_datatype]
  [NOT NULL];
```

Neither type definition sets a maximum size because there is no limit on how many elements you can store in a nested table. You can also define nested table variables that use SQL user-defined objects or PL/SQL record types. Chapter 14 shows you how to build nested table variables with user-defined object types. Chapter 7 shows you how to leverage PL/SQL record types in nested table variables.

NOTE
Your DBA has set the limit, and when you violate your PGA space allocation, you'll raise an exception.

There is one prototype for declaring a nested table collection, and there are two prototypes for defining a nested table collection. You can define a nested table collection as an initialized collection without allocating any memory, or as an initialized collection with allocated memory. You allocate memory by using a constructor that puts data into the collection.

The following are the aforementioned prototypes that you would use in a PL/SQL block:

```
var1 varray_name;
var2 varray_name := varray_name();
var3 varray_name := varray_name(value1, value2, .. ., value9, value10);
```

Calling the variable name of the nested table type without any arguments creates an empty but initialized variable. A like call of the variable name with arguments creates and allocates values to the nested table. Unless you have specified the not-null constraint, you can also allocate space by assigning null values.

The following code demonstrates how you declare a nested table of a scalar variable:

```
DECLARE
  TYPE number_table IS TABLE OF NUMBER;
  list NUMBER_TABLE := number_table(1,2,3,4,5,6,7,8);
BEGIN
  list.DELETE(2);
  FOR i IN 1..list.COUNT LOOP
    IF list.EXISTS(i) THEN
      dbms_output.put('['||list(i)||']');
    END IF;
  END LOOP;
  dbms_output.new_line;
END;
/
```

The program prints the following to the console:

```
[1][3][4][5][6][7][8]
```

It initializes the first eight elements with values and last two with nulls. The declaration allocates space for eight elements. Then, the DELETE method removes the second element from the list, but it does not remove the allocated space. The deletion makes the index non-sequential. You can reinsert a new value but only when you reuse the deleted index value. This behavior differs from a VARRAY, where you cannot remove an element once it is allocated in memory.

The COUNT method returns the number of allocated space elements in any collection type. In this case, it still returns 7, while only six elements have values. The if-block avoids referencing the deleted item because the index 2 no longer exists. Chapter 7 demonstrates another work-around for navigating sparsely populated indexes.

Associative Array Datatype   The associative array datatype is the most like a traditional C/C++ linked list. You can index an associative array with numbers or unique strings. If you choose numbers, they do not have to be sequential. This means the index of an associative array is sparsely populated. Like a nested table, an associative array is ideal when you don't know the number of items that will go in the collection before declaring it. Like lists in other programming languages, the nested table can grow in size after it is declared. Also, memory is implicitly allocated during assignment to an associative array.

There is one prototype for an associative array because you can only declare it in PL/SQL. An associative array is declared like scalar variables because is not an object type, which means it doesn't require construction. Unlike scalar variables, you cannot define an associative array because assignments are made one element at a time.

The following prototype defines an associative array of any datatype and uses a numeric index:

```
TYPE table_name IS TABLE OF [sql_datatype | plsql_datatype]
  INDEX BY PLS_INTEGER [NOT NULL];
```

The type definition is very similar to a nested table definition. It has one key difference: it specifies *how the index is kept*. An alternative prototype for associative arrays uses a variable-length string as an index:

```
TYPE table_name IS TABLE OF [sql_datatype | plsql_datatype]
   INDEX BY VARCHAR2(10) [NOT NULL];
```

Neither type definitions sets a maximum size because there is no limit on how many elements you can store in an associative array. The actual limit governs your PGA space allocation.

You can also define associative array variables that use SQL user-defined objects or PL/SQL record types. Chapter 14 shows you how to build associative array variables with user-defined object types. Chapter 7 shows you how to leverage PL/SQL record types in associative array variables.

The following is the prototype that you would use in a PL/SQL block:

```
var1 assoc_array_name;
```

The following code demonstrates declaring an associative array of a scalar variable:

```
DECLARE
  TYPE number_table IS TABLE OF NUMBER
    INDEX BY PLS_INTEGER;
  list NUMBER_TABLE;
BEGIN
  FOR i IN 1..6 LOOP
    list(i) := i;      -- Explicit assignment required for associative arrays.
  END LOOP;
  list.DELETE(2);
  FOR i IN 1..list.COUNT LOOP
    IF list.EXISTS THEN
      dbms_output.put('['||set(i)||']');
    END IF;
  END LOOP;
  dbms_output.new_line;
END;
/
```

The program prints the following to the console:

```
[1][3][4][5][6]
```

It initializes the six elements with values inside the execution block. The elements are populated by direct assignment to indexed elements of the associative array. Then, the DELETE method removes the second element from the list. Unlike in the VARRAY and nested table, deleting an element from an associative array also removes the allocated space. The deletion makes the index non-sequential. You can reinsert a new value with the deleted index value or a new index value not used. This mirrors the nested table behavior.

The COUNT method returns the number of allocated space elements in any collection type. The if-block avoids referencing the deleted item because the index 2 no longer exists. Chapter 7 demonstrates another work-around for navigating sparsely populated indexes.

System Reference Cursors

System reference cursors are pointers to result sets in *query work areas.* A query work area is a memory region (known as a *context area*) in the Oracle 11*g* Database *Process Global Area (PGA).* The query work area holds information on the query. You'll find the rows returned by a query, the number of rows processed by the query, and a pointer to the parsed query in the query work area. The query work area resides in the Oracle Shared Pool (see Appendix A).

NOTE
All cursors share the same behaviors whether they are defined as PL/ SQL reference cursor datatypes or ordinary cursors. In fact, every SQL statement is a cursor processed and tracked in a PGA context area.

You use reference cursors when you want to query data in one program and process it in another, especially when the two programs are in different programming languages. You have the option of implementing a reference cursor in two ways: one is *strongly typed* and the other is *weakly typed.* Reference cursors are a PL/SQL only datatype. You can define them in anonymous or named blocks. They are most useful when you define them in package specifications because your programs can share them.

There is one prototype but how you choose to implement the cursor defines whether it is strongly or weakly typed. The prototype is

```
TYPE reference_cursor_name IS REF CURSOR
   [RETURN catalog_object_name%ROWTYPE];
```

You create a weakly typed reference cursor by defining it without a return type. A strongly typed reference cursor has a defined return type. As a rule of thumb, you should use strongly typed reference cursors when you need to anchor a reference cursor to a catalog object. Weakly typed reference cursors are ideal when the query returns something other than a catalog object. A generic weakly typed reference cursor is already defined as SYS_REFCURSOR, and it is available anywhere in your PL/SQL programming environment.

The power of a reference cursor becomes more significant when you use them inside stored program units. You can also use reference cursors in anonymous-block programs and assign them to a SQL*Plus reference environment variable.

You define a SQL*Plus reference cursor environment variable by defining a variable and pressing ENTER. SQL*Plus statements do not require a semicolon or forward slash to run. The following creates a weakly typed SQL*Plus reference cursor:

```
SQL> VARIABLE refcur REFCURSOR
```

The following program defines and declares a reference cursor before explicitly opening it and assigning its values to an external session-level variable:

```
DECLARE
  TYPE weakly_typed IS REF CURSOR;
  quick WEAKLY_TYPED;
BEGIN
  OPEN quick FOR
    SELECT   item_title
    ,        COUNT(*)
    FROM     item
    HAVING   (COUNT(*) > 2)
    GROUP BY item_title;
  :refcur := quick;
END;
/
```

The SYS_REFCURSOR generic reference cursor can replace the locally defined reference cursor type. You can query the session-level variable to see the contents of the reference cursor with the following:

```
SELECT    :refcur
FROM      dual;
```

The query returns the following, provided you've run the seeding scripts found in the book's introduction:

```
:REFCUR
-------------------
CURSOR STATEMENT : 1
CURSOR STATEMENT : 1
ITEM_TITLE                                                    COUNT(*)
------------------------------------------------------------- ----------
Harry Potter and the Chamber of Secrets                              3
Harry Potter: Goblet of Fire                                         3
Die Another Day                                                      3
The Lord of the Rings - Two Towers                                   3
The Lord of the Rings - Fellowship of the Ring                       3
Chronicles of Narnia - The Lion, the Witch and the Wardrobe          5
Harry Potter and the Goblet of Fire                                  3
Pirates of the Caribbean - The Curse of the Black Pearl              3
Pirates of the Caribbean                                             4
The Lord of the Rings - The Return of the King                       3

10 rows selected.
```

Chapter 6 demonstrates how to use a reference cursor inside functions and procedures. Reference cursors are extremely useful datatypes when you want to pass a query work area pointer to an external program. You can pass to an external program by using the Oracle Call Interface 8 (OCI8) libraries.

Variable Scope

As discussed, PL/SQL is a blocked programming language. Program units can be named or unnamed blocks. Each programming block establishes its own program scope. Program scope includes a list of variables (identifiers) that can contain data. A program includes variables defined both in the header (only applies for named program units) and in the declaration block. They are considering local to the programming block.

Nested *anonymous* blocks are the exception to the scope rule. They have access to their containing PL/SQL block identifiers. This is true whether the containing block is anonymous or named. Figure 3-6 demonstrates the scope access of nested anonymous-block programs.

You can inadvertently override your scope access to containing blocks by reusing an identifier in a nested block. This behavior is demonstrated by the following program:

```
DECLARE
   current_block VARCHAR2(10) := 'Outer';
   outer_block   VARCHAR2(10) := 'Outer';
BEGIN
   dbms_output.put_line('[current_block]['||current_block||']');
   DECLARE
```

```
      current_block VARCHAR2(10) := 'Inner';
  BEGIN
    dbms_output.put_line('[current_block]['||current_block||']');
    dbms_output.put_line('[outer_block]['||outer_block||']');
  END;
  dbms_output.put_line('[current_block]['||current_block||']');
END;
/
```

The `current_block` and `outer_block` identifiers (local variables) are declared in the outer anonymous-block program with the value of outer. The `current_block` identifier is declared in the nested or inner block with a value of inner, while the `outer_block` identifier is not declared in the nested block.

The program renders the following output:

```
[current_block][Outer]
[current_block][Inner]
[outer_block]   [Outer]
[current_block][Outer]
```

The nested block overrides the scope of the containing block by defining the same identifier. The containing block has no visibility to the internally declared `current_block` identifier. This is the one nuance of scope that can be tricky in PL/SQL.

Another aspect of scope is passing values from one program to a named block. This is done through the formal parameter list that constitutes the signature of functions and procedures. Chapter 6 explains how these named blocks receive values as actual parameters and return values.

Summary

This chapter has explained delimiters; how you define, access, and assign values to variables; anonymous-block and named-block program units, variable types, and how variable scope works in PL/SQL programs.

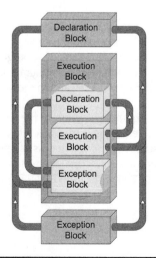

FIGURE 3-6 *PL/SQL scope reference diagram*

CHAPTER
4

Control Structures

his chapter examines the control structures in PL/SQL. Control structures let you make conditional choices, repeat operations, and access data. The IF and CASE statements let you branch program execution according to one or more conditions. Loop statements let you repeat behavior until conditions are met. Cursors let you access data one row or one set of rows at a time.

The chapter is divided into the following sections:

- Conditional statements
  - IF statements
  - CASE statements
  - Conditional compilation statements
- Iterative statements
  - Simple loop statements
  - While loop statements
  - FOR loop statements
- Cursor structures
  - Implicit cursors
  - Explicit cursors
- Bulk statements
  - COLLECT BULK statements
  - FORALL loop statements

Conditional Statements

There are three types of conditional statements in programming languages: single branching statements, multiple branching statements without fall-through, and multiple branching statements with fall-through. To fall through means to process all subsequent conditions after finding a matching CASE statement. Single branching statements are if-then-else statements. Multiple branching statements without fall-through are if-then-elsif-then-else statements, and with fall-through they are case statements. Figure 4-1 demonstrates the logical flow of the first two conditional statements. The third is not displayed because PL/SQL *does not* support fall-through, and PL/SQL implements the case statement *like* an if-then-elsif-then-else statement.

NOTE
PL/SQL uses the ELSIF *reserved word in lieu of two separate words—else if. This is a legacy from the Pascal and Ada programming languages.*

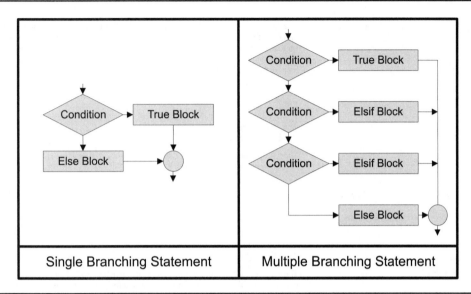

FIGURE 4-1   *Branching statement logical flows*

The diamonds in Figure 4-1 are decision trees. Decision trees represent code branching that happens because of comparison operations. Comparison operations are frequently called comparison expressions or expressions because they return a true or false value. True or false comparisons are straightforward. Not true or not false comparisons are tricky. A not true expression is met when the value is false or null. A not false expression is met when the value is true or null. When it is possible an expression may return a null value, you should enclose the expression in an NVL() built-in and provide an explicit default Boolean value.

PL/SQL supports lexical symbols, symbol sets, and identifiers as valid comparison operators. Table 4-1 contains a list and definition for symbol comparison operators. Table 4-1 expands the comparison operator list by providing the comparison operators that are identifiers. Identifiers like these are reserved words or keywords.

AND	Comparison	The AND operator allows you to combine two comparisons into one. This operator makes the combination statement true only when both individual statements are true. You also use the AND operator with the BETWEEN operator to glue the lower- and upper-range values.

```
BEGIN
  IF 1 = 1 AND 2 = 2 THEN
   dbms_output.put_line('True.');
  END IF;
END;
/
This returns:
True.
```

TABLE 4-1   *Comparison Operators*

BETWEEN	Comparison	The BETWEEN operator allows you to check whether a variable value is between two values of the same datatype. The BETWEEN operator is also an inclusive operator. Inclusive means that a match may include either of the boundary values.

```
BEGIN
  IF 1 BETWEEN 1 AND 3 THEN
    dbms_output.put_line('In the range.');
  END IF;
END;
/
```
This returns the following output:
```
In the range.
```

IN	Comparison	The IN operator allows you to check whether a variable value is in a set of comma-delimited values.

```
BEGIN
  IF 1 IN (1,2,3) THEN
    dbms_output.put_line('In the set.');
  END IF;
END;
/
```
This returns the following output:
```
In the set.
```

IS EMPTY	Comparison	The IS EMPTY operator allows you to check whether a VARRAY or NESTED TABLE collection variable is empty. Empty means that the collection was constructed without any default elements. This means no space was allocated to the SGA for elements in the collection. When no element space is allocated, the IS EMPTY comparison returns true, and it returns false when at least one element is allocated. You raise a PLS-00306 exception when the collection has not been initialized through explicit construction. Chapter 12 explains how you construct collections. You should note that this only works with collections of scalar SQL datatypes.

```
DECLARE
  TYPE list IS TABLE OF INTEGER;
  a LIST := list();
BEGIN
  IF a IS EMPTY THEN
    dbms_output.put_line('"a" is empty.');
  END IF;
END;
/
```
This returns the following output:
```
"a" is empty.
```

IS NULL	Comparison	The IS NULL operator allows you to check whether a variable value is null. The NVL() built-in can enable you to assign any Boolean or expression an explicit true or false value.

```
DECLARE
  var BOOLEAN;
BEGIN
  IF var IS NULL THEN
    dbms_output.put_line('It is null.');
  END IF;
END;
/
```
This returns the following output:
```
It is null.
```

TABLE 4-1   *Comparison Operators* (continued)

IS A SET	Comparison	The IS A SET operator allows you to check whether a variable is a VARRAY or NESTED TABLE collection variable, provided an instance of the variable has been constructed. It returns true when the variable datatype is a VARRAY or NESTED TABLE *and* the variable has been constructed. Constructed means that an instance of the collection has been created with or without members. Chapter 14 contains more on the concept of constructing a variable.

The IS A SET comparison operator returns false when the variable datatype is either a VARRAY or NESTED TABLE and the variable is not constructed. An associative array (another type of collection) is not a collection object and when you attempt to check if it is a set, you raise a PLS-00306 exception. Likewise, other variable types raise the same PLS-00306 exception. Chapter 7 explains how you construct collections. This comparison operator *only works* with collections that use scalar SQL datatypes.

If you forget the "A" in the IS A SET operator, it raises a malformed identifier PLS-00103 exception.

```
DECLARE
  TYPE list IS TABLE OF INTEGER;
  a LIST := list();
BEGIN
  IF a IS A SET THEN
    dbms_output.put_line('"a" is a set.');
  END IF;
END;
/
```

This returns the following output:

```
"a" is a set.
```

LIKE	Comparison	The LIKE operator allows you to check whether a variable value is part of another value. The comparison can be made with the SQL lexical underscore for a single-character wildcard, or % for a multiple-character wildcard. The % lexical value inside a string is not equivalent to its use as an attribute indicator in PL/SQL.

```
BEGIN
  IF 'Str%' LIKE 'String' THEN
  dbms_output.put_line('Match');
  END IF;
END;
/
```

This returns the following output:

```
Match.
```

MEMBER OF	Comparison	The MEMBER OF is a logical comparison operator. It lets you find out whether an element is a member of a collection. It only works with collections of scalar SQL datatypes. It returns true when the element exists in the collection and false when it doesn't.

```
DECLARE
  TYPE list IS TABLE OF NUMBER;
  n VARCHAR2(10) := 'One';
  a LIST := list('One', 'Two', 'Three');
BEGIN
  IF n MEMBER OF a THEN
    dbms_output.put_line('"n" is member.');
  END IF;
END;
/
```

When the left operand element is null, the operator returns false. This means that you should always check for a value before using this comparison operator. It prints the following:

```
"n" is member.
```

TABLE 4-1 *Comparison Operators* (continued)

NOT	Comparison	The NOT is a logical negation operator and allows you to check for the opposite of a Boolean state of an expression, provided it isn't null.
		
		```BEGIN```
		  ```IF NOT FALSE THEN```
		  ```dbms_output.put_line('True.');```
		  ```END IF;```
		```END;```
		```/```
		
		When the expression or value is null, the NOT changes nothing. There is no opposite of null, and *a logical negation of null is also a null*. This returns the following output because FALSE is a Boolean literal and because TRUE is the only thing not false when you exclude null values:
		
		```True.```

OR	Comparison	The OR operator allows you to combine two comparisons into one. This operator makes the combination statement true when one or the other statement is true. PL/SQL uses short-circuit evaluation, which means it stops evaluating a combination comparison when any one value is false.
		
		```BEGIN```
		  ```IF 1 = 1 OR 1 = 2 THEN```
		  ```dbms_output.put_line('True.');```
		  ```END IF;```
		```END;```
		```/```
		
		This returns the following output because of one of the two statements is true:
		
		```True.```

SUBMULTISET	Comparison	The SUBMULTISET operator lets you to check whether a VARRAY or NESTED TABLE collection is a subset of a mirrored datatype. It returns true if some to all elements in the left set are found in the right set. You should note that this operator does not check for a proper subset, which is one item less than the full set or identity set.
		
		```DECLARE```
		  ```TYPE list IS TABLE OF INTEGER;```
		  ```a LIST := list(1,2,3);```
		  ```b LIST := list(1,2,3,4);```
		```BEGIN```
		  ```IF a SUBMULTISET b THEN```
		    ```dbms_output.put_line('Subset.');```
		  ```END IF;```
		```END;```
		```/```
		
		This returns the following output:
		
		```Valid subset.```

TABLE 4-1 *Comparison Operators* (continued)

You also need to know the order of operation for comparison operators. Table 4-2 lists their order of operation. You can override the order of operation by enclosing subordinate expressions in parentheses. PL/SQL compares any expression inside parentheses as a whole result. PL/SQL applies any remaining comparison operators in an expression by their order of operation.

Single comparison expressions return a true, false, or null. Both false and null are not true when you evaluate whether an expression is true. Likewise, both true and null are not false when

Order	Operator	Definition
1	`**`	Exponentiation (see Table 3-1)
2	`+, -`	Identity and negation
3	`*, /`	Multiplication and Division
4	`+, -, ||`	Addition, subtraction, and concatenation

5	`= =, <, >, <=, >=, <>, !=, ~=, ^=,`
	`BETWEEN, IN, IS NULL, LIKE`
	Comparison	

6	`AND`	Conjunction
7	`NOT`	Logical negation
8	`OR`	Inclusion

TABLE 4-2   *Order of Operations*

you evaluate an expression as false. A null expression is never true or false. Table 4-3 maps the possible outcomes in a truth table.

Multiple comparison expressions require two-sided truth tables: one table for the conjunction operator, `AND`, and another for the inclusion operator, `OR`. The conjunction operator creates expressions where you resolve the combination of two expressions, where both are true. The whole statement is not true when one is false or null. Table 4-4 maps the possible outcomes of conjunctive truth—when X and Y expressions are true, false or null.

Multiple comparison expressions also require a two-sided truth table to examine how the inclusion operator works. Inclusion is where two things are true when one or the other is true, but because of null expressions the whole statement can be true, false, or null. Table 4-5 maps the possible outcomes of inclusive truth—when X or Y expressions are true, false or null.

X Value	Expression	Result	Negation Expression	Result
TRUE	X is TRUE	**TRUE**	X is *NOT* TRUE	**FALSE**
FALSE	X is TRUE	**FALSE**	X is *NOT* TRUE	**TRUE**
NULL	X is TRUE	**NULL**	X is *NOT* TRUE	**TRUE**

TABLE 4-3   *Single-Variable Truth Table*

X and Y	Y is TRUE	Y is FALSE	Y is NULL
X is TRUE	TRUE	FALSE	NULL
X is FALSE	FALSE	FALSE	FALSE
X is NULL	NULL	FALSE	NULL

TABLE 4-4 *X and Y are TRUE, FALSE or NULL*

The truth tables should help you plan how you will develop your branching logic in IF and CASE statements. The same logical outcomes extend to three or more expressions, but they don't render in two-dimensional tables.

This section has provided detail to support the branching subsections. Subsections examine single-branching and multiple-branching statements that use IF statements, and multiple-branching statements that use simple and searched case statements. The subsections are grouped by the IF and CASE statements.

IF Statements

The IF statement supports single-branching and multiple-branching statements. IF statements are blocks. They start with a beginning identifier, or reserved word, and end with an ending identifier and a semicolon. All statement blocks require at least one statement just as anonymous or named blocks do.

IF statements evaluate a condition. The condition can be any comparison expression, or set of comparison expressions that evaluates to a logical true or false. You can compare two literals or variables of the same type. The variables can actually have different datatypes, as long as they implicitly or you explicitly convert one of the two types to match the other. A Boolean variable can replace a comparison operation. You also can compare the results of two function calls as you would two variables or a variable and a single function call, provided it returns a Boolean variable. The valid comparison operators are in Table 3-1 in the preceding chapter, as well as in earlier Table 4-1.

X or Y	Y is TRUE	Y is FALSE	Y is NULL
X is TRUE	TRUE	TRUE	TRUE
X is FALSE	TRUE	FALSE	NULL
X is NULL	TRUE	NULL	NULL

TABLE 4-5 *X or Y are TRUE, FALSE, or NULL*

Function Calls as Expressions

When you call a function, you provide values or variables and return a result. If the function returns a variable length string, you can call it a string expression because it yields a string as a result. The result is like a string literal (covered in Chapter 3). Alternatively, function definitions can return any other scalar variable datatypes and they become expressions that yield values of those datatypes.

The following example compares a single variable and expression (or function call):

```
DECLARE
  one_thing VARCHAR2(5) := 'Three';
  FUNCTION ordinal (n NUMBER) RETURN VARCHAR2 IS
    TYPE ordinal_type IS TABLE OF VARCHAR2(5);
    ordinal ORDINAL_TYPE := ordinal_type('One','Two','Three','Four');
  BEGIN
    RETURN ordinal(n);
  END;
BEGIN
  IF one_thing = ordinal(3) THEN
    dbms_output.put_line('['||ordinal(3)||']');
  END IF;
END;
/
```

The sample program compares a variable value and function call return, or literal value and expression. They are found equal. The program prints the following provided the SQL*Plus SERVEROUTPUT is set on:

```
Three
```

The return value of a function call is an expression or a runtime value that can be compared against the content of a variable, literal value, or another function call.

If-then-else Statements

The if-then-else statement is a single branching statement. It evaluates a condition and then runs the code immediately after the condition when the condition is met. The prototype for an if-then-else statement is

```
IF [NOT] {comparison_expression | boolean_value} [[AND | OR]
          {comparison_expression | boolean_value}] THEN
  true_execution_block;
[ELSE
    false_execution_block;]
END IF;
```

You use the optional NOT (the logical negation operator) to check for a false comparison result. While there is only one [AND | OR] clause in the IF statement prototype, there is no limit to how many conditions you evaluate. The ELSE block is optional. IF statements without an ELSE block only execute code when a condition is met.

In its simplest form this is an if-then statement. The following demonstrates an if-then statement comparing two numeric literals:

```
BEGIN
  IF 1 = 1 THEN
    dbms_output.put_line('Condition met!');
  END IF;
END;
/
```

You should note that parentheses around the comparison statement aren't required. This is a convenience compared to some other programming languages where they are required, like PHP. The equivalent logic using a Boolean variable instead of the comparison operation is

```
DECLARE
  equal BOOLEAN NOT NULL := TRUE;
BEGIN
  IF equal THEN
    dbms_output.put_line('Condition met!');
  END IF;
END;
/
```

When you evaluate a Boolean variable or expression that returns a null value, the IF statement returns a false value. You should anticipate run-time behaviors that may result in a null value and use the NVL() built-in where possible to avoid unexpected outcomes. The default behavior is fine, provided you want your program to treat a null value as false.

Provided you set SERVEROUTPUT ON in SQL*Plus, either of these anonymous blocks resolves the comparison as true and prints

```
Condition met!
```

Branching out, you can build an if-then-else statement like

```
BEGIN
  IF 1 = 2 THEN
    dbms_output.put_line('Condition met!');
  ELSE
    dbms_output.put_line('Condition not met!');
  END IF;
END;
/
```

The anonymous block resolves the comparison as false and prints the else block statement:

```
Condition not met!
```

You can support variables for the literals in these examples or function calls that return matching or convertible datatypes for comparison. A single function that returns a BOOLEAN datatype also works in lieu of the Boolean example.

If-then-elsif-then-else Statements

The if-then-elsif-then-else statement is a multiple branching statement. It evaluates a series of conditions and then it runs the code immediately after the first successfully met condition. It exits the block after processing the block and ignores any subsequently successful evaluations. The prototype for an if-then-elsif-then-else statement is

```
IF    [NOT] {comparison_expression | boolean_value} [[AND | OR]
            {comparison_expression | boolean_value}] THEN
  true_if_execution_block;
[ELSIF [NOT] {comparison_expression | boolean_value} [[AND | OR]
            {comparison_expression | boolean_value}] THEN
  true_elsif_execution_block;
[ELSE
  all_false_execution_block;]
 END IF;
```

You use the optional NOT operator to check for false comparisons. While there is only one [AND | OR] clause in the IF and ELSIF statements, there is no limit to how many conditions you evaluate. The ELSE block is optional. An if-then-elsif-then-else statement without an ELSE block only executes code when a condition is met.

The following demonstrates an if-then-elsif-then-else statement where the first two comparisons are true and the third false:

```
DECLARE
   equal BOOLEAN NOT NULL := TRUE;
BEGIN
  IF 1 = 1 THEN
    dbms_output.put_line('Condition one met!');
  ELSIF equal THEN
    dbms_output.put_line('Condition two met!');
  ELSIF 1 = 2 THEN
    dbms_output.put_line('Condition three met!');
  END IF;
END;
/
```

The anonymous block resolves the first comparison as true and prints

```
Condition one met!
```

As mentioned, the if-then-elsif-then-else statement exits after the first comparison is found true. The default ELSE condition runs only when none of the conditions are met.

CASE Statements

There are two types of CASE statements in PL/SQL. Both define a selector. A selector is a variable, function, or expression that the CASE statement attempts to match in WHEN blocks. The selector immediately follows the reserved word CASE. If you don't provide a selector, PL/SQL adds a Boolean *true* as the selector. You can use any PL/SQL datatype as a selector except a BLOB, BFILE, or composite type. Chapter 3 qualifies composite types as records, collections, and user-defined object types.

The generic CASE statement prototype is

```
CASE [ TRUE | [selector_variable]]
   WHEN [criterion1 | expression1] THEN
     criterion1_statements;
   WHEN [criterion2 | expression2] THEN
     criterion2_statements;
   WHEN [criterion(n+1) | expression(n+1)] THEN
     criterion(n+1)_statements;
   ELSE
     block_statements;
END CASE;
```

Simple CASE statement selectors are variables that use or functions that return valid datatypes other than Boolean types. Searched CASE statement selectors are Boolean variables or functions that return a Boolean variable. The default selector is a Boolean *true*. A searched CASE statement can omit the selector when seeking a true expression.

Like the IF statement, CASE statements have an ELSE clause. The ELSE clause works as it does in the IF statement with one twist. You can't leave the ELSE block out, or you will raise a CASE_NOT_FOUND or PLS-06592 error when the selector is not found. PL/SQL includes this default ELSE condition when you fail to provide one and a run-time execution fails to match a WHEN block.

CASE statements are blocks. They start with a beginning identifier, or reserved word, and end with an ending identifier and a semicolon. All statement blocks require at least one statement just as anonymous or named blocks do. CASE statements require at least one statement in each WHEN block and the ELSE block.

Like the if-then-elsif-then-else statement, CASE statements evaluate WHEN blocks by sequentially checking for a match against the selector. The first WHEN block that matches the selector runs and exits the CASE block. *There is no fall-through behavior available in PL/SQL.* The ELSE block runs only when no WHEN block matches the selector.

Simple CASE Statements

The simple CASE statement sets a selector that is any PL/SQL datatype except a BLOB, BFILE, or composite type. The prototype for a simple CASE statement is

```
CASE selector_variable
   WHEN criterion1 THEN
     criterion1_statements;
   WHEN criterion2 THEN
     criterion2_statements;
   WHEN criterion(n+1) THEN
     criterion(n+1)_statements;
   ELSE
     block_statements;
END CASE;
```

Simple CASE statements *require that you provide a selector.* You can add many more WHEN blocks than shown, but the more numerous the possibilities, the less effective is this type of solution. This is a manageable solution when you typically have ten or fewer choices. Maintainability declines as the list of WHEN blocks grows.

The following example uses a NUMBER datatype as the selector:

```
DECLARE
  selector NUMBER := 0;
BEGIN
  CASE selector
    WHEN 0 THEN
      dbms_output.put_line('Case 0!');
    WHEN 1 THEN
      dbms_output.put_line('Case 1!');
    ELSE
      dbms_output.put_line('No match!');
  END CASE;
END;
/
```

The anonymous block resolves the first comparison as true because the selector contains a value of 0. It then prints

```
Case 0!
```

Therefore, the first WHEN block matches the selector value. The CASE statement ceases evaluation and runs the matching WHEN block before exiting the statement. You can substitute other PL/SQL datatypes for the selector value. The CHAR, NCHAR, and VARCHAR2 types are some possible choices.

Searched CASE Statements

The selector is implicitly set for a searched CASE statement unless you want to search for a false condition. *You must explicitly provide a false selector.* Sometimes a searched CASE selector value is dynamic based on some run-time logic. When that's the case, you can substitute a function returning a Boolean variable, provided you dynamically set the selector. The searched CASE statement only uses a Boolean selector or comparison expression.

The prototype for a searched CASE statement is

```
CASE [{TRUE | FALSE}]
  WHEN [criterion1 | expression1] THEN
    criterion1_statements;
  WHEN [criterion1 | expression1] THEN
    criterion2_statements;
  WHEN [criterion(n+1) | expression(n+1)] THEN
    criterion(n+1)_statements;
  ELSE
    block_statements;
END CASE;
```

As with the simple CASE statement, you can add many more WHEN blocks than shown, but the more numerous the possibilities, the less effective this type of solution is. The following searched CASE statement examines comparison expressions:

```
BEGIN
  CASE
    WHEN 1 = 2 THEN
```

```
      dbms_output.put_line('Case [1 = 2]');
    WHEN 2 = 2 THEN
      dbms_output.put_line('Case [2 = 2]');
    ELSE
      dbms_output.put_line('No match');
  END CASE;
END;
/
```

The anonymous block resolves the second comparison as true because the selector's default value is true and so is the comparison of twos. It then prints

```
Case [2 = 2}
```

If the CASE statement searched for a false condition, the selector would match the first WHEN block and print that 1 equals 2. You can also use a comparison expression as the selector.

Conditional Compilation Statements

Beginning with Oracle 10*g* Release 2, you can use conditional compilation. Conditional compilation lets you include debugging logic or special-purpose logic that runs only when session-level variables are set. The following command sets a PL/SQL compile time variable DEBUG equal to 1:

```
ALTER SESSION SET PLSQL_CCFLAGS = 'debug:1';
```

This command sets a PL/SQL compile time variable DEBUG equal to 1. You should note that the compile-time flag is case insensitive. You can also set compile-time variables to *true* or *false* so that they act like Boolean variables. When you want to set more than one conditional compilation flag, you need to use the following syntax:

```
ALTER SESSION SET PLSQL_CCFLAGS = 'name1:value1 [, name(n+1):value(n+1) ]';
```

The conditional compilation parameters are stored as name and value pairs in the PLSQL_CCFLAG database parameter. The following program uses the $IF, $THEN, $ELSE, $ELSIF, $ERROR, and $END directives that create a conditional compilation code block:

```
BEGIN
  $IF $$DEBUG = 1 $THEN
    dbms_output.put_line('Debug Level 1 Enabled.');
  $END
END;
/
```

Conditional code blocks differs from a normal if-then-else code blocks. Most notably, the $END directive closes the block instead of an END IF and semicolon. The $END directive ends a conditional statement. An END IF closes an IF code block. The syntax rules require that closing blocks end with a semicolon or statement terminator. Statement terminators are not conditional lexical units, and their occurrence without a preceding code statement triggers a compile-time error.

The $$ symbol denotes a PL/SQL conditional compile-time variable. The ALTER SESSION statement lets you set conditional compile-time variables. You set them in the PLSQL_CCFLAGS session variable. One or many variables are set in PLSQL_CCFLAGS. All variables are constants until the session ends or they are replaced. You replace these variables by reusing the ALTER SESSION statement. *All previous conditional compile-time variables cease to exist when you reset the* PLSQL_CCFLAGS *session variable.*

The rules governing conditional compilation are set by the SQL parser. You cannot use conditional compilation in SQL object types. This limitation also applies to nested tables and VARRAYs (scalar tables). Conditional compilation differs in functions and procedures. The behavior changes whether the function or procedure has a formal parameter list. You can use conditional compilation after the opening parenthesis of a formal parameter list, like

```
CREATE OR REPLACE FUNCTION conditional_type
( magic_number $IF $$DEBUG = 1 $THEN SIMPLE_NUMBER $ELSE NUMBER $END )
RETURN NUMBER IS
BEGIN
  RETURN magic_number;
END;
/
```

Alternatively, you can use them after the AS or IS keyword in no-parameter functions or procedures. They can also be used both inside the formal parameter list and after the AS or IS in parameter functions or procedures.

Conditional compilation can only occur after the BEGIN keyword in triggers and anonymous-block program units. Please note that *you cannot encapsulate a placeholder, or bind variable, inside a conditional compilation block.*

Iterative Statements

Iterative statements are blocks that let you repeat a statement or set of statements. There are two types of iterative statements. One guards entry into the loop before running repeatable statements. The other guards exit. An iterative statement that only guards exit guarantees that its code block is always run once and is known as a repeat until loop block. Figure 4-2 shows the execution logic for these two iteration statement types.

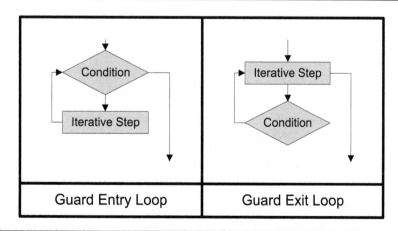

FIGURE 4-2   *Iterative statement logic flows*

The PL/SQL language supports simple, FOR, FORALL, and WHILE loops. It does not formally support a repeat until loop block. You can use the simple loop statement to mimic the behavior of a repeat until loop. Loops often work with cursors. Cursors are row-by-row or batch queries from the database, and they are covered in the section immediately after iterative statements.

Simple Loop Statements

Simple loops are explicit block structures. A simple loop starts and ends with the LOOP reserved word. They require that you manage both loop index and exit criteria. Typically, simple loops are used where easy solutions don't quite fit. Easy solutions are typically the popular FOR loop statement because it manages the loop index and exit criteria for you.

There are two prototypes for a simple loop. They differ in that one exits at the top of the loop and the other at the end of the loop. Exits are necessary unless you want an infinite loop, which is not too often. Loop exits are comparative expressions. A guard on entry loop has a branching statement first. The loop exits when the expression is no longer met. A guard on exit loop also has a branching statement, but it is the last step in the loop block. A guard on exit loop exits when the exit criteria are met. The EXIT statement immediately stops code execution and exits the loop statement. The following examples demonstrate this technique for the guard on entry and exit loops:

Guard on Entry Loop	Guard on Exit Loop
| ```
LOOP
 [counter_management_statements;]
  IF NOT entry_condition THEN
    EXIT;
  END IF;
  repeating_statements;
END LOOP;
``` | ```
LOOP
 [counter_management_statements;]
  repeating_statements;
  IF exit_condition THEN
    EXIT;
  END IF;
END LOOP;
``` |

PL/SQL simplifies writing an exit statement by providing the EXIT WHEN statement. The EXIT WHEN statement eliminates the need to write an IF statement around the EXIT statement. The following examples demonstrate this technique for the guard on entry and exit loops:

Guard on Entry Loop	Guard on Exit Loop
| ```
LOOP
 [counter_management_statements;]
  EXIT WHEN NOT entry_condition;
  repeating_statements;
END LOOP;
``` | ```
LOOP
 [counter_management_statements;]
  repeating_statements;
  EXIT WHEN exit_condition;
END LOOP;
``` |

The CONTINUE statement in Oracle 11*g* makes it imperative that you put loop index statements at the top of the loop. A CONTINUE statement stops execution in a loop iteration and returns control to the top of the loop. It is now possible that you could create an infinite loop cycling between the top of the loop and the CONTINUE statement. This can happen because the CONTINUE statement would bypass your incrementing or decrementing logic unless it is at the top of the loop. The same is true for the CONTINUE WHEN statement.

Figure 4-3 demonstrates an approach to managing the loop index. It makes some assumptions. The first assumption is that you may want to cut and paste the logic into different code components. The second assumption is that you may forget to initialize the necessary variables. All you need to do is implement two variables with consistent names to reuse this approach.

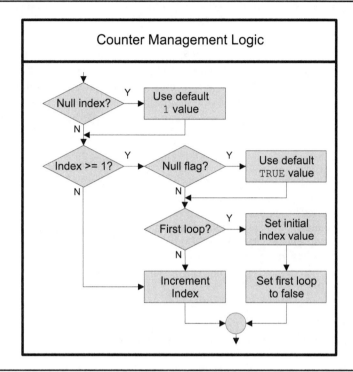

FIGURE 4-3 *Counter management logic*

The following anonymous block demonstrates a guard on entry simple loop and implements the counter management logic from Figure 4-3:

```
DECLARE
  counter NUMBER;
  first   BOOLEAN;
BEGIN
  LOOP
    -- Loop index management.
    IF NVL(counter,1) >= 1 THEN
      IF NOT NVL(first,TRUE) THEN
        counter := counter + 1;
      ELSE
        counter := 1;
        first := FALSE;
      END IF;
    END IF;
    -- Exit management.
    EXIT WHEN NOT counter < 3;
    dbms_output.put_line('Iteration ['||counter||']');
  END LOOP;
END;
/
```

This simple loop generates the following output because it guards entry after running twice:

```
Iteration [1]
Iteration [2]
```

The guard on exit simple loop is a repeat until loop. It always runs once before it checks the criteria. Leaving the guard condition at a counter value of three, you will notice that the results differ between a guard on entry loop and guard on exit loop.

An anonymous block demonstrates a guard on exit simple loop:

```
DECLARE
  counter NUMBER;
  first    BOOLEAN;
BEGIN
  LOOP
    -- Loop index management.
    IF NVL(counter,1) >= 1 THEN
      IF NOT NVL(first,TRUE) THEN
        counter := counter + 1;
      ELSE
        counter := 1;
        first := FALSE;
      END IF;
    END IF;
    dbms_output.put_line('Iteration ['||counter||']');
    -- Exit management.
    EXIT WHEN NOT counter < 3;
  END LOOP;
END;
/
```

This program does generate *three* lines of output because it guards the exit after three executions:

```
Iteration [1]
Iteration [2]
Iteration [3]
```

The output confirms what you know, that no entry check is made before performing the repeating statements. You can alter the incrementing value of the loop index in a simple loop statement by changing the literal value of 1. Both the simple and WHILE loops also afford you control over the increment interval. They also let you decrement loop indexes.

You cannot decrement index values using FOR and FORALL loops. FOR and FORALL loops also don't task you with managing the loop index because the loop index is done implicitly and *outside of your accessible programming scope.*

Skipping an index value is possible in Oracle 11*g* by using the new CONTINUE statement. The CONTINUE statement signals an immediate end to a loop iteration and returns to the first statement in the loop.

NOTE
The CONTINUE *and* CONTINUE WHEN *statements are new Oracle 11g features.*

The following anonymous block illustrates how to implement a CONTINUE statement in a simple loop:

```
DECLARE
  counter NUMBER;
  first   BOOLEAN;
BEGIN
  LOOP
    -- Loop index management.
    IF NVL(counter,1) >= 1 THEN
      IF NOT NVL(first,TRUE) THEN
        counter := counter + 1;
      ELSE
        counter := 1;
        first := FALSE;
      END IF;
    END IF;
    -- Exit management.
    EXIT WHEN NOT counter < 3;
    IF counter = 2 THEN
      CONTINUE;
    ELSE
      dbms_output.put_line('Index ['||counter||'].');
    END IF;
  END LOOP;
END;
/
```

This version of the program only prints the first index value before the program exits. The program prints the initial index 1, increments the loop index to 2, skips the printing statement, increments the loop index to 3, and then exits the loop, failing to meet the *guard on entry* condition. You can simplify your code by replacing the combination of an IF block and CONTINUE statement with the CONTINUE WHEN statement. The following shows how you would replace it:

```
CONTINUE WHEN counter = 2;
dbms_output.put_line('Index ['||counter||'].');
```

The print statement was previously in the ELSE block. The CONTINUE WHEN eliminates the need for the IF block.

Either program prints this to the console after two passes through the loop:

```
Iteration [1]
```

The simple loop becomes much more robust when combined with cursor attributes. That discussion is in the section "Cursor Structures" later in the chapter.

FOR Loop Statements

The FOR loop is a favorite of many developers because it is powerful and simple to use. A FOR loop manages the loop index and exit for you because it is part of the statement definition.

There are two types of FOR loop statements. One is a range FOR loop statement, and the other is a cursor FOR loop statement.

Range FOR Loop Statements

A range FOR loop statement is ideal when you know the starting and ending points and the range can be represented in integers. You can also use a FOR loop statement to navigate the contents of an associative array by traversing the number of elements in it. An example of navigating an associative array using a string index is provided in Chapter 7.

The prototype for a range FOR loop statement is

```
FOR range_index IN range_bottom..range_top LOOP
  repeating_statements;
END LOOP;
```

The *range index* can be any identifier that you prefer. As when writing for loops in other languages, many developers use i as a variable name. Then, they use j, k, l, and so forth as variable names when nesting loops. The range index for a range FOR loop is a PLS_INTEGER. You set the starting value when you set the *bottom of the range,* and the ending value when you set the *top of the range.* It increments by 1, and you cannot change that.

The following anonymous-block program demonstrates a FOR loop statement:

```
BEGIN
  FOR i IN 1..3 LOOP
    dbms_output.put_line('Iteration ['||i||']');
  END LOOP;
END;
/
```

This code prints

```
Iteration [1]
Iteration [2]
Iteration [3]
```

The range index variable value is printed in the square brackets. You should note that the range limits are inclusive, not exclusive. An exclusive range would have excluded 1 and 3.

There is no exit statement in the example because one isn't required. *The exit statement is implicitly placed at the top of the loop.* The conditional logic checks whether the range index is less than the top of the range, and it exits when that condition is not met. This means if you reverse the bottom and top of the range, the loop would exit before processing any statement because it would find 3 is not less than 1. Therefore, a range FOR loop statement is a guard on entry loop statement.

Cursor FOR Loop Statements

A cursor FOR loop statement is ideal when you query a database table or view. You don't usually know how many rows it will return.

This section uses an implicit cursor and the later section "Cursor Structures" demonstrates cursor FOR loops with explicit cursors. An implicit cursor is a SELECT statement defined as part of the cursor FOR loop statement. An explicit cursor is defined in the declaration block.

The prototype for a cursor FOR loop statement is

```
FOR cursor_index IN {cursor_name[(actual_parameters)] | (select_statement)} LOOP
  repeating_statements;
END LOOP;
```

The *cursor index* can be any identifier that you prefer. As when writing for loops in other languages, many developers use i as a variable name. Then, they use j, k, l, and so forth as variable names they you nest loops. The cursor index for a cursor FOR loop is a pointer to a result set in a query work area. A query work area is a memory region (known as a *context area*) in the Oracle 11*g* Database *Process Global Area (PGA)*. The query work area holds information on the query. You'll find the rows returned by a query, the number of rows processed by the query, and a pointer to the parsed query in the query work area. The query work area resides in the Oracle Shared Pool (see Appendix A).

The example code shows how to implement an implicit cursor FOR loop. It depends on your having already run the seeding code discussed in the Introduction, and returns the names of Harry Potter films in the video rental store sample database. The Introduction has instructions for creating and seeding the video rental store database. The example follows:

```
BEGIN
   FOR i IN (SELECT    COUNT(*) AS on_hand
             ,         item_title
             ,         item_rating
             FROM      item
             WHERE     item_title LIKE 'Harry Potter%'
             AND       item_rating_agency = 'MPAA'
             GROUP BY item_title
             ,         item_rating) LOOP
      dbms_output.put('('||i.on_hand||') ');
      dbms_output.put(i.item_title||' ');
      dbms_output.put_line('['||i.item_rating||']');
   END LOOP;
END;
/
```

The *cursor index* points to the row, and the component selector (period) links the row pointer to the column name or alias assigned by the implicit cursor. This prints the following from inventory:

```
Harry Potter and the Sorcerer's Stone [PG]
(3) Harry Potter and the Goblet of Fire [PG-13]
(3) Harry Potter and the Chamber of Secrets [PG]
(2) Harry Potter and the Prisoner of Azkaban [PG]
(1) Harry Potter and the Order of the Phoenix [PG-13]
```

There is also no exit statement in the example, because one isn't required. The exit statement is implicitly placed at the top of the loop. The exit condition checks whether all rows have been read. It exits when there are no more rows to read.

Explicit cursors have some obvious differences and some subtle ones. The later section "Cursor Structures" covers explicit cursors in cursor FOR loop statements.

WHILE Loop Statements

WHILE loops are explicit block structures like the simple loops. A WHILE loop starts and ends with the LOOP reserved word. Like simple loops, WHILE loops require that you manage both loop index and exit criteria. The WHILE loop is a guard on entry loop and may exclude a loop index because the entry condition explicitly checks another expression or Boolean variable.

The prototype for the WHILE loop is

```
WHILE entry_condition LOOP
  [counter_management_statements;]
  repeating_statements;
END LOOP;
```

The following example implements a WHILE loop. The WHILE loop uses a loop index value as its gate on entry criterion:

```
DECLARE
  counter NUMBER := 1;
BEGIN
  WHILE (counter < 3) LOOP
    dbms_output.put_line('Index ['||counter||'].');
    IF counter >= 1 THEN
      counter := counter + 1;
    END IF;
  END LOOP;
END;
/
```

It prints the following:

```
Index [1].
Index [2].
```

Two things differ between a simple and WHILE loop. The gate on entry counter variable must be initialized or you cannot enter the loop. This change eliminates checking for an initialized counter variable. The second difference is that you no longer check for the first versus subsequent iterations through the loop. This is eliminated because you no longer need to guarantee initialization of a counter variable.

You should note that the loop index management is the last statement in a WHILE loop. It is last because the exit criterion is the first thing evaluated at the top of the loop. This poses a logical challenge to using a CONTINUE statement in a WHILE loop because it can skip over the incrementing or decrementing index logic and create an infinite loop. A GOTO statement and a block label are actually the best solution to this problem presented by the CONTINUE statement.

The following shows you how to use sequential control with the GOTO statement and a block label:

```
DECLARE
  counter NUMBER := 1;
BEGIN
  WHILE (counter < 3) LOOP
    IF counter = 2 THEN
      GOTO loopindex;
    ELSE
      dbms_output.put_line('Index ['||counter||'].');
    END IF;
    << loopindex >>
    IF counter >= 1 THEN
```

```
      counter := counter + 1;
    END IF;
  END LOOP;
END;
/
```

The `GOTO` statement skips execution to the block label for the incrementing or decrementing logic. After running the loop index logic, control shifts to the top of the loop. This work-around guarantees that each iteration through a `WHILE` loop increments or decrements the loop index. It also avoids creating a short-circuiting infinite loop.

As you've seen, the `WHILE` loop is useful when you want to gate entry to a loop. On a downside, the `WHILE` loop limits how you skip logic when using a `CONTINUE` statement and loop index management block. The `GOTO` statement and block labels allow you to do the same thing.

Cursor Structures

Cursor structures are the return results from SQL `SELECT` statements. In PL/SQL, you can process `SELECT` statements row-by-row or as bulk statements. This section covers how you work with row-by-row statement processing cursors.

There are two types of cursors: implicit and explicit. You create an explicit cursor when you define a cursor inside a declaration block. DML statements inside any execution or exception block are implicit cursors. These include `INSERT`, `UPDATE`, and `DELETE` statements. You also create implicit cursors whenever you use a `SELECT` statement with `INTO` or `BULK COLLECT INTO` clauses, or you embed a `SELECT` statement inside a cursor `FOR` loop statement.

The balance of this section discusses implicit and explicit cursors separately. Implicit cursors come first, followed by explicit cursors. Bulk processing is covered in the next section.

Implicit Cursors

Every SQL statement in a PL/SQL block is actual an implicit cursor. You can see how many rows are changed by any statement using the `%ROWCOUNT` attribute after a Data Manipulation Language (DML) statement. `INSERT`, `UPDATE`, and `DELETE` statements are DML statements. You can also count the number of rows returned by a `SELECT` statement or query.

The following example demonstrates the `%ROWCOUNT` cursor attribute by using a single-row implicit cursor based on the `DUAL` pseudotable:

```
DECLARE
  n NUMBER;
BEGIN
  SELECT 1 INTO n FROM dual;
  dbms_output.put_line('Selected ['||SQL%ROWCOUNT||']');
END;
/
```

The reserved word `SQL` before the `%ROWCOUNT` cursor attribute stands for any implicit cursor. It also applies to bulk processing cursors when matched with a bulk cursor attribute. PL/SQL manages implicit cursors and limits your access to their attributes. Table 4-6 lists the available implicit cursor attributes.

You have three types of implicit cursors. One is an implicit bulk collection cursor, which is covered in the section "Bulk Statements" later in the chapter. The other two implicit cursors are

Attribute	Definition
%FOUND	This attribute returns TRUE when a DML statement has changed a row, or DQL has accessed one.
%ISOPEN	This attribute always returns a FALSE for any implicit cursor.
%NOTFOUND	This attribute returns TRUE when a DML statement has changed a row, or DQL can't access another.
%ROWCOUNT	This attribute returns the number of rows changed by a DML statement or the number of rows returned by a SELECT INTO statement.

TABLE 4-6   *Implicit Cursor Attributes*

the subject of this section. They are single-row and multiple-row implicit cursors that use SELECT statements.

Single-Row Implicit Cursors

The SELECT INTO statement is present in all implicit cursors that query data. It works only when a single row is returned by a select statement. You can select a column or list of columns in the SELECT clause and assign the row columns to individual variables or collectively to a record datatype.

The prototype for a single-row implicit cursor minus standard SQL WHERE, HAVING, GROUP BY, and ORDER BY clauses is

```
SELECT column1 [, column2 [, column(n+1) ]]
INTO variable1 [, variable2 [, variable(n+1) ]]
FROM table_name;
```

Both example programs use the ITEM table that is seeded in the downloadable code for the book. The first example program assigns column values to scalar variables on a one-to-one basis:

```
DECLARE
  id       item.item_id%TYPE;
  title    item.item_title%TYPE;
  subtitle item.item_subtitle%TYPE;
BEGIN
  SELECT  item_id, item_title, item_subtitle
  INTO    id, title, subtitle
  FROM    item
  WHERE   ROWNUM < 2;
  dbms_output.put_line('Selected ['||title||']');
END;
/
```

The example program anchors all variables to the target table and limits the query to one row by using the Oracle SQL ROWNUM pseudocolumn. It prints one row:

```
Selected [Around the World in 80 Days]
```

One-to-one assignments get very tiresome to type after a while. They also make your code more expensive to maintain over time. The more common convention is to assign the columns as a group to record datatypes.

The second example assigns the columns to a record datatype:

```
DECLARE
  TYPE item_record IS RECORD
  ( id        item.item_id%TYPE
  , title     item.item_title%TYPE
  , subtitle item.item_subtitle%TYPE);
  dataset ITEM_RECORD;
BEGIN
  SELECT    item_id, item_title, item_subtitle
  INTO      dataset
  FROM      item
  WHERE     rownum < 2;
  dbms_output.put_line('Selected ['||dataset.title||']');
END;
/
```

While record datatypes require an explicit construction, columns within the structure can be anchored to column datatypes. You should also note that the component selector, or period, glues the record variable to the element name.

Single-row implicit cursors are great quick fixes, but they have a weakness. It is a weakness that many developers attempt to exploit by using it to raise exceptions when cursors return more than one row. They do this because single-row implicit cursors raise an "exact fetch returned too many rows" error (ORA-01422) when returning more than one row. Better solutions are available to detect errors before fetching the data. You should explore alternatives when developing your code and where possible explicitly handle errors. Explicit cursors are typically better solutions every time.

Multiple-Row Implicit Cursors

There are two ways you can create multiple-row implicit cursors. The first is done by writing any DML statement in a PL/SQL block. DML statements are considered multiple-row implicit cursors, even though you can limit them to a single row. The second is to write an embedded query in a cursor FOR loop rather than defined in a declaration block.

The following query demonstrates an implicit cursor created by a DML statement:

```
BEGIN
  UPDATE    system_user
  SET       last_update_date = SYSDATE;
  IF SQL%FOUND THEN
    dbms_output.put_line('Updated ['||SQL%ROWCOUNT||']');
  ELSE
    dbms_output.put_line('Nothing updated!');
  END IF;
END;
/
```

As shown in Table 4-6, the `%FOUND` cursor attribute for implicit cursors only returns a Boolean true value when rows are updated. This statement should update five rows and print the `SQL%ROWCOUNT` result:

```
Updated [5]
```

You can also define multiple-row implicit cursors inside cursor `FOR` loop statements. These are select statements that have a marvelous feature: all the variables are implicitly provided in the scope of the cursor `FOR` loop.

The following demonstrates a multiple-row implicit cursor in a cursor `FOR` loop:

```
BEGIN
  FOR i IN (SELECT item_id, item_title FROM item) LOOP
    dbms_output.put_line('Item #['||i.item_id||']['||i.item_title||']');
  END LOOP;
END;
/
```

This implicit cursor is available in the scope of the cursor `FOR` loop index. The cursor index for a cursor `FOR` loop is a pointer to result set in a query work area. A query work area is a memory region (known as a *context area*) in the Oracle 11*g* Database *Process Global Area (PGA)*.

NOTE
The `SQL%ROWCOUNT` *attribute returns a null value for this type of implicit cursor.*

Explicit Cursors

As discussed earlier in this section, you create an explicit cursor when you define it inside a declaration block. Explicit cursors can be static or dynamic `SELECT` statements. Static `SELECT` statements return the same query each time with potentially different results. The results change as the data changes in the tables or views. Dynamic `SELECT` statements act like parameterized subroutines. They run different queries each time, depending on the actual parameters provided when they're opened.

You open static and dynamic explicit cursors differently, provided they are defined with formal parameters. When they do not have formal parameters, you open them with the same syntax. The actual parameters are then mapped by local variable substitution.

Explicit cursors require you to open, fetch, and close them whether you're using simple or `WHILE` loops or cursor `FOR` loop statements. You use the `OPEN` statement to open cursors, the `FETCH` statement to fetch records from cursors, and the `CLOSE` statement to close and release resources of cursors. These statements work with both dynamic and static cursors inside or outside of a looping structure. *Cursor* `FOR` loop statements implicitly open, fetch, and close cursors for you. The `OPEN`, `FETCH`, and `CLOSE` statements are key elements in the "Static Explicit Cursors" and "Dynamic Explicit Cursors" subsections where the examples use simple loops.

The prototype for the `OPEN` statement is

```
OPEN cursor_name [(parameter1 [, parameter2 [, parameter(n+1)]])];
```

There are two prototypes for the `FETCH` statement. One assigns individual columns to variables, and the other assigns a row to a record structure.

The prototype for assigning individual columns to matching variables is

```
FETCH cursor_name
INTO variable1 [, variable2 [, variable(n+1) ]];
```

The prototype for assigning rows to record structure variables is

```
FETCH cursor_name
INTO record_variable;
```

The prototype for the `CLOSE` statement is

```
CLOSE cursor_name;
```

While Table 4-6 lists the implicit cursor attributes, Table 4-7 lists the explicit cursor attributes. The attributes work the same way whether an explicit cursor is dynamic or static but differently than the limited set that work with implicit cursors. The explicit cursor attributes return different results, depending on where they are called in reference to the `OPEN`, `FETCH`, and `CLOSE` statements.

The `%FOUND` cursor attribute signals that rows are available to retrieve from the cursor and the `%NOTFOUND` attribute signals that all rows have been retrieved from the cursor. The `%ISOPEN` attribute lets you know that the cursor is already open, and is something you should consider running before attempting to open a cursor. Like implicit cursors, the `%ROWCOUNT` attribute tells you how many rows you've fetched at any given point. Only the `%ISOPEN` cursor attribute works anytime without an error. The other three raise errors when the cursor isn't open. The Table 4-7 matrix captures these changing behaviors.

The examples use simple loop statements, but you can also use explicit cursors in `WHILE` loop statements or nested inside range and cursor `FOR` loops. Static and dynamic cursors are covered in different subsections to organize the examples and highlight differences.

Static Explicit Cursors
A static explicit cursor is a SQL `SELECT` statement that doesn't change its behavior. An explicit cursor has four components: you define, open, fetch from, and close a cursor. The example program defines a cursor as a `SELECT` statement that queries the `ITEM` table. The table and seeded data are delivered in the downloadable code.

Statement	State	`%FOUND`	`%NOTFOUND`	`%ISOPEN`	`%ROWCOUNT`
OPEN	Before	Exception	Exception	FALSE	Exception
	After	NULL	NULL	TRUE	0
1st FETCH	Before	NULL	NULL	TRUE	0
	After	TRUE	FALSE	TRUE	1
Next FETCH	Before	TRUE	FALSE	TRUE	1
	After	TRUE	FALSE	TRUE	n + 1
Last FETCH	Before	TRUE	FALSE	TRUE	n + 1
	After	FALSE	TRUE	TRUE	n + 1
CLOSE	Before	FALSE	TRUE	TRUE	n + 1
	After	Exception	Exception	FALSE	Exception

TABLE 4-7 *Explicit Cursor Attributes*

The following program defines, opens, fetches from, and closes a static cursor into a series of scalar variables:

```
DECLARE
    id        item.item_id%TYPE;
    title     VARCHAR2(60);
    CURSOR c IS
      SELECT    item_id
      ,         item_title
      FROM      item;
BEGIN
  OPEN c;
  LOOP
    FETCH c
    INTO  id, title;
    EXIT WHEN c%NOTFOUND;
    dbms_output.put_line('Title ['||title||']');
  END LOOP;
  CLOSE c;
END;
/
```

The program uses the fetch of columns to variables that match their data type. One of the variables is anchored to the table and the other is literally defined. You should really choose one or the other style, but this example wanted to display both. The program exits when there are no more records to fetch and it has printed the titles to the console.

The same program can be written using a cursor FOR loop statement. The FOR loop implicitly creates variables that you can access through the cursor index. This eliminate the need for you to create them as required by the simple or WHILE loop statements. The cursor FOR loop statement also implicitly opens, fetches, and closes the cursor, like this:

```
DECLARE
    CURSOR c IS
      SELECT    item_id AS id
      ,         item_title AS title
      FROM      item;
BEGIN
  FOR i IN c LOOP
    dbms_output.put_line('Title ['||i.title||']');
  END LOOP;
END;
/
```

By comparison the cursor FOR loop is much simpler to use with a static cursor than a simple or WHILE loop statement. The implicitly declared variables inside the cursor FOR loop have no context outside of the FOR loop statement. This limitation restricts how you can use the return values from a cursor FOR loop. Simple or WHILE loop statements are more effective solutions when you want to assign return values to variables that are exchanged with other program units. Chapter 6 discusses some of these advantages while covering stored functions and procedures.

The alternative FETCH statement syntax of assigning a row of data to a record datatype is illustrated in the next program. Everything else remains the same.

The following program defines, opens, fetches from, and closes a static cursor into a record structure:

```
DECLARE
    TYPE item_record IS RECORD
    ( id        NUMBER
    , title     VARCHAR2(60));
    item ITEM_RECORD;
    CURSOR c IS
      SELECT    item_id
      ,         item_title
      FROM      item;
BEGIN
  OPEN c;
  LOOP
    FETCH c INTO item;
    EXIT WHEN c%NOTFOUND;
    dbms_output.put_line('Title ['||item.title||']');
  END LOOP;
END;
/
```

You should note that a cursor FOR loop statement does not support direct assignment of any type of variable, but you can assign values inside the FOR loop statement by using the cursor index. You can assign a record structure or an element of the record structure.

The following demonstrates assigning a record structure from the cursor index:

```
DECLARE
    TYPE item_record IS RECORD
    ( id    NUMBER
    , title VARCHAR2(60));
    explicit_item ITEM_RECORD;
    CURSOR c IS
      SELECT    item_id AS id
      ,         item_title AS title
      FROM      item;
BEGIN
  FOR i IN c LOOP
    explicit_item := i;
    dbms_output.put_line('Title ['||explicit_item.title||']');
  END LOOP;
END;
/
```

In both of these examples, it is possible that the cursor may not find any records. When an implicit or explicit cursor runs and no data is found, no error is raised. You need to manually determine if any records are found. This can be done by using an IF statement and the %NOTFOUND and %ROWCOUNT cursor attributes.

The following program prints a no data found message when the cursor fails to find any records by using a negative ITEM_ID value that shouldn't be in the data:

```
DECLARE
    TYPE item_record IS RECORD
    ( id        NUMBER
```

```
  , title    VARCHAR2(60));
  item ITEM_RECORD;
  CURSOR c IS
    SELECT    item_id
    ,         item_title
    FROM      item
    WHERE     item_id = -1;
BEGIN
  OPEN c;
  LOOP
    FETCH c INTO item;
    IF c%NOTFOUND THEN
      IF c%ROWCOUNT = 0 THEN
        dbms_output.put_line('No Data Found');
      END IF;
      EXIT;
    ELSE
      dbms_output.put_line('Title ['||item.title||']');
    END IF;
  END LOOP;
END;
/
```

The program demonstrates a *conditional exit*. The exit is reachable only when all records are read. A special message is printed only when the %ROWCOUNT returns a 0 value. This can only happen when no rows are returned by the cursor. You cannot replicate this logic inside a cursor FOR loop statement.

Dynamic Explicit Cursors

Dynamic explicit cursors are very much like static explicit cursors. They use a SQL SELECT statement. Only the SELECT statement uses variables that change the query behavior. The variables take the place of what would otherwise be literal values.

Dynamic explicit cursors have the same four components as static cursors: you define, open, fetch from, and close a dynamic cursor. The example program defines a cursor as a SELECT statement that queries the ITEM table for a range of values. Both variables are declared as local variables and assigned numeric literal values. The names of the local variables must differ from column names, or the column name values are substituted in place of the variable values.

The following program uses two local variables inside the cursor's SELECT statement:

```
DECLARE
  lowend NUMBER := 1010;
  highend NUMBER := 1020;
  TYPE item_record IS RECORD
  ( id       NUMBER
  , title    VARCHAR2(60));
  item ITEM_RECORD;
  CURSOR c IS
    SELECT    item_id
    ,         item_title
    FROM      item
    WHERE     item_id BETWEEN lowend AND highend;
```

```
BEGIN
  OPEN c;
  LOOP
    FETCH c INTO item;
    EXIT WHEN c%NOTFOUND;
    dbms_output.put_line('Title ['||item.title||']');
  END LOOP;
END;
/
```

The values for the `lowend` and `highend` variables are substituted when you open the cursor. This also works in cursor `FOR` and `WHILE` loops because the variables are substituted while opening the cursor. While this acts more or less as a static query because the variables are static constants in the program scope, you can change the program to use input parameters as follows:

```
DECLARE
… same as earlier example …
BEGIN
  lowend := TO_NUMBER(NVL(&1,1005));
  highend := TO_NUMBER(NVL(&2,1021));
  OPEN c;
  LOOP
    FETCH c INTO item;
    EXIT WHEN c%NOTFOUND;
    dbms_output.put_line('Title ['||item.title||']');
  END LOOP;
END;
/
```

You can rely on local variables, but it can be confusing and more difficult to support the code. Cursors should be defined to accept formal parameters. The next example replaces the prior by altering the cursor definition and the call to the `OPEN` statement, as

```
DECLARE
  lowend NUMBER;
  highend NUMBER;
  item_id number := 1012;
  TYPE item_record IS RECORD
  ( id        NUMBER
  , title     VARCHAR2(60));
  item ITEM_RECORD;
  CURSOR c
  ( low_id NUMBER
  , high_id NUMBER) IS
    SELECT    item_id
    ,         item_title
    FROM      item
    WHERE     item_id BETWEEN low_id AND high_id;
BEGIN
  lowend := TO_NUMBER(NVL(&1,1005));
  highend := TO_NUMBER(NVL(&2,1021));
  OPEN c (lowend,highend);
```

```
LOOP
  FETCH c INTO item;
  EXIT WHEN c%NOTFOUND;
  dbms_output.put_line('Title ['||item.title||']');
END LOOP;
END;
/
```

The range variables in the SELECT statement are no longer local variable names. They are local variables to the cursor, defined by the formal parameter in the cursor definition. You should note that these variables have no physical size, because that is derived at run time.

When you run the program, the input values &1 and &2 are assigned to local variables lowend and highend respectively. The local variables become actual parameters passed to open the cursor. The actual parameters are then assigned to the low_id and high_id cursor-scoped variables.

The same logic works when you substitute a cursor FOR loop statement. The following loop structure is equivalent to the one in the simple loop statement:

```
FOR i IN c (lowend,highend) LOOP
  item := i;
  dbms_output.put_line('Title ['||item.title||']');
END LOOP;
```

This section has explained how to use implicit and explicit cursors in your program units. You've learned that some implicit behaviors are outside of your control. You've also learned that explicit structures provide you with more control.

Bulk Statements

Bulk statements let you select, insert, update, or delete large data sets from tables or views. You use the BULK COLLECT statement with SELECT statements and the FORALL statement to insert, update, or delete large data sets.

Table 4-8 lists descriptions of the two bulk cursor attributes. The subsection "INSERT Statement" subsection under the section "FORALL Statements" illustrates how to use the %BULK_ROWCOUNT attribute. Chapter 5 covers how you use the %BULK_EXCEPTION attribute.

Bulk Attributes	Definitions
%BULK_EXCEPTIONS(i)	The %BULK_EXCEPTION(*index*) attribute lets you see whether or not a row encountered an error during a bulk INSERT, UPDATE, or DELETE statement. You access these statistics by putting them in range FOR loop statements.
%BULK_ROWCOUNT(i)	The %BULK_ROWCOUNT(*index*) attribute lets you see whether or not an element is altered by a bulk INSERT, UPDATE, or DELETE statement. You access these statistics by putting them in range FOR loop statements.

TABLE 4-8   *Bulk Cursor Attributes*

This section explains how to use the BULK COLLECT INTO and FORALL statements. The subsection "BULK COLLECT INTO Statement" discusses the uses of and differences between parallel scalar and record collections. The subsection "FORALL Statements" has independent sections on how you can use bulk INSERT, UPDATE, and DELETE statements.

BULK COLLECT INTO Statements

The BULK COLLECT INTO statement lets you select a column of data and insert it into Oracle collection datatypes. You can use a bulk collect inside a SQL statement or as part of a FETCH statement. A SQL statement bulk collection uses an implicit cursor, while a FETCH statement works with an explicit cursor. You cannot limit the number of rows returned when performing bulk collection in an implicit cursor. The FETCH statement lets you append the LIMIT statement to set the maximum number of rows read from the cursor at a time. You can use any standard or user-defined PL/SQL datatype as the target of an implicit cursor statement.

The following is a basic prototype of an implicit bulk collection statement:

```
SELECT   column1 [, column2 [, column(n+1)]]
COLLECT BULK INTO collection1 [, collection2 [, collection(n+1)]]
FROM     table_name
[WHERE   where_clause_statements];
```

Bulk collections performed as part of a FETCH statement use an explicit cursor. They have the following prototype:

```
FETCH cursor_name [(parameter1 [, parameter2 [, parameter(n+1)]])]
BULK COLLECT INTO collection1 [, collection2 [, collection(n+1)]]
[LIMIT rows_to_return];
```

The number of columns returned by the explicit cursor determines the number of scalar collection targets, or the structure of a record collection target. The SELECT statement defines the number and type of columns returned by a cursor.

You can use BULK COLLECT INTO statements to insert a series of targets or a single target. A series of targets is a set of collection variables separated by commas. The target comma-delimited collections are known as parallel collections because you generally manage them in parallel. A single target is a collection of a record structure. You cannot insert some of the columns into a collection of a record structure and others into scalar collections in the same statement call. Any attempt to do so raises a PLS-00494 error that disallows coercion into multiple record targets.

The BULK COLLECT INTO statement is much faster than a standard cursor because it has one parse, execute, and fetch cycle. Ordinary implicit INTO statement cursors or explicit cursors have more parses, executes, and fetches. Bulk operations scale better as the number or rows increase, but very large operations require database configurations to support them.

The sections "Parallel Collection Targets" and "Record Collection Targets" demonstrate bulk collections using implicit cursors. Explicit cursors are demonstrated in the last subsection along with the LIMIT statement. The LIMIT statement lets you constrain the size of bulk selections, but you can only use it with explicit cursors. The last subsection on limited collection targets demonstrates how you can work within your database operating constraints, like the PGA.

Parallel Collection Targets

Scalar collections are the only supported SQL collection datatypes. When you want to share data with external programs or web applications, you should return your bulk selections into a series of parallel collections. You can exchange these datatypes with external programs and web applications, using the Oracle Call Interface (OCI).

The example program uses an implicit BULK COLLECT INTO statement cursor, and it performs a bulk selection into a set of parallel scalar collections:

```
DECLARE
  TYPE title_collection IS TABLE OF VARCHAR2(60);
  TYPE subtitle_collection IS TABLE OF VARCHAR2(60);
  title    TITLE_COLLECTION;
  subtitle SUBTITLE_COLLECTION;
BEGIN
  SELECT  item_title
  ,       item_subtitle
  BULK COLLECT INTO title, subtitle
  FROM    item;
  -- Print one element of one of the parallel collections.
  FOR i IN 1..title.COUNT LOOP
    dbms_output.put_line('Title ['||title(i)||']');
  END LOOP;
END;
/
```

The program demonstrates how you pass a set of values into scalar collections. After you change the natural row structure to a parallel collection of column values, you should ensure the discrete collections remain synchronized. Creating and maintaining synchronized collections is difficult and tedious. You should only choose this direction when you have a critical business need to move data around using SQL datatypes.

The typical reason to opt for parallel collections is to move the data from PL/SQL to external programming languages or web applications. You should reconvert the parallel collections into a multiple dimensional collections after transferring the data. *Multiple dimension collections are typically collections of record types.*

Record Collection Targets

Current limitations on building SQL collections limits collections of records to *PL/SQL-only structures.* This means that you can only use them inside programs that run exclusively in the PL/SQL environment.

You can use a collection of PL/SQL record types as a datatype for a parameter in a stored function or procedure when you define the datatype in a PL/SQL package specification form. This limitation means that you cannot exchange the datatype with external programs. You must use parallel collections when you want to exchange them with external programs and web applications.

The example program uses an implicit BULK COLLECT INTO statement cursor, and it performs a bulk selection into a collection of a local record structure:

```
DECLARE
  TYPE title_record IS RECORD
  ( title VARCHAR2(60)
  , subtitle VARCHAR2(60));
  TYPE collection IS TABLE OF TITLE_RECORD;
  full_title COLLECTION;
BEGIN
  SELECT  item_title
```

```
    ,           item_subtitle
    BULK COLLECT INTO full_title
    FROM      item;
    -- Print one element of a structure.
    FOR i IN 1..full_title.COUNT LOOP
      dbms_output.put_line('Title ['||full_title(i).title||']');
    END LOOP;
END;
/
```

You will find the mechanics for creating and accessing datatypes defined in package specifications in Chapter 9. At some future time Oracle may let you create SQL collections of record types, but currently you are limited to scalar and user-defined object types. Access to these structures may first come from the Oracle Call Interface (OCI), since it began letting you access PL/SQL associative arrays and reference cursors in the Oracle 10g Database, Release 2.

LIMIT Constrained Collection Targets

The LIMIT statement lets you set the maximum number or rows returned by a bulk collection. It constrains the bulk collection. You can only constrain the number of rows returned by explicit cursors in a FETCH statement.

The downside to this approach is tied to how interactive applications work. Interactive applications generally require all or nothing, not just some of the records. Batch processing programs that manage large transaction processing steps are the best candidates for leveraging this approach.

Explicit cursors can return one to many columns of data from the internal SELECT statement. You choose to place those column values inside a series of scalar collection targets or a single record collection target. The next two subsections demonstrate both techniques.

Parallel Collection Targets   Parallel collection targets are scalar collection variables. Parallel collections may differ in datatype but each have the same number of rows and matching index values. You need scalar collection variables for each column returned by the explicit cursor.

The following program demonstrates how to manage a bulk collection ten rows at a time:

```
DECLARE
  -- Define scalar datatypes.
  TYPE title_collection IS TABLE OF VARCHAR2(60);
  TYPE subtitle_collection IS TABLE OF VARCHAR2(60);
  -- Define local variables.
  title    TITLE_COLLECTION;
  subtitle SUBTITLE_COLLECTION;
  -- Define a static cursor.
  CURSOR c IS
    SELECT    item_title
    ,         item_subtitle
    FROM      item;
BEGIN
  OPEN c;
  LOOP
    FETCH c BULK COLLECT INTO title, subtitle LIMIT 10;
    EXIT WHEN title.COUNT = 0;
    FOR i IN 1..title.COUNT LOOP
```

```
          dbms_output.put_line('Title ['||title(i)||']');
      END LOOP;
   END LOOP;
END;
/
```

All iterations through the loop fetch all available rows or up to ten rows of data from the open cursor. This means that the processing logic must manage all returned rows before fetching the next set of rows. The exit condition uses the Oracle Collection API COUNT() method to determine when no rows have been fetched by the cursor. This is equivalent logic to the following statement for an ordinary cursor:

```
EXIT WHEN c%NOTFOUND;
```

While ten is a small number, the idea is to limit consumed memory and minimize the number of parses, executes, and fetches. This solution support exchanges with external programs and web applications that are otherwise limited by the OCI8 library.

Record Collection Targets   Record collection targets are record collection variables. A target record collection must map exactly to the return structure of the cursor's SELECT statement. You can only use record collections inside the PL/SQL environment.

The following program demonstrates how to manage a bulk collection ten rows at a time:

```
DECLARE
   TYPE title_record IS RECORD
   ( title VARCHAR2(60)
   , subtitle VARCHAR2(60));
   TYPE collection IS TABLE OF TITLE_RECORD;
   full_title COLLECTION;
   CURSOR c IS
     SELECT    item_title
     ,         item_subtitle
     FROM      item;
BEGIN
   OPEN c;
   LOOP
     FETCH c BULK COLLECT INTO full_title LIMIT 10;
     EXIT WHEN full_title.COUNT = 0;
     FOR i IN 1..full_title.COUNT LOOP
       dbms_output.put_line('Title ['||full_title(i).title||']');
     END LOOP;
   END LOOP;
END;
/
```

The program logic is a mirror to the sample program demonstrating parallel collections except that it returns a row of data into a record collection. All iterations through the loop fetch all available rows or up to ten rows of data from the open cursor. This means that the processing logic must manage all returned rows before fetching the next set of rows. The exit condition uses the Oracle Collection API COUNT() method to determine when no rows have been fetched by the cursor. This is equivalent logic to the following statement for an ordinary cursor:

```
EXIT WHEN c%NOTFOUND;
```

While ten is a small number, the idea is to limit consumed memory and minimize the number of parses, executes, and fetches. This solution doesn't support exchanges with external programs or web applications because of OCI8 limitations.

FORALL Statements

The FORALL loop is designed to work with Oracle collections. It lets you insert, update, or delete bulk data. This section focuses on how to use the FORALL statement and forward reference collections, which Chapter 7 covers in depth.

The examples build on the bulk collection examples. They also depend on an ITEM_TEMP target table. You should create the table by using the following syntax:

```
CREATE TABLE ITEM_TEMP
( item_id   NUMBER
, item_title VARCHAR2(62)
, item_subtitle VARCHAR2(60));
```

The subsections are ordered to support the example code. You insert, update, and delete the data using FORALL statements. Then, you can drop the ITEM_TEMP table.

INSERT Statement

Bulk inserts require that you use scalar collections inside the VALUES clause. You raise an ORA-00947 not enough values error when you attempt to insert a record collection.

The following example code uses scalar collections to perform a bulk insert:

```
DECLARE
  TYPE id_collection IS TABLE OF NUMBER;
  TYPE title_collection IS TABLE OF VARCHAR2(60);
  TYPE subtitle_collection IS TABLE OF VARCHAR2(60);
  id        ID_COLLECTION;
  title     TITLE_COLLECTION;
  subtitle SUBTITLE_COLLECTION;
  CURSOR c IS
    SELECT   item_id
    ,        item_title
    ,        item_subtitle
    FROM     item;
BEGIN
  OPEN c;
  LOOP
    FETCH c BULK COLLECT INTO id, title, subtitle LIMIT 10;
    EXIT WHEN title.COUNT = 0;
    FORALL i IN id.FIRST..id.LAST
      INSERT INTO item_temp VALUES (id(i),title(i),subtitle(i));
  END LOOP;
  FOR i IN id.FIRST..id.LAST LOOP
    dbms_output.put('Inserted ['||id(i)||']');
    dbms_output.put_line('['||SQL%BULK_ROWCOUNT(i)||']');
  END LOOP;
END;
/
```

The FORALL statement reads the index of the first scalar array but could easily read the others. They should all be exactly the same. Nested tables use a 1-based integer index. In this example the low range is always 1 and the high range value is always 10. You place the scalar collection variables in the right position and index them with a subscript value. This essentially acts like an insert from another SELECT statement.

The second range FOR loop captures the ITEM_ID value and whether or not it was inserted into the table. It prints 1 when successful and 0 when unsuccessful. This illustrates how you can use the %BULK_ROWCOUNT attribute.

The real performance advantage comes by placing the COMMIT statement after the end of the loop. Otherwise, you commit for each batch of inserts. There are occasions when the size of data inserted makes it more advantageous to put the COMMIT statement as the last statement in the loop. You should examine the size factors and discuss them with your DBA.

UPDATE Statement

Bulk updates require that you use scalar collections inside the SET clause and any WHERE clause. Like the INSERT statement, you raise an ORA-00947 not enough values error when you attempt to insert a record collection.

The following example code uses scalar collections to perform a bulk update:

```
DECLARE
  TYPE id_collection IS TABLE OF NUMBER;
  TYPE title_collection IS TABLE OF VARCHAR2(60);
  id       ID_COLLECTION;
  title    TITLE_COLLECTION;
  CURSOR c IS
    SELECT   item_id
    ,        item_title
    FROM     item;
BEGIN
  OPEN c;
  LOOP
    FETCH c BULK COLLECT INTO id, title LIMIT 10;
    EXIT WHEN title.COUNT = 0;
    FORALL i IN id.FIRST..id.LAST
      UPDATE   item_temp
      SET      title = title(i)||': '
      WHERE    id = id(i);
  END LOOP;
END;
/
```

The FORALL statement reads the index of the first scalar array but could easily read the other collection index. All the index values should all be exactly the same. In this example the low range is always 1 and the high range value is always 10 because nested table indexes are 1-based numbers. You place the scalar collection variables in the SET clause or WHERE clause and index them with a subscript value. This essentially acts like a correlated update statement.

As with the INSERT statement, you should judge where the COMMIT statement belongs when updating bulk records. After the loop is better when the data chunks are small, and the penultimate loop statement is best when the chunks are large. In both cases, you should examine the size factors and discuss them with your DBA.

DELETE Statement

Bulk deletes require that you use scalar collections inside the WHERE clause. As with the INSERT or UPDATE statements, you can't use record collections.

The following example code uses scalar collections to perform a bulk delete:

```
DECLARE
  TYPE id_collection IS TABLE OF NUMBER;
  TYPE title_collection IS TABLE OF VARCHAR2(60);
  id        ID_COLLECTION;
  title     TITLE_COLLECTION;
  CURSOR c IS
    SELECT    item_id
    ,         item_title
    FROM      item;
BEGIN
  OPEN c;
  LOOP
    FETCH c BULK COLLECT INTO id, title LIMIT 10;
    EXIT WHEN title.COUNT = 0;
    FORALL i IN id.FIRST..id.LAST
      DELETE
      FROM      item_temp
      WHERE     subtitle IS NULL
      AND       id = id(i);
  END LOOP;
END;
/
```

The FORALL statement reads the index of the first scalar array but could easily read the other collection index. All the index values should be exactly the same. In this example the low range is always 1 and the high range value is always 10 because nested table indexes are 1-based numbers. You place the scalar collection variables in the WHERE clause and index them with a subscript value. This essentially acts like a correlated update statement.

As with the INSERT and UPDATE statements, you should judge where the COMMIT statement belongs when deleting bulk records. After the loop is better when the data chunks are small, and the penultimate loop statement is best when the chunks are large. In both cases, you should examine the size factors and discuss them with your DBA.

This section has demonstrated how to use bulk collections and the FORALL statement. These commands offer you performance improvements over the traditional row-by-row cursor approach. You should look for opportunities to use them to improve your application throughput.

Summary

This chapter has examined the control structures in PL/SQL. You should understand how to effectively use conditional statements and iterative statements. You should also understand how to build and manage cursors in your PL/SQL programs.

CHAPTER
5

Error Management

T his chapter covers PL/SQL error management. PL/SQL handles errors in the exception block. You'll find two types of errors in PL/SQL: compilation errors and run-time errors. You discover compilation errors when you run an anonymous block program or attempt to build a stored program unit—a function, procedure, or user-defined object type. Run-time errors are more complex because they have two potential scenarios. Run-time errors raise manageable errors in the execution or exception blocks, but you can't catch run-time errors raised in the declaration block.

You will learn about both types of errors and how to manage them in this chapter. Sections in the chapter are

- Exception types and scope

  - Compilation errors

  - Run-time errors

- Exception management built-in functions

- User-defined exceptions

  - Declaring user-defined exceptions

  - Dynamic user-defined exceptions

- Exception stack trace functions

  - Exception stack management

  - Exception stack formatting

- Database trigger exception management

This chapter is designed to be read sequentially. If you want to quickly reference something, you should consider browsing the chapter first, before targeting a specific section.

Exception Types and Scope

You have two types of errors: compilation errors and run-time errors. Compilation errors occur when you make an error typing the program or defining the program. The typing errors include forgetting a reserved word, keyword, or semicolon. These lexical errors are caught when the plain text file is parsed during compilation. Parsing is the process of reading a text file to ensure that it meets the lexical usage rules of a programming language. Run-time errors occur when actual data fails to meet the rules defined by your program unit.

Chapter 3 explains variable scope and displays how it moves from the outermost block to the innermost. While variable scope begins at the outside and narrows as we nest program units, exception handling works in the opposite direction. Exceptions in the innermost blocks are handled locally or thrown to the containing block in sequence until they arrive at the originating session. Figure 5-1 shows this exception management process.

Compilation errors are often seen quickly because they fail during the parsing phase. Some deferred errors go unhandled until you run the programs with data values that trigger the error.

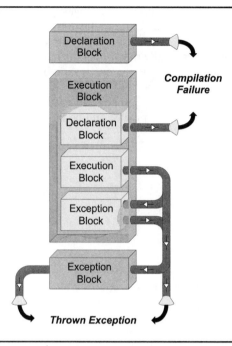

FIGURE 5-1 *Exception scope and routing*

You create deferred compilation errors when actual data values don't fit during assignment because they are too large or the wrong datatype. All compilation errors are thrown back to the session and cannot be handled by your local exception handler, but you can catch them in a wrapper (containing outer) block.

Run-time *execution* errors can always be caught and processed by the local or external exception block. Run-time errors in exception blocks can *only be caught by an outer block exception handler.* You can also opt not to catch errors and have them thrown back to the originating SQL*Plus session.

The next two subsections cover compilation and run-time errors.

Compilation Errors

Compilation errors are generally typing errors. The parsing of your PL/SQL text file into a set of interpreted instructions, known as p-code, finds lexical errors. Lexical errors occur when you misuse a delimiter, identifier, literal, or comment. You can misuse lexical units by

- Forgetting a semicolon (the statement terminator)

- Using only one delimiter when you should use two, as by failing to enclose a string literal

- Misspelling an identifier (reserved words and keywords)

- Commenting out a lexical value required by the parsing rules

There are three general patterns for error messages: prior line, current line, and declaration errors. The prior line error points to an error on the prior statement line, which is generally a missing statement terminator. Current line errors point to the column of the error or one column after the error. The difference generally means that the parser is looking for a missing lexical unit. Declaration errors point to any failure in the declaration block and generally have the actual error line as the last line of the error message.

The following program should only print a hello world message, but it fails to compile because it is missing the statement terminator on line 2:

```
SQL> BEGIN
  2    dbms_output.put_line('Hello World.')
  3  END;
  4  /
```

This raises the following error message:

```
END;
*
ERROR at line 3:
ORA-06550: line 3, column 1:
PLS-00103: Encountered the symbol "END" when expecting one of the following:
:= . ( % ;
The symbol ";" was substituted for "END" to continue.
```

This error message may look undecipherable, but it is actually quite informative when you know how to read it. The first line of the error message provides either the line where the error occurred or the line after the error. The second line places an asterisk immediately below the error location or on the first column of the line. The PLS-00103 error message raised by the example says that a lexical unit is missing immediately before the END reserved word. This typically means the error occurred one statement line before the echoed error message line. The error message also provides five possible lexical values for a missing symbol. The parser suggests using a semicolon. In this case the semicolon or statement terminator is the missing lexical unit. The semicolon should end the statement on line 2.

The next example shows a compilation error where the error occurs on the same line:

```
SQL> DECLARE
  2    a NUMBER := 0;
  3    b NUMBER;
  4    c NUMBER;
  5  BEGIN
  6    c := a  b;
  7    dbms_output.put_line('['||c||']');
  8  END;
  9  /
```

The error message displayed is

```
  c := a  b;
         *
ERROR at line 6:
ORA-06550: line 6, column 11:
```

```
PLS-00103: Encountered the symbol "B" when expecting one of the following:
. ( * @ % & = - + ; < / > at in is mod remainder not rem
<an exponent (**)> <> or != or ~= >= <= <> and or like LIKE2_
LIKE4_ LIKEC_ between || multiset member SUBMULTISET_
The symbol "." was substituted for "B" to continue.
```

The `PLS-00103` error message says that a lexical unit is missing immediately before the variable b. The asterisk on the second line below the variable b tells you that the error occurs immediately before the variable. You can fix this program by placing any arithmetic operator in between the a and b variables.

A variation on the prior error message places the asterisk immediately below where the error occurs in a statement line. The following program raises this type of error message:

```
SQL> DECLARE
  2    a NUMBER;
  3  BEGIN
  4    a = 1;
  5  END;
  6  /
```

The error message displayed is

```
  a = 1;
    *
ERROR at line 4:
ORA-06550: line 4, column 5:
PLS-00103: Encountered the symbol "=" when expecting one of the following:
:= . ( @ % ;
The symbol ":= was inserted before "=" to continue.
```

This type of error message points to the use of a comparison operator where an assignment operator should appear. This is the easiest type of error message to read and understand.

You receive a less obvious error message when you trigger an error in the declaration block. The following example tries to assign a two-character string to a one-character variable in the declaration block:

```
SQL> DECLARE
  2    a CHAR := 'AB';
  3  BEGIN
  4    dbms_output.put_line('['||a||']');
  5  END;
  6  /
```

The program raises the following error message, which provides very little information if you were trying to apply the previously discussed rules:

```
DECLARE
*
ERROR at line 1:
ORA-06502: PL/SQL: numeric or value error: character string buffer too small
ORA-06512: at line 2
```

The error points to line 1. Unlike the earlier errors, this does not point to a problem before the `DECLARE` statement. It tells you that the error occurs in the declaration block, and the last statement in the error message points to the specific line number. The last line is actually the first error written to the exception stack trace. The `ORA-06512` error on the last line of the error message points to line 2 in the program. The error occurs when the program tries to assign a string literal `'AB'` into a single character-sized variable.

This section has shown you how to read and interpret compilation errors. You should now know that there are three general types of compilation messages. One type points to the first column of a statement line when the error occurs on the prior statement line. Another type points to a column where the error occurs or one column past where the error occurs on the same line. A third points to a declaration block error and provides a line number for the actual error at the bottom of the message. You should be able to increase your speed diagnosing errors if you apply the right one of these three rules.

Run-Time Errors

Run-time errors can happen in declaration, execution, and exception PL/SQL blocks. The easiest to catch and handle are those errors thrown from an execution block because they are caught first by any local exception block and next by any containing block. On the other hand, only an external exception block can catch errors thrown from an exception block. This means that you can only handle exception block errors when they come from a nested PL/SQL program unit. That leaves errors thrown from declaration blocks. Declaration errors can't be caught or handled by a local exception block.

Exception blocks contain `WHEN` blocks. `WHEN` blocks catch specific errors or general errors. The prototype for the `WHEN` block is

```
WHEN {predefined_exception | user_defined_exception | OTHERS} THEN
    exception_handling_statement;
[RETURN | EXIT ];
```

The `WHEN` block can take an Oracle-predefined exception name, like those listed later in Table 5-2. These are specific errors. Predefined errors are known error numbers that map to names. They are defined in the `SYS.STANDARD` package. Alternatively, you can define your own exceptions by assigning the `EXCEPTION` datatype. User-defined errors are also specific errors. The section "User-Defined Errors" later in this chapter covers the process of defining these. You use the `OTHERS` reserved word when you want a `WHEN` clause to catch any exception.

You also have two built-in functions: `SQLCODE` and `SQLERRM`. Table 5-1 covers these two functions because they are used in subsequent example programs. Appendix J also covers these functions in more depth.

The subsections cover execution and exception block errors first and then declaration block errors. They're ordered that way because you need to see how the basic mechanics work before you see how they fail.

Execution and Exception Block Errors

Errors raised in the execution block are thrown to the local exception block where they are caught and managed. *Exception handler is another name for the exception block in PL/SQL.* When the local exception block fails to catch the exception and the block was called by another PL/SQL program, the exception signals to the calling program. The calling program manages the thrown exception, provided it catches and manages that type of exception. This process continues until

Function	Oracle-Predefined Errors	User-Defined Errors
SQLCODE	Returns a negative number that maps to the Oracle predefined exceptions but for one special case: the NO_DATA_FOUND exception returns a positive 100.	Returns a positive 1 if there is no EXCEPTION_INIT PRAGMA defined. If an **EXCEPTION_INIT PRAGMA** is defined, it returns a valid number in the range of negative 20001 to negative 20999.
SQLERRM	Is overloaded (a concept covered in Chapter 9) and performs as qualified: Returns the defined error code and message for a raised exception if no number is passed to it. Returns the actual number parameter as a negative integer and a non-Oracle exception message if a positive number is passed to it or a negative number that is not a predefined Oracle exception. Returns the actual number parameter as a negative integer and the Oracle-defined message if a negative number for an Oracle-predefined exception is passed.	Returns a 1 and a "User-Defined Exception" message if triggered by the **RAISE** command. Returns a valid integer in the range of negative 20001 to negative 20999 and a text message set by the **RAISE_APPLICATION_INFO** function.

TABLE 5-1   *Oracle Exception Management Built-in Functions*

an exception block catches and manages the thrown error, or an unhandled exception is returned to the SQL*Plus environment.

The following demonstrates handling an assignment error raised by trying to put a two-character string into a one-character variable:

```
DECLARE
  a VARCHAR2(1);
  b VARCHAR2(2) := 'AB';
BEGIN
  a := b;
EXCEPTION
  WHEN value_error THEN
    dbms_output.put_line('You can''t put ['||b||'] in a one character string.');
END;
/
```

Running this program, you generate the following output message when you've enabled SERVEROUTPUT in your session:

```
You can't put [AB] in a one character string.
```

The preceding example demonstrates how a local error is caught and managed by a local exception block. The exception block only manages that exception; any other exception would be ignored and thrown to the SQL*Plus session.

The following raises a NO_DATA_FOUND error inside the inner block that isn't caught until the outer block exception handler:

```
DECLARE
  a NUMBER;
BEGIN
  DECLARE
    b VARCHAR2(2);
  BEGIN
    SELECT    1
    INTO      b
    FROM dual
    WHERE 1 = 2;
    a := b;
  EXCEPTION
    WHEN value_error THEN
      dbms_output.put_line('You can''t put ['||b||'] in a one character string.');
  END;
EXCEPTION
  WHEN others THEN
    dbms_output.put_line('Caught in outer block ['||SQLERRM||'].');
END;
/
```

The raised error is an NO_DATA_FOUND exception. The inner block only checks for a VALUE_ERROR exception because it is a specific catch block. The program then throws the error to the containing block, where the general OTHERS exception catches it. The actual message prints the SQLERRM message:

```
Caught in outer block [ORA-01403: no data found].
```

You can manually raise a user-defined exception without encountering one. This technique lets you see what happens when an error is raised inside an exception block.

```
DECLARE
  a NUMBER;
  e EXCEPTION;
BEGIN
  DECLARE
    b VARCHAR2(2) := 'AB';
  BEGIN
    RAISE e;
  EXCEPTION
    WHEN others THEN
      a := b;
      dbms_output.put_line('Does not reach this line.');
  END;
EXCEPTION
  WHEN others THEN
    dbms_output.put_line('Caught in outer block ['||SQLCODE||'].');
END;
/
```

The `RAISE` statement passes control to the local exception handler. Inside the `WHEN` block it attempts to assign a multiple-character literal to a one-character string, which raises a `VALUE_ERROR` exception. An error raised inside an exception block is passed to the calling block or the SQL*Plus environment. The program generates the `SQLCODE` output from the outer block exception handler:

```
Caught in outer block [-6502].
```

This section has demonstrated the basics of run-time exception management. You should note that when you raise an error in the execution block, it is handled locally where possible. When the local exception block doesn't manage the error, it is sent to an outer block or the SQL*Plus environment. PL/SQL throws exceptions raised in an exception block to an outer block or the SQL*Plus environment.

Declaration Block Errors

The declaration block is susceptible to run-time errors. These errors occur when you make dynamic assignments in the declaration block. As a good coding practice, you should only make literal assignments inside the declaration section. You should make dynamic assignments inside the execution block because exception block errors are caught and managed by the local exception block. *Runtime assignment errors in the declaration block are not captured by the local exception block.*

The following anonymous-block program uses a dynamic assignment through a substitution variable:

```
DECLARE
  a varchar2(1) := '&1';
BEGIN
  dbms_output.put_line('Substituted variable value ['||a||']');
EXCEPTION
  WHEN others THEN
    dbms_output.put_line('Local exception caught.');
END;
/
```

The substitution of a two-character string raises the following exception:

```
DECLARE
*
ERROR at line 1:
ORA-06502: PL/SQL: numeric or value error: character string buffer too small
ORA-06512: at line 2
```

This error message indicates that *a dynamic sizing error ignores a local exception block.* You can catch the error when you enclose the declaration as an inner block in another PL/SQL block. This shifts the dynamic assignment from an outer to inner block.

The following program demonstrates enclosing the declaration error in another PL/SQL block:

```
BEGIN
  DECLARE
    a varchar2(1) := '&1';
  BEGIN
    dbms_output.put_line('Substituted variable value ['||a||']');
  EXCEPTION
```

```
    WHEN others THEN
      dbms_output.put_line('Local exception caught.');
  END;
EXCEPTION
  WHEN others THEN
    dbms_output.put_line('Outer exception caught.');
END;
/
```

When you assign a two-character string, the error is caught by the outer exception block, as shown:

```
Outer exception caught.
```

This same behavior exists in stored program units, like functions and procedures. While procedures require wrapping their calls, functions don't. If you call a function directly from SQL, it can raise an unhandled exception.

NOTE
You can call stored functions from SQL when they return a native SQL datatype.

The following function replicates the dynamic assignment problem in a stored programming unit:

```
CREATE OR REPLACE FUNCTION runtime_error
(variable_in VARCHAR2) RETURN VARCHAR2 IS
  a VARCHAR2(1) := variable_in;
BEGIN
  RETURN NULL;
EXCEPTION
  WHEN others THEN
    dbms_output.put_line('Function error.');
END;
/
```

You can call this function in SQL using a statement that queries it from the pseudotable DUAL:

```
SELECT runtime_error ('AB') FROM dual;
```

It generates the following unhandled exception:

```
SELECT runtime_error ('AB') FROM dual;
       *
ERROR at line 1:
ORA-06502: PL/SQL: numeric or value error: character string buffer too small
ORA-06512: at "PLSQL.RUNTIME_ERROR", line 3
```

This section has demonstrated that you should make dynamic assignments in execution blocks because PL/SQL doesn't catch dynamic assignment errors in local exception handlers. You've also seen that you can wrap dynamic assignments inside an outer block to catch errors.

TIP
Good PL/SQL coding practices avoid dynamic assignments in declaration blocks.

Exception Management Built-in Functions

Oracle provides a series of predefined exceptions in the STANDARD package. These are useful tools in your debugging of Oracle PL/SQL programs. Most errors raise a negative number as their error number. An ORA-01001 maps to the INVALID_CURSOR predefined exception. You find error codes by using the SQLCODE built-in function. The predefined exceptions are noted in Table 5-2.

Exception	Error	When Raised
ACCESS_INTO_NULL	ORA-06530	You encounter this when attempting to access an uninitialized object.
CASE_NOT_FOUND	ORA-06592	You encounter this when you have defined a CASE statement without an ELSE clause and none of the CASE statements meet the run-time condition.
COLLECTION_IS_NULL	ORA-06531	You encounter this when attempting to access an uninitialized NESTED TABLE or VARRAY.
CURSOR_ALREADY_OPEN	ORA-06511	You encounter this when attempting to open a cursor that is already open.
DUP_VAL_ON_INDEX	ORA-00001	You encounter this when attempting to insert a duplicate value to a table's column when there is a unique index on it.
INVALID_CURSOR	ORA-01001	You encounter this when attempting a disallowed operation on a cursor, like closing a closed cursor.
INVALID_NUMBER	ORA-01722	You encounter this when attempting to assign something other than a number to a number or when the LIMIT clause of a bulk fetch returns a non-positive number.
LOGIN_DENIED	ORA-01017	You encounter this when attempting to log in with a program to an invalid username or password.
NO_DATA_FOUND	ORA-01403	You encounter this when attempting to use the SELECT-INTO structure and the statement returns a null value, when you attempt to access a deleted element in a nested table, or when you attempt to access an uninitialized element in an index-by table (called an associative array since Oracle 10g).
NO_DATA_NEEDED	ORA-06548	You raise this error when a caller to a PIPELINED function signals no need for further rows.

TABLE 5-2 *Predefined Exceptions in the Standard Package*

Exception	Error	When Raised
NOT_LOGGED_ON	ORA-01012	You encounter this when a program issues a database call and is not connected, which is typically after the instance has disconnected your session.
PROGRAM_ERROR	ORA-06501	You encounter this all too often when an error occurs that Oracle has not yet formally trapped. This happens with a number of the Object features of the database.
ROWTYPE_MISMATCH	ORA-06504	You encounter this when your cursor structure fails to agree with your PL/SQL cursor variable, or an actual cursor parameter differs from a formal cursor parameter.
SELF_IS_NULL	ORA-30625	You encounter this error when you try to call an object type non-static member method in which an instance of the object type has not been initialized.
STORAGE_ERROR	ORA-06500	You encounter this error when the SGA has run out of memory or been corrupted.
SUBSCRIPT_BEYOND_COUNT	ORA-06533	You encounter this error when the space allocated to a NESTED TABLE or VARRAY is smaller than the subscript value used.
SUBSCRIPT_OUTSIDE_LIMIT	ORA-06532	You encounter this error when you use an illegal index value to access a NESTED TABLE or VARRAY, which means a non-positive integer.
SYS_INVALID_ROWID	ORA-01410	You encounter this error when you try to convert a string into an invalid ROWID value.
TIMEOUT_ON_RESOURCE	ORA-00051	You encounter this error when the database is unable to secure a lock to a resource.
TOO_MANY_ROWS	ORA-01422	You encounter this when using the SELECT-INTO and the query returns more than one row. It is also possible for you to get this error when a subquery returns more than one row and the comparison operator is an equality operator.

TABLE 5-2 *Predefined Exceptions in the Standard Package* (continued)

Exception	Error	When Raised
USERENV_COMMITSCN_ERROR	ORA-01725	You can only use the function USERENV('COMMMITSCN') as a top-level expression in a VALUES clause of an INSERT statement or as a right operand in the SET clause of an UPDATE statement.
VALUE_ERROR	ORA-06502	You encounter this when you try to assign a variable into another variable that is too small to hold it.
ZERO_DIVIDE	ORA-01476	You encounter this when you try to divide a number by zero.

TABLE 5-2 *Predefined Exceptions in the Standard Package* (continued)

These are very handy tools for writing exception handlers. You should use these when they meet your needs. When they don't meet your needs, you should create user-defined exceptions.

User-Defined Exceptions

User-defined exceptions can be declared two ways: you can declare an EXCEPTION variable in the declaration block, or you can build a dynamic exception in your execution block.

There are two options when you declare an EXCEPTION variable. The simplest implementation lets you declare a variable and raise it by name. The alternate implementation lets you declare the variable and map it to a valid Oracle error code. The former requires that you catch your user-defined errors using the general catch OTHERS exception. The latter lets you build specific WHEN blocks for individual errors.

You can build dynamic exceptions by calling the RAISE_APPLICATION_ERROR function. You can use a range between –20,000 and –20,999 when you raise dynamic exceptions. You assign error messages at run time when using dynamic exceptions. They also don't require you to declare EXCEPTION variables beforehand. You improve the usefulness of dynamic exceptions by declaring exception variables. Together they enhance how you catch exceptions.

NOTE
The Oracle E-Business Suite and other software applications already use numbers in this range for their exceptions, and you should try to avoid conflicts.

The subsections are divided into declaring user-defined exceptions and raising dynamic user-defined exceptions. They should be read sequentially because the second topic depends on your understanding how to declare EXCEPTION variables.

Declaring User-Defined Exceptions

You declare an exception like any other variable in PL/SQL. After declaring it, you can raise the exception but you have no way to catch it in the exception handler. The purpose behind your user-defined exception dictates which way you declare it.

The following program declares and raises an exception:

```
DECLARE
  e EXCEPTION;
BEGIN
  RAISE e;
  dbms_output.put_line('Can''t get here.');
EXCEPTION
  WHEN OTHERS THEN
    IF SQLCODE = 1 THEN
      dbms_output.put_line('This is a ['||SQLERRM||'].');
    END IF;
END;
/
```

This program raises the exception and prints

```
This is a [User-Defined Exception].
```

By default all user-defined exceptions have a `SQLCODE` value of 1. The `IF` block lets you catch user-defined errors separately inside a general `WHEN` block.

A two-step declaration process lets you declare an exception and map it to a number. The first step was declaring the `EXCEPTION` variable. The second step declares a `PRAGMA`. A `PRAGMA` is a compiler directive. You use a `PRAGMA` to direct the compiler to perform something differently. PL/SQL supports a number of `PRAGMA` directives. You use the `EXCEPTION_INIT` directive to map an exception to an error code. The first parameter of an `EXCEPTION_INIT` call is a user-defined `EXCEPTION` variable, and the second is a valid error number.

TIP
You should avoid mapping a user-defined exception to an error code that is already a predefined exception, as qualified in earlier Table 5-2.

The example program defines an `EXCEPTION` variable and maps the exception to an error number:

```
DECLARE
  a VARCHAR2(20);
  invalid_userenv_parameter EXCEPTION;
  PRAGMA EXCEPTION_INIT(invalid_userenv_parameter,-2003);
BEGIN
  a := SYS_CONTEXT('USERENV','PROXY_PUSHER');
EXCEPTION
  WHEN invalid_userenv_parameter THEN
    dbms_output.put_line(SQLERRM);
END;
/
```

The `ORA-02003` is a real error code, assigned in the implementation of the `STANDARD` package. The choice of `INVALID_USERENV_PARAMETER` also mirrors its actual definition in the `STANDARD` package body.

The code prints the standard Oracle error message:

```
ORA-02003: invalid USERENV parameter
```

Dynamic User-Defined Exceptions

Dynamic user-defined exceptions let you raise an exception, assign it a number, and manage whether or not you add the new error to a list of errors (known as an error stack). The following is the prototype for the dynamic exception function:

```
RAISE_APPLICATION_ERROR(error_number, error_message [, keep_errors])
```

The first formal parameter takes an error number in the range of –20,000 to –20,999. You raise an `ORA-21000` error when you provide any other value. The second formal parameter is an error message. The last formal parameter is optional and has a default value of `FALSE`. You instruct that the error should be added to any existing error stack when you provide an optional `TRUE` value.

The following demonstrates raising a dynamic exception without previously declaring a user-defined `EXCEPTION` variable:

```
BEGIN
  RAISE_APPLICATION_ERROR(-20001,'A not too original message.');
EXCEPTION
  WHEN others THEN
    dbms_output.put_line(SQLERRM);
END;
/
```

This catches the error using the `OTHERS` reserved word and prints

```
ORA-20001: A not too original message.
```

The next program combines declaring an `EXCEPTION` variable, mapping a user-defined error code to an `EXCEPTION` variable, and then setting the message dynamically. This demonstrates how all three can work together to provide you with control throughout your program, as shown:

```
DECLARE
  e EXCEPTION;
  PRAGMA EXCEPTION_INIT(e,-20001);
BEGIN
  RAISE_APPLICATION_ERROR(-20001,'A less than original message.');
EXCEPTION
  WHEN e THEN
    dbms_output.put_line(SQLERRM);
END;
/
```

This prints the dynamic error message from the `RAISE_APPLICATION_ERROR()` function:

```
ORA-20001: A less than original message.
```

Unlike the message files for standard Oracle errors, this message is dynamic to your PL/SQL program units. The `SQLERRM` built-in does not look the message up but simply substitutes the string literal provided to the `RAISE_APPLICATION_ERROR` function.

This section has demonstrated how to declare exceptions and use them. You have seen how to map existing Oracle errors and error message definitions to user-defined exceptions. You have also seen how to provide your own error messages dynamically.

Exception Stack Functions

The exception stack is the sequencing of errors from the triggering event to the calling block of code. PL/SQL throws an exception in the execution block when a failure occurs and runs the code in its local exception block. If the failure is in a nested or referenced PL/SQL block, it first runs a local exception handler before running the calling program unit's exception handler. It then continues running available exception blocks or returning errors to the error stack until it returns control to the outermost PL/SQL block.

When PL/SQL does not contain exception blocks, you get a propagation of line number and error codes. Beginning in Oracle 10g, you can use an exception block and the `DBMS_UTILITY` package to get line number and error codes.

There are two approaches to managing errors in PL/SQL; the choice of which to use depends on the application transaction control requirements. If you encounter an error that's fatal to the business logic of your application, you need to raise an exception. The exception should stop the business process and roll back the transaction to a state where the data is safe and consistent.

When the error is not fatal to your application business logic, you may choose to log the error in a table and allow the transaction to complete. The section "Database Trigger Exception Management" shows you how to log this type of error. While the example demonstrates how you log a non-fatal error, it does not cover defining the recovery mechanism. You must analyze what the transaction is doing to plan how you can recover the information.

The next two sections highlight management of the error stack in named PL/SQL blocks. First, you'll learn how to manage error stacks within anonymous- and named-block PL/SQL units. Then, you'll learn how to use the `FORMAT_ERROR_BACKTRACE` function.

Exception Stack Management

This section shows how to format error stacks without using the `DBMS_UTILITY` package functions—a necessary skill when you're working in Oracle 9i or some earlier release. The section also forward-references concepts covered in Chapters 6 and 7 on both stored functions and procedures, as well as collections. You'll learn how to build a standard error event management procedure, and how to test it with a set of related procedures.

Whether errors are thrown from called local or named PL/SQL blocks, the stack management process is the same. Error are raised and put in a *last_in, first_out* (LIFO) queue, which is known as a stack. As raised errors are placed on the stack, they are passed to calling program units until they reach the outermost program. The outermost program reports the error stack to the end user. The end user can be a physical person, a SQL statement, or a batch processing script external to the database.

The script creates a simple procedure that you will call from an exception block in each of the named PL/SQL stored functions and procedures later in this section:

`-- This is found in exception1.sql on the publisher's web site.`

```
CREATE OR REPLACE PROCEDURE handle_errors
```

```
( object_name            IN          VARCHAR2
, module_name            IN          VARCHAR2 := NULL
, table_name             IN          VARCHAR2 := NULL
, sql_error_code         IN          NUMBER   := NULL
, sql_error_message      IN          VARCHAR2 := NULL
, user_error_message     IN          VARCHAR2 := NULL ) IS

  -- Define a local exception.
  raised_error           EXCEPTION;

  -- Define a collection type and initialize it.
  TYPE error_stack IS TABLE OF VARCHAR2(80);
  errors                 ERROR_STACK := error_stack();

  -- Define a local function to verify object type.
  FUNCTION object_type
  ( object_name_in       IN          VARCHAR2 )
  RETURN VARCHAR2 IS
    return_type          VARCHAR2(12) := 'Unidentified';
  BEGIN
    FOR i IN ( SELECT    object_type
               FROM      user_objects
               WHERE     object_name = object_name_in ) LOOP
      return_type := i.object_type;
    END LOOP;
    RETURN return_type;
  END object_type;
BEGIN
  -- Allot space and assign a value to collection.
  errors.EXTEND;
  errors(errors.COUNT) := object_type(object_name)||' ['||object_name||']';

  -- Substitute actual parameters for default values.
  IF module_name IS NOT NULL THEN
    errors.EXTEND;
    errors(errors.COUNT) := 'Module Name: ['||module_name||']';
  END IF;
  IF table_name IS NOT NULL THEN
    errors.EXTEND;
    errors(errors.COUNT) := 'Table Name: ['||table_name||']';
  END IF;
  IF sql_error_code IS NOT NULL THEN
    errors.EXTEND;
    errors(errors.COUNT) := 'SQLCODE Value: ['||sql_error_code||']';
  END IF;
  IF sql_error_message IS NOT NULL THEN
    errors.EXTEND;
    errors(errors.COUNT) := 'SQLERRM Value: ['||sql_error_message||']';
  END IF;
  IF user_error_message IS NOT NULL THEN
    errors.EXTEND;
    errors(errors.COUNT) := user_error_message;
```

```
  END IF;

  errors.EXTEND;
  errors(errors.COUNT) := '----------------------------------------';
  RAISE raised_error;
EXCEPTION
  WHEN raised_error THEN
    FOR i IN 1..errors.COUNT LOOP
      dbms_output.put_line(errors(i));
    END LOOP;
    RETURN;
END;
/
```

The stored procedure signature includes optional formal parameters. This makes the handle_errors procedure more flexible. There is a local function that captures and verifies object source definitions. The procedure tests for not-null values before processing actual values passed through formal parameters. The EXTEND() method creates space before assigning values to lists. The method is part of the Oracle 11*g* Collection API and is covered in Chapter 7.

The following three procedures are built in descending order because of their dependencies. The error_level1 procedure calls the error_level2 procedure, which then calls the error_level3 procedure. You can build these with the following script:

-- This is found in exception2.sql on the publisher's web site.

```
CREATE OR REPLACE PROCEDURE error_level3 IS
  one_character            VARCHAR2(1);
  two_character            VARCHAR2(2)   := 'AB';
  local_object             VARCHAR2(30)  := 'ERROR_LEVEL3';
  local_module             VARCHAR2(30)  := 'MAIN';
  local_table              VARCHAR2(30)  :=  NULL;
  local_user_message       VARCHAR2(80)  :=  NULL;
BEGIN
  one_character := two_character;
EXCEPTION
  WHEN others THEN
    handle_errors( object_name => local_object
                 , module_name => local_module
                 , sql_error_code => SQLCODE
                 , sql_error_message => SQLERRM );
    RAISE;
END error_level3;
/
CREATE OR REPLACE PROCEDURE error_level2 IS
  local_object             VARCHAR2(30)  := 'ERROR_LEVEL2';
  local_module             VARCHAR2(30)  := 'MAIN';
  local_table              VARCHAR2(30)  :=  NULL;
  local_user_message       VARCHAR2(80)  :=  NULL;
BEGIN
  error_level3();
EXCEPTION
  WHEN others THEN
```

```
      handle_errors( object_name => local_object
                   , module_name => local_module
                   , sql_error_code => SQLCODE
                   , sql_error_message => SQLERRM );
    RAISE;
END error_level2;
/
CREATE OR REPLACE PROCEDURE error_level1 IS
  local_object            VARCHAR2(30) := 'ERROR_LEVEL1';
  local_module            VARCHAR2(30) := 'MAIN';
  local_table             VARCHAR2(30) :=  NULL;
  local_user_message      VARCHAR2(80) :=  NULL;
BEGIN
  error_level2();
EXCEPTION
  WHEN others THEN
    handle_errors( object_name => local_object
                 , module_name => local_module
                 , sql_error_code => SQLCODE
                 , sql_error_message => SQLERRM );
    RAISE;
END error_level1;
/
```

The script builds three stored procedures. They call each other in reverse sequence until the innermost raises an exception. You can test the propagation and format an error stack by running the following test program:

```
BEGIN
  error_level1;
END;
/
```

You'll get the following formatted error stack:

```
PROCEDURE [ERROR_LEVEL3]
Module Name: [MAIN]
SQLCODE Value: [-6502]
SQLERRM Value: [ORA-06502: PL/SQL: numeric or value error: character ...
----------------------------------------
PROCEDURE [ERROR_LEVEL2]
Module Name: [MAIN]
SQLCODE Value: [-6502]
SQLERRM Value: [ORA-06502: PL/SQL: numeric or value error: character ...
----------------------------------------
PROCEDURE [ERROR_LEVEL1]
Module Name: [MAIN]
SQLCODE Value: [-6502]
SQLERRM Value: [ORA-06502: PL/SQL: numeric or value error: character ...
----------------------------------------
begin
*
ERROR at line 1:
```

```
ORA-06502: PL/SQL: numeric or value error: character string buffer too small
ORA-06512: at "PLSQL.ERROR_LEVEL1", line 14
ORA-06512: at line 2
```

You have now covered how to format your error stack in PL/SQL to demonstrate an exception stack trace through named procedures. The method does require a bit of effort but clearly illustrates how you find the propagation path to trace, diagnose, and fix problems in the data or application code.

Error Stack Formatting

This section shows how to format error stack management with the functions in the DBMS_UTILITY package. There was a user_error_message formal parameter in the handle_errors procedure that went unused. You will use it to manage the output from the DBMS_UTILITY package's FORMAT_ERROR_BACKTRACE function.

The handle_errors procedure remains the same in the following discussion. However, the three procedures illustrating exception propagation have changed slightly, as noted next:

```
-- This is found in exception3.sql on the publisher's web site.

CREATE OR REPLACE PROCEDURE error_level3 IS
  one_character            VARCHAR2(1);
  two_character            VARCHAR2(2)   := 'AB';
  local_object             VARCHAR2(30)  := 'ERROR_LEVEL3';
  local_module             VARCHAR2(30)  := 'MAIN';
  local_table              VARCHAR2(30)  :=  NULL;
  local_user_message       VARCHAR2(80)  :=  NULL;
BEGIN
  one_character := two_character;
EXCEPTION
  WHEN others THEN
    handle_errors(object_name => local_object
                 ,module_name => local_module
                 ,sql_error_code => SQLCODE
                 ,sql_error_message => SQLERRM
                 ,user_error_message => DBMS_UTILITY.FORMAT_ERROR_BACKTRACE);
    RAISE;
END error_level3;
/
CREATE OR REPLACE PROCEDURE error_level2 IS
  local_object             VARCHAR2(30)  := 'ERROR_LEVEL2';
  local_module             VARCHAR2(30)  := 'MAIN';
  local_table              VARCHAR2(30)  :=  NULL;
  local_user_message       VARCHAR2(200) :=  NULL;
BEGIN
  error_level3();
EXCEPTION
  WHEN others THEN
    handle_errors(object_name => local_object
                 ,module_name => local_module
                 ,sql_error_code => SQLCODE
                 ,sql_error_message => SQLERRM
```

```
                            ,user_error_message => DBMS_UTILITY.FORMAT_ERROR_BACKTRACE);
     RAISE;
END error_level2;
/
CREATE OR REPLACE PROCEDURE error_level1 IS
  local_object          VARCHAR2(30)  := 'ERROR_LEVEL1';
  local_module          VARCHAR2(30)  := 'MAIN';
  local_table           VARCHAR2(30)  :=  NULL;
  local_user_message    VARCHAR2(200) :=  NULL;
BEGIN
  error_level2();
EXCEPTION
  WHEN others THEN
    handle_errors(object_name => local_object
                 ,module_name => local_module
                 ,sql_error_code => SQLCODE
                 ,sql_error_message => SQLERRM
                 ,user_error_message => DBMS_UTILITY.FORMAT_ERROR_BACKTRACE);
     RAISE;
END error_level1;
/
```

Like the prior example, the script builds three stored procedures. They call each other in reverse sequence until the innermost raises an exception. You can test the propagation and format an error stack by running the following test program:

```
BEGIN
  error_level1;
END;
/
```

You'll get the following formatted error stack:

```
PROCEDURE [ERROR_LEVEL3]
Module Name: [MAIN]
SQLCODE Value: [-6502]
SQLERRM Value: [ORA-06502: PL/SQL: numeric or value error: character ...
ORA-06512: at "PLSQL.ERROR_LEVEL3", line 9
----------------------------------------
PROCEDURE [ERROR_LEVEL2]
Module Name: [MAIN]
SQLCODE Value: [-6502]
SQLERRM Value: [ORA-06502: PL/SQL: numeric or value error: character ...
ORA-06512: at "PLSQL.ERROR_LEVEL3", line 17
ORA-06512: at "PLSQL.ERROR_LEVEL2", line 7
----------------------------------------
PROCEDURE [ERROR_LEVEL1]
Module Name: [MAIN]
SQLCODE Value: [-6502]
SQLERRM Value: [ORA-06502: PL/SQL: numeric or value error: character ...
ORA-06512: at "PLSQL.ERROR_LEVEL2", line 15
ORA-06512: at "PLSQL.ERROR_LEVEL1", line 7
----------------------------------------
```

```
BEGIN
*
ERROR at line 1:
ORA-06502: PL/SQL: numeric or value error: character string buffer too small
ORA-06512: at "PLSQL.ERROR_LEVEL1", line 15
ORA-06512: at line 2
```

The DBMS_UTILITY.FORMAT_ERROR_BACKTRACE package function provides you with a more effective tool to trace, diagnose, and fix problems. The only tedious part is matching the line numbers of the exceptions to the line numbers of the stored programs. You can do this by leveraging the data dictionary.

For example, if you would like to find the source error that occurred at line 12 in the error_level3 procedure, the following query finds the responsible line of code:

```
COL line FORMAT 999
COL text FORMAT A60

SELECT    line
,         text
FROM      user_source
WHERE     name = 'ERROR_LEVEL3'
AND       line = 9;
```

The output shows the following:

```
LINE TEXT
----- --------------------------------
    9    one_character := two_character;
```

The FORMAT_ERROR_BACKTRACE function in the DBMS_UTILITY package lets you quickly identify an error's location. You now know how to manage error stacks with or without the FORMAT_ERROR_BACKTRACE function.

Database Trigger Exception Management

Database triggers are event-driven programs. If you're unfamiliar with database triggers, see Chapter 10. Triggers are activated when a transactional program unit calls a database object, like a table or view. Database triggers may sometimes call other stored functions, procedures, and packages. When triggers call other stored objects, those program units *cannot* contain any transaction control language (TCL) commands, like **SAVEPOINT**, **ROLLBACK**, and **COMMIT**.

Database triggers solve two types of problems: how to handle critical errors and non-critical errors. You raise an exception and stop processing when encountering critical errors. You raise and record exceptions but allow processing to continue for non-critical errors.

The next two subsections cover how you manage critical and non-critical exceptions in database triggers. The sample programs are Data Manipulation Language (DML) triggers. They show concepts that also apply to other trigger types. The examples use the code and data found in the introduction. You can download it from the publisher's web site.

Database Trigger Order of Precedence

There is *no order* of precedence when you have multiple triggers registered against the same object, like a table or view. If you have several things that should happen in some sequence, then you should write them in one or more stored program units and call them sequentially in a single event trigger.

When you have mutually exclusive things that must occur, you'll need to disable the other trigger or delete it before enabling or creating the other. In a production system, you should write dynamic SQL to disable one trigger and enable the other before running the code. Chapter 11 covers dynamic SQL. Dropping and creating triggers can nominally fragment the database. Likewise, you should clean up after the transaction, leaving the default trigger enabled.

Critical Error Database Triggers

Database triggers stop execution by raising critical errors when you can't allow processing to continue. Business rules dictate what is critical or non-critical. They decide whether a transaction can harm the data. Any transaction that harms the data is a critical error and must be stopped before it can complete.

Database constraints are terrific for guaranteeing integrity of a data model. The sample data model supports a foreign key constraint on all foreign keys. This means any insert to a table that violates the foreign key constraint raises an exception. The processing load of foreign key constraints generally makes them too expensive to implement in real applications. The alternative to using foreign key constraints involves building the logic into the application programs. Sometimes you may elect to put this protective logic in database triggers.

Database constraints are also limited as to what they can constrain. You can't use a database constraint to guarantee there are only two authorized signers on an account. The *foreign key* constraints control relationship values, while *check* and *unique* constraints control range values. A foreign key constraint guarantees a value is found in a list of values from a column defined with a *primary key* constraint. A check constraint limits a value to a range of values but does not limit the recurrence of repeating values in multiple rows. A unique constraint makes sure that only one row contains any given value, like a specific foreign key value. Therefore, database constraints can only constrain data to meet certain conditions and value ranges in tables or views.

Database triggers let you define complex business rules that aren't supported by database constraints. Business rules are sometimes very complex. For example, there is no database constraint that works when a business rule defines that there can only be two authorized signers. This business rule says that for every row in the member table there can only be two related rows in the contact table. Only a database triggers can let you audit and enforce this type of relationship constraint between two tables.

NOTE
A data model communicates this limitation by limiting the maximum cardinality in a relationship to 2. This would appear as 0..2 *on a UML drawing.*

Raised Exceptions for Critical Errors

You build a DML trigger to enforce this type of relationship between the `member` and `contact` tables. The trigger can use a cursor that identifies when more than one row exists to trigger a dynamic user-defined exception. The trigger lets you insert one or two rows in the `contact` table but disallows a third. The following script implements the trigger for this logic:

-- This is found in create_contact_t1.sql on the publisher's web site.

```
CREATE OR REPLACE TRIGGER contact_t1
BEFORE INSERT ON contact
FOR EACH ROW
DECLARE
  CURSOR c ( member_id_in NUMBER ) IS
    SELECT null
    FROM    contact c
    ,       member m
    WHERE   c.member_id = m.member_id
    AND     c.member_id = member_id_in
    HAVING COUNT(*) > 1;
BEGIN
  FOR i IN c (:new.member_id) LOOP
    RAISE_APPLICATION_ERROR(-20001,'Already two signers.');
  END LOOP;
END;
/
```

The cursor retrieves no value from the tables but retrieves a one-row cursor containing a null value. This opens the `FOR` loop statement and raises the dynamic user-defined exception when an insert tries to add a third dependent row to the `contact` table.

This insert statement violates the constraint provided both seeding scripts have run:

```
INSERT INTO contact
VALUES
( contact_s1.nextval
, 1002
,(SELECT   common_lookup_id
  FROM     common_lookup
  WHERE    common_lookup_table = 'CONTACT'
  AND      common_lookup_column = 'CONTACT_TYPE'
  AND      common_lookup_type = 'CUSTOMER')
,'Sweeney','Irving','M'
, 2, SYSDATE, 2, SYSDATE);
```

It raises the following exception from the `contact_t1` trigger:

```
( contact_s1.nextval
  *
ERROR at line 2:
ORA-20001: Already two signers.
ORA-06512: at "PLSQL.CONTACT_T1", line 11
ORA-04088: error during execution of trigger 'PLSQL.CONTACT_T1'
```

The exception provides *your dynamic exception message.* It also returns two system-generated exception messages. The system-generated messages tell you what raised the error message. This approach immediately communicates to the end user that he or she has violated a business rule.

The downside to this type of trigger is that you haven't captured the end-user error. Businesses often want to both prevent errors and capture employee actions. Many video stores let parents restrict what their children can rent, for instance, not allowing them to rent MPAA R-rated movies or ESRB M-rated games. Sometimes children may attempt to rent materials that are disallowed by their parents. A raised exception like that shown previously prevents the rental but does not let the video store collect a record of the attempted rental.

Raised and Recorded Exceptions for Critical Errors

Autonomous triggers can both capture events and raise critical exceptions to stop activities. You use another PRAGMA (precompiler instruction) to define a trigger as autonomous. The AUTONOMOUS_TRANSACTION directive says that the trigger should run in a separate transaction scope. This allows the trigger to commit an action to the database while also repudiating the DML statement that fired the trigger.

You need a place to store the information from the attempt. Use the following script to build the nc_error table for that purpose:

```
-- This is found in create_nc_error.sql on the publisher's web site.
```

```
CREATE TABLE nc_error
( error_id               NUMBER          CONSTRAINT pk_nce   PRIMARY KEY
, module_name            VARCHAR2(30)    CONSTRAINT nn_nce_1 NOT NULL
, table_name             VARCHAR2(30)
, class_name             VARCHAR2(30)
, error_code             VARCHAR2(9)
, sqlerror_message       VARCHAR2(2000)
, user_error_message     VARCHAR2(2000)
, last_update_date       DATE            CONSTRAINT nn_nce_2 NOT NULL
, last_updated_by        NUMBER          CONSTRAINT nn_nce_3 NOT NULL
, creation_date          DATE            CONSTRAINT nn_nce_4 NOT NULL
, created_by             NUMBER          CONSTRAINT nn_nce_5 NOT NULL);
```

After building a repository for attempted activities, you should write a stored procedure to process the insert statement. This is important for two reasons. First, the logic is easy to wrap or protect from prying eyes. Second, the logic won't clutter your database trigger.

The following record_errors procedure writes data to the non-critical error repository:

```
-- This is found in create_record_errors.sql on the publisher's web site.
```

```
CREATE OR REPLACE PROCEDURE record_errors
( module_name          IN        VARCHAR2
, table_name           IN        VARCHAR2 := NULL
, class_name           IN        VARCHAR2 := NULL
, sqlerror_code        IN        VARCHAR2 := NULL
, sqlerror_message     IN        VARCHAR2 := NULL
, user_error_message   IN        VARCHAR2 := NULL ) IS

  -- Declare anchored record variable.
```

```
  nc_error_record NC_ERROR%ROWTYPE;

BEGIN

  -- Substitute actual parameters for default values.
  IF module_name IS NOT NULL THEN
    nc_error_record.module_name := module_name;
  END IF;
  IF table_name IS NOT NULL THEN
    nc_error_record.table_name := module_name;
  END IF;
  IF sqlerror_code IS NOT NULL THEN
    nc_error_record.sqlerror_code := sqlerror_code;
  END IF;
  IF sqlerror_message IS NOT NULL THEN
    nc_error_record.sqlerror_message := sqlerror_message;
  END IF;
  IF user_error_message IS NOT NULL THEN
    nc_error_record.user_error_message := user_error_message;
  END IF;

  -- Insert non-critical error record.
  INSERT INTO nc_error
  VALUES
  ( nc_error_s1.nextval
  , nc_error_record.module_name
  , nc_error_record.table_name
  , nc_error_record.class_name
  , nc_error_record.sqlerror_code
  , nc_error_record.sqlerror_message
  , nc_error_record.user_error_message
  , 2
  , SYSDATE
  , 2
  , SYSDATE);
EXCEPTION
  WHEN others THEN
    RETURN;
END;
/
```

The stored procedure signature includes optional formal parameters. This makes the `record_errors` procedure more flexible. There is a local function that captures and verifies object source definitions.

You can make a few changes to the `contact_t1` trigger, and define a new trigger that guarantees writing the attempt while disallowing the DML action. The `contact_t2` trigger contains these changes, and its definition is

```
CREATE OR REPLACE TRIGGER contact_t2
BEFORE INSERT ON contact
```

```
FOR EACH ROW
DECLARE
  PRAGMA AUTONOMOUS_TRANSACTION;
  CURSOR c ( member_id_in NUMBER ) IS
    SELECT null
    FROM   contact c
    ,      member m
    WHERE  c.member_id = m.member_id
    AND    c.member_id = member_id_in
    HAVING COUNT(*) > 1;
BEGIN
  FOR i IN c (:new.member_id) LOOP
    record_errors( module_name => 'CREATE_CONTACT_T2'
                 , table_name => 'MEMBER'
                 , class_name => 'MEMBER_ID ['||:new.contact_id||']'
                 , sqlerror_code => 'ORA-20001'
                 , user_error_message => 'Too many contacts per account.');
  END LOOP;
  COMMIT;
  RAISE_APPLICATION_ERROR(-20001,'Already two signers.');
END;
/
```

The program adds the AUTONONMOUS_TRANSACTION PRAGMA, a call to the record_errors stored procedure, and a COMMIT statement; it then raises a user-defined exception message. The commit comes after the loop, which is nothing more than a convenient structure to implicitly open and close a cursor for each row. The commit only affects the call to the record_errors procedure. After the commit, a raised exception stops the transaction that fired the trigger.

This familiar insert statement violates the business rule imposed by the trigger:

```
INSERT INTO contact
VALUES
( contact_s1.nextval
, 1002
,(SELECT    common_lookup_id
  FROM      common_lookup
  WHERE     common_lookup_table = 'CONTACT'
  AND       common_lookup_column = 'CONTACT_TYPE'
  AND       common_lookup_type = 'CUSTOMER')
,'Sweeney','Irving','M'
, 2, SYSDATE, 2, SYSDATE);
```

It raises the following exception from the contact_t2 trigger:

```
INSERT INTO contact
*
ERROR at line 1:
ORA-20001: Already two signers.
ORA-06512: at "PLSQL.CONTACT_T2", line 19
ORA-04088: error during execution of trigger 'PLSQL.CONTACT_T2'
```

When you query the `nc_error` table, you find that the attempt has been captured. The following formatting and query lets you check the data:

```
COL module_name FORMAT A17
COL user_error_message FORMAT A30

SELECT    error_id
,         module_name
,         user_error_message
FROM      nc_error;
```

You should see the following output:

```
ERROR_ID MODULE_NAME       USER_ERROR_MESSAGE
---------- ----------------- ------------------------------
        28 CREATE_CONTACT_T3 Too many contacts per account.
```

These examples have shown you how to build triggers to stop processing. One stops the insertion of data and raises an error, while the other does that and captures the attempt to insert the data as well. You implement these types of triggers when it is critical to not violate a business rule.

Non-Critical Error Database Triggers

Database triggers work differently with non-critical errors. They raise and record exceptions but allow processing to continue for non-critical errors. This requires that you provide a database table to record non-critical errors.

In the last section, you built the `nc_error` table. If you skipped that section, you can use the following the `create_nc_error.sql` script to build the table. The same table can store attempts for critical and non-critical errors. The table definition is

```
Name                                     Null?    Type
---------------------------------------- -------- --------------
ERROR_ID                                 NOT NULL NUMBER
MODULE_NAME                              NOT NULL VARCHAR2(30)
TABLE_NAME                                        VARCHAR2(30)
CLASS_NAME                                        VARCHAR2(30)
SQLERROR_CODE                                     VARCHAR2(9)
SQLERROR_MESSAGE                                  VARCHAR2(2000)
USER_ERROR_MESSAGE                                VARCHAR2(2000)
LAST_UPDATED_BY                          NOT NULL NUMBER
LAST_UPDATE_DATE                         NOT NULL DATE
CREATED_BY                               NOT NULL NUMBER
CREATION_DATE                            NOT NULL DATE
```

The same `record_errors` procedure defined to manage critical error attempts works with both critical and non-critical event triggers. This is no accident. There is no `COMMIT` statement in the `record_errors` procedure, and so you can call it in autonomous or dependent transaction scope triggers. The procedure definition is

```
PROCEDURE record_errors
  Argument Name                  Type                     In/Out Default?
  ------------------------------ ------------------------ ------ --------
  MODULE_NAME                    VARCHAR2                 IN
  TABLE_NAME                     VARCHAR2                 IN     DEFAULT
```

CLASS_NAME	VARCHAR2	IN	DEFAULT
SQLERROR_CODE	VARCHAR2	IN	DEFAULT
SQLERROR_MESSAGE	VARCHAR2	IN	DEFAULT
USER_ERROR_MESSAGE	VARCHAR2	IN	DEFAULT

The stored procedure signature includes optional formal parameters. This makes the `record_errors` procedure more flexible. There is a local function that captures and verifies object source definitions.

After creating the new procedure, you can run the script that builds the `contact_t3` trigger. The stored procedure lets you wrap or protect from prying eyes how non-critical errors are handled, and it doesn't clutter your database trigger. Appendix F shows you how to wrap your PL/SQL code.

The `create_contact_t3.sql` script automatically deletes the `contact_t1` and/or `contact_t2` triggers when they exist. The reason for this precaution is that you can't guarantee which trigger fires first when there's more than one. You want to guarantee what you're testing. In this case, you're testing a non-critical error handling trigger.

The trigger creation script follows:

```
-- This is found in create_contact_t3.sql on the publisher's web site.

CREATE OR REPLACE TRIGGER contact_t3
BEFORE INSERT ON contact
FOR EACH ROW
DECLARE
  CURSOR c ( member_id_in NUMBER ) IS
    SELECT null
    FROM   contact c
    ,      member m
    WHERE  c.member_id = m.member_id
    AND    c.member_id = member_id_in
    HAVING COUNT(*) > 1;
BEGIN
  FOR i IN c (:new.member_id) LOOP
    record_errors( module_name => 'CREATE_CONTACT_T2'
                , table_name => 'MEMBER'
                , class_name => 'MEMBER_ID ['||:new.contact_id||']'
                , sqlerror_code => 'ORA-20001'
                , user_error_message => 'Too many contacts per account.');
  END LOOP;
END;
/
```

The trigger calls the `record_errors` procedure, which inserts the data into your target table. There is no commit in the `record_errors` procedure because it is designed to work only with a trigger or other PL/SQL block that manages transaction scope and issues a COMMIT statement.

You can now reuse the familiar INSERT statement to the `contact` table:

```
INSERT INTO contact
VALUES
( contact_s1.nextval
, 1002
,(SELECT   common_lookup_id
```

```
FROM      common_lookup
WHERE     common_lookup_table = 'CONTACT'
AND       common_lookup_column = 'CONTACT_TYPE'
AND       common_lookup_type = 'CUSTOMER')
,'Sweeney','Irving','M'
, 2, SYSDATE, 2, SYSDATE);
```

This time, the trigger does not raise any exception. It adds a third row and violates the non-critical business rule. The INSERT statement did fire the trigger, and the trigger calls the procedure and wrote the error data. At least, all that happened when you committed the data after the INSERT statement. The non-critical error was managed as a dependent transaction inside the transaction scope of the original insert into the contact table.

These sections have demonstrated how you can manage critical and non-critical errors with database triggers. You've been exposed to a number of parts, like procedures and triggers, and they are covered in more detail in Chapters 6 and 10, respectively.

Summary

This chapter has explained how you work with PL/SQL error management. It has described the differences between compilation errors and run-time errors. You have also learned about the unhandled behavior of run-time errors that occur in declaration blocks, and how to handle raised errors in both the execution and exception blocks.

PART
II

PL/SQL Programming

CHAPTER
6

Functions and Procedures

s you've seen in previous chapters, there are two types of subroutines: functions and procedures. You use these to build database tier libraries to encapsulate application functionality, which is then co-located on the database tier for efficiency.

This chapter covers these areas:

- Function and procedure architecture
- Transaction scope
- Calling subroutines
- Functions
    - Creation options
    - Pass-by-value functions
    - Pass-by-reference functions
- Procedures
    - Pass-by-value procedures
    - Pass-by-reference functions

Oracle 11*g* supports subroutines that are stored as functions and procedures in the database. They are named PL/SQL blocks. You can deploy them as standalone subroutines or as components in packages. Packages and object types can contain both functions and procedures. Anonymous blocks can also have local functions and procedures defined in their declaration blocks. You can also nest functions and procedures inside other functions and procedures.

You publish functions and procedures as standalone units or within packages and object types. This means that they are defined in the package specification or object type, not the package body or object type body. They're local subroutines when you define functions or procedures inside package bodies or object type bodies. Local subroutines aren't published subroutines. Likewise, subroutines defined in the declaration block of anonymous block programs are local subroutines.

You deploy collections of related functions and procedures in packages and object types. Packages and object types serve as library containers in the database. Packages act as primary library containers because you don't have to create instances to use them, whereas some subroutines in object types require you to create instances to use them. Packages also let you overload functions and procedures. Chapter 9 covers packages.

User-defined object types are SQL datatypes. Inside Object types, functions and procedures can be defined as class- or instance-level subroutines. Class functions and procedures are static subroutines, and you can access them the same way you use functions and procedures in packages. Instance-level subroutines are only accessible when you create an instance of an object type. Chapter 14 covers object types.

The sections work sequentially to build a foundation of concepts. If you wish to skip ahead, browsing from the beginning may provide clarity to later sections.

Function and Procedure Architecture

As described in Chapter 3, functions and procedures are named PL/SQL blocks. You can also call them subroutines or subprograms. They have headers in place of the DECLARE statement. The header defines the function or procedure name, a list of formal parameters, and a return datatype for functions. Formal parameters define variables that you can send to subroutines when you call them. You use both formal parameters and local variables inside functions and procedures. While functions return a datatype, procedures don't. At least, procedures don't formally list a return datatype, because they return a void. The void is explicitly defined in other programming languages, like C, C#, Java, and C++. Procedures can return values through their formal parameter list variables when they are passed by reference.

There are four types of generic subroutines in programming languages. The four types are defined by two behaviors, whether they return a formal value or not and whether their parameter lists are passed by value or reference.

You set formal parameters when you define subroutines. You call subroutines with actual parameters. Formal parameters define the list of possible variables, and their positions and datatypes. Formal parameters do not assign values other than a default value, which makes a parameter optional. Actual parameters are the values you provide to subroutines when calling them. You can call subroutines without an actual parameter when the formal parameter has a default value. Subroutines may be called without actual parameters if all their formal parameters are defined as optional.

Subroutines are black boxes. They're called that because black boxes hide their implementation details and only publish what you can send into them or receive from them. Table 6-1 describes and illustrates these subroutines.

Subroutines are functions when they return output and procedures when they don't. Functions return output as values represented as SQL or PL/SQL datatypes. Chapter 3 describes the characteristics of PL/SQL datatypes, and Appendix B discusses SQL datatypes. Pass-by-value functions are sometimes called expressions because you submit values that are returned as a result. When the return datatype is a SQL type, you can call the function inside a SQL statement.

The "Black Box"

The *black box* (the term comes from the engineering lexicon) is part of verification and validation. Verification is a process that examines whether you built something right. Validation checks whether you built the right thing. For example, you validate that the manufacturing line is producing iPod nanos, and then you verify that they're making them to the new specification.

Integration testing validates whether components work as a part. You can't see how the product works. You only know what it should do when you provide input, like a function that should add two numbers. If one plus one equals two, then the function appears to work against expectations. This is black box testing.

Black box testing is the process of validation. Verification requires peering into the black box to inspect how it behaves. This type of testing is white box testing because you can see how things actually work—step by step. Unit testing verifies that your function or procedure builds the thing right. An example would be verifying that you're using the right formula to calculate the future value of money using compounding interest.

Subroutine Description	Subroutine Illustration
Pass-by-value functions: They receive copies of values when they are called. These functions return a single output variable upon completion. The output variable can be a scalar or compound variable. They can also perform external operations, like SQL statements to the database.	
Pass-by-reference functions: They receive references to variables when they are called. The references are actual parameters to the function. Like other functions, they return a single output value, which can be a scalar or compound variable. Unlike functions that work with values, this type of function can also change the values of actual parameters. They return their actual parameter references upon completion to the calling program. They can also perform external operations, like SQL statements to the database.	
Pass-by-value procedures: They receive copies of values when they are called. Procedures do not return an output variable. They only perform internal operations on local variables or external operations, like SQL statements to the database.	
Pass-by-reference procedures: They receive references to variables when they are called. Procedures do not return an output variable. Like pass-by-reference functions, they can change the value of actual parameters. They return their actual parameter references upon completion to the calling program. They can also perform external operations, like SQL statements to the database.	

TABLE 6-1   *List of Subroutine Types*

NOTE
Datatypes are defined in the database catalog two ways. They can be defined as native or user-defined SQL types, or as user-defined PL/SQL types inside package specifications.

You can use functions as right operands in assignments because their result is a value of a datatype defined in the database catalog. Both pass-by-value and pass-by-reference functions fill this role equally inside PL/SQL blocks. You can use pass-by-reference functions in SQL statements only when you manage the actual parameters before and after the function call. You can also use the CALL statement with the INTO clause to return SQL datatypes from functions.

NOTE
Technically, you only need to handle SQL session bind variables before the SQL call to a pass-by-reference function.

Figure 6-1 shows how you can assign the return value from a function in a PL/SQL block. SQL statements typically use pass-by-value functions because they don't manage reference output. Most SQL function calls submit columns or literals as actual parameters and expect a scalar return value. A SQL function call mimics a SQL expression, which is a SQL query that returns only one column and one row.

What Are PL/SQL Expressions?
Expressions are values, like character, date, numeric, and string literals. Beyond literal values, expressions are variable assignments or function return values. The following UML illustration shows several types of expressions.

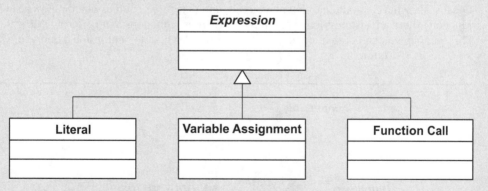

Although the term "expression" can be confusing, it generally refers to the return value from a function call in PL/SQL. In SQL, you may encounter a SQL expression, which is another label for a scalar subquery. Scalar subqueries return one row with a single column value. The simple rule is that an expression always means a value or something that has a value or returns a value.

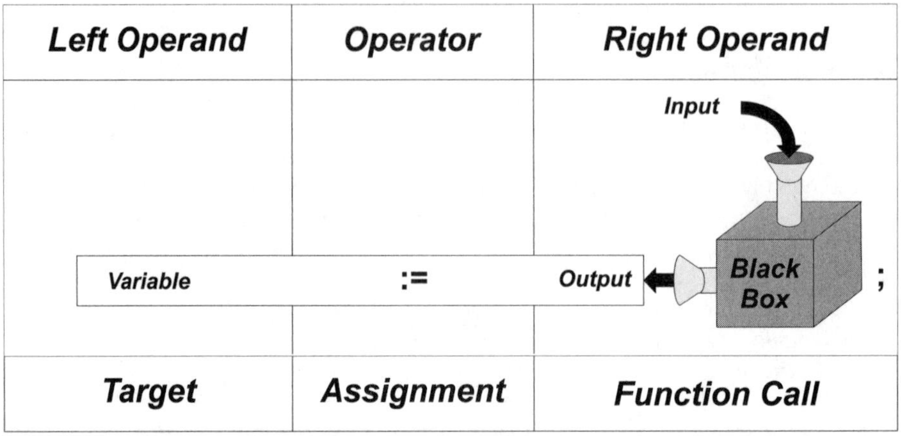

Left Operand	Operator	Right Operand
		Input
Variable	:=	Output ◄─ Black Box ;
Target	Assignment	Function Call

FIGURE 6-1 *Assignment of a function result*

Procedures can't serve as right operands. Procedures also must have run-time scope set inside a calling PL/SQL block. You cannot call procedures in SQL statements. However, you can use the `CALL` or `EXECUTE` statements to run procedures in SQL*Plus. Procedures are also self-contained units, whereas functions can only run as part of an assignment, comparative evaluation, or SQL statement.

PL/SQL functions or procedures can also run SQL statements inside their black boxes. These actions are not represented in the previous diagrams. Figure 6-2 shows a modified pass-by-value function that actually updates the database. This gets more complex for pass-by-reference functions because they have an output, reference output, and database action as outcomes of a single function. There are also restrictions on how you can use functions that perform DML statements. For example, you can't use a function that performs a DML statement inside a query, or you raise an `ORA-14551` error.

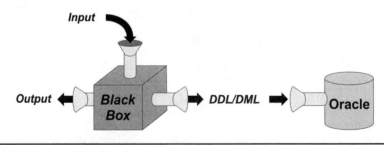

FIGURE 6-2 *Pass-by-value functions with read-write to the database*

NOTE
You can include SQL statements in functions.

As a rule, many developers use procedures to perform database actions but limit functions to queries or calculations. They do this more or less because procedures were once the only way to write changes to the database. Oracle 10*g* forward supports autonomous transactions, which have changed the rules. You should now only call a procedure when you can guarantee that it *doesn't run* autonomously, *isn't called* across the OCI, or *doesn't act* as a distributed transaction. Otherwise, you are assuming that the procedure worked when all you know is that it was called, which is optimistic processing. *If you call a function to perform database changes and it returns a Boolean value signaling success or failure, you are using pessimistic processing.*

Figure 6-3 demonstrates how to call a function to verify completion. This is the general transaction pattern for many external applications. You should strongly consider implementing it as a standard for both server-side wrappers (the *pass-by-value* version also works with Java code, as shown in Chapter 15).

PL/SQL qualifies functions and procedures as pass-by-value or pass-by-reference subroutines by the mode of their formal parameter lists. PL/SQL supports three modes: *read-only, write-only,* and *read-write.* The IN mode is the default and designates a formal parameter as read-only. OUT mode designates a write-only parameter, and IN OUT mode designates a read-write parameter mode. Table 6-2 presents the details of these available parameter modes.

By default Oracle 11*g* programs send copies of all parameters to subroutines when they call them. This may seems strange because it is contrary to the concept of pass-by-reference subroutines. However, it is exactly what you'd expect for a pass-by-value subroutine.

When subroutines complete successfully, they copy OUT or IN OUT mode parameters back into external variables. This approach guarantees the contents of an external variable are unchanged before a subroutine completes successfully. This eliminates the possibility of writing partial result sets because an error terminates a subroutine. When an exception is thrown by a subroutine, you have an opportunity to attempt recovery or write variables to log files.

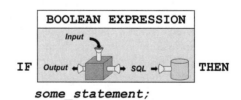

some_statement;

END IF;

FIGURE 6-3   *Pessimistic functions guarantee outcomes of SQL statements.*

Mode	Description
IN	The IN mode is the default mode. It means a formal parameter is *read-only*. When you set a formal parameter as read-only, you can't alter it during the execution of the subroutine. You *can* assign a default value to a parameter, making the parameter optional. You use the IN mode for all formal parameters when you want to define a pass-by-value subroutine.
OUT	The OUT mode means a formal parameter is *write-only*. When you set a formal parameter as write-only, there is no initial physical size allocated to the variable. You allocate the physical size and value inside your subroutine. You can't assign a default value, which would make an OUT mode formal parameter optional. If you attempt that, you raise a PLS-00230 error. The error says that an OUT or IN OUT mode variable cannot have a default value. Likewise, you cannot pass a literal as an actual parameter to an OUT mode variable because that would block writing the output variable. If you attempt sending a literal, you'll raise an ORA-06577 error with a call from SQL*Plus, and a PLS-00363 error inside a PL/SQL block. The SQL*Plus error message states the output parameter is not a bind variable, which is a SQL*Plus session variable. The PL/SQL error tells you that the expression (or more clearly literal) cannot be an assignment target. You use an OUT mode with *one or more* formal parameters when you want a *write-only* pass-by-reference subroutine.
IN OUT	The IN OUT mode means a formal parameter is *read-write*. When you set a formal parameter as read-write, the actual parameter provides the physical size of the actual parameter. While you can change the contents of the variable inside the subroutine, *you can't change or exceed the actual parameter's allocated size.* You *can't assign* a default value making an IN OUT mode parameter optional. If you attempt that, you raise a PLS-00230 error. The error says that an OUT or IN OUT mode variable cannot have a default value. Likewise, you cannot pass a literal as an actual parameter to an OUT mode variable because that would block writing the output variable. If you attempt sending a literal, you'll raise an ORA-06577 error with a call from SQL*Plus, and a PLS-00363 error inside a PL/SQL block. The SQL*Plus error message states the output parameter is not a bind variable, which is a SQL*Plus session variable. The PL/SQL error tells you that the expression (or more clearly literal) cannot be an assignment target. You use an IN OUT mode with one or more formal parameters when you want a *read-write* pass-by-reference subroutine.

TABLE 6-2 *Subroutine Parameter Modes*

You can override the default behavior of passing copies of variables when calling functions and procedures for local transactions. This means you use fewer resources and actually pass a reference, not a copy of data. You cannot override that default behavior when calling the program unit via a database link or external procedure call. You override the copy behavior by using the NOCOPY hint.

The NOCOPY hint doesn't override the copy rule when

- An actual parameter is an element of an associative array. The NOCOPY hint works when you pass a complete associative array but not a single element.

- An actual parameter is NOT NULL constrained.

- An actual parameter is constrained by scale.

- An actual parameter is an implicitly defined record structure, which means you used either the %ROWTYPE or %TYPE anchor.

- An actual parameter is an implicitly defined record structure from a FOR loop, which fails because the native index has restricted scope to the loop structure.

- An actual parameter requires implicit type casting.

The examples in this chapter and the book use the definer rights model. It is the more common solution, but you'll find a complete comparative analysis of both models in Chapter 4 of *Expert Oracle PL/SQL*. Chapter 9 discusses the design implications of using the definer and invoker rights models.

The Oracle 11*g* Database brings changes in how name and positional notation work in both SQL and PL/SQL. They actually now work the same way in both SQL and PL/SQL. This fixes a long-standing quirk in the database.

What Is Local Data?

Oracle classifies local data as materialized views, synonyms, tables, or views. Tables and materialized views are physically stored data. Views are run-time queries drawn from tables, materialized views, and other views. Synonyms to data are pointers to materialized views, synonyms, tables, or views.

You can write to a local materialized view, table, view, or synonym from a stored subprogram collocated in the same schema. Synonyms can point to objects in the same schema or another schema. When the object is defined in another schema, you must have privileges to read or write to them for a synonym to translate correctly to the object. A local synonym can resolve a schema, component selector (the period or dot), and object name into a local schema name.

Transaction Scope

As discussed in Chapter 2, transaction scope is a thread of execution—a process. You establish a session when you connect to the database. What you do during your session is visible only to you until commit any changes to the database. After you commit the changes, other sessions can see the changes you've made.

During a session, you can run one or more PL/SQL programs. They execute serially, or in sequence. The first program can alter the data or environment before the second runs, and so on. This is true because your session is the main transaction. All activities depend on one or more prior activities. You can commit work, making all changes permanent, or reject work, repudiating all or some changes.

Transaction scope is fairly straightforward when working with process-centric workflows but a bit more complex when you rely on functions and procedures. Functions and procedures have one of two types of scope. They are dependently scoped by default, which means that they run in the transaction scope of the main process—the calling program. However, you can set functions or procedures to run in their own scope by defining them as autonomous transactions.

Autonomous transactions can commit their local work independently of the calling program. This makes all changes permanent, notwithstanding the main program control rules.

Autonomous transactions are great when you want something to happen notwithstanding the success or failure of something else. They're useful when you want to write data in a trigger before raising an exception that causes the main program's failure. However, they're dangerous for the same reason. You can inadvertently write data states when you don't want them written.

You should note that transaction scope is controlled by using the `SAVEPOINT`, `ROLLBACK`, and `COMMIT` commands. Both the later sections "Functions" and "Procedures" demonstrate autonomous subroutines.

Calling Subroutines

Prior to Oracle 11*g*, you were able to use both positional and named notation when calling subroutines in PL/SQL program units, but unable to use named notation in SQL calls to functions. Oracle 11*g* has fixed that shortfall and introduced mixed notation calls too.

Positional notation means that you provide a value for each variable in the formal parameter list. The values must be in sequential order and must also match the datatype. Named notation means that you pass actual parameters by using their formal parameter name, the association operator (=>), and the value. Named notation lets you only pass values to required parameters, which means you accept the default values for any optional parameters.

The new mixed notation means that you can now call subroutines by a combination of positional and named notation. This becomes very handy when parameter lists are defined with all mandatory parameters first, and optional parameters next. It lets you name or avoid naming the mandatory parameters, and it lets you skip optional parameters where their default values work. It does not solve exclusionary notation problems. Exclusionary problems occur with positional notation when optional parameters are interspersed with mandatory parameters, and when you call some but not all optional parameters.

The following function lets you experiment with these different approaches. The function accepts three optional parameters and returns the sum of three numbers:

```
CREATE OR REPLACE FUNCTION add_three_numbers
  ( a NUMBER := 0, b NUMBER := 0, c NUMBER := 0 ) RETURN NUMBER IS
```

```
BEGIN
  RETURN a + b + c;
END;
/
```

   The first three subsections show you how to make positional, named, and mixed notation function calls. The last one demonstrates how to make exclusionary notation calls.

Positional Notation

You use positional notation to call the function as follows:

```
BEGIN
  dbms_output.put_line(add_three_numbers(3,4,5));
END;
/
```

Named Notation

You call the function using named notation by

```
BEGIN
  dbms_output.put_line(add_three_numbers(c => 4,b => 5,c => 3));
END;
/
```

Mixed Notation

You call the function by a mix of both positional and named notation by

```
BEGIN
  dbms_output.put_line(add_three_numbers(3,c => 4,b => 5));
END;
/
```

   There is a restriction on mixed notation. All positional notation actual parameters must occur first and in the same order as they are defined by the function signature. *You cannot provide a position value after a named value without raising an exception.*

Exclusionary Notation

As mentioned, you can also exclude one or more of the actual parameters when the formal parameters are defined as optional. All parameters in the add_three_numbers function are optional. The following example passes a value to the first parameter by positional reference, and the third parameter by named reference:

```
BEGIN
  dbms_output.put_line(add_three_numbers(3,c => 4));
END;
/
```

   When you opt to not provide an actual parameter, it acts as if you're passing a null value. This is known as exclusionary notation. Oracle has recommended for years that you should list optional parameters last in function and procedure signatures. They've also recommended that you sequence optional variables so that you never have to skip an optional parameter in the list. These recommendations exist to circumvent errors when making positional notation calls.

You can't really skip an optional parameter in a positional notation call. This is true because all positional calls are in sequence by datatype, but you can provide a comma-delimited null value when you want to skip an optional parameter in the list. However, Oracle 11*g* now lets you use mixed notation calls. You can now use positional notation for your list of mandatory parameters, and named notation for optional parameters. This lets you skip optional parameters without naming all parameters explicitly.

SQL Call Notation

Previously, you had only one choice. You had to list all the parameters in their positional order because you couldn't use named reference in SQL. This is fixed in Oracle 11*g*; now you can call them just as you do from a PL/SQL block. The following demonstrates mixed notation in a SQL call:

```
SELECT add_three_numbers(3,c => 4,b => 5) FROM dual;
```

As when using earlier releases, you can only call functions that have IN mode–only variables from SQL statements. You cannot call a function from SQL when any of its formal parameters are defined as IN OUT or OUT mode–only variables without handling the actual parameter in SQL*Plus as a session bind variable. This is true because you must pass a variable reference when a parameter has an OUT mode.

Functions

As mentioned, you have pass-by-value and pass-by-reference functions in PL/SQL. Both types of functions return output values. Function output values can be any SQL or PL/SQL datatype. You can use functions that return SQL datatypes inside SQL statements. Functions returning PL/SQL datatypes *only* work inside PL/SQL blocks.

One exception to these general rules is that you cannot call a stored function that contains a DML operation from inside a SQL query. If you do, it raises an ORA-14551 error saying that it can't perform a DML inside a query. However, you can call a function that performs a DML operation inside inserts, updates, and deletes.

Functions can also contain nested named blocks, which are local functions and procedures. You define named blocks in the declaration block of the function. You can likewise nest anonymous blocks in the execution block.

The following illustrates a named block function prototype:

```
FUNCTION function_name
[( parameter1     [IN][OUT] [NOCOPY] sql_datatype | plsql_datatype
, parameter2      [IN][OUT] [NOCOPY] sql_datatype | plsql_datatype
, parameter(n+1) [IN][OUT] [NOCOPY] sql_datatype | plsql_datatype )]

RETURN { sql_data_type | plsql_data_type }
[ AUTHID [ DEFINER | CURRENT_USER ]]
[ DETERMINISTIC | PARALLEL_ENABLED ]
[ PIPELINED ]
[ RESULT_CACHE [ RELIES_ON table_name ]] IS
  declaration_statements
```

```
BEGIN
  execution_statements
  RETURN variable;
[EXCEPTION]
  exception_handling_statements
END [function_name];
/
```

You call functions by providing any required parameters as a list of arguments inside opening and closing parentheses. No parentheses are required when functions aren't defined with required parameters. This differs from most other programming languages. Calls in other languages require an empty set of opening and closing parentheses.

The prototype for a function call with actual parameters from SQL*Plus is

```
CALL function_name(parameter1, parameter2, parameter(n+1))
INTO target_variable_name;
```

When there aren't any mandatory formal parameters, the prototype differs, as shown:

```
CALL function_name INTO target_variable_name;
```

Assignments inside PL/SQL blocks with mandatory parameters look like

```
target_variable_name := function_name(parameter1, parameter2, parameter(n+1));
```

The assignment prototype drops the parentheses when unnecessary:

```
target_variable_name := function_name;
```

You can also return a function value as an expression, and then use it as an actual parameter to another function. This is done by using the following prototype:

```
external_function_name(function_name(parameter1, parameter2, parameter(n+1)));
```

There are several optional configurations you can use when creating functions. The default model of operation is definer rights. You can define a function to support an invoker rights model by including the AUTHID as CURRENT_USER. The definer rights model runs with the privileges of the owning schema and is best suited for a centralized computing model. The invoker rights model requires you to maintain multiple copies of tables or views in different schemas or databases. The invoker rights model best supports distributed computing models. Chapter 9 discusses definer and invoker rights models.

You can also guarantee the behavior of a function, which make it possible to use them in SQL statements, function-based indexes, and materialized views. You can also configure functions to return pipelined tables and, in Oracle 11g, shared result sets from the cache in the SGA.

As discussed, you can define formal parameters in one of three modes. They are IN mode for read-only parameters, OUT mode for write-only parameters, and IN OUT mode for read-write parameters. You build a pass-by-value function when you define *all* parameters as IN mode, and a pass-by-reference function when you defined *one or more* as OUT or IN OUT mode parameters.

The next three sections discuss how you can create functions. The first section examines the optional clauses that let you create functions for various purposes. The second section examines pass-by-value functions, and the third discusses pass-by-value functions.

Creation Options

You create functions for SQL statements, function-based indexes, and materialized views by using the `DETERMINISTIC` or `PARALLEL_ENABLED` clauses. The `DETERMINISTIC` and `PARALLEL_ENABLED` clauses replace the older `RESTRICT_REFERENCES` precompiler instructions that limited what functions could do when they were in packages. The new clauses let you assign the same restrictions to functions in packages, and they also let you assign them to standalone stored functions.

Backward Compatibility Issues for Functions

Functions were restricted subroutines before Oracle 8*i* (8.1.6). You had to define them with a guarantee of performance, which was known as their level of purity. The guarantees limited whether functions could read or write to package variables or to the database.

These limits can still be imposed on functions *inside* packages by using the `RESTRICT_REFERENCES PRAGMA` options listed in Table 6-3. A `PRAGMA` is a precompiler instruction. Any attempt to use a `RESTRICT_REFERENCES PRAGMA` inside a standalone function raises an `PLS-00708` error.

You must define `PRAGMA` restrictions in *package specifications*, not in package bodies. There should only be one `PRAGMA` per function. You can include multiple options in any `RESTRICT_REFERENCES` precompiler instruction. The `TRUST` option can be added to restricting `PRAGMA` instructions when you want to enable a restricted function to call other unrestricted functions. The `TRUST` option disables auditing whether called functions adhere to the calling program unit's restrictions—sharing the same level of purity, or guarantee of performance.

NOTE
You should consider replacing these restricting precompiler instructions in older package specifications with a DETERMINISTIC *or* PARALLEL_ENABLED *clause.*

Backward compatibility is nice but seldom lasts forever. You should replace these old precompiler instructions by defining functions with the new syntax. This means making functions `DETERMINISTIC` when they are used by function-based indexes. Likewise, you should define functions as `PARALLEL_ENABLED` when they may run in parallelized operations.

The `PIPELINED` clause lets you build functions that return pipelined tables. Pipelined tables act like pseudo–reference cursors and are built using modified PL/SQL collection types. They let you work with PL/SQL collections of record structures without defining them as instantiable user-defined object types. You can also read the collections in SQL statements as you would an inline view.

Oracle 11*g* introduces the cross-session result cache. You implement this feature by defining functions with the `RESULT_CACHE` clause. The cross-session result cache stores the actual parameters and result for each call to these functions. A second call to the function with the same actual parameters finds the result in the cross-session cache and thereby avoids rerunning the code. The result is stored in the SGA. When the result cache runs out of memory, it ages out least used function call results.

DETERMINISTIC Clause

The `DETERMINISTIC` clause lets you guarantee that a function always works the same way with any inputs. This type of guarantee requires that a function doesn't read or write data from external sources, like packages or database tables. *Only deterministic functions work in materialized views and function-based indexes.* They are also recommended solutions for user-defined functions that

Option	Description
RNDS	The RNDS option guarantees a function *reads no data state*. This means you cannot include a SQL query of any type in the function. It also cannot call any other named block that includes a SQL query. A PLS-00452 error is raised during compilation if you have a query inside the function's program scope that violates the PRAGMA restriction.
WNDS	The WNDS option guarantees a function *writes no data state*. This means you cannot include SQL statements that insert, update, or delete data. It also cannot call any other named block that includes a SQL query. A PLS-00452 error is raised during compilation if you have a DML statement inside the function's program scope that violates the PRAGMA restriction.
RNPS	The RNPS option guarantees a function *reads no package state*, which means that it does not read any package variables. This means you cannot access a package variable in the function. It also cannot call any other named block reads package variables. A PLS-00452 error is raised during compilation if you have a query inside the function's program scope that violates the PRAGMA restriction.
WNPS	The WNPS options guarantees a function *writes no data state*, which means that it does not write any values to package variables. This means you cannot change package variables or call another named block that changes them. A PLS-00452 error is raised during compilation if you have a statement inside the function's program scope that violates the PRAGMA restriction.
TRUST	The TRUST option instructs the function not to check whether called programs enforce other RESTRICT_REFERENCES options. The benefit of this option is that you can slowly migrate code to the new standard. The risks include changing the behavior or performance of SQL statements. For reference, the other options also guard conditions necessary to support function-based indexes and parallel query operations.

TABLE 6-3   *Precompiler Options for Package Functions*

you plan to use in SQL statement clauses, like WHERE, ORDER BY, or GROUP BY; or SQL object type methods, like MAP or ORDER.

Deterministic functions typically process parameters in the exact same way. This means that no matter what values you submit, the function works the same way. They should *not* have internal dependencies on package variables or data from the database. The following pv function is deterministic and calculates the present value of an investment:

-- This is found in pv.sql on the publisher's web site.

```
CREATE OR REPLACE FUNCTION pv
( future_value    NUMBER
, periods         NUMBER
, interest        NUMBER )
RETURN NUMBER DETERMINISTIC IS
```

```
BEGIN
  RETURN future_value / ((1 + interest)**periods);
END pv;
/
```

Assume you want to know how much to put in a 6% investment today to have $10,000 in five years. You can test this function by defining a bind variable, using a `CALL` statement to put the value in the bind variable, and querying the result against the `DUAL` table, like

```
VARIABLE result NUMBER
CALL pv(10000,5,6) INTO :result;
COLUMN money_today FORMAT 9,999.90
SELECT :result AS money_today FROM dual;
```

The function call uses positional notation but could also use named notation or mixed notation. It prints the formatted present value amount:

```
MONEY_TODAY
-----------
   7,472.58
```

You use deterministic functions inside materialized views and function-based indexes. Both materialized views and function-based indexes must be rebuilt when you change the internal working of deterministic functions.

PARALLEL_ENABLE Clause

`PARALLEL_ENABLE` lets you designate a function to support parallel query capabilities. This type of guarantee requires that a function doesn't read or write data from external sources, like packages or database tables. You should consider designating functions as safe for parallel operations to improve throughput, but the Oracle 11*g* optimizer may run undesignated functions when it believes they are safe for parallel operations. Java methods and external C programs are *never* deemed safe for parallel operations.

Materialized Views

Unlike a standard view in a relational database, a *materialized view* is a cached result set. As a cached result set, it is stored as a concrete table.

Materialized views are more responsive to queries because they don't demand resources to dynamically build the view each time. The trade-off is that materialized views are often slightly out of date because underlying data *may change from when the view is cached to when it is accessed.*

You can use function-based indexes in materialized views provided they use deterministic functions. Deterministic functions always produce the same result value when called with any set of actual parameters. They also guarantee that they don't modify package variables or data in the database.

Consider using materialized views when the underlying table data changes *infrequently,* and query speed is important. Materialized views are possible solutions when developing data warehouse fact tables.

The following function supports parallel SQL operations and merges last name, first name, and middle initial into a single string:

```
-- This is found in merge.sql on the publisher's web site.
CREATE OR REPLACE FUNCTION merge
( last_name      VARCHAR2
, first_name     VARCHAR2
, middle_initial VARCHAR2 )
RETURN VARCHAR2 PARALLEL_ENABLE IS
BEGIN
  RETURN last_name ||', '||first_name||' '||middle_initial;
END;
/
```

You can use the function safely in database queries, like

```
SELECT    merge(last_name,first_name,middle_initial) AS full_name
FROM      contact
ORDER BY last_name, first_name, middle_initial;
```

This query depends on the code discussed in the introduction and returns

```
FULL_NAME
-----------------
Sweeney, Ian M
Sweeney, Irving M
Sweeney, Meaghan
Vizquel, Doreen
Vizquel, Oscar
Winn, Brian
Winn, Randi
```

Parallel operations do not always occur when you use the PARALLEL_ENABLE hint. Parallel operations are more expensive with small data sets. The Oracle 11*g* optimizer judges when to run operations in parallel mode. Also, sometimes the optimizer runs functions in parallel when they're not marked as parallel enabled. It makes this decision after checking whether the function can support the operation. It is a good coding practice to enable functions for parallel operation when they qualify.

PIPELINED Clause

The PIPELINED clause provides improved performance when functions return collections, like nested tables or VARRAYs. You'll also note performance improvements when returning system reference cursors by using the PIPELINED clause. Pipelined functions also let you return aggregate tables. Aggregate tables act like collections of PL/SQL record structures. They only work in SQL statements.

This section discusses collection concepts. Chapter 6 covers collections for those new to PL/SQL. Collections are arrays and lists of scalar and compound variables. Pipelined functions *only* work with VARRAY and nested table collections. These two types of collections are indexed by sequential numbers. You can also build collections of user-defined SQL object types, which are treated like single-dimensional arrays of number, strings, or dates. Chapter 14 covers object types and includes a shadow box demonstrating how to use pipelined functions.

The easiest implementation of a pipelined function involves a collection of scalar values defined by a SQL datatype. You define a NUMBERS datatype as a VARRAY of number by using the following command:

```
CREATE OR REPLACE TYPE numbers AS VARRAY(10) OF NUMBER;
/
```

The 10 in parentheses after the VARRAY sets the maximum number of elements in the collection. VARRAY datatypes are very similar to arrays. Arrays in most programming languages are initialized with a fixed size or memory allocation.

After you create the collection datatype, you can describe it at the SQL command line:

```
SQL> DESCRIBE NUMBERS
 NUMBERS VARRAY(10) OF NUMBER
```

NOTE
When you create types in the database, the DDL command acts like a PL/SQL block. These commands require a semicolon to end the statement and a forward slash to execute it (or compile it into the database).

A pipelined function depends on available SQL or PL/SQL collection datatypes. These types are limited to VARRAY or nested table collections. You can define SQL collection types of scalar variables or user-defined object types.

The following defines a pipelined function that returns an array of ordinal numbers:

```
-- This is found in create_pipelined1.sql on the publisher's web site.
CREATE OR REPLACE FUNCTION pipelined_numbers
RETURN NUMBERS
PIPELINED IS
  list NUMBERS := numbers(0,1,2,3,4,5,6,7,8,9);
BEGIN
  FOR i IN 1..list.LAST LOOP
    PIPE ROW(list(i));
  END LOOP;
  RETURN;
END;
/
```

The function returns the NUMBERS user-defined SQL datatype from the data catalog. The function declares a local collection of NUMBERS by initializing the collection. You initialize a collection by calling the user-defined SQL datatype name with a list of scalar variables. Inside the FOR loop, you assign elements from the collection to the pipe.

You can then query the results as follows:

```
SELECT * FROM TABLE(pipelined_numbers);
```

The output is a single column with the ordinal numbers from 0 to 9.

Pipelined functions can also use PL/SQL collection types, provided you implement them as VARRAY or nested table collections. PL/SQL collection types can hold scalar variables or user-defined object types like their SQL equivalents. They can also be collections of record structures. This means they are similar to system reference cursors.

Unlike system reference cursors, they cannot be defined as SQL or PL/SQL datatypes. They can only be defined as PL/SQL datatypes. In order to return these types in stored functions, they must be defined inside a package specification. At the very least, you must define the record type in a package specification even when you implement a pipelined standalone function. Chapter 9 covers packages in more detail.

The following package specification defines a record structure, a collection of the record structure, and a function returning the collection type:

```
-- This is found in create_pipelined2.sql on the publisher's web site.
CREATE OR REPLACE PACKAGE pipelined IS
  -- Define a PL/SQL record type and Collection of the record type.
  TYPE account_record IS RECORD
  ( account       VARCHAR2(10)
  , full_name     VARCHAR2(42));
  TYPE account_collection IS TABLE OF account_record;

  -- Define a pipelined function.
  FUNCTION pf RETURN account_collection PIPELINED;
END pipelined;
/
```

The function is implemented in the package body:

```
-- This is found in create_pipelined2.sql on the publisher's web site.
CREATE OR REPLACE PACKAGE BODY pipelined IS
  -- Implement a pipelined function.
  FUNCTION pf
  RETURN account_collection
  PIPELINED IS
    -- Declare a collection control variable and collection variable.
    counter NUMBER := 1;
    account ACCOUNT_COLLECTION := account_collection();

    -- Define a cursor.
    CURSOR c IS
      SELECT   m.account_number
      ,        c.last_name || ', '||c.first_name full_name
      FROM     member m JOIN contact c ON m.member_id = c.member_id
      ORDER BY c.last_name, c.first_name, c.middle_initial;
  BEGIN
    FOR i IN c LOOP
      account.EXTEND;
      account(counter).account   := i.account_number;
      account(counter).full_name := i.full_name;
      PIPE ROW(account(counter));
      counter := counter + 1;
    END LOOP;
    RETURN;
  END pf;
END pipelined;
/
```

The package body implements the `pf` function. Inside the function, a local variable is declared using the `account_collection` PL/SQL collection type. Both `VARRAY` and nested table collections are internal objects, and they require explicit construction. The constructor is the name of the collection type without any actual parameters when you want to declare an empty collection. Collections require you to allocate space before adding elements to a collection. The `EXTEND` method allocates space for one element, and then values are assigned to components of that indexed element. The record element is then added as a row in the `PIPE`.

You can call the function using the package name, component selector, and function name, as shown:

```
SELECT * FROM TABLE(pipelined.pf);
```

This returns rows from the record structure as an aggregate table:

```
ACCOUNT     FULL_NAME
----------  ----------------
B293-71447  Sweeney, Ian
B293-71446  Sweeney, Irving
B293-71447  Sweeney, Meaghan
B293-71446  Vizquel, Doreen
B293-71446  Vizquel, Oscar
B293-71445  Winn, Brian
B293-71445  Winn, Randi
```

It may appear that you're limited to packages because that's where the return type is located. While PL/SQL datatypes are not available in the data dictionary, they are available to other PL/SQL program units when they're published in a package specification.

The standalone function definition implements the same pipelined function outside of the package:

```
-- This is found in create_pipelined2.sql on the publisher's web site.
CREATE OR REPLACE FUNCTION pf
RETURN pipelined.account_collection
PIPELINED IS
  -- Declare a collection control variable and collection variable.
  counter NUMBER := 1;
  account PIPELINED.ACCOUNT_COLLECTION := pipelined.account_collection();

  -- Define a cursor.
  CURSOR c IS
    SELECT   m.account_number
    ,        c.last_name || ', '||c.first_name full_name
    FROM     member m JOIN contact c ON m.member_id = c.member_id
    ORDER BY c.last_name, c.first_name, c.middle_initial;
BEGIN
  FOR i IN c LOOP
    account.EXTEND;
    account(counter).account   := i.account_number;
    account(counter).full_name := i.full_name;
    PIPE ROW(account(counter));
    counter := counter + 1;
  END LOOP;
```

```
    RETURN;
END pf;
/
```

The differences are in how you reference the PL/SQL collection type. You must use the package name, component selector, and datatype name. However, you can call the function by referencing only the function name, like

```
SELECT * FROM TABLE(pf);
```

Pipelined Results Are Limited to SQL Scope

There is a temptation to pass the return value from a pipelined function to another PL/SQL module because it isn't clear that these aggregate tables are designed only for use in SQL statements. You receive a `PLS-00653` error when you try to pass a pipelined function result to another PL/SQL program as an actual parameter. A `PLS-00653` error states that "aggregate/table functions are not allowed in PL/SQL scope." *Pipelined table results are only accessible in SQL scope.*

The following procedure passes compilation checks because it refers to a valid PL/SQL collection type:

```
-- This is found in create_pipelined2.sql on the publisher's web site.
CREATE OR REPLACE PROCEDURE read_pipe
( pipe_in pipelined.account_collection ) IS
BEGIN
  FOR i IN 1..pipe_in.LAST LOOP
    dbms_output.put(pipe_in(i).account);
    dbms_output.put(pipe_in(i).full_name);
  END LOOP;
END read_pipe;
/
```

This seems a logical segue to control the reading of a pipelined table. The following demonstrates how you would call the procedure, by passing the result set of a call to the pipelined `pf` function:

```
EXECUTE read_pipe(pf);
```

This raises the following error message:

```
BEGIN read_pipe(pf); END;
          *
ERROR at line 1:
ORA-06550: line 1, column 10:
PLS-00653: aggregate/table functions are not allowed in PL/SQL scope
```

The error occurs because the actual datatype passed to the procedure is a pipelined aggregate or table with equivalent values but not a PL/SQL collection datatype. Fortunately, the error message gives you great feedback when you know that a pipelined aggregate table *isn't* a PL/SQL collection type.

You can use pipelined functions to build views, like this:

```
CREATE OR REPLACE VIEW pipelined_view AS
SELECT r.account, r.full_name FROM TABLE(pf) r;
```

Views built by calls to pipelined functions require instead-of triggers to manage inserts, updates, and deletes. At least, you build the instead-of trigger when you want to allow DML operations. Chapter 10 covers how to implement an instead-of trigger.

Pipelined functions are designed to let you use collections of scalar variables or record structures. The previously demonstrated pipelined functions convert the PL/SQL collection into an aggregate table. You cannot reuse the pipelined table in another PL/SQL scope, but you can use it in SQL scope queries.

You have learned how to use pipelined functions and their strengths and weaknesses. They're great tools when you want to get data into a query or view that requires procedural logic.

RESULT_CACHE Clause

The RESULT_CACHE clause is *new* in the Oracle 11*g* Database. It indicates that a function is cached only once in the SGA and available across sessions. Both the actual parameters of prior calls and results are available in the result cache. The RESULT_CACHE clause instructs the PL/SQL engine to check the result cache for function calls with matching actual parameters. A matching function call also stores the result, and the cache returns the result and skips re-running the function. This means the function only runs when new parameters are sent to it.

NOTE
Cross-session functions only work with IN *mode formal parameters.*

The prototype for the RESULT_CACHE clause has an optional RELIES_ON clause. The RELIES_ON clause is critical because it ensures any change to the underlying table invalidates the result cache. This also means any DML transactions that would change result sets. The RELIES_ON clause ensures that the cache is dynamic, representing the current result set. *You can list any number of dependent tables in the* RELIES_ON *clause, and they're listed as comma-delimited names.*

The next example depends on the downloadable code from the publisher's web site. You can find a description of the code in the Introduction. Also, this example uses a collection, which forward-references material in Chapter 6.

This statement lets you build a collection of VARCHAR2 values:

```
-- This is found in result_cache.sql on the publisher's web site.
CREATE OR REPLACE TYPE strings AS TABLE OF VARCHAR2(60);
/
```

This function implements a cross-session result cache with the RELIES_ON clause:

```
-- This is found in result_cache.sql on the publisher's web site.
CREATE OR REPLACE FUNCTION get_title
( partial_title VARCHAR2 ) RETURN STRINGS
RESULT_CACHE RELIES_ON(item) IS
  -- Declare a collection control variable and collection variable.
  counter      NUMBER  := 1;
  return_value STRINGS := strings();

  -- Define a parameterized cursor.
```

```
    CURSOR get_title
    ( partial_title VARCHAR2 ) IS
    SELECT    item_title
    FROM      item
    WHERE     UPPER(item_title) LIKE '%'||UPPER(partial_title)||'%';
BEGIN
    -- Read the data and write it to the collection in a cursor FOR loop.
    FOR i IN get_title(partial_title) LOOP
      return_value.EXTEND;
      return_value(counter) := i.item_title;
      counter := counter + 1;
    END LOOP;
    RETURN return_value;
END get_title;
/
```

Probably the most important detail of the foregoing `get_title` function is that you should *start your counter at 1, not 0.* The function uses the counter as the collection index value, and collection indexes should be positive integers. An index with a non-positive integer raises an `ORA-06532` error stating that the subscript is out of range.

NOTE
The `RELIES_ON` clause can accept one or a list of actual parameters.

You can test the `get_title` function with the following anonymous block program:

```
-- This is found in result_cache.sql on the publisher's web site.
DECLARE
  list STRINGS;
BEGIN
  list := get_title('Harry');
  FOR i IN 1..list.LAST LOOP
    dbms_output.put_line('list('||i||') : ['||list(i)||']');
  END LOOP;
END;
/
```

After calling the result caching function, you insert, delete, or update dependent data. Then, you'll find new result sets are displayed. This change ensures that stale data never misleads the user. The `RELIES_ON` clause ensures the integrity of the result set, but it does cost you some processing overhead.

TIP
You should consider excluding the `RELIES_ON` clause to improve transactional efficiency in data warehouse implementations.

Result-cached functions also have some restrictions. Result-cached functions must meet the following criteria:

- They cannot be defined in a module that uses invoker's rights or in an anonymous block.

- They cannot be a pipelined table function.

- They cannot have pass-by-reference semantics, like `IN OUT` or `OUT` mode parameters.

- They cannot use formal parameters with a `BLOB`, `CLOB`, `NCLOB`, `REF CURSOR`, collection, object, or record datatype.

- They cannot return a variable with a `BLOB`, `CLOB`, `NCLOB`, `REF CURSOR`, collection, object, or record datatype.

Also, Oracle recommends that result-cached functions should not modify the database state, modify the external state (by using the `DBMS_OUTPUT` package), or send email (through the `UTL_SMTP` package). Likewise, the function should not depend on session-specific settings or contexts.

These sections have covered the available options for defining functions. These skills are assumed when discussing pass-by-value functions.

Pass-by-Value Functions

Pass-by-value functions receive copies of values when they are called. These functions return a single output variable upon completion, and they can perform external operations. The external operations can be physical reads and writes to the operating system or SQL statements against the database. Refer back to Table 6-1 for an illustration of the pass-by-value function.

As discussed, you can define pass-by-value functions as deterministic or parallel-enabled when the functions don't alter package variables or database values. You can also define functions to return pipelined tables that mimic SQL or PL/SQL collections. The results of pipelined functions require that you use them in SQL scope. All functions except those created with pipelined results support result caches.

The basic structure of a pass-by-value program takes a list of inputs, which are also known as formal parameters. *Functions return a single output variable.* Output variables can be scalar values, structures, collections, pipelined tables, or user-defined object types. This means that a single variable can contain many things when it is a compound datatype.

Whether functions interact with the file system or database does not impact how they act inside your PL/SQL code block. You can use a function to assign a result to a variable, or return a variable as an expression. Earlier Figure 6-1 illustrates using a function as a right operand in an assignment operation.

You can use a function that returns a variable as an expression when you put it inside a call to another PL/SQL built-in function, like

```
EXECUTE dbms_output.put_line(TO_CHAR(pv(10000,5,6),'9,999.90'));
```

When `SERVEROUTPUT` is enabled, this outputs

```
7,472.58
```

The example uses the `pv` function described in the section "DETERMINISTIC Clause" section earlier in this chapter, and it uses the `TO_CHAR` built-in function (see Appendix J for details). A call to the `pv` function becomes an expression to the `TO_CHAR` function, and the result of the `TO_CHAR` function then becomes an expression and actual parameter to the `PUT_LINE` procedure of the `DBMS_OUTPUT` package. These are typical calls and uses of pass-by-value functions.

PL/SQL pass-by-value functions are defined by the following six rules:

- All formal parameters must be defined as *write-only* variables by using the `IN` mode.

- All formal parameters are locally scoped variables that *cannot* be changed during execution inside the function.

- Any formal parameter can use any valid SQL or PL/SQL datatype. Only functions with parameter lists that use SQL datatypes work in SQL statements.

- Any formal parameter may have a default initial value.

- The formal return variable can use any valid SQL or PL/SQL datatype, but pipelined return tables must be used in SQL statements. You can't access pipelined table results in another PL/SQL scope.

- Any system reference cursor cast from a SQL query into a function is not writable, and therefore it must be passed through an IN mode parameter.

System Reference Cursors

All cursor result sets are static structures stored in the Oracle SGA. Cursors variables are actually references or handles. The handle points to an internally cached result set from a query. You populate cursor variables by fetching records, typically by using an

```
OPEN cursor_name FOR select_statement;
```

You access cursors by using a reference or handle that lets you scroll their content. You scroll through them by using the FETCH cursor INTO variable syntax. Once you declare an implicit or explicit cursor structure, you can then assign its reference to a SQL cursor datatype. You can also return these cursor variables as function return types or as IN OUT or OUT reference variables in function and procedure signatures. The result sets are *read-only* structures.

The following shows how to return a cursor using a function:

```
-- This is found in cursor_management.sql on the publisher's web site.
CREATE OR REPLACE FUNCTION get_full_titles
RETURN SYS_REFCURSOR IS
  titles SYS_REFCURSOR;
BEGIN
  OPEN titles FOR
    SELECT  item_title, item_subtitle
    FROM    item;
  RETURN titles;
END;
/
```

The function uses the predefined SYS_REFCURSOR, which is a weakly typed system reference cursor. A weakly typed reference cursor can assume any record structure at run time, whereas a strongly typed reference cursor is anchored to a database catalog object.

The OPEN clause creates a reference in the SGA for the cursor. You can then pass the reference to another PL/SQL block as a cursor variable, as shown in the following anonymous block:

```
-- This is found in cursor_management.sql on the publisher's web site.
DECLARE
  -- Define a type and declare a variable.
  TYPE full_title_record IS RECORD
  ( item_title    item.item_title%TYPE
  , item_subtitle item.item_subtitle%TYPE);
  full_title FULL_TITLE_RECORD;
```

```
  -- Declare a system reference cursor variable.
  titles SYS_REFCURSOR;
BEGIN
  -- Assign the reference cursor function result.
  titles := get_full_titles;

  -- Print one element of one of the parallel collections.
  LOOP
    FETCH titles INTO full_title;
    EXIT WHEN titles%NOTFOUND;
    dbms_output.put_line('Title ['||full_title.item_title||']');
  END LOOP;
END;
/
```

NOTE
There is never an open statement before the loop when a cursor is passed into a subroutine, because they are already open. Cursor variables are actually references that point into a specialized cursor work area in the SGA.

The receiving or processing block needs to know what record type is stored in the cursor. Some use this requirement to argue that you should only use strongly typed reference cursors. In PL/SQL-only solutions, they have a point.

The other side of the argument can be made for weakly typed reference cursors when you query them through external programs using the OCI libraries. In these external languages you can dynamically discover the structure of reference cursors and manage them discretely through generic algorithms. Appendix C shows how to do so using the `ReferenceCursor.php` program.

Calculating the future value of a bank deposit illustrates how to write a pass-by-value function. The following builds the `fv` function, which calculates an annual interest rate compounded daily:

```
-- This is found in fv.sql on the publisher's web site.
CREATE OR REPLACE FUNCTION fv
( current_value   NUMBER := 0
, periods         NUMBER := 1
, interest        NUMBER)
RETURN NUMBER DETERMINISTIC IS
BEGIN
  -- Compounded Daily Interest.
  RETURN current_value * (1 + ((1 + ((interest/100)/365))**365 -1)*periods);
END fv;
/
```

The function defines three formal parameters. Two are optional parameters because they have default values. The default values are the current balance of the account and the 365 days of the year (for non-leap years). The third parameter is mandatory because no value is provided. As discussed, the `IN` mode is the default, and you do not have to specify it when defining functions.

As a general practice, mandatory parameters come before optional parameters. This is critical when actual parameters are submitted in positional order. Oracle 11*g* supports positional order, named notation order, and mixed notation.

After defining an output variable, you use the CALL statement to run the function using named notation:

```
VARIABLE future_value NUMBER
CALL fv(current_value => 10000, periods => 5, interest => 4)
INTO :future_value
/
```

You can then select the future value of $10,000 after five years at 4% annual interest compounded daily, by using

```
SELECT :future_value FROM dual;
```

Alternatively, you can format with SQL*Plus and call the function in SQL with this statement:

```
COLUMN future_value FORMAT 99,999.90
SELECT fv(current_value => 10000, periods => 5, interest => 4) FROM dual;
```

Both the CALL statement and SQL query return a result of $12,040.42. The compounding of interest yields $40.42 more than an annual rate. There might be an extra penny or two, depending on where the leap year falls in the five years, but the function doesn't manage that nuance in the calculation.

Pass-by-value functions disallow any attempt to reassign a value to a formal parameter during run time. You raise a PLS-00363 error that tells you the expression (formal parameter) can't be used as an assignment target.

Functions also let you process DML statements inside them. There are some people that feel you shouldn't use functions to perform DML statements because, historically, procedures were used. The *only downside* of embedding a DML statement inside a function is that you can't call that function inside a query. If you call a function that performs a DML statement from a query, you raise an ORA-14551 error. The error message says you can't have a DML operation inside a query.

The following function inserts a row by calling the autonomous add_user function:

```
-- This is found in create_add_user.sql on the publisher's web site.
CREATE OR REPLACE FUNCTION add_user
( system_user_id      NUMBER
, system_user_name    VARCHAR2
, system_group_id     NUMBER
, system_user_type    NUMBER
, last_name           VARCHAR2
, first_name          VARCHAR2
, middle_initial      VARCHAR2
, created_by          NUMBER
, creation_date       DATE
, last_updated_by     NUMBER
, last_update_date    DATE ) RETURN BOOLEAN IS
  -- Set function to perform in its own transaction scope.
  PRAGMA AUTONOMOUS_TRANSACTION;
  -- Set default return value.
  retval BOOLEAN := FALSE;
BEGIN
  INSERT INTO system_user
  VALUES
```

```
( system_user_id, system_user_name, system_group_id, system_user_type
, last_name, first_name, middle_initial
, created_by, creation_date, last_updated_by, last_update_date );
    -- Save change inside its own transaction scope.
    COMMIT;
    -- Reset return value.
    retval := TRUE;
    RETURN retval;
END;
/
```

Autonomous program units perform their operations in a separate transactional scope, which means their behavior is isolated from the calling transaction scope. This anonymous-block program demonstrates how you use a function as an expression in an `IF` statement when it performs a DML operation in an autonomous function:

```
-- This is found in create_add_user.sql on the publisher's web site.
BEGIN
    IF add_user( 6,'Application DBA', 1, 1
                ,'Brown','Jerry',''
                , 1, SYSDATE, 1, SYSDATE) THEN
        dbms_output.put_line('Record Inserted');
        ROLLBACK;
    ELSE
        dbms_output.put_line('No Record Inserted');
    END IF;
END;
/
```

The rollback doesn't undo the insertion because it only applies to the current transaction scope. The `add_user` function is an autonomous transaction and therefore writes changes in an independent transaction scope. When the function returns a Boolean true value, the value has already been written and made permanent. You can subsequently query the row, and you will find the row is still there even when the calling scope failed or was rolled back.

> **TIP**
> *You can't pass a system reference cursor as an* `IN` *mode actual*
> *parameter and subsequently open them, because they're already*
> *open.*

This section has explained how to use pass-by-value functions. The next section builds on this information and explores pass-by-reference functions.

Recursive Functions

Recursive functions are a useful tool to solve some complex problems, like advanced parsing. A recursive function calls one or more copies of itself to resolve a problem by converging on a result. Recursive functions look backward in time, whereas non-recursive functions look forward in time. Recursive functions are a specialized form of pass-by-value functions.

Non-recursive programs take some parameters and begin processing, often in a loop, until they achieve a result. This means they start with something and work with it until they find a result by applying a set of rules or evaluations. This means non-recursive programs solve problems moving forward in time.

Recursive functions have a base case and a recursive case. The base case is the anticipated result. The recursive case applies a formula that includes one or more calls back to the same function. One recursive call is known as a linear or straight-line recursion. Recursive cases that make two or more recursive calls separated by an operator are non-linear. Linear recursion is much faster than non-linear recursion, and the more recursive calls, the higher the processing costs. Recursive functions use the recursive case only when the base case isn't met. A result is found when a recursive function call returns the base case value. This means recursive program units solve problems moving backward in time, or one recursion after another.

Solving factorial results is a classic problem for linear recursion. The following function returns the factorial value for any number:

```
-- This is found in recursion.sql on the publisher's web site.
CREATE OR REPLACE FUNCTION factorial
( n BINARY_DOUBLE ) RETURN BINARY_DOUBLE IS
BEGIN
  IF n <= 1 THEN
    RETURN 1;
  ELSE
    RETURN n * factorial(n - 1);
  END IF;
END factorial;
/
```

The base case is met when the `IF` statement resolves as true. The recursive case makes only a single call to the same function. Potentially, the recursive case can call many times until it also returns the base case value of 1. Then, it works its way back up the tree of recursive calls until an answer is found by the first call.

Fibonacci numbers are more complex because recursion requires two calls for each recursion. The following function demonstrates non-linear recursion:

```
-- This is found in recursion.sql on the publisher's web site.
CREATE OR REPLACE FUNCTION Fibonacci
( n BINARY_DOUBLE ) RETURN BINARY_DOUBLE IS
BEGIN
  IF n <= 2 THEN
    RETURN 1;
  ELSE
    RETURN fibonacci(n - 2) + fibonacci(n - 1);
  END IF;
END fibonacci;
/
```

The addition operator has a lower order of precedence than a function call. Therefore, the recursive call on the left is processed first until it returns an expression. Then, the recursive call on the right is resolved to an expression. The addition happens after both recursive calls return expressions.

This discussion has demonstrated how you can implement recursion. You should note that recursion lends itself to pass-by-value functions because you only want the base case returned. While you can call recursive function using pass-by-reference semantics, you shouldn't. Recursive parameters should not be altered during execution because that creates a mutating behavior in the recursive case.

You should explore recursion when you want to parse strings or you are checking for syntax rules. Chapter 16 uses recursion to write an asymmetrical nested HTML table (naturally, you can substitute the table tags for `<div>` tags). It is much more effective than trying to move forward through the string.

Pass-by-Reference Functions

Pass-by-reference functions receive copies of values when they are called, unless you override the default behavior by using the `NOCOPY` hint. The `NOCOPY` hint only works with certain functions that meet restrictive criteria. These functions return a single output variable upon completion. They also can perform external operations, like SQL statements. At run time, they can return new values for actual parameters to calling program units. If they use the `NOCOPY` hint and pass references, the function may alter any value pointed to by the reference. External operations can be physical reads and writes to the operating system or SQL statements against the database. Refer back to Table 6-1 for an illustration of the pass-by-reference function.

You use pass-by-reference functions when you want to perform an operation, return a value from the function, and alter one or more actual parameters. These functions can only act inside the scope of another program or environment. The SQL*Plus environment lets you define session-level variables (also known as bind variables) that you can use when you call these types of functions. You cannot pass *literals* (like dates, numbers, or strings) or *expressions* (like function return values) into a parameter defined as `OUT` or `IN OUT` mode.

PL/SQL pass-by-reference functions are defined by the following six rules:

- At least one formal parameters must be defined as a *read-only or read-write* variable by using the `OUT` or `IN OUT` mode respectively.

- All formal parameters are locally scoped variables that you can change during operations inside the function.

- Any formal parameter can use any valid SQL or PL/SQL datatype. Only functions with parameter lists that use SQL datatypes work in SQL statements.

- Any `IN` mode formal parameters can have a default initial value.

- The formal return variable can use any valid SQL or PL/SQL datatype, but pipelined return tables must be use in SQL statements. You can't access pipelined table results in another PL/SQL scope.

- Any system reference cursor cast from a SQL query into a function is not writable and therefore must be passed through an `IN` mode parameter.

The following pass-by-reference function demonstrates returning a value while altering the input variable:

```
-- This is found in create_counting1.sql on the publisher's web site.
CREATE OR REPLACE FUNCTION counting
( number_in IN OUT NUMBER ) RETURN VARCHAR2 IS
  -- Declare a collection control variable and collection variable.
  TYPE numbers IS TABLE OF VARCHAR2(5);
  ordinal NUMBERS := numbers('One','Two','Three','Four','Five');
  -- Define default return value.
  retval VARCHAR2(9) := 'Not Found';
```

```
BEGIN
  -- Replace a null value to ensure increment.
  IF number_in IS NULL THEN
    number_in := 1;
  END IF;
  -- Increment actual parameter when within range.
  IF number_in < 4 THEN
    retval := ordinal(number_in);
    number_in := number_in + 1;
  ELSE
    retval := ordinal(number_in);
  END IF;
  RETURN retval;
END;
/
```

The function guarantees the `number_in` index value isn't null and doesn't exceed 4. The index value reads an ordinal number from the nested table collection. You can test the function with the following anonymous block:

```
-- This is found in create_counting1.sql on the publisher's web site.
DECLARE
  counter NUMBER := 1;
BEGIN
  FOR i IN 1..5 LOOP
    dbms_output.put('Counter ['||counter||']');
    dbms_output.put_line('['||counting(counter)||']');
  END LOOP;
END;
/
```

The counter variable is always printed before making the call to the function. This means you see the initial value and matching ordinal number string together. The output is

```
Counter [1][One]
Counter [2][Two]
Counter [3][Three]
Counter [4][Four]
Counter [4][Four]
```

As you can see in the output, the IN OUT mode actual parameter is only incremented until the value is 4. The last call in the anonymous block reuses the prior unchanged index value because the function only increments values less than four.

A read-only (OUT mode) formal parameter can't work in this type of call because the new value is never read. The initial IF statement sets the `number_in` to 1 each time you call the program with a null actual parameter. OUT mode parameters are always null values on entry.

The counting function is recreated with an OUT mode parameter in this:

```
-- This is found in create_counting1.sql on the publisher's web site.
CREATE OR REPLACE FUNCTION counting
( number_out OUT NUMBER ) RETURN VARCHAR2 IS
  TYPE numbers IS TABLE OF VARCHAR2(5);
  ordinal NUMBERS := numbers('One','Two','Three','Four','Five');
  retval VARCHAR2(9) := 'Not Found';
```

```
BEGIN
  -- Replace a null value to ensure increment.
  IF number_out IS NULL THEN
    number_out := 1;
  END IF;
  -- Increment actual parameter when within range.
  IF number_out < 4 THEN
    retval := ordinal(number_out);
    number_out := number_out + 1;
  ELSE
    retval := ordinal(number_out); -- Never run because number_out is always null.
  END IF;
  RETURN retval;
END;
/
```

The new counting function uses an `OUT` mode parameter. The parameter is renamed appropriately to `number_out`. At call time, the value of `number_out` is always a null value. This means it is always reset to 1, found less than 4, and reset to 2.

This familiar anonymous block lets you test the new function:

```
DECLARE
  counter NUMBER := 1;
BEGIN
  FOR i IN 1..5 LOOP
    dbms_output.put('Counter ['||counter||']');
    dbms_output.put_line('['||counting(counter)||']');
  END LOOP;
END;
/
```

The counter is initially 1, and is always returned as 2, which means you get the following output:

```
Counter [1][One]
Counter [2][One]
Counter [2][One]
Counter [2][One]
Counter [2][One]
```

The section has covered how you define and use a pass-by-reference function. You should recognize that there are two types of pass-by-reference parameters. One type has a value on entry and exit: `IN OUT` mode variables. The other always has a null value on entry and should have a value on exit: `OUT` mode parameters.

Procedures

Procedures cannot be right operands or called from SQL statements. They do support using `IN`, `OUT`, and `IN OUT` mode formal parameters.

Like functions, procedures can also contain nested named blocks. Nested named blocks are local functions and procedures that you define in the declaration block. You can likewise nest anonymous blocks in the execution block or procedures.

The following illustrates a named block procedure prototype:

```
PROCEDURE procedure_name
[( parameter1     [IN][OUT] [NOCOPY] sql_datatype | plsql_datatype
, parameter2     [IN][OUT] [NOCOPY] sql_datatype | plsql_datatype
, parameter(n+1) [IN][OUT] [NOCOPY] sql_datatype | plsql_datatype )]
[ AUTHID DEFINER | CURRENT_USER ] IS
  declaration_statements
BEGIN
  execution_statements
[EXCEPTION]
  exception_handling_statements
END [procedure_name];
/
```

You can define procedures with or without formal parameters. Formal parameters in procedures can be either *pass-by-value* or *pass-by-reference* variables in stored procedures. *Pass-by-reference* variables have both and IN and OUT mode. As when working with functions, you create it as a *pass-by-value* procedure when you don't specify the parameter mode because it uses the default IN mode.

Compiling (creating or replacing) the procedure implicitly assigns the IN mode phrase when none is provided. Like functions, formal parameters in procedures also support optional default values for IN mode parameters.

The AUTHID clause sets the execution authority model. The default is definer rights. Definer rights means any one with execution privileges on the procedure acts as if they are the owner of that same schema. CURRENT_USER overrides the default and sets the execution authority to invoker rights. Invoker rights authority means that you call procedures to act on your local data, and it requires that you replicate data objects in any participating schema. Chapter 9 provides a broader comparison of definer and invoker rights.

As in functions, the *declaration* block is between the IS and BEGIN phrases, while other blocks mirror the structure of anonymous-block programs. Procedures require an execution environment, which means you must call them from SQL*Plus or another program unit. The calling program unit can be another PL/SQL block or an external program using the OCI or JDBC.

Procedures are used most frequently to perform DML statements and transaction management. You can define procedures to act in the current transaction scope or an independent transaction scope. As with functions, you use the PRAGMA AUTONOMOUS_TRANSACTION to set a procedure so that it runs as an independent transaction.

Pass-by-Value Procedures

Pass-by-value procedures receive copies of values when they are called. These procedures do not return an output variable like a function. They only perform external operations, like SQL statements to the database or external file read or write operations. Refer back to Table 6-1 for an illustration of the pass-by-value procedure.

As discussed, you can define pass-by-value procedures to run autonomously in a separate transaction scope, or you can accept the default and have them run in the current transaction scope. Pass-by-value procedures frequently run in the current transaction scope. They organize database DML statements, like insert statements to multiple tables.

PL/SQL pass-by-value procedures are defined by the following five rules:

■ All formal parameters must be defined as *write-only* variables by using the IN mode.

■ All formal parameters are locally scoped variables that *cannot* be changed during execution inside the procedure.

- Any formal parameter can use any valid SQL or PL/SQL datatype.

- Any formal parameter may have a default initial value.

- Any system reference cursor cast from a SQL query into a function is not writable and therefore must be passed through an IN mode parameter. This includes those passed as explicit cursor variables and those cast using the CURSOR function. As mentioned in the section "System Reference Cursors" earlier in this chapter, cursor variables are actually references or handles. The handles point to internally cached result sets, which are read-only structures.

The add_contact procedure demonstrates a procedure that inserts values into one or three tables. The procedure uses the call parameters to determine the target insert tables. As described in the Introduction, the seeding script creates a video store. All tables inside the video store use surrogate primary keys, along with copies of the primary key values as foreign keys. The add_contact does not accept surrogate primary keys, but it uses them inside the procedure. This is one of the benefits of putting related inserts into a single procedure.

The add_contact procedure shows you how to use a pass-by-value procedure to manage multiple DML statements across a single transaction scope:

```
-- This is found in create_add_contact1.sql on the publisher's web site.
CREATE OR REPLACE procedure add_contact
( member_id          NUMBER
, contact_type       NUMBER
, last_name          VARCHAR2
, first_name         VARCHAR2
, middle_initial     VARCHAR2 := NULL
, address_type       NUMBER   := NULL
, street_address     VARCHAR2 := NULL
, city               VARCHAR2 := NULL
, state_province     VARCHAR2 := NULL
, postal_code        VARCHAR2 := NULL
, created_by         NUMBER
, creation_date      DATE     := SYSDATE
, last_updated_by    NUMBER
, last_update_date   DATE     := SYSDATE) IS
  -- Declare surrogate key variables.
  contact_id         NUMBER;
  address_id         NUMBER;
  street_address_id NUMBER;

  -- Define autonomous function to secure any surrogate key values.
  FUNCTION get_sequence_value (sequence_name VARCHAR2) RETURN NUMBER IS
    PRAGMA AUTONOMOUS_TRANSACTION;
    id_value  NUMBER;
    statement VARCHAR2(2000);
  BEGIN
    -- Build and run dynamic SQL in a PL/SQL block.
    statement := 'BEGIN'                                  ||CHR(10)
              || '  SELECT  '||sequence_name||'.nextval'||CHR(10)
              || '  INTO    :id_value'                    ||CHR(10)
              || '  FROM    dual;'                        ||CHR(10)
              || 'END;';
```

```
      EXECUTE IMMEDIATE statement USING OUT id_value;
      RETURN id_value;
   END get_sequence_value;
BEGIN
   -- Set savepoint to guarantee all or nothing happens.
   SAVEPOINT add_contact;

   -- Assign next value from sequence and insert record.
   contact_id := get_sequence_value('CONTACT_S1');
   INSERT INTO contact VALUES
   ( contact_id
   , member_id
   , contact_type
   , last_name
   , first_name
   , middle_initial
   , created_by
   , creation_date
   , last_updated_by
   , last_update_date);

   -- Check before inserting data in ADDRESS table.
   IF address_type IS NOT NULL   AND
      city IS NOT NULL            AND
      state_province IS NOT NULL AND
      postal_code IS NOT NULL     THEN
      -- Assign next value from sequence and insert record.
      address_id := get_sequence_value('ADDRESS_S1');
      INSERT INTO address VALUES
      ( address_id
      , contact_id
      , address_type
      , city
      , state_province
      , postal_code
      , created_by
      , creation_date
      , last_updated_by
      , last_update_date);

      -- Check before inserting data in STREET_ADDRESS table.
      IF street_address IS NOT NULL THEN
        -- Assign next value from sequence and insert record.
        street_address_id := get_sequence_value('STREET_ADDRESS_S1');
        INSERT INTO street_address VALUES
        ( street_address_id
        , address_id
        , street_address
        , created_by
        , creation_date
        , last_updated_by
        , last_update_date);
```

```
    END IF;
  END IF;
EXCEPTION
  WHEN others THEN
    ROLLBACK TO add_contact;
    RAISE_APPLICATION_ERROR(-20001,SQLERRM);
END add_contact;
/
```

You submit data to the `add_contact` procedure, and it inserts data into one or three tables. All formal parameters use `IN` mode parameters. This means that you can't assign anything to these variables inside the procedure. This is one reason local procedure variables manage the primary and foreign keys.

The procedure manages all primary and foreign keys, ensuring they're available as required during execution of the procedure. It sets a `SAVEPOINT` at the beginning and rolls back any transaction component if there is any raised error. It raises a user-defined error when an exception occurs. The autonomous function has no impact on the transactional integrity because querying a sequence in the same or a different transaction scope increments a sequence. Sequences are *never* reset by a `ROLLBACK` statement.

The local `get_sequence_value` function uses Native Dynamic SQL (NDS) so that a single function can access the sequences supporting primary keys. The procedure gets new primary keys before attempting any of the `INSERT` statements.

You can test the procedure by calling it, as demonstrated in the following anonymous block program:

```
-- This is found in create_add_contact1.sql on the publisher's web site.
DECLARE
  -- Declare surrogate key variables.
  member_id NUMBER;

  -- Declare local function to get type.
  FUNCTION get_type
  ( table_name  VARCHAR2
  , column_name VARCHAR2
  , type_name   VARCHAR2) RETURN NUMBER IS
    retval NUMBER;
  BEGIN
    SELECT    common_lookup_id
    INTO      retval
    FROM      common_lookup
    WHERE     common_lookup_table = table_name
    AND       common_lookup_column = column_name
    AND       common_lookup_type = type_name;
    RETURN retval;
  END get_type;

  -- Define autonomous function to secure surrogate key values.
  FUNCTION get_member_id RETURN NUMBER IS
    PRAGMA AUTONOMOUS_TRANSACTION;
    id_value NUMBER;
```

```
    BEGIN
      SELECT member_s1.nextval INTO id_value FROM dual;
      RETURN id_value;
    END;
BEGIN
  -- Set savepoint to guarantee all or nothing happens.
  SAVEPOINT add_member;

  -- Declare surrogate key variables.
  member_id := get_member_id;
  INSERT INTO member VALUES
  ( member_id
  ,(SELECT common_lookup_id
    FROM   common_lookup
    WHERE  common_lookup_table = 'MEMBER'
    AND    common_lookup_column = 'MEMBER_TYPE'
    AND    common_lookup_type = 'GROUP')
  , '4563-98-71'
  , '5555-6363-1212-4343'
  ,(SELECT common_lookup_id
    FROM   common_lookup
    WHERE  common_lookup_table = 'MEMBER'
    AND    common_lookup_column = 'CREDIT_CARD_TYPE'
    AND    common_lookup_type = 'VISA_CARD')
  , 3
  , SYSDATE
  , 3
  , SYSDATE);
  -- Call procedure to insert records in related tables.
  add_contact( member_id => member_id
             , contact_type => get_type('CONTACT','CONTACT_TYPE','CUSTOMER')
             , last_name => 'Rodriguez'
             , first_name => 'Alex'
             , address_type => get_type('ADDRESS','ADDRESS_TYPE','HOME')
             , street_address => 'East 161st Street'
             , city => 'Bronx'
             , state_province => 'NY'
             , postal_code => '10451'
             , created_by => 3
             , last_updated_by => 3);
EXCEPTION
  WHEN others THEN
    ROLLBACK TO add_member;
    RAISE_APPLICATION_ERROR(-20002,SQLERRM);
END;
/
```

The anonymous block inserts a row to the member table and then calls the procedure to insert data into the contact, address, and street_address tables. The procedure call uses named notation calling the add_contact procedure.

Pass-by-value procedures let you perform tasks in the database or external resources. They also let you manage primary and foreign keys in a single program scope.

Pass-by-Reference Procedures

Pass-by-reference procedures receive references to variables when they are called. Procedures do not return output variables. This type of procedure can change the values of actual parameters. They return their actual parameter references upon completion to the calling program. They can also perform external operations, like SQL statements to the database. Refer back to Table 6-1 for an illustration of the pass-by-reference procedure.

As discussed, you can define pass-by-reference procedures to run autonomously. Then, they execute in a separate transaction scope. You can also accept the default and run them in the current transaction scope. They organize database DML statements to move data between the program and the database, or they send data to external program units.

PL/SQL pass-by-reference procedures are defined by the following five rules:

- At least one formal parameter must be defined as a *read-only or read-write* variable by using the OUT or IN OUT mode respectively.

- All formal parameters are locally scoped variables that you can change during operations inside the procedure.

- Any formal parameter can use any valid SQL or PL/SQL datatype.

- Any IN mode formal parameters can have a default initial value.

- Any system reference cursor cast from a SQL query into a procedure is not writable and therefore must be passed through an IN mode parameter.

Pass-by-value programs let you put sequences of multiple DML statements into a single transaction and program scope. You are able to share values, like primary and foreign keys, inside of the black box when using them. As noted in the prior section, the add_contact procedure shows how you can implement a set of conditional INSERT statements.

Sometimes you want to build smaller reusable program units. For example, each insert statement could be put into its own stored procedure. You accomplish that by implementing pass-by-reference procedures. These new procedures expand the parameter lists by using both primary and foreign key parameters. The parameter list change makes the procedures capable of exchanging values between programs.

The example re-implements the prior pass-by-value section solution as a set of pass-by-reference procedures. The first step removes the local get_sequence_value function and builds it as a standalone function in the database, as shown:

```
-- This is found in create_add_contact2.sql on the publisher's web site.
CREATE OR REPLACE FUNCTION get_sequence_value
(sequence_name VARCHAR2) RETURN NUMBER IS
  PRAGMA AUTONOMOUS_TRANSACTION;
```

```
  id_value  NUMBER;
  statement VARCHAR2(2000);
BEGIN
  -- Build dynamic SQL statement as anonymous block PL/SQL unit.
  statement := 'BEGIN'                              ||CHR(10)
            || '  SELECT  '||sequence_name||'.nextval'||CHR(10)
            || '  INTO    :id_value'                ||CHR(10)
            || '  FROM    dual;'                    ||CHR(10)
            || 'END;';

  -- Execute dynamic SQL statement.
  EXECUTE IMMEDIATE statement USING OUT id_value;
  RETURN id_value;
END get_sequence_value;
/
```

This version of the function uses native dynamic SQL (NDS) to build and run the SELECT statement that gets the sequence value. Chapter 11 covers NDS.

After building the standalone function, you need to build a procedure to add a row to the contact table. The new add_contact procedure only adds a row to the contact table. It also has a different formal parameter list. The primary key for the table is returned as an OUT mode *(write-only)* variable, which lets you reuse the primary key as a foreign key, which is what you'll do in a subsequent procedure. You should also note that the member_id foreign key is passed as a value.

Inlining Subroutine Calls

Inlining is a compiler behavior that copies an external subroutine into another program. This is done to avoid the overhead of frequently calling an external subroutine. While leaving the decision to the compiler is always an option, you can designate when you would like to suggest an external call be copied inline.

You designate a subroutine call for inlining by using the following prototype:

```
PRAGMA INLINE(subroutine_name, 'YES'|'NO')
```

The compiler ultimately makes the decision whether to inline the subroutine because precompiler instructions are only hints. There are other factors that make inlining some subroutines undesirable. This pragma affects any call to the function or procedure when it precedes the call. It also impacts every call to CASE, CONTINUE-WHEN, EXECUTE IMMEDIATE, EXIT-WHEN, LOOP, and RETURN statements.

The behavior of the PRAGMA INLINE precompiler hint changes, depending on the setting of the PLSQL_OPTIMIZE_LEVEL session variable. Subprograms are inlined when PLSQL_OPTIMIZE_LEVEL is set to 2 and only given a high priority when set to 3. If the PLSQL_OPTIMIZE_LEVEL is set to 1, subprograms are only inlined when the compiler views it as necessary.

The pass-by-reference `add_contact` procedure follows:

```
-- This is found in create_add_contact2.sql on the publisher's web site.
CREATE OR REPLACE procedure add_contact
( contact_id            OUT NUMBER    -- Primary key after insert.
, member_id          IN    NUMBER    -- Foreign key preceding insert.
, contact_type       IN    NUMBER
, last_name          IN    VARCHAR2
, first_name         IN    VARCHAR2
, middle_initial     IN    VARCHAR2 := NULL
, created_by         IN    NUMBER
, creation_date      IN    DATE     := SYSDATE
, last_updated_by    IN    NUMBER
, last_update_date   IN    DATE     := SYSDATE) IS
BEGIN
  -- Set savepoint so that all or nothing happens.
  SAVEPOINT add_contact;

  -- Suggest inlining the get_sequence_value function.
  PRAGMA INLINE(get_sequence_value,'YES');

  -- Assign next value from sequence and insert record.
  contact_id := get_sequence_value('CONTACT_S1');
  INSERT INTO contact VALUES
  ( contact_id
  , member_id
  , contact_type
  , last_name
  , first_name
  , middle_initial
  , created_by
  , creation_date
  , last_updated_by
  , last_update_date);
EXCEPTION
  WHEN others THEN
    ROLLBACK TO add_contact;
    RAISE_APPLICATION_ERROR(-20001,SQLERRM);
END add_contact;
/
```

The `add_contact` procedure provides a `PRAGMA INLINE` hint to suggest that the compiler inline the `get_sequence_value` function. This is something you should consider when program units call other stored subroutines. It is not included in the subsequent examples, but you would likely include it in production code.

The next procedure controls the insert into the address and `street_address` tables. It defines the foreign key value as an `IN` mode *(read-only)* variable, just as the `add_contact` procedure defined the `member_id` foreign key.

The `add_address` procedure is

```
-- This is found in create_add_contact2.sql on the publisher's web site.
CREATE OR REPLACE procedure add_address
( address_id              OUT NUMBER   -- Primary key after insert.
, contact_id          IN      NUMBER   -- Foreign key preceding insert.
, address_type        IN      NUMBER   := NULL
, street_address       IN      VARCHAR2 := NULL
, city                IN      VARCHAR2 := NULL
, state_province      IN      VARCHAR2 := NULL
, postal_code         IN      VARCHAR2 := NULL
, created_by          IN      NUMBER
, creation_date       IN      DATE     := SYSDATE
, last_updated_by     IN      NUMBER
, last_update_date    IN      DATE     := SYSDATE) IS

  -- Declare surrogate key variables.
  street_address_id NUMBER;
BEGIN
  -- Set savepoint so all or nothing happens.
  SAVEPOINT add_address;

  -- Check data is present for insert to ADDRESS table.
  IF address_type IS NOT NULL    AND
     city IS NOT NULL            AND
     state_province IS NOT NULL AND
     postal_code IS NOT NULL     THEN

    -- Assign next value from sequence and insert record.
    address_id := get_sequence_value('ADDRESS_S1');
    INSERT INTO address VALUES
    ( address_id
    , contact_id
    , address_type
    , city
    , state_province
    , postal_code
    , created_by
    , creation_date
    , last_updated_by
    , last_update_date);

    -- Check data is present for insert to ADDRESS table.
    IF street_address IS NOT NULL THEN
      -- Assign next value from sequence and insert record.
      street_address_id := get_sequence_value('STREET_ADDRESS_S1');
      INSERT INTO street_address VALUES
      ( street_address_id
      , address_id
      , street_address
      , created_by
```

```
      , creation_date
      , last_updated_by
      , last_update_date);
    END IF;
  END IF;
EXCEPTION
  WHEN others THEN
    ROLLBACK TO add_address;
    RAISE_APPLICATION_ERROR(-20001,SQLERRM);
END add_address;
/
```

After building the standalone function and two procedures, you rewrite the anonymous block to make independent calls to the `add_contact` and `add_address` procedures. The anonymous block follows:

```
-- This is found in create_add_contact2.sql on the publisher's web site.
DECLARE
  -- Declare surrogate key variables.
  member_id  NUMBER;
  contact_id NUMBER;
  address_id NUMBER;

  -- Declare local function to get type.
  FUNCTION get_type
  ( table_name  VARCHAR2
  , column_name VARCHAR2
  , type_name   VARCHAR2) RETURN NUMBER IS
    retval NUMBER;
  BEGIN
    SELECT    common_lookup_id
    INTO      retval
    FROM      common_lookup
    WHERE     common_lookup_table = table_name
    AND       common_lookup_column = column_name
    AND       common_lookup_type = type_name;
    RETURN retval;
  END get_type;

  -- Define autonomous function to secure surrogate key values.
  FUNCTION get_member_id RETURN NUMBER IS
    PRAGMA AUTONOMOUS_TRANSACTION;
    id_value NUMBER;
  BEGIN
    SELECT member_s1.nextval INTO id_value FROM dual;
    RETURN id_value;
  END;
BEGIN
  -- Declare surrogate key variables.
  member_id := get_member_id;
  INSERT INTO member VALUES
```

```
( member_id
,(SELECT common_lookup_id
  FROM   common_lookup
  WHERE  common_lookup_table = 'MEMBER'
  AND    common_lookup_column = 'MEMBER_TYPE'
  AND    common_lookup_type = 'GROUP')
, '4563-98-71'
, '5555-6363-1212-4343'
,(SELECT common_lookup_id
  FROM   common_lookup
  WHERE  common_lookup_table = 'MEMBER'
  AND    common_lookup_column = 'CREDIT_CARD_TYPE'
  AND    common_lookup_type = 'VISA_CARD')
, 3
, SYSDATE
, 3
, SYSDATE);

-- Call procedure to insert records in related tables.
add_contact( member_id => member_id
           , contact_id => contact_id  -- This is an OUT mode variable.
           , contact_type => get_type('CONTACT','CONTACT_TYPE','CUSTOMER')
           , last_name => 'Rodriguez'
           , first_name => 'Alex'
           , created_by => 3
           , last_updated_by => 3);

-- Call procedure to insert records in related tables.
add_address( address_id => address_id
           , contact_id => contact_id  -- This is an OUT mode variable.
           , address_type => get_type('ADDRESS','ADDRESS_TYPE','HOME')
           , street_address => 'East 161st Street'
           , city => 'Bronx'
           , state_province => 'NY'
           , postal_code => '10451'
           , created_by => 3
           , last_updated_by => 3);
END;
/
```

The call to the `add_contact` returns a value for the primary key column. The subsequent call to the `add_address` procedure uses that value as a foreign key value. Whether you implement a pass-by-value or pass-by-reference procedure depends on many factors. The choice is often between reusability and manageability.

Smaller units, like pass-by-reference procedures, are more reusable, but they're harder to manage. They can exist for every table or view in your application. Lager units, like pass-by-value procedures, let you manage complex processes in a single black box. They tend to implement what are sometimes called workflow units. Pass-by-value procedures are generally more process-centric than data-centric wrappers and less expensive to maintain. However, you should note that pass-by-reference procedures are ideal for supporting stateless web-based applications.

The best rule of thumb is probably that all procedures should focus on process-centric activities. Then, you can choose which subroutine best suits your task on an exception basis.

You have now reviewed the four types of supported subroutines in PL/SQL. Examples have been provided that show you how to use each. The challenge now lies in how you design your applications.

Summary

You should now have an understanding of transaction scope and how to implement functions and procedures. This should include appreciating when to choose a function over a procedure and vice versa.

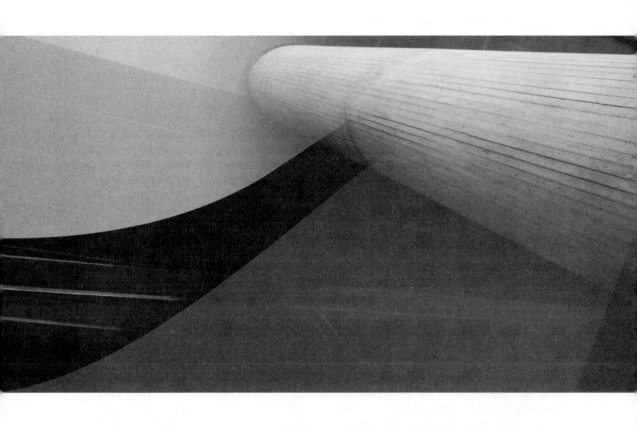

CHAPTER
7

Collections

here are three types of collections in the Oracle Database 11*g* family of products. They are the varray, nested table, and associative array datatypes. Collections are powerful structures because they enable you to develop programs that manage large sets of data in memory.

You can build collections of any SQL or PL/SQL datatype. Collections of SQL datatypes work in both SQL and PL/SQL environments but collections of PL/SQL datatypes do not. They only work in PL/SQL.

This chapter explains how to define and work with collections in PL/SQL. There is also some coverage of using collections as database columns. It covers these topics:

- Collection types
    - Varrays
    - Nested tables
    - Associative arrays
- Collection set operators
- Collection API

Collections are programming structures that hold sets of like things. Collections fall into two categories: arrays and lists. Arrays typically have a physical size allocated when you define them, while lists have no physical limit imposed. Naturally, the memory available for processing in the SGA curtails the maximum size of some very large lists.

These lists are often indexed by a series of sequential numbers that start with 0 or 1 and increase one value at a time. Using sequential numeric index values ensures that you can use the index to traverse a complete list by incrementing or decrementing one at a time in a loop. Alternatively, lists can be indexed by non-sequential numbers or unique strings. Lists are called associative arrays when they can be indexed by non-sequential numbers or unique strings.

Figure 7-1 illustrates a collection of strings as an inverted tree, which represents a single-dimensional collection. It uses a sequentially numbered index and would work with any SQL datatype or PL/SQL scalar or user-defined object type. The caveat on PL/SQL datatypes is that they can only be used in the context of PL/SQL blocks.

The index values become the identifier to access individual elements inside of a collection variable. As discussed in Chapter 3, variable names are identifiers, and that includes variable names that include index values.

You can create pseudo-multidimensional collections when you use a user-defined SQL object type as the base element of a collection. However, user-defined object types require specialized constructors and both static and instance access methods. Chapter 14 covers object types and demonstrates how to build collections of object types.

Multidimensional collections are not supported as SQL datatypes. You can, however, build multidimensional collections as PL/SQL datatypes. Multidimensional collection elements are record structures. You can access record structures inside PL/SQL, or you can build pipelined functions to access their contents in SQL. Chapter 6 demonstrates how to use pipelined functions to convert multidimensional collections to aggregate tables for use in SQL statements.

While Figure 7-2 shows the record elements as SQL datatypes, you can also use PL/SQL datatypes. The PL/SQL record types can also be collections of other PL/SQL record types. The syntax as you nest collections becomes more complex. You should consider why you require nested collections and compare other strategies before adopting them as your solution.

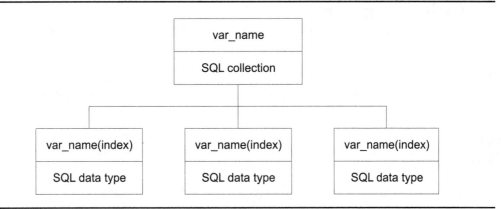

FIGURE 7-1 *An inverted tree diagram of a single-dimensional SQL datatype collection*

You can also create multiple dimension arrays, known as multilevel collections. You do this by including collections as elements inside collections.

The sections are organized to build on concepts as you work through the chapter. If you want to skip ahead, please browse the earlier sections to see if something might catch your eye and help you with the subsequent material.

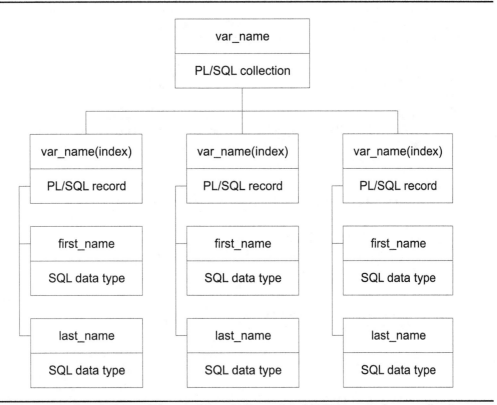

FIGURE 7-2 *An inverted tree diagram of a multidimensional PL/SQL record type collection*

Collection Types

The VARRAY and NESTED TABLE collections can be defined as both SQL and PL/SQL datatypes. As SQL datatypes, they are single-dimensional arrays of scalar values or object types. They can also define user-specified column datatypes. Both the VARRAY and NESTED TABLE datatypes are structures indexed by sequential integers (using 1-based integers). Sequentially indexed structures disallow gaps in the index values, and are also known as densely populated structures. While the VARRAY has a fixed number of elements when defined, the NESTED TABLE does not.

NOTE
Oracle varray and nested table collections are indexed by 1-based numbering.

The associative array, previously known as a PL/SQL table, is *only* a PL/SQL datatype. Associative array datatypes can only be referenced in a PL/SQL scope. They are typically defined in package specifications when they are to be used externally from an anonymous or named block program. Associative array datatypes support both numeric and string indexes. Numeric indexes for associative arrays do not need to be sequential and are non-sequential structures. Non-sequential structures can have gaps in index sequences and are known as sparsely populated structures. Associative arrays are dynamically sized and, like the NESTED TABLE datatype, have no fixed size.

All three have access to the Oracle Collection API, but each uses a different set of methods. The recent changes to OCI8 enable it to support scalar, arrays of scalar, and reference cursor variables to external languages, like C, C++, C#, Java, and PHP. The VARRAY and NESTED TABLE datatypes require that you use the OCI-Collection class to access them externally from the SQL*Plus environment. OCI8 also has a new function that supports passing by reference a PL/SQL table.

Table 7-1 provides a comparison of the collection types. You should note that while size is dynamic, the SGA and PGA memory regions are constrained by database initialization parameters. When you work with these collection types, you gain tremendous throughput, provided you don't exhaust your memory resources.

Deciding on the collection type that best meets your programming need is critical. You should carefully consider the strengths and weaknesses of each collection type. Here is a thumbnail guide to selecting the right collection:

- Use a varray when the physical size of the collection is static and the collection may be used in tables. Varrays are the closest thing to arrays in other programming languages, such as Java, C, C++, or C#.

- Use nested tables when the physical size is unknown due to run-time variations and when the type may be used in tables. Nested tables are like lists and bags in other programming languages.

- Use associative arrays when the physical size is unknown due to run-time variations and when the type will not be used in tables. Associative arrays are ideal for standard programming solutions, such as using maps and sets.

Collection Type	Description	Subscript	Size
Associative arrays (index-by tables)	Associative array is the name introduced in Oracle 10*g* for a familiar structure. You may have known these as index-by tables in Oracle 8 to Oracle 9*i* and possibly as PL/SQL tables in Oracle 7. They have mutated forward in Oracle 11*g* and deserve a new name. They are still sparsely populated arrays, which means the numbering does not have to be sequential, only unique. They now support subscripts that are unique integers or strings. This change moves a familiar and powerful structure from a sparsely populated pseudo-array or array list to a standard structured programming language datatype, known as lists or maps.	Sequential or non-sequential integers or unique strings	Dynamic
NESTED TABLES	NESTED TABLES were introduced in Oracle 8. They are initially defined as densely populated arrays but may become sparsely populated as records are deleted. They may be stored in permanent tables and accessed by SQL. They also may be dynamically extended and act more like traditional programming bags and sets than arrays. Another corollary would be the *ArrayList* class introduced in Java 5. They may contain a scalar variable or user-defined object type when they are used as SQL datatypes. SQL scope collections are single-dimensional lists of valid SQL datatypes. They may also contain a list of one or more compound datatypes (PL/SQL record structures) when they work exclusively in a PL/SQL scope.	Sequential integers	Dynamic

TABLE 7-1   *Collection Type Comparison*

Collection Type	Description	Subscript	Size
Varrays	Varrays were introduced in Oracle 8. They are densely populated arrays and behave like traditional programming arrays. They may be stored in permanent tables and accessed by SQL. At creation they have a fixed size that cannot change. Like the Nested Tables, varrays may contain a scalar variable or user-defined object type when they are used as SQL datatypes. As mentioned earlier, SQL scope collections are single-dimensional lists of valid SQL datatypes. Varrays may also contain a list of one or more compound datatypes (PL/SQL record structures) when they work exclusively in a PL/SQL scope.	Sequential integers	Fixed

TABLE 7-1 *Collection Type Comparison* (continued)

While Table 7-1 introduced collections in alphabetical order, you will cover them in descending alphabetical order. The discussion will start with varrays and end with associative arrays. Coverage will include access methods in both SQL and PL/SQL. It is hard to imagine how you would use them in PL/SQL without knowing how to leverage these methods in your tables.

The subsections cover the VARRAY, NESTED TABLE, and associative array datatypes, and the Oracle Collection API. These sections are designed to be read in order but should support an experienced developer poking around for targeted explanations.

Varrays

Varrays are single-dimensional structures of Oracle 11*g* SQL or PL/SQL datatypes. You can use varrays in table, record, and object definitions, and you can then access them in SQL or PL/SQL. They are arrays in the traditional sense of programming languages because they have a fixed size and use a sequential numeric index. They are like arrays in Java, C, C++, and C#.

Defining and Using Varrays as PL/SQL Program Constructs

The syntax to define a varray in a PL/SQL program unit is

```
TYPE type_name IS {VARRAY | VARYING ARRAY} (size_limit)
  OF element_type [ NOT NULL ];
```

The *type name* is often a string followed by an underscore and the word varray. Many programmers and configuration management people find it a useful pattern to improve code readability. It is also the convention used in the chapter.

Either VARRAY or VARYING ARRAY syntax may be used, but the former is much more common. The size limit is a required value. It is a positive integer giving the maximum number of elements in the varray. *Element type* may be any Oracle 11*g* datatype or a user-defined datatype. Allowing null values in varrays is the default. If null values should be disallowed, you must exclude them with the NOT NULL clause.

The following example program demonstrates defining, declaring, and initializing a varray of integers in a PL/SQL program unit. An integer is a subtype of the Oracle 11*g* number datatype.

Subscript index values begin at 1, not 0. This is consistent with the long-standing behavior of index-by tables in Oracle 8 to Oracle 9*i* and PL/SQL tables in Oracle 7. Most programming languages, including Java, C, C++, and C#, use subscript index values that begin with 0.

```
-- This is in create_varray1.sql on the publisher's web site.
DECLARE
  -- Define a varray with a maximum of 3 rows.
  TYPE integer_varray IS VARRAY(3) OF INTEGER;

  -- Declare the varray with null values.
  varray_integer INTEGER_VARRAY := integer_varray(NULL,NULL,NULL);
BEGIN
  -- Print initialized null values.
  dbms_output.put_line('Varray initialized as nulls.');
  dbms_output.put_line('---------------------------');
  FOR i IN 1..3 LOOP
    dbms_output.put      ('Integer Varray ['||i||'] ');
    dbms_output.put_line('['||varray_integer(i)||']');
  END LOOP;

  -- Assign values to subscripted members of the varray.
  varray_integer(1) := 11;
  varray_integer(2) := 12;
  varray_integer(3) := 13;

  -- Print initialized null values.
  dbms_output.put      (CHR(10)); -- Visual line break.
  dbms_output.put_line('Varray initialized as values.');
  dbms_output.put_line('---------------------------');
  FOR i IN 1..3 LOOP
    dbms_output.put_line('Integer Varray ['||i||'] '
    ||                   '['||varray_integer(i)||']');
  END LOOP;
END;
/
```

The example program defines a local scalar collection, declares an initialized collection variable, prints the null value collection elements, assigns values to the elements, and reprints the collection element values. You should also see how to initialize a collection, access the contents of a collection element, and assign a value to a collection element in the sample program.

Here is the output from the program:

```
Varray initialized as nulls.
---------------------------
Integer Varray [1] []
Integer Varray [2] []
Integer Varray [3] []
```

```
Varray initialized as values.
------------------------------
Integer Varray [1] [11]
Integer Varray [2] [12]
Integer Varray [3] [13]
```

If you skip any of the steps, you will encounter exceptions. The one that most new developers encounter is an uninitialized collection, ORA-06531. It occurs because you must at least initialize a null element varray by calling the collection type as shown here:

```
varray_integer INTEGER_VARRAY := integer_varray();
```

This exception fails to allocate space to any elements in the varray. The example program initializes the varray with null values because nulls are allowed. It is also possible to initialize the variable with values. You initialize the variable by using the varray type name and parentheses around the values. When you initialize a varray, you set the actual number of initialized rows. Using the Collection API COUNT method returns the number of elements with allotted space. Use of this method will be shown in the next example program.

The maximum number of elements in the varray is three. The program allocates memory and an index value only when you initialize elements. You can test this by editing the program and changing the initialization from three null values to two. When you run the program, you raise an ORA-06533 exception inside the first range FOR loop. The message says that you've attempted to access a subscript beyond the count of elements. The exception means that subscript 3 is unavailable. It does not exist. While you defined the varray as three elements in size, you initialized it as only two elements in size. Therefore, the variable has only two valid subscripts, 1 and 2.

If you encountered the error, you might check the Oracle 11*g* documentation. You would find that there is a Collection API EXTEND method for collections and that it is overloaded. The Collections API *requires us to initialize a row and then assign a value.*

You add a row using the Collection API EXTEND method without an actual parameter or with a single actual parameter. If you use the single parameter, it is the number of elements to initialize. It cannot exceed the difference between the number of possible and actual elements defined by the varray. You will read more on using these methods in the section "Oracle 11*g* Collection API" at the end of this chapter.

The following program illustrates initialization with zero rows in the declaration section. Then, it demonstrates dynamic initialization and assignment in the execution section:

```
-- This is in create_varray2.sql on the publisher's web site.
DECLARE
  -- Define a varray of integer with 3 rows.
  TYPE integer_varray IS VARRAY(3) OF INTEGER;

  -- Declare an array initialized as a no-element collection.
  varray_integer INTEGER_VARRAY := integer_varray();
BEGIN
  -- Allocate space as you increment the index.
  FOR i IN 1..3 LOOP
    varray_integer.EXTEND;       -- Allocates space in the collection.
    varray_integer(i) := 10 + i; -- Assigns a value to the indexed value.
  END LOOP;

  -- Print initialized array.
```

```
    dbms_output.put_line('Varray initialized as values.');
    dbms_output.put_line('----------------------------');
    FOR i IN 1..3 LOOP
      dbms_output.put      ('Integer Varray ['||i||'] ');
      dbms_output.put_line('['||varray_integer(i)||']');
    END LOOP;
END;
/
```

Like the earlier example, this program defines a local collection type. The difference is that this program does not allocate space and populate nulls during the declaration of the variable. It actually creates a no-element collection. You must allot space with the EXTEND method of the Collection API before you can add an element to this type of collection. This is what's done inside the range FOR loop.

The output from the program is

```
Varray initialized as values.
----------------------------
Integer Varray [1] [11]
Integer Varray [2] [12]
Integer Varray [3] [13]
```

You now have the fundamentals to build varray structures within PL/SQL program units. The power and management utilities of the collection methods will enhance your ability to use these. While this section has touched on the Collection API methods to illustrate initialization issues, they are covered in depth later in the chapter. By working through the examples there, you will be able to see how you can apply these methods across collection types.

Defining and Using Varrays as Object Types in SQL

The syntax to define an object type of varray in the database is

```
CREATE OR REPLACE TYPE type_name  AS {VARRAY | VARYING ARRAY} (size_limit)
OF element_type [ NOT NULL ];
```

As discussed, the type name is often a string followed by an underscore and the word varray. Many programmers and configuration management people find this a useful pattern to improve code readability. It is also the convention used in the chapter for PL/SQL structure and object types.

As with a PL/SQL type structure, either VARRAY or VARYING ARRAY syntax may be used. The former is much more common. The size limit is a required value. It is a positive integer, the maximum number of elements in the varray. The element type may be any Oracle 11*g* datatype or a user-defined datatype. Allowing null values in varrays is the default. If null values should be disallowed, you must exclude them with the NOT NULL clause.

The following creates a user-defined object type of varray with a limit of three elements:

```
-- This is in create_varray3.sql on the publisher's web site.
CREATE OR REPLACE TYPE integer_varray AS VARRAY(3) OF INTEGER;
/
```

The following anonymous-block PL/SQL program then uses the varray object type by declaring and initializing a variable based on the SQL datatype:

```
-- This is in create_varray3.sql on the publisher's web site.
DECLARE
```

```
    varray_integer INTEGER_VARRAY := integer_varray(NULL,NULL,NULL);
BEGIN
  -- Assign values to replace the null values.
  FOR i IN 1..3 LOOP
    varray_integer(i) := 10 + i;
  END LOOP;

  -- Print the initialized values.
  dbms_output.put_line('Varray initialized as values.');
  dbms_output.put_line('----------------------------');
  FOR i IN 1..3 LOOP
    dbms_output.put      ('Integer Varray ['||i||'] ');
    dbms_output.put_line('['||varray_integer(i)||']');
  END LOOP;
END;
/
```

The example is a mirror of the prior program except for the fact that the variable is now a SQL user-defined collection datatype. It prints the following output:

```
Varray initialized as values.
----------------------------
Integer Varray [1] [11]
Integer Varray [2] [12]
Integer Varray [3] [13]
```

The benefit of defining the varray object type is that it may be referenced from any programs that have permission to use it, whereas a PL/SQL varray type structure is limited to the program unit. Program units may be anonymous-block programs like the example or stored procedures or packages in the database. Only the latter enables reference by other PL/SQL programs that have permissions to the package. Please refer to Chapter 9 for details on creating and using packages.

All the varrays to this point leverage the default behavior that allows null values. It is always a bit clearer to start with the default behavior. After you master the basic syntax and default for defining, declaring, and initializing varrays, there is a question that needs to be resolved: When, why, and how do you allow or disallow null rows?

This is a good question. In the small example programs in the book, it seems that it may not matter too much. In fact, it does matter a great deal. Varrays are the closest structure related to standard programming language arrays. Arrays are structures that require attentive management. As a rule of thumb, arrays should always be dense. Dense means that there should not be any gaps in the sequencing of index values. It also means you should not have gaps in data. You should not allow nulls when you want a varray to act like a standard array structure.

Allowing nulls in varrays ensures that you may encounter them in the data stream. Oracle 11*g* does not allow you to create gaps in index values. If you *do not* want to write a host of error-handling routines for arrays with missing data, you should consider overriding the default behavior. Disallow null values in varrays to simplify data access and error handling.

You will now learn how to disallow null values in varrays. The main impact of doing so is felt when you initialize them. For example, if you redefined the varray object type used in the preceding program to disallow null values, the program would fail. You raise a PLS-00567 exception because you're trying to pass a null to a not-null-constrained column.

A problem with programming books is that concepts need to be illustrated with an economy of space. To do so, they are limited to small, workable examples. Small workable arrays seldom illustrate the real world and the high demands placed on these structures.

When you use varrays as arrays, it will be to do large transaction processing in memory because the I/O costs are too high. You will define varrays that contain hundreds of elements. Some may be dynamically defined by counting rows in a table before being built as dynamic structures.

When you initialize varrays that contain 100 percent of the data, doing so is straightforward because the constructor can do that. However, when you initialize varrays that contain less than all the data, adding elements requires additional programming.

You should create a SQL collection type that disallows null values for the next example. The following builds the required datatype:

```
-- This is in create_varray4.sql on the publisher's web site.
CREATE OR REPLACE TYPE integer_varray
  AS VARRAY(100) OF INTEGER NOT NULL;
/
```

The following example allocates the 100 possible records. It does so without initializing the data as null values by leveraging the LIMIT method of the Collection API. You will find the Collection API covered later in the chapter.

```
-- This is in create_varray4.sql on the publisher's web site.
DECLARE
  varray_integer INTEGER_VARRAY := integer_varray();
BEGIN
  FOR i IN 1..varray_integer.LIMIT LOOP
    varray_integer.EXTEND;
  END LOOP;
    dbms_output.put      ('Integer Varray Initialized ');
    dbms_output.put_line('['||varray_integer.COUNT||']');
END;
/
```

This program creates a varray collection by allocating space without explicitly assigning null values. However, when you read the elements in the varray they are treated as null values. It prints the following:

```
Integer Varray Initialized [100]
```

You have developed skills with using varrray object types. The next section will use those varray object types to define tables that use them as column datatypes.

Defining and Using Varrays as Column Datatypes in Tables

The power of varrays is not limited to procedural programming. Varrays provide Oracle 8 through Oracle 11*g* with unique capabilities for representing data. This is why Oracle's database became known as an object relational database management system (ORDBMS). It is a standard that many have moved to adopt.

Relational databases work on a principal of normalization. *Normalization* is the process of grouping related data into sets that are unique. It relies on two basic premises. One is that data may be positioned by semantic evaluation into third normal form or higher. Another is that data may be positioned by domain key normal form. For the purposes of the discussion on Oracle 11*g* collections, this book advocates at a minimum that each table meets third normal form, which means

- Tables should include a primary key that uniquely identifies each row.

- Tables should not contain any multipart columns, like collections in comma-delimited strings.

- Tables should not contain any transitive dependencies, which means you've designed a single table where you should have at least another table for each transitive dependency.

A transitive dependency means that columns of data rely on one or more columns before they rely on the primary key. This type of dependency means that you can put two subjects (domains) into a table and potentially create deletion anomalies. *The simple rule of thumb is to design and build tables that contain a single subject, have a unique key, and place all data in a single row.*

The book uses a surrogate key as the primary key. A *surrogate key* is an artificial key, that is, a key or column that it is not part of the data in the row. The alternative is a natural key, which is a column or set of columns that uniquely identifies every row in a table. Copies of the primary key are placed in columns of related tables as foreign key values. Joins between tables use the values in the primary and foreign keys to match rows in SQL statements.

The benefit of using a surrogate key is that an evolving understanding of the table may change the column or columns that uniquely define a natural key. When a natural key evolves, it changes the owning table and any related tables that contain a natural foreign key. It also changes every SQL statement join between that table and other tables. *A surrogate key avoids this maintenance nightmare because the only thing you'll need to change is the table's unique index*, which should contain the surrogate key first, followed by all columns of the natural key.

Multivalued Columns

Many database modeling books say you should absolutely never have any multivalued columns. Multivalued columns contain a collection of like things. In a purely relational model, this was true because they didn't support collection or object types as base SQL types. Oracle 11*g* does support these types, and so have prior releases.

Technically, an ID-dependent relationship requires that dependent tables hold only the primary key of the determinant table. This means you can only have a one-to-one binary relationship for ID-dependent tables, and not have a one-to-many binary relationship. The work-around has been to build a composite key in the ID-dependent table by using the inherited primary key and another column that defines uniqueness for the related rows in the relationship. This added column creates a function dependency, which means there is a filter when you go from the determinant table to the dependent table. The filter moving the other way, from the data to the key, is a transitive dependency. This type of design violates the definition of third normal form.

Defining collection columns solves this problem because the index value acts as the filtering column, and the column's identity is preserved inside the same row with the determinant record. Multivalued columns are natural solutions in a relational model when you can store them as collection types because they are one thing in the context of a row—a collection of like things.

The UML static class diagram in Figure 7-3 represents the data model for this chapter. UML static class diagrams replace traditional Entity Relation Diagrams (ERDs). Most traditional ERD diagrams use an information engineering model, colloquially called crow's feet. An IE model would have the crow's foot on the `addresses` side of the relationship.

The drawing presents three tables that support code in this chapter but do not directly fit within the video store example. You can download this code from the publisher's web site as given in the Introduction to this book.

The `strings` datatype is a collection of `VARCHAR2` values. There are two typical alternatives to putting the data into a collection column. You can assume that customers in the data model will never have more than two street addresses, and then create two columns for street address, labeled `street_address1` and `street_address2`. This is a form of denormalization. Alternatively, you can adhere to normalization and build a separate table for street addresses.

The ability to include the list in the base table reduces the complexity of physical implementation. It eliminates the need to join the base table and the subordinate table. This changes because the latter becomes a list within a row of the base table. This is actually a solid way to implement what's known as an ID-dependent relationship that supports a one-to-many binary relationship.

Defining Varrays in Database Tables

The `create_addressbook.sql` script changes the table definition to the new model. The following varray object type definition is provided, which supports globalization by using a Unicode standard.

```
-- This is in create_addressbook.sql on the publisher's web site.
CREATE OR REPLACE TYPE strings
  AS VARRAY(3) OF VARCHAR2(30 CHAR);
/
```

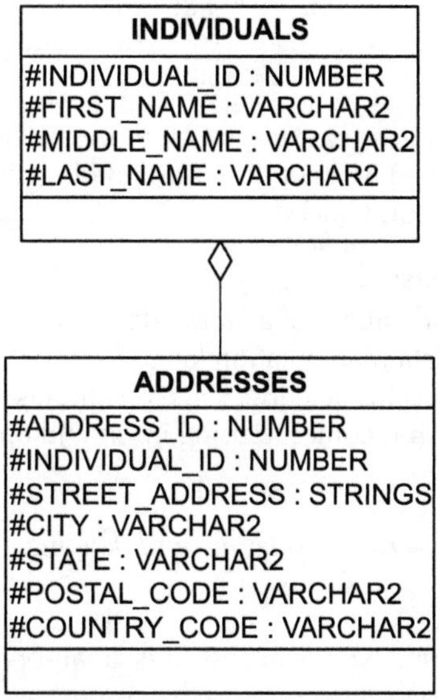

INDIVIDUALS

#INDIVIDUAL_ID : NUMBER
#FIRST_NAME : VARCHAR2
#MIDDLE_NAME : VARCHAR2
#LAST_NAME : VARCHAR2

ADDRESSES

#ADDRESS_ID : NUMBER
#INDIVIDUAL_ID : NUMBER
#STREET_ADDRESS : STRINGS
#CITY : VARCHAR2
#STATE : VARCHAR2
#POSTAL_CODE : VARCHAR2
#COUNTRY_CODE : VARCHAR2

FIGURE 7-3 *UML static class diagram (ERD modeling in UML)*

NOTE
*If this type doesn't replace the earlier one of the same name in
Chapter 6, you'll raise an* ORA-22913 *error when you build the
addresses table. The error code means you don't have a correct
definition for the datatype. You should drop and re-create the correct
type.*

After you create the object type, the addresses table is redefined to conform to the new
UML static class diagram. As you can see, the diagram implements a varray of a known database
catalog type. The table also maintains referential integrity through database constraints. This was
also done in the base case.

```
-- This is in create_addressbook.sql on the publisher's web site.
CREATE TABLE individuals
( individual_id          INTEGER              NOT NULL
, first_name             VARCHAR2(30 CHAR)    NOT NULL
, middle_name            VARCHAR2(30 CHAR)
, last_name              VARCHAR2(30 CHAR)    NOT NULL
, title                  VARCHAR2(10 CHAR)
, CONSTRAINT indiv_pk    PRIMARY KEY(individual_id));

CREATE TABLE addresses
( address_id             INTEGER              NOT NULL
, individual_id          INTEGER              NOT NULL
, street_address         STRINGS              NOT NULL
, city                   VARCHAR2(20 CHAR)    NOT NULL
, state                  VARCHAR2(20 CHAR)    NOT NULL
, postal_code            VARCHAR2(20 CHAR)    NOT NULL
, country_code           VARCHAR2(10 CHAR)    NOT NULL
, CONSTRAINT addr_pk     PRIMARY KEY(address_id)
, CONSTRAINT addr_indiv_fk FOREIGN KEY(individual_id)
  REFERENCES individuals  (individual_id));
```

You will notice that the street_address column uses the strings collection type. The
varray is a single-dimensioned array of three variable-length strings. The variable-length strings
are defined as noted to support Unicode.

Using Varrays in Database Tables
After creating a table with a column of a varray datatype, you need to know how to use it. Using
it requires understanding data manipulation language (DML) access methods to varrays. Varrays
present no unique conditions for deleting, since deletion is at the row level. However, there are
substantive differences when it comes to using insert and update statements.

NOTE
*DML access involves inserting, updating, and deleting data
from tables.*

Insert statements have one type of access. It is an all-or-nothing approach to the datatype.
Insert statements allocate space necessary to the construction of the varray. For example, in the

three-element array for `street_address`, it is possible to insert one to three rows of data. When the insert is made to the row, an instance of the collection type is built with the number of rows used.

```
-- This is in varray_dml1.sql on the publisher's web site.
INSERT INTO individuals VALUES
( individuals_s1.nextval, 'John', 'Sidney', 'McCain', 'Mr.');

INSERT INTO addresses VALUES
( 1
, individuals_s1.currval
, strings
  ('Office of Senator McCain'
  ,'450 West Paseo Redondo'
  ,'Suite 200')
,'Tucson'
,'AZ'
,'85701'
,'USA');
```

The example program inserts a full set of three rows into the varray datatype. It is important to note that in the values clause, the varray datatype name is used as the constructor name. The constructor uses the syntax previously presented with a list of comma-delimited actual parameters in a set of parentheses.

If you were to query the `street_address` column from the table, you would see a return set of the constructor with its actual parameters. This is illustrated by running a query like the following:

```
-- This is in varray_dml1.sql on the publisher's web site.
SELECT    street_address
FROM      addresses;
```

The shortened output from the query is noted.

```
-- This is found running varray_dml1.sql from the publisher's web site.
STREET_ADDRESS
-------------------------------
ADDRESS_VARRAY('Office of Senator McCain','450 West Paseo ...
```

This type of output is not very useful. It is also very different than what you might expect. Using data query language (DQL) to select a result from a varray datatype requires specialized syntax. You need to define a nested table collection structure to actually access the varray data meaningfully. If you are unfamiliar with the concept of nested tables, you may wish to fast forward a few pages to the "Nested Tables" section.

NOTE
DQL is a new acronym to some. Select statements were previously classified as DML statements because they can lock rows with optional clauses.

The following example illustrates how you build a nested table collection for the immediate problem at hand. Later in the chapter you will cover this in more detail when studying nested tables. Here, it illustrates a rather unintuitive syntax for querying the data.

```
-- This is in varray_dml1.sql on the publisher's web site.
-- Create a PL/SQL table datatype.
CREATE OR REPLACE TYPE varray_nested_table IS TABLE OF VARCHAR2(30 CHAR);
/

-- Use SQL*Plus to format the output.
COL column_value FORMAT A30

-- Print formatted elements from aggregate table.
SELECT nested.column_value
FROM   addresses a
,      TABLE(CAST(a.street_address AS VARRAY_NESTED_TABLE)) nested
WHERE  address_id = 1;
```

The TABLE keyword can be interchanged with the older THE keyword, but Oracle recommends you use TABLE. In the example program, a nested table collection is built to mirror the element definition for the varray. Nested tables are not upwardly bound as are varrays but can be used to temporarily hold the contents of varrays. Using a nested table is the *only* way to meaningfully display the contents of a varray using a select statement. The CAST function allows you to convert the varray to a nested table, which can then be managed as an aggregate table.

The formatted output from the query is

```
-- This is found running varray_dml1.sql from the publisher's web site.
COLUMN_VALUE
---------------
Office of Senator McCain
450 West Paseo Redondo
Suite 200
```

You must ensure that your varray is a mirror of your nested table structure. If they are not datatype mirrors, you will encounter an ORA-00932 error. The error complains that the source for the CAST is the wrong type to convert to a nested table.

You can also update varray and nested table columns as shown in this statement:

```
-- This is in varray_dml2.sql on the publisher's web site.
UPDATE    addresses
SET       street_address =
              strings('Office of Senator McCain'
                     ,'2400 E. Arizona Biltmore Cir.'
                     ,'Suite 1150')
WHERE     address_id = 1;
```

The update statement assigns the value of a newly constructed strings collection type. Using the same complex select statement to query the new data, you will see the following output:

```
-- This is found running varray_dml2.sql from the publisher's web site.
COLUMN_VALUE
---------------
```

```
Office of Senator McCain
2400 E. Arizona Biltmore Cir.
Suite 1150
```

You cannot update a portion of a varray column by any direct or indirect method in SQL. You *must* update portions of varray collections by using PL/SQL programs. The following anonymous-block program enables the update of first element of the varray collection:

```
-- This is in varray_dml3.sql on the publisher's web site.
DECLARE
  TYPE address_type IS RECORD
  ( address_id          INTEGER
  , individual_id       INTEGER
  , street_address      STRINGS
  , city                VARCHAR2(20 CHAR)
  , state               VARCHAR2(20 CHAR)
  , postal_code         VARCHAR2(20 CHAR)
  , country_code        VARCHAR2(10 CHAR));
  address               ADDRESS_TYPE;

  CURSOR get_street_address
    (address_id_in      INTEGER) IS
    SELECT   *
    FROM     addresses
    WHERE    address_id = address_id_in;
BEGIN
  -- Access the cursor.
  OPEN  get_street_address(1);
  FETCH get_street_address INTO  address;
  CLOSE get_street_address;

  -- Reset the first element of the varray type variable.
  address.street_address(1) := 'Office of Senator John McCain';

  -- Update the entire varray column value.
  UPDATE   addresses
  SET      street_address = address.street_address
  WHERE    address_id = 1;
END;
/
```

The example program reads the full row and nested varray. It then updates only the first element of the collection, and then rewrites the collection to the same row.

You can see that it has only changed the first element of the varray collection column. This is done using our nested table syntax, which was discussed in a prior example. The results are in the following output file:

```
-- This is found running varray_dml3.sql from the publisher's web site.
COLUMN_VALUE
---------------
Office of Senator John McCain
2400 E. Arizona Biltmore Cir.
Suite 1150
```

Another update scenario remains for you to examine. This example shows how a varray collection column may be grown from one element to two or more elements. Adding elements to a varray collection column requires PL/SQL. This is like the case of updating a single element of the varray collection column. You should recall from the prior discussion that an insert statement constructs a varray collection column.

The insert statement for this example inserts only one element into the `street_address` column, initializing only one element in the varray collection for the row. The following example shows the insert statement:

```
-- This is in varray_dml4.sql on the publisher's web site.
INSERT INTO individuals VALUES
( individuals_s1.nextval, 'John', 'Sidney', 'McCain', 'Mr.');

INSERT INTO addresses VALUES
( 2
, individuals_s1.currval
, strings('Office of Senator Kennedy')
, 'Boston'
, 'MA'
, '02203'
, 'USA');
```

You can use the following solution to add the missing elements to the varray collection column:

```
-- This is in varray_dml4.sql on the publisher's web site.
DECLARE
  TYPE address_type IS RECORD
  ( address_id          INTEGER
  , individual_id       INTEGER
  , street_address      STRINGS
  , city                VARCHAR2(20 CHAR)
  , state               VARCHAR2(20 CHAR)
  , postal_code         VARCHAR2(20 CHAR)
  , country_code        VARCHAR2(10 CHAR));
  address               ADDRESS_TYPE;

  -- Define a cursor to return the %ROWTYPE value.
  CURSOR get_street_address
    (address_id_in      INTEGER) IS
    SELECT    *
    FROM      addresses
    WHERE     address_id = address_id_in;
BEGIN
  -- Access the cursor.
  OPEN  get_street_address(2);
  FETCH get_street_address INTO  address;
  CLOSE get_street_address;

  -- Add elements.
  address.street_address.EXTEND(2);
  address.street_address(2) := 'JFK Building';
  address.street_address(3) := 'Suite 2400';
```

```
  -- Update the varray column value.
  UPDATE    addresses
  SET       street_address = address.street_address
  WHERE     address_id = 2;
END;
/
```

The example program reads the full row and nested varray. It then updates only the second and third elements of the nested collection.

You can see that the column now has three elements, using our nested table syntax again. The following output file shows the results:

```
-- This is found running varray_dml4.sql from the publisher's web site.
COLUMN_VALUE
---------------
Office of Senator Kennedy
JFK Building
Suite 2400
```

You have now covered the features of varrays in Oracle 11g. You have seen that varrays are highly structured collection types. The advantages and disadvantages of varrays have been covered. Moreover, you will now know when and how to use this collection type.

The discussion on varrays has set a foundation for moving to the next collection type, nested tables. You saw in the select statements that varrays depend on nested table structures in some cases. While varrays have a place in database design, they do present challenges that can be avoided by using unbounded nested tables. You may conclude that varrays are better suited to PL/SQL processing than they are to defining tables.

Nested Tables

Like varrays, nested tables are single-dimensional structures of Oracle 11g SQL or PL/SQL datatypes. You can use them table, record, and object definitions and access them in SQL and PL/SQL. You can also use nested tables in table, record, and object definitions. They are accessible in both SQL and PL/SQL. Unlike varrays, they differ from traditional arrays in programming languages such as Java, C, C++, and C#. The difference is that they have no initial maximum size and therefore their size is unconstrained except for available memory in the SGA. The closest corollaries to standard programming languages are bags and sets.

Defining Nested Tables as Object Types as PL/SQL Program Constructs

The syntax to define a PL/SQL nested table collection type is

```
TYPE type_name IS TABLE OF element_type [ NOT NULL ];
```

As discussed, the type name is often a string followed by an underscore and the word table. Some programming traditions prefer the suffix of tab to that of table. It does not matter what you choose to do. It does matter that you do it consistently.

The following example program demonstrates defining, declaring, and initializing a nested table of cards in a PL/SQL program unit. The cards will be limited to a single suit. They will be defined as variable-length strings:

```
-- This is in create_nestedtable1.sql on the publisher's web site.
DECLARE
    -- Define a nested table type.
```

```
  TYPE card_table IS TABLE OF VARCHAR2(5 CHAR);

  -- Declare a nested table with null values.
  cards CARD_TABLE := card_table(NULL,NULL,NULL);
BEGIN

  -- Print initialized null values.
  dbms_output.put_line('Nested table initialized as null values.');
  dbms_output.put_line('-------------------------------------');
  FOR i IN 1..3 LOOP
    dbms_output.put      ('Cards Varray ['||i||'] ');
    dbms_output.put_line('['||cards(i)||']');
  END LOOP;

  -- Assign values to subscripted members of the nested table.
  cards(1) := 'Ace';
  cards(2) := 'Two';
  cards(3) := 'Three';

  -- Print initialized null values.
  dbms_output.put      (CHR(10)); -- Visual line break.
  dbms_output.put_line('Nested table initialized as 11, 12 and 13.');
  dbms_output.put_line('-------------------------------------');
  FOR i IN 1..3 LOOP
    dbms_output.put_line('Cards ['||i||'] '||'['||cards(i)||']');
  END LOOP;
END;
/
```

The example program defines a local nested table collection, declares an initialized collection variable, prints the null value collection elements, assigns values to the elements, and reprints the collection element values. Here is the output from `create_nestedtable1.sql` program:

```
-- This is found running create_nestedtable1.sql from the publisher's web site.
Nested table initialized as nulls.
-----------------
Cards Varray [1] []
Cards Varray [2] []
Cards Varray [3] []

Nested table initialized as Ace, Two and Three.
-----------------------
Cards [1] [Ace]
Cards [2] [Two]
Cards [3] [Three]
```

If you fail to initialize the collection, you raise an ORA-06531 exception, which tells you a collection is not initialized. When you initialize a varray, you set the actual number of initialized rows. You can use the Collection API COUNT method to see how many rows have been initialized so that you don't read past the number of elements. Nested tables act like varrays when you attempt to access an element before allocating it space and an index value, and they raise an ORA-06533 exception. The exception means that subscript is unavailable because it does not exist. When you defined the nested table as three rows in size, you set its size. Therefore, the variable has three valid subscripts, 1, 2, and 3.

If you encountered the error, you might check the Oracle 11*g* documentation. You would find that there is the Collection API EXTEND method to allocate space, and that it is overloaded. It is also covered later in this chapter, in the section "Collection API."

As discussed in the varrays section, use of the Collection API EXTEND(n, i) method to insert a row beyond the subscripted range will fail. It will raise the subscript beyond count error.

You add a row using the Collection API EXTEND method without an actual parameter or with a single actual parameter. If you use the single parameter, it is the number of rows to initialize. It cannot exceed the difference between the number of possible and actual rows for the varray. More information on using these methods is in the section "Collection API."

The following program illustrates initialization with zero rows in the declaration section. Then it demonstrates dynamic initialization and assignment in the execution section.

```
-- This is in create_nestedtable2.sql on the publisher's web site.
DECLARE
  -- Define a nested table.
  TYPE card_suit IS TABLE OF VARCHAR2(5 CHAR);

  -- Declare a no-element collection.
  cards CARD_SUIT := card_suit();
BEGIN
  -- Allocate space as you increment the index.
  FOR i IN 1..3 LOOP
    cards.EXTEND;
    IF    i = 1 THEN
      cards(i) := 'Ace';
    ELSIF i = 2 THEN
      cards(i) := 'Two';
    ELSIF i = 3 THEN
      cards(i) := 'Three';
    END IF;
  END LOOP;

  -- Print initialized collection.
  dbms_output.put_line('Nested table initialized as Ace, Two and Three.');
  dbms_output.put_line('-----------------------------------------------');
  FOR i IN 1..3 LOOP
    dbms_output.put      ('Cards ['||i||'] ');
    dbms_output.put_line('['||cards(i)||']');
  END LOOP;
END;
/
```

The example program defines a local nested table collection and declares a no-element collection. Inside the execution block, the program initializes and prints the element values.

The output is shown here:

```
-- This is found running create_nestedtable2.sql from the publisher's web site.
Nested table initialized as Ace, Two and Three.
-----------------------
Cards [1] [Ace]
```

```
Cards [2] [Two]
Cards [3] [Three]
```

You now have the fundamentals to build nested table structures within PL/SQL program units. The power and management utilities of the collection methods will enhance your ability to use these. This section has further touched on the same Collection API methods used in the varray discussion. They help illustrate initialization issues and are covered in depth later in the chapter. By using these in simple examples, you will be able to see opportunities to apply the methods across collection types.

Defining and Using Nested Tables as Object Types in PL/SQL

The syntax to define a SQL collection type of nested tables in the database is

```
CREATE OR REPLACE TYPE type_name
  AS TABLE OF element_type [ NOT NULL ];
```

The type name is often a string followed by an underscore and the word table. As discussed, many programmers and configuration management people find it a useful pattern to improve code readability. It is also the convention used in the chapter for PL/SQL structure and object types.

The element type may be any Oracle 11*g* SQL datatype, user-defined subtype, or object type. Allowing null values in nested tables is the default. If null values should be disallowed, it must be specified when they are defined.

The following example program demonstrates defining a nested table collection type. The first step creates a SQL nested table collection type in the schema:

```
-- This is in create_nestedtable3.sql on the publisher's web site.
CREATE OR REPLACE TYPE card_table
  AS TABLE OF VARCHAR2(5 CHAR);
/
```

The anonymous-block PL/SQL program then uses it by declaring and initializing a variable.

```
-- This is in create_nestedtable3.sql on the publisher's web site.
DECLARE
  -- Declare a nested table with null values.
  cards CARD_TABLE := card_table(NULL,NULL,NULL);
BEGIN
  -- Print initialized null values.
  dbms_output.put_line('Nested table initialized as nulls.');
  dbms_output.put_line('---------------------------------');
  FOR i IN 1..3 LOOP
    dbms_output.put      ('Cards Varray ['||i||'] ');
    dbms_output.put_line('['||cards(i)||']');
  END LOOP;

  -- Assign values to subscripted members of the table.
  cards(1) := 'Ace';
  cards(2) := 'Two';
  cards(3) := 'Three';

  -- Print initialized values.
  dbms_output.put      (CHR(10)); -- Visual line break.
```

```
  dbms_output.put_line('Nested table initialized as Ace, Two and Three.');
  dbms_output.put_line('--------------------------------------------');
  FOR i IN 1..3 LOOP
    dbms_output.put_line('Cards ['||i||'] '||'['||cards(i)||']');
  END LOOP;
END;
/
```

The example program declares an initialized collection variable, prints the null value collection elements, assigns values to the elements, and reprints the collection element values. Here is the output from the `create_nestedtable1.sql` program:

-- This is found running create_nestedtable3.sql from the publisher's web site.
```
Nested table initialized as null values.
--------------------
Cards Varray [1] []
Cards Varray [2] []
Cards Varray [3] []

Nested table initialized as Ace, Two and Three.
----------------------
Cards [1] [Ace]
Cards [2] [Two]
Cards [3] [Three]
```

The benefit of defining the nested table object type is that it may be referenced from any programs that have permission to use it, whereas a PL/SQL nested table type structure is limited to the program unit. Program units may be anonymous-block programs like the example or stored procedures or packages in the database. Only the latter enables reference by other PL/SQL programs that have permissions to the package. Please refer to Chapter 9 for details on creating and using packages.

The nested table type uses the default behavior that allows null values. After you master the basic syntax and defaults for defining, declaring, and initializing varrays, there is a question that needs to be resolved. When, why, and how do you allow or disallow null rows?

This is a good question and one that you initially covered in the varray section. In these small example programs, it seems that it may not matter too much, though it will matter when you implement nested table collections. Nested tables start as dense arrays, like varrays. However, it is possible to remove elements from nested tables. As elements are removed, nested tables become sparse, meaning that there are gaps in the sequencing of index values.

While index sequencing has gaps, logically there should not be any data gaps. If your application design allows nulls in nested tables, you should carefully review it. You should consider why you want to allow nulls in a nested table, because there should never be data gaps in nested tables.

Allowing nulls in nested tables guarantees you will encounter them in the data stream. Combined with index sequence gaps, allowing null values will increase the amount of required error handling. You should consider overriding the default behavior and disallowing null values in nested tables. Essentially, nested tables and varrays are ill-suited to fill the traditional programming role of lists or maps. If you need the functionality of a list or map, you should use an associative array.

You will now learn how to disallow null values in nested tables. The main impact of disallowing them comes when initializing them. This is a mirror of the issue you saw in varrays earlier. For example, if you redefined the nested table object type used in the previous program to disallow null values, the program would fail. As when using the varray, you raise a PLS-00567 exception because you're trying to pass a null to a NOT NULL–constrained column.

When you use nested tables as bags or sets, you will define structures that contain hundreds of rows. Some may be dynamically defined by counting rows in a table before being built as dynamic structures.

When you initialize nested tables that contain 100 percent of the data, doing so is straightforward because the constructor can do that. However, when you initialize nested tables that contain less than all the data, adding rows will require some additional programming techniques. These are more or less equivalent to what you worked through with varrays.

The following example allocates a full playing deck of cards. To do so, you will work with varrays that contain the value sets. You will use varrays because the problem is a natural fit to traditional structured arrays. There are thirteen cards in a suit and there are four suits. We will see the use of these structures as in the following program along with nested loops. If you are not comfortable with loop structures, you can review them in Chapter 4.

The first step involves creating three SQL collection types:

```sql
-- This is in create_nestedtable4.sql on the publisher's web site.
CREATE OR REPLACE TYPE card_unit_varray AS VARRAY(13) OF VARCHAR2(5 CHAR);
/
CREATE OR REPLACE TYPE card_suit_varray AS VARRAY(4) OF VARCHAR2(8 CHAR);
/
CREATE OR REPLACE TYPE card_deck_table AS TABLE OF VARCHAR2(17 CHAR);
/
```

Then, you can use these in the following anonymous block:

```sql
-- This is in create_nestedtable4.sql on the publisher's web site.
DECLARE
  -- Declare counter.
  counter INTEGER := 0;

  -- Declare and initialize a card suit and unit collections.
  suits CARD_SUIT_VARRAY :=
    card_suit_varray('Clubs','Diamonds','Hearts','Spades');
  units CARD_UNIT_VARRAY :=
    card_unit_varray('Ace','Two','Three','Four','Five','Six','Seven'
                    ,'Eight','Nine','Ten','Jack','Queen','King');

  -- Declare and initialize a null nested table.
  deck CARD_DECK_TABLE := card_deck_table();
BEGIN
  -- Loop through the four suits, then thirteen cards.
  FOR i IN 1..suits.COUNT LOOP
    FOR j IN 1..units.COUNT LOOP
      counter := counter + 1;
      deck.EXTEND;
      deck(counter) := units(j)||' of '||suits(i);
    END LOOP;
  END LOOP;
```

```
  -- Print initialized values.
  dbms_output.put_line('Deck of cards by suit.');
  dbms_output.put_line('--------------------');
  FOR i IN 1..counter LOOP
    dbms_output.put_line('['||deck(i)||']');
  END LOOP;
END;
/
```

The example program builds two varrays, which are used to build a deck of cards. Dynamic space allocation occurs for the nested table, while the varrays are statically allocated.

The redacted output is shown here:

 -- This is found running create_nestedtable4.sql from the publisher's web site.

```
Deck of cards by suit.
-----------
[Ace of Clubs]
[Two of Clubs]
[Three of Clubs]
...
The remainder is redacted to conserve space.
...
[Jack of Spades]
[Queen of Spades]
[King of Spades]
```

You have developed skills using nested table collections as object types. The next section will use nested table collections and define tables that use them as column datatypes.

Defining and Using Nested Tables as Column Datatypes in Tables

After creating a table with a column of a nested table datatype, you need to know how to use it. Using it requires understanding DML access methods and how they work with nested tables. Nested tables, like varrays, present no unique conditions for deleting, since deletion is at the row level. However, there are substantive differences when it comes to using insert and update statements.

The differences are less than those encountered with varrays on updates. Nested tables provide a more intuitive access set for DML. Since the ERD represents street_address as a list, there is no need to redefine it. A varray or nested table is an implementation of a list.

While DML is more intuitive, you do lose some flexibility on database constraints. When you worked with varrays earlier in the chapter, you were able to define a collection column and set the constraint to disallow null values. This was a new feature in Oracle 10g. Varrays are now stored as inline structures, enabling a NOT NULL constraint. By contrast, nested tables as column values do not let you use a NOT NULL constraint. This is true when you define the table type with the default or override the default to disallow nulls. When you attempt to use a table type in a table definition and set the column constraint to NOT NULL, it will raise an ORA-02331 error.

NOTE
If you use the oerr tool to check an ORA-02331 error, it will tell you that it applies to varrays. This is no longer true.

You can test the limitation on database constraints easily. Create a nested table datatype like the following:

```
CREATE OR REPLACE TYPE address_table AS TABLE OF VARCHAR2(30 CHAR) NOT NULL;
/
```

You'll see the following error raised if you run the script inserting null values in the column:

```
, street_address          ADDRESS_TABLE       NOT NULL
                                                   *
ERROR at line 4:
ORA-02331: cannot create constraint on column of datatype Named Table Type
```

The table creation fails because the nested table type disallows using the NOT NULL constraint. Nested tables are not constrainable by definition. You should consider this when you use a nested table. You are storing a table that is only referenced through the parent table. Placing a NOT NULL column constraint is inconsistent with a nested table type.

A NOT NULL constraint on a nested table column is equivalent to mandating a row be inserted in the nested table before defining it. This is impossible. A NOT NULL constraint in this case acts like a database referential integrity constraint and is therefore disallowed. NOT NULL constraints for nested tables become application design considerations when inserting or updating rows.

After reading this section, you want to consider why you would use a varray in table definitions. You will see that nested tables provide a more natural access method to elements within DML update statements.

The create_addressbook2.sql script builds the environment for this section. You should run it before attempting to use any of the following scripts.

Like varrays covered earlier, insert statements have one type of access. It is an all-or-nothing approach to the datatype. Insert statements allocate space necessary to the construction of the nested table. For example, in a nested table implementation of street_address, it is possible to insert one to any number of rows of data. When the insert is made to the row, an instance of the collection type is constructed with the number of rows chosen. As you see, the syntax to insert a nested table is a mirror to that used for a varray. The single exception is the name of the collection type used in the constructor.

```
-- This is found in nestedtable_dml1.sql on the publisher's web site.
INSERT INTO individuals VALUES
( individuals_s1.nextval, 'John', 'Sidney', 'McCain', 'Mr.');
```

```
INSERT INTO addresses VALUES
( addresses_s1.nextval
, individuals_s1.currval
, strings
  ('Office of Senator McCain'
  ,'450 West Paseo Redondo'
  ,'Suite 200')
,'Tucson'
,'AZ'
,'85701'
,'USA');
```

The example program inserts a full set of three rows into the nested table datatype. It is important to note that in the values clause, the nested table datatype name is used as the constructor name. The constructor uses the syntax previously presented with a list of comma-delimited actual parameters in a set of parentheses.

If you were to query the `street_address` column from the table, you would see a return set of the constructor with its actual parameters. This is illustrated by running a query like the following:

```
-- This is found in nestedtable_dml1.sql on the publisher's web site.
SELECT    street_address
FROM      addresses;
```

The shortened output from the query is noted.

```
-- This is found running nestedtable_dml1.sql from the publisher's web site.
STREET_ADDRESS
-------------------------------
ADDRESS_TABLE('Office of Senator McCain', '450 West Paseo ...
```

This type of output is not very useful. It is also very different than what you might expect. Using data query language (DQL) to select a result from a nested table datatype requires specialized syntax. Fortunately, unlike when you implemented the varray by casting to a nested table, you can directly access nested tables in DQL.

The following example formats the output with SQL*Plus. It then selects the column values from the nested table one row at a time. A bit more intuitive than the varray DQL covered, it is still complex.

```
-- This is found in nestedtable_dml1.sql on the publisher's web site.
-- Use SQL*Plus to format the output.
COL column_value FORMAT A30

-- Print formatted elements from aggregate table.
SELECT nested.column_value
FROM   addresses a
,       TABLE(a.street_address) nested
WHERE  address_id = 1;
```

The `TABLE` keyword translates the nested table into an aggregate table like a pipelined function. The formatted output from the query is

```
-- This is found running nestedtable_dml1.sql from the publisher's web site.
 COLUMN_VALUE
---------------
Office of Senator McCain
450 West Paseo Redondo
Suite 200
```

The DQL to access the values in a nested table returns a row set. A problem with a row set is merging the row set with other data in SQL. Since other elements returned in a normal selection will have one occurrence per row, representing the data is difficult. You are better served reading these inside PL/SQL blocks.

PL/SQL helps you ease limitations. You will build a function to return a single variable-length string with row breaks. If you need to review the details of building stored functions, please check Chapter 6. Likewise, you should check the Collection API later in this chapter for details on the COUNT method.

The following function takes the row returns and creates a single variable-length string. You will find it a useful example, especially in the case of building mailing addresses:

```
-- This is found in nestedtable_dml1.sql on the publisher's web site.
CREATE OR REPLACE FUNCTION many_to_one
(street_address_in ADDRESS_TABLE) RETURN VARCHAR2 IS
  retval VARCHAR2(2000) := '';
BEGIN
  -- Read all elements in the nested table, and delimit with a line break.
  FOR i IN 1..street_address_in.COUNT LOOP
    retval := retval || street_address_in(i) || CHR(10);
  END LOOP;
  RETURN retval;
END many_to_one;
/
```

The function takes a nested table and translates it into a multiple-line string. Using SQL*Plus to format the column, you can query the formatted string:

```
-- This is found in nestedtable_dml1.sql on the publisher's web site.
-- Use SQL*Plus to format the output.
COL address_label FORMAT A30

-- Print a mailing label.
SELECT   i.first_name || ' '
||       i.middle_initial || ' '
||       i.last_name || CHR(10)
||       many_to_one(a.street_address)
||       city || ', '
||       state || ' '
||       postal_code address_label
FROM     addresses a
,        individuals i
WHERE    a.individual_id = i.individual_id
AND      i.individual_id = 1;
```

The formatted output from the query is

```
-- This is found in nestedtable_dml1.sql on the publisher's web site.
ADDRESS_LABEL
---------------
John   McCain
Office of Senator McCain
450 West Paseo Redondo
Suite 200
Tucson, AZ 85701
```

As you have seen earlier in the chapter, PL/SQL is the only way to update varrays unless changing the entire content. This is not the case with nested tables. A key advantage of nested tables is that you can update individual row elements. These updates can be done directly in DML update statements.

You use the following example program to replace the entire content of the `street_address` nested table datatype:

```
-- This is found in nestedtable_dml2.sql on the publisher's web site.
UPDATE    addresses
SET       street_address =
              address_table('Office of Senator McCain'
                           ,'2400 E. Arizona Biltmore Cir.'
                           ,'Suite 1150')
WHERE     address_id = 1;
```

The update statement assigns the value of a newly constructed `address_table` collection type. It does so by constructing an instance of a nested table. This is done through a construction process, where actual parameters are passed inside parentheses and delimited by commas.

Using the same complex select statement to query the new data, you will see the following output:

```
-- This is found in nestedtable_dml2.sql on the publisher's web site.
COLUMN_VALUE
---------------
Office of Senator McCain
2400 E. Arizona Biltmore Cir.
Suite 1150
```

You can update a portion of a nested table column directly in SQL. Alternatively, you may use two approaches in PL/SQL. This is an improvement over the lack of direct update capability for the varray column.

The following program will update the first row in the `street_address` nested table. It will add the senator's first name to the variable-length string:

```
-- This is found in nestedtable_dml3.sql on the publisher's web site.
UPDATE    TABLE(SELECT   street_address
                FROM     addresses
                WHERE    address_id = 1)
SET       column_value = 'Office of Senator John McCain'
WHERE     column_value = 'Office of Senator McCain';
```

The formatted output from the query is

```
-- This is found running nestedtable_dml3.sql from the publisher's web site.
COLUMN_VALUE
---------------
Office of Senator John McCain
450 West Paseo Redondo
Suite 200
```

Alternatively, you can use PL/SQL to do the update. Two approaches you can choose from in PL/SQL are

- A direct update of a row in the nested table
- An update of all the row contents for a nested table column

The update of all row contents is a mirror to the approach used earlier for varrays. You should check the example provided earlier in the chapter for that approach. Next you will see how to update a row in a nested table column directly. The example uses dynamic SQL and bind variables. Both are covered in Chapter 11.

```
-- This is found in nestedtable_dml3.sql on the publisher's web site.
DECLARE
  -- Define old and new values.
  new_value VARCHAR2(30 CHAR) := 'Office of Senator John McCain';
  old_value VARCHAR2(30 CHAR) := 'Office of Senator McCain';

  -- Build SQL statement to support bind variables.
  sql_statement VARCHAR2(100 CHAR)
    := 'UPDATE    THE (SELECT   street_address '
    || '                FROM     addresses '
    || '                WHERE    address_id = 21) '
    || 'SET       column_value = :1 '
    || 'WHERE     column_value = :2';
BEGIN
  -- Use dynamic SQL to run the update statement.
  EXECUTE IMMEDIATE sql_statement USING new_value, old_value;
END;
/
```

The program lets you use bind variables rather than substitution variables to create a dynamic update statement. The USING clause supports IN, OUT, and IN OUT modes like the functions and procedures covered in the prior chapter. The default is IN mode, which is as close as you can come with an UPDATE statement to what you do when you want to explicitly pass parameters into cursors.

NOTE
The bind variables are numerically numbered placeholders. Position-specific variables or strings reference them with the USING clause.

The formatted output from the query is the same as shown in the last example. It is not redisplayed to save space.

Updates can only be done for elements within a nested table. If you want to add an element to a nested table column value, you must use PL/SQL. The following program shows you how to add two rows of data.

The insert statement is the same except for the type definition to the one you used in the varray update discussion. It inserts only one element into the street_address column, initializing only one element in the nested table collection for the row. The following example shows the insert statement:

```
-- This is found in nestedtable_dml4.sql on the publisher's web site.
INSERT INTO individuals VALUES
( individuals_s1.nextval, 'Edward', 'Moore', 'Kennedy', 'Mr.');

INSERT INTO addresses VALUES
( addresses_s1.nextval
, individuals_s1.currval
, address_table('Office of Senator Kennedy')
```

```
, 'Boston'
, 'MA'
, '02203'
, 'USA');
```

You can use the following solution to add the missing elements to the nested table collection column. You should note there is only one difference between a varray and nested table. That difference is the datatype.

-- **This is found in nestedtable_dml4.sql on the publisher's web site.**

```
DECLARE
  TYPE address_type IS RECORD
  ( address_id          INTEGER
  , individual_id       INTEGER
  , street_address      ADDRESS_VARRAY
  , city                VARCHAR2(20 CHAR)
  , state               VARCHAR2(20 CHAR)
  , postal_code         VARCHAR2(20 CHAR)
  , country_code        VARCHAR2(10 CHAR));
  address               ADDRESS_TYPE;

  -- Define a cursor to return the %ROWTYPE value.
  CURSOR get_street_address
    (address_id_in      INTEGER) IS
    SELECT  *
    FROM    addresses
    WHERE   address_id = address_id_in;
BEGIN
  -- Access the cursor.
  OPEN  get_street_address(2);
  FETCH get_street_address INTO  address;
  CLOSE get_street_address;

  -- Add elements.
  address.street_address.EXTEND(2);
  address.street_address(2) := 'JFK Building';
  address.street_address(3) := 'Suite 2400';

  -- Update the varray column value.
  UPDATE    addresses
  SET       street_address = address.street_address
  WHERE     address_id = 2;
END;
/
```

The example program reads the full row and the nested table. It then updates only the second and third elements of the nested collection.

The following output file shows the results:

-- **This is found running nestedtable_dml4.sql from the publisher's web site.**

```
COLUMN_VALUE
---------------
Office of Senator Kennedy
```

```
JFK Building
Suite 2400
```

You have now covered the features of nested tables in Oracle 11*g*. You have seen that nested tables are structured collection types. The advantages and disadvantages of nested tables have been covered and contrasted against varrays. Moreover, you will now know when and how to use this collection type.

Associative Arrays

Associative arrays are single-dimensional structures of an Oracle 11*g* datatype or a user-defined record/object type. As discussed at the beginning of the section, they were previously known as PL/SQL tables. This section focuses on single-dimensional structures of the associative array.

Associative arrays *cannot* be used in tables. They may be used only as programming structures. They can be accessed only in PL/SQL. They are like the other collection types and different than arrays in the traditional sense of programming languages such as Java, C, C++, and C#. They are close cousins to lists and maps. They do not have the capability of linked lists but may be made to act that way through a user-defined programming interface.

It is important to note some key issues presented by associative arrays. These issues drive a slightly different approach to illustrating their use. Associative arrays

- Do not require initialization and have no constructor syntax. They do not need to allocate space before assigning values, which eliminates using the Collection API `EXTEND` method.

- Can be indexed numerically up to and including Oracle 11*g*. In Oracle 11*g*, they can also use unique variable-length strings.

- Can use any integer as the index value, which means any negative, positive, or zero whole number.

- Are implicitly converted from equivalent `%ROWTYPE`, record type, and object type return values to associative array structures.

- Are the key to using the `FORALL` statement or `BULK COLLECT` clause, which enables bulk transfers of records from a database table to a programming unit.

- Require special treatment when using a character string as an index value in any database using globalized settings, such as the `NLS_COMP` or `NLS_SORT` initialization parameters.

TIP
Unique strings as indexes can encounter sorting differences when the National Language Support (NLS) character set changes during operation of the database.

You will start by seeing the expanded definition techniques provided in Oracle 11*g*. Then examine their principal uses as PL/SQL programming structures.

Defining and Using Associative Arrays as PL/SQL Program Constructs

The syntax to define an associative array in PL/SQL has two possibilities. One is

```
CREATE OR REPLACE TYPE type_name AS TABLE OF element_type [ NOT NULL ]
INDEX BY [ PLS_INTEGER | BINARY_INTEGER | VARCHAR2(size) ];
```

The same issues around enabling or disabling null values in nested tables apply to associative arrays. As a rule, you should ensure that data in an array is not null. You can do that by enabling the constraint when defining an associative array, or you can do it programmatically. It is a decision that you will need to make on a case-by-case basis.

You can use a negative, positive, or zero number as the index value for associative arrays. Both PLS_INTEGER and BINARY_INTEGER types are unconstrained types that map to call specifications in C/C++, C#, and Java in Oracle 11*g*.

You can use variable-length strings up to four thousand characters in length as columns in tables. The VARCHAR2 type supports the Unicode physical size for globalized implementation. This means that you may store half or one-third of the characters depending on your Unicode implementation. Please cross reference the NCHAR, NCLOB, and NVARCHAR2 datatypes in Chapter 3 for more information on Unicode size management.

The other possible syntax to define an associate array is

```
CREATE OR REPLACE TYPE type_name AS TABLE OF element_type [ NOT NULL ]
INDEX BY key_type;
```

The key_type alternative enables you to use VARCHAR2, STRING, or LONG datatypes in addition to PLS_INTEGER and BINARY_INTEGER datatypes. Both VARCHAR2 and STRING require a size definition. The LONG datatype does not, because it is by definition a variable length string of 32,760 bytes.You should refer to Chapter 3 for coverage of LONG datatypes.

As discussed, associative arrays do not require initialization and do not have a constructor syntax. This is a substantive difference from the other two collection types: varrays and nested tables. It is a tremendous advantage to using associative arrays in PL/SQL. This is especially true because the basic structure of associative arrays with an integer index has not changed much since their implementation in Oracle 7, release 7.3.

If you attempt to construct an associative array, you will raise a PLS-00222 exception. The following program attempts to construct an associative array:

```
-- This is found in create_assocarray1.sql on the publisher's web site.
DECLARE
  -- Define an associative array.
  TYPE card_table IS TABLE OF VARCHAR2(5 CHAR)
    INDEX BY BINARY_INTEGER;

  -- Declare and attempt to construct an associative array.
  cards CARD_TABLE := card_table('A','B','C');
BEGIN
  NULL;
END;
/
```

It will raise the following error messages:

```
-- This is found running create_assocarray1.sql from the publisher's web site.
  cards CARD_TABLE := card_table('A','B','C');
                             *
ERROR at line 8:
```

```
ORA-06550: line 8, column 23:
PLS-00222: no function with name 'CARD_TABLE' exists in
           this scope
ORA-06550: line 8, column 9:
PL/SQL: Item ignored
```

The failure occurs because the INDEX BY clause has built an associative array, not a nested table. While a nested table type definition implicitly defines a constructor, an associative array does not.

In our previous discussion, the object constructor was qualified as a function. Other collection types, varrays and nested tables, are object types that implicitly define constructor functions. An associative array is a structure, not an object type. Therefore, it does not have an implicitly built constructor function and fails when you attempt to call the function.

Likewise, you cannot navigate an associative array until it contains elements. The following example program demonstrates the failure:

```
-- This is found in create_assocarray2.sql on the publisher's web site.
DECLARE
  -- Define an associative array of strings.
  TYPE card_table IS TABLE OF VARCHAR2(5 CHAR)
    INDEX BY BINARY_INTEGER;

  -- Define an associative array variable.
  cards CARD_TABLE;
BEGIN
    DBMS_OUTPUT.PUT_LINE(cards(1));
END;
/
```

It will raise the following exception, which is quite different from those of other collection types. As described previously, you get an uninitialized collection error from varrays and nested tables. Associative arrays raise a no data found exception. The no data found error occurs because associative array elements are built through direct element assignment.

```
-- This is found running create_assocarray2.sql from the publisher's web site.
DECLARE
*
ERROR at line 1:
ORA-01403: no data found
ORA-06512: at line 13
```

As a rule of thumb, you want to avoid the possibility of this error. The following program provides a mechanism to avoid encountering the error:

```
-- This is found in create_assocarray3.sql on the publisher's web site.
DECLARE
  -- Define an associative array of strings.
  TYPE card_table IS TABLE OF VARCHAR2(5 CHAR)
    INDEX BY BINARY_INTEGER;

  -- Define an associative array variable.
  cards CARD_TABLE;
```

```
BEGIN
  IF cards.COUNT <> 0 THEN
    DBMS_OUTPUT.PUT_LINE(cards(1));
  ELSE
    DBMS_OUTPUT.PUT_LINE('The cards collection is empty.');
  END IF;
END;
/
```

The Collection API COUNT method returns a zero value under only two conditions:

■ When a varray or nested table collection is initialized and no space is allocated to elements

■ When an associative array has no assigned elements

Since the second condition is met, the program returns the message from the else statement. The output follows:

```
-- This is found running create_assocarray3.sql from the publisher's web site.
The cards collection is empty.
```

The Collection API EXTEND method will fail to allocate space to an associative array. The following program illustrates the attempt:

```
-- This is found in create_assocarray4.sql on the publisher's web site.
DECLARE
  -- Define an associative array of strings.
  TYPE card_table IS TABLE OF VARCHAR2(5 CHAR)
    INDEX BY BINARY_INTEGER;

  -- Define an associative array variable.
  cards CARD_TABLE;
BEGIN
  IF cards.COUNT <> 0 THEN
    DBMS_OUTPUT.PUT_LINE(cards(1));
  ELSE
    cards.EXTEND;
  END IF;
END;
/
```

The attempt to extend an associative array raises a PLS-00306 exception. The exception states that you're calling it with the wrong number or types of arguments. It actually means that the component select can't find the method attached to the associative array. The Collection API EXTEND method can only operate on varrays and nested tables.

You have developed an appreciation of why associative arrays cannot be constructed like varrays and nested tables. You will now experiment with defining and initializing associative arrays.

Initializing Associative Arrays

As discussed, you can build associative arrays with a number index or a unique variable-length string. Number indexes must be integers, which are positive, negative, and zero numbers. Unique variable-length strings can be VARCHAR2, STRING, or LONG datatypes.

You see how to assign elements to a numerically indexed associative array in the following example:

```
-- This is found in create_assocarray5.sql on the publisher's web site.
DECLARE
  -- Define a varray of twelve strings.
  TYPE months_varray IS VARRAY(12) OF STRING(9 CHAR);

  -- Define an associative array of strings.
  TYPE calendar_table IS TABLE OF VARCHAR2(9 CHAR) INDEX BY BINARY_INTEGER;

  -- Declare and construct a varray.
  month MONTHS_VARRAY :=
    months_varray('January','February','March','April','May','June'
               ,'July','August','September','October','November','December');

  -- Declare an associative array variable.
  calendar CALENDAR_TABLE;
BEGIN
  -- Check if calendar has no elements, then add months.
  IF calendar.COUNT = 0 THEN
    DBMS_OUTPUT.PUT_LINE('Assignment loop:');
    DBMS_OUTPUT.PUT_LINE('----------------');
    FOR i IN month.FIRST..month.LAST LOOP
      calendar(i) := '';
      DBMS_OUTPUT.PUT_LINE('Index ['||i||'] is ['||calendar(i)||']');
      calendar(i) := month(i);
    END LOOP;

    -- Print assigned element values.
    DBMS_OUTPUT.PUT(CHR(10));
    DBMS_OUTPUT.PUT_LINE('Post-assignment loop:');
    DBMS_OUTPUT.PUT_LINE('---------------------');
    FOR i IN calendar.FIRST..calendar.LAST LOOP
      DBMS_OUTPUT.PUT_LINE('Index ['||i||'] is ['||calendar(i)||']');
    END LOOP;
  END IF;
END;
/
```

The preceding example illustrates moving the contents of a varray to an associative array. In this example, both structures have a numeric index value.

Its output prints a line for each month for both collection types. The following is a shortened copy of the output:

```
-- This is found running create_assocarray5.sql from the publisher's web site.
Assignment loop:
--------
Index [1] is []
Index [2] is []
...
Index [11] is []
```

```
Index [12] is []

Post-assignment loop:
-----------
Index [1] is [January]
Index [2] is [February]
...
Index [11] is [November]
Index [12] is [December]
```

If you decide, in Oracle 11*g,* to use a variable-length string as an index value, the process changes. The standard range FOR loop works to assign values from the varray to the associative array. However, the same type of range FOR loop will fail to read the associative array. The problem is the assignment inside the FOR loop. You must change the index value as

Numeric Index Assignment	**String Index Assignment**
`calendar(i) := '';`	`calendar(month(i)) := '';`

The counter variable is i in the preceding program. A counter variable is defined as a PLS_INTEGER. Thus, the variable-length string index value cannot be cast to an integer because it is not an integer. Therefore, it raises an ORA-06502 conversion error. The same example worked previously because the counter variable was cast as a VARCHAR2 when initializing members and cast back to an INTEGER when reading the associative array.

TIP
Associative arrays do not have a navigational syntax equivalent to their namesake in JavaScript. You cannot treat an associative array as a cursor by using a cursor FOR-loop structure.

This presents you with a problem. A non-numeric index value requires you to know where to start and how to increment. The Collection API FIRST and NEXT methods provide the tools. Details of the Collection API are covered later in the chapter if you want more on these methods now.

You can use the approach demonstrated in the following example program to solve the problem. In the second range FOR loop, the logic to traverse a unique string index is provided:

```
-- This is found in create_assocarray6.sql on the publisher's web site.
DECLARE
  -- Define variables to traverse a string indexed associative array.
  current VARCHAR2(9 CHAR);
  element INTEGER;

  -- Define required collection datatypes.
  TYPE months_varray IS VARRAY(12) OF STRING(9 CHAR);.
  TYPE calendar_table IS TABLE OF VARCHAR2(9 CHAR) INDEX BY VARCHAR2(9 CHAR);

  -- Declare a varray.
  month MONTHS_VARRAY :=
    months_varray('January','February','March','April','May','June'
              ,'July','August','September','October','November','December');

  -- Declare empty associative array.
```

```
    calendar CALENDAR_TABLE;
BEGIN
  -- Check if calendar has no elements.
  IF calendar.COUNT = 0 THEN
    -- Print assignment output title.
    DBMS_OUTPUT.PUT_LINE('Assignment loop:');
    DBMS_OUTPUT.PUT_LINE('----------------');
    FOR i IN month.FIRST..month.LAST LOOP
      calendar(month(i)) := TO_CHAR(i);
      DBMS_OUTPUT.PUT_LINE('Index ['||month(i)||'] is ['||i||']');
    END LOOP;

    -- Print assigned output title.
    DBMS_OUTPUT.PUT(CHR(10));
    DBMS_OUTPUT.PUT_LINE('Post-assignment loop:');
    DBMS_OUTPUT.PUT_LINE('---------------------');
    FOR i IN 1..calendar.COUNT LOOP
      IF i = 1 THEN
        -- Assign the first character index to a variable.
        current := calendar.FIRST;
        -- Use the derived index to find the next index.
        element := calendar(current);
      ELSE
        -- Check if next index value exists.
        IF calendar.NEXT(current) IS NOT NULL THEN
          -- Assign the character index to a variable.
          current := calendar.NEXT(current);
          -- Use the derived index to find the next index.
          element := calendar(current);
        ELSE
          -- Exit loop since last index value is read.
          EXIT;
        END IF;
      END IF;

      -- Print an indexed element from the array.
      DBMS_OUTPUT.PUT_LINE('Index ['||current||'] is ['||element||']');
    END LOOP;
  END IF;
END;
/
```

The preceding example illustrates moving the contents of a varray with a numeric index to an associative array with a unique string index.

The IF statement checks whether or not the range for-loop counter is equal to 1. This finds our first record to start traversing the associative array. You use the Collection API FIRST method to return the first unique string index value. The program assigns the unique string index value to the current variable, and then it uses the current variable to find the data value and assign it to the element variable. At this point, it exits the if-then-else statement and prints the values, as described later.

On your second pass through the range FOR loop, the IF statement check will fail. It will then go to the ELSE statement and encounter the nested if-then-else statement. The IF statement uses the Collection API NEXT to check whether there is another record in the associative array. If there is another record in the associative array, it will use the current variable to find the next index value. Then, it assigns the value to replace the value in the current variable. When there are no more records, it exits.

It prints the indexes and values from calendar associative array with the DBMS_OUTPUT package. The program generates the following output stream. Again, it has been edited to conserve space:

-- This is found running create_assocarray6.sql from the publisher's web site.

```
Assignment loop:
--------
Index [January] is [1]
Index [February] is [2]

Index [November] is [11]
Index [December] is [12]

Post-assignment loop:
-----------
Index [April] is [4]
Index [August] is [8]
Index [December] is [12]
Index [February] is [2]
Index [January] is [1]
Index [July] is [7]
Index [June] is [6]
Index [March] is [3]
Index [May] is [5]
Index [November] is [11]
Index [October] is [10]
Index [September] is [9]
```

You can see that the population sequence of the associative array differs from how it can be traversed. The Collection API FIRST, NEXT, and PRIOR methods work from hash maps for the unique strings. Sorting is dependent on the NLS_COMP and NLS_SORT database parameters in globalized databases.

As a result of this sorting behavior, unique string index values present some interesting considerations. If you need to keep track of original ordering, you will need to use a record or object type that provides a surrogate key. The surrogate key can maintain your original ordering sequence.

You have developed an appreciation of standard initialization methods for associative arrays. You have also explored key issues that you should avoid. Moreover, you have learned how to initialize and traverse associative arrays.

Collection Set Operators

Oracle 11g delivers collection set operators. They act and function like SQL set operators in select statements. The difference is that they are used in assignments between collections of matching signature types. They only work with varrays and nested tables because they require numeric index values. You have to migrate associative arrays into varrays or nested tables before using set operators, and the *collections must contain scalar SQL datatypes.* You will raise a wrong number or types of argument error, or a `PLS-00306` exception, if you use set operators to compare collections of user-defined object types. Table 7-2 describes the multiset operators.

Multiset Operator	Description
CARDINALITY	The `CARDINALITY` operator counts the number of elements in a collection. It makes no attempt to count only unique elements, but you can combine it with the `SET` operator to count unique elements. The prototype is: `CARDINALITY(collection)`
EMPTY	The `EMPTY` operator acts as an operand, as you would check whether a variable is null or is not null. The comparative syntax is: `variable_name IS [NOT] EMPTY`
MEMBER OF	The `MEMBER OF` operator lets you check if the left operand is a member of the collection used as the right operand. The comparative syntax is: `variable_name MEMBER OF collection_name`
MULTISET EXCEPT	The `MULTISET EXCEPT` operator removes one set from another. It works like the SQL `MINUS` set operator. The prototype is: `collection MULTISET EXCEPT collection`
MULTISET INTERSECT	The `MULTISET INTERSECT` operator evaluates two sets and returns one set. The return set contains elements that were found in both original sets. It works like the SQL `INTERSECT` set operator. The prototype is: `collection MULTISET INTERSECT collection`
MULTISET UNION	The `MULTISET UNION` operator evaluates two sets and returns one set. The return set contains all elements of both sets. Where duplicate elements are found, they are returned. It functions like the SQL `UNION ALL` set operator. You may use the `DISTINCT` operator to eliminate duplicates. The `DISTINCT` operator follows the `MULTISET UNION` operator rule. It functions like the SQL `UNION` operator. The prototype is: `collection MULTISET UNION collection`
SET	The `SET` operator removes duplicates from a collection, and thereby creates a set of unique values. It acts like a `DISTINCT` operator sorting out duplicates in a SQL statement. The operator prototype is: `SET(collection)` You can also use the `SET` operator as an operand, as you would check whether a variable is null or is not null. The comparative syntax is: `variable_name IS [NOT] A SET`

TABLE 7-2 *Set Operators for Collections*

Multiset Operator	Description
SUBMULTISET	The SUBMULTISET operator identifies if a set is a subset of another set. It returns true when the left operand is a subset of the right operand. The true can be misleading if you're looking for a proper subset, which contains at least one element less than the superset. The function returns true because any set is a subset of itself. There is no test for a proper subset without also using the CARDINALITY operator to compare whether the element counts of both sets are unequal. The prototype is: *collection* SUBMULTISET OF collection

TABLE 7-2 *Set Operators for Collections* (continued)

Sets are displayed as comma-delimited lists of values. The following SQL nested table type and function let you format the results of the set operators into a comma-delimited set.

```
-- This is found in multiset.sql on the publisher's web site.
CREATE OR REPLACE TYPE list IS TABLE OF NUMBER;
/

CREATE OR REPLACE FUNCTION format_list(set_in LIST) RETURN VARCHAR2 IS
  retval VARCHAR2(2000);
BEGIN
  IF set_in IS NULL THEN
    dbms_output.put_line('Result: <Null>');
  ELSIF set_in IS EMPTY THEN
    dbms_output.put_line('Result: <Empty>');
  ELSE  -- Anything not null or empty.
    FOR i IN set_in.FIRST..set_in.LAST LOOP
      IF i = set_in.FIRST THEN
        IF set_in.COUNT = 1 THEN
          retval := '('||set_in(i)||')';
        ELSE
          retval := '('||set_in(i);
        END IF;
      ELSIF i <> set_in.LAST THEN
        retval := retval||', '||set_in(i);
      ELSE
        retval := retval||', '||set_in(i)||')';
      END IF;
    END LOOP;
  END IF;
  RETURN retval;
END format_list;
/
```

The `format_list` function only works with numeric indexes because collection set operators are limited to varrays and nested tables, which are only indexed by integers. The set operator examples all use this function to format output.

CARDINALITY Operator

The `CARDINALITY` operator lets count the elements in a collection. If there are unique elements, they are counted once for each copy in the collection. The following example shows you how to exclude matching elements:

```
DECLARE
  a LIST := list(1,2,3,3,4,4);
BEGIN
  dbms_output.put_line(CARDINALITY(a));
END;
/
```

The program prints the number 6 because there are four elements in the collection. You can count only the unique values by combining the `CARDINALITY` and `SET` operators, as shown here:

```
DECLARE
  a LIST := list(1,2,3,3,4,4);
BEGIN
  dbms_output.put_line(CARDINALITY(SET(a)));
END;
/
```

The program now prints the number 4 because there are four unique elements in the set derived from the six-element collection. This section has demonstrated how you can use the `CARDINALITY` operator to count elements in collections or sets.

EMPTY Operator

The `EMPTY` operator is covered in the `SET` subsection.

MEMBER OF Operator

The `MEMBER OF` operator lets you find if the left operand is a member of the collection used as the right operand. As with other set operators, the collections must use standard scalar datatypes. This example demonstrates how you find if an element exists in a collection:

```
DECLARE
  TYPE list IS TABLE OF VARCHAR2(10);
  n VARCHAR2(10) := 'One';
  a LIST := list('One','Two','Three');
BEGIN
  IF n MEMBER OF a THEN
    dbms_output.put_line('"n" is member.');
  END IF;
END;
/
```

The `MEMBER OF` operator compares and returns a Boolean true type when it finds the left operand value in the right operand collection. The left operand datatype must match the base datatype of the scalar collection.

MULTISET EXCEPT Operator

The `MULTISET EXCEPT` operator lets you find the elements remaining from the first set after removing any matching elements from the second set. The operator ignores any elements in the second set not found in the first. The following example shows you how to exclude matching elements:

```
DECLARE
  a LIST := list(1,2,3,4);
  b LIST := list(4,5,6,7);
BEGIN
  dbms_output.put_line(format_list(a MULTISET EXCEPT b));
END;
/
```

Only the element 4 exists in both sets. The operation therefore removes 4 from the first set. The following output is generated by the block:

```
(1,  2,  3)
```

This section has demonstrated how you can use set operators to exclude elements from one set when they are in another.

MULTISET INTERSECT Operator

The `MULTISET INTERSECT` operator lets you find the intersection or matching values between two sets. The following example shows you how to create a set of the intersection between two sets:

```
DECLARE
  a LIST := list(1,2,3,4);
  b LIST := list(4,5,6,7);
BEGIN
  dbms_output.put_line(format_list(a MULTISET INTERSECT b));
END;
/
```

Only one element from both sets matches, and that's the number 4. The following output is generated by the block:

```
(1,  2,  3)
```

This section has demonstrated how you can use set operators to create sets of the intersection between two sets.

MULTISET UNION Operator

The `MULTISET UNION` operator performs a `UNION ALL` operation on two collections. The following example demonstrates how to combine the sets into one set:

```
DECLARE
  a LIST := list(1,2,3,4);
  b LIST := list(4,5,6,7);
BEGIN
  dbms_output.put_line(format_list(a MULTISET UNION b));
END;
/
```

The operation result of the `MULTISET UNION` is passed as an actual parameter to the `format_list` function. The function converts it into the string

```
(1, 2, 3, 4, 4, 5, 6, 7)
```

You'll notice that both sets contain the integer 4, and the resulting set has two copies of it. You can eliminate the duplication and mimic a `UNION` operator by appending the `DISTINCT` operator:

```
DECLARE
  a LIST := list(1,2,3,4);
  b LIST := list(4,5,6,7);
BEGIN
  dbms_output.put_line(format_list(a MULTISET UNION DISTINCT b));
END;
/
```

Alternatively, you can take the result of the `MULTISET UNION DISTINCT` operation and pass it as an argument to the `SET` operator to eliminate duplicates.

```
DECLARE
  a LIST := list(1,2,3,4);
  b LIST := list(4,5,6,7);
BEGIN
  dbms_output.put_line(format_list(SET(a MULTISET UNION b)));
END;
/
```

Both the `DISTINCT` and `SET` operators produce the following output:

```
(1, 2, 3, 4, 5, 6, 7)
```

This section has demonstrated how you can use the set operations with collection to create supersets of two sets with or without duplicate values.

SET Operator

The `SET` operator acts on a single input, which is another set. It removes any duplicates from the set and returns a new set with unique values. The following example demonstrates how to pare a set into unique elements:

```
DECLARE
  a LIST := list(1,2,3,3,4,4,5,6,6,7);
BEGIN
  dbms_output.put_line(format_list(SET(a)));
END;
/
```

The original set contains ten elements, but three are duplicated. The `SET` operator removes all duplicates and generates a new set with seven unique elements.

```
(1, 2, 3, 4, 5, 6, 7)
```

You can also use `SET` as an operand in comparison statements:

```
DECLARE
  a LIST := list(1,2,3,4);
  b LIST := list(1,2,3,3,4,4);
  c LIST := list();
  FUNCTION isset (set_in LIST) RETURN VARCHAR2 IS
  BEGIN
    IF set_in IS A SET THEN
      IF set_in IS NOT EMPTY THEN
        RETURN 'Yes - a unique collection.';
      ELSE
        RETURN 'Yes - an empty collection.';
      END IF;
    ELSE
      RETURN 'No - a non-unique collection.';
    END IF;
  END isset;
BEGIN
  dbms_output.put_line(isset(a));
  dbms_output.put_line(isset(b));
  dbms_output.put_line(isset(c));
END;
/
```

NOTE
*Always remember to use empty parentheses when you build empty
collections. If you forget the parentheses because you don't need them
to call some functions or procedures, you'll raise an* ORA-00330
error—invalid use of type name.

The program returns

```
Yes - a unique collection.
No  - a non-unique collection.
Yes - an empty collection.
```

This anonymous block demonstrates that the IS A SET comparison returns true when the
collection is either unique or empty. You must use the IS EMPTY comparison to capture empty
collections, as done in the format_set function previously shown.

This section has demonstrated how you can use set operators to create sets of the intersection
between two sets.

SUBMULTISET Operator

The SUBMULTISET operator compares the left operand against the right operand to determine if
the left operand is a subset of the right operand. It returns a Boolean true when it finds all elements
in the left set are also in the right set.

The following example demonstrates how to determine if a set is a subset of another:

```
DECLARE
  a LIST := list(1,2,3,4);
  b LIST := list(1,2,3,3,4,5);
```

```
    c LIST := list(1,2,3,3,4,4);
BEGIN
  IF a SUBMULTISET c THEN
    dbms_output.put_line('[a] is a subset of [c]');
  END IF;
  IF NOT b SUBMULTISET c THEN
    dbms_output.put_line('[b] is not a subset of [c]');
  END IF;
END;
/
```

It prints

```
[a] is a subset of [c]
[b] is not a subset of [c]
```

This demonstrates that all elements of set a are in set c and all elements in set b are not. You should note that this function looks for subsets, not proper subsets. A proper subset differs because it contains at least one element less than the set.

NOTE
The set operators only work when the collections are lists of scalar variables. They return a PLS-00306 *exception when you attempt to use a user-defined object type.*

Collection API

Oracle 8i introduced the Collection API. The Collection API is provided to give simplified access to collections. These methods did simplify access before Oracle 11g. Unfortunately, they were not critical to master. The shift from Oracle 9i index-by tables to Oracle 11g associative arrays makes them critical for you to understand. You covered the reason working with associative arrays. The FIRST, LAST, NEXT, and PRIOR methods are the only way to navigate unique string indexes.

The Collection API methods are really not methods in a truly object-oriented sense. They are functions and procedures. Three, EXTEND, TRIM, and DELETE, are procedures. The rest are functions.

Table 7-3 summarizes the Oracle 11g Collection API.

Method	Description
COUNT	The COUNT method returns the number of elements with allocated space in VARRAY and NESTED TABLE datatypes. The COUNT method returns all elements in associative arrays. The return value of the COUNT method can be smaller than the return value of LIMIT for the VARRAY datatypes. It has the following prototype: pls_integer COUNT

TABLE 7-3 *Oracle 11g Collection API*

Method	Description
DELETE	The DELETE method lets you delete members from the collection. It has two formal parameters; one is mandatory and the other is optional. Both parameters accept PLS_INTEGER, VARCHAR2, and LONG variable types. Only one actual parameter, n, is interpreted as the index value to delete from the collection. When you supply two actual parameters, the function deletes everything from the parameter n to m, inclusively. It has the following prototypes: void DELETE(n) void DELETE(n,m)
EXISTS	The EXISTS method checks to find an element with the supplied index in a collection. It returns true when the element is found and false otherwise. The element may contain a value or a null value. It has one mandatory parameter, and the parameter can be a PLS_INTEGER, VARCHAR2, or LONG type. It has the following prototype: boolean EXISTS(n)
EXTEND	The EXTEND method allocates space for one or more new elements in a VARRAY or NESTED TABLE collection. It has two optional parameters. It adds space for one element by default without any actual parameter. A single optional parameter designates how many physical spaces should be allocated, but it is constrained by the LIMIT value for VARRAY datatypes. When two optional parameters are provided, the first designates how many elements should be allocated space and the second designates the index it should use to copy the value to the newly allocated space. It has the following prototypes: void EXTEND void EXTEND(n) void EXTEND(n,i)
FIRST	The FIRST method returns the lowest subscript value in a collection. It can return a PLS_INTEGER, VARCHAR2, or LONG type. It has the following prototype: mixed FIRST
LAST	The LAST method returns the highest subscript value in a collection. It can return a PLS_INTEGER, VARCHAR2, or LONG type. It has the following prototype: mixed LAST
LIMIT	The LIMIT method returns the highest possible subscript value in a collection. It can only return a PLS_INTEGER type and can only be used by a VARRAY datatype. It has the following prototype: mixed LIMIT
NEXT(n)	The NEXT method returns the next higher subscript value in a collection when successful or a false. The return value is a PLS_INTEGER, VARCHAR2, or LONG type. It requires a valid index value as an actual parameter. It has the following prototype: mixed NEXT(n)

TABLE 7-3   *Oracle 11g Collection API (continued)*

Method	Description
PRIOR(*n*)	The PRIOR method returns the next lower subscript value in a collection when successful or a false. The return value is a PLS_INTEGER, VARCHAR2, or LONG type. It requires a valid index value as an actual parameter. It has the following prototype: `mixed PRIOR(n)`
TRIM	The TRIM method removes a subscripted value from a collection. It has one optional parameter. Without an actual parameter, it removes the highest element form the array. An actual parameter is interpreted as the number of elements removed from the end of the collection. It has the following prototypes: `void TRIM` `void TRIM(n)`

TABLE 7-3   *Oracle 11g Collection API* (continued)

You will examine each of the methods in alphabetical order. Some examples include multiple Collection API methods. As in the coverage of the collection types, it is hard to treat the Collection API methods in isolation. Where a single example fully covers multiple methods, it will be cross-referenced; sometimes it may be forward-referenced. Under each Collection API method, you will be referred to appropriate example code. You will examine each of the Collection API methods in example programs. It should be noted that only the EXISTS method will fail to raise an exception if the collection is empty.

There are five standard collection exceptions. They are described in Table 7-4.

Collection Exception	Raised By
COLLECTION_IS_NULL	An attempt to use a null collection.
NO_DATA_FOUND	An attempt to use a subscript that has been deleted or is a nonexistent unique string index value in an associative array.
SUBSCRIPT_BEYOND_COUNT	An attempt to use a numeric index value that is higher than the current maximum number value. This error applies only to varrays and nested tables. Associative arrays are not bound by the COUNT return value when adding new elements.
SUBSCRIPT_OUTSIDE_LIMIT	An attempt to use a numeric index value outside of the LIMIT return value. This error only applies to varrays and nested tables. The LIMIT value is defined one of two ways. Varrays set the maximum size, which becomes their limit value. Nested tables and associative arrays have no fixed maximum size, so the limit value is set by the space allocated by the EXTEND method.
VALUE_ERROR	An attempt is made to use a type that cannot be converted to a PLS_INTEGER, which is the datatype for numeric subscripts.

TABLE 7-4   *Collection Exceptions*

COUNT Method

The COUNT method is really a function. It has no formal parameter list. It returns the number of elements in the array. The following example program illustrates that it returns a PLS_INTEGER value:

```
DECLARE
   TYPE number_table IS TABLE OF INTEGER;
   number_list NUMBER_TABLE := number_table(1,2,3,4,5);
BEGIN
   DBMS_OUTPUT.PUT_LINE('How many elements? ['||number_list.COUNT||']');
END;
/
```

The example program defines a local scalar collection, declares a collection variable, and uses the COUNT function to find out how many elements are in the collection. It generates the following output:

```
How many elements? [5]
```

DELETE Method

The DELETE method is really a procedure. It is an overloaded procedure. If the concept of overloading is new to you, please check Chapter 9.

It has one version that takes a single formal parameter. The parameter must be a valid subscript value in the collection. This version will remove the element with that subscript. It is illustrated in the EXISTS method example program.

The other version takes two formal parameters. Both parameters must be valid subscript values in the collection. This version deletes a continuous, inclusive range of elements from a collection. The following example program illustrates a range delete from a collection:

```
DECLARE
   TYPE number_table IS TABLE OF INTEGER;
   number_list NUMBER_TABLE;

   -- Define local procedure to check and print elements.
   PROCEDURE print_list(list_in NUMBER_TABLE) IS
   BEGIN
     -- Check whether subscripted elements are there.
     DBMS_OUTPUT.PUT_LINE('-----------------------------');
     FOR i IN list_in.FIRST..list_in.LAST LOOP
       IF list_in.EXISTS(i) THEN
         DBMS_OUTPUT.PUT_LINE('List ['||list_in(i)||']');
       END IF;
     END LOOP;
   END print_list;
BEGIN
   -- Construct collection when one doesn't exist.
   IF NOT number_list.EXISTS(1) THEN
     number_list := number_table(1,2,3,4,5);
   END IF;

   -- Print initialized contents.
```

```
  DBMS_OUTPUT.PUT_LINE('Nested table before a deletion');
  print_list(number_list);

  -- Delete a elements from 2, 3 and 4.
  number_list.DELETE(2,4);

  -- Print revised contents.
  DBMS_OUTPUT.PUT_LINE(CHR(10)||'Nested table after a deletion');
  print_list(number_list);
END;
/
```

The example program defines a local scalar collection, defines an uninitialized collection variable, initializes the collection variable, and deletes three elements from the middle of the collection. The display portion of the program uses a local procedure to print the current content of a collection.

TIP
The DBMS_OUTPUT.PUT_LINE *procedure can't print a line return if you pass it a null string. You send a* CHR(10)*, or line feed, when you want to print a line break in your output file.*

It generates the following output:

```
Nested table before a deletion
-----------------------------
List [1]
List [2]
List [3]
List [4]
List [5]

Nested table after a deletion
-----------------------------
List [1]
List [5]
```

EXISTS Method

The EXISTS method is really a function. It has only one formal parameter list that it supports. It takes a subscript value. The subscript may be a number or a unique string. The latter subscript index applies only to Oracle 11*g* associative arrays.

As mentioned, EXISTS is the *only* Collection API method that will not raise a COLLECTION_IS_NULL exception for a null element collection. Null element collections have two varieties: first, varrays and nested tables constructed with a null constructor, and second, associative arrays that have zero elements initialized.

The following program illustrates the EXISTS method. A portion of the program is redacted because it was used in a prior example program.

```
DECLARE
  TYPE number_table IS TABLE OF INTEGER;
  number_list NUMBER_TABLE;
```

```
  -- Define local procedure to check and print elements.
  PROCEDURE print_list(list_in NUMBER_TABLE) IS
  BEGIN
    -- Check whether subscripted elements are there.
    DBMS_OUTPUT.PUT_LINE('------------------------------');
    FOR i IN list_in.FIRST..list_in.LAST LOOP
      IF list_in.EXISTS(i) THEN
        DBMS_OUTPUT.PUT_LINE('List ['||list_in(i)||']');
      END IF;
    END LOOP;
  END print_list;
BEGIN
  -- Construct collection when one doesn't exist.
  IF NOT number_list.EXISTS(1) THEN
    number_list := number_table(1,2,3,4,5);
  END IF;

  -- Print initialized contents.
  DBMS_OUTPUT.PUT_LINE('Nested table before a deletion');
  print_list(number_list);

  -- Delete element 2.
  number_list.DELETE(2);

  -- Print revised contents.
  DBMS_OUTPUT.PUT_LINE(CHR(10)||'Nested table after a deletion');
  print_list(number_list);
END;
/
```

The example program defines a local scalar collection, defines an uninitialized collection variable, initializes the collection variable, and deletes the second element from the collection. The display portion of the program uses a local procedure to print the current content of a collection. *Most importantly, the* EXIST *method checks whether an element exists without raising an exception.*

It generates the following output:

```
Nested table before a deletion
------------------------------
List [1]
List [2]
List [3]
List [4]
List [5]

Nested table after a deletion
------------------------------
List [1]
List [3]
List [4]
List [5]
```

EXTEND Method

The EXTEND method is really a procedure. It is an overloaded procedure. If the concept of overloading is new to you, please check Chapter 9 on packages or Chapter 14 on objects.

It has one version that takes no formal parameters. When used without formal parameter(s), EXTEND allocates space for a new element in a collection. However, if you attempt to EXTEND space beyond a LIMIT in a varray, it will raise an exception.

A second version takes a single formal parameter. The parameter must be a valid integer value. EXTEND with a single actual parameter will allocate space for that number of elements specified by the actual parameter. As with the version without a parameter, attempting to EXTEND space beyond a LIMIT in a varray will raise an exception. This method is illustrated in the following example.

The last version takes two formal parameters. Both parameters must be valid integers. The second must also be a valid subscript value in the collection. This version allocates element space equal to the first actual parameter. Then, it copies the contents of the referenced subscript found in the second actual parameter.

The following program illustrates the EXTEND method with one and two formal parameters. A portion of the program is redacted because it was used in a prior example program.

```
DECLARE
  TYPE number_table IS TABLE OF INTEGER;
  number_list NUMBER_TABLE;

  -- Define local procedure to check and print elements.
  PROCEDURE print_list(list_in NUMBER_TABLE) IS
  BEGIN
    -- Check whether subscripted elements are there.
    DBMS_OUTPUT.PUT_LINE('-----------------------------');
    FOR i IN list_in.FIRST..list_in.LAST LOOP
      IF list_in.EXISTS(i) THEN
        DBMS_OUTPUT.PUT_LINE('List ['||list_in(i)||']');
      END IF;
    END LOOP;
  END print_list;
BEGIN
  -- Construct collection when one doesn't exist.
  IF NOT number_list.EXISTS(1) THEN
    number_list := number_table(1,2,3,4,5);
  END IF;

  -- Print initialized contents.
  DBMS_OUTPUT.PUT_LINE('Nested table before a deletion');
  print_list(number_list);

  -- Add two null value members at the end of the list.
  number_list.EXTEND(2);

  -- Add three members at the end of the list and copy the contents of item 4.
  number_list.EXTEND(3,4);

  -- Print revised contents.
```

```
   DBMS_OUTPUT.PUT_LINE(CHR(10)||'Nested table after a deletion');
   print_list(number_list);
END;
/
```

The example program defines a local scalar collection, defines an uninitialized collection variable, initializes the collection variable, adds two null value elements, and adds three elements with the value from the element indexed by 4. The display portion of the program uses a local procedure to print the current content of a collection. *The* EXTEND method allocates space to nested tables and allows you to copy contents from one element to a set of elements.

It generates the following output:

```
Nested table before a deletion
-------------------------------
List [1]
List [2]
List [3]
List [4]
List [5]

Nested table after a deletion
-------------------------------
List [1]
List [2]
List [3]
List [4]
List [5]
List []
List []
List [4]
List [4]
List [4]
```

FIRST Method

The FIRST method is really a function. It returns the lowest subscript value used in a collection. If it is a numeric index, it returns a PLS_INTEGER. If it is an associative array, it returns a VARCHAR2 or LONG datatype. You *cannot* use the FIRST method in a range FOR loop when the index is non-numeric.

The FIRST method is illustrated in the example program for the DELETE method. That example uses a numeric index. The following example demonstrates the FIRST method with a non-numeric or unique string index. As discussed, non-numeric indexes in *associative arrays* are new in Oracle 11*g* functionality. The INDEX BY clause lets you tell the difference between a nested table and an associative array because the clause only works with associative arrays.

```
DECLARE
   TYPE number_table IS TABLE OF INTEGER INDEX BY VARCHAR2(9 CHAR);
   number_list NUMBER_TABLE;
BEGIN
   -- Add elements with unique string subscripts.
   number_list('One') := 1;
   number_list('Two') := 2;
   number_list('Nine') := 9;
```

```
-- Print the first index and next.
DBMS_OUTPUT.PUT_LINE('FIRST Index ['||number_list.FIRST||']');
DBMS_OUTPUT.PUT_LINE('NEXT Index ['||number_list.NEXT(number_list.
FIRST)||']');

-- Print the last index and prior.
DBMS_OUTPUT.PUT_LINE(CHR(10)||'LAST  Index ['||number_list.LAST||']');
DBMS_OUTPUT.PUT_LINE('PRIOR Index ['||number_list.PRIOR(number_list.
LAST)||']');
END;
/
```

The example program defines a local scalar collection, defines an uninitialized collection variable, assigns elements to the associative array, and prints the FIRST, NEXT, LAST, and PRIOR index values. If you raised your eyebrows at the output, you did not catch this earlier. When using a unique string as an index value, the ordering of values is based on the NLS environment. Therefore, you generate the following output, which is ordered alphabetically:

```
FIRST Index [Nine]
NEXT  Index [One]

LAST  Index [Two]
PRIOR Index [One]
```

LAST Method

The LAST method is really a function. It returns the highest subscript value used in a collection. If it is a numeric index, it returns a PLS_INTEGER. If it is an associative array, it returns a VARCHAR2 or LONG datatype. You *cannot* use the LAST method in a range FOR loop when the index is non-numeric.

The LAST method is illustrated in the example program for the DELETE method. That example uses a numeric index. The example in the FIRST method also demonstrates the LAST method with a non-numeric or unique string index. As discussed, non-numeric indexes in associative arrays are new in Oracle 11*g* functionality.

LIMIT Method

The LIMIT method is really a function. It returns the highest possible subscript value used in a varray. It has no value for the other two collection types. It returns a PLS_INTEGER.

The example program that follows illustrates the LIMIT method:

```
DECLARE
    TYPE number_varray IS VARRAY(5) OF INTEGER;
    number_list NUMBER_VARRAY := number_varray(1,2,3);

    -- Define a local procedure to check and print elements.
    PROCEDURE print_list(list_in NUMBER_VARRAY) IS
    BEGIN
        -- Print all subscripted elements.
        DBMS_OUTPUT.PUT_LINE('--------------------------');
        FOR i IN list_in.FIRST..list_in.COUNT LOOP
            DBMS_OUTPUT.PUT_LINE('List Index ['||i||'] '||
```

```
                              'List Value ['||list_in(i)||']');
    END LOOP;
  END print_list;
BEGIN
  -- Print initial contents.
  DBMS_OUTPUT.PUT_LINE('Varray after initialization');
  print_list(number_list);

  -- Extend with null element to the maximum limit size.
  number_list.EXTEND(number_list.LIMIT - number_list.LAST);

  -- Print revised contents.
  DBMS_OUTPUT.PUT_LINE(CHR(10));
  DBMS_OUTPUT.PUT_LINE('Varray after extension');
  print_list(number_list);
END;
/
```

The example program defines a local scalar collection, defines an uninitialized collection variable, initializes the collection variable, and then extends space for as many null element values as possible. This prints the following output:

```
Varray after initialization
----------------------------
List Index [1] List Value [1]
List Index [2] List Value [2]
List Index [3] List Value [3]

Varray after extension
----------------------------
List Index [1] List Value [1]
List Index [2] List Value [2]
List Index [3] List Value [3]
List Index [4] List Value []
List Index [5] List Value []
```

NEXT Method

The NEXT method is really a function. It returns the next subscript value used in a collection. If there is no higher subscript value, it returns a null. If it is a numeric index, it returns a PLS_INTEGER. If it is an associative array, it returns a VARCHAR2 or LONG datatype.

The NEXT method is illustrated in the example program for the DELETE method. That example uses a numeric index. The example in the FIRST method also demonstrates the NEXT method with a non-numeric or unique string index. As discussed, non-numeric indexes in associative arrays are new in Oracle 11*g* functionality.

PRIOR Method

The PRIOR method is really a function. It returns the prior subscript value used in a collection. If there is no lower subscript value, it returns a null. If it is a numeric index, it returns a PLS_INTEGER. If it is an associative array, it returns a VARCHAR2 or LONG datatype.

The `PRIOR` method is illustrated in the example program for the `DELETE` method. That example uses a numeric index. The example in the `FIRST` method also demonstrates the `PRIOR` method with a non-numeric or unique string index. As discussed, non-numeric indexes in associative arrays are new in Oracle 11*g* functionality.

TRIM Method

The `TRIM` method is really a procedure. It is an overloaded procedure. If the concept of overloading is new to you, please check Chapter 9.

It has one version that takes no formal parameters. When used without formal parameter(s), `TRIM` deallocates space for an element in a collection. However, if you attempt to `TRIM` space below zero elements, it will raise an exception.

The other version takes a single formal parameter. The parameter must be a valid integer value. `TRIM` with a single actual parameter will deallocate space for the number of elements specified by the actual parameter. As with the version without a parameter, attempting to `TRIM` space below zero elements will raise an exception.

The example program that follows illustrates the `TRIM` method:

```
DECLARE
  TYPE number_varray IS VARRAY(5) OF INTEGER;
  number_list NUMBER_VARRAY := number_varray(1,2,3,4,5);

  -- Define a local procedure to check and print elements.
  PROCEDURE print_list(list_in NUMBER_VARRAY) IS
  BEGIN
    -- Print all subscripted elements.
    DBMS_OUTPUT.PUT_LINE('---------------------------');
    FOR i IN list_in.FIRST..list_in.COUNT LOOP
      DBMS_OUTPUT.PUT_LINE('List Index ['||i||'] '||
                           'List Value ['||list_in(i)||']');
    END LOOP;
  END print_list;
BEGIN
  -- Print initialized collection.
  DBMS_OUTPUT.PUT_LINE('Varray after initialization');
  print_list(number_list);

  -- Trim one element from the end of the collection.
  number_list.TRIM;

  -- Print collection minus last element.
  DBMS_OUTPUT.PUT(CHR(10));
  DBMS_OUTPUT.PUT_LINE('Varray after a trimming one element');
  print_list(number_list);

  -- Trim three elements from the end of the collection.
  number_list.TRIM(3);

  -- Print collection minus another three elements.
  DBMS_OUTPUT.PUT(CHR(10));
```

```
   DBMS_OUTPUT.PUT_LINE('Varray after a trimming three elements');
   print_list(number_list);
END;
/
```

The example program defines a local scalar collection, declares an initialized collection variable, prints the contents, trims the last element, prints the smaller contents, trims the last three elements, and prints what's left. This prints the following output:

```
Varray after initialization
--------------------------
List Index [1] List Value [1]
List Index [2] List Value [2]
List Index [3] List Value [3]
List Index [4] List Value [4]
List Index [5] List Value [5]

Varray after a trimming one element
---------------------------
List Index [1] List Value [1]
List Index [2] List Value [2]
List Index [3] List Value [3]
List Index [4] List Value [4]

Varray after a trimming three elements
---------------------------
List Index [1] List Value [1]
```

You have now gone through the complete Oracle 11*g* Collection API. It is time to summarize what you have covered in the chapter.

Summary

You have covered the definition and use of varrays, nested tables, and associative arrays, which are the Oracle 11*g* collection types. You have worked through examples in SQL DML and PL/SQL that use Oracle 11*g* collections. Finally, you worked through the details of the Collections API.

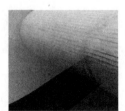

CHAPTER
8

Large Objects

arge objects (LOBs) are powerful data structures that let you store text, images, music, and video in the database. Oracle 11*g* dramatically changes the LOB landscape by reengineering how large objects work. They're now faster and more secure *(SecureFiles)*. You can now define `BLOB`, `CLOB`, or `NCLOB` columns as SecureFiles when you create a table or alter it.

LOBs can hold up to a maximum of 8 to 128 terabytes, depending on how you configure your database. A call to the `GET_STORAGE_LIMIT` function in the `DBMS_LOB` package tells you your database maximum LOB size. You can store character large objects in `CLOB` columns, and binary large objects inside the database as `BLOB` columns or outside the database as `BFILE` (binary file) columns. `BFILE` columns actually store a locator that points to the physical location of an external file.

This chapter explains how to use PL/SQL to work with the different LOB datatypes. It covers these topics:

- Character large objects
  - PL/SQL reading files and writing CLOB or NCLOB columns
  - Uploading CLOBs to the database
- Binary large objects
  - PL/SQL reading files and writing BLOB columns
  - Uploading BLOBs to the database
- SecureFiles
- External BFILEs
- Creating and using virtual directories
- The DBMS_LOB package

The concepts governing how you use `BLOB`, `CLOB`, and `NCLOB` datatypes are very similar. `CLOB` and `NCLOB` datatypes are covered first, since they let you focus on managing transactions with large blocks of text. The `BLOB` datatype comes second, because the concepts leverage those covered for character large objects. `BLOB`s store binary documents, like Adobe *PDF (Portable Document Format)* files, images, and movies, inside the database. Access and display of the `BLOB` files is supplemented by using the PHP programming language to render images in web pages. SecureFiles follow the ordinary and internally stored datatypes because they add features to `CLOB`s.

After SecureFiles, you learn how to set up, configure, read, and maintain `BFILE` datatypes. They require more effort in some ways because the catalog only stores locator data, and you have to guarantee their physical presence in the file system. The `DBMS_LOB` package is last because not all the functions are necessary to show how to use large objects. Each section builds on the one before it, but you should be able to use them individually as quick references, too.

Character Large Objects: CLOB and NCLOB Datatypes

The `CLOB` and `NCLOB` datatypes can define a column in a table or nested table. It has a maximum physical size between 8 and 128 terabytes. The `CLOB` datatype lets you store large text files. The text file can serve many purposes, such as a chapter in a book, a book in a library, or an XML fragment. This section examines text as a work unit. You can refer to the Oracle XML DB Developer's Guide for direction on using these types to support XML.

NOTE
The size variability for CLOB *datatypes is managed by the* db_block_size *database initialization parameter. The default 8KB block size limits a* CLOB *to 8 terabytes.*

CLOB columns are usually stored separately from the rest of the row in a table. Only the descriptor or locator is physically stored in the column. The locator points to where the physical contents of a CLOB are stored and provides a reference to a private work area in the SGA. This work area allows us to scroll through the content and write new chunks of data. Some reference materials use the term descriptor to refer to the BLOB, CLOB, and NCLOB locator, but they use locator when working with external BFILEs. Oracle 11*g* documentation begins to consistently label both as locators.

The CLOB datatype is an object type. As an object type, it requires implicit or explicit construction of an object instance. You can implicitly construct a CLOB variable by direct assignment of a number or character type. When you assign a number to a CLOB datatype, the number is first cast to a character datatype, and then the character datatype is converted to a CLOB datatype. Unfortunately, character conversions for CHAR, NCHAR, NVARCHAR, and VARCHAR2 datatypes are constrained by the SQL or PL/SQL environments. *SQL allows you to convert character streams up to 4,000 bytes, whereas PL/SQL lets you convert 32,767 bytes of character data at one time.*

The following examples review how you declare a CLOB variable:

```
var1 CLOB;                      -- Declare a null reference to a CLOB.
var1 CLOB := empty_clob();      -- Declare an empty CLOB.
var2 CLOB := 'some_string';     -- Declare a CLOB with a string literal.
```

CLOB columns differ from scalar datatypes because they are not limited to NULL or NOT NULL states. BLOBs, CLOBs, and NCLOBs are either NULL, empty, or populated as qualified in Table 8-1.

You insert an empty CLOB or NCLOB by calling the empty_clob() constructor as an expression in the VALUES clause of an INSERT statement. The only change for BLOB datatypes is the substitution of empty_blob() constructor. Appendix J demonstrates the basic uses of the

Initializing an Object

You declare a scalar variable by assigning a type and value. You call a function by passing actual parameters. However, you declare an object instance by calling a specialized function that initializes an object type. Initialized object types are objects or object instances.

You call the initialization process: constructing an object. Construction occurs by calling a specialized function that typically shares the name of the object type and returns an instance of the object. This specialized function is called a constructor. Object programming lingo uses the words initializing and constructing interchangeably. Both words mean giving life to an object type by creating an instance of an object.

State	Description
NULL	The column in a table row contains a null value.
Empty	The column contains a LOB locator (or descriptor) that is an empty instance. You can verify an empty LOB by calling the `DBMS_LOB.GETLENGTH` function. The function returns a zero value for an empty `BLOB`, `CLOB`, or `NCLOB` column.
Populated	The column contains a LOB locator, and a call to `DBMS_LOB.GETLENGTH` function returns a positive integer value for a `BLOB`, `CLOB`, or `NCLOB` column.

TABLE 8-1   *Possible BLOB, CLOB, and NCLOB Data States*

`EMPTY_BLOB` and `EMPTY_CLOB` functions. While this section's examples use a `CLOB` datatype, you could substitute a `NCLOB` datatype and they would also work. More or less, `CLOB` and `NCLOB` are interchangeable in regard to this section.

The initial assignment of an `EMPTY_CLOB` function call is generally the most effective in terms of resources when the object is truly large. You'll find the suggestion in the *Oracle Database Large Objects Developer's Guide*.

The following statement inserts an `empty_clob()` constructor in the `item_desc` column of the `item` table:

```
-- This is found in create_store.sql on the publisher's web site.

INSERT INTO item VALUES
( item_s1.nextval
,'ASIN: B00003CXI1'
,(SELECT   common_lookup_id
  FROM     common_lookup
  WHERE    common_lookup_type = 'DVD_WIDE_SCREEN')
,'Harry Potter and the Sorcer''s Stone'
,'Two-Disc Special Edition'
, empty_clob()
, NULL,'PG','MPAA','28-MAY-2002'
, 3, SYSDATE, 3, SYSDATE);
```

Once you've inserted an empty `CLOB`, you can update it several ways. A basic update using SQL limits you to a string of 4,000 bytes. A SQL statement example follows:

```
UPDATE item
SET    item_desc = 'Harry Potter is seemingly an ordinary eleven-year-old boy, '
WHERE  item_title = 'Harry Potter and the Sorcerer''s Stone'
AND    item_type IN
         (SELECT common_lookup_id
          FROM   common_lookup
          WHERE  common_lookup_table = 'ITEM'
          AND    common_lookup_column = 'ITEM_TYPE'
          AND    REGEXP_LIKE(common_lookup_type,'^(DVD|VHS)*'))
```

This UPDATE statement set the item_desc column equal to a string less than 4,000 bytes. The subquery against the common_lookup table uses a regular expression to find all common_lookup_type columns that start with either uppercase DVD or VHS. You can find more on regular expressions in Appendix E.

If you transfer the UPDATE statement to the inside of a PL/SQL block, you can assign a 32,767-byte string to the CLOB column. However, you must then use the WRITEAPPEND procedure from the DBMS_LOB package to append additional data to the column after the initial write. This approach is probably the easiest and most widely available PL/SQL code snippet on the web writing a CLOB column. The solution uses the DBMS_LOB package to read a file. Then, it loads the data to the CLOB in 32,767-byte chunks through the DBMS_LOB.WRITEAPPEND procedure. Appendix J contains a similar use of the DBMS_LOB.WRITEAPPEND procedure.

The problem with this approach is that it doesn't leverage the RETURNING INTO clause, which you can add to any INSERT or UPDATE DML statements. You transform INSERT or UPDATE statements into function calls by adding this clause.

The RETURING clause declares a formal OUT mode parameter as the target of the INTO predicate. The clause anchors a column descriptor to the OUT mode variable. The actual parameter must be a declared CLOB or NCLOB variable. It effectively opens a stream resource into the large object column that lets you circumvent the size limitations of SQL and PL/SQL. Figure 8-1 shows the process of how the RETURNING INTO clause works.

You have the ability to write to the CLOB or NCLOB column from the beginning of either an INSERT or UPDATE statement (which opens the stream) until the end of the transaction scope. A COMMIT or ROLLBACK statement ends the transaction scope inside SQL or a PL/SQL block and closes the large object stream. Another nuance would be the termination of an autonomous block, which may also commit the write.

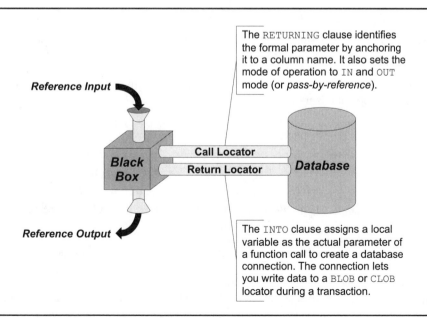

FIGURE 8-1 *The implicit LOB locator function architecture*

The following INSERT and UPDATE statement prototypes demonstrate a specialized approach to managing LOB datatypes. The RETURNING keyword of the RETURNING INTO clause is awkward at first, but *it means channeling out the column reference into a local variable.*

INSERT Statement

The INSERT statement initializes a CLOB column, and then it returns the locator through the RETURNING INTO clause into a local variable. The local variable is passed by reference and has an OUT mode of operation. You can check Chapter 6 for details on the OUT mode operation, but essentially it disallows the submission of a value to a formal parameter in a function signature. In the INSERT statement, the assignment inside the values clause acts as part of an IN mode operation. The insert also starts a transaction scope. You can add to or replace the contents pointed to by the locator during the scope of this transaction.

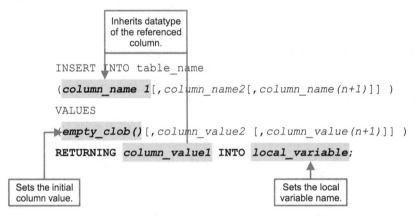

UPDATE Statement

The UPDATE statement sets a CLOB column value with EMPTY_CLOB function, and then it returns the column locator through the RETURNING INTO clause into a local variable. The local variable is passed by reference and has an OUT mode of operation. Like the INSERT statement, an update also starts a transaction scope. You can add to or replace the contents pointed to by the locator during the scope of this transaction.

```
              Sets the initial
              column value.
UPDATE table_name
SET    column_name1 = column_value1
[,     column_name2 = empty_clob()
[,     column_name(n+1) = column_value(n+1)]] )
RETURNING column_value2 INTO local_variable;
     Inherits datatype
     of the referenced              Sets the local
     column.                        variable name.
```

Ultimately, reading and writing in chunks is necessary for files that are hundreds of megabytes, gigabytes, or terabytes in size but not for files that are less than 100 megabytes. Some developers resort to C, C++, C#, Java, or PHP to accomplish reading and writing small CLOB files. PL/SQL supports your writing these files without relying on external files. The first subsection shows you how to read external files and write them as CLOB columns. The solution in this section uses PL/SQL exclusively. The subsequent subsection provides a PHP example that shows you how to upload a file, write the data stream directly to a CLOB column, and then read the column contents into a web page.

NOTE
The examples in this section work with the item *table from the companion programs found on the publisher's web site. The introduction covers the code tree for this book.*

The following subsections discuss methods for reading and writing CLOB or NCLOB columns to database columns. The first one discusses a database server solution, and the second provides you with a PL/SQL procedure to support uploading CLOB or NCLOB across the remotely.

PL/SQL Reading Files and Writing CLOB or NCLOB Columns

The DBMS_LOB package provides all the tools required to load large objects directly when they exceed the byte stream limitations of SQL or PL/SQL. The first step requires that you define a virtual directory. This is done for you when you run the create_user.sql script from the publisher's web site (found in the introduction). A virtual directory is an internal directory alias that points to a canonical path.

In this example, you create a virtual directory that points to your local temporary directory. You must connect as the SYSTEM user to define virtual directories. The following commands work on your specific operating system:

Linux or Unix

```
CREATE DIRECTORY generic AS '/tmp';
```

Windows

```
CREATE DIRECTORY generic AS 'C:\Windows\temp';
```

After you create the virtual directory, you need to grant read permissions on the directory to the plsql user. The syntax is

```
GRANT READ ON DIRECTORY generic TO plsql;
```

The next steps are reading the file and writing the data to the CLOB column. While a couple small snippets could show concepts, a single working code example is provided. This way, you can cut and paste it right in to your applications. The example uses NDS (Native Dynamic SQL). You should check Chapter 11 if you're curious about the mechanics of NDS.

The following load_clob_from_file procedure demonstrates how you do this:

```
-- This is found in load_clob_from_file.sql on the publisher's web site.
CREATE OR REPLACE PROCEDURE load_clob_from_file
( src_file_name      IN VARCHAR2
, table_name         IN VARCHAR2
, column_name        IN VARCHAR2
, primary_key_name   IN VARCHAR2
, primary_key_value  IN VARCHAR2 ) IS
  -- Define local variables for DBMS_LOB.LOADCLOBFROMFILE procedure.
  des_clob    CLOB;
```

```
  src_clob    BFILE := BFILENAME('GENERIC',src_file_name);
  des_offset NUMBER := 1;
  src_offset NUMBER := 1;
  ctx_lang    NUMBER := dbms_lob.default_lang_ctx;
  warning     NUMBER;
  -- Define a pre-reading size.
  src_clob_size NUMBER;
  -- Define local variable for Native Dynamic SQL.
  stmt VARCHAR2(2000);
BEGIN
  -- Opening source file is a mandatory operation.
  IF dbms_lob.fileexists(src_clob) = 1 AND NOT dbms_lob.isopen(src_clob) = 1 THEN
    src_clob_size := dbms_lob.getlength(src_clob);
    dbms_lob.open(src_clob,DBMS_LOB.LOB_READONLY);
  END IF;
  -- Assign dynamic string to statement.
  stmt := 'UPDATE '||table_name||' '
       || 'SET    '||column_name||' = empty_clob() '
       || 'WHERE  '||primary_key_name||' = '||''''||primary_key_value||''' '
       || 'RETURNING '||column_name||' INTO :locator';
  -- Run dynamic statement.
  EXECUTE IMMEDIATE stmt USING OUT des_clob;
  -- Read and write file to CLOB, close source file and commit.
  dbms_lob.loadclobfromfile( dest_lob     => des_clob
                           , src_bfile    => src_clob
                           , amount       => dbms_lob.getlength(src_clob)
                           , dest_offset  => des_offset
                           , src_offset   => src_offset
                           , bfile_csid   => dbms_lob.default_csid
                           , lang_context => ctx_lang
                           , warning      => warning );
  dbms_lob.close(src_clob);
  IF src_clob_size = dbms_lob.getlength(des_clob) THEN
    $IF $$DEBUG = 1 $THEN
      dbms_output.put_line('Success!');
    $END
    COMMIT;
  ELSE
    $IF $$DEBUG = 1 $THEN
      dbms_output.put_line('Failure.');
    $END
    RAISE dbms_lob.operation_failed;
  END IF;
END load_clob_from_file;
/
```

The procedure takes arguments that let you use it against any table that has a single CLOB column and one column primary key. The DBMS_LOB.OPEN procedure call opens the external file and reads it into a BFILE datatype. The BFILENAME function secures the canonical directory path from the database catalog and appends the filename. The BFILENAME function returns a canonical filename. The dynamic UPDATE statement sets the CLOB column to an empty_clob(). Then, the UPDATE statement returns the designated column into an output variable. The :locator bind variable is the output variable in the NDS statement. You assign the CLOB locator to the des_clob variable when the NDS statement runs.

NOTE
An UPDATE *statement that uses a* RETURNING INTO *changes the target column value for all updated rows.*

All the preceding actions read the source file and thread to a CLOB column locator into the program scope. With these two resource handlers, the call to LOADCLOBFROMFILE procedure transfers the contents of the open file to the CLOB locator. This read-and-write operation is not subject to the 32,767-byte handling limitation of PL/SQL. It is also an approach that lets you read large chunks of files directly into CLOB columns. The source file offset (src_offset) and destination CLOB column offset (dest_offset) values let you parse chunks out of the file and place them in the CLOB column. All you need to do is add the logic for a loop, since the sample files are relatively small but larger than 4,000 bytes (which limits a direct assignment inside an UPDATE statement).

You can test this stored procedure by running the following anonymous-block program:

```
-- This is found in load_clob_from_file.sql on the publisher's web site.
BEGIN
  FOR i IN (SELECT item_id
            FROM   item
            WHERE  item_title = 'The Lord of the Rings - Fellowship of the Ring'
            AND    item_type IN
                     (SELECT common_lookup_id
                      FROM   common_lookup
                      WHERE  common_lookup_table = 'ITEM'
                      AND    common_lookup_column = 'ITEM_TYPE'
                      AND    REGEXP_LIKE(common_lookup_type,'^(dvd|vhs)*','i')))
  LOOP
     -- Call reading and writing CLOB procedure.
     load_clob_from_file( src_file_name       => 'LOTRFellowship.txt'
                        , table_name          => 'ITEM'
                        , column_name         => 'ITEM_DESC'
                        , primary_key_name    => 'ITEM_ID'
                        , primary_key_value   => TO_CHAR(i.item_id));
  END LOOP;
END;
/
```

The call to the load_clob_from_file procedure is made for every item_id value that meets the business rule, which is defined by the regular expression search. The regular expression gets all DVD and VHS rows where the item_title is "The Lord of the Rings – Fellowship of the Ring" and item_type maps to a string value starting with a DVD or VHS substring. Appendix E explains more on how you can leverage regular expressions in your Oracle 11*g* PL/SQL code.

You can run the following formatting and query to confirm that the three rows now have CLOB columns with data streams longer than 4,000 bytes.

```
-- Format column for output.
COL item_id    FORMAT 9999
COL item_title FORMAT A50
COL size       FORMAT 9,999,990

-- Query column size.
```

```
SELECT  item_id
,       item_title
,       dbms_lob.getlength(item_desc) AS "SIZE"
FROM    item
WHERE   dbms_lob.getlength(item_desc) > 0;
```

It yields the following three rows:

```
ITEM_ID ITEM_TITLE                                        SIZE
---------- ----------------------------------------------- ------
      1037 The Lord of the Rings - Fellowship of the Ring  5,072
      1038 The Lord of the Rings - Fellowship of the Ring  5,072
      1039 The Lord of the Rings - Fellowship of the Ring  5,072
```

This section has shown you how to load directly from files into CLOB columns. The same rules apply for NCLOBs. There's a slight difference in how you handle BLOB columns. The difference is covered in the section "PL/SQL Reading Files and Writing BLOB Columns" later in the chapter. You have also learned how to use the DBMS_LOB package to read external files. You should note that there are fewer security restrictions than those required to process UTL_FILE or external Java file I/O operations.

Uploading CLOBs to the Database

Like PL/SQL, external programming languages work with the same limitations for uploading and writing CLOB or NCLOB columns. You must choose whether you enter small chunks (32,767 bytes) or large chunks of 1MB or beyond. This section assumes you want to upload and write large chunks through external programs.

The following solution creates a PL/SQL procedure that can support any external web programming language that works with the Oracle JDBC or OCI8 libraries. It allows you to reset and add a complete CLOB column value, but you should remember truly huge files should be written as chunks.

```
-- This is found in create_web_clob_loading.sql on the publisher's web site.
CREATE OR REPLACE PROCEDURE web_load_clob_from_file
( item_id_in IN      NUMBER
, descriptor IN OUT CLOB ) IS
BEGIN
  -- A FOR UPDATE makes this a DML transaction.
  UPDATE      item
  SET         item_desc = empty_clob()
  WHERE       item_id = item_id_in
  RETURNING item_desc INTO descriptor;
END web_load_clob_from_file;
/
```

This procedure lets you open a CLOB locator and access it from a remote program file. There are three key features in this procedure. First, the formal parameter is a CLOB locator with an IN OUT mode access. Second, the RETURNING INTO clause provides a local variable gateway into the SET clause variable. Third, the lack of a COMMIT in the stored procedure leaves the CLOB locked and DML transaction scope open for the external web program.

These sections have demonstrated how to read and write CLOB and NCLOB columns on the database tier and through external programs.

Binary Large Objects: BLOB Datatype

The BLOB datatype can define a column in a table or nested table. Like the CLOB datatype, it has a maximum physical size between 8 and 128 terabytes. The BLOB datatype lets you store large binary files, like images, music tracks, movies, or Portable Document Format (PDF) files. This section examines how you can upload, write, and read BLOB datatypes.

NOTE
Like the CLOB datatype, the BLOB datatype has a maximum column size set by the db_block_size database initialization parameter. The default 8KB block size limits a BLOB to 8 terabytes.

BLOB columns are usually stored separately from the rest of the row in a table. Only the descriptor or locator is physically stored in the column. The locator points to where the physical contents of a BLOB are stored and provides a reference to a private work area in the SGA. This work area allows us to read and write new chunks of data. Some refer to a BLOB handle as a descriptor and reserve the moniker locator for when they work with external BFILEs. Either works, but Oracle 11*g* documentation begins to consistently label both as locators. The book bows to that convention and calls them locators.

Like the CLOB datatype, the BLOB datatype is an object type. It requires implicit or explicit construction. You can implicitly construct a BLOB variable by assigning a null, an empty_blob() constructor, or a hexadecimal string. Chapter 3 covers the initialization and assignment of values to BLOB datatypes. You may also check the sidebar "Initializing an Object" earlier in this chapter for more information on constructing an object.

The following examples review how you declare a BLOB variable:

```
var1 BLOB;                    -- Declare a null reference to a BLOB.
var1 BLOB := empty_blob();    -- Declare an empty BLOB.
var2 BLOB := '43'||'41'||'52'; -- Declare a hexadecimal BLOB for CAR.
```

There are two ways to populate BLOB columns. You can load a server-side file by calling the OPEN, LOADBLOBFROMFILE, and CLOSE procedures found in the DBMS_LOB package. You can use an external programming language like Java or PHP. Java uses the JDBC libraries to write a binary stream to a BLOB column, and PHP uses the OCI8 libraries to write a binary stream.

BLOB columns differ from scalar datatypes for the same reason that CLOB columns differ. They are also not limited to NULL or NOT NULL states. BLOBs, CLOBs, and NCLOBs are either NULL, empty, or populated as qualified earlier in Table 8-1.

As in the case of the CLOB columns, there is a problem with this approach. It doesn't leverage the RETURNING INTO clause, which you can add to any INSERT or UPDATE DML statements. You transform INSERT or UPDATE statements into function calls by adding this clause.

The RETURING clause declares a formal OUT mode parameter as the target of the INTO predicate. The clause anchors a column descriptor to the OUT mode variable. The actual parameter must be a declared BLOB variable. It effectively opens a stream resource into the large object column that lets you circumvent the size limitations of SQL and PL/SQL. Figure 8-1 earlier in this chapter shows the process of how the RETURNING INTO clause works.

You have the ability to write to the BLOB column from the beginning of either an INSERT or UPDATE statement (which opens the stream) until the end of the transaction scope. A COMMIT or ROLLBACK statement ends the transaction scope inside SQL or a PL/SQL block and closes the large object stream. Another nuance would be the termination of an autonomous block, which may also commit the write.

The following INSERT and UPDATE statement prototypes demonstrate a specialized approach to managing LOB datatypes. They are mirror images to those that work with CLOB and NCLOB datatypes but for the empty_blob() constructor. The RETURING keyword of the RETURNING INTO clause *means channeling out the column reference into a local variable.*

INSERT Statement

The INSERT statement initializes a BLOB column, and then it returns the locator through the RETURNING INTO clause into a local variable. The local variable is passed by reference and has an OUT mode of operation. You can check Chapter 6 for details on the OUT mode operation, but essentially it disallows the submission of a value to a formal parameter in a function signature. In the INSERT statement, the assignment inside the values clause acts as part of an IN mode operation. The insert also starts a transaction scope. You can add to or replace the contents pointed to by the locator during the scope of this transaction.

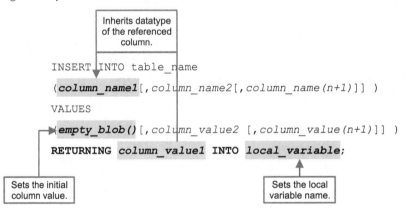

UPDATE Statement

The UPDATE statement assumes column_name2 is a BLOB datatype. It sets the BLOB column's value, and then it returns the locator through the RETURNING INTO clause to a local variable. The local variable is passed by reference and has an OUT mode of operation. Like the INSERT statement, the UPDATE statement starts a transaction scope. You can add to or replace the contents pointed to by the locator during the scope of this transaction.

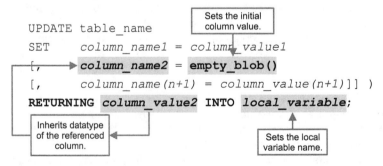

The next two sections demonstrate how you read files larger than the PL/SQL limitation for character data and write them to BLOB columns. The first one demonstrates how you can write a PL/SQL module to load a BLOB. Unfortunately, you can't read a BLOB from the database into SQL*Plus as anything other than a binary string *(not too much fun to most people)*. The reading and display examples use PHP to demonstrate how it is uploaded, written to the database, and rendered in a web page.

PL/SQL Reading Files and Writing BLOB Columns

The DBMS_LOB package provides all the tools required to load large objects directly when they exceed the buffer limitations for SQL or PL/SQL. The first step requires you define a virtual directory. This was done for you if you ran the create_user.sql script from the publisher's web site. As mentioned in the section "PL/SQL Reading Files and Writing CLOB or NCLOB Columns," however, this virtual database directory must point to a canonical path. As in the CLOB example, you need to create a virtual directory that maps to your operating system temporary directory.

You must connect as the SYSTEM user to define virtual directories. If you created this virtual directory in the last section, you can skip redefining them here. The following commands work depending on your specific operating system:

Linux or Unix

```
CREATE DIRECTORY generic AS '/tmp';
```

Windows

```
CREATE DIRECTORY generic AS 'C:\Windows\temp';
```

After you create the virtual directory, you need to grant read permissions on the directory to the plsql user. The syntax is

```
GRANT READ ON DIRECTORY generic TO plsql;
```

The next steps are reading the file and writing the data to the BLOB column. While a couple small snippets could show concepts, a single working code example is provided. The example uses NDS (Native Dynamic SQL), which makes a forward reference to material covered in Chapter 11.

The following load_blob_from_file procedure demonstrates how you do this:

```
-- This is found in load_blob_from_file.sql on the publisher's web site.
CREATE OR REPLACE PROCEDURE load_blob_from_file
( src_file_name      IN VARCHAR2
, table_name         IN VARCHAR2
, column_name        IN VARCHAR2
, primary_key_name   IN VARCHAR2
, primary_key_value  IN VARCHAR2 ) IS
  -- Define local variables for DBMS_LOB.LOADBLOBFROMFILE procedure.
  des_blob    BLOB;
  src_blob    BFILE := BFILENAME('GENERIC',src_file_name);
  des_offset  NUMBER := 1;
  src_offset  NUMBER := 1;
  -- Define a pre-reading size.
  src_blob_size NUMBER;
  -- Define local variable for Native Dynamic SQL.
  stmt VARCHAR2(2000);
BEGIN
  -- Opening source file is a mandatory operation.
  IF dbms_lob.fileexists(src_blob) = 1 AND NOT dbms_lob.isopen(src_blob) = 1 THEN
    src_blob_size := dbms_lob.getlength(src_blob);
    dbms_lob.open(src_blob,DBMS_LOB.LOB_READONLY);
```

```
  END IF;
     -- Assign dynamic string to statement.
  stmt := 'UPDATE '||table_name||' '
       || 'SET    '||column_name||' = empty_blob() '
       || 'WHERE  '||primary_key_name||' = '''''||primary_key_value||''' '
       || 'RETURNING '||column_name||' INTO :locator';
  -- Run dynamic statement.
  EXECUTE IMMEDIATE stmt USING OUT des_blob;
  -- Read and write file to BLOB.
  dbms_lob.loadblobfromfile( dest_lob      => des_blob
                           , src_bfile     => src_blob
                           , amount        => dbms_lob.getlength(src_blob)
                           , dest_offset   => des_offset
                           , src_offset    => src_offset );
  -- Close open source file.
  dbms_lob.close(src_blob);
  -- Commit write.
  IF src_blob_size = dbms_lob.getlength(des_blob) THEN
    $IF $$DEBUG = 1 $THEN
      dbms_output.put_line('Success!');
    $END
    COMMIT;
  ELSE
    $IF $$DEBUG = 1 $THEN
      dbms_output.put_line('Failure.');
    $END
    RAISE dbms_lob.operation_failed;
  END IF;
END load_blob_from_file;
/
```

The procedure takes arguments that let you use it against any table that has a single BLOB column and one column primary key. After validating the file exists and isn't open, the DBMS_LOB.OPEN procedure call opens the external file and reads it into a BFILE datatype. The BFILENAME function secures the canonical directory path from the database catalog and appends the filename. The BFILENAME function returns a canonical filename. The dynamic UPDATE statement sets the BLOB column to an empty_blob() and then returns the column into an output variable. The :locator bind variable is the output variable in the NDS statement. The program returns a BLOB locator and assigns it to the des_blob variable when the NDS statement runs. The external file size is compared against the uploaded BLOB column before committing the transaction. Conditional code blocks signal successful or unsuccessful completion of the procedure when you've set PLSQL_CCFLAGS option in the session as qualified in Chapter 4.

All the preceding actions read the source file and destination BLOB column locator into the program scope. With these two resource handlers, the call to LOADBLOBFROMFILE procedure transfers the contents of the open file to the BLOB locator. This read-and-write operation lets you put large chunks of files directly into BLOB columns. The source file offset (src_offset) and destination BLOB column offset (dest_offset) values let you parse chunks out of the file and place them in the BLOB column. You can add a loop to approach the upload a chunk at a time for very large binary files, like movies.

You can test this stored procedure by running the following anonymous-block program:

```
-- This is found in load_blob_from_file.sql on the publisher's web site.
BEGIN
```

```
   FOR i IN (SELECT item_id
             FROM    item
             WHERE   item_title = 'Harry Potter and the Sorcerer''s Stone'
             AND     item_type IN
              (SELECT common_lookup_id
               FROM    common_lookup
               WHERE   common_lookup_table = 'ITEM'
               AND     common_lookup_column = 'ITEM_TYPE'
               AND     REGEXP_LIKE(common_lookup_type,'^(dvd|vhs)*','i'))) LOOP
     -- Call procedure for matching rows.
     load_blob_from_file( src_file_name      => 'HarryPotter1.png'
                        , table_name         => 'ITEM'
                        , column_name        => 'ITEM_BLOB'
                        , primary_key_name   => 'ITEM_ID'
                        , primary_key_value  => TO_CHAR(i.item_id) );
   END LOOP;
END;
/
```

The call to the `load_blob_from_file` procedure is made for every `item_id` value that meets the business rule, which is defined by the regular expression search. The regular expression gets all DVD and VHS rows where the `item_title` is "Harry Potter and the Socerer's Stone"; the apostrophe is backquoted to treat the embedded the single quote as an embedded apostrophe. The `item_type` maps to a string value starting with a DVD or VHS substring, which means images are loaded into all the target columns for any matching rows. Appendix E explains more on how regular expressions work in Oracle 11*g*.

You can run the following formatting and query to confirm that the two rows now have BLOB columns with binary data streams longer.

```
-- Format column for output.
COL item_id    FORMAT 9999
COL item_title FORMAT A50
COL size       FORMAT 9,999,990

-- Query column size.
SELECT item_id
,      item_title
,      dbms_lob.getlength(item_blob) AS "SIZE"
FROM   item
WHERE  dbms_lob.getlength(item_blob) > 0;
```

It yields the following three rows:

```
ITEM_ID ITEM_TITLE                                          SIZE
------- -------------------------------------------------- -------
   1021 Harry Potter and the Sorcerer's Stone              121,624
   1022 Harry Potter and the Sorcerer's Stone              121,624
```

This section has shown you how to load directly from files into BLOB columns. You have also learned revisited how to use the DBMS_LOB package to read external files. You should note that there is less security restriction than that required to perform UTL_FILE or external Java file I/O operations.

Uploading BLOBs to the Database

As discussed in the parallel section for CLOB columns, external programming languages work with the same limitations for uploading and writing BLOB columns. You must choose which language and approach work best for your organization. This section assumes you want to upload the entire image as a binary file.

The following solution creates a PL/SQL procedure that can support any external web programming language that works with the Oracle JDBC or OCI8 libraries. It allows you to reset and add a complete BLOB column value, but you should remember that truly huge files should be written as chunks.

```
-- This is found in create_web_blob_loading.sql on the publisher's web site.
CREATE OR REPLACE PROCEDURE web_load_blob_from_file
( item_id_in IN      NUMBER
, descriptor IN OUT BLOB ) IS
BEGIN
  -- A FOR UPDATE makes this a DML transaction.
  UPDATE     item
  SET        item_blob = empty_blob()
  WHERE      item_id = item_id_in
  RETURNING item_blob INTO descriptor;
END web_load_blob_from_file;
/
```

This procedure lets you open a BLOB locator and access it from a PHP library file. There are three key features in this procedure. First, the formal parameter is a BLOB locator with an IN OUT mode access. Second, the RETURNING INTO clause provides a local variable gateway into the SET clause variable. Third, the lack of a COMMIT leaves the BLOB locked and DML transaction scope open for external web programs.

These sections have demonstrated how to read and write BLOB columns on the database tier and through external programs.

SecureFiles

SecureFiles are specialized large objects. They are declared with special storage parameters that let you encrypt, compress, and deduplicate them.

Oracle 11*g* lets you store SecureFiles in BLOB, CLOB, and NCLOB columns. SecureFiles let you encrypt, compress, and deduplicate LOBs. They work on a principle of Transparent Data Encryption (TDE) and use an Oracle Wallet as the encryption key.

NOTE
This is available only in the Oracle 11g Enterprise Edition.

TDE lets you choose a non-default encryption algorithm. You can choose from the following:

- 3DES168

- AES128

- AES192 (default)

- AES256

You can check whether your instance is configured to work with SecureFiles by querying the v$parameter view. The query and SQL*Plus formatting are

```
COLUMN name FORMAT A14
COLUMN value FORMAT A14
SELECT name, value FROM v$parameter WHERE name LIKE 'db_securefile';
```

You should have at least the following to work with SecureFiles:

```
NAME            VALUE
-------------- --------------
db_securefile   PERMITTED
```

The next step requires that you set up an encryption password in an Oracle 11*g* Wallet. The easiest way to configure the Wallet is to run the Oracle 11*g* Wallet Manager.

The commands are noted here:

Linux or Unix

```
# $ORACLE_HOME/bin/owm
```

Windows

```
C:> %ORACLE_HOME%\bin\launch.exe "oracle_canonical_path\bin" owm.cl
```

The menu command is probably easier. It is: Start | Programs | Oracle – Oracle Home | Integrated Management Tools | Wallet Manager. Inside the Wallet Manager you can build an encryption key. You should save it to the default location, which is

Linux or Unix

```
/etc/ORACLE/WALLETS/username
```

Windows

```
%USERPROFILE%\ORACLE\WALLETS
```

The %USERPROFILE% maps to the user name on a Windows platform. On some platforms you must put directions into the sqlnet.ora file, which you'll find in the /network/admin *(reverse the slashes for Windows)* directory off the Oracle Home. The wallet filename is ewallet.p12.

You should enter the following in the sqlnet.ora file:

```
ENCRYPTION_WALLET_LOCATION =
    (SOURCE =
     (METHOD = FILE)
     (METHOD_DATA = (DIRECTORY=<canonical_path>\wallet)))
```

After creating the Wallet password, you should create a special tablespace for your SecureFiles, like

```
CREATE TABLESPACE securefiles
DATAFILE '<canonical_path>\sec_file.dbf' SIZE 5M
EXTENT MANAGEMENT LOCAL
SEGMENT SPACE MANAGEMENT AUTO;
```

Keeping in harmony with the video store example, you'll add a secure file CLOB column to the item table. The following syntax allows you to create the new column as a secure file:

```
ALTER TABLE item ADD (sec_file CLOB) LOB(sec_file)
STORE AS SECUREFILE sec_file (TABLESPACE securefile);
```

You can now alter and encrypt the column:

```
ALTER TABLE item MODIFY LOB(sec_file) (ENCRYPT USING '3DES168');
```

You now have an encrypted column in the item table. Any internally stored LOB supports SecureFiles, but you should put them in their own tablespace.

Binary Files: BFILE Datatype

The BFILE (binary file) datatype works differently than its counterpart BLOB, CLOB, and NCLOB datatypes. The largest differences are that BFILE values are *read-only* LOB datatypes and stored externally from the database. Unlike BLOB, CLOB, and NCLOB datatypes, the BFILE has a maximum physical size set by the operating system.

External BFILEs represent data that doesn't fit nicely into standard datatypes, such as images, PDF files, Microsoft Office documents, and QuickTime movies. These external files are related to business elements inside the database by storing an external file descriptor in a BFILE column. They are generally served to Internet or intranet customers through web browsers. Web browsers use the MIME content-type to interpret how they should render these documents, which generally require browser plug-ins to manage access and display.

The first subsection explores how you configure and use the database to leverage external files that are referenced as BFILE columns. You will set up another virtual directory (like those in the earlier sections), define a BFILE locator, and examine how virtual directories limit your access to the canonical filenames of external BFILE source files. Synchronizing the Apache and Oracle virtual directories, while an administrative headache, is a traditional deployment strategy when using external BFILE source files.

The second subsection shows you how to extend the database catalog and read canonical filenames, which simplifies how you call external files from server-side programs. This is useful when you want to store files internally in the database. Appendix D also shows you how to leverage canonical filename resolution from the database, including how to read BFILE source files into server-side JServlets.

Creating and Using Virtual Directories

Virtual directories are like synonyms; they point to another thing— a physical directory on the operating system. The virtual and physical directory names are stored in the database catalog and viewable in the dba_directories view. Database users can view them when they have been granted the SELECT privilege on the view or the SELECT_CATALOG_ROLE role. By default, the SYSTEM user accesses the dba_directories view through the SELECT_CATALOG_ROLE role.

You typically create virtual directories as the SYSTEM user or as another database user that enjoys the DBA role privilege. Alternatively, the SYSTEM user can grant the CREATE ANY DIRECTORY privilege to a user. This alleviates a burden from the DBA but can lead to a proliferation of virtual directories and potential naming conflicts. You should generally disallow users other than the DBA to create virtual directories.

All virtual directories are actually owned by the SYS user. The physical directory is always the canonical path, which means a fully qualified directory path. A Linux or Unix canonical path starts at a mount point and ends at the desired directory. A Windows canonical file path starts at the physical drive letter and as in Linux or Unix ends at the desired directory.

You should connect as the SYSTEM user and define an image virtual directory. The following commands work on your specific operating system:

Linux or Unix

```
CREATE DIRECTORY images AS '/var/www/html/images';
```

Windows

```
CREATE DIRECTORY images AS 'C:\Program Files\Apache Group\Apache2\htdocs\images';
```

After you create the virtual directory, as the SYSTEM user you need to grant read permissions on the directory to the plsql user. The syntax is

```
GRANT READ ON DIRECTORY images TO plsql;
```

The next steps typically involve creating a virtual alias and directory in your Apache httpd.conf file. If you wish to configure the Apache virtual alias and directory, you can check the sidebar "Creating an Apache Virtual Alias and Directory." There are very good reasons to set virtual alias and directories in Apache. As a rule, you must mirror the definition in the Apache alias and virtual directory with the configuration of the Oracle database virtual directory. The rule exists *(rumor has it)* because the DBMS_LOB package FILEGETNAME procedure provides only the base filename; it doesn't provide a means to find canonical filenames. Canonical filenames are the combination of canonical paths and base filenames.

Creating an Apache Virtual Alias and Directory

Two Apache configuration steps are required when you want to enable a new virtual directory. You need to configure an alias and directory in your httpd.conf file, as follows for your respective platform.

Linux

```
Alias /images/ "/var/www/html/images"

<Directory "/var/www/html/images">
  Options None
  AllowOverride None
  Order allow,deny
  Allow from all
</Directory>
```

Windows

```
Alias /images/ "C:/Program Files/Apache Group/Apache2/htdocs/images/"

<Directory "C:/Program Files/Apache Group/Apache2/htdocs/images">
  Options None
  AllowOverride None
```

```
    Order allow,deny
    Allow from all
</Directory>
```

After you make these changes in your Apache configuration file, you must stop and start your Apache instance. You use the Apache service on a Windows system and the apachectl shell script on Linux or Unix systems.

As seen in the sections "PL/SQL Reading Files and Writing CLOB or NCLOB Columns" and "Reading Files and Writing BLOB Columns," you can open a file in your PL/SQL block without knowing the canonical path. This happens because the OPEN procedure in the DBMS_LOB package resolves it for you. When you read the file through the virtual directory by using the OPEN procedure, you must provide a separate module to render images in web pages. This is required because the file has been converted into a raw byte stream when opened for reading. Whenever you read the file as a byte stream, you must convert the file back into an image when rendering it in a web page. The section "PHP Uploading Files and Writing BLOB Columns" earlier in this chapter discusses why the conversion is required.

You should copy the Raiders3.png file from the publisher's web site and put it in your platform-specific physical directory that maps to your images virtual directory in the database. You can find that physical system directory (or *canonical path*) by writing the following query as the SYSTEM user:

```
SELECT * FROM dba_directories WHERE directory_name = 'IMAGES';
```

After you've configured the virtual directory and put the Raiders3.png file in the correct directory, you should insert a BFILE locator into a database column for testing. You can use the following statement to update a column with a BFILE locator:

```
UPDATE item
item_photo = BFILENAME('IMAGES','Raiders3.png')
WHERE   item_id = 1055;
```

You need to commit the update. If you forget that step, later you may get a browser error telling you the image can't be displayed because it contains errors. This is the standard error when the BFILE column returns a null or empty stream.

```
COMMIT;
```

You can verify that the file exists and the virtual directory resolves. Confirming the existence of the file before attempting to open it provides your program with more control. The following anonymous block lets you confirm the file existence and get its file size.

Naturally, you must enable SERVEROUTPUT in SQL*Plus to see any output:

```
SQL> SET SERVEROUTPUT ON SIZE 1000000
```

Then, you can run this anonymous-block program.

```
DECLARE
    file_locator BFILE;
BEGIN
    SELECT item_photo INTO file_locator FROM item WHERE item_id = 1055;
```

```
  IF dbms_lob.fileexists(file_locator) = 1 THEN
    dbms_output.put_line('File is: ['||dbms_lob.getlength(file_locator)|| ']');
  ELSE
    dbms_output.put_line('No file found.');
  END IF;
END;
/
```

The `DBMS_LOB.FILEEXISTS` function was built to work in both SQL and PL/SQL. Since SQL does not support a native Boolean datatype, the function returns a 1 when it finds a file and 0 when it fails. The anonymous block should return the following:

```
File is: [126860]
```

If you've successfully added both an images alias and a virtual directory to your Apache `httpd.conf` file, you should be able to display the file by using the following URL:

```
http://<hostname>.<domain_name>/images/Raiders3.png
```

Figure 8-2 depicts the image file found by the URL. You should note both the difference and similarity between the browser titles of Figures 8-2 and 8-3. Figure 8-3 says that a PHP program produced the image, whereas Figure 8-2 says that an image was read from the server. Both use parentheses to identify the rendered PNG image and its pixel dimensions.

While the database can read the file without an Apache alias and virtual directory, the reading process converts it to a byte stream. This puts the complexity of making an image reference on par with reading a `BLOB` column from the database. You will need to convert the byte stream back into a file. This is true whether you're using C, C++, C#, Java, or PHP to accomplish the task.

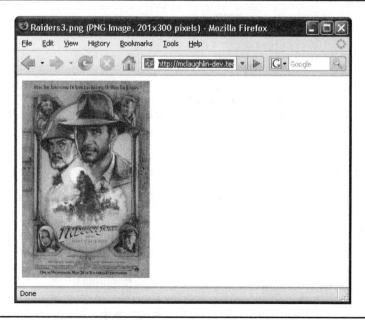

FIGURE 8-2   *PNG file rendered as an image (201 × 300 pixels)*

The following `ConvertFileToImage.php` program demonstrates how you read an external file through a virtual database directory, convert it from a file into a byte stream, and convert it from a byte stream to an image. This program can read a physical file from any virtual database directory because the program leverages the database catalog to resolve the physical file location.

```php
-- This is found in ConvertFileToImage.php on the publisher's web site.
<?php
  // Return successful attempt to connect to the database.
  if ($c = @oci_new_connect("plsql","plsql","orcl")) {
    // Declare input variables.
    (isset($_GET['id'])) ? $id = (int) $_GET['id'] : $id = 1021;
    // Declare a SQL SELECT statement returning a CLOB.
    $stmt = "SELECT item_photo FROM item WHERE item_id = :id";
    // Parse a query through the connection.
    $s = oci_parse($c,$stmt);
    // Bind PHP variables to the OCI types.
    oci_bind_by_name($s,':id',$id);
    // Execute the PL/SQL statement.
    if (oci_execute($s)) {
      // Return a LOB descriptor and free resource as the value.
      while (oci_fetch($s)) {
        for ($i = 1;$i <= oci_num_fields($s);$i++)
          if (is_object(oci_result($s,$i))) {
            if ($size = oci_result($s,$i)->size()) {
              $data = oci_result($s,$i)->read($size); }
            else
              $data = " "; }
          else {
            if (oci_field_is_null($s,$i))
              $data = " ";
            else
              $data = oci_result($s,$i); }}
      // Free statement resources.
      oci_free_statement($s);
      // Print the header first.
      header('Content-type: image/png');
      imagepng(imagecreatefromstring($data)); }
    // Disconnect from database.
    oci_close($c); }
  else {
    // Assign the OCI error and format double and single quotes.
    $errorMessage = oci_error();
    print htmlentities($errorMessage['message'])."<br />"; }
?>
```

The program reads the `BFILE` locator, which then implicitly opens the `BFILE` into a binary stream. The binary stream is read by the OCI8 `read()` method, converted to a file resource by the `imagecreatefromstring()` function, and converted to an image by the `imagepng()` function. Figure 8-3 shows the displayed image from this program.

Another approach to rendering image files involves what's known as structural coupling between the virtual Apache and database directories. This means that you define the database virtual directory as *images* when you also define the Apache alias as *images*. This lets you build a relative

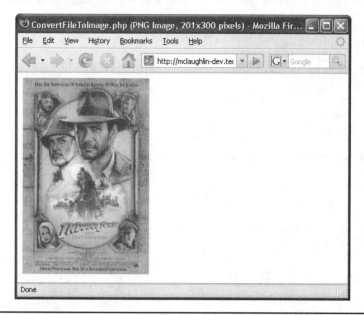

FIGURE 8-3 *BFILE column rendered as a PNG image (201 × 300 pixels)*

path to the image file location in the `src` element of the `img` tag. It also avoids the issue of converting a binary stream back into a file.

The first step in accomplishing this type of approach requires a wrapper function around the `FILEGETNAME` procedure of the `DBMS_LOB` package. The `get_bfilename` function delivers that wrapper. You may reuse this program for other tables because it uses NDS (Native Dynamic SQL) to query and return the data. The encapsulation of the `SELECT` statement inside the anonymous block lets you capture the return value easily. You will find more on NDS in Chapter 11.

```
-- This is found in get_bfilename.sql on the publisher's web site.
CREATE OR REPLACE FUNCTION get_bfilename
( table_name         VARCHAR2
, column_name        VARCHAR2
, primary_key_name   VARCHAR2
, primary_key_value VARCHAR2)
RETURN VARCHAR2 IS
  -- Define a locator.
  locator            BFILE;
  -- Define alias and filename.
  dir_alias VARCHAR2(255);
  directory VARCHAR2(255);
  file_name VARCHAR2(255);
  -- Define local variable for Native Dynamic SQL.
  stmt        VARCHAR2(2000);
  delimiter VARCHAR2(1) := '/';
  -- Define a local exception for size violation.
  directory_num EXCEPTION;
  PRAGMA EXCEPTION_INIT(directory_num,-22285);
BEGIN
```

```
-- Wrap the statement in an anonymous block to create and OUT mode variable.
stmt := 'BEGIN '
     || 'SELECT '||column_name||' '
     || 'INTO :locator '
     || 'FROM '||table_name||' '
     || 'WHERE '||primary_key_name||' = '||''''||primary_key_value||''';'
     || 'END;';
-- Return a scalar query result from a dynamic SQL statement.
EXECUTE IMMEDIATE stmt USING OUT locator;
-- Check for available locator.
IF locator IS NOT NULL THEN
  dbms_lob.filegetname(locator,dir_alias,file_name);
END IF;
-- Return filename.
RETURN delimiter||LOWER(dir_alias)||delimiter||file_name;
EXCEPTION
  WHEN directory_num THEN
  RETURN NULL;
END get_bfilename;
/
```

The `dir_alias` is the virtual database directory name. The function returns the `dir_alias`, a / (forward slash), and a base filename. Assuming that you're using the `Raiders3.png` file, you can call the standalone function through a query:

```
SELECT get_bfilename('ITEM','ITEM_PHOTO','ITEM_ID','1055') AS directory
FROM   dual;
```

It should return:

```
DIRECTORY
--------------------
/images/Raiders3.png
```

The `QueryRelativeBFILE.php` program uses the `get_bfilename` return value as the `src` element of the `img` tag. This works *only when the Apache alias also points to the same location.* The query inside the PHP program makes a call to the `get_bfilename` function and returns the value as the third element in the query. The PHP program assumes that the virtual path is the only string returned with a leading / forward slash. You probably want to explore other alternatives when you can have more than one image location in a single row of data.

The `QueryRelativeBFILE.php` follows:

```
-- This is found in QueryRelativeBFILE.php on the publisher's web site.
<?php
  // Declare input variables.
  (isset($_GET['id']))    ? $id = (int) $_GET['id'] : $id = 1021;
  // Call the local function.
  query_insert($id);
  // Query results after an insert.
  function query_insert($id) {
    // Return successful attempt to connect to the database.
    if ($c = @oci_connect("plsql","plsql","orcl")) {
      // Declare a SQL SELECT statement returning a CLOB.
      $stmt = "SELECT   item_title
             ,          item_desc
```

```
                ,              get_bfilename('ITEM','ITEM_PHOTO','ITEM_ID',:id)
             FROM        item
             WHERE       item_id = :id";
  // Parse a query through the connection.
  $s = oci_parse($c,$stmt);
  // Bind PHP variables to the OCI types.
  oci_bind_by_name($s,':id',$id);
  // Execute the PL/SQL statement.
  if (oci_execute($s)) {
    // Return a LOB descriptor as the value.
    while (oci_fetch($s)) {
      for ($i = 1;$i <= oci_num_fields($s);$i++)
        if (is_object(oci_result($s,$i))) {
          if ($size = oci_result($s,$i)->size())
            if (oci_field_type($s,$i) == 'CLOB')
              $data = oci_result($s,$i)->read($size);
          else
            $data = " "; }
        else {
          if (oci_field_is_null($s,$i))
            $title = " ";
          else
            if (substr(oci_result($s,$i),0,1) == '/')
              $photo = oci_result($s,$i);
            else
              $title = oci_result($s,$i); }
    } // End of the while(oci_fetch($s)) loop.
    // Free statement resources.
    oci_free_statement($s);
    // Format HTML table to display BLOB photo and CLOB description.
    $out = '<table border="1" cellpadding="5" cellspacing="0">';
    $out .= '<tr>';
    $out .= '<td align="center" class="e">'.$title.'</td>';
    $out .= '</tr>';
    $out .= '<tr><td class="v">';
    $out .= '<div>';
    $out .= '<div style="margin-right:5px;float:left">';
    $out .= '<img src="'.$photo.'">';
    $out .= '</div>';
    $out .= '<div style="position=relative;">'.$data.'</div>';
    $out .= '</div>';
    $out .= '</td></tr>';
    $out .= '</table>'; }
  // Print the HTML table.
  print $out;
  // Disconnect from database.
  oci_close($c); }
else {
  // Assign the OCI error and format double and single quotes.
  $errorMessage = oci_error();
  print htmlentities($errorMessage['message'])."<br />"; }}
?>
```

While the `QueryRelativeBFILE.php` works for web-based solutions, it fails to work for server-side programs that require the canonical filename, which is always an absolute value. It is less expensive in terms of machine resources because it only reads the image file and serves it to the Apache server. The problems with this approach are twofold. First, you have an administrative duty to synchronize the two virtual directories. Second, any user can view the source and determine some information about your physical file structure. As a security precaution, consuming a small amount of overhead to obfuscate *(hide)* the location of files is a good thing. Likewise, eliminating the job of synchronizing Apache and Oracle 11*g* virtual directories makes your application less expensive to maintain. Figure 8-4 shows the output from of this relative image query.

This section has shown you how to configure and use virtual directories to support external `BFILE` locators. It has also compared the process of using Apache alias and virtual directories to the process of using the database to resolve of external file locations. The next section shows you how to remake the rules, and how to access the canonical path names and filenames stored in the database catalog.

Reading Canonical Path Names and Filenames

This section demonstrates how you can modify the database catalog and enable your programs to translate `BFILE` locator to secure both the canonical path name and filename. You must open permissions to secure the virtual directory information owned by the `SYS` user. As a rule of thumb, you should grant access to `SYS` objects with care and allow *only* the minimum access required when building your database applications. This generally translates to a two-step process. First, grant the privilege from `SYS` to `SYSTEM`. Second, encapsulate the privilege by writing a stored function or procedure *(and don't forget to wrap the source from prying eyes, too).*

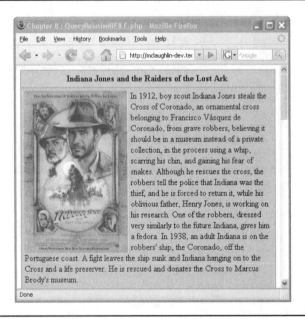

FIGURE 8-4   *Rendered page from the QueryRelativeBFILE.php program*

The data required for capturing canonical paths is found in the dba_directories view. The SYSTEM user only has privileges through the SELECT_CATALOG_ROLE role, which limits the SYSTEM user access to the dba_directories view. Role privileges disallow a user to build a stored function or procedure that queries the catalog view. Hence, the SYSTEM user can't access the dba_directories view through the SELECT_CATALOG_ROLE role.

You need to connect as the privileged SYS user as follows:

```
sqlplus '/ as sysdba'
```

This will require the database administrator password. This is typically the same as the SYSTEM password. Sometimes the passwords differ because a company chooses to monitor the gatekeeper more closely as a result of Sarbane-Oxley compliance. After connecting as the SYS user, you should grant the minimum necessary privilege, which is SELECT on the specific view.

The grant command is

```
GRANT select ON dba_directories TO system;
```

Now, you should connect as the SYSTEM user and create the get_directory_path function, as follows:

```
-- This is found in get_directory_path.sql on the publisher's web site.
CREATE OR REPLACE FUNCTION get_directory_path
( virtual_directory IN VARCHAR2 )
RETURN VARCHAR2 IS
  -- Define return variable.
  directory_path VARCHAR2(256) := 'C:\';
  -- Define dynamic cursor.
  CURSOR get_directory (virtual_directory VARCHAR2) IS
    SELECT   directory_path
    FROM     sys.dba_directories
    WHERE    directory_name = virtual_directory;
  -- Define a local exception for name violation.
  directory_name EXCEPTION;
  PRAGMA EXCEPTION_INIT(directory_name,-22284);
BEGIN
  OPEN  get_directory (virtual_directory);
  FETCH get_directory
  INTO  directory_path;
  CLOSE get_directory;
  -- Return filename.
  RETURN directory_path;
EXCEPTION
  WHEN directory_name THEN
  RETURN NULL;
END get_directory_path;
/
```

The get_directory_path takes a virtual directory as its only formal parameter. It uses the virtual directory to find the canonical path. You can use the FILEGETNAME procedure in the DBMS_LOB package to find the virtual directory. It returns the canonical path and base filename for any BFILE locator.

The `get_canonical_bfilename` uses NDS (Native Dynamic SQL) to return a BFILE column. This way you write one function for any number of possible BFILE columns. The only problem with this example is that it depends on a single-column primary key for all target tables. You should compile the `get_canonical_bfilename` function in the SYSTEM schema after you've compiled the `get_directory_path` function.

```
-- This is found in get_canonical_bfilename.sql on the publisher's web site.
CREATE OR REPLACE FUNCTION get_canonical_bfilename
( table_name          IN      VARCHAR2
, bfile_column_name IN      VARCHAR2
, primary_key        IN      VARCHAR2
, primary_key_value IN      VARCHAR2
, operating_system  IN      VARCHAR2 := 'WINDOWS')
RETURN VARCHAR2 IS
  -- Declare default delimiter.
  delimiter          VARCHAR2(1) := '\';
  -- Define statement variable.
  stmt               VARCHAR2(200);
  -- Define a locator.
  locator            BFILE;
  -- Define alias and filename.
  dir_alias          VARCHAR2(255);
  directory          VARCHAR2(255);
  file_name          VARCHAR2(255);
  -- Define a local exception for size violation.
  directory_num EXCEPTION;
  PRAGMA EXCEPTION_INIT(directory_num,-22285);
BEGIN
  -- Assign dynamic string to statement.
  stmt := 'BEGIN '
       || ' SELECT '||bfile_column_name||' '
       || ' INTO :column_value '
       || ' FROM   '||table_name||' '
       || ' WHERE '||primary_key||'='||''''||primary_key_value||''''||';'
       || 'END;';
  -- Run dynamic statement.
  EXECUTE IMMEDIATE stmt USING OUT locator;
  -- Check for available locator.
  IF locator IS NOT NULL THEN
    dbms_lob.filegetname(locator,dir_alias,file_name);
  END IF;
  -- Check operating system and swap delimiter when necessary.
  IF operating_system <> 'WINDOWS' THEN
    delimiter := '/';
  END IF;
  -- Create a canonical filename.
  file_name := get_directory_path(dir_alias) || delimiter || file_name;
  -- Return filename.
  RETURN file_name;
EXCEPTION
  WHEN directory_num THEN
```

```
   RETURN NULL;
END get_canonical_bfilename;
/
```

The dir_alias *(database virtual directory)*, directory *(canonical directory)*, and file_name *(base filename)* variables must be defined as 255 character–long strings before calling the FILEGETNAME procedure from the DBMS_LOB package. The balance of the function concatenates *(glues)* the canonical path and base filename together into a canonical filename.

While you may choose to grant this to only one or a select handful of scheme *(or users)*, you should consider making it a public grant like this:

```
GRANT EXECUTE ON get_canonical_bfilename TO PUBLIC;
```

Assuming you'll want to build a synonym because that's how the example works, as the SYSTEM user you need to grant the CREATE ANY SYNONYM privilege to the plsql user. The syntax is

```
GRANT CREATE ANY SYNONYM TO plsql;
```

You also need to create synonyms for any tables or views that the SYSTEM user should be able to query. In this example, only the item table from the video store is required:

```
CREATE SYNONYM item ON plsql.item;
```

While this synonym can't translate until the reciprocal grant is made, you'll do that in a moment. Reconnect as the plsql user:

```
SQL> connect plsql/plsql@orcl
```

and create the synonym:

```
CREATE SYNONYM get_canonical_bfilename FOR system.get_canonical_bfilename;
```

Then, grant the SELECT privilege to the SYSTEM user:

```
GRANT SELECT ON item TO SYSTEM;
```

Now you can call the get_canonical_bfilename and get the canonical filename for the Raiders3.png file:

```
CALL get_canonical_bfilename('ITEM','ITEM_PHOTO','ITEM_ID','1055' INTO :directory;
```

It returns the operating system specific values (provided you've set it up earlier):

Linux or Unix

```
/var/www/html/images/Raiders3.png
```

Windows

```
C:\Program Files\Apache Group\Apache2\htdocs\images\Raiders3.png
```

This approach avoids configuring the Apache alias and virtual directory. It is also a handy alternative in some organizations where control of virtual paths is strictly regulated and restricted. However, it still requires you to read and convert the binary stream into an image or document. At least this is true for web pages. Other server-side programs can leverage this mechanism to read images directly from their physical location. Appendix D has an example that uses this approach to reading files.

Two programs let you implement this type of solution much as you implemented a read of both CLOB and BLOB columns in the section "PHP Uploading Files and Writing BLOB Columns" earlier in this chapter. Before working through these steps, you should download the Raiders3.txt file from the publisher's web site, and load it to the database with one of the tools introduced earlier in this chapter.

The file upload is more complex than the previous examples because the file directory is no longer guaranteed to be a subdirectory of the directory containing an uploading web page. Therefore, we'll focus on the two scripts that are required to read and display the externally stored BFILE and internally stored CLOB description.

The QueryItemBFILE.php script reads the title and CLOB description from the item table, and the script calls the ReadCanonicalFileToImage.php script inside a src element of an img tag. The program follows:

```php
-- This is found in QueryItemBFILE.php on the publisher's web site.
<?php
  // Declare input variables.
  (isset($_GET['id']))      ? $id = (int) $_GET['id'] : $id = 1021;
  // Call the local function.
  query_insert($id);
  // Query results after an insert.
  function query_insert($id) {
    // Return successful attempt to connect to the database.
    if ($c = @oci_connect("plsql","plsql","orcl")) {
      // Declare a SQL SELECT statement returning a CLOB.
      $stmt = "SELECT item_title, item_desc FROM item WHERE item_id = :id";
      // Parse a query through the connection.
      $s = oci_parse($c,$stmt);
      // Bind PHP variables to the OCI types.
      oci_bind_by_name($s,':id',$id);
      // Execute the PL/SQL statement.
      if (oci_execute($s)) {
        // Return a LOB descriptor as the value.
        while (oci_fetch($s)) {
          for ($i = 1;$i <= oci_num_fields($s);$i++)
            if (is_object(oci_result($s,$i))) {
              if ($size = oci_result($s,$i)->size())
                $data = oci_result($s,$i)->read($size);
              else
                $data = " "; }
            else {
              if (oci_field_is_null($s,$i))
                $title = " ";
              else
                $title = oci_result($s,$i); }}
        // Free statement resources.
        oci_free_statement($s);
        // Format HTML table to display BLOB photo and CLOB description.
        $out = '<table border="1" cellpadding="5" cellspacing="0">';
```

```
       $out .= '<tr>';
       $out .= '<td align="center" class="e">'.$title.'</td>';
       $out .= '</tr>';
       $out .= '<tr><td class="v">';
       $out .= '<div>';
       $out .= '<div style="margin-right:5px;float:left">';
       $out .= '<img src="ReadCanonicalFileToImage.php?id='.$id.'">';
       $out .= '</div>';
       $out .= '<div style="position=relative;">'.$data.'</div>';
       $out .= '</div>';
       $out .= '</td></tr>';
       $out .= '</table>'; }
    // Print the HTML table.
    print $out;
    // Disconnect from database.
    oci_close($c); }
  else {
    // Assign the OCI error and format double and single quotes.
    $errorMessage = oci_error();
    print htmlentities($errorMessage['message'])."<br />"; }}
?>
```

The program reads and assigns the CLOB column to the $data variable, and the item_title column to the $title variable. You should note that there aren't any changes required to the Apache alias or virtual directory configuration for this solution.

MIME Content Types and Configuring Zend Core for Oracle

Two principles define how you display images to web pages when you read them from BLOB columns as raw byte streams. The first principle involves how web browsers read images from files. They read files through asynchronous threads by referencing the src element in an img tag. The src element provides a URL or relative reference inside the directory hierarchy of the web server. The second principle concerns how browsers read image files. They read image files by comparing their file extensions and assigning a MIME content-type (Multipart Internet Mail Extension). You can find a comprehensive list of MIME content-types at the IANA (Intenet Assigned Numbers Authority):

```
www.iana.org/assignments/media-types/application/
```

This standard web browser process implicitly creates an XHTML header when reading an image. It derives the MIME content-type from the file extension. An alternative approach as shown in the example PHP code calls the PHP header() function and then a set of functions to convert the raw stream into a resource and then an image file, as shown:

```
header('Content-type: image/png');
imagepng(imagecreatefromstring($data));
```

This set of steps creates an image that the browser can read into another web page. You call the converting PHP program through a src element in an img tag. This graphics format requires some additional configuration of the standard installation of Zend Core for Oracle.

You should enable the *exif* and *gd* extensions to work with the PNG (Portable Network Graphic) images found on the publisher's web site with this code. It enables you to access the required libraries to display the BLOB raw stream as an image without first writing it to a file.

You should connect to the Administration console at the following URL:

```
http://<hostname>.<domain_name>/ZendCore/login.php?goto=
```

After authenticating, the following illustration shows the console image for enabling these extensions:

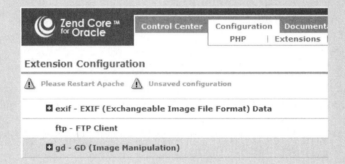

Then, you should also enable the *mbstring* extension, which handles multibyte character processing on Microsoft Windows operating systems. The following illustration shows you the Zend Core Administration console. This is found on the same web page as the previous configuration step.

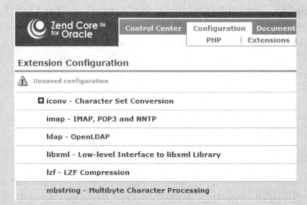

This general process can work with Microsoft Word, Excel, PowerPoint, and Portable Document Format (PDF) files. You have some additional management steps, depending on which you choose to implement.

The `ReadCanonicalFileToImage.php` program is

```
-- This is found in ReadCanonicalFileToImage.php on the publisher's web site.
<?php
  // Return successful attempt to connect to the database.
  if ($c = @oci_new_connect("plsql","plsql","orcl")) {
    // Declare input variables.
    (isset($_GET['id']))    ? $id = $_GET['id'] : $id = 1021;
    // Declare a SQL SELECT statement returning a CLOB.
    $stmt = "SELECT get_canonical_bfilename('ITEM','ITEM_PHOTO','ITEM_ID',:id)
             FROM   dual";
    // Parse a query through the connection.
    $s = oci_parse($c,$stmt);
    // Bind PHP variables to the OCI types.
    oci_bind_by_name($s,':id',$id);
    // Execute the PL/SQL statement.
    if (oci_execute($s)) {
      // Return a LOB descriptor and free resource as the value.
      while (oci_fetch($s)) {
        for ($i = 1;$i <= oci_num_fields($s);$i++)
          if ((!is_object(oci_result($s,$i))) && (!oci_field_is_null($s,$i)))
            $data = oci_result($s,$i);
          else
            $data = " "; }

      // Print the header first.
      header('Content-type: image/png');
      imagepng(imagecreatefromstring(file_get_contents($data))); }
    // Disconnect from database.
    oci_close($c); }
  else {
    // Assign the OCI error and format double and single quotes.
    $errorMessage = oci_error();
    print htmlentities($errorMessage['message'])."<br />"; }
?>
```

The `ReadCanonicalFileToImage.php` program renders the image by reading the canonical filename. The program then uses the PHP `file_get_contents()` function to read the file into a binary string. The `imagecreatefromstring()` function coverts the binary stream to a resource, and the `imagepng()` function converts the resource into a file. Figure 8-5 shows the displayed image from this program.

You have learned how to work with external files—BFILE datatypes. The examples have taught you how to leverage the locator and extend the database catalog to secure both canonical path names and filenames.

FIGURE 8-5 *Rendered page from the QueryPhotoBFILE.php program*

DBMS_LOB Package

Discussions earlier in the chapter rely on elements of the DBMS_LOB package. These include functions, procedures, and package specification constants. This section summarizes the balance of the features in the DBMS_LOB package, and it is divided into seven subsections. The subsections are: package constants, package exceptions, opening and closing methods *(a term that encompasses functions and procedures),* manipulation methods, introspection methods, BFILE methods, and Temporary LOB methods.

Package Constants

There are several package constants that you can use when working with functions and procedures in the DBMS_LOB package. They are qualified in Table 8-2.

These constants have various uses inside the package. They should be used in lieu of their numeric equivalents because, while unlikely, Oracle reserves the right to change the values.

There are also four package specification types. Two are structures. Structures are a list of variables organized by position and datatype. They act like rows of data. The other two types are associative arrays of the base structures. Both the types and structures are limited to uses in your PL/SQL blocks. They are covered next in pairs, the base structure and associative array.

BLOB_DEDUPLICATE_REGION Record Structures

The BLOB_DEDUPLICATE_REGION type is a record composed of five fields, as qualified in Table 8-3. The BLOB_DUPLICATE_REGION_TAB type is an associative array indexed by PLS_INTEGER.

Name	Classification	Type	Value
CALL	General	PLS_INTEGER	12
DEFAULT_CSID	General	INTEGER	0
DEFAULT_LANG_CTX	General	INTEGER	0
FILE_READONLY	General	BINARY_INTEGER	0
LOBMAXSIZE	General	INTEGER	1.84467
LOB_READONLY	General	BINARY_INTEGER	0
LOB_READWRITE	General	BINARY_INTEGER	1
NO_WARNING	General	INTEGER	0
SESSION	General	PLS_INTEGER	10
TRANSACTION	General	PLS_INTEGER	11
WARN_INCONVERTIBLE_CHAR	General	INTEGER	1
OPT_COMPRESS	Option Type	PLS_INTEGER	1
OPT_DEDUPLICATE	Option Type	PLS_INTEGER	4
OPT_ENCRYPT	Option Type	PLS_INTEGER	2
COMPRESS_OFF	Option Value	PLS_INTEGER	0
COMPRESS_ON	Option Value	PLS_INTEGER	1
ENCRYPT_OFF	Option Value	PLS_INTEGER	0
ENCRYPT_ON	Option Value	PLS_INTEGER	1
DEDUPLICATE_OFF	Option Value	PLS_INTEGER	0
DEDUPLICATE_ON	Option Value	PLS_INTEGER	1

TABLE 8-2   *DBMS_LOB Package Constants*

Position	Field Name	Datatype
1	LOB_OFFSET	INTEGER
2	LEN	INTEGER
3	PRIMARY_LOB	BLOB
4	PRIMARY_LOB_OFFSET	NUMBER
5	MIME_TYPE	VARCHAR2(80)

TABLE 8-3   *Field Map of the BLOB_DEDUPLICATE_REGION Record Structure*

Position	Field Name	Datatype
1	LOB_OFFSET	INTEGER
2	LEN	INTEGER
3	PRIMARY_LOB	CLOB
4	PRIMARY_LOB_OFFSET	NUMBER
5	MIME_TYPE	VARCHAR2(80)

TABLE 8-4   *Field Map of the CLOB_DEDUPLICATE_REGION Record Structure*

CLOB_DEDUPLICATE_REGION Record Structures

The CLOB_DEDUPLICATE_REGION type is a record composed of five fields, as qualified in Table 8-4. The CLOB_DUPLICATE_REGION_TAB type is an associative array indexed by PLS_INTEGER.

Package Exceptions

There are eight exceptions defined in the DBMS_LOB package. They are covered in Table 8-5. You should try to leverage these exceptions where appropriate in your own code before you create new user-defined exceptions.

Opening and Closing Methods

The opening and closing methods apply to all LOB datatypes. You have a function to check whether a file is already open, and procedures to open and close LOB datatypes.

CLOSE Procedure

You call the CLOSE procedure to close a LOB. This is a pass-by-reference procedure for the LOB locator parameter. It requires that you define an appropriate LOB variable in the block where you call the procedure. You can't close a LOB unless it is already opened without raising an ORA-22289 exception.

The overloaded procedure has the following prototypes:

```
CLOSE(bfile_locator)
CLOSE(blob_locator)
CLOSE(blob_locator)
```

You can find examples of the CLOSE function in the sections "PL/SQL Reading Files and Writing CLOB Columns" and "PL/SQL Reading Files and Writing BLOB Columns." They're in the load_clob_from_file.sql and load_blob_from_file.sql files.

ISOPEN Function

You call the ISOPEN function to check if a LOB is already open. You should use this function instead of the FILEISOPEN function because FILEISOPEN only checks for opened files using the input BFILE locator. The function is written to run in both SQL and PL/SQL environments. It returns a 1 when successful and a 0 when unsuccessful because there aren't any Boolean types in SQL.

The overloaded function has the following prototypes:

```
ISOPEN(bfile_locator)
ISOPEN(blob_locator)
ISOPEN(clob_locator)
```

Exception Name	Error Code	Definition
ACCESS_ERROR	ORA-22925	The ACCESS_ERROR exception occurs when you attempt to write more than the maximum size allowed for a LOB column.
INVALID_ARGVAL	ORA-21560	The INVALID_ARGVAL exception occurs when you pass a null value or a value outside of the 1–4GB range.
INVALID_LOCATOR	ORA-22275	The INVALID_LOCATOR exception occurs when you pass an invalid LOB locator value.
INVALID_DIRECTORY	ORA-22287	The INVALID_DIRECTORY exception occurs when you attempt to read from or write to a virtual database directory that no longer translates to a valid file system directory.
NOEXIST_DIRECTORY	ORA-22285	The NOEXIST_DIRECTORY exception occurs when you attempt to read from or write to a virtual database directory that doesn't exist.
NOPRIV_DIRECTORY	ORA-22286	The NOPRIV_DIRECTORY exception occurs when you attempt to read from or write to a virtual database directory and you've not been granted the appropriate access privilege.
OPEN_TOOMANY	ORA-22290	The OPEN_TOOMANY exception occurs when you attempt to open more files than are allowed for the instance.
OPERATION_FAILED	ORA-22288	The OPERATION_FAILED exception occurs when you attempt to access a file that doesn't exist, or a file to which the Oracle user doesn't have read or write privileges.
UNOPENED_FILE	ORA-22289	The UNOPENED_FILE exception occurs when you try to perform operations on an external file before you've opened it.

TABLE 8-5   *DBMS_LOB Package Exceptions*

You can find examples of the ISOPEN function in the sections "PL/SQL Reading Files and Writing CLOB Columns" and "PL/SQL Reading Files and Writing BLOB Columns." They're in the load_clob_from_file.sql and load_blob_from_file.sql files.

OPEN Procedure

You call the OPEN procedure to open a LOB. This is a pass-by-reference procedure for the LOB locator parameter. It requires that you define an appropriate LOB variable in the block where you call the procedure. You can open BLOB, CLOB, or NCLOB files in read-only or read-write mode, and BFILE in read-only mode. While you don't have to use the constants, it is safer to do so. You should use the LOB_READONLY or LOBREADWRITE constants for read-only or read-write mode respectively. The open mode uses a default of DBMS_LOB.LOB_READONLY, and the actual parameter is optional.

The overloaded procedure has the following prototypes:

```
OPEN(bfile_locator [, open_mode<MI><MI> ])
OPEN(blob_locator [, open_mode ])
OPEN(clob_locator [, open_mode ])
```

You can find examples of the OPEN function in the sections "PL/SQL Reading Files and Writing CLOB Columns" and "PL/SQL Reading Files and Writing BLOB Columns." You'll find them in the `load_clob_from_file.sql` and `load_blob_from_file.sql` files.

Manipulation Methods

The manipulation methods are a collection of functions and procedures that allow you to read, write, and alter the content of LOBs. Several new features have been added in Oracle 11*g*, including compression, deduplication, and secure file encryption.

Many methods are overloaded to work with all LOB datatypes, while some only work with BLOB, CLOB, and NCLOB datatypes. The following subsections cover these manipulation methods and point out when a method is limited in scope.

You must create a transaction context by using an INSERT or UPDATE statement to use these manipulation methods against LOB columns. The RETURNING INTO clause opens the transaction scope, and a COMMIT statement closes it. You use the locator returned by these statements as the gateway to copying one LOB to another of an equivalent type.

APPEND Procedure

You call the APPEND procedure to append to a BLOB, CLOB, or NCLOB datatype. The APPEND procedure is a pass-by-reference procedure for the LOB locator parameter. It allows you to add the contents of *another LOB* at the end of a LOB column. The WRITEAPPEND procedure does the same thing, except it accepts a RAW or VARCHAR2 stream to append to a BLOB or CLOB column, respectively.

The overloaded procedure has the following prototypes:

```
APPEND(blob_locator, new_lob_stream)
APPEND(clob_locator, new_lob_stream)
```

CONVERTTOBLOB Procedure

You call the CONVERTTOBLOB procedure to convert a CLOB or NCLOB to a BLOB datatype. The CONVERTTOBLOB procedure is a pass-by-reference procedure for the LOB locator, destination and source offset, and language context parameters.

The procedure has the following prototype:

```
CONVERTTOBLOB(destination_blob_locator, source_clob_locator, amount
             ,destination_offset, source_offset, blob_csid, language_context
             ,warning)
```

CONVERTTOCLOB Procedure

You call the CONVERTTOCLOB procedure to convert a BLOB to a CLOB or NCLOB datatype. The CONVERTTOCLOB procedure is a pass-by-reference procedure for the LOB locator, destination and source offset, and language context parameters.

The procedure has the following prototype:

CONVERTTOCLOB(*destination_clob_locator*, *source_blob_locator*, *amount*
                  ,*destination_offset*, *source_offset*, *clob_csid*, *language_context*
                  ,*warning*)

COPY Procedure

You call the COPY procedure to copy a BLOB to another BLOB or a CLOB or NCLOB to another equivalent character LOB datatype. The COPY procedure is a pass-by-reference procedure for the destination LOB locator parameter.

The overloaded procedure has the following prototypes:

COPY(*destination_clob_locator*, *source_clob_locator*, *amount*
       ,*destination_offset*, *source_offset*)
COPY(*destination_blob_locator*, *source_blob_locator*, *amount*
       ,*destination_offset*, *source_offset*)

ERASE Procedure

You call the ERASE procedure to erase a chunk of a BLOB, or CLOB, or NCLOB datatype. The ERASE procedure is a pass-by-reference procedure for the LOB locator and amount parameters. The default offset is 1, and the offset is an optional parameter.

The overloaded procedure has the following prototypes:

ERASE(*blob_locator*, *amount* [, *offset*])
ERASE(*clob_locator*, *amount* [, *offset*])

FRAGMENT_DELETE Procedure

You call the FRAGMENT_DELETE procedure to delete a chunk of a BLOB, or CLOB, or NCLOB datatype. The FRAGMENT_DELETE procedure is a pass-by-reference procedure for the LOB locator parameter.

The overloaded procedure has the following prototypes:

ERASE(*blob_locator*, *amount*, *offset*)
ERASE(*clob_locator*, *amount*, *offset*)

FRAGMENT_INSERT Procedure

You call the FRAGMENT_INSERT procedure to insert a chunk of data (or a stream) to a BLOB, or CLOB, or NCLOB datatype. This procedure is a pass-by-reference procedure for the LOB locator parameter.

The overloaded procedure has the following prototypes:

FRAGMENT_INSERT(*blob_locator*, *amount*, *offset*, *raw_buffer*)
FRAGMENT_INSERT(*clob_locator*, *amount*, *offset*, *character_buffer*)

FRAGMENT_MOVE Procedure

You call the FRAGMENT_MOVE procedure to move a chunk of data (or a stream) to another location in the same LOB. This function only works with BLOB, or CLOB, or NCLOB datatypes. The FRAGMENT_MOVE procedure is a pass-by-reference procedure for the LOB locator parameter.

The overloaded procedure has the following prototypes:

FRAGMENT_MOVE(*blob_locator*, *amount*, *source_offset*, *destination_offset*)
FRAGMENT_MOVE(*clob_locator*, *amount*, *source_offset*, *destination_offset*)

FRAGMENT_REPLACE Procedure

You call the FRAGMENT_REPLACE procedure to move a chunk of data (or a stream) to replace a chunk of data in the same LOB. This function only works with BLOB, or CLOB, or NCLOB datatypes. The FRAGMENT_REPLACE procedure is a pass-by-reference procedure for the LOB locator parameter.

The overloaded procedure has the following prototypes:

```
FRAGMENT_MOVE(blob_locator, old_amount, new_amount, offset, buffer)
FRAGMENT_MOVE(clob_locator, old_amount, new_amount, offset, buffer)
```

ISSECUREFILE Function

You call the ISSECUREFILE function in Oracle 11*g* or newer to determine if a BLOB, CLOB, or NCLOB is configured as a secure file. This function only works in a PL/SQL scope because it returns a BOOLEAN datatype, and it is a pass-by-value function.

The overloaded function has the following prototypes:

```
ISSECUREFILE(blob_locator)
ISSECUREFILE(clob_locator)
```

The following anonymous block demonstrates how to use this new function:

```
DECLARE
  audit_blob BLOB;
  CURSOR c IS
    SELECT NVL(item_blob,empty_blob) FROM item WHERE item_id = 1021;
BEGIN
  OPEN c;
  FETCH c INTO audit_blob;
  IF dbms_lob.issecurefile(audit_blob) THEN
    dbms_output.put_line('A secure file.');
  ELSE
    dbms_output.put_line('Not a secure file.');
  END IF;
  CLOSE c;
END;
/
```

The ISSECUREFILE function requires that the BLOB column be initialized. If you attempt to apply this function to invalid LOB locator, it raises an ORA-22275 error. There is an opportunity to find this error anytime a row leaves the BLOB column non-initialized or null. It is a good coding practice to enclose it in an NVL function call providing an empty_blob() or empty_clob() constructor. By so doing, you evaluate for secure files without the risk of raising a null exception. This approach ensures both non-secure files and null values are managed by the ELSE clause. The approach also lets you suppresses run-time errors triggered by an invalid LOB locator exception.

NOTE
This isn't documented in the DBMS_LOB *package specification in the initial production release of Oracle 11g.*

LOADBLOBFROMFILE Procedure

You call the LOADBLOBFROMFILE procedure to copy a physical file, treated as a BFILE, to a BLOB datatype. The LOADBLOBFROMFILE procedure is a pass-by-reference procedure for the destination LOB locator and the destination and source offset parameters. You must always call the OPEN procedure before this file, or you will raise an ORA-22889 for an unopened file.

The procedure has the following prototype:

```
LOADBLOBFROMFILE(destination_clob_locator, source_bfile, amount
                ,destination_offset, source_offset)
```

LOADCLOBFROMFILE Procedure

You call the LOADCLOBFROMFILE procedure to copy a physical file, treated as a BFILE, to a CLOB datatype. The LOADCLOBFROMFILE procedure is a pass-by-reference procedure for the destination LOB locator, the destination and source offset, and language context parameters. You must always call the OPEN procedure before this file, or you will raise an ORA-22889 for an unopened file.

The procedure has the following prototype:

```
LOADCLOBFROMFILE(destination_clob_locator, source_bfile, amount
                ,destination_offset, source_offset, bfile_csid
                ,language_context, warning)
```

LOADFROMFILE Procedure

You call the LOADFROMFILE procedure to copy a physical file, treated as a BFILE, to a BLOB, CLOB or NCLOB datatype. The LOADFROMFILE procedure is a pass-by-reference procedure for the destination LOB locator parameter. You must always call the OPEN procedure before this file, or you will raise an ORA-22889 for an unopened file. The destination and source offset parameters use a default value of 1, and are therefore optional parameters.

The overloaded procedure has the following prototypes:

```
LOADFROMFILE(destination_clob_locator, source_bfile, amount
            [,destination_offset [, source_offset ]])
LOADFROMFILE(destination_blob_locator, source_bfile, amount
            [,destination_offset [, source_offset ]])
```

While this procedure works, you should consider using the LOADBLOBFROMFILE or LOADCLOBFROMFILE procedures first. They provide more control, and you can set language context for CLOB columns.

SETOPTIONS Procedure

You call the SETOPTIONS procedure to override the storage option of SecureFiles, or BLOB, CLOB, and NCLOB datatypes, in Oracle 11*g*. The SETOPTIONS procedure is a pass-by-reference procedure for the LOB locator parameter. You must always create a transaction to access a specific LOB locator.

The Oracle 11*g* documentation says you can change either the default column compression or deduplication settings. The documentation did not say, at time of writing, that you could override the default column encryption. However, encryption is one of three new constants added to the DBMS_LOB package in Oracle 11*g*. Full utility of these features may await a bug fix or the second release of Oracle 11*g*.

> **NOTE**
> *At the time of this writing, calling the* SETOPTIONS *procedure against the Oracle 11g (11.1.0.6.0) release raises an* ORA-43857 *exception for "an unsupported object type for SECUREFILE LOB operation."*

The overloaded procedure has the following prototypes:

```
SETOPTIONS(blob_locator, option_type, option)
SETOPTIONS(clob_locator, option_type, option)
```

TRIM Procedure

You call the TRIM procedure to remove unwanted content from CLOB, NCLOB, or BLOB datatypes. The TRIM procedure is a pass-by-reference procedure for the LOB locator parameter and requires a transaction context to change a LOB column value.

The overloaded procedure has the following prototypes:

```
TRIM(blob_locator, new_length)
TRIM(clob_locator, new_length)
```

WRITE Procedure

You call the WRITE procedure to write data to a CLOB, NCLOB, or BLOB datatype beginning at a specified offset. The default offset is 1. Beginning in Oracle 11*g*, you should consider using the FRAGMENT_INSERT or FRAGMENT_REPLACE procedures over the WRITE procedure.

The overloaded procedure has the following prototypes:

```
WRITE(blob_locator, amount, offset, raw_buffer)
WRITE(clob_locator, amount, offset, character_buffer)
```

WRITEAPPEND Procedure

You call the WRITEAPPEND procedure to append data to the end of a CLOB, NCLOB, or BLOB datatype. Appendix J demonstrates the behaviors of this procedure in the sections "EMPTY_BLOB Function" and "EMPTY_CLOB Function."

The overloaded procedure has the following prototypes:

```
WRITEAPPEND(blob_locator, amount, raw_buffer)
WRITEAPPEND(clob_locator, amount, character_buffer)
```

Introspection Methods

Introspection methods let you discover something about the value in the instance of a datatype. Some of these methods should look familiar because they're staples in working with strings.

COMPARE Function

You call the COMPARE function to check whether two LOBs of the same datatype are equal, or two LOB *fragments* of the same datatype are equal. The function is a pass-by-value module. It works with BLOB, CLOB, NCLOB, or BFILE datatypes. The COMPARE function works in both SQL and PL/SQL environments. It returns a 0 when the two are equal and a 1 when they're not.

The overloaded function has the following prototypes:

```
COMPARE(bfile_locator_1, bfile_locator_2, amount [, offset_1 [, offset_2 ]])
COMPARE(blob_locator_1, blob_locator_2 [, amount [, offset_1 [, offset_2 ]]])
COMPARE(clob_locator_1, clob_locator_2 [, amount [, offset_1 [, offset_2 ]]])
```

You should notice from the prototypes that the size for comparison is optional for BLOB, CLOB, and NCLOB but it is required for BFILE datatypes. The simplest way to compare two values is with a SQL statement, like

```
SELECT CASE
          WHEN DBMS_LOB.COMPARE(i1.item_blob,i2.item_blob) = 0 THEN
          THEN 'True'
          ELSE 'False'
       END AS compared
FROM item i1 CROSS JOIN item i2 WHERE i1.item_id = 1021 AND i2.item_id = 1022;
```

This statement returns true if you've uploaded the same image of Harry Potter to both rows (as done in the `load_blob_from_file.sql` script). Otherwise, it returns false.

GETCHUNKSIZE Function

You call the GETCHUNKSIZE function to check the read and write chunk size. This is typically the block size *(as determined by the* db_block_size database parameter) minus a handling value. If you're db_block_size is set to 8K (8,192 bytes), then the chunk size will be 8,132 bytes. The function works with BLOB, CLOB, NCLOB, or BFILE datatypes.

The overloaded procedure has the following prototypes:

```
GETCHUNKSIZE(bfile_locator)
GETCHUNKSIZE(blob_locator)
GETCHUNKSIZE(clob_locator)
```

The simplest way to call this function is

```
SELECT DBMS_LOB.GETCHUNKSIZE(i1.item_blob)
FROM item i1
WHERE i1.item_id = 1021;
```

In most cases, it returns 8,132 bytes because the default db_block_size parameter value is 8,192 bytes. The query should work provided you inserted the Harry Potter image into the BLOB column for this row.

GET_DEDUPLICATED_REGIONS Procedure

You call the GET_DEDUPLICATED_REGIONS procedure to check for deduplicated regions in Oracle SecureFiles. This is a new procedure in Oracle 11*g*. The function works with BLOB, CLOB, or NCLOB datatypes. It is a pass-by-reference procedure for the associative array of structures, which are implementations of the record structures covered earlier in the "Package Constants" subsection of this chapter.

The overloaded procedure has the following prototypes:

```
GET_DEDUPLICATED_REGIONS(blob_locator, blob_deduplicated_table)
GET_DEDUPLICATED_REGIONS(clob_locator, clob_deduplicated_table)
```

GETLENGTH Function

You call the GETLENGTH function to get the length of a LOB. The function works with BLOB, CLOB, NCLOB, or BFILE datatypes. It is a pass-by-value function and essential in many regards for working with LOB columns. Appendix J contains several examples, like the one found in the "BFILE Function" subsection.

The overloaded function has the following prototypes:

```
GETLENGTH(bfile_locator)
GETLENGTH(blob_locator)
GETLENGTH(clob_locator)
```

GETOPTIONS Function

You call the GETOPTIONS function to examine the storage options of SecureFiles, which are BLOB, CLOB, or NCLOB datatypes in Oracle 11*g*. This function is a pass-by-reference function for the LOB locator parameter. You must always create a transaction to access a specific LOB locator. Again, full utility of these features may await a bug fix or the second release of the Oracle 11*g*.

> **NOTE**
> *At the time of this writing, calling the* GETOPTIONS *procedure against the Oracle 11g (11.1.0.6.0) release raises "an* ORA-43856 *exception for an unsupported object type for SECUREFILE LOB operation."*

The overloaded function has the following prototypes:

```
GETOPTIONS(blob_locator, option_type)
GETOPTIONS(clob_locator, option_type)
```

GET_STORAGE_LIMIT Function

You call the GET_STORAGE_LIMIT function to get the maximum storage length of a LOB. The function works with BLOB, CLOB, or NCLOB datatypes. It is a pass-by-value function.

The overloaded function has the following prototypes:

```
GET_STORAGE_LIMIT(blob_locator)
GET_STORAGE_LIMIT(clob_locator)
```

INSTR Function

You call the INSTR function to find the position where a byte pattern begins in a LOB. The function works with BLOB, CLOB, NCLOB, or BFILE datatypes. It is a pass-by-value function. The offset and nth_occurrence parameters have a default value of 1, which makes them optional.

The overloaded function has the following prototypes:

```
INSTR(bfile_locator, raw_byte_pattern [, offset [, nth_occurrence ]])
INSTR(blob_locator, raw_byte_pattern [, offset [, nth_occurrence ]])
INSTR(clob_locator, character_pattern [, offset [, nth_occurrence ]])
```

READ Procedure

You call the READ procedure to read data from a CLOB, NCLOB, or BLOB datatype beginning at a specified offset. There is no default offset value and it is a mandatory actual parameter.

The procedure is pass-by-reference for the locator and buffer. The overloaded procedure has the following prototypes:

```
READ(bfile_locator, amount, offset, raw_buffer)
READ(blob_locator, amount, offset, raw_buffer)
READ(clob_locator, amount, offset, character_buffer)
```

SUBSTR Function

You call the SUBSTR function to read data from a CLOB, NCLOB, or BLOB datatype beginning at a specified offset. The default for the amount and offset is 1. This is a pass-by-value function that returns a RAW datatype for BFILE and BLOB datatypes and VARCHAR2 datatype for CLOB or NCLOB datatypes. The function is subject to the character stream limits of the environment where you use it. This means that the SUBSTR function can return a 4,000-byte length string in SQL and a 32,767-byte string in PL/SQL.

The overloaded function has the following prototypes:

```
SUBSTR(bfile_locator [, amount [, offset ]])
SUBSTR(blob_locator [, amount [, offset ]])
SUBSTR(clob_locator [, amount [, offset ]])
```

BFILE Methods

The BFILE methods only support external and read-only BFILE datatypes. Some of the BFILE methods have recommended alternatives. Oracle hasn't deprecated any methods in the DBMS_LOB package but they've superseded some methods by new DBMS_LOB methods. Recommendations that you call alternative methods are noted in their respective subsections.

FILECLOSE Procedure

You call the FILECLOSE procedure to close a BFILE. This is a pass-by-reference procedure for the LOB locator parameter. It requires that you define an appropriate LOB variable in the block where you call the procedure. You can't close a LOB unless it is already opened without raising an ORA-22289 exception. Oracle recommends you use the CLOSE procedure instead of the FILECLOSE procedure.

The procedure has the following prototype:

```
FILECLOSE(bfile_locator)
```

FILECLOSEALL Procedure

You call the FILECLOSEALL procedure to close all open files. This function has no formal parameter.

The procedure has the following prototype:

```
FILECLOSEALL
```

FILEEXISTS Function

You call the FILEEXISTS function to check if a file exists on the file system. It relies on the virtual database directory translation to a physical directory on the file system. You can use this function in SQL or PL/SQL environments, and it returns a 1 if true and 0 when false.

The function has the following prototype:

```
FILEEXISTS(bfile_locator)
```

FILEGETNAME Procedure

You call the `FILEGETNAME` procedure to find the base filename in a `BFILE` locator. You must call the procedure only after you initialize all three actual parameter values to `VARCHAR2(255)` strings. The definition of space for declared variables is required because the virtual database directory and base filename formal parameters are `OUT` mode variables, which must be sized before calling a pass-by-reference function or procedure.

The procedure has the following prototype:

```
FILEGETNAME(bfile_locator, virtual_database_directory, base_file_name)
```

You can refer to the example in the `get_bfilename` function for the details of how to use this function. That is found in the section "Creating and Using Virtual Directories" earlier in this chapter.

FILEISOPEN Function

You call the `FILEISOPEN` function to check if a `BFILE` is already open. You should not use this function because it is only provided for backward compatibility. The alternative is the `ISOPEN` function. This function, like the `ISOPEN` function, is written to run in both SQL and PL/SQL environments. It returns a 1 when successful and a 0 when unsuccessful because there aren't any Boolean types in SQL.

The function has the following prototype:

```
FILEISOPEN(bfile_locator)
```

You can find examples in the sections "PL/SQL Reading Files and Writing CLOB Columns" or "PL/SQL Reading Files and Writing BLOB Columns." You'll find them in the `load_clob_from_file.sql` and `load_blob_from_file.sql` files.

FILEOPEN Procedure

You call the `FILEOPEN` procedure to open a `BFILE`. This is a pass-by-reference procedure for the LOB locator parameter. It requires that you define an appropriate LOB variable in the block where you call the procedure. Oracle recommends you use the `OPEN` procedure instead of the `FILEOPEN` procedure. The option open mode parameter has a default value of `DBMS.LOB_READONLY`.

The procedure has the following prototype:

```
FILEOPEN(bfile_locator [, open_mode ])
```

Temporary LOB Methods

Temporary LOB datatypes are not linked to a physical location in the database. The LOB locator points to a memory location where the temporary LOB is written.

CREATETEMPORARY Function

You call the `CREATETEMPORARY` procedure to create a temporary `BLOB`, `CLOB`, or `NCLOB` in memory. Temporary LOBs are time-bound entities, and you should constrain their existence to the smallest time slice possible. The optional duration parameter is bound by the `DBMS_LOB.SESSION` constant, which is the length of the session.

The overloaded procedure has the following prototypes:

```
CREATETEMPORTY(blob_locator, cache [, duration ])
CREATETEMPORTY(clob_locator, cache [, duration ])
```

ISTEMPORARY Function
You call the `ISTEMPORARY` function to free resources that held a temporary `BLOB` or `CLOB` variable. This is an important function and should be used each time you manage a temporary LOB. It works with `BLOB`, `CLOB`, or `NCLOB` datatypes. The `ISTEMPORARY` function works in both SQL and PL/SQL environments. It returns a 1 when successful and a 0 when not.
The overloaded function has the following prototypes:

```
ISTEMPORARY(blob_locator)
ISTEMPORARY(clob_locator)
```

FREETEMPORARY Function
You call the `FREETEMPORARY` procedure to free the memory consumed for a temporary `BLOB`, `CLOB`, or `NCLOB` in memory. This is an important function and should be used each time you manage a temporary LOB.
The overloaded procedure has the following prototypes:

```
FREETEMPORTY(blob_locator)
FREETEMPORTY(clob_locator)
```

This section has reviewed the methods of the `DBMS_LOB` package. Several new methods were added Oracle 11*g*, and there may yet be more to simplify the access and management of LOBs.

Summary
You have covered how PL/SQL works with `BLOB`, `CLOB`, and `NCLOB` internally stored large objects, and how to define these base types as SecureFiles. You have also seen how to use and leverage internal locators to external `BFILE` files. Image retrieval has been demonstrated by using the PHP programming language. Appendix D contains similar examples using the Java programming language.

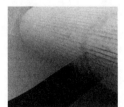

CHAPTER
9

Packages

 ackages are the backbone of Oracle 11g application development. They let you group functions and procedures as components into libraries. Inside these package libraries you can have shared variables, types, and components. Components are functions and procedures. Unlike standalone stored functions and procedures covered in Chapter 6, stored packages divide their declaration from their implementation. Package specifications publish the declaration, and package bodies implement the declaration.

This chapter explains how to declare, implement, leverage, and manage stored packages. The sections are as follows:

- Package architecture
  - Forward referencing
  - Overloading
- Package specification
  - Variables
  - Types
  - Components: functions and procedures
- Package body
  - Variables
  - Types
  - Components: functions and procedures
- Definer and invoker rights
  - Grants and synonyms
  - Remote calls
- Managing packages through the database catalog
  - Finding, validating, and describing packages
  - Checking dependencies
  - Comparing validation methods: timestamp versus signature

The chapter is set up to help someone new to the concepts master them. However, if you're already familiar with the general concepts, you should also be able to target reference material to support your current projects. Chapter 14 covers object types. Object types differ from packages because their behavior is divided into two states: static and instance level. Static methods *mirror* the behavior of functions and procedures in packages. Instance-level methods only work when you create an instance of an object type. Instance methods only act on attributes of the object instance.

Package Architecture

Packages are stored libraries in the database. They are owned by the user schema where they're created, like tables and views. This ownership makes packages schema-level objects in the database catalog, like standalone functions and procedures.

Package specifications declare variables, datatypes, functions, and procedures. The declaration publishes them to the local schema. You use package variables and datatypes in other PL/SQL blocks by calling them from other PL/SQL blocks. Calling blocks can be inside or outside of the package where they're declared.

All users, other than the owner, must be granted the EXECUTE privilege on a package to call its published components. This mimics the same rules for tables, views, SQL datatypes, or standalone modules (like standalone functions and procedures). Published components have context inside the package, just as a standalone component has context inside a user's schema.

The Oracle 11*g* security model lets you grant the EXECUTE privilege on any package to all users *(through a grant to public)*. This effectively makes it possible to grant public access to packages. Alternatively, you can restrict access to packages when you choose to do so. These security tools let you narrow privileges to targeted audiences.

You define *(declare and implement)* package-only scope functions and procedures in package bodies. Package-only scope functions and procedures can access anything in the package specification. They can also access anything declared before them in the package body. However, they don't know anything declared after them in the package body.

This is true because PL/SQL uses a single-pass parser. Parsers place identifiers into a temporary name space as they read through the source code. A parser fails when identifiers are referenced before they are declared. This is why identifiers are declared in a certain order in PL/SQL declaration sections. Typically, you declare identifiers in the following order: datatypes, variables, exceptions, functions, and procedures.

The sequencing of identifiers solves many but not all problems with forward referencing. Sometimes a component implementation requires access before another component exists. While you could shift the order of some components to fix to this sequencing problem, it is often more effective to declare a forward reference stub. A forward reference declares a subroutine without implementing it. You can do this in any declaration block.

Forward Referencing

The concept of *forward referencing* is rather straightforward. You can't send a text message to new acquaintances from a conference if you didn't get their cell phone numbers. In the same vein, you can't call a function or procedure until you know its name and formal parameter list.

The following example would demonstrate that A can't call B until B has been declared, or placed in scope. If you comment out the forward referencing stub for procedure B, the program raises a "PLS-00313: 'B' not declared in this scope" error. The parser would raise the error because it wouldn't find a declaration of procedure B in its list of identifiers. The forward referencing stub declares procedure B before it is defined *(or implemented)*.

```
DECLARE
  PROCEDURE b (caller VARCHAR2);   -- This is a forward referencing stub.
  PROCEDURE a (caller VARCHAR2) IS
    procedure_name VARCHAR2(1) := 'A';
  BEGIN
    dbms_output.put_line('Procedure "A" called by ['||caller||']');
```

```
    b(procedure_name);
  END;
  PROCEDURE b (caller VARCHAR2) IS
    procedure_name VARCHAR2(1) := 'B';
  BEGIN
    dbms_output.put_line('Procedure "B" called by ['||caller||']');
  END;
BEGIN
  a('Main');
END;
/
```

This prints

```
Procedure "A" called by [Main]
Procedure "B" called by [A]
```

The execution block knows everything in its declaration block or external declaration block(s). The forward referencing stub lets the PL/SQL single-pass parser put the procedure B declaration in its list of identifiers. It is added before the parser reads procedure A because single-pass parsers read from the top down. When the parser reads procedure A, it knows of the declaration of procedure B. The parser then validates the call to B and looks for the implementation of B later in the program to compile the code successfully. The parser raises a PLS-00328 error if the subprogram is missing after reading the complete source code.

NOTE
Java uses a two-pass parser and lets you avoid forward declarations.

Package specifications exist to declare implementations. Package bodies provide implementations of the declarations found in the package specifications.

Figure 9-1 depicts the package specification and body. It shows you that the package specification acts as an interface to the package body. You can declare variables, types, and components inside both the package specification and the body. Those declared in the package specification are published, while those declared only in the package body are local components. Named blocks defined inside component implementations are private modules, or part of the *black box* of local functions or procedures.

Types can be referenced by external PL/SQL blocks. You can assign values to package variables or use their values. Constants are specialized variables that disallow assignments. You can only use the values of constants as right operands. External PL/SQL blocks call package functions and procedures when they're declared in a package specification. Components declared only in the package body call published components through their package declarations.

Chapter 3 discusses scalar and composite datatypes that are available in anonymous and named blocks. All these are available in packages because they're named blocks. You can use any scalar or compound variable that is available in your package specification or body. You can also create user-defined datatypes in your SQL environment or package. User-defined datatypes are publicly available when you define them in the package specification to any other PL/SQL block. They are privately available when you define them in the package body to PL/SQL blocks implemented in the package body.

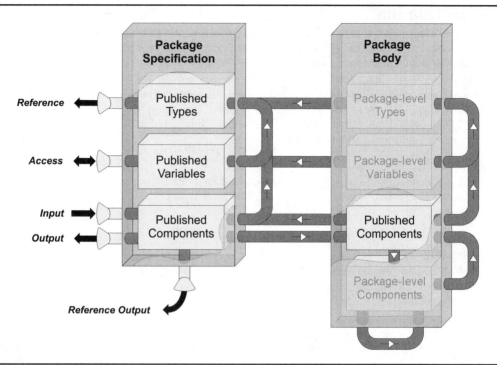

FIGURE 9-1 *PL/SQL package architecture*

As with functions and procedures, you can declare variables, types, and components in your package specification or body. Unlike when using standalone functions and procedures, you can access and use datatypes from your package specification in other PL/SQL blocks. You only need to preface the components with the package name and the component selector *(that's the period)* before the datatype, as shown in the following call:

```
EXECUTE some_package.some_procedure(some_package.some_variable);
```

NOTE
Package types may include shared cursors. Shared cursors are mutually exclusive structures during run time in Oracle 11g, which means they can only be run by a single process at any time.

The next two sections cover how you define and implement packages. How you implement variables and types is the same, whether you're using a package specification or package body. You'll also find that while functions and procedures do everything that they did in Chapter 6, they also support overloading.

Overloading

Overloading means that you create more than one function or procedure with the same identifier *(or component name)* but different signatures. Function and procedure signatures are defined by their respective formal parameter lists. An overloaded component differs in either the number of parameters or the datatypes of parameters in respective positions. While PL/SQL supports named, mixed, and positional notation (Oracle 11*g* forward), formal parameters are *only* unique by position and datatype. Parameter names do not make formal parameter lists unique.

For example, you cannot overload the `adding` function that uses two numbers by simply changing the formal parameter names, like this:

```
CREATE OR REPLACE PACKAGE not_overloading IS
FUNCTION adding (a NUMBER, b NUMBER) RETURN NUMBER;
FUNCTION adding (one NUMBER, two NUMBER) RETURN BINARY_INTEGER;
END not_overloading;
/
```

NOTE
PL/SQL allows you to overload functions and procedures by simply renaming variables, but at run time the ambiguity raises a `PLS-00307` *exception.*

You can compile this package specification and implement its package body without raising a compile-time error. However, you can't call the overloaded function without finding that too many declarations of the function exist. The ambiguity between declarations raises the `PLS-00307` exception. The return datatype for functions is not part of their signature. A change in the return datatype for functions does not alter their unique signatures because *the return type isn't part of the signature.*

Redefining the package declaration like this lets you call either implementation of the `adding` function. The datatypes now differ between the two declarations.

```
CREATE OR REPLACE PACKAGE overloading IS
FUNCTION adding (a NUMBER, b NUMBER) RETURN NUMBER;
FUNCTION adding (a VARCHAR2, b VARCHAR2) RETURN BINARY_INTEGER;
END not_overloading;
/
```

Figure 9-2 shows you how overloading works inside the *black box.* In the first signature, the second parameter is a `CLOB` and the third a `DATE`, while their positions are reversed in the second signature. A drawing of the sample adding function would show two round funnels for the `VARCHAR2` parameters, and two square funnels for the `NUMBER` parameters.

You call an overloaded function or procedure name with a list of actual parameters. Inside the black box the run-time engine identifies the sequence and datatypes of the actual parameters. It matches the calls against possible candidates. When it finds a matching candidate, the actual parameters are sent to that version of the function or procedure.

This information is stored in the database catalog. You can see it in the `ALL_ARGUMENTS`, `DBA_ARGUMENTS`, or `USER_ARGUMENTS` view. If there isn't a signature that matches a function call, the PL/SQL run-time engine returns an `ORA-06576` error. The error says you've called an invalid function or procedure.

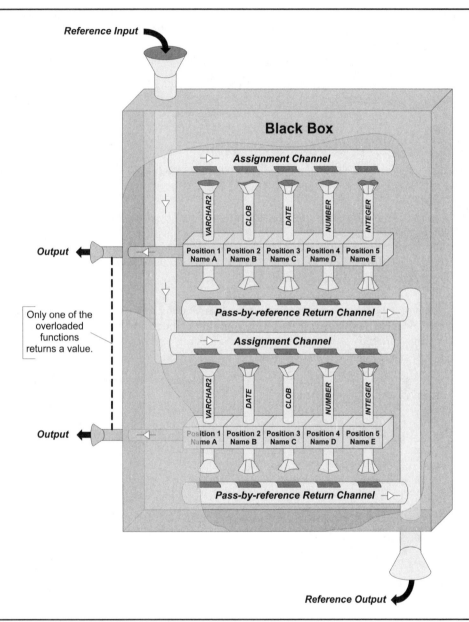

FIGURE 9-2 *Overloading the black box*

Package Specification

The package specification declares a package as a black box to a user's schema. The declaration publishes the available functions and procedures. After compiling a package specification, you can use the SQL*Plus DESCRIBE command to see the functions and procedures inside a package.

Unfortunately, the variables and datatypes are not visible when you describe a package. You must determine those by inspecting the package specification found in the `text` column of the `user_source` administration view.

You can query the source by using a query and SQL*Plus formatting like this:

```
-- Set page break to maximum SQL*Plus value.
SET PAGESIZE 49999
-- Set column formatting for 80 column display.
COLUMN line FORMAT 99999 HEADING "Line#"
COLUMN text FORMAT A73   HEADING "Text"
-- Query any source in the user's account.
SELECT line, text FROM user_source WHERE UPPER(name) = UPPER('&input_name');
```

NOTE
Oracle 11g and previous releases store all metadata by default in uppercase strings. You can override that default behavior in Oracle 11g, as described in the sidebar "Case-Sensitive Table and Column Names" of Appendix B. The UPPER *function around the column name ensures you'll always match uppercase strings.*

The prototype for a package specification lists all components as optional because it is possible to build a package without any components. The prototype shows the possibilities for package variables, types, and subroutines *(functions and procedures)*.

The package specification prototype is

```
CREATE [OR REPLACE] PACKAGE package_name [AUTHID {DEFINER | CURRENT_USER}] IS
  [PRAGMA SERIALLY_REUSABLE;]
  [variable_name    [CONSTANT] scalar_datatype [:= value];]
  [collection_name [CONSTANT] collection_datatype [:= constructor];]
  [object_name     [CONSTANT] object_datatype [:= constructor];]

  [TYPE record_structure IS RECORD
  ( field_name1     datatype
  [,field_name2     datatype
  [,field_name(n+1) datatype]]);]

  [CURSOR cursor_name
  [(parameter_name1     datatype
  [,parameter_name2     datatype
  [,parameter_name(n+1) datatype]])] IS
    select_statement;]

  [TYPE ref_cursor IS REF CURSOR [RETURN { catalog_row | record_structure }];]

  [user_exception_name EXCEPTION;
  [PRAGMA EXCEPTION_INIT(user_exception_name,-20001);]]

  [FUNCTION function_name
  [( parameter1    [IN][OUT] [NOCOPY] sql_datatype | plsql_datatype
  [, parameter2    [IN][OUT] [NOCOPY] sql_datatype | plsql_datatype
  [, parameter(n+1) [IN][OUT] [NOCOPY] sql_datatype | plsql_datatype )]
```

```
    RETURN { sql_data_type | plsql_data_type }
    [ DETERMINISTIC | PARALLEL_ENABLED ]
    [ PIPELINED ]
    [ RESULT_CACHE [ RELIES_ON (table_name) ]];]

    [ PRAGMA RESTRICT_REFERENCES ({ DEFAULT | function_name }
                                  , option1 [, option2 [, option(n+1) ]]); ]

    [PROCEDURE procedure_name
    [( parameter1      [IN][OUT] [NOCOPY] sql_datatype | plsql_datatype
    [, parameter2      [IN][OUT] [NOCOPY] sql_datatype | plsql_datatype
    [, parameter(n+1)  [IN][OUT] [NOCOPY] sql_datatype | plsql_datatype)]];]
END package_name;
/
```

NOTE
The OR REPLACE *clause is very important because without it you must drop the package specification before attempting to re-declare it.*

The SERIALLY_REUSABLE PRAGMA *(precompiler instruction)* can be used only in a package context. You must use it in both the package specification and the body. This practice differs from the PRAGMA instructions covered earlier for exceptions, functions, and procedures. The SERIALLY_REUSABLE PRAGMA is important when you want to share variables because it guarantees their starting state each time they're called.

The CONSTANT qualifier lets you designate variables as read-only and static variables. While this fact is not mentioned earlier chapters, you can also designate any variable as a CONSTANT in any declaration block. A constant can't be used as an assignment target in any package where it is defined. Constants become more important when you share them through package specifications.

NOTE
You cannot use package variables as assignment targets when they're defined as constants. Any attempt to assign a value to a constant raises a PLS-00363 *exception.*

Package exceptions are helpful development tools because they can be referenced by other program units. All you need do to use it in other programs is prepend the package name and component selector to the exception.

For example, you would declare an exception like

```
sample_exception EXCEPTION;
PRAGMA EXCEPTION_INIT(sample_exception,-20003);
```

Chapter 5 demonstrates how you can leverage exceptions. You declare them in packages just as you do in standalone functions and procedures, or anonymous blocks.

The section "System Reference Cursor" in Chapter 3 only discusses strongly and weakly typed reference cursors. There, the chapter covers strongly typed reference cursors as datatypes anchored to a catalog object, like a table or view. Package specifications let you share record type definitions with other PL/SQL blocks. This feature lets you share record types with other PL/SQL blocks and anchor reference cursors to package-defined record types.

Schema-Level Programs

Stored functions, procedures, packages, and objects are schema-level programs. Only schema-level programs can be defined as programs with definer rights or invoker rights. The default model of operation is *definer rights,* which means the code runs with the permissions available to the owner of the schema. You can define schema-level programs as invoker rights models by including the `AUTHID` as `CURRENT_USER`. An invoker rights model runs with the permissions of the schema that calls the component.

The definer rights model runs with the privileges of the owning schema and is best suited for a centralized computing model. The `AUTHID` as `DEFINER` sets a schema-level program as a definer rights model, but it is unnecessary because that's the default. The invoker rights model requires you to maintain multiple copies of tables or views in different schemas or databases.

Package specifications define packages. The package body only implements the declaration from the package specification. The package specification is the schema-level program. You can define a package as having definer or invoker rights, but all components of the package inherit a single mode of operation.

You raise a `PLS-00157` exception when you try to set the mode of operation for functions and procedures when they're inside packages. Functions and procedures defined inside packages *are not* schema-level programs. They're actually nested components of packages. They inherit the operational mode of the package.

The nested function definition also shows the potential for pipelined and cached result sets. You should remember to use a collection as the return type of pipelined functions. If you forget, the compilation cycle raises a `PLS-00630` exception telling you must return a supported collection.

NOTE
The cached result set feature works for standalone (schema-level) functions but doesn't appear to work for functions inside packages. At the time of this writing, it raises a `PLS-00999` exception.

Table 6-3 in Chapter 6 covers the precompiler options that restrict function performance. The package specification introduces a `DEFAULT` mode, which means apply the limitations to all functions defined in the package. Again, these precompiler options that restrict function behaviors and the `TRUST` option are more for backward compatibility than they are for new development.

The next three subsections discuss variables, types, and components. They point out changes in behavior between serially or non–serially reusable packages. Non–serially reusable packages are the default. Types are subdivided into structures, cursors, and collections.

Variables

Packages are non–serially reusable by default. This means that a second user isn't guaranteed the same package after a first user calls a package. The default works well when you don't declare shared variables or cursors in a package specification because the functions and procedures are reusable. At least, they're reusable when they don't depend on package variables. Moreover, you should always make packages serially reusable when they contain shared variables.

You define a package as serially reusable by placing the SERIALLY_REUSABLE PRAGMA in the package specification. The PRAGMA changes the basic behavior of package variables. A serially reusable package creates a new *(fresh)* copy of the package when it is called by another program unit, whereas a default *(non–serially reusable)* package reuses variables.

```
PRAGMA SERIALLY_REUSABLE;
```

While you declare variables like any other anonymous or named block, they are not hidden inside the black box. Package-level variables are accessible from other PL/SQL block programs. This means package-level variables are shared. They are also subject to change by one or more programs. The duration of package-level variables varies in any session. The length of time can extend through the life of a connection or can be shortened when other packages displace it in the SGA. Older and less-used packages can age out of the SGA because that's how the least-used algorithm works.

The least-used algorithm acts more or less like a garbage collector for the database. It is very similar to the garbage collector in a JVM (Java Virtual Machine).

You can access shared constants or variables from package specifications. Constants have fixed values whether you declare the package as serially or non–serially reusable. Variables don't have a fixed value in either case. A serially reusable package guarantees the initial values of variables because a call to the package always gets a new copy of the package. A non–serially reusable package doesn't guarantee the initial value because it can't. A non–serially reusable package variable returns either the initial or last value of a variable. The last value is returned when the package still resides in the SGA from a prior call in the same session.

The following example creates a shared_variables package specification and demonstrates the behavior of a non–serially reusable package specification. The package defines a constant and a variable. You can use the package specification to test the behavior of shared variables.

```
-- This is found in create_shared_variables.sql on the publisher's web site.
CREATE OR REPLACE PACKAGE shared_variables IS
  protected    CONSTANT NUMBER := 1;
  unprotected           NUMBER := 1;
END shared_variables;
/
```

The change_unprotected procedure changes the state of the package-level variable and then prints the unprotected variable value. It takes one formal parameter, which can be any number.

```
-- This is found in create_shared_variables.sql on the publisher's web site.
CREATE OR REPLACE PROCEDURE change_unprotected (value NUMBER) IS
  PRAGMA AUTONOMOUS_TRANSACTION;
BEGIN
  shared_variables.unprotected := shared_variables.unprotected + value;
  dbms_output.put_line('Unprotected ['||shared_variables.unprotected||']');
END change_unprotected;
/
```

NOTE
You can access package specification variables from PL/SQL blocks but not from SQL commands.

You can test the durability of the shared package-level variable by running this command twice or more:

```
EXECUTE change_unprotected(2);
```

It will print 3 initially, 5 next, and so on until the package ages out of the SGA. The function prints 3 again, only when you call the package specification after it has aged out of the SGA. You can recompile the specification to reset values. You use the following command to reset the `shared_variables` package:

```
ALTER PACKAGE shared_variables COMPILE SPECIFICATION;
```

The procedure always returns 3 when you redefine it as serially reusable. This is true because each call to the package gets a fresh copy. Serially reusable packages re-initialize the values of shared variables. The only difference between a serially reusable variable and a constant is that a constant can never change its value while the variable can. The change is lost on any subsequent call to the package when the package is serially reusable. As a rule of thumb, package specification variables *should always be constants.*

Types

There are two generalized types that you define in packages. You can declare static or dynamic datatypes. Datatypes are typically PL/SQL structures, collections, reference cursors, and cursors. All of these can be dynamic or static datatypes. They are dynamic when their declaration anchors their type to a row or column definition. You use the `%ROWTYPE` to anchor to a row and `%TYPE` to anchor to a column, as qualified in Table 9-1. Types are static when they rely on explicitly declared SQL datatypes, such as `DATE`, `INTEGER`, `NUMBER`, or `VARCHAR2`.

As a general rule, package specifications are independent of other schema-level objects. You build dependencies when you anchor package specification–declared types to catalog objects, like tables and views. If something changes in the dependent table or view, the package specification becomes invalid. As discussed later, in the section "Managing Packages in the Database Catalog," changes in package specifications can create a *cascade reaction* that invalidates numerous package bodies and standalone schema-level programs.

Attribute	Description
`%ROWTYPE`	The `%ROWTYPE` anchors the datatype of a variable to the row structure of a database catalog object *(table or view),* or PL/SQL record structure. The new variable inherits both the position and datatype of the columns found in the referenced table or view when you anchor to a catalog object. The new variable inherits both the position and datatype of the explicit PL/SQL record structure, which may inherit indirectly from one or more catalog objects.
`%TYPE`	The `%TYPE` anchors the datatype of a variable to a column datatype found in a database catalog object, like a table or view.

TABLE 9-1   *Anchoring Attributes*

Pseudotypes or Attributes

The %ROWTYPE and %TYPE act as pseudotypes because they inherit the base catalog type for a table or column respectively. More importantly, they implicitly anchor PL/SQL variable datatypes to the database catalog. They are also known as attributes because they're preceded by the attribute indicator *(the % symbol)*. The important point to remember is that these attributes inherit a datatype and anchor a variable's datatype to the database catalog.

Beyond the dynamic or static condition of package types, a shared cursor is a package cursor. Shared cursors are dynamic in so far as they return different data sets over time. Other package datatypes don't inherit anything beyond the default values that may be assigned during their declaration.

You can use any PL/SQL record and collection types that you declare in a package specification as a formal parameter or function return datatype of a named PL/SQL block. You can't use these PL/SQL datatypes in SQL statements. PL/SQL blocks that reference package-level record and collections are dependent on the package. If the package specification becomes invalid, so do the external program units that depend on the package declarations.

Chapter 6 contains an example using this technique in the section "Pipelined Clause." There it declares a pipelined package specification that contains a record and collection type. The collection type is dependent on the record structure. The standalone pf pipelined function returns an *aggregate table* to the SQL environment. The standalone function uses the package-level collection type, which implicitly relies on the package-level record structure. This example demonstrates how you can use record and collection types found in package specifications in other PL/SQL blocks.

Declaring shared cursors in the package specification anchors a cursor to the tables or views referenced by its SELECT statement. This makes the package specification dependent on any referenced tables or views. A change to the tables or views can invalidate the package specification and all package bodies that list the invalid specification as a dependent.

Shared cursors can be queried simultaneously by different program units. The first program that opens the cursor, gains control of the cursor until it is released by a CLOSE cursor command. *Prior to Oracle 11g these were not read consistent and required that you declare the package serially reusable to ensure they performed as read-consistent cursors.* Any attempt to fetch from an open shared cursor by another process is denied immediately. A cursor already open, ORA-06511, exception should be thrown, but the error message can be suppressed when the calling program runs as an autonomous transaction. Autonomous transactions suppress the other error and raise an ORA-06519 exception. Unfortunately, PL/SQL doesn't have a WAIT *n (seconds)* command syntax that would allow you to wait on an open cursor. This is probably one reason some developers avoid shared cursors.

NOTE
If you need this feature, you could kludge something together with the DBMS_LOCK.SLEEP procedure.

The following demonstrates a shared cursor package specification definition:

```
CREATE OR REPLACE PACKAGE shared_cursors IS
  CURSOR item_cursor IS SELECT item_id, item_title FROM item;
END shared_cursors;
/
```

You can then access in an anonymous or named block, as follows:

```
BEGIN
  FOR i IN shared_types.item_cursor LOOP
    dbms_output.put_line('['||i.item_id||']['||i.item_title||']');
  END LOOP;
END;
/
```

NOTE
You can also reference any package specification collection type by prepending the package name and component selector.

There's the temptation to use a reference cursor defined by a record structure. You may choose that development direction because you don't want to create a view. The following declares a strongly typed PL/SQL-only reference cursor:

```
CREATE OR REPLACE PACKAGE shared_types IS
  CURSOR item_cursor IS SELECT item_id, item_title FROM item;
  TYPE item_type IS RECORD
  ( item_id      item.item_id%TYPE
  , item_title item.item_title%TYPE);
END shared_types;
/
```

You can now use the reference cursor but not with the package-level cursor. *Reference cursors support only explicit cursors.* You can test the shared package-level record structure and cursor by first creating a SQL session-level (or *bind*) variable, like

```
VARIABLE refcur REFCURSOR
```

Then, you can run the following anonymous-block program:

```
DECLARE
  TYPE package_typed IS REF CURSOR RETURN shared_types.item_type;
  quick PACKAGE_TYPED;
BEGIN
  OPEN quick FOR SELECT item_id, item_title FROM item;
  :refcur := quick;
END;
/
```

The package_typed variable uses the package specification datatype to create a strong reference cursor that is dependent on a package-level datatype as opposed to a schema-level table or view. The record structure *is a catalog object declared in the context of the package.*

The anonymous block returns the cursor results into the bind variable. You can query the bind variable reference cursor as follows:

```
SELECT :refcur FROM dual;
```

The query will return the results from the explicit query in the FOR clause. You should note that the OPEN *reference cursor* FOR *sql_statement;* fails if you change the query so that it returns a different set of datatypes or columns.

NOTE
The substitution of a dynamic reference for a literal query raises a
PLS-00455 *exception, which is a "cursor such-and-such and cannot*
be used in a dynamic SQL OPEN *statement."*

Shared record structures, collections, and reference cursors are the safest types to place in package specifications. They become accessible to anyone with the EXECUTE privilege on the package, but they aren't part of the output when you describe a package. As mentioned in the beginning of the section "Package Specification," you must query the source to find the available package specification types.

Components: Functions and Procedures

The components in package specifications are functions or procedures. They have slightly different behaviors than their respective schema-level peers. Package specification functions and procedures are merely *forward referencing* stubs. They define the namespace for a function or procedure and their respective signatures. Functions also define their return types.

The package specification information is recorded in the USER_ARGUMENTS, ALL_ARGUMENTS, and DBA_ARGUMENTS catalog views. These catalog views are covered in the section "Checking Dependencies" later in the chapter.

You define a function stub as follows:

```
FUNCTION a_function (a NUMBER := 1, b NUMBER) RETURNS NUMBER;
```

You declare a procedure stub like this:

```
PROCEDURE a_procedure (a NUMBER := 1, b NUMBER);
```

The sample declarations assign a default to the first formal parameter, which makes it optional. When there's an optional parameter before one or more mandatory parameters, you should use named notation. You can use a positional call, provided you pass a null value in the position of the optional parameter.

The package specification is also where you provide any PRAGMA instructions for package-level functions and procedures. Two PRAGMA instructions can apply to either the whole package or all functions in a package. The SERIALLY_REUSABLE precompiler instruction must be placed in both the package specification and the body. The RESTRICT_REFERENCES precompiler instruction applies to all functions when you use the keyword DEFAULT instead of a function name.

The following precompiler instruction restricts the behavior of all functions in the package, and it guarantees they can't write any database state:

```
CREATE OR REPLACE PACKAGE financial IS
   FUNCTION fv (current NUMBER, periods NUMBER, interest NUMBER) RETURN NUMBER;
   FUNCTION pv (future  NUMBER, periods NUMBER, interest NUMBER) RETURN NUMBER;
   PRAGMA RESTRICT_REFERENCES(DEFAULT, WNDS);
END financial;
/
```

Chapter 6 contains the implementation of the fv and pv functions declared in the package specification. They don't write data states, and their implementations would succeed in a package body.

Package Body

The package body contains the implementations declared in the package specification. Everything must match exactly, including default values for formal parameters. Prior to Oracle 9*i*, you could declare formal parameters in the specification, but they weren't enforced in the package body. This is something you should check in your code before migrating from Oracle 8*i* to newer releases *(if you haven't already done so)*.

The package body prototype is very similar to the package specification prototype. The package body can declare almost everything that the specification sets except one thing. You can't define PRAGMA instructions for functions inside a package body. Any attempt raises a PLS-00708 error that says you must put them in the package specification.

You can use EXCEPTION_INIT PRAGMA instructions for package-level exceptions provided they're distinct from those declared in your package specification. You can also override a variable that is declared in the package specification. You do this by declaring the variable again in the package body. When you do this, you make both copies of this variable inaccessible to your package body. Any reference inside a package body to the doubly declared variable raises a PLS-00371 exception when you attempt to compile the package body. The exception tells you that at most one declaration for the variable is permitted. The intent appears to indicate that you shouldn't take advantage of this behavior, and successful compilation of the package body may be a bug.

The prototype for a package body follows:

```
CREATE [OR REPLACE] PACKAGE package_name [AUTHID {DEFINER | CURRENT_USER}] IS
  [PRAGMA SERIALLY_REUSABLE;]
  [variable_name    [CONSTANT] scalar_datatype [:= value];]
  [collection_name [CONSTANT] collection_datatype [:= constructor];]
  [object_name      [CONSTANT] object_datatype [:= constructor];]

  [TYPE record_structure IS RECORD
  ( field_name1      datatype
  [,field_name2      datatype
  [,field_name(n+1) datatype]]);]

  [CURSOR cursor_name
  [(parameter_name1      datatype
  [,parameter_name2      datatype
  [,parameter_name(n+1) datatype]])] IS
    select_statement;]

  [TYPE ref_cursor IS REF CURSOR [RETURN { catalog_row | record_structure }];]

  [user_exception_name EXCEPTION;
  [PRAGMA EXCEPTION_INIT(user_exception_name,-20001);]]

  -- This is a forward referencing stub to a function implemented later.
  [FUNCTION function_name
  [( parameter1     [IN][OUT] [NOCOPY] sql_datatype | plsql_datatype
  [, parameter2     [IN][OUT] [NOCOPY] sql_datatype | plsql_datatype
  [, parameter(n+1) [IN][OUT] [NOCOPY] sql_datatype | plsql_datatype )]
  RETURN { sql_data_type | plsql_data_type }
```

```
[ DETERMINISTIC | PARALLEL_ENABLED ]
[ PIPELINED ]
[ RESULT_CACHE [ RELIES_ON (table_name) ]];]

-- This is a forward referencing stub to a procedure implemented later.
[PROCEDURE procedure_name
[( parameter1     [IN][OUT] [NOCOPY] sql_datatype | plsql_datatype
[, parameter2     [IN][OUT] [NOCOPY] sql_datatype | plsql_datatype
[, parameter(n+1) [IN][OUT] [NOCOPY] sql_datatype | plsql_datatype])];]

[FUNCTION function_name
[( parameter1     [IN][OUT] [NOCOPY] sql_datatype | plsql_datatype
[, parameter2     [IN][OUT] [NOCOPY] sql_datatype | plsql_datatype
[, parameter(n+1) [IN][OUT] [NOCOPY] sql_datatype | plsql_datatype )]
RETURN { sql_data_type | plsql_data_type }
[ DETERMINISTIC | PARALLEL_ENABLED ]
[ PIPELINED ]
[ RESULT_CACHE [ RELIES_ON (table_name) ]] IS
[ PRAGMA AUTONOMOUS_TRANSACTION;]        -- Check rules in Chapter 6.
   some_declaration_statement;           -- Check rules in Chapter 6.
 BEGIN
   some_execution_statement;             -- Check rules in Chapter 6.
[EXCEPTION
   WHEN some_exception THEN
   some exception_handling_statement;] -- Check rules in Chapter 5.
 END [function_name];]

[PROCEDURE procedure_name
[( parameter1     [IN][OUT] [NOCOPY] sql_datatype | plsql_datatype
[, parameter2     [IN][OUT] [NOCOPY] sql_datatype | plsql_datatype
[, parameter(n+1) [IN][OUT] [NOCOPY] sql_datatype | plsql_datatype])] IS
[ PRAGMA AUTONOMOUS_TRANSACTION;]        -- Check rules in Chapter 6.
   some_declaration_statement;           -- Check rules in Chapter 6.
 BEGIN
   some_execution_statement;             -- Check rules in Chapter 6.
[EXCEPTION
   WHEN some_exception THEN
   some exception_handling_statement;] -- Check rules in Chapter 5.
 END [procedure_name];]
END [package_name];
/
```

The SERIALLY_REUSABLE PRAGMA (precompiler instructions) must be included in the package body if the package specification uses it. This practice differs from the PRAGMA instructions covered earlier.

The next three subsections discuss how you can implement variables, types, and components in your package bodies. They point out changes in behavior between serially or non–serially reusable packages. As mentioned, packages are non–serially reusable by default. As in the section "Package Specification" earlier, types are subdivided into structures, cursors, and collections.

Variables

Package-level variables declared in package bodies differ from those declared in package specifications. You can't access package-level variables outside of the package. Only functions and procedures published by the package specification can access package-level variables. This makes these variables very much like instance variables because they retain their state between calls to the package functions and procedures. At least, they retain their state from the point of the first call until the end of the session or they age out of the SGA.

The following package specification creates a function and procedure. The get function returns the value of a package body variable. The set procedure lets you reset a package body variable's value. This package is non–serially reusable, which means it retains variable values until it ages out of the SGA.

The package specification is

```
-- This is found on create_package_variables on the publisher's web site.
CREATE OR REPLACE PACKAGE package_variables IS
  -- Declare package components.
  PROCEDURE set(value VARCHAR2);
  FUNCTION get RETURN VARCHAR2;
END package_variables;
/
```

Package specifications don't know what variables are implemented in package bodies. The implementation details are known exclusively to the package body. Published functions and procedures can access any package-level components. They are also available to any user who is granted the EXECUTE privilege on the package.

The package body declares a package-level variable. It also provides the implementation for the function and procedure. The published components have access to everything declared in the package. You can call them without prepending the package name and component selector *(that period again)* from inside the package.

The package body follows:

```
-- This is found on create_package_variables on the publisher's web site.
CREATE OR REPLACE PACKAGE BODY package_variables IS
  -- Declare package scope variable.
  variable VARCHAR2(20) := 'Initial Value';
  -- Define function
  FUNCTION get RETURN VARCHAR2 IS
  BEGIN
    RETURN variable;
  END get;
  -- Define procedure.
  PROCEDURE set(value VARCHAR2) IS
  BEGIN
    variable := value;
  END set;
END package_variables;
/
```

The get function returns the package-level variable. The set procedure resets the package-level variable. After you compile the program, you can test the behavior by declaring a session-level (bind) variable. Call the `get` function to return a value into the bind variable. You can then query the bind variable:

```
VARIABLE outcome VARCHAR2(20)
CALL package_variables.get() INTO :outcome;
SELECT :outcome AS outcome FROM dual;
```

The output is

```
OUTCOME
--------------
Initial Value
```

Execute the `set` procedure to reset the variable's value. Call the `get` function again before you re-query the bind variable. The test results are

```
EXECUTE package_variables.set('New Value');
CALL package_variables.get() INTO :outcome;
SELECT :outcome AS outcome FROM dual;
```

The output is

```
OUTCOME
--------------
New Value
```

If you rerun the `create_package_variables.sql` file to repeat the test in the same session, it works differently. You would print "New Value" first, not "Initial Value," because the package hasn't aged out of the SGA. The DDL command replaces a package specification only when there's a change between the original and new package specifications. Otherwise, it simply skips the process. The next DDL command in the file checks the package body for a change. When it doesn't find a change, it skips the replace command and runs the test scripts.

You can force a change and refresh variables by running an `ALTER` command to recompile the package specification. After recompilation, all variables are returned to their initial values. You can alter the package before rerunning the script, and see the same results shown.

The syntax to recompile only a package specification is

```
ALTER PACKAGE package_variables COMPILE SPECIFICATION;
```

If you change the package from non–serially reusable to serially reusable, the test results change. Each call to a serially reusable package body gets a new copy of both the package specification and the body. The package-level variable is always the same.

You should consider declaring packages as non–serially reusable libraries. If you adopt that policy, you should declare only constants in the package specification. Declare variables only in the package body or inside the functions and procedures as local variables.

Types

As with the package specification, you can declare dynamic or static datatypes in package bodies. Datatypes are typically PL/SQL structures, collections, reference cursors, and cursors. You can declare dynamic datatypes by anchoring them to row or column declarations (refer back to Table 9-1). You declare static datatypes when types are explicitly declared as SQL datatypes.

Singleton Design Pattern

A Singleton design pattern lets you construct only one instance of an object. It guarantees any subsequent attempt to construct an instance fails until the original object instance is discarded. This pattern is widely used in OO programming languages, like C++, C#, or Java.

You can guarantee a single instance of a package in any session, too. To do so, you simply embed a call to a locally scoped function or procedure as the first step in *all published* functions and procedures. The locally scoped function or procedure holds a local variable that should match a package-level control variable. If the values match, the local function or procedure changes the package-level variable to lock the package.

You also need another locally scoped function or procedure as the last step in all published functions and procedures. The last step resets all package variables to their initial state. The easiest way is to accomplish this is to write a procedure that resets the default values for package variables. You call the resetting procedure as the last statement in your published function or procedure.

Don't forget to reset the control variable with the other package variables. If you forget to reset the control variable, the package would be locked until the end of the session or when it ages out of the SGA.

Package bodies are dependent on their package specification. They are also dependent on other schema-level objects that they use in their implementation of components. The behaviors of types in the package body are consistent with those of the package specification with one exception: PL/SQL blocks outside of the package body can't access elements declared in the package body.

Components: Functions and Procedures

Components are implementation of published functions or procedures, or they are declarations or definitions of package-only functions or procedures. You can also declare local components inside published or package-only functions or procedures.

Declaring something before the implementation is called forward referencing (or a prototype). When you define local components, you provide both their declaration and implementation. Sometimes you need to declare a component before you're ready to implement it. You do this by providing a forward referencing stub for a function or procedure.

Components can only specify whether they are autonomous or local transactions. Local transactions run inside a pre-existing transaction scope. Autonomous transactions run discretely in their own transaction scope. By default, all functions and procedures are local transactions unless you declare them as autonomous transactions. The AUTONOMOUS_TRANSACTION PRAGMA declares a function or procedure as autonomous.

Only published functions or procedures can be called from PL/SQL blocks that are external to the package. Package-level functions can be called by three types of components. You can call them from published, package-level, or local components. Local components are declared and implemented *(or defined)* inside a published or package-level component. Another option is to define a local component inside another local component. Chapter 6 covers the rules governing how you declare and implement functions and procedures.

The components package specification declares only a *getter* function and *setter* procedure. A *getter* component simply gets something from the black box, while a *setter* component sets an initial value or resets an existing value inside the black box. These are stock terms in OO programming. As you've discovered earlier in this chapter, they also apply well to PL/SQL packages that are declared as non–serially reusable.

The `components` package specification is

```
-- This is found in create_components.sql on the publisher's web site.
CREATE OR REPLACE PACKAGE components IS
  PROCEDURE set (value VARCHAR2); -- Declare published procedure.
  FUNCTION get RETURN VARCHAR2;   -- Declare published function.
END components;
/
```

Functions are almost always declared before procedures in PL/SQL, but their sequencing is meaningless inside a package specification. It is meaningful when you declare them as local functions and procedures because of forward referencing possibilities.

The `components` package body adds a package-level function and procedure, and two shared variables. One variable is provided to demonstrate how you would implement a Singleton pattern in a PL/SQL package. The other variable contains a value that should always have an initial value.

The `components` package body is

```
-- This is found in create_components.sql on the publisher's web site.
CREATE OR REPLACE PACKAGE BODY components IS
  -- Declare package scoped shared variables.
  key NUMBER := 0;
  variable VARCHAR2(20) := 'Initial Value';
  -- Define package-only function and procedure.
  FUNCTION locked RETURN BOOLEAN IS
    key NUMBER := 0;
  BEGIN
    IF components.key = key THEN
      components.key := 1;
      RETURN FALSE;
    ELSE
      RETURN TRUE;
    END IF;
  END locked;
  PROCEDURE unlock IS
    key NUMBER := 1;
  BEGIN
    IF components.key = key THEN
      components.key := 0;            -- Reset the key.
      variable := 'Initial Value'; -- Reset initial value of shared variable.
    END IF;
  END unlock;
  -- Define published function and procedure.
  FUNCTION get RETURN VARCHAR2 IS
  BEGIN
    RETURN variable;
  END get;
  PROCEDURE set (value VARCHAR2) IS
  BEGIN
    IF NOT locked THEN
      variable := value;
```

```
      dbms_output.put_line('The new value until release is ['||get||'].');
      unlock;
    END IF;
  END set;
END components;
/
```

The key action occurs in the `set` procedure. It locks the package to change, changes a shared variable, gets a copy of the temporary value *(also known as a transitive value)* of the shared variable, and unlocks the package. The unlock procedure resets the control key and resets the shared package variable.

You can test this by first creating a session or bind variable:

```
VARIABLE current_content VARCHAR2(20)
```

After setting bind variable, you call the function and return the value into the bind variable. A select statement lets you see the initial package value, as shown:

```
CALL components.get() INTO :current_content;
SELECT :current_content AS contents FROM dual;
```

It returns the following:

```
CONTENTS
------------------
Initial Value
```

The temporary value is printed to console when you call the `set` procedure. At least, it is printed when you've enable `SERVEROUTPUT` first.

```
SET SERVEROUTPUT ON SIZE 1000000
EXECUTE components.set('New Value');
```

The output should look like this:

```
The new value until release is [New Value].
```

A subsequent call to the `get` function returns the original value of the package variable. The `components` package implements a Singleton pattern for shared package variables.

The locked function and unlock procedure ensure that the package state is always the same. You are able to call the `set` procedure to change a variable, see the change with a call to the `get` function. This is not possible when the package is serially reusable. A call to the `get` function inside the `set` function always grabs a new copy of the package when the package is declared serially reusable.

The `components` package demonstrates an approach to managing shared package variables between calls. In this example, the shared package variable behaves like an instance variable in a user-defined object. As mentioned earlier in this chapter, Chapter 14 covers user-defined objects. Clearly, this is a lot of work to share a variable and guarantee that the next call to the package finds the same initial value.

Aside from showing you how to implement the Singleton pattern, this code demonstrates how you call package-level components through published declarations. Package-level declarations are hidden package elements. You can't see them when you describe a package.

Definer vs. Invoker Rights

Earlier references have touched on the concepts of the definer and invoker rights. These are models of operation. The default model of operation for stored programs is definer rights. Definer rights programs act on catalog objects that are declared in the same schema. They perform with all the privileges of the schema owner.

A definer rights model does not dictate that all declared catalog objects are owned by the same schema as the package owner. It is possible that synonyms point to catalog objects owned by another user, where that other user has granted privileges to on their catalog objects. Catalog objects can be functions, packages, procedures, materialized views, sequences, tables, or views. Figure 9-3 shows you a visual representation of a definer rights model where all the catalog objects are owned by the same user.

A schema is a container of stored programs. The schema grants access to stored programs, or *black boxes,* though privileges. External users may create synonyms to simplify call statements to external programs. Synonyms only translate *(resolve)* when grants, stored programs, and catalog objects are valid in the owning schema. The combination of synonyms and grants lets external users call programs with inputs and retrieve output from stored programs in another schema. They also allow a call syntax that mirrors what it would be in the owning schema, provided you declare synonym names that match the target functions or procedures.

The definer rights model is ideal when you want to deploy a single set of stored programs that act on local catalog objects. Alternatively, it also works when you want to have all access centralized in a single schema. The centralized access model is a bit more complex because the access schema may contain synonyms that point to stored programs in other schemas. The stored programs in turn have definer rights on catalog objects in their own schema.

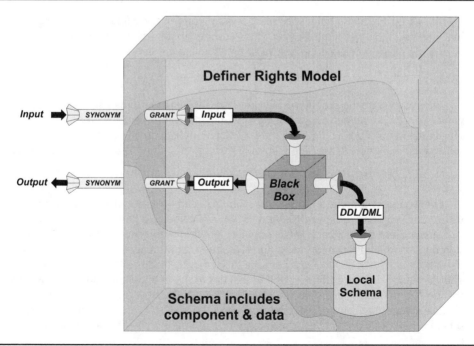

FIGURE 9-3   *Definer rights model of operation with local catalog objects*

NOTE
A centralized access schema is exactly how the Oracle E-Business Suite runs.

Grants and Synonyms

Assume you have a package named manage_items declared and implemented as a definer rights program in your plsql schema. You want to create a second schema called purchasing and let the purchasing user access the manage_items package. There are two steps required to make access seamless to the manage_items package.

The first step requires you to connect as the plsql user and grant the EXECUTE privilege on the manage_items package to the new purchasing schema. The following command grants that privilege:

```
GRANT EXECUTE ON manage_items TO purchasing;
```

After you grant the EXECUTE privilege on the package, the purchasing user can access the package. However, the purchasing user must prepend the plsql schema name and a component selector to see the package, as follows:

```
SQL> DESCRIBE plsql.manage_items
```

CAUTION
You have limited privileges when grants are made through roles. Functions and procedures that contain SQL statements may fail at run time when grants are not explicit privileges.

You can dispense with the schema name and component selector by creating a SYNONYM in the purchasing schema. A SYNONYM translates an alias to a fully qualified reference, like plsql.manage_items. You create a synonym using the same name as the package as follows:

```
CREATE SYNONYM manage_items FOR plsql.manage_items;
```

After you create the synonym, you can describe the package by using the SYNONYM. This lets you dispense with prepending the schema name and component selector to packages or any other catalog object. You can grant the EXECUTE privilege to all other users by substituting the schema name with PUBLIC. The following grants permissions to all other database users:

```
GRANT EXECUTE ON manage_items TO PUBLIC;
```

Grants and synonyms are powerful tools. You can find GRANT definitions in the user_tab_privs administrative view. SYNONYM values are in the USER_SYNONYMS view.

More or less, the definer rights model lets individual users act on subsets of data that are stored in a common repository. The stored programs control access and authentication by using the DBMS_APPLICATION_INFO package to set the CLIENT_INFO column in V$SESSION. They stripe the data by adding a column that ties to the user's organization or business entity. The section "Compound Triggers" in Chapter 10 demonstrates how use the CLIENT_INFO column.

The invoker rights model requires you to set the AUTHID value to CURRENT_USER in any schema-level program. This approach requires that you identify all catalog objects that are dependencies of invoker rights programs. After identifying the dependencies, you must replicate those catalog objects to any schema that wants to call the invoker rights programs. This requirement is due to the fact that *invoker rights modules resolve by using the caller's privileges, not the definer's privileges.*

> **NOTE**
> *Database triggers and functions called from within views are always executed with definer rights and run with the privileges of the user who owns the triggering table or view.*

You choose an invoker rights mode of operation to support distributed data repositories. A single code repository can use grants and synonyms to bridge transactions across a network. They accomplish this by using a DB_LINK. A DB_LINK lets you resolves a network alias through the tnsnames.ora file to find another Oracle database. Appendix A describes how to configure and use the tnsnames.ora file.

The invoker rights model best supports data that is stored in a separate user schema. It is also ideal for distributed database solutions when they're running in the same instance. There are significant limitations to remote calls when making remote procedure calls that use database links.

Remote Calls

Remote calls are made from one database instance to another. You make remote calls through database links (DB_LINK). A user must have the CREATE DATABASE LINK privilege to create a database link. You grant as the SYSTEM user the privilege by using the following syntax:

```
GRANT CREATE DATABASE LINK TO schema_name;
```

After granting this to a schema, you can create a database link to another schema. The prototype to create a DB_LINK is

```
CREATE DATABASE LINK db_link_name
CONNECT TO schema_name IDENTIFIED BY schema_password
USING 'tns_names_alias'
```

A database link is a static object in the database. It stores the schema name and password to resolve a remote connection. You must update database links whenever the remote database changes its schema's password. Database links can reference other database instances or a different schema of the same database.

The examples in this sidebar use a DB_LINK named loopback, which allows you to reconnect to the same instance. You don't need to change anything in the tnsnames.ora file to make a loopback database link work. However, there are some rules on the calls that you can make using a remote connection. You can call schema-level components provided that they don't require arguments.

For example, you call a remote status function by using the following syntax when using the loopback database link:

SQL

```
SELECT status@loopback FROM dual;
```

PL/SQL

```
BEGIN
  dbms_output.put_line('Status ['||status@loopback||']');
END;
/
```

The remote schema-level component can contain DDL or DML statements. You cannot return a handle to a LOB. Any attempt to do so raises an ORA-22992 exception that says you can't use a LOB locator selected from a remote table.

Managing Packages in the Database Catalog

As databases grow, so do the stored programs that support them. Whether you choose to implement a definer or invoker rights solution, understanding what you've added to your schema is very important. The next three sections show you how to find, manage, and validate packages and their dependencies in the Oracle 11*g* database.

Finding, Validating, and Describing Packages

The all_objects, dba_objects, and user_objects administrative views let you find packages. They also let you validate whether a package specification or body is valid or invalid. Rather than create new code artifacts, the example uses the pipelined package and pf function created in the section "PIPELINED Clause" of Chapter 6.

The following query lets you see that they are created and valid. The SQL*Plus column formatting ensures the output is readable in one 80-column screen.

```
COLUMN object_name FORMAT A10
SELECT   object_name
,        object_type
,        last_ddl_time
,        timestamp
,        status
FROM     user_objects
WHERE    object_name IN ('PIPELINED','PF');
```

This query should return data like this:

```
OBJECT_NAME          OBJECT_TYPE          LAST_DDL_ TIMESTAMP            STATUS
-------------------- -------------------- --------- ------------------- ------
PF                   FUNCTION             03-JAN-08 2008-01-03:22:50:23 VALID
PIPELINED            PACKAGE              03-JAN-08 2008-01-03:22:50:19 VALID
PIPELINED            PACKAGE BODY         03-JAN-08 2008-01-03:22:50:20 VALID
```

If you put an extraneous character in the pipelined package body, it will fail when you run it. After attempting to compile an incorrect package body, re-query the data and you should see something like this:

```
OBJECT_NAM OBJECT_TYPE          LAST_DDL_ TIMESTAMP            STATUS
---------- -------------------- --------- ------------------- -------
PF         FUNCTION             03-JAN-08 2008-01-03:22:50:23 VALID
PIPELINED  PACKAGE              03-JAN-08 2008-01-03:22:50:19 VALID
PIPELINED  PACKAGE BODY         03-JAN-08 2008-01-03:22:53:34 INVALID
```

The invalid package body does not invalidate the pf function, which is dependent on the pipelined package. The reason is that the pf function is dependent on the package specification, not the package body. As mentioned earlier, the package specification is the schema-level component. You should fix the pipelined package body and recompile it before attempting the next step.

If you now put an extraneous character in the pipelined package specification, it fails when you try to compile it. Re-querying the data from the USER_SOURCE view tells you that the dependent package body and pf function are also invalid.

```
OBJECT_NAM  OBJECT_TYPE        LAST_DDL_ TIMESTAMP            STATUS
----------  -----------------  --------- -------------------  -------
PF          FUNCTION           03-JAN-08 2008-01-03:22:50:23 INVALID
PIPELINED   PACKAGE            03-JAN-08 2008-01-03:23:06:10 INVALID
PIPELINED   PACKAGE BODY       03-JAN-08 2008-01-03:22:53:34 INVALID
```

You can rebuild the pipelined package by running the create_pipelined2.sql script found on the publisher's web site. You would find that the pf function is still invalid in the database catalog after you recompiled the package specification and body (but not the case if you reran the script).

You can validate it by an explicit compilation statement like

```
ALTER FUNCTION pf COMPILE;
```

Or, you can simply call the function, which validates that its dependent objects are valid before running the statement. This is known as a *lazy compile* but is actually called automatic recompilation.

```
SELECT * FROM TABLE(pf);
```

You can describe the package as you would a table or view from SQL*Plus:

```
SQL> DESCRIBE pipelined
```

It returns the following:

```
FUNCTION PF RETURNS ACCOUNT_COLLECTION
```

You may notice that the record and collection type declared in the package specification aren't displayed. This is normal. As stated in the section "Package Specification" earlier in the chapter, you must query the all_source, dba_source, or user_source to find the complete package declaration. Wrapped package bodies will be returned from that query as gibberish that you should discard.

This section has shown you how to find, validate, and describe packages. The next section explores tracking dependencies.

Checking Dependencies

The all_dependencies, dba_dependencies, and user_dependencies administrative view let you examine dependencies between stored programs. As done in the previous section, the example here uses the pipelined package and pf function created in the section "PIPELINED Clause" of Chapter 6.

The following query lets you see the dependencies for the `pf` function. The SQL*Plus column formatting ensures the output is readable in one 80-column screen.

```
COLUMN name FORMAT A10
COLUMN type FORMAT A8
COLUMN referenced_name FORMAT A30
COLUMN referenced_type FORMAT A10
COLUMN dependency_type FORMAT A4
SELECT   name
,        type
,        referenced_name
,        referenced_type
,        dependency_type
FROM     user_dependencies
WHERE    name = 'PF';
```

The output returned is displayed in the following illustration. The `pf` function has a direct hard dependency on the pipelined package and two direct hard dependencies on the contact and member tables. The two tables are referenced in the `FROM` clause of the `CURSOR` declared in the `pf` function.

NAME	TYPE	REFERENCED_NAME	REFERENCED	DEPE
PF	FUNCTION	STANDARD	PACKAGE	HARD
PF	FUNCTION	SYS_STUB_FOR_PURITY_ANALYSIS	PACKAGE	HARD
PF	FUNCTION	PLITBLM	SYNONYM	HARD
PF	FUNCTION	CONTACT	TABLE	HARD
PF	FUNCTION	MEMBER	TABLE	HARD
PF	FUNCTION	PIPELINED	PACKAGE	HARD

6 rows selected.

These dependencies are set because of the cursor in the function.

This dependency is on record type found in the package specification.

This section has shown you how to find the dependencies between stored programs. You can also refer to Appendix H that covers the PL/Scope tool. Together you can understand what your dependencies are and their respective frequency.

Comparing Validation Methods: Timestamp vs. Signature

Stored programs are validated or invalidated by using a timestamp or signature method. The timestamp model is the default for most Oracle databases. The timestamp method compares the `last_ddl_time` column, which you can check in the `all_objects`, `dba_objects`, or `user_objects` view. When the base object has a newer timestamp than the dependent object, the dependent object will be recompiled.

Dates and timestamps always provide some interesting twists and turns. When you are working in a distributed situation and the two database instances are in different time zones, the comparison may be invalid. You may also encounter unnecessary recompilations when distributed servers are in the same time zone. Dependent objects are sometimes compiled even when the change in `last_ddl_time` column didn't result in a change of the base object.

Another complication with time stamp validation occurs when PL/SQL is distributed between the server and Oracle Forms. In this case, a change in the base code can't trigger recompilation because it isn't included in the run-time version of the Oracle Form.

The alternative to timestamp validation is the signature model. This model works by comparing the signature of schema-level and package-level functions and procedures. You must alter the database as a privileged user to convert the database to signature model validation. You would use the following command syntax:

```
ALTER SYSTEM SET REMOTE_DEPENDENCIES_MODE = SIGNATURE;
```

NOTE
You must hold the ALTER SYSTEM *privilege to issue this command.*

This command changes the remote_dependencies_mode parameter in your spfile. ora or pfile.ora configuration file. If you want the change to be permanent, you should change it in your configuration file.

The signature model works by checking whether the base object signature changes between compilation events. If there is a change, it will force compilation of dependent packages. You can find the signature information in the all_arguments, dba_arguments, and user_arguments views.

NOTE
Remote procedure calls can raise an ORA-04062 *exception when a remote database uses timestamp, not signature, mode.*

The timestamp model is ideal for centralized environments. The signature model is sometimes more effective for some centralized development environments but generally a preferred solution in distributed database applications.

Summary
This chapter has shown you why packages are the backbone of Oracle 11*g* application development. You've learned how to group functions and procedures into libraries that include overloading. You've also learned the difference between package and local variables, types, and components, and you've seen how to plan and manage these features.

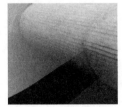

CHAPTER
10

Triggers

D atabase *triggers* are specialized stored programs. They are not called directly but are triggered by events in the database. They run between the time you issue a command and the time you perform the database management system action. You can write triggers in PL/SQL or Java. Triggers can capture events that create, modify, or drop objects, and they can capture inserts to, updates of, and deletes from tables or views. They can also monitor changes in the state of the database or schema, and the actions of users.

This chapter covers the following:

- Introduction to triggers

- Trigger architecture

- Data Definition Language triggers

- Data Manipulation Language triggers

- Compound triggers

- Instead-of triggers

- System or database event triggers

- Trigger restrictions

The sections lay a foundation and develop ideas sequentially. They should also serve as a quick reference if you want to focus on writing a specific trigger type quickly. For example, you can go to the section "Data Manipulation Language Triggers" to learn how to write triggers for inserts, updates, and deletes.

Introduction to Triggers

Database *triggers* are specialized stored programs. As such, they are defined by very similar DDL rules. Likewise, triggers can call SQL statements and PL/SQL functions and procedures. You can choose to implement triggers in PL/SQL or Java. You can check Chapter 14 and Appendix D for clarification of syntax on writing Java libraries to support your triggers.

Database triggers differ from stored functions and procedures because you can't call them directly. Database triggers are fired when a triggering event occurs in the database. This makes them very powerful tools in your efforts to manage the database. You are able to limit or redirect actions through triggers.

You can do the following with triggers:

- Control the behavior of DDL statements, as by altering, creating, or renaming objects

- Control the behavior of DML statements, like inserts, updates, and deletes

- Enforce referential integrity, complex business rules, and security policies

- Control and redirect DML statements when they change data in a view

- Audit information of system access and behavior by creating transparent logs

On the other hand, you can't control the sequence of or synchronize calls to triggers, and this can present problems if you rely too heavily on triggers. The only control you have is to designate them as before or after certain events. Oracle 11*g* delivers compound triggers to help you manage larger events, like those triggering events that you would sequence.

There are risks with triggers. The risks are complex because while SQL statements fire triggers, triggers call SQL statements. A trigger can call a SQL statement that in turn fires another trigger. The subsequent trigger could repeat the behavior and fire another trigger. This creates *cascading triggers*. Oracle 11*g* and earlier releases limit the number of cascading trigger to 32, after which an exception is thrown.

The following summarizes the five types of triggers and their uses:

- **Data Definition Language triggers**   These triggers fire when you create, change, or remove objects in a database schema. They are useful to control or monitor DDL statements. An *instead-of create* table trigger provides you with a tool to ensure table creation meets your development standards, like including storage or partitioning clauses. You can also use them to monitor poor programming practices, such as when programs *create* and *drop* temporary tables rather than use Oracle collections. Temporary tables can fragment disk space and degrade database performance over time.

- **Data Manipulation Language triggers**   These triggers fire when you *insert, update,* or *delete* data from a table. You can fire them once for all changes on a table, or for each row change, using *statement-* or *row-level* trigger types, respectively. DML triggers are useful to control DML statements. You can use these triggers to audit, check, save, and replace values before they are changed. Automatic numbering of numeric *primary keys* is frequently done by using a row-level DML trigger.

- **Compound triggers**   These triggers acts as both statement- and row-level triggers when you *insert, update,* or *delete* data from a table. This trigger lets you capture information at four timing points: (a) before the firing statement; (b) before each row change from the firing statement; (c) after each row change from the firing statement; and (d) after the firing statement. You can use these types of triggers to audit, check, save, and replace values before they are changed when you need to take action at both the statement and row event levels.

- **Instead-of triggers**   These triggers enable you to stop performance of a DML statement and redirect the DML statement. INSTEAD OF triggers are often used to manage how you write to non-updatable views. The INSTEAD OF triggers apply business rules and directly *insert, update,* or *delete* rows in tables that define updatable views. Alternatively, the INSTEAD OF triggers *insert, update,* or *delete* rows in designated tables unrelated to the view.

- **System or database event triggers**   These triggers fire when a system activity occurs in the database, like the logon and logoff event triggers. They are useful for auditing information of system access. These triggers let you track system events and map them to users.

Triggers have some restrictions that are important to note. The largest one is that the trigger body can be no longer than 32,760 bytes. That's because trigger bodies are stored in LONG datatypes columns. This means you should consider keeping your trigger bodies small. You do that by placing the coding logic in other schema-level components, like functions, procedures, and packages. Another advantage of moving the coding logic out of the trigger body is that you can't wrap it when it's in trigger bodies, as explained in Appendix F.

Each of these triggers has a set of rules that govern its use. You will cover all five triggers in their respective sections. The next section describes the architecture of database triggers.

Privileges Required to Use Triggers

You must have the CREATE TRIGGER system privilege to create a trigger on an object that you own. If the object is owned by another user, you'll need that user to grant you the ALTER privilege on the object. Alternatively, the privileged user can grant you the ALTER ANY TABLE and CREATE ANY TRIGGER privileges.

You have definer permissions on your own schema-level components, but you must have EXECUTE permission when you call a schema-level component owned by another user. You should document any required privileges during development to streamline subsequent implementation.

Database Trigger Architecture

Database triggers are defined in the database like packages. They're composed of two pieces: the database trigger declaration and the body. The declaration states how and when a trigger is called. You can't call a trigger directly. They are triggered *(called)* by a firing event. Firing events are DDL or DML statements or database or system events. Database triggers implement an object-oriented observer pattern, which means they listen for an event and then take action.

Trigger declarations consist of four parts: a trigger name, a statement, a restriction, and an action. The first three define the trigger declaration, and the last defines the trigger body. A trigger name must be unique among triggers but can duplicate the name of any other object in a schema because triggers have their own namespace. A trigger statement identifies the event or statement type that fires the trigger. A trigger restriction, such as a WHEN clause or INSTEAD OF clause, limits when the trigger runs. A trigger action is a trigger body.

NOTE
A namespace is a unique list of identifiers maintained in the database catalog.

A database trigger declaration is valid unless you remove the object that it observes. A database trigger declaration also creates a run-time process when an event fires it. The trigger body is not as simple. A trigger body can depend on other tables, views, or stored programs. This means that you can invalidate a trigger body by removing a dependency. Dependencies are local schema objects, but those include synonyms that may resolve across the network. You invalidate a trigger when the trigger body becomes invalid. Trigger bodies are specialized anonymous-block programs. You can call and pass them parameters only through the trigger.

The linkage becomes acute when you define a DDL trigger on the create event. As discussed in the section "Data Definition Language Triggers," an invalid trigger body for a CREATE trigger disables your ability to recreate the missing dependency. Similar behaviors occur for other DDL events, like ALTER and DROP.

You can recompile triggers after you replace any missing dependencies. The syntax is:

```
ALTER TRIGGER trigger_name COMPILE;
```

Triggering events communicate directly with the trigger. You have no control over or visibility into how that communication occurs. You have no data other than that which is available through the system-defined event attributes (see the section "Event Attribute Functions" later in this chapter for more information on DDL, statement-level DML, and system and database event triggers). You do have access to the new and old pseudo-record types in row-level DML and INSTEAD OF triggers. The structure of these types is dynamic and defined at run time. The trigger declaration inherits the declaration of these values from the DML statement that fires it.

DML row-level and INSTEAD OF triggers call their trigger bodies differently than statement-level triggers. When an event fires this type of trigger, the trigger declaration spawns a run-time program unit. The run-time program unit is the real "trigger" in this process. The trigger makes available new and old pseudo-record structures by communicating with the DML statement that fired it. The trigger code block can access these pseudo-record structures by calling them as bind variables. The trigger code block is an anonymous PL/SQL block that is only accessible through a trigger declaration.

As discussed in Chapter 3, Table 3-1, bind variables allow you to reach outside of a program's scope. You can access variables defined in the calling program's scope. The :in and :out variables are bind variables inside trigger bodies. They let the trigger code block communicate with the trigger session. Only row-level triggers can reference these pseudo-record structure bind variables. Row-level trigger code blocks can read and write through these bind variables, as shown in Figure 10-1.

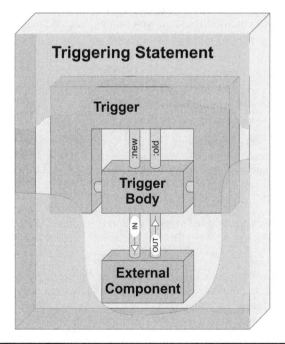

FIGURE 10-1   *Trigger architecture*

You can also call external standalone or package functions and procedures from trigger bodies. When you call programs from the trigger body, the called programs are *black boxes.* This means that external stored programs can't access the `:new` and `:old` bind variables. You do have the option to pass them by value or reference to other stored functions and procedures.

Oracle 11*g* introduces compound triggers. This new trigger changes the landscape of writing triggers. You can now fire a compound trigger, capture row-level statement information, accumulate it in a global trigger collection, and access that data in the `AFTER STATEMENT` timing block. You can read this in detail in the section "Compound Triggers."

You can define multiple triggers on any object or event. Oracle 11*g* provides you with no way to synchronize which trigger fires first, second, or last. This limit is because triggers are interleaved, that is, because program units work independently as discrete processes. Triggers can slow down your application interface, especially row-level statements. You should be careful when and where you deploy triggers to solve problems.

Data Definition Language Triggers

Data Definition Language triggers fire when you create, change, or remove objects in a database schema. They are useful to control or monitor DDL statements. Table 10-1 lists the data definition events that work with DDL triggers. These triggers support both `BEFORE` and `AFTER` event triggers and work at the database or schema level.

You often use DDL triggers to monitor significant events in the database. Sometimes you use them to monitor errant code. Errant code can perform activities that corrupt or destabilize your database. More often, you use these in development, test, and stage systems to understand and monitor the dynamics of database activities.

NOTE
A stage system is used for end-user testing and load balancing metrics before deployment to production.

DDL triggers are very useful when you patch your application code. They can let you find potential changes between releases. You can also use the instead-of create trigger during an upgrade to enforce table creation storage clauses or partitioning rules.

CAUTION
The overhead of these types of triggers should be monitored carefully in production systems.

These triggers can also track the creation and modification of tables by application programs that lead to database fragmentation. They are also effective security tools when you monitor `GRANT` and `REVOKE` privilege statements. The following sections list and describe in detail the event attribute functions you can use to supplement your DDL trigger.

DDL Event	Description
ALTER	You ALTER objects by changing something about them, like their constraints, names, storage clauses, or structure.
ANALYZE	You ANALYZE objects to compute statistics for the cost optimizer.
ASSOCIATE STATISTICS	You ASSOCIATE STATISTICS to link a statistic type to a column, function, package, type, domain index, or index type.
AUDIT	You AUDIT to enable auditing on an object or system.
COMMENT	You COMMENT to document column or table purposes.
CREATE	You CREATE objects in the database, like objects, privileges, roles, tables, users, and views.
DDL	You use the DDL event to represent any of the primary data definition events. It effectively says any DDL event acting on anything.
DISASSOCIATE STATISTICS	You DISASSOCIATE STATISTICS to unlink a statistic type from a column, function, package, type, domain index, or index type.
DROP	You DROP objects in the database, like objects, privileges, roles, tables, users, and views.
GRANT	You GRANT privileges or roles to users in the database. The privileges enable a user to act on objects, like objects, privileges, roles, tables, users, and views.
NOAUDIT	You NOAUDIT to disable auditing on an object or system.
RENAME	You RENAME objects in the database, like columns, constraints, objects, privileges, roles, synonyms, tables, users, and views.
REVOKE	You REVOKE privileges or roles from users in the database. The privileges enable a user to act on objects, like objects, privileges, roles, tables, users, and views.
TRUNCATE	You TRUNCATE tables, which drops all rows from a table and resets the high-water mark to the original storage clause initial extent value. Unlike the DML DELETE statement, the TRUNCATE command can't be reversed by a ROLLBACK command. You can use the new flashback to undo the change.

TABLE 10-1 *Available Data Definition Events*

Event Attribute Functions

The following is a list of system-defined event attribute functions:

- ORA_CLIENT_IP_ADDRESS
- ORA_DATABASE_NAME

- ORA_DES_ENCRYPTED_PASSWORD

- ORA_DICT_OBJ_NAME

- ORA_DICT_OBJ_NAME_LIST

- ORA_DICT_OBJ_OWNER

- ORA_DICT_OBJ_OWNER_LIST

- ORA_DICT_OBJ_TYPE

- ORA_GRANTEE

- ORA_INSTANCE_NUM

- ORA_IS_ALTER_COLUMN

- ORA_IS_CREATING_NESTED_TABLE

- ORA_IS_DROP_COLUMN

- ORA_IS_SERVERERROR

- ORA_LOGIN_USER

- ORA_PARTITION_POS

- ORA_PRIVILEGE_LIST

- ORA_REVOKEE

- ORA_SERVER_ERROR

- ORA_SERVER_ERROR_DEPTH

- ORA_SERVER_ERROR_MSG

- ORA_SERVER_ERROR_NUM_PARAMS

- ORA_SERVER_ERROR_PARAM

- ORA_SQL_TXT

- ORA_SYSEVENT

- ORA_WITH_GRANT_OPTION

- SPACE_ERROR_INFO

ORA_CLIENT_IP_ADDRESS

The ORA_CLIENT_IP_ADDRESS function takes no formal parameters. It returns the client IP address as a VARCHAR2 datatype.

You can use it like this:

```
DECLARE
  ip_address VARCHAR2(11);
BEGIN
  IF ora_sysevent = 'LOGON' THEN
    ip_address := ora_client_ip_address;
```

```
    END IF;
END;
```

ORA_DATABASE_NAME

The `ORA_DATABASE_NAME` function takes no formal parameters. It returns the database name as a `VARCHAR2` datatype.

You can use it like this:

```
DECLARE
    database VARCHAR2(50);
BEGIN
    database := ora_database_name;
END;
```

ORA_DES_ENCRYPTED_PASSWORD

The `ORA_DES_ENCRYPTED_PASSWORD` function takes no formal parameters. It returns the DES-encrypted password as a `VARCHAR2` datatype. This is equivalent to the value in the `SYS.USER$` table `PASSWORD` column in Oracle 11*g*. Passwords are no longer accessible in the `DBA_USERS` or `ALL_USERS` views.

You can use it like this:

```
DECLARE
    password VARCHAR2(60);
BEGIN
    IF ora_dict_obj_type = 'USER' THEN
        password := ora_des_encrypted_password;
    END IF;
END;
```

ORA_DICT_OBJ_NAME

The `ORA_DICT_OBJ_NAME` function takes no formal parameters. It returns an object name as a `VARCHAR2` datatype. The object name represents the target of the DDL statement.

You can use it like this:

```
DECLARE
    database VARCHAR2(50);
BEGIN
    database := ora_obj_name;
END;
```

ORA_DICT_OBJ_NAME_LIST

The `ORA_DICT_OBJ_NAME_LIST` function takes one formal parameter. The formal parameter is also returned because it is passed by reference as an `OUT` mode list of `VARCHAR2` variables. The formal parameter datatype is defined in the `DBMS_STANDARD` package as `ORA_NAME_LIST_T`. The `ORA_NAME_LIST_T` is a table of `VARCHAR2(64)` datatypes. The *function returns the number of elements in the list* as a `PLS_INTEGER` datatype. The `name_list` contains the list of object names touched by the triggering event.

You can use it like this:

```
DECLARE
    name_list DBMS_STANDARD.ORA_NAME_LIST_T;
    counter      PLS_INTEGER;
```

```
BEGIN
  IF ora_sysevent = 'ASSOCIATE_STATISTICS' THEN
    counter := ora_dict_obj_name_list(name_list);
  END IF;
END;
```

ORA_DICT_OBJ_OWNER

The ORA_DICT_OBJ_OWNER function takes no formal parameters. It returns an owner of the object acted upon by the event as a VARCHAR2 datatype.

You can use it like this:

```
DECLARE
  owner VARCHAR2(30);
BEGIN
  database := ora_dict_obj_owner;
END;
```

ORA_DICT_OBJ_OWNER_LIST

The ORA_DICT_OBJ_OWNER_LIST function takes one formal parameter. The formal parameter is also returned because it is passed by reference as an OUT mode list of VARCHAR2 variables. The formal parameter datatype is defined in the DBMS_STANDARD package as ORA_NAME_LIST_T. The ORA_NAME_LIST_T is a table of VARCHAR2(64) datatypes. The *function returns the number of elements in the list* indexed by a PLS_INTEGER datatype.

In the example, the owner_list contains the list of object owners, where their statistics were analyzed by a triggering event. You can use it like this:

```
DECLARE
  owner_list DBMS_STANDARD.ORA_NAME_LIST_T;
  counter    PLS_INTEGER;
BEGIN
  IF ora_sysevent = 'ASSOCIATE_STATISTICS' THEN
    counter := ora_dict_obj_owner_list(owner_list);
  END IF;
END;
```

ORA_DICT_OBJ_TYPE

The ORA_DICT_OBJ_TYPE function takes no formal parameters. It returns the datatype of the dictionary object changed by the event as a VARCHAR2 datatype.

You can use it like this:

```
DECLARE
  type VARCHAR2(19);
BEGIN
  database := ora_dict_obj_type;
END;
```

ORA_GRANTEE

The ORA_GRANTEE function takes one formal parameter. The formal parameter is also returned because it is passed by reference as an OUT mode list of VARCHAR2 variables. The formal parameter datatype is defined in the DBMS_STANDARD package as ORA_NAME_LIST_T. The ORA_NAME_

LIST_T is a table of VARCHAR2(64) datatypes. The *function returns the number of elements in the list* indexed by a PLS_INTEGER datatype. The user_list contains the list of users granted privileges or roles by the triggering event.

You can use it like this:

```
DECLARE
  user_list DBMS_STANDARD.ORA_NAME_LIST_T;
  counter   PLS_INTEGER;
BEGIN
  IF ora_sysevent = 'GRANT' THEN
    counter := ora_grantee(user_list);
  END IF;
END;
```

ORA_INSTANCE_NUM

The ORA_INSTANCE_NUM function takes no formal parameters. It returns the current database instance number as a NUMBER datatype.

You can use it like this:

```
DECLARE
  instance NUMBER;
BEGIN
  instance := ora_instance_num;
END;
```

ORA_IS_ALTER_COLUMN

The ORA_IS_ALTER_COLUMN function takes one formal parameter, which is a column name. The function returns a *true* or *false* value as a BOOLEAN datatype. It is true when the column has been altered, and it is false when it hasn't been changed. This function worked with the traditional uppercase catalog information, but in Oracle 11*g* you need to match the catalog case if you opted to save any tables in a case-sensitive format. The example uses a case-insensitive string as an actual parameter.

You can use it like this:

```
DECLARE
  TYPE column_list IS TABLE OF VARCHAR2(32);
  columns COLUMN_LIST := column_list('CREATED_BY','LAST_UPDATED_BY');
BEGIN
  IF ora_sysevent = 'ALTER' AND
     ora_dict_obj_type = 'TABLE' THEN
    FOR i IN 1..columns.COUNT THEN
      IF ora_is_alter_column(columns(i)) THEN
        INSERT INTO logging_table
        VALUES (ora_dict_obj_name||'.'||columns(i)||' changed.');
      END IF;
    END LOOP;
  END IF;
END;
```

This is very useful if you want to guard against changing standard *who-audit* columns, like CREATED_BY, CREATION_DATE, LAST_UPDATED_BY, or LAST_UPDATE_DATE. These are security columns generally used to identify who last touched the data through the standard application programming interface (API). Any change to columns like these can destabilize an API.

ORA_IS_CREATING_NESTED_TABLE

The ORA_IS_CREATING_NESTED_TABLE function takes no formal parameters. It returns a *true* or *false* value as a BOOLEAN datatype when you create a table with a nested table.

You can use it like this:

```
BEGIN
  IF ora_sysevent = 'CREATE' AND
     ora_dict_obj_type = 'TABLE' AND
     ora_is_creating_nested_table THEN
       INSERT INTO logging_table
       VALUES (ora_dict_obj_name||'.'||' created with nested table.');
  END IF;
END;
```

ORA_IS_DROP_COLUMN

The ORA_IS_DROP_COLUMN function takes one formal parameter, which is a column name. The function returns a *true* or *false* value as a BOOLEAN datatype. It is true when the column has been dropped, and it returns false when it hasn't been dropped. This function worked with the traditional uppercase catalog information, but in Oracle 11*g* you need to match the catalog case if you opted to save any tables in a case-sensitive format. The example uses a case-insensitive string as an actual parameter.

You can use it like this:

```
DECLARE
  TYPE column_list IS TABLE OF VARCHAR2(32);
  columns COLUMN_LIST := column_list('CREATED_BY','LAST_UPDATED_BY');
BEGIN
  IF ora_sysevent = 'DROP' AND
     ora_dict_obj_type = 'TABLE' THEN
     FOR i IN 1..columns.COUNT THEN
       IF ora_is_drop_column(columns(i)) THEN
         INSERT INTO logging_table
         VALUES (ora_dict_obj_name||'.'||columns(i)||' changed.');
       END IF;
     END LOOP;
  END IF;
END;
```

This function is very useful if you want to guard against changing standard *who-audit* columns, like those discussed for the ORA_IS_DROP_COLUMN function earlier in this table.

ORA_IS_SERVERERROR

The ORA_IS_SERVERERROR function takes one formal parameter, which is an error number. It returns a *true* or *false* value as a BOOLEAN datatype when the error is on the error stack.

You can use it like this:

```
BEGIN
  IF ora_is_servererror(4082) THEN
    INSERT INTO logging_table
```

```
      VALUES ('ORA-04082 error thrown.');
  END IF;
END;
```

ORA_LOGIN_USER

The ORA_LOGIN_USER function takes no formal parameters. The function returns the current schema name as a VARCHAR2 datatype.

You can use it like this:

```
BEGIN
  INSERT INTO logging_table
  VALUES (ora_login_user||' is the current user.');
END;
```

ORA_PARTITION_POS

The ORA_PARTITION_POS function takes no formal parameters. The function returns the numeric position with the SQL text where you can insert a partition clause. This is only available in an INSTEAD OF CREATE trigger.

You can use the following, provided you add your own partitioning clause:

```
DECLARE
  sql_text  ORA_NAME_LIST_T;
  sql_stmt  VARCHAR2(32767);
  partition VARCHAR2(32767) := 'partitioning_clause';
BEGIN
  FOR i IN 1..ora_sql_txt(sql_text) LOOP
    sql_stmt := sql_stmt || sql_text(i);
  END LOOP;
  sql_stmt := SUBSTR(sql_text,1,ora_partition_pos - 1)||' '
            || partition||' '||SUBSTR(sql_test,ora_partition_pos);
  -- Add logic to prepend schema because this runs under SYSTEM.
  sql_stmt := REPLACE(UPPER(sql_stmt),'CREATE TABLE '
                     ,'CREATE TABLE '||ora_login_user||'.');
  EXECUTE IMMEDIATE sql_stmt;
END;
```

The coding sample requires that you grant the owner of the trigger the CREATE ANY TRIGGER privilege. You should consider a master privileged user for your application, and avoid using the SYSTEM schema.

ORA_PRIVILEGE_LIST

The ORA_PRIVILEGE_LIST function takes one formal parameter. The formal parameter is also returned because it is passed by reference as an OUT mode list of VARCHAR2 variables. The formal parameter datatype is defined in the DBMS_STANDARD package as ORA_NAME_LIST_T. The ORA_NAME_LIST_T is a table of VARCHAR2(64) datatypes. The *function returns the number of elements in the list* indexed by a PLS_INTEGER datatype. The priv_list contains the list of privileges or roles granted by the triggering event.

You can use it like this:

```
DECLARE
  priv_list DBMS_STANDARD.ORA_NAME_LIST_T;
  counter   PLS_INTEGER;
```

```
BEGIN
  IF ora_sysevent = 'GRANT' OR
     ora_sysevent = 'REVOKE' THEN
    counter := ora_privilege_list(priv_list);
  END IF;
END;
```

ORA_REVOKEE

The ORA_REVOKEE function takes one formal parameter. The formal parameter is also returned because it is passed by reference as an OUT mode list of VARCHAR2 variables. The formal parameter datatype is defined in the DBMS_STANDARD package as ORA_NAME_LIST_T. The ORA_NAME_LIST_T is a table of VARCHAR2(64) datatypes. The *function returns the number of elements in the list* indexed by a PLS_INTEGER datatype. The priv_list contains the list of users that had privileges or roles revoked by the triggering event.

You can use it like this:

```
DECLARE
  revokee_list DBMS_STANDARD.ORA_NAME_LIST_T;
  counter      PLS_INTEGER;
BEGIN
  IF ora_sysevent = 'REVOKE' THEN
    counter := ora_revokee(priv_list);
  END IF;
END;
```

ORA_SERVER_ERROR

The ORA_SERVER_ERROR function takes one formal parameter, which is the position on the error stack, where 1 is the top of the error stack. It returns an error number as a NUMBER datatype.

You can use it like this:

```
DECLARE
  error NUMBER;
BEGIN
  FOR i IN 1..ora_server_error_depth LOOP
    error := ora_server_error(i);
  END LOOP;
END;
```

ORA_SERVER_ERROR_DEPTH

The ORA_SERVER_ERROR_DEPTH function takes no formal parameters. The function returns the number of errors on the error stack as a PLS_INTEGER datatype. The code samples for the ORA_SERVER_ERROR and ORA_SERVER_ERROR_MSG functions demonstrate how you can use it.

ORA_SERVER_ERROR_MSG

The ORA_SERVER_ERROR_MSG function takes one formal parameter, which is the position on the error stack, where 1 is the top of the error stack. It returns an error message text as a VARCHAR2 datatype.

You can use it like this:

```
DECLARE
  error VARCHAR2(64);
BEGIN
  FOR i IN 1..ora_server_error_depth LOOP
    error := ora_server_error_msg(i);
  END LOOP;
END;
```

ORA_SERVER_ERROR_NUM_PARAMS

The `ORA_SERVER_ERROR_NUM_PARAMS` function takes no formal parameters. The function returns the count of any substituted strings from error messages as a `PLS_INTEGER` datatype. For example, an error format could be "Expected %s, found %s." The code sample for `ORA_SERVER_ERROR_PARAM` function shows how you can use it.

ORA_SERVER_ERROR_PARAM

The `ORA_SERVER_ERROR_PARAM` function takes one formal parameter, which is the position in an error message, where 1 is the first occurrence of a string in the error message. It returns an error message text as a `VARCHAR2` datatype.

You can use it like this:

```
DECLARE
  param VARCHAR2(32);
BEGIN
  FOR i IN 1..ora_server_error_depth LOOP
    FOR j IN 1..ora_server_error_num_params(i) LOOP
      param := ora_server_error_param(j);
    END LOOP;
  END LOOP;
END;
```

ORA_SQL_TXT

The `ORA_SQL_TXT` function takes one formal parameter. The formal parameter is also returned because it is passed by reference as an `OUT` mode list of `VARCHAR2` variables. The formal parameter datatype is defined in the `DBMS_STANDARD` package as `ORA_NAME_LIST_T`. The `ORA_NAME_LIST_T` is a table of `VARCHAR2(64)` datatypes. The function returns the number of elements in the list indexed by a `PLS_INTEGER` datatype. The list contains the substrings of the processed SQL statement that triggered the event. The coding example is shown with the `ORA_PARTITION_POS` function.

ORA_SYSEVENT

The `ORA_SYSEVENT` function takes no formal parameters. The function returns the system event that was responsible for firing the trigger as a `VARCHAR2` datatype.

You can use it like this:

```
BEGIN
  INSERT INTO logging_table
  VALUES (ora_sysevent||' fired the trigger.');
END;
```

ORA_WITH_GRANT_OPTION

The ORA_WITH_GRANT_OPTION function has no formal parameters. The function returns a *true* or *false* value as a BOOLEAN datatype. It returns *true* when privileges are granted with *grant option*.

You can use it like this:

```
BEGIN
    IF ora_with_grant_option THEN
        INSERT INTO logging_table
        VALUES ('ORA-04082 error thrown.');
    END IF;
END;
```

SPACE_ERROR_INFO

The SPACE_ERROR_INFO function uses six formal pass-by-reference parameters. They are all OUT mode parameters. The prototype is

```
space_error_info( error_number OUT NUMBER
                , error_type OUT VARCHAR2
                , object_owner OUT VARCHAR2
                , table_space_name OUT VARCHAR2
                , object_name OUT VARCHAR2
                , sub_object_name OUT VARCHAR2)
```

This function returns *true* when the triggering event is related to an *out-of-space* condition, and it fills in all the outbound parameters. You implement this with a logging table that supports at least the six OUT parameters. When the function returns *false,* the OUT mode variables are null.

You can use it like this:

```
DECLARE
    error_number      NUMBER;
    error_type        VARCHAR2(12);
    object_owner      VARCHAR2(30);
    tablespace_name   VARCHAR2(30);
    object_name       VARCHAR2(128);
    subobject_name    VARCHAR2(30);
BEGIN
    IF space_error_info( error_number, error_type
                       , object_owner, tablespace_name
                       , object_name, subobject_name) THEN
        INSERT INTO logging_table
        VALUES ( … implementation_dependent … );
    END IF;
END;
```

Building DDL Triggers

The prototype for building DDL triggers is

```
CREATE [OR REPLACE] TRIGGER trigger_name
{BEFORE | AFTER | INSTEAD OF} ddl_event ON {DATABASE | SCHEMA}
[WHEN (logical_expression)]
[DECLARE]
  declaration_statements;
```

```
BEGIN
  execution_statements;
END [trigger_name];
/
```

You can use the INSTEAD OF clause only when auditing a creation event. Before triggers make sure the contents of the trigger body occur before the triggering DDL command, while after triggers run last. See the section "ORA_PARTITION_POS" earlier in this chapter for an implementation of an INSTEAD OF CREATE trigger that appends a partitioning table.

The DDL example trigger requires that you create the audit_creations table and audit_creations_s1 sequence before the trigger. If you forget to create one or both, you can't create either after you attempt to compile the database trigger. This limitation exists because you have a valid trigger declaration but an invalid trigger body. You must drop or disable the trigger *(declaration)* before you can create anything in the schema.

You should note that the table and trigger share the same name. This is possible because there are two namespaces in Oracle databases, one for triggers and another for everything else.

You create the table and sequence as follows:

```
CREATE TABLE audit_creation
( audit_creation_id NUMBER
, audit_owner_name   VARCHAR2(30) CONSTRAINT audit_creation_nn1 NOT NULL
, audit_obj_name     VARCHAR2(30) CONSTRAINT audit_creation_nn2 NOT NULL
, audit_date         DATE         CONSTRAINT audit_creation_nn3 NOT NULL
, CONSTRAINT audit_creation_p1   PRIMARY KEY (audit_creation_id));

CREATE SEQUENCE audit_creation_s1;
```

Now you can create the audit_creation system trigger. This trigger shows you the behavior of a DDL trigger when dependencies become unavailable to the trigger:

```
CREATE OR REPLACE TRIGGER audit_creation
BEFORE CREATE ON SCHEMA
BEGIN
  INSERT INTO audit_creation VALUES
  (audit_creation_s1.nextval,ORA_DICT_OBJ_OWNER,ORA_DICT_OBJ_NAME,SYSDATE);
END audit_creation;
/
```

The following DDL statement triggers the system trigger, which inserts data from the trigger attribute functions. It creates a synonym called mythology that doesn't translate to anything real, but it does create an event that fires the trigger.

The DDL statement is

```
CREATE SYNONYM mythology FOR plsql.some_myth;
```

You can query the results of the trigger using the following SQL*Plus formatting and statement:

```
COL audit_creation_id FORMAT 99999999 HEADING "Audit|Creation|ID #"
COL audit_owner_name  FORMAT A6 HEADING "Audit|Owner|Name"
COL audit_obj_name    FORMAT A8 HEADING "Audit|Object|Name"
COL audit_obj_name    FORMAT A9 HEADING "Audit|Object|Name"
SELECT * FROM audit_creation;
```

The query returns

```
Audit Audit  Audit
   Creation Owner  Object    Audit
       ID # Name   Name      Date
--------- ------ --------- ---------
       21 PLSQL  MYTHOLOGY 17-NOV-08
```

You have now seen how to implement a DDL trigger. The next section examines DML triggers.

Data Manipulation Language Triggers

DML triggers can fire *before* or *after* INSERT, UPDATE, and DELETE statements. DML triggers can be *statement-* or *row-level* activities. *Statement-level* triggers fire and perform a statement or set of statements once no matter how many rows are affected by the DML event. *Row-level* triggers fire and perform a statement or set of statements for *each* row changed by a DML statement.

A *principal caveat* of triggers that manage data changes is that you cannot use SQL Data Control Language (DCL) in them, unless you declare the trigger as autonomous. When triggers run inside the scope of a transaction, they disallow setting a SAVEPOINT or performing either a ROLLBACK or COMMIT statement. Likewise, they can't have a DCL (also known as TCL) statement in the execution path of any function or procedure that they call.

The prototype for building DML triggers is

```
CREATE [OR REPLACE] TRIGGER trigger_name
{BEFORE | AFTER}
{INSERT | UPDATE | UPDATE OF column1 [, column2 [, column(n+1)]] | DELETE}
ON table_name
[FOR EACH ROW]
[WHEN (logical_expression)]
[DECLARE]
  [PRAGMA AUTONOMOUS_TRANSACTION;]
  declaration_statements;
BEGIN
  execution_statements;
END [trigger_name];
/
```

The BEFORE or AFTER clause determines whether the trigger fires *before* or *after* the change is written to your local copy of the data. You can define a BEFORE or AFTER clause on tables but not views. While the prototype shows either an insert, update, update of *(a column)*, or delete, you can also use an inclusion, OR, operator between the events. Using one OR between two events creates a single trigger that runs for two events. You can create a trigger that supports all four possible events with multiple inclusion operators.

There are two options for DML triggers. You can declare them as *statement*-level triggers, which are also known as *table*-level triggers, or you can declare them as *row*-level triggers.

You have a FOR EACH ROW clause, a WHEN clause, and new and old pseudo-records in row-level triggers. The FOR EACH ROW clause specifies that the trigger should fire for each row as opposed to once per statement. The WHEN clause acts as a filter specifying when the trigger fires. Unlike when working with other stored program units, you must qualify a DECLARE block when you declare local variables, types, or cursors in a trigger.

Triggers require the `DECLARE` block in trigger bodies because the declaration of a trigger is separate from the trigger body. Trigger bodies are like anonymous-block PL/SQL programs. They are called by the trigger, and the trigger implicitly manages parameter passing. Trigger bodies don't support substitution variables, like anonymous blocks. They support *bind* variables, but only in the context of row-level triggers. There is no parameter passing to statement-level triggers.

Statement- and *row*-level triggers have different purposes and approaches. The trigger types are covered in the next two subsections.

Statement-Level Triggers

Statement-level triggers are also known as table-level triggers because they're triggered by a change to a table. Statement-level triggers capture and process information when a user inserts, updates, or deletes one or more rows in a table. You can also restrict *(filter)* `UPDATE` statement triggers by constraining them to fire only when a specific column value changes. You can restrict the trigger by using a `UPDATE OF` clause. The clause can apply to a *column name* or a *comma-delimited list of column names.*

You can't use a `WHEN` clause in a statement-level trigger. You also can't reference the `new` or `old` pseudo-records without raising an `ORA-04082` exception. The exception is a compile-time error, and it tells you that `new` or `old` references aren't allowed in table-level triggers.

You can implement statement-level triggers on inserting, updating, or deleting events. Statement-level triggers don't let you collect transaction details. You have access to only the type of event and values returned by event attribute functions. The `UPDATE OF` clause lets you filter the triggering event to a specific column change.

The *statement*-level example uses an `UPDATE OF` *column name* event. The trigger depends on your running the `create_store.sql` script from the publisher's web site. You can find a reference to it in the introduction.

The trigger logs events in the `price_type_log` table. It must be created before you compile the trigger. The following statement creates the table:

```
-- This is found in create_price_type_trigger.sql on the publisher's web site.
CREATE TABLE price_type_log
( price_id      NUMBER              CONSTRAINT price_type_log_nn1 NOT NULL
, user_id       VARCHAR2(32)        CONSTRAINT price_type_log_nn2 NOT NULL
, action_date   DATE                CONSTRAINT price_type_log_nn3 NOT NULL
, CONSTRAINT    price_type_log_p1 PRIMARY KEY (price_id))
/
```

After creating the table, you can create the trigger. It is possible that the trigger can fail if you've already declared another `price_t1` trigger on another table. The `REPLACE` command only works when the `CREATE OR REPLACE TRIGGER` command works against the same table. You raise an `ORA-04095` exception when a trigger name already exists for another table.

The following trigger works in Oracle 10*g* or 11*g*. Oracle 10*g* doesn't support references to sequence `.nextval` or `.currval` pseudo-columns in SQL statements when they're inside a PL/SQL block.

This backward-compatible trigger is not found in the script on the publisher's web site.

```
CREATE OR REPLACE TRIGGER price_t1
AFTER UPDATE OF price_type ON price
DECLARE
  price_id NUMBER;
```

```
BEGIN
  SELECT price_log_s1.nextval INTO price_id FROM dual;
  INSERT INTO price_type_log
  VALUES (price_log_s1.nextval,USER,SYSDATE);
END price_t1;
/
```

Oracle 11*g does* support references to sequence `.nextval` or `.currval` pseudo-columns in SQL statements when they're inside PL/SQL blocks. The following is included:

```
-- This is found in create_price_type_trigger.sql on the publisher's web site.
CREATE OR REPLACE TRIGGER price_t1
AFTER UPDATE OF price_type ON price
BEGIN
  -- This statement only works in Oracle 11g forward.
  INSERT INTO price_type_log VALUES (price_log_s1.nextval,USER,SYSDATE);
END price_t1;
/
```

You can trigger this by running the following UPDATE statement that changes nothing because it simply reassigns the current value of `price_type` column to itself:

```
UPDATE price p
SET    p.price_type = p.price_type
WHERE  EXISTS (SELECT NULL
               FROM   price q
               WHERE  q.price_id = p.price_id);
```

The following query shows that the trigger fired and wrote audit information to the `price_type_log` table:

```
SELECT * FROM price_type_log;
```

This subsection has shown you how to use statement-level DML triggers. The next section shows you how to write row-level triggers.

Row-Level Triggers

Row-level triggers let you capture new and prior values from each row. This information can let you audit changes, analyze behavior, and recover prior data without performing a database recovery operation.

There are two *pseudo*-records when you use the FOR EACH ROW clause in a *row-level* trigger. They both refer to the columns referenced in the DML statement. The pseudo-records are composite variables; new or old are the pseudo-record variable names in the WHEN clause, and :new and :old are the *bind* variables in the trigger body. They differ because the trigger declaration and body are separate PL/SQL blocks. The new and old pseudo-records are declared in scope by the row-level trigger declaration. The trigger declaration is the calling block, and the trigger body is the called block. *Bind* variables are passed *by reference* between PL/SQL blocks when an event fires a trigger in a database session. The elements of the pseudo-record are pseudo-fields.

The new or old pseudo-records are session-level composite variables. They're implicitly declared in the scope of the triggering event, which is the DML statement. Triggers do not have formal signatures like standalone functions or procedures, but they have access to column values changed by DML statements. These column values are the elements of the pseudo-records, or pseudo-fields. Pseudo-field values are those columns inserted by an INSERT statement, set by an UPDATE statement, or destroyed by a DELETE statement.

You access pseudo-fields by referencing the new or old pseudo-records, a component selector, and a *column name* in the WHEN clause. Inside a trigger body, you preface the *pseudo*-records with a colon (:). The colon let you reference the externally scoped pseudo-records in the trigger body. The DML statement declares the list of column names *(pseudo-fields)*.

The following example demonstrates a trigger that replaces a whitespace in a last name with a dash for hyphenated names.

```
CREATE OR REPLACE TRIGGER contact_insert_t1
   BEFORE INSERT ON contact         Checks the local
                                    transaction pseudo-field
   FOR EACH ROW
   WHEN (REGEXP_LIKE(new.last_name,' '))
BEGIN
   :new.last_name:= REGEXP_REPLACE(:new.last_name,' ','-',1,1);
END contact_insert_t1;
/                                        Reads external
     Writes external                     pseudo-field
     pseudo-field
```

The WHEN clause checks whether the value of the pseudo-field for the last_name column in the contact table contains a whitespace. If the condition is met, the trigger passes control to the trigger body. The trigger body has one statement; the REGEXP_REPLACE function takes a copy of the pseudo-field as an actual parameter. REGEXP_REPLACE changes any whitespace in the string to a dash, and it returns the modified value as a result. The result is assigned to the pseudo-field, and becomes the value in the INSERT statement. This is an example of using a DML trigger to enforce a business policy of entering all last names as hyphenated.

The trigger depends on your having run the create_store.sql script, as discussed in the introduction. After compiling the trigger in your test schema, you can test the trigger by running the following insert:

```
INSERT INTO contact
VALUES (contact_s1.nextval, 1001, 1003
,       'Zeta Jones','Catherine',NULL
,        3, SYSDATE, 3, SYSDATE);
```

It converts the last name to a hyphenated last name. You query last_name from the contact table to see the actual inserted value:

```
SELECT last_name FROM contact WHERE last_name LIKE 'Zeta%';
```

You should have the following results:

```
LAST_NAME
--------------------
Zeta-Jones
```

The only problem with the trigger is that a user can simply update the column to remove the dash from the `last_name` column. You can prevent that in a single trigger by using the inclusion OR operator, like

```
CREATE OR REPLACE TRIGGER contact_insert_t1
  BEFORE INSERT OR UPDATE OF last_name ON contact
  FOR EACH ROW
  WHEN (REGEXP_LIKE(new.last_name,' '))
BEGIN
  :new.last_name := REGEXP_REPLACE(:new.last_name,' ','-',1,1);
END contact_insert_t1;
/
```

The trigger is now fired on any INSERT statement and *only* for UPDATE statements that change the `last_name` column. It is always better to build triggers that work with multiple DML events when you take the same type of action.

Another common use for a DML trigger is automatic numbering for a primary key column. As you know, Oracle doesn't support automatic numbering, like Microsoft Access or SQL Server. You create a sequence and a trigger to manage automatic numbering.

While you can create this type of trigger with or without a WHEN clause, the WHEN clause filters when the trigger should or shouldn't run. A WHEN clause let you *insert* a manual primary key value, which can synchronize pseudo-columns `.nextval` and `.currval` for *primary* and *foreign keys* during a single transaction insert.

Rather than build a multiple table example, you will examine automatic numbering from the perspective of logging new connections to and disconnections from the database. The balance of the code for this example is in the section "Data Definition Language Triggers." The DDL triggers that monitor login and logout events call a `user_connection` package that logs to a `connection_log` table. The table definition is

```
CREATE TABLE connection_log
( event_id               NUMBER(10)
, event_user_name        VARCHAR2(30) CONSTRAINT log_event_nn1 NOT NULL
, event_type             VARCHAR2(30) CONSTRAINT log_event_nn2 NOT NULL
, event_date             DATE         CONSTRAINT log_event_nn3 NOT NULL
, CONSTRAINT connection_log_p1     PRIMARY KEY (event_id));
```

The *row-level* trigger `connection_log_t1` demonstrates the proper way to write a pseudo-automatic numbering trigger for Oracle 10*g*:

```
-- This is found in create_signon_trigger.sql on the publisher's web site.
CREATE OR REPLACE TRIGGER connection_log_t1
  BEFORE INSERT ON connection_log
  FOR EACH ROW
  WHEN (new.event_id IS NULL)
BEGIN
  SELECT    connection_log_s1.nextval
  INTO      :new.event_id
  FROM      dual;
END;
/
```

The `connection_log_t1` trigger demonstrates managing a sequence, but it also shows you how to `SELECT INTO` a pseudo-field variable. You should really modify the trigger when deploying it on an Oracle 11*g* database because you no longer have to select a sequence value into a variable from the pseudo-table dual. You can simply assign it directly.

The *row-level* trigger `connection_log_t2` demonstrates the proper way to write a pseudo-automatic numbering trigger for Oracle 11*g*:

```
CREATE OR REPLACE TRIGGER connection_log_t1
  BEFORE INSERT ON connection_log
  FOR EACH ROW
  WHEN (new.event_id IS NULL)
BEGIN
  :new.event_id := connection_log_s1.nextval;
END;
/
```

The `connection_log_t1` and `connection_log_t2` triggers fire only when you fail to provide a primary key value during an `INSERT` statement.

These row-level triggers illustrate two processing rules. One rule is that you can reference a *pseudo*-row column as an *ordinary* variable in the `WHEN` clause because the actual trigger fires in the same memory scope as the DML transaction. The other rule is that you must reference a *pseudo*-row column as a *bind* variable inside the actual trigger scope, where it is running in a different memory space. The *pseudo*-rows `NEW` and `OLD` are *pass-by-reference* structures, and they contain your active DML session variable values when arriving at the trigger body. The `new` and `old` *pseudo*-record variables also receive any changes made in the trigger body when they are returned to your active DML session.

All the `old` pseudo-record columns are null when you execute an `INSERT` statement, and the `new` pseudo-record columns are null when you run a `DELETE` statement. Both `new` and `old` pseudo-records are present during `UPDATE` statements, but only for those columns referenced by the `SET` clause.

This subsection has shown you how to write *row-level* triggers. It demonstrates how to use the new and old pseudo-record in your `WHEN` clause and trigger body.

This section has covered how to use DML triggers and examined both *statement-* and *row-level* trigger implementation. You should be able to use DML triggers by drawing on what you have learned in this section.

Compound Triggers

Compound triggers acts as both statement- and row-level triggers when you *insert, update,* or *delete* data from a table. You can use a compound trigger to capture information at four timing points: (a) before the firing statement; (b) before each row change from the firing statement; (c) after each row change from the firing statement; and (d) after the firing statement. You can use these types of triggers to audit, check, save, and replace values before they are changed when you need to take action at both the statement and row event levels.

Prior to compound triggers, you went to great lengths to mimic this behavior and ran the risk of a memory leak with the failure of an after statement trigger. A compound trigger functions like a multithreaded process. There is a declaration section for the trigger as a whole, and each *timing point section* has its own local declaration section. Timing point sections are subordinate trigger blocks of the compound trigger.

You can use a compound trigger when you want the behavior of both statement-level and row-level triggers. They can be defined on either a table or a view. Compound triggers don't support filtering actions with the WHEN clause or the use of the autonomous transaction PRAGMA. You can use the UPDATE OF *column name* filter as a governing event in updates. Also, the firing order of compound triggers is not guaranteed because they can be interleaved *(mixed between)* with the firing of standalone triggers.

TIP
You can always call out to a stored function or procedure that runs autonomously.

Compound triggers don't support an EXCEPTION block, but you can implement EXCEPTION blocks in any of the subordinate timing point blocks. The GOTO command is restricted to a single timing point block, which means you can't call between timing blocks. You can use the :new and :old pseudo-records in the row-level statement blocks but nowhere else.

The minimum implementation of a compound trigger requires that you implement at least one timing point block. Only DML statements trigger compound triggers. Also, compound triggers don't fire when (a) the DML statement doesn't change any rows and (b) the trigger hasn't implemented at least a BEFORE STATEMENT or AFTER STATEMENT block. Compound triggers have significant performance advantages when your DML statements use bulk operations.

The prototype for a compound trigger is

```
CREATE [OR REPLACE] TRIGGER trigger_name
FOR {INSERT | UPDATE | UPDATE OF column1 [, column2 [, column(n+1)]] | DELETE}
ON table_name
COMPOUND TRIGGER
[BEFORE STATEMENT IS
  [declaration_statement;]
 BEGIN
   execution_statement;
 END BEFORE STATEMENT;]
[BEFORE EACH ROW IS
  [declaration_statement;]
 BEGIN
   execution_statement;
 END BEFORE EACH ROW;]
[AFTER EACH ROW IS
  [declaration_statement;]
 BEGIN
   execution_statement;
 END AFTER EACH ROW;]
[AFTER STATEMENT IS
  [declaration_statement;]
 BEGIN
   execution_statement;
 END AFTER STATEMENT;]
END [trigger_name];
/
```

The example rewrites the insert event row-level trigger from the section "Row-Level Triggers" as a compound trigger. The code follows:

```
-- This is found in create_signon_trigger.sql on the publisher's web site.
CREATE OR REPLACE TRIGGER compound_connection_log_t1
  FOR INSERT ON connection_log
  COMPOUND TRIGGER
  BEFORE EACH ROW IS
  BEGIN
    IF :new.event_id IS NULL THEN
      :new.event_id := connection_log_s1.nextval;
    END IF;
  END BEFORE EACH ROW;
END;
/
```

You should note three key elements about compound triggers. You can't filter events in this type of trigger by using a WHEN clause. As mentioned, :new and :old pseudo-records are only available in the BEFORE EACH ROW and AFTER EACH ROW timing blocks. Variables declared in the global declaration block retain their value through the execution of all timing blocks that you've implemented.

You can collect row-level information in either the BEFORE EACH ROW or AFTER EACH ROW timing points and transfer that information to a global collection declared in the trigger body. Then, you can perform bulk operations with the collection contents in the AFTER STATEMENT timing point. If you don't write the data to another table, you could raise a maximum number of recursive calls error, ORA-00036.

The next example demonstrates collecting information in the row-level timing points, transferring it to a global collection, and processing it as a bulk transaction in the AFTER STATEMENT timing block. This example depends on your running the create_store.sql script, which is described in the introduction. The first step requires creating a log repository, which is done by creating the following table and sequence:

```
-- This is found in create_compound_trigger.sql on the publisher's web site.
CREATE TABLE price_event_log
( price_log_id       NUMBER
, price_id           NUMBER
, created_by         NUMBER
, creation_date      DATE
, last_updated_by    NUMBER
, last_update_date   DATE );

CREATE SEQUENCE price_event_log_s1;
```

The trigger populates created_by and last_updated_by columns as part of the applications "*who-audit*" information. It assumes that you're striping the data, which means you need to set a CLIENT_INFO value for the session. The physical CLIENT_INFO section is found in the V$SESSION view. You can read more on these concepts in the sidebar "Reading and Writing Session Metadata" later in this chapter.

The following sets the CLIENT_INFO value to 3, which is a valid system_user_id in the system_user table:

```
EXEC dbms_application_info.set_client_info('3');
```

The trigger depends on the state of the CLIENT_INFO column, but as you might imagine, it can't control it. Therefore, the trigger assigns a –1 when the CLIENT_INFO value is missing during its execution.

The following defines the compound trigger with both BEFORE EACH ROW and AFTER STATEMENT timing blocks:

```
-- This is found in create_compound_trigger on the publisher's web site.
CREATE OR REPLACE TRIGGER compound_price_update_t1
  FOR UPDATE ON price
  COMPOUND TRIGGER
    -- Declare a global record type.
    TYPE price_record IS RECORD
    ( price_log_id      price_event_log.price_log_id%TYPE
    , price_id          price_event_log.price_id%TYPE
    , created_by        price_event_log.created_by%TYPE
    , creation_date     price_event_log.creation_date%TYPE
    , last_updated_by   price_event_log.last_updated_by%TYPE
    , last_update_date price_event_log.last_update_date%TYPE );
    -- Declare a global collection type.
    TYPE price_list IS TABLE OF PRICE_RECORD;
    -- Declare a global collection and initialize it.
    price_updates  PRICE_LIST := price_list();
  BEFORE EACH ROW IS
    -- Declare or define local timing point variables.
    c       NUMBER;
    user_id NUMBER := NVL(TO_NUMBER(SYS_CONTEXT('userenv','client_info')),-1);
  BEGIN
    -- Extend space and assign dynamic index value.
    price_updates.EXTEND;
    c := price_updates.LAST;
    price_updates(c).price_log_id := price_event_log_s1.nextval;
    price_updates(c).price_id := :old.price_id;
    price_updates(c).created_by := user_id;
    price_updates(c).creation_date := SYSDATE;
    price_updates(c).last_updated_by := user_id;
    price_updates(c).last_update_date := SYSDATE;
  END BEFORE EACH ROW;
  AFTER STATEMENT IS
  BEGIN
    -- Bulk insert statement.
    FORALL i IN price_updates.FIRST..price_updates.LAST
      INSERT INTO price_event_log
      VALUES
      ( price_updates(i).price_log_id
      , price_updates(i).price_id
      , price_updates(i).created_by
      , price_updates(i).creation_date
      , price_updates(i).last_updated_by
      , price_updates(i).last_update_date );
  END AFTER STATEMENT;
END;
/
```

The BEFORE EACH ROW timing block collects row-level data and stores it in a global collection, which can then be read from another timing block. The numeric index for the collection is dynamic and leverages the Collection API LAST method. If you'd like to check how that works, please refer to Chapter 7, where it is covered.

The AFTER STATEMENT timing block reads the global collection and performs a bulk insert of the data to the log table. The next time the trigger is fired, the global collection is empty because the compound trigger implementation is serialized.

You can test the trigger by running the following UPDATE statement:

```
UPDATE price
SET    last_updated_by = NVL(TO_NUMBER(SYS_CONTEXT('userenv','client_info')),-1);
```

Then, you can query the price_event_log table:

```
SELECT * FROM price_event_log;
```

This example has shown you how to capture row-level data, save it in a global collection, and reuse it in a statement-level statement.

Reading and Writing Session Metadata

The process of writing to and reading from the session CLIENT_INFO column requires you to use the DBMS_APPLICATION_INFO package. You use the SET_CLIENT_INFO procedure in the DBMS_APPLICATION_INFO package to write data into the 64-character CLIENT_INFO column found in the V$SESSION view. The following anonymous PL/SQL block assumes that the CREATED_BY and LAST_UPDATED_BY columns should be 3:

```
BEGIN
   -- Write value to V$SESSION.CLIENT_INFO column.
   DBMS_APPLICATION_INFO.SET_CLIENT_INFO('3');
END;
/
```

You can now read this value by calling the READ_CLIENT_INFO procedure. You should enable SERVEROUTPUT using SQL*Plus to see the rendered output when you run the following program:

```
DECLARE
  client_info       VARCHAR2(64);
BEGIN
   -- Read value from V$SESSION.CLIENT_INTO column.
   DBMS_APPLICATION_INFO.READ_CLIENT_INFO(client_info);
   DBMS_OUTPUT.PUT_LINE('[ '||client_info||']');
END;
/
```

User-defined session columns let you store unique information related to user credentials from your Access Control List (ACL). You assign a session column value during user authentication. Then, the session CLIENT_INFO column allows you to manage multiple user interactions in a single schema. Authenticated users can access rows from tables when their session CLIENT_INFO column value matches a striping column value in the table.

This section has explained the new Oracle 11*g* compound triggers and shown you how to implement them. They allow you to mix the benefits and operations of statement- and row-level triggers in a single trigger.

Instead-of Triggers

You can use the `INSTEAD OF` trigger to intercept `INSERT`, `UPDATE`, and `DELETE` statements and replace those instructions with alternative procedural code. Non-updatable views generally have `INSTEAD OF` triggers to accept the output and resolve the issues that make the view non-updatable.

The prototype for building an `INSTEAD OF` trigger is

```
CREATE [OR REPLACE] TRIGGER trigger_name
INSTEAD OF {dml_statement }
ON {object_name | database | schema}
FOR EACH ROW
[WHEN (logical_expression)]
[DECLARE]
  declaration_statements;
BEGIN
  execution_statements;
END [trigger_name];
/
```

`INSTEAD OF` triggers are powerful alternatives that resolve how you use complex and non-updatable views. When you know how the `SELECT` statement works, you can write procedural code to update the data not directly accessible through non-updatable views.

You can only deploy an `INSTEAD OF` DML trigger against a view. There is no restriction as to whether the view is updatable or non-updatable, but generally `INSTEAD OF` triggers are built for non-updatable views.

The following view is supported by the data model provided on the publisher's web site. It is also a non-updatable view because of the `DECODE` statement, as shown:

```
-- This is found in create_insteadof_trigger.sql on the publisher's web site.
CREATE OR REPLACE VIEW account_list AS
  SELECT c.member_id
  ,       c.contact_id
  ,       m.account_number
  ,       c.first_name
  ||      DECODE(c.middle_initial,NULL,' ',' '||c.middle_initial||' ')
  ||      c.last_name FULL_NAME
  FROM contact c JOIN member m ON c.member_id = m.member_id;
```

Without an `INSTEAD OF` trigger, a DML statement against this view can raise an ORA-01776 exception that says you're disallowed from modifying more than one base table through a join. You could also raise an ORA-01779 exception that tells you you're disallowed to modify a column because it fails to map to a non-key-preserved table.

You can create an `INSTEAD OF` trigger that would allow you to update or delete from this view. However, the view doesn't have enough information to support `INSERT` statements to either base table. Without redefining the view, there is also no programmatic way to fix these shortcomings.

The following is an INSTEAD OF INSERT trigger. It raises an exception for any insertion attempt to the non-updatable view.

```
CREATE OR REPLACE TRIGGER account_list_insert
  INSTEAD OF INSERT ON account_list
  FOR EACH ROW
BEGIN
  RAISE_APPLICATION_ERROR(-20000,'Not enough data for insert!');
END;
/
```

After compiling the trigger, an INSERT statement run against the view now raises the following exception stack:

```
INSERT INTO account_list
            *
ERROR at line 1:
ORA-20000: Not enough data for insert!
ORA-06512: at "PLSQL.ACCOUNT_LIST_INSERT", line 2
ORA-04088: error during execution of trigger 'PLSQL.ACCOUNT_LIST_INSERT'
```

The question here is, do you want to define three INSTEAD OF event triggers or one? Some developers opt for multiple INSTEAD OF triggers as opposed to one that does everything. You should consider defining one trigger for inserting, updating, and deleting events. Table 10-2 qualifies the INSERTING, UPDATING, and DELETING functions from the DBMS_STANDARD package. These functions let you determine the type of DML event and write one trigger that manages all three DML events.

Certain required fields for an insert to either the member or contact tables are missing from the view. There is also a programmatic way to fix these shortcomings.

Function Name	Return Datatype	Description
DELETING	BOOLEAN	The DELETING function returns a Boolean true when the DML event is deleting.
INSERTING	BOOLEAN	The INSERTING function returns a Boolean true when the DML is inserting.
UPDATING	BOOLEAN	The UPDATING function returns a Boolean true when the DML is updating.

TABLE 10-2   *Data Manipulation Language Event Functions*

You can build a complete trigger for all DML statements by using the event function from Table 10-2. The following provides an example INSTEAD OF trigger:

```
-- This is found in create_insteadof_trigger.sql on the publisher's web site.
CREATE OR REPLACE TRIGGER account_list_dml
  INSTEAD OF INSERT OR UPDATE OR DELETE ON account_list
  FOR EACH ROW
DECLARE
  -- Source variable.
  source account_list.full_name%TYPE := :new.full_name;
  -- Parsed variables.
  fname   VARCHAR2(43);
  mname   VARCHAR2(1);
  lname   VARCHAR2(43);
  -- Check whether all dependents are gone.
  FUNCTION get_dependents (member_id NUMBER) RETURN BOOLEAN IS
    rows NUMBER := 0;
    CURSOR c (member_id_in NUMBER) IS
      SELECT COUNT(*) FROM contact WHERE member_id = member_id_in;
  BEGIN
    OPEN c (member_id);
    FETCH c INTO rows;
    IF rows > 0 THEN
      RETURN FALSE;
    ELSE
      RETURN TRUE;
    END IF;
  END get_dependents;
BEGIN
  IF INSERTING THEN -- On insert event.
    RAISE_APPLICATION_ERROR(-20000,'Not enough data for insert!');
  ELSIF UPDATING THEN -- On update event.
    -- Assign source variable.
    source := :new.full_name;
    -- Parse full_name for elements.
    fname := LTRIM(REGEXP_SUBSTR(source,'(^|^ +)([[:alpha:]]+)',1));
    mname := REGEXP_SUBSTR(
               REGEXP_SUBSTR(
                 source,'( +)([[:alpha:]]+)(( +|. +))',1),'([[:alpha:]])',1);
    lname := REGEXP_SUBSTR(
               REGEXP_SUBSTR(
                 source,'( +)([[:alpha:]]+)( +$|$)',1),'([[:alpha:]]+)',1);
    -- Update name change in base table.
    UPDATE contact
    SET    first_name = fname
    ,      middle_initial = mname
    ,      last_name = lname
    WHERE  contact_id = :old.contact_id;
  ELSIF DELETING THEN -- On delete event.
```

```
     DELETE FROM contact WHERE member_id = :old.member_id;
     -- Only delete the parent when there aren't any more children.
     IF get_dependents(:old.member_id) THEN
       DELETE FROM member WHERE member_id = :old.member_id;
     END IF;
   END IF;
END;
/
```

Some tricks or risks are inherent in this type of trigger. Risks are bad in triggers because they should be foolproof. One potential flaw in *this* trigger is the assignment of the pseudo-field :new. full_name in the declaration section. The database doesn't check when you compile the trigger if the size of the source variable is large enough to handle possible assignments. This is a critical place to use type anchoring as discussed in Chapter 9.

The account_list_dml trigger anchors the source variable to the assigned column value, which ensures you won't raise ORA-06502, ORA-06512, and ORA-04088 errors. An assignment in the DECLARE block of a trigger body does raise a run-time exception, like standalone anonymous-block programs.

This trigger fires on any DML event against the non-updatable view, and it handles the insert, update, or deletion to the base tables where appropriate. As mentioned, there wouldn't be enough information to perform INSERT statements to the base tables. The trigger raises a user-defined exception when someone attempts to insert a new record through the view. There is enough information to *update* the name, but as you can tell, it isn't a trivial bit of work. You should know that the regular expression for the middle name won't work if you have leading whitespace before the first name. The DELETE statement only touches one table unless all dependent rows in the contact table have been deleted first, because you never want to leave orphaned rows in a dependent table.

This section has shown you how to write individual-event and multiple-event INSTEAD OF triggers. You should try to write all DML events in a single INSTEAD OF trigger because they're much easier to maintain.

Non-Updatable Views
Views are non-updatable when they contain any of the following constructs:

- Set operators
- Aggregate functions
- CASE or DECODE statements
- CONNECT BY, GROUP BY, HAVING, or START WITH clauses
- The DISTINCT operator
- Joins (with exceptions when they contain the joining key)

You also cannot reference any pseudo-columns or expressions when you update a view.

System or Database Event Triggers

System triggers enable you to audit *server startup* and *shutdown, server errors,* and *user logon* and *logoff* activities. They are convenient for tracking the duration of connections per user and the uptime of the database server.

The prototype for building a database SYSTEM trigger is

```
CREATE [OR REPLACE] TRIGGER trigger_name
{BEFORE | AFTER} database_event ON {database | schema}
[DECLARE]
  declaration_statements;
BEGIN
  execution_statements;
END [trigger_name];
/
```

The *logon* and *logoff* triggers monitor the duration of connections. The DML statements for these triggers are in the user_connection package. Both the connecting_trigger and the disconnecting_trigger call procedures in the user_connection package to insert *logon* and *logoff* information per user.

The connecting_trigger provides an example of a system trigger that monitors users' logons to the database, as shown:

```
-- This is found in create_system_triggers.sql on the publisher's web site.
CREATE OR REPLACE TRIGGER connecting_trigger
  AFTER LOGON ON DATABASE
BEGIN
  user_connection.connecting(sys.login_user);
END;
/
```

The disconnecting_trigger provides an example of a system trigger that monitors users' logoffs from the database, as shown:

```
-- This is found in create_system_triggers.sql on the publisher's web site.
CREATE OR REPLACE TRIGGER disconnecting_trigger
  BEFORE LOGOFF ON DATABASE
BEGIN
  user_connection.disconnecting(sys.login_user);
END;
/
```

Both triggers are compact and call methods of the user_connection package. This package requires the connection_log table, which is

```
-- This is found in create_system_triggers.sql on the publisher's web site.
CREATE TABLE connection_log
( event_id            NUMBER
, event_user_name     VARCHAR2(30) CONSTRAINT log_event_nn1 NOT NULL
, event_type          VARCHAR2(14) CONSTRAINT log_event_nn2 NOT NULL
, event_date          DATE         CONSTRAINT log_event_nn3 NOT NULL
, CONSTRAINT connection_log_p1    PRIMARY KEY (event_id));
```

The package body declares two procedures. One supports the *logon* trigger, and the other supports the *logoff* trigger. The package specification is

```
-- This is found in create_system_triggers.sql on the publisher's web site.
CREATE OR REPLACE PACKAGE user_connection AS
  PROCEDURE connecting (user_name IN VARCHAR2);
  PROCEDURE disconnecting (user_name IN VARCHAR2);
END user_connection;
/
```

The implementation of the `user_connection` package body is

```
-- This is found in create_system_triggers.sql on the publisher's web site.
CREATE OR REPLACE PACKAGE BODY user_connection AS
  PROCEDURE connecting (user_name IN VARCHAR2) IS
  BEGIN
    INSERT INTO connection_log (event_user_name, event_type, event_date)
    VALUES (user_name,'CONNECT',SYSDATE);
  END connecting;
  PROCEDURE disconnecting (user_name IN VARCHAR2) IS
  BEGIN
    INSERT INTO connection_log (event_user_name, event_type, event_date)
    VALUES (user_name,'DISCONNECT',SYSDATE);
  END disconnecting;
END user_connection;
/
```

You may notice that the `connection_log` table has four columns but the `INSERT` statement only uses three. This is possible because the `connection_log_t1` trigger automatically assigns the next value from the `connection_log_s1` sequence. You can find the source of the `connection_log_t1` trigger in the section "Row-Level Triggers" in this chapter.

This section has demonstrated how you can build system triggers.

Trigger Restrictions

There are several restrictions on how you implement triggers in Oracle 11*g*. They are fairly consistent between releases, but Oracle 11*g* has relaxed some mutating table restrictions. Restrictions have been covered in earlier sections when they apply to only one type of trigger.

The following subsections cover the remaining restrictions.

Maximum Trigger Size

A trigger body can be no longer than 32,760 bytes, as noted in the section "Introduction to Triggers" at the beginning of this chapter. This size limitation means that you should consider keeping your trigger bodies small in size. You can accomplish this without losing any utility by moving coding logic into other schema-level components, such as functions, procedures, and packages. An advantage of moving the coding logic out of the trigger body is that you can reuse the code. You can also wrap schema-level objects, whereas you can't wrap trigger bodies. Appendix F discusses wrapping your PL/SQL code from prying eyes.

SQL Statements

Nonsystem trigger bodies can't contain DDL statements. They also can't contain Data Control Language (DCL) or Transaction Control Language (TCL) commands, like `ROLLBACK`, `SAVEPOINT`, or `COMMIT`. This rule holds true for the schema-level components that you call from nonsystem trigger bodies when the trigger runs within the scope of the triggering statement.

If you declare a trigger as autonomous, nonsystem trigger bodies can contain Data Control Language commands because they don't alter the transaction scope. They act outside of it. You enable a trigger to work outside the scope of a triggering statement by putting the following in its `DECLARE` block:

```
PRAGMA AUTONOMOUS_TRANSACTION;
```

A larger problem with SQL statements exists with remote transactions. If you call a remote schema-level function or procedure from a trigger body, it is possible that you may encounter a timestamp or signature mismatch. A mismatch invalidates the trigger and causes the triggering SQL statement to fail.

LONG and LONG RAW Datatypes

The `LONG` and `LONG RAW` datatypes are legacy components. No effort is spent on updating them, and you should migrate to LOBs at your earliest opportunity.

You can't declare a local variable in a trigger with the `LONG` or `LONG RAW` datatype. However, you can insert into a `LONG` or `LONG RAW` column when the value can be converted to a constrained datatype, like a `CHAR` or `VARCHAR2`. The maximum length is 32,000 bytes.

Row-level triggers cannot use a *:new* or *:old* pseudo-record, or row of data, when the column is declared as a `LONG` or `LONG RAW` datatype.

Mutating Tables

A *mutating* table is one undergoing change. Change can come from an `INSERT`, `UPDATE`, or `DELETE` statement, or from a `DELETE CASCADE` constraint.

This type of error can only happen on row-level triggers.

You can't query or modify tables when they're changing. This makes sense if you think about it. If a trigger fires because of a change on a table, it can't see the change until it is final. While you can access the `new` and `old` pseudo-records, you can't read the state of the table. Any attempt to do so raises an `ORA-04091` exception.

The following demonstrates how mutating errors can occur. You create a `mutant` table, as follows:

```
CREATE TABLE mutant
( mutant_id      NUMBER
, mutant_name    VARCHAR2(20));
```

You can then insert the four primary ninja turtles:

```
INSERT INTO mutant VALUES (mutant_s1.nextval,'Donatello');
INSERT INTO mutant VALUES (mutant_s1.nextval,'Leonardo');
INSERT INTO mutant VALUES (mutant_s1.nextval,'Michelangelo');
INSERT INTO mutant VALUES (mutant_s1.nextval,'Raphael');
```

After inserting the data, you can build the following trigger:

```
CREATE OR REPLACE TRIGGER mutator
AFTER DELETE ON mutant
FOR EACH ROW
```

```
DECLARE
  rows NUMBER;
BEGIN
  SELECT COUNT(*) INTO rows FROM mutant;
  dbms_output.put_line('[rows] has '||rows||']');
END;
/
```

The trigger body attempts to get the number of rows but it can't find the number of rows because the record set is not final. This restriction exists to prevent the trigger from seeing inconsistent data.

You can fire the trigger by running the following command to delete Michelangelo from the mutant table. The DELETE statement is

```
DELETE FROM MUTANT WHERE mutant_name = 'Michelangelo';
```

After running that statement, the DELETE statement raises the following error stack:

```
DELETE FROM mutant WHERE mutant_name = 'Michelangelo'

ERROR at line 1:
ORA-04091: table PLSQL.MUTANT is mutating, trigger/function may not see it
ORA-06512: at "PLSQL.MUTATOR", line 4
ORA-04088: error during execution of trigger 'PLSQL.MUTATOR'
```

A trigger rolls back the trigger body instructions and triggering statement when it encounters a mutating table. You should be careful to avoid mutating table errors now that you understand why they can occur.

System Triggers

System triggers can present interesting problems. Most problems relate to limitations or constraints imposed by event attribute functions. Some of the event attribute functions may be undefined for certain DDL events. You should refer back to the section "Event Attribute Functions" earlier in this chapter to understand exactly what to expect from event attribute functions.

Event attribute functions are declared and implemented in the Oracle STANDARD package. You can also encounter a problem creating objects after a system trigger fails to compile. This occur for a CREATE event trigger when a CREATE event fires the trigger and the trigger body is invalid due to a missing object dependency. The missing dependency invalidates the trigger and marks it as invalid. When you try to create the missing object, the CREATE event trigger raises an ORA-04098 error and disallows the DDL statement. You must drop the invalid trigger, fix the object dependency, and recompile the trigger to proceed.

You can use the audit_creation trigger created in the section "Data Definition Language Triggers" to illustrate this restriction. If you drop the audit_creation table, the audit_creation trigger becomes invalid. Subsequently, you raise an ORA-04098 while attempting to create this missing table. You can't proceed until you drop the trigger, or you disable it. You disable the trigger by running the following command:

```
ALTER TRIGGER audit_creations DISABLE;
```

You can now create the table, and the trigger should re-validate when it is called. If the trigger is still invalid, you can compile it with this syntax:

```
ALTER TRIGGER audit_new_stuff COMPILE;
```

This section has covered some trigger restrictions. You should check the individual sections for restrictions that are specific to certain trigger types.

Summary

This chapter has reviewed the five types of database triggers. It has explained triggers and their architecture.

PART
III

PL/SQL Advanced Programming

CHAPTER
11

Dynamic SQL

ative Dynamic SQL (NDS) delivered in Oracle 9*i*, improved in 10*g* and 11*g*, provides a replacement for all but one feature of the `DBMS_SQL` package. NDS is the future and you should consider moving any remaining `DBMS_SQL` code forward at the earliest opportunity. NDS and the `DBMS_SQL` package let you create and execute SQL at run time.

This chapter is divided into three principal areas:

- Dynamic SQL architecture

- Native Dynamic SQL (NDS)

  - Dynamic statements

  - Dynamic statements with inputs

  - Dynamic statements with inputs and outputs

  - Dynamic statements with an unknown number of inputs

- DBMS_SQL package

  - Dynamic statements

  - Dynamic statements with input variables

  - Dynamic statements with input and output variables

Dynamic SQL statements are a powerful technology that lets you write and execute queries as your programs run. This means the DDL and DML statements can change as your programming needs change.

The architecture of dynamic statements applies to both NDS and `DBMS_SQL`. It is covered first, and you should at least examine it before going straight to the NDS or `DBMS_SQL` sections. NDS is covered first because you can use it to handle everything except dynamic statements where you don't know the number and datatypes of output values. You must work with the `DBMS_SQL` package to manage those. The `DBMS_SQL` package is covered next because there's often a lot of old code that gets migrated and supported for years.

Dynamic SQL Architecture

Dynamic SQL delivers the flexibility to solve many problems. It allows you to write what are known as lambda-style functions. You declare lambda-style functions like other functions, but they can have an unknown parameter list and return type. Dynamic SQL provides this functionality to the PL/SQL programming language.

While you have two approaches, you should consider that Oracle 11*g* has improved NDS, and that `DBMS_SQL` is provided for backward compatibility. Both solutions allow you to build dynamic programs. You should choose which approach best meets your future needs.

You have essentially two architectures that apply in both cases. You can glue strings together, or you can implement placeholders. The gluing of strings is susceptible to SQL injection attacks. SQL injection attacks prey on the issues surrounding quoting strings. Implementing placeholders makes your dynamic SQL immune to these attacks. You probably know these placeholders as bind variables. They act as formal parameters to dynamic statements, but they're not quite as tidy as the signatures of functions and procedures.

You use NDS or the DBMS_SQL package to build dynamic SQL statements. At compile time none of the elements in the dynamic statement are validated against objects in the database. This lets you write statements that will work with future components, or work for multiple components. The decision about what these dynamic statements will do rests with how you call them.

The process of running a dynamic statement involves four steps. First, the statement is parsed at run time. Second, statements with placeholders map the actual parameters to the formal parameters. Third, it executes the statement. Fourth, it returns values to the calling statement. The process for DBMS_SQL is a bit more complex, but you can find the process flow chart in the *Oracle Database PL/SQL Packages and Types Reference*.

Native Dynamic SQL (NDS)

NDS is a powerful and simple tool. It is easy to use and deploy. It generally meets most needs for lambda-style functions. This section is divided into three parts. First, you cover dynamic statements, which are gluing strings together to make dynamic statements. Second, you learn how to use input bind variables. Third, you learn how to return data from NDS statements.

Dynamic Statements

This section shows you how to run dynamic statements. These statements are static shells when you define your programs. You use them to build statement at run time. These types of statements implement Method 1 from the DBMS_SQL package (see Table 11-1 for a list of these methods).

You write DDL statements in dynamic SQL to avoid failures during compilation. An example would be a statement that should perform only when an object exists. Without dynamic SQL statements, the program unit could fail due to missing objects in the database.

The reasons for dynamic DML statements are different. More often than not, it is tied to checking something in the current session before you perform a statement. For example, you may read the CLIENT_INFO value from the session to check for authentication, roles, and privileges in an end-user application.

The subsections demonstrate dynamic DDL and DML statements.

Dynamic DDL Statement

A frequently performed task in standalone scripts requires you to check whether something is in the database before you act on it. You don't want to run a DROP statement on a table or sequence that doesn't exist because it would raise an error.

The following anonymous block shows you how to conditionally drop a sequence. It uses a FOR loop to check whether the sequence exists, and then it creates and runs a dynamic DDL statement.

You should enable the SQL*Plus SERVEROUTPUT environment variable before testing this code, if you want to see a confirmation message. You can run this anonymous block successfully whether there is or isn't a sample_sequence. The sample program creates the sequence, validates it exists in the user_sequences view, and then run this anonymous block. After that, it queries the user_sequences to confirm it's no longer there.

```
-- This is found in create_nds1.sql on the publisher's web site.
BEGIN
  -- Use a loop to check whether to drop a sequence.
  FOR i IN (SELECT null
            FROM   user_objects
            WHERE  object_name = 'SAMPLE_SEQUENCE') LOOP
    EXECUTE IMMEDIATE 'DROP SEQUENCE sample_sequence';
    dbms_output.put_line('Dropped [sample_sequence].');
```

```
  END LOOP;
END;
/
```

NDS is simple and direct. You simply query to see if the table is there; when it's not there, you drop it. The execute immediate runs the command.

Dynamic DML Statement

Dynamic DML statements are often simply strings assembled at run time. They can be inserted as function or procedure parameters. The problem with gluing strings together from inputs is that they're subject to *SQL injection attacks*. The DBMS_ASSERT package lets you validate input parameters against SQL injection attacks.

The following procedure lets you dynamically build an INSERT statement to the item table:

```
-- This is found in create_nds2.sql on the publisher's web site.
CREATE OR REPLACE PROCEDURE insert_item
( table_name     VARCHAR2
, asin           VARCHAR2
, item_type      VARCHAR2
, item_title     VARCHAR2
, item_subtitle  VARCHAR2 := ''
, rating         VARCHAR2
, agency         VARCHAR2
, release_date   VARCHAR2 ) IS
  stmt VARCHAR2(2000);
BEGIN
  stmt := 'INSERT INTO '||dbms_assert.simple_sql_name(table_name)||' VALUES '
       || '( item_s1.nextval '
       || ','||dbms_assert.enquote_literal('ASIN'||CHR(58)||asin)
       || ',(SELECT    common_lookup_id '
       || '  FROM      common_lookup '
       || '  WHERE     common_lookup_type = '
       ||             dbms_assert.enquote_literal(item_type)||')'
       || ','||dbms_assert.enquote_literal(item_title)
       || ','||dbms_assert.enquote_literal(item_subtitle)
       || ', empty_clob() '
       || ', NULL '
       || ','||dbms_assert.enquote_literal(rating)
       || ','||dbms_assert.enquote_literal(agency)
       || ','||dbms_assert.enquote_literal(release_date)
       || ', 3, SYSDATE, 3, SYSDATE)';
       dbms_output.put_line(stmt);
  EXECUTE IMMEDIATE stmt;
END insert_item;
/
```

The item table could be hard-coded in the string, but it is a parameter to highlight the QUALIFIED_SQL_NAME function. The QUALIFIED_SQL_NAME function compares the string against the namespace value in the schema. It raises an ORA-44004 error when the actual parameter is incorrect. The ENQUOTE_LITERAL function puts containing quotes around string literals in SQL statements. This function is superior to the older style where you backquote the quotes like '''*some_string*''' to get a delimited string literal, '*some_string*'.

You can test the program with the following anonymous block:

```
-- This is found in create_nds2.sql on the publisher's web site.
BEGIN
   insert_item (table_name => 'ITEM'
               ,asin => 'B0000503VC'
               ,item_title => 'Monty Python and the Holy Grail'
               ,item_subtitle => 'Special Edition'
               ,rating => 'PG'
               ,agency => 'MPAA'
               ,release_date => '23-OCT-2001');
END;
/
```

It successfully enters a new item in the `item` table.

SQL Injection Attacks

SQL injection attacks are attempts to fake entry by using unbalanced quotes in SQL statements. Dynamic SQL is a place where some hacker might try to exploit your code.

Oracle now has the DBMS_ASSERT package to help you prevent SQL injection attacks. DBMS_ASSERT has the following functions:

- The ENQUOTE_LITERAL function takes a string input and adds leading and trailing single quotes to the output string.

- The ENQUOTE_NAME function takes a string input and promotes it to uppercase before adding leading and trailing double quotes to the output string. There's an optional parameter Boolean parameter that lets you disable capitalization when you set it to false.

- The NOOP function takes a string input and returns the same value as an output without any validation. The NOOP function is overloaded and can manage a VARCHAR2 or CLOB datatype.

- The QUALIFIED_SQL_NAME function validates the input string as a valid schema-object name. This function lets you validate your functions, procedure, packages, and user-defined objects. The actual parameter evaluates in lowercase, mixed case, or uppercase.

- The SCHEMA_NAME function takes a string input and validates whether it is a valid schema name. The actual parameter needs to be uppercase for this to work properly. So, you should pass the actual parameter inside a call to the UPPER function covered in Appendix J.

- The SIMPLE_SQL_NAME function validates the input string as a valid schema-object name. This function lets you validate your functions, procedure, packages, and user-defined objects.

- The SQL_OBJECT_NAME function validates the input string as a valid schema-object name. This function lets you validate your functions, procedures, and packages. At the time of writing it raised an ORA-44002 error when checking a user-defined object type.

You can find more about the DBMS_ASSERT package in the *Oracle Database PL/SQL Packages and Types Reference*. Oracle NDS is immune to SQL injection attacks when you use bind variables as opposed to gluing things together.

Dynamic Statements with Inputs

A dynamic statement with input variables takes you one step beyond gluing strings together. This lets you write a statement with placeholders. The placeholders act like formal parameters, but they're interspersed inside the SQL statement. You pass actual parameters into statements by placing them as arguments to the USING clause. You return values through the RETURNING INTO clause by default.

Placeholders are positional based on their location in the SQL statement, or the PL/SQL call parameter. You must have an actual parameter in the USING clause for each placeholder. The USING clause takes a comma-delimited list of parameters. They are IN mode *(pass-by-value)* unless you specify otherwise. You override the default mode of operation by setting any parameter to IN OUT or OUT mode.

You use IN mode parameters when the executing a SQL statement. The IN OUT or OUT mode requires that you enclose the SQL statement inside an anonymous block, or you call a PL/SQL function or procedure. The Oracle 11*g* documentation makes the following recommendations with placeholder variables:

- If a dynamic SQL SELECT statement returns at most one row, you should return the value through an INTO clause. This requires that you either (a) open the statement as a reference cursor, or (b) enclose the SQL statement inside an anonymous block. The former does not use an IN OUT or OUT mode parameter in the USING clause, while the latter requires it.

- If a dynamic SQL SELECT statement returns more than one row, you should return the value through a BULK COLLECT INTO clause. Like the INTO clause, the bulk collection requires that you either (a) open the statement as a reference cursor, or (b) enclose the SQL statement inside an anonymous block. The former does not use an IN OUT or OUT mode parameter in the USING clause, while the latter requires it.

- If a dynamic SQL statement is a DML with input-only placeholders, you should put them in the USING clause.

- If a dynamic SQL statement is a DML and uses a RETURNING INTO clause, you should put the input values in the USING clause and the output values in the NDS RETURNING INTO clause.

- If the dynamic SQL statement is a PL/SQL anonymous block or CALL statement, then you should put both input and output parameters in the USING clause. All parameters listed in the USING clause are IN mode only. You must override the default and designate them as IN OUT or OUT.

The examples in this section demonstrate all approaches with SQL statements and calling a PL/SQL anonymous block. As a rule of thumb, you should avoid enclosing a NDS statement in an anonymous block because the RETURNING INTO clause is superior and simpler.

The following example re-writes the insert_item procedure from the prior section. This one uses bind variables:

```
-- This is found in create_nds3.sql on the publisher's web site.
CREATE OR REPLACE PROCEDURE insert_item
( asin          VARCHAR2
, item_type     VARCHAR2
```

```
, item_title     VARCHAR2
, item_subtitle VARCHAR2 := ''
, rating         VARCHAR2
, agency         VARCHAR2
, release_date   DATE ) IS
  stmt VARCHAR2(2000);
BEGIN
  stmt := 'INSERT INTO item VALUES '
       || '( item_s1.nextval '
       || ',''ASIN''||CHR(58)||:asin '
       || ',(SELECT   common_lookup_id '
       || '  FROM     common_lookup '
       || '  WHERE    common_lookup_type = :item_type)'
       || ', :item_title '
       || ', :item_subtitle '
       || ', empty_clob() '
       || ', NULL '
       || ', :rating '
       || ', :agency '
       || ', :release_date '
       || ', 3, SYSDATE, 3, SYSDATE)';
  EXECUTE IMMEDIATE stmt
  USING asin, item_type, item_title, item_subtitle, rating, agency, release_date;
END insert_item;
/
```

You may have noticed a couple of changes. Foremost is that all the DBMS_ASSERT package calls were removed. Bind variables inherit the datatype from the actual parameter passed through the USING clause. This is why there are no delimiting quotes around the variables that would otherwise be string literals. The next change you may notice is the removal of the table name substitution. You can't substitute a table name as a *bind variable* without raising an ORA-00903 error at run time. The last change is the datatype of the release_date parameter; it is now a DATE type.

The EXECUTE IMMEDIATE statement uses all variables passed as actual parameters through the USING clause as IN mode–only variables. Like formal parameters in functions and procedures, the IN mode is the default. You need to specify OUT mode when you want variables results returned to the local program scope.

If the list of parameters is fewer than the actual number of placeholders, you raise an ORA-01008. The error says that not all variables are bound. The using clause replace the old BIND_VALUE and BIND_ARRAY procedures in the DBMS_SQL package.

The following anonymous block lets you test the replacement insert_item procedure:

```
-- This is found in create_nds3.sql on the publisher's web site.
BEGIN
  insert_item (asin => 'B000050VC'
             ,item_type => 'DVD_FULL_SCREEN'
             ,item_title => 'Monty Python and the Holy Grail'
             ,item_subtitle => 'Special Edition'
             ,rating => 'PG'
             ,agency => 'MPAA'
             ,release_date => '23-OCT-2001');
END;
/
```

Bind variables are generally a preferred choice over gluing strings together, but both have their purposes. They're preferred because bind variables make your code immune to SQL injection attacks.

Dynamic Statements with Inputs and Outputs

The ability to bind inputs is powerful and simple using NDS. The terrific thing about getting output variables is that it is *so simple.* This is a refreshing change over the verbose DBMS_SQL approach that you can find in the section "Dynamic Statements with Input and Output Variables" later in this chapter.

```
-- This is found in create_nds4.sql on the publisher's web site.
DECLARE
   -- Define explicit record structure.
   TYPE title_record IS RECORD
   ( item_title     VARCHAR2(60)
   , item_subtitle  VARCHAR2(60));
   -- Define dynamic variables.
   title_cursor  SYS_REFCURSOR;
   title_row     TITLE_RECORD;
   stmt          VARCHAR2(2000);
BEGIN
   -- Set statement.
   stmt := 'SELECT  item_title, item_subtitle '
        || 'FROM    item '
        || 'WHERE   SUBSTR(item_title,1,12) = :input';
   -- Open and read dynamic cursor, then close it.
   OPEN title_cursor FOR stmt USING 'Harry Potter';
   LOOP
     FETCH title_cursor INTO title_row;
     EXIT WHEN title_cursor%NOTFOUND;
     dbms_output.put_line(
       '['||title_row.item_title||']['||title_row.item_subtitle||']');
   END LOOP;
   CLOSE title_cursor;
END;
/
```

The NDS statement is dynamic, accepting a single input bind variable. The OPEN FOR statement simply appends the USING clause to accept filtering criteria. The USING clause in this context is IN mode only. If you attempt to specify an OUT mode operation, the parser raises a PLS-00254 error.

You output the results of the query as you would any other reference cursor statement. Chapter 6 contains a sidebar on system reference cursors.

A bulk operation is also possible in NDS. Chapter 4 has a section called "Bulk Statements" that you may cross-reference while working through the bulk processing examples. You simply call the FETCH BULK COLLECT INTO statement. This is demonstrated in the next query:

```
-- This is found in create_nds5.sql on the publisher's web site.
DECLARE
   -- Define explicit record structure.
   TYPE title_record IS RECORD
```

```
( item_title      VARCHAR2(60)
, item_subtitle   VARCHAR2(60));
TYPE title_collection IS TABLE OF TITLE_RECORD;
-- Define dynamic variables.
title_cursor      SYS_REFCURSOR;
titles            TITLE_COLLECTION;
stmt              VARCHAR2(2000);
BEGIN
  -- Set statement.
  stmt := 'SELECT  item_title, item_subtitle '
       || 'FROM    item '
       || 'WHERE   SUBSTR(item_title,1,12) = :input';
  -- Open and read dynamic cursor, then close it.
  OPEN title_cursor FOR stmt USING 'Harry Potter';
  FETCH title_cursor BULK COLLECT INTO titles;
  FOR i IN 1..titles.COUNT LOOP
    dbms_output.put_line(
      '['||titles(i).item_title||']['||titles(i).item_subtitle||']');
  END LOOP;
  CLOSE title_cursor;
END;
/
```

The FETCH BULK COLLECT INTO moves the entire cursor return set into the collection variable. In a larger program scope you could return the collection record set to another PL/SQL block, or a pipelined function as described in Chapter 6. You can also reference the section "FORALL Statements" in Chapter 4 to see how you could then use bulk inserts to process the resulting collection.

The last item to cover is how you use NDS to handle input and output variables. You declare actual parameters as OUT mode variables in the USING clause. This approach requires two things. You enclose the SQL statement in an anonymous-block PL/SQL program, and you return the variable through a RETURNING INTO clause in the dynamic statement.

The next two scripts depend on your adding another row to the item table. This anonymous block uses the insert_item procedure that you build by running the create_nds3.sql script.

```
-- This is found in create_nds3.sql on the publisher's web site.
BEGIN
  insert_item (asin => 'B000G6BLWE'
              ,item_type => 'DVD_FULL_SCREEN'
              ,item_title => 'Young Frankenstein'
              ,rating => 'PG'
              ,agency => 'MPAA'
              ,release_date => '05-SEP-2006');
END;
/
```

The following example demonstrates reading and writing through a CLOB locator with a dynamic SQL statement. Oracle 11*g* documentation recommends this approach. It has a couple benefits. First, all input bind variables are passed through the USING clause, and all output bind variables are returned through the RETURNING INTO clause. Second, there is no need to create an enclosing anonymous PL/SQL block for the statement.

The recommended script is

```
-- This is found in create_nds6.sql on the publisher's web site.
DECLARE
   -- Define explicit record structure.
   target  CLOB;
   source  VARCHAR2(2000) := 'A Mel Brooks comedy classic!';
   movie   VARCHAR2(60) := 'Young Frankenstein';
   stmt    VARCHAR2(2000);
BEGIN
   -- Set statement.
   stmt := 'UPDATE   item '
        || 'SET      item_desc = empty_clob() '
        || 'WHERE    item_id = '
        || '             (SELECT item_id '
        || '              FROM    item '
        || '              WHERE   item_title = :input) '
        || 'RETURNING item_desc INTO :descriptor';
   EXECUTE IMMEDIATE stmt USING movie RETURNING INTO target;
   dbms_lob.writeappend(target,LENGTH(source),source);
   COMMIT;
END;
/
```

The :input placeholder receives the single actual parameter from the USING clause. The statement RETURNING INTO clause returns the :descriptor placeholder to the target local variable. As qualified in Chapter 8, the LOB locator is a special connection to a work area that lets you read from and write to a CLOB variable. The locator acts like an IN OUT mode variable. This is a very simple and direct approach compared to the alternative. The alternative would have you replace the RETURNING INTO clause with an IN OUT mode parameter in the USING clause, which would require you to enclose the SQL statement in a PL/SQL anonymous block.

You could also write a standalone procedure to manage this UPDATE statement. The procedure would look like this:

```
-- This is found in create_nds7.sql script on the publisher's web site.
CREATE OR REPLACE PROCEDURE get_clob
( item_title_in  VARCHAR2, item_desc_out IN OUT CLOB ) IS
BEGIN
   UPDATE   item
   SET      item_desc = empty_clob()
   WHERE    item_id =
               (SELECT item_id
                FROM   item
                WHERE  item_title = item_title_in)
   RETURNING item_desc INTO item_desc_out;
END get_clob;
/
```

After creating the procedure, you can then use NDS to call the stored procedure. This *works more like a call through the OCI than NDS.* It does provide you with the ability to dynamically marshal call parameters by filtering them through some procedural logic.

The following calls the stored procedure and writes a new string to the CLOB column. The actual call semantic is enclosed in an anonymous block, which is required when you want to use IN OUT or OUT mode placeholders.

```
-- This is found in create_nds7.sql on the publisher's web site.
DECLARE
  -- Define explicit record structure.
  target  CLOB;
  source  VARCHAR2(2000) := 'A Mel Brooks classic movie!';
  movie   VARCHAR2(60)  := 'Young Frankenstein';
  stmt    VARCHAR2(2000);
BEGIN
  -- Set statement
  stmt := 'BEGIN '
       || '  get_clob(:input,:output); '
       || 'END;';
  EXECUTE IMMEDIATE stmt USING movie, IN OUT target;
  dbms_lob.writeappend(target,LENGTH(source),source);
  COMMIT;
END;
/
```

The USING clause maps the local movie variable to the :input placeholder, and the target variable to the :output placeholder. The call to the standalone procedure returns a CLOB locator. You use the CLOB locator as the first actual parameter to the DBMS_LOB.WRITEAPPEND procedure. It writes the contents of the local source variable to CLOB column *courtesy of the placeholder.*

You can't replace the IN OUT mode variable with a RETURNING INTO clause because it would fail. The attempt raises an ORA-06547 error. The error tells you that the RETURING INTO clause can only be used with an INSERT, UPDATE, or DELETE statement.

NOTE
This fails if you have more than one row in the table that meets the criteria. You should delete any extra copies to test this.

You can confirm any of the writes by running the following query:

```
SELECT item_desc FROM item WHERE item_title = 'Young Frankenstein';
```

You'll see

```
ITEM_DESC
--------------------------
A Mel Brooks classic movie!
```

Dynamic Statements with an Unknown Number of Inputs

This section shows you how to create statements that run with an unknown number of placeholders. It demonstrates what is known as DBMS_SQL Method 4 approach, which allows you to bind a variable number of input placeholders.

The following shows you how to build an unknown number of inputs, while returning a known list of columns. You still need to use Method 4 and DBMS_SQL when you have a variable list of outputs.

```
-- This is found in create_nds8.sql on the publisher's web site.
DECLARE
  -- Declare explicit record structure and table of structure.
  TYPE title_record IS RECORD
  ( item_title      VARCHAR2(60)
  , item_subtitle   VARCHAR2(60));
  TYPE title_table IS TABLE OF title_record;
  -- Declare dynamic variables.
  title_cursor  SYS_REFCURSOR;
  title_rows    TITLE_TABLE;
  -- Declare DBMS_SQL variables.
  c             INTEGER := dbms_sql.open_cursor;
  fdbk          INTEGER;
  -- Declare local variables.
  counter       NUMBER := 1;
  column_names  DBMS_SQL.VARCHAR2_TABLE;
  item_ids      DBMS_SQL.NUMBER_TABLE;
  stmt          VARCHAR2(2000);
  substmt       VARCHAR2(2000) := '';
BEGIN
  -- Find the rows that meet the criteria.
  FOR i IN (SELECT 'item_ids' AS column_names
            ,            item_id
            FROM    item
            WHERE   REGEXP_LIKE(item_title,'^Harry Potter')) LOOP
    column_names(counter) := counter;
    item_ids(counter) := i.item_id;
    counter := counter + 1;
  END LOOP;
  -- Dynamically create substatement.
  IF item_ids.COUNT = 1 THEN
    substmt := 'WHERE item_id IN (:item_ids)';
  ELSE
    substmt := 'WHERE item_id IN (';
    FOR i IN 1..item_ids.COUNT LOOP
      IF i = 1 THEN
        substmt := substmt ||':'||i;
      ELSE
        substmt := substmt ||',:'||i;
      END IF;
    END LOOP;
    substmt := substmt || ')';
  END IF;
  -- Set statement.
  stmt := 'SELECT  item_title, item_subtitle '
       || 'FROM    item '
       ||  substmt;
```

```
-- Parse the statement with DBMS_SQL.
dbms_sql.parse(c,stmt,dbms_sql.native);
-- Bind the bind variable name and value.
FOR i IN 1..item_ids.COUNT LOOP
  dbms_sql.bind_variable(c,column_names(i),item_ids(i));
END LOOP;
-- Execute using DBMS_SQL.
fdbk := dbms_sql.execute(c);
-- Convert the cursor to NDS.
title_cursor := dbms_sql.to_refcursor(c);
-- Open and read dynamic cursor, then close it.
FETCH title_cursor BULK COLLECT INTO title_rows;
FOR i IN 1..title_rows.COUNT LOOP
  dbms_output.put_line(
    '['||title_rows(i).item_title||']['||title_rows(i).item_subtitle||']');
END LOOP;
-- Close the System Reference Cursor.
CLOSE title_cursor;
END;
/
```

The program dynamically builds a SQL SELECT statement. The query looks like the following:

```
SELECT item_title, item_subtitle FROM item
WHERE  item_id IN (:1,:2,:3,:4,:5,:6,:7,:8,:9,:10,:11,:12,:13,:14)
```

The loop binds the list of numeric placeholders with the values in the item_ids associative array. The call to DBMS_SQL.TO_REFCURSOR function converts the DBMS_SQL cursor to a standard weakly typed system reference cursor. It also closes the original DBMS_SQL cursor. If you try to close the DBMS_SQL cursor after conversion, you raise an ORA-29471 error. The error message says that you're denied access because the package no longer owns the resource.

After converting to the system reference cursor, you simply use the standard NDS features to bulk-fetch the record set. You can also convert back from NDS to DBMS_SQL by using the TO_CURSOR_NUMBER function.

This section has shown you how to use NDS. You should note two things: NDS is simple to implement and simple to use. The next section describes the older and more complex DBMS_SQL.

DBMS_SQL Package

Oracle introduced the DBMS_SQL package in Oracle 7. It gave you a way to store object code in the database that would dynamically build SQL statements. It was an innovative solution because it works around the problem of how PL/SQL checks dependencies. Prior to DBMS_SQL, you could not store a SQL statement unless the table existed with the same definition.

DBMS_SQL was enhanced to support collections in Oracle 8i. The package has grown through successive releases up to Oracle 9i. As discussed in the section "Native Dynamic SQL (NDS)" earlier in the chapter, the direction shifted to NDS with the release of Oracle 9i.

The DBMS_SQL package provides several overloaded procedures. If you were to run a describe command on the DBMS_SQL package, you would find a copy of each of these overloaded procedures for the types listed. The section "DBMS_SQL Package Definition" documents the constants, type, functions, and procedures.

DBMS_SQL still has one major feature that is not delivered in NDS. It can manage dynamic statements when the number and datatype of column returns are unknown before run time. This feature is possible because of two DBMS_SQL procedures. The procedures are DESCRIBE_COLUMNS and DESCRIBE_COLUMNS2.

Like the NDS approach, DBMS_SQL supports string concatenation and bind variables. If you need a refresher on bind variables, please check Chapter 2. Unlike NDS, the DBMS_SQL package requires explicit grants.

Oracle qualifies four types of dynamic SQL statements. You use certain functions and procedures with each method type. Table 11-1 lists the methods, their definitions, and the DBMS_SQL functions and procedures you use with each.

The next four subsections examine the DBMS_SQL package. The first three demonstrate the features and use of dynamic SQL with the DBMS_SQL package. The last section documents the package constants, types, functions, and procedures.

Dynamic Statements

This section shows you how to run dynamic statements. These statements are static when you define your programs. They are constructed at run time. These types of statements implement Method 1 from Table 11-1.

You write DDL statements in dynamic SQL to avoid failures during compilation. An example would be a statement that should only perform when an object exists. Without dynamic SQL statements, the program unit could fail due to missing objects in the database.

The reasons for dynamic DML statements are different. More often than not, they are tied to checking something in the current session before you perform a statement. For example, you may

---

DBMS_SQL Grants and Privileges

The DBMS_SQL package is owned by the SYS schema. It is sometimes necessary to grant permissions to the SYSTEM user first. Then, you can grant permissions to the individual users rather than provisioning them through roles. You generally need access to the DBMS_SQL and DBMS_SYS_SQL packages.

You grant permissions from the SYS account to the SYSTEM user with the following two statements:

```
GRANT EXECUTE ON dbms_sys_sql TO system WITH GRANT OPTION;
GRANT EXECUTE ON dbms_sql TO system WITH GRANT OPTION;
```

After granting the proper privileges to the SYSTEM user, you can grant them to your plsql user to run the sample programs. You grant the following privileges as the system user:

```
GRANT EXECUTE ON sys.dbms_sys_sql TO plsql;
GRANT EXECUTE ON sys.dbms_sql TO plsql;
```

You should now be able to run the scripts in this file, provided you've also installed the video store example discussed in the introduction.

Method	Description	Functions or Procedures
1	Method 1 supports DML or DDL statements that are static. Static statements have no inputs or outputs when they're defined. Method 1 also does not support DQL statements.	EXECUTE OPEN_CURSOR PARSE
2	Method 2 supports DML statements that are dynamic, which means they have bind variables. This method requires that you know the number and datatype of bind variables at statement definition. Method 2 also does not support DQL statements.	BIND_ARRAY BIND_VARIABLE EXECUTE OPEN_CURSOR PARSE
3	Method 3 supports DML statements that are dynamic, which means they have bind variables. It also supports the RETURNING INTO clause. The RETURNING INTO clause lets you retrieve columns and LOB locators from DML statements. This method requires that you know the number and datatype of bind variables at statement definition. Method 3 supports DQL statements, provided you know the number and datatypes at statement definition.	BIND_ARRAY BIND_VARIABLE COLUMN_VALUE DEFINE_COLUMN EXECUTE EXECUTE_AND_FETCH FETCH_ROWS OPEN_CURSOR PARSE VARIABLE_VALUE
4	Method 4 supports DML statements that are dynamic, which means they have bind variables. It also supports the RETURNING INTO clause. The RETURNING INTO clause lets you retrieve columns and LOB locators from DML statements. This method does not require advanced knowledge of the number and datatype of bind variables at statement definition. Method 4 supports DQL statements without requiring you to know the number and datatype of columns at statement definition.	BIND_ARRAY BIND_VARIABLE COLUMN_VALUE DEFINE_COLUMN DESCRIBE_COLUMNS DESCRIBE_COLUMNS2 DESCRIBE_COLUMNS3 EXECUTE EXECUTE_AND_FETCH FETCH_ROWS OPEN_CURSOR PARSE VARIABLE_VALUE

TABLE 11-1 *DBMS_SQL Methods of Operation*

read the CLIENT_INFO value from the session to check for authentication, roles, and privileges in an end-user application.

The subsections demonstrate dynamic DDL and DML statements, respectively.

Dynamic DDL Statement

A frequently performed task in standalone scripts requires you to check whether something is in the database before you act on it. You don't want to run a DROP statement on a table or sequence that doesn't exist.

The following anonymous block shows you how to conditionally drop a sequence. It uses a FOR loop to check whether the sequence exists, and then it creates and runs a dynamic DDL statement.

You should enable the SQL*Plus `SERVEROUTPUT` environment variable before testing this code, if you want to see the confirmation message. The code follows:

```
-- This is found in create_dbms_sql1.sql on the publisher's web site.
DECLARE
   -- Define local DBMS_SQL variables, and open cursor.
   c       INTEGER := dbms_sql.open_cursor;
   fdbk    INTEGER;
   stmt    VARCHAR2(2000);

BEGIN
   -- Use a loop to check whether to drop a sequence.
   FOR i IN (SELECT null
             FROM    user_objects
             WHERE   object_name = 'SAMPLE_SEQUENCE') LOOP
      -- Build, parse, and execute SQL statement, then close cursor.
      stmt := 'DROP SEQUENCE sample_sequence';
      dbms_sql.parse(c,stmt,DBMS_SQL.NATIVE);
      fdbk := dbms_sql.execute(c);
      dbms_sql.close_cursor(c);
      dbms_output.put_line('Dropped Sequence [SAMPLE_SEQUENCE].');
   END LOOP;
END;
/
```

The declaration block defines three variables for `DBMS_SQL` statements. One holds the database cursor number; by tradition more than anything else it is named `c` for *cursor*. You're welcome to change it to something more meaningful to you, but you'll see it in all the sample programs. `c` is defined, not declared, by calling the `DBMS_SQL.OPEN_CURSOR` function. The next variable is `fdbk` *(another acronym)*, which stands for *feedback*. It is used to capture the return value from the `DBMS_SQL.EXECUTE` function. The third name almost makes sense: `stmt` means *statement*.

The execution block assigns a valid DDL statement to the `stmt` variable. Then, the `DBMS_SQL.PARSE` ties the cursor number and statement together and runs the statement using the current database version's execution semantics.

You can test the program by creating a `sample_sequence` with the following syntax:

```
CREATE SEQUENCE sample_sequence;
```

You can confirm the sequence is there and working by querying the database catalog, or incrementing the sequence. This verifies the presence of the sequence by incrementing it:

```
SELECT sample_sequence.nextval FROM dual;
```

Run the conditional drop statement and you see this message:

```
Dropped Sequence [SAMPLE_SEQUENCE].
```

You have now seen how to implement a dynamic DDL statement using the DBMS_SQL package. If you check back in the section "Native Dynamic SQL (NDS)," you'll see this approach is more typing for little or no return.

Dynamic DML Statement

Dynamic DML statements are often created as strings at run time. They often audit some state or behavior before deciding how to build the DML statement. This section discusses DBMS_SQL Method 1, which allows only strings or patchworks of strings.

The example uses a code block that changes the column values for an INSERT statement. Authenticated users enter one type of data, while unauthenticated users enter another.

You could check the value of the CLIENT_INFO variable in the session, and then choose the value to insert into the LAST_UPDATED_BY column of a table. Chapter 10 has a sidebar "Reading and Writing Session Metadata" that explains how you can set and get the CLIENT_INFO value for your session.

The example checks if the value has been set. If not set, it substitutes a –1 for the LAST_UPDATED_BY column. That would be an illegal user, and entering it conditionally lets you track manual SQL entries to a production database. Actually, it should update both the CREATED_BY and LAST_UPDATED_BY columns for completeness, but you'll do that in a subsequent example with bind variables.

```
-- This is found in create_dbms_sql2.sql on the publisher's web site.
DECLARE
  -- Define local DBMS_SQL variables, and open cursor.
  c       INTEGER := dbms_sql.open_cursor;
  fdbk    INTEGER;
  stmt1 VARCHAR2(2000);
  stmt2 VARCHAR2(20) := '-1,SYSDATE)';
  -- V$SESSION.CLIENT_INFO variable.
  client VARCHAR2(64);
BEGIN
  stmt1 := 'INSERT INTO item VALUES '
        || '( item_s1.nextval '
        || ',''ASIN''||CHR(58)||' B000VBJEEG'''
        || ',(SELECT   common_lookup_id '
        || '  FROM     common_lookup '
        || '  WHERE    common_lookup_type = ''DVD_WIDE_SCREEN'') '
        || ',''Ratatouille'''
        || ',''''''
        || ', empty_clob() '
        || ', NULL '
        || ',''G'''
        || ',''MPAA'''
        || ',''06-NOV-2007'''
        || ', 3, SYSDATE,';
  -- Get the current CLIENT_INFO value and conditionally append to string.
  dbms_application_info.read_client_info(client);
```

```
IF client IS NOT NULL THEN
  stmt1 := stmt1 || client || ',SYSDATE)';
ELSE
  stmt1 := stmt1 || stmt2;
END IF;
  -- Build, parse, and execute SQL statement, then close cursor.
  dbms_sql.parse(c,stmt1,dbms_sql.native);
  fdbk := dbms_sql.execute(c);
  dbms_sql.close_cursor(c);
  dbms_output.put_line('Rows Inserted ['||fdbk||']');
END;
/
```

Unless you set the CLIENT_INFO column value, this script should insert one row with a –1 in the LAST_UPDATED_BY column. As you can tell from the statement, typing SQL statements into a variable is tedious and a backquoting feat when successful. You raise an ORA-01756 error, which says "quoted string not properly terminated," when you fail to get all the single quotes matched.

Colons inside dynamic SQL statements are indicators of placeholders. When DBMS_SQL.PARSE parses a statement string, it marks placeholders as bind values targets. If you fail to call either the BIND_ARRAY or BIND_VARIABLE procedure before you execute the parsed statement, it would fail due to the missing bind variable. You bind *scalar* variables by calling the BIND_VARIABLE procedure, and you bind *nested tables* by calling the BIND_ARRAY procedure.

You should use CHR(58) in lieu of the colon when you want to insert a colon as text, because the parser doesn't interpret it as a bind variable. While the parsed output string contains a colon, the parsing process didn't trigger a substitution.

All the DBMS_SQL command syntax mirrors the syntax in the DDL example in the preceding section. You have now seen how to create and implement dynamic SQL statements by creating and executing conditionally constructed strings.

Dynamic Statements with Input Variables

The prior section demonstrated how you dynamically piece strings together to build a statement. That is a cumbersome process, and as you might guess, there is a better way. This section discusses DBMS_SQL Method 2, which allows you to bind variables into statements.

You generally know the statement structure of your DML statements when you write a PL/SQL block. You can actually write your dynamic statements like a function, with input values. You call these input variables placeholders instead of formal parameters. Inside the statements they act as bind variables, and you may find many people calling them that.

It is much easier to write a DDL or DML statement that uses placeholders than gluing strings together through concatenation. DBMS_SQL Method 2 from Table 11-1 provides this feature. Table 11-2 lists some errors that can occur when using placeholders and bind variables.

You should also note that you can implement a PL/SQL block with DBMS_SQL. The only caveat is that you terminate the string with a semicolon. This is a departure from how ordinary SQL statements work. The difference occurs because the closing semicolon terminates the PL/SQL block. A semicolon acts as an execution instruction for a SQL statement. You will see an example of this approach in the next section, "Dynamic Statements with Input and Output variables."

Error Code	Description and Fix
ORA-00928	You raise an ORA-00928 error when you put placeholders inside the overriding signature of an INSERT statement. The signature is the formal parameter list between the table name and VALUES clause. The generic "missing SELECT keyword" message can be misleading.
ORA-06502	You raise an ORA-06502 error when an explicit size is required for a CHAR, RAW, or VARCHAR2 variable. You need to include the output size when you call the BIND_VARIABLE_CHAR or BIND_VARIABLE_RAW procedures. The generic "PL/SQL: numeric or value error" message can be misleading.
ORA-01006	You raise an ORA-01006 error when you enclose placeholders for VARCHAR2 datatypes in quotes. The BIND_VARIABLE function binds the value and datatype to the statement, which eliminates the need for delimiting quotes. The generic "bind variable does not exist" message is a complete misnomer, but now you know how to fix it.
PLS-00049	You raise a PLS-00049 error when a placeholder receives an unexpected datatype that can't be implicitly converted to the target datatype. You need to ensure any assignments are explicitly made with the correct datatype. Don't rely on implicit type conversion and you'll never be disappointed. The "bad bind variable" message isn't clear, but it's spot on because you've sent the wrong datatype.

TABLE 11-2   *Errors That Can Occur When Using DBMS_SQL*

The following example re-implements the INSERT statement from the prior section. This time it uses replacement variables. The anonymous block is rewritten as a standalone procedure. After creating the procedure, you can insert new items into the item table through the procedure.

The following is the standalone procedure that implements IN mode placeholders or bind variables:

```
-- This is found in create_dbms_sql3.sql on the publisher's web site.
CREATE OR REPLACE PROCEDURE insert_item
( asin     VARCHAR2
, title    VARCHAR2
, subtitle VARCHAR2 := NULL
, itype    VARCHAR2 := 'DVD_WIDE_SCREEN'
, rating   VARCHAR2
, agency   VARCHAR2
, release  DATE ) IS
  -- Define local DBMS_SQL variables.
  c      INTEGER := dbms_sql.open_cursor;
  fdbk   INTEGER;
  stmt   VARCHAR2(2000);
  -- Variable to get OUT parameter value.
  client VARCHAR2(64);
```

```
BEGIN
  stmt := 'INSERT INTO item VALUES '
      || '( item_s1.nextval '
      || ',''ASIN''||CHR(58)|| :asin'
      || ',(SELECT   common_lookup_id '
      || '  FROM     common_lookup '
      || '  WHERE    common_lookup_type = :itype) '
      || ',:title'
      || ',:subtitle'
      || ', empty_clob() '
      || ', NULL '
      || ',:rating'
      || ',:agency'
      || ',:release'
      || ',:created_by,SYSDATE,:last_updated_by,SYSDATE)';
  -- Call and dynamically set the session for the CLIENT_INFO value.
  dbms_application_info.read_client_info(client);
  IF client IS NOT NULL THEN
    client := TO_NUMBER(client);
  ELSE
    client := -1;
  END IF;
  -- Parse and execute the statement.
  dbms_sql.parse(c,stmt,dbms_sql.native);
  dbms_sql.bind_variable(c,'asin',asin);
  dbms_sql.bind_variable(c,'itype',itype);
  dbms_sql.bind_variable(c,'title',title);
  dbms_sql.bind_variable(c,'subtitle',subtitle);
  dbms_sql.bind_variable(c,'rating',rating);
  dbms_sql.bind_variable(c,'agency',agency);
  dbms_sql.bind_variable(c,'release',release);
  dbms_sql.bind_variable(c,'created_by',client);
  dbms_sql.bind_variable(c,'last_updated_by',client);
  fdbk := dbms_sql.execute(c);
  dbms_sql.close_cursor(c);
  dbms_output.put_line('Rows Inserted ['||fdbk||']');
END insert_item;
/
```

The placeholders are represented in bold text inside the dynamic INSERT statement. You should note that they don't have delimiting single quotes around them. This is because the value and datatype are bound to the statement, and the delimiters are unnecessary. If you forget and include the delimiting internal quotes in the statement, an ORA-01006 error is raised at run time. You need to remove the single quotes, or enclose the statement in a PL/SQL block.

As the number of bind variables increase, so do the calls to BIND_VARIABLE procedure. This section has shown you how to use Method 2 dynamic SQL, which lets you substitute input variables.

Dynamic Statements with Input and Output Variables

This section shows you how to implement placeholders that either input or output data from SQL statements. It demonstrates DBMS_SQL Method 3, which allows you to IN and OUT mode bind variables in SQL statements.

Debugging Tips for DBMS_SQL with SELECT Statements

It is critical when working with scalar variable-length strings that you provide a physical size to the DBMS_SQL.DEFINE_COLUMNS procedure. You must also do so when returning a scalar RAW datatype. If you forget to provide the physical size, the DBMS_SQL package raises a PLS-00307 error. The error says "too many declarations of DEFINE_COLUMN match this call." The error is actually a bit tricky because it involves how implicit casting works when calling this function.

You can make your life easier by simply providing the fourth parameter, which is the length of a CHAR, RAW, or VARCHAR2 datatype.

Dynamic SELECT statements work in Method 3, provided you know at compile time how many columns are retrieved. In this section you work with a set of scalar return values and a single scalar input value.

You are performing *row-by-row* queries when you manage scalar output values. You process *parallel arrays* when you return multiple columns from a SELECT statement into associative arrays through *bulk* processing. You need to be very attentive to managing how you navigate through these to ensure your index values are always equal. Failure to keep the index in synchronization means you're looking at columns from different rows.

This syntax is probably among the most tedious for the DBMS_SQL package, regardless of whether you're returning one, row-by-row, or bulk statement values. You should consider the Native Dynamic SQL OPEN FOR clause for these types of operation because it's simpler.

The *row-by-row* and *bulk* processing examples are covered in separate subsections.

Row-by-Row Statement Processing

The sample program shows you how to process single- and multiple-row returns from a dynamic SELECT statement. These examples depend on the item table that is built by the create_store.sql discussed in the introduction to this book.

The single-row statement is

```
-- This is found in create_dbms_sql4.sql on the publisher's web site.
DECLARE
  c                       INTEGER := dbms_sql.open_cursor;
  fdbk                    INTEGER;
  statement               VARCHAR2(2000);
  item_id                 NUMBER := 1081;
  item_title              VARCHAR2(60);
  item_subtitle           VARCHAR2(60);
BEGIN
  -- Build and parse SQL statement.
  statement := 'SELECT item_title, item_subtitle '
            || 'FROM item WHERE item_id = :item_id';
  dbms_sql.parse(c,statement,dbms_sql.native);
  -- Define column mapping, execute statement, and copy results.
  dbms_sql.define_column(c,1,item_title,60);    -- Define OUT mode variable.
  dbms_sql.define_column(c,2,item_subtitle,60); -- Define OUT mode variable.
  dbms_sql.bind_variable(c,'item_id',item_id);  -- Bind IN mode variable.
  fdbk := dbms_sql.execute_and_fetch(c);
  dbms_sql.column_value(c,1,item_title);        -- Copy query column to variable.
  dbms_sql.column_value(c,2,item_subtitle);     -- Copy query column to variable.
```

```
    -- Print return value and close cursor.
    dbms_output.put_line('['||item_title||']['||NVL(item_subtitle,'None')||']');
    dbms_sql.close_cursor(c);
END;
/
```

This approach lets you enter the SELECT columns natively in the statement because they're OUT mode variables. You need to define the columns before executing the statement, and then copy the column values to a local variable after fetching them. You reference columns by position and local variables by name. This differs for the IN mode variable, which uses a semicolon to identify it as a replacement variable *(or bind variable)*.

This query should return

```
[We Were Soldiers][None]
```

You've now seen how to return a single row, but more often than not you return more than one row. The following example performs a row-by-row query and prints the contents of the returned rows:

```
-- This is found in dbms_sql5.sql on the publisher's web site.
DECLARE
  c                        INTEGER := dbms_sql.open_cursor;
  fdbk                     INTEGER;
  statement                VARCHAR2(2000);
  item1                    NUMBER := 1003;
  item2                    NUMBER := 1013;
  item_title               VARCHAR2(60);
  item_subtitle            VARCHAR2(60);
BEGIN
  -- Build and parse SQL statement.
  statement := 'SELECT item_title, item_subtitle '
            || 'FROM item '
            || 'WHERE item_id BETWEEN :item1 AND :item2 '
            || 'AND item_type = 1014';
  dbms_sql.parse(c,statement,dbms_sql.native);
  -- Define column mapping and execute statement.
  dbms_sql.define_column(c,1,item_title,60);     -- Define OUT mode variable.
  dbms_sql.define_column(c,2,item_subtitle,60); -- Define OUT mode variable.
  dbms_sql.bind_variable(c,'item1',item1);       -- Bind IN mode variable.
  dbms_sql.bind_variable(c,'item2',item2);       -- Bind IN mode variable.
  fdbk := dbms_sql.execute(c);
  -- Read results.
  LOOP
    EXIT WHEN dbms_sql.fetch_rows(c) = 0;        -- No more results.
    -- Copy and print.
    dbms_sql.column_value(c,1,item_title);       -- Copy column to variable.
    dbms_sql.column_value(c,2,item_subtitle);    -- Copy column to variable.
    dbms_output.put_line('['||item_title||']['||NVL(item_subtitle,'None')||']');
  END LOOP;
  dbms_sql.close_cursor(c);
END;
/
```

You define the column mapping once for each column, and bind variables once. You need to copy each row's column values to the local variable to process them, as shown in the preceding loop.

With the SQL*Plus SERVEROUTPUT environment variable set, this should print

```
[Casino Royale][None]
[Die Another Day][None]
[Die Another Day][2-Disc Ultimate Version]
[Golden Eye][Special Edition]
[Golden Eye][None]
[Tomorrow Never Dies][None]
[Tomorrow Never Dies][Special Edition]
[The World Is Not Enough][2-Disc Ultimate Edition]
[The World Is Not Enough][None]
```

You've now seen how to process *single-* and *multiple-*row returns from a SELECT statement. The next section shows you how to manage bulk SELECT operations.

Bulk Statement Processing
The idea of bulk processing is often a better solution than row-by-row statements. You should use NDS for this behavior, not DBMS_SQL. The BULK COLLECT INTO clause would only work in the context of a PL/SQL block. The DBMS_SQL bulk binding process isn't designed to support SQL statements inside anonymous blocks. If you attempt that type of unsupported work-around, you'll ultimately raise a PLS-00497 error.

DBMS_SQL Package Definition
The DBMS_SQL package has been in the product since Oracle 7. Changes and fixes have made it a very stable and robust component in the database. It is popular notwithstanding the release of Native Dynamic SQL (NDS) in Oracle 9*i*. In Oracle 11*g,* the only thing you can't do in NDS is work with statements that have an unknown set of columns at run time. The DBMS_SQL package lets you manage these statements.

This section covers the constants, variables, functions, and procedures found in the DBMS_SQL package. You can go to the appropriate subsection to check on component definitions.

DBMS_SQL Constants
There are three constants. They're designed to support DBMS_SQL.PARSE procedure. You really should only use NATIVE from Oracle 8 forward. Table 11-3 defines the constants.

DBMS_SQL Datatypes
The DBMS_SQL package supports associative arrays *(the old PL/SQL tables)* that are indexed by binary integers for the following base scalar types: BFILE, BINARY_DOUBLE, BLOB, CLOB, DATE, INTERVAL_DAY_TO_SECOND, INTERVAL_YEAR_TO_MONTH, NUMBER, TIME, TIMESTAMP,

Constant Name	Description	Value
NATIVE	You should use the NATIVE constant from Oracle 8 forward. It is an INTEGER datatype and indicates the parsing language.	1
V6	You shouldn't use the V6 constant any more.	0
V7	You should use the V7 constant only if you're running the desupported Oracle 7 release.	2

TABLE 11-3 *DBMS_SQL Available Constants*

TIMESTAMP_WITH_LTZ, and UROWID. These associative array datatypes use a naming pattern of *<scalar_type>*_TABLE. They are designated as Bulk SQL Types in the *Oracle Database PL/SQL Packages and Types References*.

A DBMS_SQL.VARCHAR2_TABLE datatype is also described in the same reference as a general type. It behaves consistently with the bulk datatypes.

The DBMS_SQL package also supports three record structures:

- The desc_rec supports the DESCRIBE_COLUMNS procedure. The procedure uses it to describe columns for a cursor opened and parsed by the DBMS_SQL package.

```
TYPE desc_rec IS RECORD ( col_type              BINARY_INTEGER := 0
,                          col_max_len           BINARY_INTEGER := 0
,                          col_name              VARCHAR2(32)   := "
,                          col_name_len          BINARY_INTEGER := 0
,                          col_schema_name       VARCHAR2(32)   := "
,                          col_schema_name_len   BINARY_INTEGER := 0
,                          col_precision         BINARY_INTEGER := 0
,                          col_scale             BINARY_INTEGER := 0
,                          col_charsetid         BINARY_INTEGER := 0
,                          col_charsetform       BINARY_INTEGER := 0
,                          col_null_ok           BOOLEAN        := TRUE);
```

- The desc_rec2 supports the DESCRIBE_COLUMNS2 procedure. The procedure uses it to describe columns for a cursor opened and parsed by the DBMS_SQL package.

```
TYPE desc_rec2 IS RECORD ( col_type              BINARY_INTEGER := 0
,                          col_max_len           BINARY_INTEGER := 0
,                          col_name              VARCHAR2(32767):= "
,                          col_name_len          BINARY_INTEGER := 0
,                          col_schema_name       VARCHAR2(32)   := "
,                          col_schema_name_len   BINARY_INTEGER := 0
,                          col_precision         BINARY_INTEGER := 0
,                          col_scale             BINARY_INTEGER := 0
,                          col_charsetid         BINARY_INTEGER := 0
,                          col_charsetform       BINARY_INTEGER := 0
,                          col_null_ok           BOOLEAN        := TRUE);
```

- The desc_rec3 supports the DESCRIBE_COLUMNS3 procedure. The procedure uses it to describe columns for a cursor opened and parsed by the DBMS_SQL package.

```
TYPE desc_rec3 IS RECORD ( col_type              BINARY_INTEGER := 0
,                          col_max_len           BINARY_INTEGER := 0
,                          col_name              VARCHAR2(32767):= "
,                          col_name_len          BINARY_INTEGER := 0
,                          col_schema_name       VARCHAR2(32)   := "
,                          col_schema_name_len   BINARY_INTEGER := 0
,                          col_precision         BINARY_INTEGER := 0
,                          col_scale             BINARY_INTEGER := 0
,                          col_charsetid         BINARY_INTEGER := 0
,                          col_charsetform       BINARY_INTEGER := 0
,                          col_null_ok           BOOLEAN        := TRUE
,                          col_type_name         VARCHAR2(32)   := "
,                          col_type_name_len     BINARY_INTEGER := 0);
```

There are also associative arrays for each of the record types. These record structures and associative arrays are used for Method 4 processing, which involves an unknown set of columns at compile time.

DBMS_SQL Functions and Procedures

The functions and procedures of the DBMS_SQL package have endured over the years. They are still widely used, while virtually everything can run through NDS. Some of the reasoning is related to backward compatibility or coding standards that try to keep things the same. Clearly, Oracle 11*g* continues the trend toward deprecating the DBMS_SQL package somewhere in the future.

Whether for maintenance or replacement with NDS, the following synopses should help you quickly check the functions and procedures of the DBMS_SQL package. If you run into permission issues, please check the sidebar "DBMS_SQL Grants and Privileges" earlier in this chapter.

BIND_ARRAY Procedure The BIND_ARRAY procedure supports bulk DML operations. The function binds a nested table collection into a SQL statement. You can choose a collection from a list of base SQL datatypes. It is an overloaded procedure. There are two types of signatures, and all parameters use an IN mode of operation.

Prototype 1

```
bind_array( cursor_number NUMBER
          , column_name    VARCHAR2
          , collection     <datatype_list> )
```

Prototype 2

```
bind_array( cursor_number NUMBER
          , column_name    VARCHAR2
          , collection     <datatype_list>
          , index1         NUMBER
          , index2         NUMBER )
```

The collection is an associative array, indexed by a BINARY_INTEGER. You can choose the base scalar variable from: BFILE, BLOB, CLOB, DATE, NUMBER, ROWID, TIME, TIMESTAMP, TIME WITH TIME ZONE, or VARCHAR2. This function also supports nested tables, VARRAYs, and user-defined object types through the OCI libraries.

BIND_VARIABLE Procedure The BIND_VARIABLE procedure supports row-by-row DML operations. The function binds a wide variety of datatypes into a SQL statement. It is an overloaded procedure with a single type of signature, and all parameters in the signature use an IN mode of operation.

Prototype

```
bind_variable( cursor_number  NUMBER
             , column_name     VARCHAR2
             , variable_value <datatype_list> )
```

The datatype list includes any of these SQL datatypes: BFILE, BINARY_DOUBLE, BINARY_FLOAT, BLOB, CLOB, DATE, INTERVAL YEAR TO MONTH, INTERVAL YEAR TO SECOND, NUMBER, REF OF STANDARD, ROWID, TIME, TIMESTAMP, TIMESTAMP WITH TIME ZONE, TIME WITH TIME ZONE, or VARCHAR2.

BIND_VARIABLE_CHAR Procedure   The BIND_VARIABLE_CHAR procedure supports row-by-row DML operations. The function binds a CHAR datatype into a SQL statement. It is an overloaded procedure with two signatures, and all parameters use an IN mode of operation.

Prototype 1

```
bind_variable_char( cursor_number  NUMBER
                  , column_name    VARCHAR2
                  , variable_value CHAR )
```

Prototype 2

```
bind_variable_char( cursor_number  NUMBER
                  , column_name    VARCHAR2
                  , variable_value CHAR
                  , out_value_size NUMBER )
```

BIND_VARIABLE_RAW Procedure   The BIND_VARIABLE_RAW procedure supports row-by-row DML operations. The function binds a RAW datatype into a SQL statement. It is an overloaded procedure with two signatures, and all parameters use an IN mode of operation.

Prototype 1

```
bind_variable_raw( cursor_number  NUMBER
                 , column_name    VARCHAR2
                 , variable_value CHAR )
```

Prototype 2

```
bind_variable_raw( cursor_number  NUMBER
                 , column_name    VARCHAR2
                 , variable_value CHAR
                 , out_value_size NUMBER )
```

BIND_VARIABLE_ROWID Procedure   The BIND_VARIABLE_ROWID procedure supports row-by-row DML operations. The function binds a ROWID datatype into a SQL statement. It is not an overloaded procedure with a single signature, and all parameters use an IN mode of operation.

Prototype

```
bind_variable_rowid( cursor_number  NUMBER
                   , column_name    VARCHAR2
                   , variable_value ROWID )
```

CLOSE_CURSOR Procedure   The CLOSE_CURSOR procedure closes an open DBMS_SQL cursor. It is not an overloaded procedure, and it has one signature. The cursor number is passed by reference as an IN OUT mode variable.

Prototype

```
close_cursor( cursor_number  NUMBER )
```

COLUMN_VALUE Procedure   The COLUMN_VALUE procedure supports bulk and row-by-row DQL operations. The function binds the output from a SELECT statement into an OUT mode variable. The variable can be a scalar variable or a nested table of a scalar variable. The cursor name and position are IN mode variables, while the variable or collection value and column error and actual length are OUT mode variables. The procedure has three overloaded signatures.

Prototype 1

```
column_value( cursor_number  NUMBER
            , position        NUMBER
            , variable_value <datatype_list> )
```

Prototype 2

```
column_value( cursor_number  NUMBER
            , position        NUMBER
            , collection      <datatype_list> )
```

Prototype 3

```
column_value( cursor_number  NUMBER
            , position        NUMBER
            , collection      <datatype_list>
            , column_error    NUMBER
            , actual_length   NUMBER )
```

The datatype can be a *scalar* or *associative array* variable of any of these SQL datatypes: BFILE, BLOB, CLOB, DATE, NUMBER, ROWID, TIME, TIMESTAMP, TIME WITH TIME ZONE, or VARCHAR2.

The prototype signature five parameters are restricted to an *associative array* of a DATE, NUMBER, or VARCHAR2 scalar datatype. This function also supports associative arrays *nested tables,* VARRAYs, and user-defined object types through the OCI libraries.

COLUMN_VALUE_CHAR Procedure   The COLUMN_VALUE_CHAR procedure supports row-by-row DQL operations. The function binds the output from a SELECT statement for a CHAR column into an OUT mode variable. It is an overloaded procedure, and it has two signatures.

Prototype 1

```
column_value_char( cursor_number  NUMBER
                 , position        NUMBER
                 , variable_value CHAR )
```

Prototype 2

```
column_value_char( cursor_number  NUMBER
                 , position        NUMBER
                 , variable_value CHAR
                 , column_error    NUMBER
                 , actual_length   NUMBER )
```

COLUMN_VALUE_LONG Procedure   The COLUMN_VALUE_LONG procedure supports row-by-row DQL operations. The function binds the output from a SELECT statement for a LONG column into an OUT mode variable. It is not an overloaded procedure, and it has one signature.

Prototype

```
column_value_long( cursor_number  NUMBER
                 , position        NUMBER
                 , variable_value LONG )
```

COLUMN_VALUE_RAW Procedure   The COLUMN_VALUE_RAW procedure supports row-by-row DQL operations. The function binds the output from a SELECT statement for a RAW column into an OUT mode variable. It is an overloaded procedure, and it has two signatures.

Prototype 1

```
column_value_raw( cursor_number  NUMBER
                , position        NUMBER
                , variable_value RAW )
```

Prototype 2

```
column_value_raw( cursor_number  NUMBER
                , position        NUMBER
                , variable_value RAW
                , column_error    NUMBER
                , actual_length   NUMBER )
```

COLUMN_VALUE_ROWID Procedure   The COLUMN_VALUE_ROWID procedure supports row-by-row DQL operations. The function binds the output from a SELECT statement for a ROWID column into an OUT mode variable. It is an overloaded procedure, and it has two signatures.

Prototype 1

```
column_value_rowid( cursor_number  NUMBER
                  , position        NUMBER
                  , variable_value ROWID )
```

Prototype 2

```
column_value_rowid( cursor_number  NUMBER
                  , position        NUMBER
                  , variable_value ROWID
                  , column_error    NUMBER
                  , actual_length   NUMBER )
```

DEFINE_ARRAY Procedure   The DEFINE_ARRAY procedure supports bulk DQL operations. The function defines (or maps) a nested table to columns of a SELECT statement. You must use this before calling the COLUMN_VALUE procedure. It is an overloaded procedure, and it has one type of signature.

Prototype

```
define_array( cursor_number  NUMBER
            , position        NUMBER
```

```
         , collection      <datatype_list>
         , count           NUMBER
         , lower_bound     NUMBER )
```

The `count` parameter sets the maximum number of elements returned. The `lower_bound` parameter sets the starting point, which is typically 1.

The datatype can be an *associative array* variable of any of these SQL datatypes: `BFILE`, `BLOB`, `CLOB`, `DATE`, `NUMBER`, `ROWID`, `TIME`, `TIMESTAMP`, `TIME WITH TIME ZONE`, or `VARCHAR2`.

DEFINE_COLUMN Procedure   The `DEFINE_COLUMN` procedure supports row-by-row DQL operations. The function defines (or maps) column values to columns of a `SELECT` statement. You must use this before calling the `COLUMN_VALUE` procedure. It is an overloaded procedure, and it has one type of signature.

Prototype

```
define_column( cursor_number  NUMBER
             , position        NUMBER
             , variable_value <datatype_list> )
```

The datatype can be a *scalar* variable of any of these SQL datatypes: `BFILE`, `BLOB`, `CLOB`, `DATE`, `NUMBER`, `ROWID`, `TIME`, `TIMESTAMP`, `TIME WITH TIME ZONE`, or `VARCHAR2`.

DEFINE_COLUMN_CHAR Procedure   The `DEFINE_COLUMN_CHAR` procedure supports row-by-row DQL operations. The function defines (or maps) column values to columns of a `SELECT` statement. You must use this before calling the `COLUMN_VALUE` procedure. It is not an overloaded procedure, and it has one signature.

Prototype

```
define_column_char( cursor_number  NUMBER
                   , position       NUMBER
                   , variable_value CHAR )
```

DEFINE_COLUMN_LONG Procedure   The `DEFINE_COLUMN_LONG` procedure supports row-by-row DQL operations. The function defines (or maps) column values to columns of a `SELECT` statement. You must use this before calling the `COLUMN_VALUE` procedure. It is not an overloaded procedure, and it has one signature.

Pro]totype

```
define_column_long( cursor_number  NUMBER
                   , position       NUMBER
                   , variable_value LONG )
```

DEFINE_COLUMN_RAW Procedure   The `DEFINE_COLUMN_RAW` procedure supports row-by-row DQL operations. The function defines (or maps) column values to columns of a `SELECT` statement. You must use this before calling the `COLUMN_VALUE` procedure. It is not an overloaded procedure, and it has one signature.

Prototype

```
define_column_raw( cursor_number  NUMBER
                 , position        NUMBER
                 , variable_value RAW )
```

DEFINE_COLUMN_ROWID Procedure   The DEFINE_COLUMN_ROWID procedure supports row-by-row DQL operations. The function defines (or maps) column values to columns of a SELECT statement. You must use this before calling the COLUMN_VALUE procedure. It is not an overloaded procedure, and it has one signature.

Prototype

```
define_column_rowid( cursor_number  NUMBER
                   , position        NUMBER
                   , variable_value ROWID )
```

DESCRIBE_COLUMNS Procedure   The DESCRIBE_COLUMNS procedure supports bulk and row-by-row DQL and DML operations. The function describes columns for a cursor opened and parsed by the DBMS_SQL package. It works only with column names that are 30 characters or smaller in Oracle 10*g* but works with 32-character column names in Oracle 11*g*. It is not an overloaded procedure, and it has one signature.

Prototype

```
describe_columns( cursor_number     NUMBER
                , column_count       NUMBER
                , record_collection DBMS_SQL.DESC_TAB )
```

DBMS_SQL.DESC_TAB datatype is an associative array of the DBMS_SQL.DESC_REC record datatype. The DESC_REC record datatype contains the metadata about the column values. The information is a subset of what you would find in the user_tables view.

DESCRIBE_COLUMNS2 Procedure   The DESCRIBE_COLUMNS2 procedure supports bulk and row-by-row DQL and DML operations. The function describes columns for a cursor opened and parsed by the DBMS_SQL package. It only works with column names that are up to 32,760 bytes in length from Oracle 10*g* forward. It is not an overloaded procedure, and it has one signature.

Prototype

```
describe_columns2( cursor_number     NUMBER
                 , column_count       NUMBER
                 , record_collection DBMS_SQL.DESC_TAB2 )
```

DBMS_SQL.DESC_TAB2 datatype is an associative array of the DBMS_SQL.DESC_REC2 record datatype. The DESC_REC2 record datatype contains the same metadata about the column values as the DESC_REC but allows for a larger column name. The information is a subset of what you would find in the USER_TABLES view.

DESCRIBE_COLUMNS3 Procedure   The DESCRIBE_COLUMNS3 procedure supports bulk and row-by-row DQL and DML operations. The function describes columns for a cursor opened and parsed by the DBMS_SQL package. It only works with column names that are up to 32,760 bytes in length from Oracle 10*g* forward. It is not an overloaded procedure, and it has one signature.

Prototype

```
describe_columns3( cursor_number     NUMBER
                 , column_count      NUMBER
                 , record_collection DBMS_SQL.DESC_TAB3 )
```

DBMS_SQL.DESC_TAB3 datatype is an associative array of the DBMS_SQL.DESC_REC3 record datatype. The DESC_REC3 record datatype contains the same metadata about the column values as the DESC_REC2, plus it adds the datatype name and name length to the record structure. The information is a broader subset of what you would find in the user_tables view.

EXECUTE Function   The EXECUTE function runs the statement associated with an open DBMS_SQL cursor. It returns the number of rows touched by DML statements. You should ignore the return value when it runs a DDL statement because it is a meaningless value *(technically an undefined value)*. This function is not overloaded, and it has one signature. The parameter uses an IN mode of operation.

Prototype

```
execute( cursor_number  NUMBER ) RETURN NUMBER
```

EXECUTE_AND_FETCH Function   The EXECUTE_AND_FETCH function runs the statement associated with an open DBMS_SQL cursor and fetches one or more rows from a cursor. The function is more or less like running the EXECUTE and FETCH_ROWS functions in tandem. The function returns the number or rows touched by DML statements. You should ignore the return value when it runs a DDL statement because it is a meaningless value *(technically an undefined value)*.

The optional exact parameter is false by default, which lets you return more than one row. You can return only one row when you override the default value of the exact parameter. Oracle 7 forward does not support an exact fetch option for LONG datatype columns.

The function is not overloaded. It also has one signature. The parameter uses an IN mode of operation.

Prototype

```
execute_and_fetch( cursor_number  NUMBER
                 , exact_fetch    BOOLEAN DEFAULT FALSE ) RETURN NUMBER
```

FETCH_ROWS Function   The FETCH_ROWS function fetches a row or set of rows from a given cursor. You can run the FETCH_ROWS function until all rows are read. The COLUMN_VALUE function reads the fetch row into a local variable. The local variable can be a *scalar* or *nested table* datatype. The cursor number is passed by using an IN mode of operation.

The FETCH_ROWS function returns the number of rows fetched, or a –1. The latter means that all rows have been read.

Prototype

```
fetch_rows( cursor_number  NUMBER ) RETURN NUMBER
```

IS_OPEN Function   The IS_OPEN function checks whether a cursor is open. It returns true when the cursor is open and false when it's not. The function is not overloaded. It also has one signature. The parameter uses an IN mode of operation.

Prototype

```
execute( cursor_number  NUMBER ) RETURN BOOLEAN
```

LAST_ERROR_POSITION Function   The LAST_ERROR_POSITION function returns the byte offset in a SQL statement text where an error occurred. Unlike other things that start with a 1, this checks the string with the first position being 0. You must call this function after the PARSE call but before any execution function call.

Prototype

```
last_error_position RETURN NUMBER
```

LAST_ROW_COUNT Function   The LAST_ROW_COUNT function returns the cumulative number of rows fetch from a query. You get the cumulative number when you call the LAST_ROW_COUNT function after an EXECUTE_AND_FETCH or FETCH_ROWS call. If you call this function after an EXECUTE function, you get zero.

Prototype

```
last_row_count RETURN NUMBER
```

LAST_ROW_ID Function   The LAST_ROW_ID function returns the ROWID value of the last row fetched from a query. You get the ROWID when you call the LAST_ROW_COUNT function after an EXECUTE_AND_FETCH or FETCH_ROWS call.

Prototype

```
last_row_id RETURN ROWID
```

LAST_SQL_FUNCTION_CODE Function   The LAST_SQL_FUNCTION_CODE function returns SQL function code for the statement. You can find these codes in the *Oracle Call Interface Programmer's Guide.* This must be called immediately after you run the SQL statement, or the return value is undefined.

Prototype

```
last_sql_function_code RETURN INTEGER
```

OPEN_CURSOR Function   The OPEN_CURSOR function opens a cursor in the database and returns the cursor's number. You must call the CLOSE_CURSOR function to close the cursor and release the resource.

Prototype

```
open_cursor RETURN INTEGER
```

PARSE Procedure   The PARSE procedure parses a given statement string. All statements are parsed immediately. DML statements queue on a call to EXECUTE or EXECUTE_AND_FETCH functions. DDL statements are run immediately after they're successfully parsed. It is an overloaded procedure, and it has five types of signatures.

Prototype 1

```
parse( cursor_number  NUMBER
     , statement      {CLOB | VARCHAR2}
     , language_flag  NUMBER )
```

Prototype 2

```
parse( cursor_number  NUMBER
     , statement      {CLOB | VARCHAR2}
     , language_flag  NUMBER
     , edition        VARCHAR2 )
```

Prototype 3

```
parse( cursor_number  NUMBER
     , statement      {VARCHAR2S | VARCHAR2A}
     , language_flag  NUMBER
     , lower_bound    NUMBER
     , upper_bound    NUMBER
     , language_flag  NUMBER )
```

Prototype 4

```
parse( cursor_number  NUMBER
     , statement      {VARCHAR2S | VARCHAR2A}
     , language_flag  NUMBER
     , lower_bound    NUMBER
     , upper_bound    NUMBER
     , language_flag  NUMBER
     , edition        VARCHAR2 )
```

Prototype 5

```
parse( cursor_number                NUMBER
     , statement                    {CLOB | VARCHAR2 | VARCHAR2S | VARCHAR2A}
     , language_flag                NUMBER
     , edition                      VARCHAR2
     , apply_crossedition_trigger   VARCHAR2
     , fire_apply_trigger           BOOLEAN )
```

The VARCHAR2S datatype is a nested table collection of 256-byte strings. The VARCHAR2A datatype is a nested table collection of 32,767-byte strings.

TO_CURSOR_NUMBER Function   The TO_CURSOR_NUMBER function converts a NDS cursor to a DBMS_SQL cursor. It can be useful when you open a cursor of indefinite columns and want to process it by using the DBMS_SQL package. It takes a single IN mode cursor reference, and it returns a generic reference cursor.

Prototype

```
to_cursor_number( reference_cursor REF CURSOR ) RETURNS NUMBER
```

TO_REFCURSOR Function   The `TO_REFCURSOR` function converts a `DBMS_SQL` cursor number to a NSD reference cursor. It can be useful when you open a cursor in `DBMS_SQL` and want to process it by using NDS. It takes a single `IN` mode cursor number, and it returns a cursor number.

Prototype

```
to_refcursor( cursor_number NUMBER ) RETURNS REF CURSOR
```

VARIABLE_VALUE Procedure   The `VARIABLE_VALUE` procedure supports bulk and row-by-row DML operations. It is used to transfer a variety of datatype results back through a `RETURNING INTO` clause. The function binds a wide variety of datatypes into a SQL statement. It is an overloaded procedure with a single type of signature. The cursor and column name are passed by value as `IN` mode operations. The variable value is returned because it is passed as an `OUT` mode variable.

Prototype

```
variable_variable( cursor_number  NUMBER
                 , column_name     VARCHAR2
                 , variable_value <datatype> )
```

The datatype list includes *scalar* or *associative arrays* of scalar variables. You can use any of the following scalar datatypes: `BFILE, BINARY_DOUBLE, BINARY_FLOAT, BLOB, CLOB, DATE, INTERVAL YEAR TO MONTH, INTERVAL YEAR TO SECOND, NUMBER, REF OF STANDARD, ROWID, TIME, TIMESTAMP, TIMESTAMP WITH TIME ZONE, TIME WITH TIME ZONE,` or `VARCHAR2`. This function also supports associate arrays (PL/SQL tables), `VARRAY`s, and user-defined object types through the OCI libraries.

VARIABLE_VALUE_CHAR Procedure   The `VARIABLE_VALUE_CHAR` procedure supports row-by-row DML operations. It is used to transfer `CHAR` datatype results back through a `RETURNING INTO` clause. It is not an overloaded procedure. The cursor and column name are passed by value as `IN` mode operations. The variable value is returned because it is passed as an `OUT` mode variable.

Prototype

```
variable_value_char( cursor_number  NUMBER
                    , column_name     VARCHAR2
                    , variable_value CHAR )
```

VARIABLE_VALUE_RAW Procedure   The `VARIABLE_VALUE_RAW` procedure supports row-by-row DML operations. It is used to transfer `CHAR` datatype results back through a `RETURNING INTO` clause. It is not an overloaded procedure. The cursor and column name are passed by value as `IN` mode operations. The variable value is returned because it is passed as an `OUT` mode variable.

Prototype

```
variable_value_raw( cursor_number  NUMBER
                   , column_name     VARCHAR2
                   , variable_value RAW )
```

VARIABLE_VALUE_ROWID Procedure   The `VARIABLE_VALUE_ROWID` procedure supports row-by-row DML operations. It is used to transfer `CHAR` datatype results back through a `RETURNING INTO` clause. It is not an overloaded procedure. The cursor and column name are passed by value as `IN` mode operations. The variable value is returned because it is passed as an `OUT` mode variable.

Prototype

```
variable_value_rowid( cursor_number  NUMBER
                    , column_name    VARCHAR2
                    , variable_value ROWID )
```

This section has reviewed the functions and procedures in the `DBMS_SQL` package. You should find most of them in the `DBMS_SQL` examples.

Summary
This chapter has shown you how to leverage NDS and the `DBMS_SQL` package to create and execute dynamic SQL statements. You should now have a foundation on how you can use them in your PL/SQL applications.

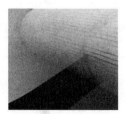

CHAPTER
12

Intersession
Communication

ntersession communication is the ability to communicate between different user connections. Sessions are individual work areas. Sessions begin when you connect and end when you disconnect from the Oracle 11*g* database. You have several approaches that enable you to communicate between sessions. The DBMS_PIPE and DBMS_ALERT built-in utilities are the focus of the chapter.

You will cover the following topics. The chapter assumes you read it sequentially. It also assumes you have read the preceding eleven chapters. If you feel comfortable with an area, consider moving straight to it. However, the chapter assumes you have mastery of earlier sections.

- Introducing intersession communication

- DBMS_PIPE built-in package

- DBMS_ALERT built-in package

Introducing Intersession Communication

Intersession communication is the ability to communicate between different user connections. When users connect to the database, they establish sessions. The duration of a session starts at connection and ends at disconnection. During the session users are in full control of their resources. Resources are anything that they own directly or have access permissions to perform, for example, using DQL, DML, or PL/SQL execution against resources.

You can communicate between sessions in Oracle 11*g* using several approaches. They each have pluses and minuses. Synchronizing discrete sessions in real time and configuring intersession communication quickly are pluses. Event propagation delays like those common with Advanced Queuing (AQ) solutions are a minus. Two types of intersession communication involve permanent or semipermanent objects in the database. The other two types involve SGA memory segments, called *named pipes*. A synopsis of methods follows.

Requiring Permanent or Semipermanent Structures

Permanent or semipermanent structures enable you to do the following:

- You can leverage the Advanced Queuing facility introduced in Oracle 8 with the DBMS_AQADM and DBMS_AQ packages. These involve setting up advanced queuing for each of the participants. Then, you use messages to exchange information between the sessions. This technology underpins Oracle's implementation of workflow applications.

- You can use tables, grants, and synonyms to exchange data between sessions. The solution is simple but subject to transaction control limitations: a transaction must complete and commit permanently the change to the database. The solution more or less involves implementing triggers to restrict DML operations based on other table values.

For more information on advanced queues, you should check the Oracle Streams Concepts and Administration or Oracle Streams Advanced Queuing User's Guide for 11*g* Release 1.

Not Requiring Permanent or Semipermanent Structures

Here you can do the following:

■ You can use the DBMS_PIPE built-in package. DBMS_PIPE uses dynamic memory structures in the SGA called *pipes.* They are very similar to Unix pipes. Pipes may be local, private, or publicly accessible. They act as first-in, first-out (FIFO) queues. Transaction control issues do not bind them. You can use pipes to send and receive data between sessions asynchronously.

■ You can use the DBMS_ALERT built-in package. DBMS_ALERT also uses a memory structure in the SGA. While the structure is not formally referred to as a pipe, it works as a public pipe. These are likewise similar to Unix pipes. They are publicly accessible pipes, or FIFO queues. These pipes are populated on event triggers and subject to transaction control limits. The alert pipes communicate between sessions asynchronously at the conclusion of an event. Events are anything that you can build a trigger against, like a DML or system action (check Chapter 10 for more on triggers). Unlike DBMS_PIPE, the DBMS_ALERT built-in package works on a publish-and-subscribe paradigm. It publishes notifications. Then it enables subscribers to register their interest in the alert and receive the alert notifications.

Comparing Intersession Communication Approaches

You should understand when and where to use these approaches. As a rule of thumb, you do not want to use permanent or semipermanent structures to exchange information when they can be avoided. Using these types of structures incurs file access, which can slow your application down. Intersession communication should be done in memory where possible.

Both DBMS_PIPE and DBMS_ALERT work in memory. They do not have permanent or semipermanent structures in the database. The structures are designed to support intersession communication. Pipes can be defined to support intersession communication in two ways: Pipes can support communication between two or more sessions of a single user. Alternatively, they can support communication between two or more users. Alerts also support two or more sessions of a single user.

DBMS_ALERT works best as an asynchronous transaction control mechanism. The DBMS_ALERT notifies subscribers of an event. The subscribers can then take action on events. DBMS_ALERT implements a publish-and-subscribe paradigm. When you use a publish-and-subscribe process, polling daemons are simplified or eliminated. Polling daemons (pronounced dee·mu*h* n) *run as background processes.* They consume varying resources, depending on how you implement them. If you eliminate polling daemons, you reduce resource demands on the database and physical machine.

DBMS_PIPE can help you mimic Unix pipes or POSIX-compliant threads. Unix pipes allow you to move data between two active processes. Unix pipes control communication at the process level. C/C++ also lets you control threading activities with mutex variables, which work at the process and thread levels. Both provide higher programming language equivalents to operating system semaphores.

DBMS_PIPE is ideal for passing information to external processes that may monitor or control system resources. For example, DBMS_PIPE can

■ Enable you to use *local pipes* to control a single program's execution.

■ Enable you to use *private pipes* to control concurrent programs run by the single user.

■ Enable you to use *public pipes* to control concurrent programs run by multiple users.

The DBMS_PIPE Built-in Package

In Oracle 11*g*, DBMS_PIPE is a privileged package owned by the SYS user. You or your DBA must grant EXECUTE permission on the DBMS_PIPE package to the PLSQL user as well as another user of your choice—some of the examples and exercises in this chapter require two users. You create the USERA and USERB users to run the examples in this chapter. The users require EXECUTE permission on the DBMS_PIPE package.

TIP
You or your DBA should probably grant execute permission with the grant option to SYSTEM. *Then, the* SYSTEM *user should grant execute permission to the* PLSQL, USERA, *and* USERB *users manually. Alternatively, you can run the* create_user.sql *script found on the publisher's website.*

Introducing the DBMS_PIPE Package

The architecture of DBMS_PIPE is key to understanding its use. You need to understand three perspectives presented by DBMS_PIPE. The perspectives are represented by access privileges. Also, the structures used to temporarily store the data are memory structures in the PGA or the SGA.

DBMS_PIPE has session local, user private, and public pipe variations. It is possible that using multiple types in the same session can cause problems. Typically, the problems relate to inadvertent destruction of the session local pipe contents. The session local pipe acts as a private buffer. Unfortunately, the same private buffer serves as the access to and from user private and public pipes. The private buffer is a PGA pipe and is inaccessible by named reference externally to the session. Private and public pipes are SGA structures.

You will now examine each of the access methods. Local pipes are first. The local pipe is only a buffer. The buffer can contain only one element. You write a variable-length string to the local buffer. Then you may read the string from the buffer. If the element is not read locally or forwarded to a named private or public pipe before the next write, the original value is lost. Figure 12-1 depicts a local pipe read-and-write operation. Forwarding the element will be covered later.

Having learned how to use the local read-and-write buffer, you will examine a private user pipe read-and-write operation. Private user pipes are accessible to all sessions of the user who created the pipe. Before writing to the private pipe, you must write the data to the local buffer. Then, you send the contents of the local buffer to the private pipe. The contents of the private pipe can then be read to a local session buffer. The local session buffer can then be read and assigned to a variable. Figure 12-2 illustrates a private user pipe.

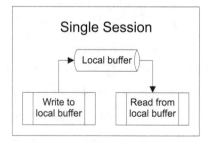

FIGURE 12-1   *Session local buffer read-and-write operation*

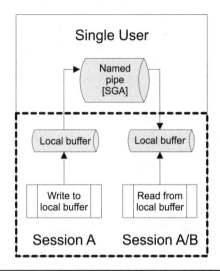

FIGURE 12-2 *Private pipe read-and-write operation*

Figure 12-2 shows that there are one or two sessions when using a private user pipe. It is possible that the same user session creating a private pipe can write to and read from it. As discussed, the local pipe is a buffer that contains only one value. A private pipe may contain any number of values in a FIFO queue. Therefore, a session that needs to write a series of data values may write to and read from a private pipe.

Alternatively, the same user can have two or more sessions and share the FIFO queue. This scenario presents some interesting issues because any session created by the user who owns the queue can write to or read from it. There is no way to track which session wrote to the pipe unless you tokenize the variable-length string.

In the tokenized string scenario, it is possible for the wrong session to read a message. If you implement this architecture, you will need to ensure the code puts the message back into the queue. Unfortunately, it will be out of sequence once it's read and replaced. This behavior is a natural consequence of FIFO queues. When using FIFO queues, you should not depend solely on sequencing of data. As an alternative, you can use a set of tokenized messages. A set of

Tokenizing Strings

Tokenizing a variable-length string means that you build a string that contains a delimiter and substrings. The delimiter separates substrings. You can tokenize a string by using a comma, for instance. The first value before the comma can contain a string that identifies the originating, or writing, session. The next delimited string can contain the destination, or reading, session. The last substring can contain the value substring or a series of delimited substrings.

An American telephone number is traditionally a tokenized number. The parentheses around the first three digits identify them as an area code. A comma-separated list is also a tokenized string. You can also sequence a set of tokenized strings by embedding index values in them.

tokenized messages is a series of delimited substrings that include index values. They are typically sent as sequential messages but may be jumbled in transmission and reassembled by the recipient. This type of use is similar to how packets are transmitted across networks. You can get much more complex in specific solutions, but that topic belongs in another book.

The premise of a private pipe is not too different from that of a public pipe. In fact, all the activity described in a private user pipe can be done in a public pipe. A public pipe is also the default pipe created. You must override the default behavior to create a private user pipe. Figure 12-3 shows a public pipe.

Moreover, public pipes are designed for sharing between two users. Figure 12-3 depicts two sessions, which would occur for multiple users sharing a public pipe. All read and write operations mirror the previously described behaviors.

You should now have a high-level view of what DBMS_PIPE uses as memory structures. This architectural view will be important as we cover the procedures and functions of the DBMS_PIPE built-in.

Defining the DBMS_PIPE Package

The DBMS_PIPE package contains procedures and functions that let you manage intersession private and public pipes. Typically, procedures would be limited to PL/SQL execution and functions enabled for SQL and PL/SQL. The CREATE_PIPE function has limited utility in SQL because the PRIVATE formal parameter is a Boolean datatype, and Boolean datatypes cannot be used in SQL. Since the default value for the PRIVATE formal parameter is true, you must use PL/SQL to create a public pipe.

The subsections qualify the DBMS_PIPE package functions and procedures. These sections examine how you create, manage, write to, and read from database pipes. They also qualify when you can use them from SQL.

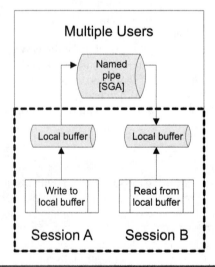

FIGURE 12-3   *Public pipe read-and-write operation*

CREATE_PIPE Function

The CREATE_PIPE function returns an INTEGER datatype and has limited SQL access. It takes three formal parameters:

- PIPENAME is positionally the first and is a mandatory parameter. It is defined as a VARCHAR2 datatype. Its maximum size should be 128 bytes. You should not use ORA$ as a preface to any of your pipes because those are reserved by Oracle Corporation for its own use.

- MAXPIPESIZE is positionally the second and an optional formal parameter. It has an INTEGER datatype. The default value is 8192.

- PRIVATE is positionally the third and an optional parameter. It has a BOOLEAN datatype. The default value is TRUE, which maps to a default private pipe.

If a privileged user calls the CREATE_PIPE function and the pipe already exists, it will not alter the existing pipe. It will return a zero value. The zero value indicates successful completion, but in this case nothing was created; it was ignored.

The CREATE_PIPE function prototype is

CREATE_PIPE(*pipe_name* [, *maxpipe_size* [, *private*]])

You may attempt to re-create a public pipe as another user. It will appear to work, but in reality the command is ignored.

If you lack permission to create the object, you raise an ORA-23322 exception.

NEXT_ITEM_TYPE Function

The NEXT_ITEM_TYPE function takes no formal parameters. It is accessible by SQL. It reads the contents of the local pipe or buffer. It returns an INTEGER that maps to values shown in Table 12-1.

The NEXT_ITEM_TYPE has the following prototype:

NEXT_ITEM_TYPE(*message_item*)

If you empty the local buffer, you will raise an ORA-06556 exception when attempting to secure a return value.

Integer Return	Meaning
0	An empty buffer
6	A NUMBER datatype
9	A VARCHAR2 datatype
11	A ROWID datatype
12	A DATE datatype
23	A RAW datatype

TABLE 12-1 *NEXT_ITEM_TYPE Function Return Types and Meaning*

PACK_MESSAGE Procedure

The PACK_MESSAGE procedure takes a single formal parameter. It is not accessible from SQL. The parameter can be a DATE, NCHAR, NUMBER, or VARCHAR2 datatype.

It has the prototype

```
PACK_MESSAGE(message_item)
```

PACK_MESSAGE takes the value of the actual parameter and puts it into the local pipe or buffer.

PACK_MESSAGE_RAW Procedure

The PACK_MESSAGE_RAW procedure takes a single formal parameter. It is not accessible from SQL. The parameter is a RAW datatype. It has the prototype

```
PACK_MESSAGE_ROWID(message_item)
```

PACK_MESSAGE_RAW takes the value of the actual parameter and puts it into the local pipe or buffer.

PACK_MESSAGE_ROWID Procedure

The PACK_MESSAGE_ROWID procedure takes a single formal parameter. It is not accessible from SQL. The parameter is a ROWID datatype. It has the prototype

```
PACK_MESSAGE_ROWID(message_item)
```

PACK_MESSAGE_ROWID takes the value of the actual parameter and puts it into the local pipe or buffer.

PURGE Procedure

The PURGE procedure takes a single formal parameter. It is not accessible from SQL. The parameter is a VARCHAR2 datatype and must be a valid private or public pipe name. It has the following prototype:

```
PURGE(pipe_name)
```

RECEIVE_MESSAGE Function

The RECEIVE_MESSAGE function takes one or two formal parameters. It is accessible from SQL. The first positional parameter is a VARCHAR2 datatype and must be a valid private or public pipe name. The second positional and optional parameter is an INTEGER datatype. Unless you can allow your program to hang for 1,000 days, you should override this value to a suitably lower count in seconds.

The RECEIVE_MESSAGE prototype is

```
RECEIVE_MESSAGE(pipe_name [, time_out_value])
```

It reads the contents of the named pipe and transfers it to the local buffer. It returns an INTEGER that maps to the values shown in Table 12-2.

REMOVE_PIPE Function

The REMOVE_PIPE function takes one formal parameter. It is accessible from SQL. It is a VARCHAR2 datatype and must be a valid private or public pipe name. The prototype is

```
REMOVE_PIPE(pipe_name)
```

Integer Return	Meaning
0	Successful completion
1	A time-out without a reply
2	A pipe message too large for the buffer, which should never happen
3	An interrupt of some kind

TABLE 12-2 *RECEIVE_MESSAGE Function Return Types and Meaning*

It returns a 0 for successful completion. If you lack permission to remove the object, you raise an ORA-23322 exception. If the user who created the named pipe is not known, the DBA has one of two choices. The DBA can shut down and restart the instance to get rid of the conflicting named pipe. Alternatively, as SYSDBA, you can remove the offending named pipe.

RESET_BUFFER Procedure

The RESET_BUFFER procedure takes no formal parameter. It is not accessible from SQL. It removes the contents of the local buffer.

SEND_MESSAGE Function

The SEND_MESSAGE function takes one to three formal parameters. It is accessible from SQL. The first positional parameter is a VARCHAR2 datatype and must be a valid private or public pipe name. The second positional sets the time-out length for the message and is an optional INTEGER parameter. Unless you can allow your program to hang for 1,000 days, you should override this value to a suitably lower count in seconds. The third positional and optional parameter is an INTEGER representing the total size of all messages placed in the pipe. This number *must* be *equal to* or *less than* the value used when creating the named pipe.

The SEND_MESSAGE prototype is

```
SEND_MESSAGE(pipe_name [, time_out_value [, max_pipe_size]])
```

It writes the contents of the local buffer to the named pipe. It returns an INTEGER that maps to the values shown in Table 12-3.

If you lack permission to access the pipe, you raise an ORA-23322 exception. The error means you cannot write to that pipe.

Integer Return	Meaning
0	Successful completion
1	A time-out without a reply
2	A pipe message too large for the buffer, which should never happen
3	An interrupt of some kind

TABLE 12-3 *SEND_MESSAGE Function Return Types and Meaning*

UNIQUE_SESSION_NAME Function

The `UNIQUE_SESSION_NAME` function takes *no formal parameter*. It is accessible from SQL. It returns a `VARCHAR2` string that represents the current session.

UNPACK_MESSAGE Procedure

The `UNPACK_MESSAGE` procedure takes a single formal parameter. It is not accessible from SQL. The parameter can be a `DATE`, `NCHAR`, `NUMBER`, or `VARCHAR2` datatype. The prototype is

```
UNPACK_MESSAGE(DATE | NCHAR | NUMBER | VARCHAR2)
```

`UNPACK_MESSAGE` takes the value from the local pipe or buffer and returns it as the `OUT` mode value of the actual parameter.

UNPACK_MESSAGE_RAW Procedure

The `UNPACK_MESSAGE_RAW` procedure takes a single formal parameter. It is not accessible from SQL. The parameter must be a `RAW` datatype. The prototype is

```
UNPACK_MESSAGE_RAW(RAW)
```

`UNPACK_MESSAGE_RAW` takes the value from the local pipe or buffer and returns it as the `OUT` mode value of the actual parameter.

UNPACK_MESSAGE_ROWID Procedure

The `UNPACK_MESSAGE_ROWID` procedure takes a single formal parameter. It is not accessible from SQL. The parameter must be a `ROWID` datatype. The prototype is

```
UNPACK_MESSAGE_ROWID(ROWID)
```

`UNPACK_MESSAGE_ROWID` takes the value from the local pipe or buffer and returns it as the `OUT` mode value of the actual parameter.

Having reviewed the `DBMS_PIPE` package, you work with `DBMS_PIPE` examples in the next section.

Working with the DBMS_PIPE Package

In this section, you will work with the following:

- Sending to and receiving from the local pipe or buffer
- Creating pipes
- Reading and writing from pipes
- Putting a wrapper around `DBMS_PIPE`

These topics will help prepare you to use `DBMS_PIPE` successfully. The topics also should prepare you to experiment with the package.

If you do not have a PLSQL account with the correct permissions, you can run the `create_intersession_user.sql` script to build one. You will find it in the code for this chapter on the publisher's web site.

Sending to and Receiving from the Local Pipe or Buffer

The local buffer is very important. You can write programs that will return an anomalous result if you do not understand how to use the local buffer. Only the session that writes to the local buffer can access the local buffer.

The following program shows how to write to the local buffer:

```
-- This is found in write_local.sql on the publisher's web site.
DECLARE
  message   VARCHAR2(30 CHAR);
  success   INTEGER;
BEGIN
  message := DBMS_PIPE.UNIQUE_SESSION_NAME;
  DBMS_PIPE.RESET_BUFFER;
  DBMS_PIPE.PACK_MESSAGE(message);
  DBMS_OUTPUT.PUT_LINE('Written to pipe ['||message||']');
END;
/
```

The sample program resets the local buffer and packs a new message in it. The next program unpacks the buffer, reads the data, and prints the contents of the pipe to the console.

```
-- This is found in read_local.sql on the publisher's web site.
DECLARE
  message   VARCHAR2(30 CHAR);
  success   INTEGER;
BEGIN
  DBMS_PIPE.UNPACK_MESSAGE(message);
  DBMS_OUTPUT.PUT_LINE('Message ['||message||']');
END;
/
```

You have learned how to write to and read from the local buffer. If you attempted to receive the contents from a named pipe in this session between writing to and reading from the local buffer, you may raise a pipe is empty exception. This can occur because the data is only in the local pipe.

The following SQL query reads the contents of a nonexistent named pipe. What it really does is attempt to transfer the contents of a nonexistent named pipe to the local buffer. If you insert the following SQL statement between the write_local.sql and read_local.sql programs, it will return a 1.

A 1 indicates the pipe is empty. When the RECEIVE_MESSAGE function returns any value, it has done one of two things: it has returned the contents of a named pipe or a null into the local buffer.

```
-- This is found in read_local_error.sql on the publisher's web site.
SELECT   DBMS_PIPE.RECEIVE_MESSAGE('NOWHERE',0)
FROM     dual;
```

You can test this behavior by running the read_local_error.sql script. The script produces the following output error messages:

```
-- This is generated by read_local_error.sql on the publisher's web site.
```

```
DECLARE
*
ERROR at line 1:
ORA-06556: the pipe is empty, cannot fulfill the
          unpack_message request
ORA-06512: at "SYS.DBMS_PIPE", line 78
ORA-06512: at line 10
```

You have seen that sequencing of commands is critical to having something in the local buffer. Also, you have seen that a call to the RECEIVE_MESSAGE function will fail but write a null to the local buffer.

You will now learn how to create named pipes.

Creating Pipes

There are two types of named pipes: one is a private named pipe; the other is a public named pipe. The former is the default type for named pipes.

You will learn how to build a named private pipe and public pipe. You should ensure you run this as the PLSQL user, since the pipe name is hard-coded. The following example demonstrates creating a private pipe:

```
-- This is found in create_pipe1.sql on the publisher's web site.
DECLARE
  message_pipe VARCHAR2(30) := 'PLSQL$MESSAGE_INBOX';
  message_size INTEGER       := 20000;
  retval INTEGER;
BEGIN
  -- Define a private pipe.
  retval := DBMS_PIPE.CREATE_PIPE(message_pipe, message_size);
  IF (retval = 0) THEN
    DBMS_OUTPUT.PUT_LINE('MESSAGE_INBOX pipe is created.');
  END IF;
EXCEPTION
  WHEN others THEN
    DBMS_OUTPUT.PUT_LINE(SQLERRM);
    RETURN;
END;
/
```

The program creates a named private pipe owned by the PLSQL schema. The private pipe is empty.

Unfortunately, there is no convenient way to display defined pipes. If you connect as another user (like USERA) and attempt to run the create_pipe1.sql script, it will raise two errors. The attempt to use DBMS_PIPE.REMOVE_PIPE will result in an untrapped error. This is the default error message:

```
-- This is generated by create_pipe1.sql on the publisher's web site.
DECLARE
*
ERROR at line 1:
ORA-23322: Privilege error accessing pipe
ORA-06512: at "SYS.DBMS_SYS_ERROR", line 86
ORA-06512: at "SYS.DBMS_PIPE", line 130
ORA-06512: at line 4
```

The attempt to create a named pipe owned by the PLSQL user will raise SQLERRM only. It does so because it is managed in the exception handler. It raises the following exception:

```
-- This is generated by create_pipe1.sql on the publisher's web site.
ORA-23322: Privilege error accessing pipe
```

You have learned that the user who created the private named pipes is the only one who can alter them. Any other user will receive a privilege error when attempting to remove or re-create a private named pipe. You will now see the differences between creating private and publicly accessible pipes.

The following example should be run as the PLSQL user. If you fail to run it as the user that owns the current private pipe, it fails with an exception. The first block removes the private pipe, and the second shows you how to create a public pipe:

```
-- This is found in create_pipe2.sql on the publisher's web site.
DECLARE
  retval INTEGER := DBMS_PIPE.REMOVE_PIPE('PLSQL$MESSAGE_INBOX');
BEGIN
 NULL;
END;
/
DECLARE
  message_pipe VARCHAR2(30)  := 'PLSQL$MESSAGE_INBOX';
  message_size INTEGER       := 20000;
  message_flag BOOLEAN       := TRUE;
  retval INTEGER;
BEGIN
  -- Define a public pipe.
  retval := DBMS_PIPE.CREATE_PIPE(message_pipe
                                 ,message_size
                                 ,message_flag);
  IF (retval = 0) THEN
    DBMS_OUTPUT.PUT_LINE('MESSAGE_INBOX pipe is created.');
  END IF;
EXCEPTION
  WHEN others THEN
    DBMS_OUTPUT.PUT_LINE(SQLERRM);
    RETURN;
END;
/
```

The first program deletes a public pipe. If you fail to remove a named pipe before trying to create a variation using the same name, it will raise an ORA-23322 error. There is unfortunately no equivalent to the SQL create or replace command syntax for database objects in the DBMS_PIPE package.

After deleting the pipe, you can recreate it. The second creates a public pipe and writes a message into it.

The next test assumes you have run create_pipe2.sql as the PLSQL user. If you connect as USERA, you will find that you can rerun the create_pipe2.sql statement without raising an exception.

It appears that the public pipe is re-created under a new user because no exception was raised. This is not the case. A zero, or success, is returned when the public pipe already exists with the same signature. (A *signature* is a collection of formal parameter[s] that define a function, method, or procedure.)

The lack of a raised exception is misleading. Unfortunately, that's the way DBMS_PIPE. CREATE_PIPE works when the same signature is used. You can test the lack of a privilege error by running create_pipe1.sql in the PLSQL schema and then running create_pipe2.sql in another user's schema.

It will raise the following exception:

```
ORA-23322: Privilege error accessing pipe
```

If you attempt to run create_pipe1.sql in the USERA schema, you will raise an exception. The reason it now returns a privilege exception is straightforward: USERA is attempting to modify the signature for the pipe, making it private when it is public. USERA cannot override the pipe created in that name because it is not the user who created it.

While it would have taken too much space in the book, a create_pipe3.sql script can be found on the publisher's web site. It has all the appropriate error trapping and good coding practices. You should take a look at how it works. Much of the anonymous block logic is migrated into the DBMS_PIPE wrapper discussed later in this chapter.

You have learned how to create private and public pipes. You have also seen that the privileges error can sometimes be suppressed. The next section will show how to read from and write to named pipes.

Writing to and Reading from Pipes

Private and public pipes are written to and read from in the same way. You write data by placing it in the local buffer and sending it to the named pipe. Then, you read data by the inverse process. You receive data from a named pipe into the local buffer and then read data from the local buffer.

You will examine two programs. One will write data to a named pipe. The other will read from a named pipe. You should use the PLSQL schema to write and read the data. However, you can read the data from any other user who has the execute privilege on DBMS_PIPE, provided you last ran create_pipe2.sql in the PLSQL schema, which builds a public pipe.

The following program writes to a named pipe:

```
-- This is found in write_pipe.sql on the publisher's web site.
DECLARE
  line_return VARCHAR2(1) := CHR(10);
  flag        INTEGER;
BEGIN
  -- Purge pipe content.
  dbms_pipe.purge('PLSQL$MESSAGE_INBOX');
  DBMS_OUTPUT.PUT_LINE('Input Message to Pipe');
  DBMS_OUTPUT.PUT_LINE('--------------------');
  FOR i IN 1..3 LOOP
    DBMS_OUTPUT.PUT_LINE('Message ['||i||']');
    DBMS_PIPE.PACK_MESSAGE('Message ['||i||']'||line_return);
    flag := DBMS_PIPE.SEND_MESSAGE('PLSQL$MESSAGE_INBOX');
  END LOOP;
  IF (flag = 0) THEN
    DBMS_OUTPUT.PUT_LINE('Message sent to PLSQL$MESSAGE_INBOX.');
  END IF;
END;
/
```

The program writes a tokenized message to standard out for each message it writes to the pipe. It outputs the following to the console:

```
-- This is generated by write_pipe.sql on the publisher's web site.
Input Message to Pipe
---------------------
Message [1]
Message [2]
Message [3]
Message sent to PLSQL$MESSAGE_INBOX.
```

You can read the data from the named pipe by inverting the write process. The process is demonstrated in the following program:

```
-- This is found in read_pipe.sql on the publisher's web site.
DECLARE
  line_return VARCHAR2(1)     := CHR(10);
  message     VARCHAR2(4000);
  output      VARCHAR2(4000);
  flag        INTEGER;
BEGIN
  DBMS_PIPE.RESET_BUFFER;
  DBMS_OUTPUT.PUT(line_return);
  DBMS_OUTPUT.PUT_LINE('Output Message from Pipe');
  DBMS_OUTPUT.PUT_LINE('------------------------');
  FOR i IN 1..3 LOOP
    flag := DBMS_PIPE.RECEIVE_MESSAGE('PLSQL$MESSAGE_INBOX',0);
    -- Read message from local buffer.
    DBMS_PIPE.UNPACK_MESSAGE(message);
    output := output || message;
  END LOOP;
  IF (flag = 0) THEN
    DBMS_OUTPUT.PUT(output);
    DBMS_OUTPUT.PUT_LINE('Message received from PLSQL$MESSAGE_INBOX.');
  END IF;
END;
/
```

The sample program uses the DBMS_PIPE.RESET_BUFFER procedure to clear the local buffer. While unnecessary when nothing is done with the buffer contents before retrieving from a named pipe, this procedure can cause erroneous data to be retrieved from the local buffer. It is a good programming practice to use it before reading from a named pipe.

It then uses DBMS_PIPE.RECEIVE_MESSAGE to move the contents from the named pipe to the local buffer. It uses a second parameter of zero. This forces an immediate read on the pipe. Unless you override the time-out of 1,000 days, your program could hang on an empty pipe instead of returning an error message.

The program outputs this:

```
-- This is generated by write_pipe.sql on the publisher's web site.
Output Message from Pipe
------------------------
Message [1]
Message [2]
```

```
Message [3]
Message received from PLSQL$MESSAGE_INBOX.
```

You should notice that the output from the pipe is ordered the same as when it was written. This is a property of a FIFO queue. As you learned earlier in the chapter, all pipes are FIFO queues.

You have learned how to create private and public pipes. Moreover, you can now write to and read from pipes. The PACK_MESSAGE_RAW, PACK_MESSAGE_ROWID, UNPACK_MESSAGE_RAW, and UNPACK_MESSAGE_ROWID procedures are not covered because they work like the PACK_MESSAGE and UNPACK_MESSAGE procedures.

Two other commands have also not been covered in earlier examples; the NEXT_ITEM_TYPE and UNIQUE_SESSION_NAME functions are covered in the following example program:

```
-- This is found in next_item_type.sql on the publisher's web site.
DECLARE
  session     VARCHAR2(30) := DBMS_PIPE.UNIQUE_SESSION_NAME;
  line_return VARCHAR2(1) := CHR(10);
  message     VARCHAR2(4000);
  output      VARCHAR2(4000);
  flag        INTEGER;
  code        INTEGER;
  message1    INTEGER      := 1776;
  message2    DATE         := TO_DATE('04-JUL-1776');
  message3    VARCHAR2(30 CHAR) := 'John Adams';
  message11   INTEGER;
  message12   DATE;
  message13   VARCHAR2(30 CHAR);
BEGIN
  -- Write the messages to a pipe.
  DBMS_PIPE.PURGE('PLSQL$MESSAGE_INBOX');
  DBMS_OUTPUT.PUT_LINE('Input Message to Pipe');
  DBMS_OUTPUT.PUT_LINE('Session: ['||session||']');
  DBMS_OUTPUT.PUT_LINE('-------------------------------');
  -- Process message1.
  DBMS_OUTPUT.PUT_LINE(message1||'[NUMBER]');
  DBMS_PIPE.PACK_MESSAGE(message1);
  flag := DBMS_PIPE.SEND_MESSAGE('PLSQL$MESSAGE_INBOX');
  -- Process message2.
  DBMS_OUTPUT.PUT_LINE(message2||'[DATE]');
  DBMS_PIPE.PACK_MESSAGE(message2);
  flag := DBMS_PIPE.SEND_MESSAGE('PLSQL$MESSAGE_INBOX');
  -- Process message3.
  DBMS_OUTPUT.PUT_LINE(message3||'[VARCHAR2]');
  DBMS_PIPE.PACK_MESSAGE(message3);
  flag := DBMS_PIPE.SEND_MESSAGE('PLSQL$MESSAGE_INBOX');
  IF (flag = 0) THEN
    DBMS_OUTPUT.PUT_LINE('Message sent to PLSQL$MESSAGE_INBOX.');
  END IF;
  DBMS_OUTPUT.PUT(line_return);
  -- Read the messages from a pipe.
  DBMS_OUTPUT.PUT_LINE('Output Message from Pipe');
  DBMS_OUTPUT.PUT_LINE('Session: ['||session||']');
  DBMS_OUTPUT.PUT_LINE('-------------------------------');
```

```
    FOR i IN 1..3 LOOP
      DBMS_PIPE.RESET_BUFFER;
      flag := DBMS_PIPE.RECEIVE_MESSAGE('PLSQL$MESSAGE_INBOX',0);
      code := DBMS_PIPE.NEXT_ITEM_TYPE;
      CASE code
        WHEN 6 THEN -- Buffer is a NUMBER.
          DBMS_PIPE.UNPACK_MESSAGE(message11);
          output := output || message11 ||'[NUMBER]'||line_return;
        WHEN 9 THEN -- Buffer is a VARCHAR2.
          DBMS_PIPE.UNPACK_MESSAGE(message13);
          output := output || message13 ||'[VARCHAR2]'||line_return;
        WHEN 12 THEN -- Buffer is a DATE.
          DBMS_PIPE.UNPACK_MESSAGE(message12);
          output := output || message12 ||'[DATE]'||line_return;
      END CASE;
    END LOOP;
    -- Print messages.
    IF (flag = 0) THEN
      DBMS_OUTPUT.PUT(output);
      DBMS_OUTPUT.PUT_LINE('Message received from PLSQL$MESSAGE_INBOX.');
    END IF;
END;
/
```

This program demonstrates sending three messages in sequence with different datatypes. Then, it uses the return type from DBMS_PIPE.NEXT_ITEM_TYPE to read and manage the different datatypes. The following is the output from the next_item_type.sql script. It shows the datatype in square brackets to the right of the value sent in and received from the pipe.

 -- This is generated by next_item_type.sql on the publisher's web site.
```
Input Message to Pipe
Session: [ORA$PIPE$00F2AFC20001]
-------------------------------
1776[NUMBER]
04-JUL-76[DATE]
John Adams[VARCHAR2]
Message sent to PLSQL$MESSAGE_INBOX.

Output Message from Pipe
Session: [ORA$PIPE$00F2AFC20001]
-------------------------------
1776[NUMBER]
04-JUL-76[DATE]
John Adams[VARCHAR2]
Message received from PLSQL$MESSAGE_INBOX.
```

TIP
The PACK_MESSAGE *and* UNPACK_MESSAGE *procedures are overloaded in the* DBMS_PIPE *package. They can use* DATE, NUMBER, *and* VARCHAR2 *datatypes. You must ensure you evaluate datatypes before reading them from the local buffer when you use more than* VARCHAR2 *datatypes.*

The preceding program has highlighted how you manage DATE, NUMBER, and VARCHAR2 into and out of database pipes. The DBMS_PIPE.NEXT_ITEM_TYPE function provides the tool to read out different datatypes.

You will now see how some of the complexity of DBMS_PIPE can be hidden from your users.

Putting a Wrapper Around DBMS_PIPE

You probably noticed that working with DBMS_PIPE is a bit tedious. Much of the problem is because of the awkward mix of functions and procedures. Functions require return variables, and procedures, the UNPACK_MESSAGE procedure, for instance, require active actual parameter values.

Access to these can be simplified by writing a PL/SQL stored procedure that hides the complexity of the DBMS_PIPE package. The following package provides a wrapper to exchange messages between all users on the system. The package builds two pipes for any user by using the create_pipe3.sql script mentioned earlier in the chapter. These pipes are named USER$MESSAGE_INBOX and USER$MESSAGE_OUTBOX, respectively.

The package specification creates two functions: SEND_MESSAGE and RECEIVE_MESSAGE. These wrap the complexity of the DBMS_PIPE package.

The package body implements the two published functions and creates a local function GET_USER. It returns the user name for the current session. This eliminates any formal parameters for the RECEIVE_MESSAGE function.

The MESSENGER package provides the ability to send and receive messages in SQL or PL/SQL. It manages only VARCHAR2 datatypes. The MESSENGER package provides a glimpse into building components based on the DBMS_PIPE package. The following contains the package specification and body:

```
-- This is found in create_messenger.sql on the publisher's web site.
CREATE OR REPLACE PACKAGE messenger IS
  FUNCTION send_message
    (user_name      VARCHAR2
    ,message        VARCHAR2
    ,message_box    VARCHAR2 DEFAULT 'MESSAGE_INBOX')
    RETURN INTEGER;

  FUNCTION receive_message
    RETURN VARCHAR2;
END messenger;
/
CREATE OR REPLACE PACKAGE BODY messenger IS
  FUNCTION get_user
    RETURN VARCHAR2 IS
  BEGIN
    FOR i IN (SELECT user FROM dual) LOOP
      return i.user;
    END LOOP;
  END get_user;

  FUNCTION send_message
    (user_name      VARCHAR2
    ,message        VARCHAR2
    ,message_box    VARCHAR2 DEFAULT 'MESSAGE_INBOX')
```

```
    RETURN INTEGER IS
    message_pipe    VARCHAR2(100 CHAR);
  BEGIN
    DBMS_PIPE.RESET_BUFFER;
    message_pipe := UPPER(user_name) || '$' || UPPER(message_box);
    DBMS_PIPE.PACK_MESSAGE(message);
    -- Return 0 for sent message and 1 for unsent message.
    IF (DBMS_PIPE.SEND_MEESAGE(message_pipe) = 0) THEN
      RETURN 0;
    ELSE
      RETURN 1;
    END IF;
  END send_message;

  FUNCTION receive_message
    RETURN VARCHAR2 IS
    message         VARCHAR2(4000 CHAR) :=  NULL;
    message_box     VARCHAR2(100 CHAR);
    inbox           VARCHAR2(14 CHAR) := 'MESSAGE_INBOX';
    timeout         INTEGER := 0;
    return_code     INTEGER;
  BEGIN
    DBMS_PIPE.RESET_BUFFER;
    message_box := get_user || '$' || inbox;
    return_code := DBMS_PIPE.RECEIVE_MESSAGE(message_box,timeout);
    CASE return_code
      WHEN 0 THEN
        DBMS_PIPE.UNPACK_MESSAGE(message);
      WHEN 1 THEN
        message := 'The message pipe is empty.';
      WHEN 2 THEN
        message :=
          'The message is too large for variable.';
      WHEN 3 THEN
        message :=
          'An interrupt occurred, contact the DBA.';
    END CASE;
    -- Return the message.
    RETURN message;
  END receive_message;
END messenger;
/
```

As a rule, programs are explained in text. For a package like this, a text description is unproductive. You can see the package lets you exchange messages with other users, provided they have execute privileges to the wrapper MESSENGER package or a separate copy in their user source code.

The specification for the package follows:

```
-- This is generated by SQL*Plus DESCRIBE MESSENGER.
FUNCTION RECEIVE_MESSAGE RETURNS VARCHAR2
FUNCTION SEND_MESSAGE RETURNS NUMBER(38)
```

Argument Name	Type	In/Out	Default?
USER_NAME	VARCHAR2	IN	
MESSAGE	VARCHAR2	IN	
MESSAGE_BOX	VARCHAR2	IN	DEFAULT

The following program illustrates sending and receiving a message using the wrapper MESSENGER package:

```
-- This is found in use_messenger.sql on the publisher's web site.
DECLARE
  FUNCTION get_user
    RETURN VARCHAR2 IS
  BEGIN
    FOR i IN (SELECT user FROM dual) LOOP
      return i.user;
    END LOOP;
  END get_user;
BEGIN
  -- Send message.
  IF (MESSENGER.SEND_MESSAGE(get_user,'Hello World!') = 0) THEN
    DBMS_OUTPUT.PUT_LINE(MESSENGER.RECEIVE_MESSAGE);
  END IF;
END;
/
```

You can use this package or create your own to experiment with DBMS_PIPE. You have now covered the DBMS_PIPE package and a key feature—intersession messaging. You will now learn about DBMS_ALERT.

DBMS_ALERT Built-in Package

DBMS_ALERT is the second intersession communication tool provided by Oracle 11*g*. It builds on the behavior of DBMS_PIPE and leverages the DBMS_PIPE package.

Introducing the DBMS_ALERT Package

DBMS_ALERT is an asynchronous transaction control mechanism. It publishes an event. Other users become subscribers by registering their interest in the named alert. DBMS_ALERT implements a publish-and-subscribe paradigm.

As mentioned at the beginning of the chapter, a publish-and-subscribe process eliminates polling daemons. Polling daemons run as background processes. They loop until they find an event. The event triggers the polling daemon to signal, spawn another program activity, or terminate. There are three components to polling daemons: One is the monitoring loop. Another is the signal processing detection. Finally, there is the activity or termination logic triggered by receiving a signal.

If you eliminate polling daemons, you can reduce resource demands on the database and physical machine. Unfortunately, there are good business reasons for using polling daemons. DBMS_ALERT provides a means of automating the monitoring loop and signal processing detection components. DBMS_ALERT implements public pipes through using the DBMS_PIPE package.

DBMS_ALERT also uses the DBMS_PIPE memory structure in the SGA. While the structure is not formally referred to as a pipe, it works as a public pipe. As discussed earlier in the chapter, they are publicly accessible pipes or FIFO queues similar to Unix pipes. These pipes are populated on event triggers and subject to transaction control limits. Moreover, alert pipes communicate between sessions asynchronously after a transaction occurs, and they implement a publish-and-subscribe paradigm. It publishes notifications. Then it enables subscribers to register to receive event notifications.

Defining the DBMS_ALERT Package

The DBMS_ALERT package contains *only* procedures. Procedures are limited to PL/SQL execution. The DBMS_ALERT procedures support only VARCHAR2 datatype pipes. Like the MESSENGER package provided earlier in the chapter, DBMS_ALERT is a wrapper package to the DBMS_PIPE package. There is one exception. DBMS_ALERT maintains a new memory structure that enables the publish-and-subscribe process. That memory structure contains a list of pipes and those who are interested in their receipt.

REGISTER Procedure

The REGISTER procedure takes a single formal parameter, NAME, which accepts a valid SIGNAL name. Unfortunately, you don't raise an exception when you register for a signal name that doesn't exist. It has the prototype

```
REGISTER(signal_name)
```

You use REGISTER to subscribe to one or more alerts. It is important to note that you must keep track of which alerts you subscribe to because there isn't a tool to check them.

REMOVE Procedure

The REMOVE procedure takes a single formal parameter, NAME, which accepts a valid SIGNAL name. Like the REGISTER procedure, the REMOVE procedure fails to raise an exception when unsubscribing from an alert. The prototype is

```
REMOVE(signal_name)
```

You use REMOVE to unsubscribe interest in one or more alerts. Also, like the REGISTER procedure, the REMOVE procedure does not track when you unsubscribe to an alert. You must keep a list of your own.

REMOVEALL Procedure

The REMOVEALL procedure has no formal parameter. It has the prototype

```
REMOVEALL
```

You unsubscribe from all alerts when you call the REMOVEALL procedure. It is the cleanest way to reset your listening state for alerts.

SET_DEFAULTS Procedure

The SET_DEFAULTS procedure sets only default, and that is the sensitivity parameter. The procedure takes an INTEGER as its single formal parameter. The prototype is

```
SET_DEFAULTS(event_polling_in_seconds)
```

The polling default is five seconds. Although you can reset it, you should be careful because you increase the likelihood of missing a signal. Signals are perishable events, erased by subsequent events.

SIGNAL Procedure

The SIGNAL procedure takes two formal parameters: the NAME and MESSAGE parameters. The NAME parameter accepts a valid SIGNAL name. A SIGNAL name must be no longer than 30 characters. The MESSAGE parameter accepts a valid VARCHAR2 name. The prototype for the procedure is

 SIGNAL(*signal_name*, *signal_message*)

The MESSAGE parameter size is limited to 1,800 bytes. This means that you have 600 characters in a 3-byte UTF8 Unicode character set. The VARCHAR2 datatype doesn't support the 2-byte AL16UTF16 character set because it is reserved for NCHAR, NCLOB, and NVARCHAR2 dataypes.

> **CAUTION**
> *You should not use ORA$ as a preface to any of your alerts because it is reserved by Oracle Corporation for their own use.*

WAITONE Procedure

The WAITONE procedure takes four formal parameters, as described in Table 12-4.

When using the WAITONE procedure, you need to ensure that the variable is equal to or larger than the actual message sent. If you size the variable too small, you may not receive an alert.

Parameter	Mandatory or Optional	Description
NAME	Mandatory	The NAME parameter is positionally the first paramater, and it accepts an IN mode VARCHAR2 datatype that represents the SIGNAL name.
MESSAGE	Mandatory	The MESSAGE parameter is positionally the second parameter, and it is an OUT mode VARCHAR2 datatype containing the 1,800 byte message text.
STATUS	Mandatory	The STATUS parameter is positionally the third parameter, and it is also an OUT mode INTEGER datatype. The STATUS parameter returns a zero when successful and one due to a failure.
TIMEOUT	Optional	The TIMEOUT parameter is positionally the last parameter. It is an IN mode INTEGER datatype that sets the length of time to wait on an alert, which is expressed in seconds.

TABLE 12-4 *Four Formal Parameters of the WAITONE Procedure*

In addition, you should note that since DBMS_ALERT uses DBMS_LOCK it is possible to receive a status four from DBMS_LOCK. This occurs when you try to override an existing lock.

You have reviewed the idea, utility, and specifics of the DBMS_ALERT package. In the next section, you will see how DBMS_ALERT works.

Working with the DBMS_ALERT Package

In this section, you will work with the following:

- Building a trigger to signal an alert

- Registering interest in an alert

- Waiting on an alert

- Triggering an alert

- Analyzing the impact of transaction-based alerts

These topics will help prepare you to use DBMS_ALERT successfully. The topics also should prepare you to experiment with the package. Before running any of these scripts, you should run create_messages_table.sql. It will build necessary database tables to support the examples.

Building a Trigger to Signal an Alert

These topics will help prepare you to use DBMS_ALERT successfully. The topics also should prepare you to experiment with the package. Before running any of these scripts, you should run create_messages_table.sql. It will build necessary database tables to support the examples.

The following row-level trigger allows you to see how to capture inserts, updates, and deletes from a table. As you work with the trigger and DBMS_ALERT, you will find there are some design issues to consider. This trigger is our signaling device. Any call to DBMS_ALERT.SIGNAL should be found in a database trigger. If it is not in a trigger, you are leveraging DBMS_ALERT in an unintended way.

```
-- This is found in create_signal_trigger.sql on the publisher's web site.
CREATE OR REPLACE TRIGGER signal_messages
AFTER
INSERT OR UPDATE OR DELETE
OF message_id
  ,message_source
  ,message_destination
  ,message
ON messages
FOR EACH ROW
BEGIN
  IF :old.message_id IS NULL THEN -- Check for no previous row - an inserts.
    -- Signal Event and insert message.
    DBMS_ALERT.SIGNAL('EVENT_MESSAGE_QUEUE'
                  ,:new.message_source||':Insert');
    INSERT
    INTO    messages_alerts
    VALUES  (:new.message_source||':Insert');
```

```
  ELSIF :new.message_id IS NULL THEN  -- Check for no current row - a deletes.
    DBMS_ALERT.SIGNAL('EVENT_MESSAGE_QUEUE'
                    ,:old.message_source||':Delete');
    INSERT
    INTO      messages_alerts
    VALUES    (:old.message_source||':Delete');
  ELSE - Handle all others - updates.
    IF :new.message_source IS NULL THEN
      DBMS_ALERT.SIGNAL('EVENT_MESSAGE_QUEUE'
                      ,:new.message_source||':Update#1');
      INSERT
      INTO      messages_alerts
      VALUES    (:new.message_source||'Update#1');
    ELSE
      DBMS_ALERT.SIGNAL('EVENT_MESSAGE_QUEUE'
                      ,:old.message_source||':Update#2');
      INSERT
      INTO      messages_alerts
      VALUES    (:old.message_source||':Update#2');
    END IF;
  END IF;
END;
/
```

The sample trigger fires on DML events to the messages table. The trigger checks if the `:old`
`.message_id` does not exist. This condition is met whenever a new row is inserted into the target
table. If this condition is met, it signals an alert to `EVENT_MESSAGE_QUEUE` and inserts a matching
message into the `messages_alert` table: the `:new.message_id` does not exist. This condition
is met whenever a row is deleted from the target table. If this condition is met, it again signals the
event and writes a record. The ELSE block handles the same behavior for `UPDATE` statements. You
have built your signaling device. It will publish the message. The next section will examine how
you subscribe to see the published message.

Registering Interest in an Alert

When you register your interest in an alert, you are subscribing to an alert. You register within the
scope of a session. This means that each session that is interested in a published alert must subscribe.

The following example program subscribes to a named alert:

```
-- This is found in register_interest.sql on the publisher's web site.
BEGIN
  DBMS_ALERT.REGISTER('EVENT_MESSAGE_QUEUE');
END;
/
```

The sample program registers interest in the `EVENT_MESSAGE_QUEUE` alert.

You have now registered interest in the `EVENT_MESSAGE_QUEUE` alert. Alternatively, you
have subscribed to the alert. Every time the alert fires after an insert, update, or delete, you will
receive a message if you are waiting to handle its receipt.

Waiting on an ALERT

After you have registered your interest in an alert, you may or may not receive an alert. Part of a
publish-and-subscribe paradigm requires you to wait to receive a message. It is very much like

a baseball pitcher's and catcher's relationship. If the catcher is not there and the pitcher throws the ball, the ball will not be caught.

In the following program, you will learn to catch the ball. The program shows you how to wait on a single alert. You should also note that the SENSITIVITY, or polling rate, discussed earlier is the default. The default is checking every five seconds.

```
-- This is found in waitone.sql on the publisher's web site.
DECLARE
  -- Define OUT mode variables required from WAITONE.
  message          VARCHAR2(30 CHAR);
  status           INTEGER;
BEGIN
  -- Register interest in an alert.
  DBMS_ALERT.WAITONE('EVENT_MESSAGE_QUEUE', message, status, 30);
  IF (STATUS <> 0) THEN
    DBMS_OUTPUT.PUT_LINE('A timeout has happened.');
  ELSE
    DBMS_OUTPUT.PUT_LINE('Alert Messages Received');
    DBMS_OUTPUT.PUT_LINE('----------------------');
    DBMS_OUTPUT.PUT_LINE(message);
  END IF;
END;
/
```

The sample program uses DBMS_ALERT.WAITONE procedure to create a polling loop for 30 seconds. Given a five-second default interval, the polling loop will run six times before ending. A time-out occurs when no alert was received. If the time-out does not occur before an alert is received, it will print the alert. Otherwise, nothing is printed.

You should run this without doing anything to trigger the alert. It will show you a time-out message:

```
-- This is generated by waitone.sql on the publisher's web site.
A timeout has happened.
```

You have worked through subscribing to an alert. Unfortunately, there was no alert signaled before the scheduled time-out. The next section will show you how to trigger events.

Triggering an Alert

After you have built a trigger and registered interest in another session where you are waiting for a signaled alert, you can trigger the alert. That means you need two sessions connected to the PLSQL user to do this. In one session, you need to start the waitone.sql script discussed previously. In the other session, you need to run the following program before the thirty seconds has expired. If thirty seconds is too short a time, then you should modify waitone.sql to allow yourself more time.

The following program will trigger an alert:

```
-- This is found in trigger_alerts1.sql on the publisher's web site.
-- Insert a new row.
INSERT
INTO     messages
VALUES (4,'PLSQL','USERA','Insert, Shazaam.');
-- Upgrade a row.
```

```
UPDATE    messages
SET       message = 'Update, Shazaam.'
WHERE     message_id = 2;
-- Delete a row.
DELETE    messages
WHERE     message_id = 3;
-- Commit the changes.
COMMIT;
```

The preceding program inserted, updated, and deleted rows from the `messages` table. After making all three changes, it committed the changes.

The `waitone.sql` script will now return the following formatted output:

```
-- This is generated by waitone.sql on the publisher's web site.
Alert Messages Received
-----------------------
PLSQL:Delete

MESSAGE
-----------------------
PLSQL:Insert
PLSQL:Update#2
PLSQL:Delete
```

You can see the benefit of doing the `INSERT` statement within the `signal_messages` trigger. It sends the messages and inserts a duplicate into a table. The commit for the external transaction commits the writes to the `messages_alerts` table. As you can see, there are three messages, but the `DBMS_ALERT` subscription returned only the last one. The other two messages were lost. This is why the output for alert messages received shows only the last DML change made.

In the next section, you will analyze why you lost two messages with `DBMS_ALERT`. You may already have guessed the answer. If so, you have two choices at this point. You can skip the next section or confirm your analysis.

Analyzing the Impact of Transaction-Based Alerts

The general answer is that the polling loop returns immediately with any alert message. In the preceding script, the commit occurs only once at the end of the program. Actually, three messages were sent by `DBMS_ALERT.SIGNAL`. The second message overwrote the value of the first, and the third, the value of the second. The third value was actually the only value published because it was the last value signaled before the commit.

`DBMS_ALERT` operates much like `DBMS_PIPE`. Individual signals are stuffed into a private pipe that acts like a local buffer. Imitating a local buffer, the private pipe can contain only one signal value. Therefore, only the last private pipe value is signaled to the subscribers.

The following program will trigger three alerts:

```
-- This is found in trigger_alert2.sql on the publisher's web site.
-- Insert a new row.
INSERT
INTO      messages
VALUES (4,'PLSQL','USERA','Insert, Shazaam.');
-- Commit the change.
```

```
COMMIT;
-- Upgrade a row.
UPDATE    messages
SET       message = 'Update, Shazaam.'
WHERE     message_id = 2;
-- Commit the change.
COMMIT;
-- Delete a row.
DELETE    messages
WHERE     message_id = 3;
-- Commit the change.
COMMIT;
```

The preceding program inserted, updated, and deleted rows from the `messages` table. It committed each change before making another.

You can now rerun the `waitone.sql` program in one session and `trigger_alerts2.sql` in another. The `waitone.sql` script will generate the following results:

```
-- This is generated by waitone.sql on the publisher's web site.
Alert Messages Received
-----------------------
PLSQL:Insert

MESSAGE
-----------------------
PLSQL:Insert
PLSQL:Update#2
PLSQL:Delete
```

As you can see, only the first signaled message is received by the polling program `waitone.sql`. The reason is that the polling program is a simple illustration of how you catch the signal. The commit terminates the transaction. Termination of the transaction triggers the signaling of the alert.

The presentation has laid a foundation for you. More elegant solutions can be developed. You develop them by nesting the polling logic into signal management programming logic.

Summary

You have covered both mechanisms for accomplishing intersession communication, DBMS_ALERT and DBMS_PIPE. The DBMS_PIPE package gives you more freedom of latitude but requires more programming management, while the DBMS_ALERT package is very limited in scope because of how it is linked to transaction processing.

The chapter has provided coverage of both utilities. Advanced Queuing also provides these features and is part of work-flow solutions. Advanced Queuing is best when communication delays between sessions *are not critical.* You should be able to leverage the material to rapidly build intersession communication solutions.

CHAPTER
13

External Procedures

xternal routines are delivered in Oracle 11*g* through external *procedures.* They enable the database to communicate with external applications through PL/SQL. While it is nontrivial to configure the database to support them, external procedures provide a critical framework.

You will cover the following topics. The chapter assumes you read it sequentially. It also assumes you have read the preceding twelve chapters.

- Introducing external procedures

- Working with external procedures

The introduction to this book provides scripts that create a user account, create a data model, and then seed the data model. You need to run them before working through the examples in the chapter.

Introducing External Procedures

External routines provide the ability to communicate between the database and external programs written in C, C++, COBOL, FORTRAN, PL/1, Visual Basic, and Java. There is one caveat: the language must be callable from C. While the surgeon general has not provided a warning, other languages can present different challenges than PL/SQL. The chapter focuses on implementations of C and Java libraries as external routines.

Development teams may want to isolate programming logic from the database. External routines are the natural solution. They are ideal for computation-intensive programs, providing an interface between external data sources and the database. Unlike stand-alone Oracle Pro*C programs, they are callable from PL/SQL.

You will work with a C shared library and a Java class library in this chapter. The C and Java examples have been made as small and narrow in scope as possible to conserve space while you focus on PL/SQL programming. You can find more on stored Java classes in Chapter 15. Appendix D also offers a Java Primer for those new to Java.

External routines leverage the Oracle Net Services transport layer. You will need to work through a number of architectural and configuration issues to run the basic samples. It is helpful if you have some formal background in C or Java, but it is not necessary. This chapter is important because PL/SQL programmers can be expected to explain the process to C and Java programmers. You will also write the PL/SQL library definitions, which become the gateways to these libraries. These are often called "PL/SQL wrappers."

NOTE
The documentation for this chapter is spread far and wide. The key configuration references are from Appendix A in the Advanced Application Developer's Guide, Chapter 4 in the Heterogeneous Connectivity Administrator's Guide, *and Chapter 13 in the* Net Services Administrator's Guide.

You will now work with implementing external procedures.

Working with External Procedures

As discussed, external procedures enable you to communicate through PL/SQL with external programs. The external programs can call back to an Oracle database using the Oracle Call Interface (OCI). They can also communicate with external databases such as Sybase, IBM DB2, and Microsoft SQL Server. External procedures are ideal to work with external applications. External applications can use other databases or file systems as data repositories. Moreover, any combination of these is supported.

You will now learn about the architecture for external procedures. Then you will learn the setup issues for Oracle Networking and the heterogeneous service agent. When you have learned how to configure your environment, you will then work with building and accessing C and Java libraries from PL/SQL.

Defining the extproc Architecture

Oracle built an extensible architecture for external procedures. It is flexible to support any programming language that is callable by the C programming language. For example, you can call a C++ program using the `extern` command in C. However, callbacks into the database by the external programming languages are limited to those supported by OCI. OCI supports C, C++, COBOL, FORTRAN, PL/1, Visual Basic, Perl, PHP, and Java.

Whatever programming language you choose to implement must support building a shared library. Likewise, the platform must support shared libraries. Shared libraries, also called dynamic link libraries (DLLs), are code modules that can be leveraged by your program. Java shared libraries are called libunits. When you access shared libraries from PL/SQL, the libraries are loaded dynamically at run time as external procedures. By default, each remote procedure call uses a discrete and dedicated `extproc` agent to access the shared library. Alternatively, you can configure a multithreaded agent through the Oracle Heterogeneous Services. If you do so, you can share the `extproc` agent among any number of database sessions.

External procedures use the PL/SQL library definition to exchange data between the PL/SQL run-time engine and shared libraries. The PL/SQL library definition acts as a wrapper to the shared library. It defines the external call specification and maps PL/SQL datatypes to native language equivalents. The map between data types is used to translate data types when exchanging information. Figure 13-1 illustrates the external procedure architecture.

A call to a PL/SQL wrapper translates types. Then, the wrapper sends a signal across Oracle Net Services. Oracle Net Services receives the signal and spawns or forks an `extproc` agent process. It is the `extproc` agent that accesses the shared library. The `extproc` agent forks a Remote Procedure Call (RPC) to the shared library. The shared library result is returned to the `extproc` agent by the RPC. The `extproc` agent then returns the result to the PL/SQL wrapper. Next, the PL/SQL wrapper receives and translates the data types from the local language to the native PL/SQL data types. Ultimately, the PL/SQL wrapper returns the value to the calling PL/SQL program.

As you can see from Figure 13-1, there are two potential failure points to dynamic execution. The decision diamonds in the process flow chart qualify potential failure points. Both failure points are linked to the listener. The second failure point can also be missing libraries in the defined locations.

One failure point exists when a separate `extproc` agent listener is not configured or is incorrectly configured. The other failure point arises in two possible cases. One case is when the `extproc` listener fails to resolve the connection. Another case is when a physical shared library is not found where defined in the PL/SQL library definition.

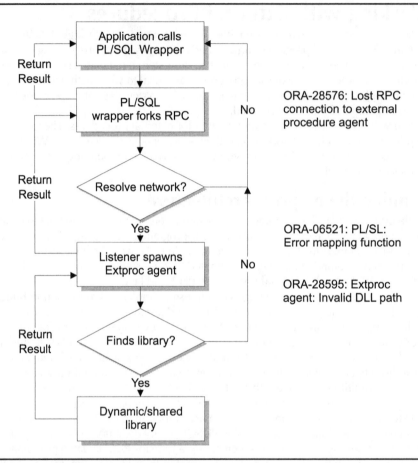

FIGURE 13-1 *External procedure architecture*

Configuring the heterogeneous multithreaded agent is complex. However, it enables you to share a single extproc agent among multiple database sessions. Benefits of this implementation are a reduction in resources required to dynamically fork extproc agents. The default behavior of external procedures is to fork a new extproc agent for each external procedure call. The default works but consumes too many resources too frequently. When you have many sessions using external libraries, you should use a multithreaded extproc agent. Figure 13-2 looks at how a multithreaded extproc agent works.

As shown in the diagram, multiple database sessions can connect through the heterogeneous multithreaded extproc agent, which fits into the extproc agent niche in Figure 13-1. Once the signal arrives at the agent, the monitor thread puts the connection into a FIFO queue. The monitor thread maintains load-balancing information; using that information, the monitor thread passes the connection to the first available dispatcher thread, which puts the request into another FIFO queue. Task threads read the dispatcher FIFO queues and process requests. Each task thread sends the result back to the requesting session. You will cover more about the multithreaded agent later in this chapter.

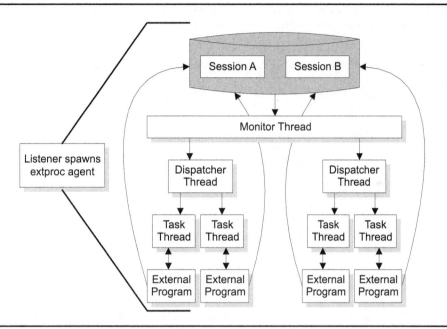

FIGURE 13-2   *Multithreaded agent architecture*

You have developed an understanding of the basic architecture of external procedures. The next section will show you how to set up and configure Oracle Net Services to support external procedures.

Defining extproc Oracle Net Services Configuration

External procedures use Oracle Net Services to fork or link signals to the extproc agent. As discussed, the extproc agent can be the default stand-alone unit or a multithreaded extproc agent. Unfortunately, configuring your listener.ora and tnsnames.ora files is a manual process.

The standard listener built by the Net Configuration Assistant on installation does not provide a complete extproc agent listener. Net Configuration Assistant likewise does not provide an automated way to create an extproc agent listener. The standard listener includes an extproc handler service in the standard listener. This is not adequate for implementing the extproc agent. You must set up an exclusive listener for external procedures.

As a PL/SQL developer, configuring Oracle Net Services may not be something you do often. It is also possible your DBA may be unfamiliar with the nuances required to support extproc agents. This section provides the steps required to configure Oracle Net Services to support extproc agents.

The listener.ora file can be found in one of two locations. It can be found in the directory pointed to by the $TNS_ADMIN environment variable. Alternatively, the default location is in the $ORACLE_HOME/network/admin directory. The standard listener.ora file contains two entries: one is the LISTENER and the other is the SID_LIST_LISTENER.

The LISTENER describes an address list or set of address lists. Addresses consist of a protocol definition and a key value, or else a protocol definition, a host name, and a port number. The Oracle 11*g* standard fresh install LISTENER entry in the listener.ora file follows:

```
-- This is found in listener1.ora on the publisher's web site.
LISTENER =
  (DESCRIPTION_LIST =
    (DESCRIPTION =
      (ADDRESS_LIST =
        (ADDRESS = (PROTOCOL = IPC)
                   (KEY = EXTPROC1521)
        )
      )
      (ADDRESS_LIST =
        (ADDRESS = (PROTOCOL = TCP)
                   (HOST = <host_name>.<domain_name>)
                   (PORT = 1521)
        )
      )
    )
  )
```

The standard listener.ora file has a problem supporting the extproc agent. The problem is that the listener has two ADDRESS_LIST parameters using different protocols. The first listens for Internal Procedure Calls (IPCs). The second listens for TCP messages, like RPCs. This is the principal reason why a separate listener is required for extproc IPC calls.

NOTE
Oracle 11g lists the KEY *parameter value as* EXTPROC<listener_port>; *whereas previously only* EXTPROC *was listed.*

The SID_LIST_LISTENER, the second entry in the standard listener.ora file, contains the SID description. The Oracle 11*g* standard SID_DESC is defined by the SID_NAME, ORACLE_HOME, and PROGRAM parameter definitions. The SID_NAME parameter is defined as PLSExtProc, which is used as the extproc identifier. The ORACLE_HOME parameter defines the Oracle home directory. Finally, the PROGRAM parameter defines the extproc agent as the program. The Oracle 11*g* standard SID_LIST_LISTENER entry in the listener.ora file follows:

```
-- This is found in listener1.ora on the publisher's web site.
SID_LIST_LISTENER =
  (SID_LIST =
    (SID_DESC =
      (SID_NAME = PLSExtProc)
      (ORACLE_HOME = <oracle_home_directory>)
      (PROGRAM = extproc)
    )
  )
```

The standard SID_LIST_LISTENER is another mix of two purposes in one definition. The SID_NAME and PROGRAM parameters are there to support the extproc agent signals. The ORACLE_HOME parameter is provided for both the TCP listener and extproc IPC services. These two services run under a single standard listener, although they really are suited to separate listeners. The clincher is that *external procedures require their own listener.*

NOTE
Oracle provides the preceding caveat for the extproc *listener in Appendix A of the* Oracle Database Advanced Application Developer's Guide, *Release 11g.*

The standard listener.ora file works in tandem with the standard tnsnames.ora file. The listener.ora and tnsnames.ora files are used by Oracle Net Services. The standard tnsnames.ora file provides two service names. One is CODE, which maps to the standard listener to the database. The other is EXTPROC_CONNECTION_DATA, which maps to the extproc agent. The following is an example of the standard tnsnames.ora file:

```
-- This is found in tnsnames1.ora on the publisher's web site.
CODE =
  (DESCRIPTION =
    (ADDRESS = (PROTOCOL = TCP)
               (HOST = <host_name>.<domain_name>)
               (PORT = 1521)
    )
    (CONNECT_DATA =
      (SERVER = DEDICATED)
      (SERVICE_NAME = <database_sid>)
    )
  )

EXTPROC_CONNECTION_DATA =
  (DESCRIPTION =
    (ADDRESS_LIST =
      (ADDRESS = (PROTOCOL = IPC)
                 (KEY = EXTPROC)
      )
    )
    (CONNECT_DATA =
      (SID = PLSExtProc)
      (PRESENTATION = RO)
    )
  )
```

The tnsnames.ora service names provide connection aliases that enable users and programs to connect to the listener. They resolve requests for connections by matching the tnsnames.ora ADDRESS parameter to the address in a running listener. Then they use the CONNECTION_DATA parameters to connect a database or agent. The extproc agent is not the only agent supported by Oracle 11g. You can define any number of heterogeneous servers that enable communication between Oracle and other databases.

On any case-insensitive system, these files resolve extproc across Oracle Net Services. They fail on a case-sensitive system. The KEY parameter in the listener.ora file is lowercase, while the KEY value in the tnsnames.ora is uppercase. The two will fail to resolve. You can see if your system contains the error by using the tnsping utility.

For example, run `tnsping` with the following:

```
$ tnsping EXTPROC_CONNECTION_DATA
```

If you get the following, everything is correctly configured:

```
TNS Ping Utility for Linux: Version 11.1.0.6.0 - Production on 22-AUG-2007
Copyright (c) 1997, 2007, Oracle.  All rights reserved.
Used parameter files:
/u03/oracle/11g/11.1.0/network/admin/sqlnet.ora
Used TNSNAMES adapter to resolve the alias
Attempting to contact (DESCRIPTION = (ADDRESS_LIST = (ADDRESS = (PROTOCOL =
IPC)(KEY = EXTPROC1521))) (CONNECT_DATA = (SID = PLSExtProc) (PRESENTATION = RO)))
OK (0 msec)
```

If you get a `TNS-12541` error when using `tnsping`, the likelihood is that there is a mismatch between the `ADDRESS` parameter values in the `listener.ora` and `tnsnames.ora` files.

Before you are introduced to working files, you need to learn about the `PROGRAM` and `ENV` parameters in `listener.ora` files. The `PROGRAM` parameter must specify a valid executable in the `$ORACLE_HOME/bin` directory. The program can access only libraries found in the `$ORACLE_HOME/lib` directory by default. You can change the default by doing any of the following:

- Define `EXTPROC_DLLS` to enable loading of shared libraries. You have three choices for using `EXTPROC_DLLS`. They are shown in Table 13-1.

- Define the `$LD_LIBRARY_PATH` for the `extproc` agent.

- Define the `$PATH` for the `extproc` agent.

- Define the `$APL_ENV_FILE` to specify a set of environment variables for the external `extproc` agent.

Syntax	Description	Security Level
DLL:DLL	Allows the `extproc` agent to load any of the specified shared libraries located in the `$ORACLE_HOME/lib` directory.	Medium
ONLY:DLL:DLL	Allows `extproc` to run any entered DLLs from specified directories.	High (recommended)
ANY	Allows `extproc` to load any DLL. It disables DLL checking.	Low

TABLE 13-1 *Options for EXTPROC_DLLS*

The following `listener.ora` file separates the two listeners. It also defines an external library that you will work with later in the chapter. You can use it as an example to build your own `listener.ora` file.

```
-- This is found in listener2.ora on the publisher's web site.
LISTENER =
  (DESCRIPTION_LIST =
    (DESCRIPTION =
      (ADDRESS_LIST =
        (ADDRESS = (PROTOCOL = TCP)
                   (HOST = <host_name>.<domain_name>)
                   (PORT = 1521)
        )
      )
    )
  )

SID_LIST_LISTENER =
  (SID_LIST =
    (SID_DESC =
      (SID_NAME = <database_name>)
      (ORACLE_HOME = <oracle_home_directory>)
    )
  )

CALLOUT_LISTENER =
  (DESCRIPTION_LIST =
    (DESCRIPTION =
      (ADDRESS_LIST =
        (ADDRESS = (PROTOCOL = IPC)
                   (KEY = extproc)
        )
      )
    )
  )

SID_LIST_CALLOUT_LISTENER =
  (SID_LIST =
    (SID_DESC =
      (SID_NAME = PLSExtProc)
      (ORACLE_HOME = <oracle_home_directory>)
      (PROGRAM = extproc)
      (ENV = "EXTPROC_DLLS=ONLY:
              <oracle_home_directory>/customlib/writestr1.so
             ,LD_LIBRARY_PATH=<oracle_home_directory>/lib")
    )
  )
```

The sample `listener.ora` file has a standard `LISTENER` TCP listener on port 1521. You should note that the IPC `ADDRESS` information has been removed from the standard listener. The sample file also has a standard `SID_LIST_LISTENER`. You should notice that the `SID_NAME` parameter value is no longer `PLSExtProc`, which was used for the `extproc` agent. It uses the database name. You should also notice that the `PROGRAM` parameter and value are no longer in the `SID_LIST_LISTENER`.

The second address was removed from the standard listener and put in a separate listener, and the `CALLOUT_LISTENER` IPC listener uses a `KEY` parameter value of `extproc`. As a result of this change, the `SID_NAME` parameter has a value of `PLSExtProc`, and it should map to a case-sensitive equivalent `SID` parameter value in the `tnsnames.ora` service name. Also, the `PROGRAM` parameter is there with a new `ENV` parameter. The `ENV` parameter provides the recommended security implementation that allows access to only a specified library and the `LD_LIBRARY_PATH` for the external procedure.

The new `listener.ora` requires a new `tnsnames.ora` file. The following file works with the new `listener.ora` previously covered:

```
-- This is found in tnsnames2.ora on the publisher's web site.
CODE =
  (DESCRIPTION =
    (ADDRESS = (PROTOCOL = TCP)
               (HOST = <host_name>.<domain_name>)
               (PORT = 1521)
    )
    (CONNECT_DATA =
      (SERVER = DEDICATED)
      (SERVICE_NAME = CODE)
    )
  )

EXTPROC_CONNECTION_DATA =
  (DESCRIPTION =
    (ADDRESS_LIST =
      (ADDRESS = (PROTOCOL = IPC)
                 (KEY = extproc)
      )
    )
    (CONNECT_DATA =
      (SID = PLSExtProc)
      (PRESENTATION = RO)
    )
  )
```

The sample `tnsnames.ora` file has a `CODE` alias that uses an `ADDRESS` pointing to the database and a `CONNECT_DATA` parameter supporting a dedicated connection. The `CONNECT_DATA` parameter `SERVER` has a dedicated value, which means a dedicated server connection. The sample file also has an `EXTPROC_CONNECTION_DATA` alias that uses a single `ADDRESS` to an IPC and `CONNECT_DATA` to the `extproc` SID.

You now have working `listener.ora` and `tnsnames.ora` files. You will need to shut down the listener services, copy the files into the new locations, and restart the listener. The following are the steps to take to replace the listener, by platform.

Microsoft Windows

1. As the Oracle user, source your environment, navigate to your system services, and shut down the Oracle listener.

2. Copy the original `listener.ora` and `tnsnames.ora` files in the `%ORACLE_HOME%\ network\admin` directory to `listener.ora.orig` and `tnsnames.ora.orig`.

3. Copy the new `listener2.ora` and `tnsnames2.ora` files into the `%ORACLE_HOME%\ network\admin` directory and rename them as `listener.ora` and `tnsnames.ora`, respectively.

4. As the Oracle user, source your environment, navigate to your system services, and start up the Oracle listener. In Windows, you will need to rebuild the original service and build a new service for the second listener.

5. Verify that you have two listener processes running by using the Task Manager. You will find the running services under the Processes tab.

Unix

1. As the Oracle user, source your environment and shut down the Oracle listener. You can use the following on a generic demonstration database:

    ```
    $ lsnrctl stop LISTENER
    ```

2. Copy the original `listener.ora` and `tnsnames.ora` files in the `$ORACLE_HOME/ network/admin` directory to `listener.ora.orig` and `tnsnames.ora.orig`.

3. Copy the new `listener2.ora` and `tnsnames2.ora` files into the `$ORACLE_HOME/ network/admin` directory and rename them as `listener.ora` and `tnsnames.ora`, respectively.

4. As the Oracle user, source your environment and start up the Oracle listener and `extproc` agent listener. You can use the following syntax, based on a generic demonstration database:

    ```
    $ lsnrctl start LISTENER
    $ lsnrctl start CALLOUT_LISTENER
    ```

5. Verify that you have two listener processes running by using the ps utility, as shown:

    ```
    $ ps -ef | grep -v grep | grep tnslsnr
    ```

At this point, you should have a `LISTENER` for the database and a `CALLOUT_LISTENER` for the `extproc` agent. You should also have a background process running for the `extproc` agent. In Microsoft Windows, you can check with the Task Manager for an `extprocPLSExtProc` process. In Unix, you can use the `ps` utility to find it.

Assuming you have successfully started the two listeners, you need to confirm whether or not it can communicate to the `extproc` agent. There are two steps to validating whether or not it is working. After sourcing your environment files, you should first use the `tnsping` utility as you did earlier in the chapter to test the network connection. You will use the `EXTPROC_CONNECTION_DATA` alias to check connectivity. Run `tnsping` with the following:

```
$ tnsping EXTPROC_CONNECTION_DATA
```

If you get the following, everything is correctly configured:

```
TNS Ping Utility for Linux: Version 11.1.0.6.0 - Production on 22-AUG-2007
Copyright (c) 1997, 2007, Oracle.  All rights reserved.
Used parameter files:
/u03/oracle/11g/11.1.0/network/admin/sqlnet.ora
```

If you get a `TNS-12541` error when using `tnsping`, the likelihood is that there is a *mismatch* between the `ADDRESS` parameter values in the `listener.ora` and `tnsnames.ora` files. Please check if there is a typo in either the `listener.ora` or `tnsnames.ora` file. You must resolve any `TNS-12541` error before continuing with the examples in the chapter.

Assuming you have successfully used the tnsping utility, the second step is to attempt to connect to the `extproc` agent TNS alias. Use this to attempt to connect to the `extproc` agent TNS alias:

```
$ sqlplus plsql/plsql@EXTPROC_CONNECTION_DATA
```

It should always fail. You should get the following output:

```
SQL*Plus: Release 11.1.0.6.0 - Production on Wed Aug 22 16:15:50 2007
Copyright (c) 1982, 2007, Oracle.  All rights reserved.
ERROR:
ORA-28547: connection to server failed, probable Net8 admin error
```

This is the correct behavior. It is actually telling you that the SQL*Plus connection is rejected by the `extproc` agent. The connection must have attempted to start and been rejected for you to receive this message.

You have now learned how to configure your listener to support the `extproc` agent. The next section will demonstrate an alternative to spawning a dedicated `extproc` agent for each database session.

Defining the Multithreaded External Procedure Agent

As discussed in the review of architecture, configuring the heterogeneous multithreaded agent is complex. However, it enables you to share a single `extproc` agent among multiple database sessions. Implementing a multithreaded external procedure agent reduces resources required to dynamically fork `extproc` agents.

The default behavior of external procedures is to fork a new `extproc` agent for each external procedure call. This default works but consumes too many resources too frequently. When you have many sessions using external libraries, you should use a multithreaded `extproc` agent. This section will show you how to configure and use the multithreaded `extproc` agent.

Before you begin to learn how to configure the multithreaded external procedure agent, there are three things to note about it:

- The external library must be thread-safe.

- The agent process, the database server, and the listener process must be on the same host.

- The agent process must run from the same database instance that issues the external procedure call.

When using the multithreaded external procedure agent, you must start the agent separately from the database. The multithreaded external procedure agent is an implementation of Oracle Heterogeneous Connectivity Services. The `agtctl` executable to start and manage sessions is the Agent Control utility. You will find it in the `$ORACLE_HOME/hs` directory.

If you attempt to use this tool without setting either the `$AGTCTL_ADMIN` or `$TNS_ADMIN` environment variable, you will generate the following error message:

```
$ agtctl

AGTCTL: Release 11.1.0.6.0 - Production on Wed Aug 22 07:57:24 2007

Copyright (c) 1982, 2007, Oracle.  All rights reserved.

ORA-28591: agent control utility: unable to access parameter file
ORA-28591: agent control utility: unable to access parameter file
```

It is recommended that you set the `$AGTCTL_ADMIN` environment variable to point to the `$ORACLE_HOME/hs/admin` directory. Any environment variables configured in the ENV parameter within your `extproc` listener must be in the sourced environment of the Oracle user when running `agtctl`.

The `agtctl` utility has two interfaces. One is the single-line command mode, and the other is the `agtctl` shell mode. There is no GUI interface to the `agtctl` utility. There is no text configuration file for this utility. It maintains parameter values in the `$ORACLE_HOME/hs/admin/initagt.dat` control file, which is a binary file maintained by the `agtctl` utility. Before you run the `agtctl` utility, the file will not exist. Table 13-2 provides a synopsis of the command structure.

There are six initialization parameters. All have default behaviors that can be overridden by using the `agtctl set` command. Table 13-3 provides the initialization parameters and their default values and descriptions.

Command Syntax	Description
delete agent_sid	Deletes an `agent_sid` entry.
Exit	Exits the `agtctl` file.
Help	Displays available commands.
set *parameter_name* parameter_value	Sets a configuration parameter.
Show parameter_name	Shows a parameter's value.
shutdown agent_sid	Shuts down an *agent_sid* multithreaded agent.
startup agent_sid	Starts an *agent_sid* multithreaded agent.
unset *parameter_name* parameter_value	Unsets a configuration parameter.

TABLE 13-2   *Commands for the agtctl Utility*

Parameter	Default Value	Description
listener_address	(ADDRESS_LIST = (ADDRESS = (PROTOCOL = IPC) (KEY = PNPKEY)) (ADDRESS = (PROTOCOL = IPC) (KEY= \<oracle_sid>) (ADDRESS = (PROTOCOL = TCP) (HOST = 127.0.0.1) (PORT = 1521)))	Address list for the agent controller listener. The \<oracle_sid> value is the \<service_name> parameter in the tnsnames.ora entry for the database.
max_dispatchers	1	Maximum number of dispatchers.
max_sessions	5	Maximum number of sessions.
max_task_threads	2	Maximum number of threads.
shutdown_address	(ADDRESS_LIST = (ADDRESS = (PROTOCOL = IPC) (KEY = extproc)))	Address on which agtctl listens for shutdown instruction.
tcp_dispatchers	0	Number of dispatchers listening on TCP. All other dispatchers listen on IPC.

TABLE 13-3 *Initialization Parameters for the agtctl Utility*

You will now configure the extproc multithreaded agent using the agtctl shell mode. The following steps will enable one hundred sessions and four dispatchers before starting the extproc multithreaded agent:

```
AGTCTL> set agent_sid CALLOUT_LISTENER
AGTCTL> set max_dispatchers 4
AGTCTL> set max_sessions 100
AGTCTL> show max_dispatchers
4
AGTCTL> show max_sessions
100
AGTCTL> startup extproc
```

In Unix, you can use the ps utility to see the multithreaded external procedure agent. The task manager in Microsoft Windows will also let you see the process. Here is the Unix command:

```
$ ps -ef | grep -v grep | grep extprocCALLOUT
```

The output from this command is

```
oracle    4635    1  0 18:41 ?    00:00:01 extprocCALLOUT_LISTENER -mt
```

You can now shut down the multithreaded external procedure agent by using the shutdown command. Shutdown without an argument acts like a shutdown of the database, which means it allows transactions in progress to complete. Shutdown immediate will cause in-progress external procedure calls to abort. This is the immediate command:

```
AGTCTL> shutdown immediate
```

When you start the `extproc` multithreaded agent, all new external procedure calls will route through the multithreaded agent. However, any calls previously started with dynamic stand-alone `extproc` agents will continue to completion.

When you shut down the `extproc` multithreaded agent, it stops taking new requests. This means all processing transactions should complete normally unless you stop the agent with the immediate clause. The immediate clause forces all running threads to stop. After you shutdown the multithreaded agent, the external procedure monitoring thread rejects new calls. Dynamic `extproc` agents are then spawned for any new external procedure calls.

You have now learned how to start, configure, and stop the multithreaded external procedure agent. You have seen how you can seamlessly move between dedicated dynamic `extproc` sessions and a background multithreaded agent. The next section will demonstrate how you create an external C shared library.

Working with a C Shared Library

As discussed when you covered the `extproc` architecture, Oracle built an extensible architecture for external procedures. It is flexible to support any programming language that is callable by the C programming language. For example, you can call a C++ program using the `extern` command in C. You could call another C program from the shared library. It could then call back into the database. The second C program would use embedded SQL to access data. Using embedded SQL requires use of the Oracle Pro*C precompiler and the Oracle Call Interface (OCI). Both the Pro*C precompiler and OCI tools require a solid working knowledge of C or C++.

Defining the C Shared Library

You will now define a simple C shared library. You will use the following C program as a dynamic link library (DLL) or shared library. The structure of this program has been chosen to avoid having to introduce you to the extensive details of Oracle Pro*C precompiler and OCI functionality. You will need to have a C compiler installed on your platform to compile this example.

Compiling a C program has several nuances. A C compiler does several things. It preprocesses the source code by breaking it down into tokens while validating syntax. Then, it compiles the program into assembly programming code and uses an assembler to create object code. After creating the object code, the compiler then links other object code into the program to create a stand-alone program unit.

The following program includes standard library header files but does not link libraries:

```
-- This is found in writestr1.c on the publisher's web site.
/* Include standard IO. */
#include <stdio.h>

/* Declare a writestr function. */
void writestr(char *path, char *message)
{
```

```
   /* Declare a FILE variable. */
   FILE *file_name;

   /* Open the file in write-only mode. */
   file_name = fopen(path,"w");

   /* Write to file the message received. */
   fprintf(file_name,"%s\n",message);

   /* Close the file. */
   fclose(file_name);
}
```

The program includes the `stdio.h` file, which is called a header file. `stdio.h` contains the definitions required to do basic I/O operations in C programs. The `#include <stdio.h>` statement tells the C precompiler to include the contents of `/usr/include/stdio.h` file in the program. The program writes a new file with a string message passed by an actual parameter to the library.

It should be noted that the `writestr1.c` program does not have a `main()` function. A `main()` function is required for a stand-alone C program. This program can be used only as a DLL or shared library.

If you attempt a generic compilation of a library file that lacks a `main()` function, it will raise an error. For example, if `writestr1.c` were a stand-alone program, you would compile it into object code like this:

```
$ cc -o writestr.o writestr1.c
```

This will raise an error because there is no `main()` function in the program. The error message follows:

```
/usr/lib/gcc-lib/i386-redhat-linux7/2.96/../../../crt1.o(.text+0x18): In function
'_start':
: undefined reference to 'main'
collect2: ld returned 1 exit status
```

It is assumed that you have a C or C++ Development IDE if you are working on the Microsoft Windows platform. Since each IDE works a bit differently, you will have to understand how to use your IDE to compile the program as a DLL.

If you are working on Unix, you live in the command-line world. The following examples illustrate the two methods for creating a C shared library in Unix. The first example will work on the Sun Microsystems C compiler. The second example is the most common approach and supported on Linux.

Unix C Compiler that supports the –G option

```
cc -G -o writestr1.so writestr1.c
```

Unix C Compiler that supports the –shared option

```
cc -shared -o writestr1.so writestr1.c
   - OR -
gcc -shared -o writestr1.so writestr1.c
```

TIP
If you are using IBM AIX and the IBM C compiler, you need to ensure that you have a symbolic link named cc *that points to* xlc. *The IBM C compiler will attempt to include proprietary libraries that are not referenced in the sample program. It will not attempt to include those libraries when the calling executable is a symbolic* cc.

You should now have a C shared library. Now, you or your DBA should create a custom library directory off your $ORACLE_HOME. Please name it *customlib* if you want to be consistent with the examples in this chapter. You should ensure the permissions for the directory is read, write, and execute for owner and read and execute for group and user.

If you are not the DBA but a member of the DBA group, copying the file and executing it will work. If are not in the DBA group, please have your DBA change the group ownership of the file to the DBA group. It will not prevent you from executing the shared library, but it is a check-in mechanism. Any files not in the DBA group would be considered development or stage program units.

You have now created a DLL/shared library and positioned it where a database external procedure can call it. Next, you will define the PL/SQL library definition and wrapper.

Defining and Calling the PL/SQL Library Wrapper

You have configured your network; learned how to start, configure, and shut down a multithreaded and stand-alone extproc agent; and created a C DLL or shared library. Now you need to define a PL/SQL library definition and wrapper so that you can pass information from the database to your C program.

PL/SQL Library Definition

The first step is to define the external library in the database. You do this after you have decided where to place your library. $ORACLE_HOME/customlib is used for the C external procedure example. As discussed, using a custom library requires configuration of the EXTPROC_DLLS value in the ENV parameter. The ENV parameter is found in the listener.ora file. Alternatively, you can put your libraries in the $ORACLE_HOME/bin or $ORACLE_HOME/lib directory and not configure the EXTPROC_DLLS value. If you have customized where you place your libraries, please synchronize the directory path for the library with your listener.ora file.

The PL/SQL library prototype is

```
CREATE [OR REPLACE] LIBRARY <library_name> AS | IS
'<file_specification>'
AGENT '<agent_dblink>';
/
```

The create_library1.sql and create_library2.sql files use Dynamic Native SQL (DNS) to build the library creation DLL. This was done to simplify your submission of a directory path. The command is provided in the comments section for the programs and noted in the following:

```
-- This is found in create_library1.sql on the publisher's web site.
CREATE OR REPLACE LIBRARY library_write_string AS
'<oracle_home_directory>/<custom_library>/<file_name>.<file_ext>';
/
```

The PL/SQL library role defines the name of the library and the physical location where the library will be found. There is no validation of whether or not the file is physically located where you have specified. The library name is the access point for your PL/SQL wrapper. You will now learn about the PL/SQL library wrapper.

PL/SQL Library Wrapper

The principal role of the PL/SQL library wrapper is to define an interface between the database and the external procedure. The interface defines how the formal parameters map between PL/SQL and C data types. It also defines any context and the location of the external procedure or library. When you create a PL/SQL library wrapper, there is no check whether or not the shared library is in the directory. You need to have a management process to ensure check-in and version control.

Oracle provides additional derived types to support OCI. The table columns show the source of the types. The table also shows you the default conversion type. Table 13-4 maps PL/SQL and C data types.

In your small example, data types are converted only from PL/SQL to C, but the library definition supports bidirectional conversions. The bidirectional support is independent of the external shared library. Whether the external C library returns data or not, the PL/SQL library wrapper has defined it as bidirectional.

There are some differences beyond mapping between PL/SQL and C data types. They are qualified here:

- A variable can be NULL in PL/SQL, but there is no equivalent of a null value in C. When a variable can be NULL, you must use another variable to notify that a variable is null or not. This second variable is known as an indicator. You use OCI_IND_NULL and OCI_IND_NOTNULL to check whether the indicator variable is null or not. The indicator value is passed by value unless you override that behavior and pass by reference. An advanced consideration for an indicator variable is that it can have a type descriptor object (TDO) for composite objects and collections.

- Both C and PL/SQL need to know the length of character strings when they are exchanged. This is problematic because there is no standard means of determining the length of RAW or STRING parameter types. You can use the LENGTH or VSIZE functions to determine the length of a formal parameter. It is important to note that LENGTH is passed into the external procedure by value when the mode is IN. It is passed by reference when using mode OUT. You should use VSIZE when dealing with binary strings.

- CHARSETID and CHARSETFORM are subject to globalization complexity if the extproc agent database is running in a different database. The calling database NLS_LANG and NLS_CHAR values are the expected values for the extproc agent. If this is not the case for the extproc agent, you need to use the OCI attribute names to set these for the program. The OCI attributes are OCI_ATTR_CHARSET_ID and OCI_ATTR_CHARSET_FORM. Both CHARSETID and CHARSETFORM are passed by value for IN mode and by reference for OUT mode.

The generalized format for creating a C library wrapper procedure is noted here:

```
CREATE [OR REPLACE] PROCEDURE name [parameter_list]
AS EXTERNAL
LIBRARY_NAME library_name
NAME "<external_library_name>"
AGENT IN [parameter_list]
WITH CONTEXT
PARAMETER [parameter_list];
```

PL/SQL	Native C	Oracle	Default
BINARY_INTEGER BOOLEAN PLS_INTEGER	[UNSIGNED] CHAR [UNSIGNED] SHORT [UNSIGNED] INT [UNSIGNED] LONG	SB1, SB2, SB4 UB1, UB2, UB4 SIZE_T	INT
NATURAL NATURALN POSITIVE POSITIVEN SIGNTYPE	[UNSIGNED] CHAR [UNSIGNED] SHORT [UNSIGNED] INT [UNSIGNED] LONG	SB1, SB2, SB4 UB1, UB2, UB4 SIZE_T	[UNSIGNED] INT
FLOAT REAL	FLOAT		FLOAT
DOUBLE PRECISION	DOUBLE		DOUBLE
CHAR CHARACTER LONG NCHAR NVARCHAR2 ROWID VARCHAR VARCHAR2		STRING OCISTRING	STRING
LONG RAW RAW		RAW OCIRAW	RAW
BFILE BLOB CLOB NCLOB		OCILOBLOCATOR	OCILOBLOCATOR
NUMBER DEC DECIMAL INT INTEGER NUMERIC SMALLINT		OCINUMBER	OCINUMBER
DATE		OCIDATE	OCIDATE
TIMESTAMP TIMESTAMP WITH TIME ZONE TIMESTAMP WITH LOCAL TIME ZONE		OCIDATETIME	OCIDATETIME
INTERVAL DAY TO SECOND INTERVAL YEAR TO MONTH		OCIINTERVAL	OCIINTERVAL
Composite Object Types: ADTs		dvoid	dvoid
Composite Object Types: Collections (VARRAYS, NESTED TABLES)		OCICOLL	OCICOLL

TABLE 13-4   *Mapping PL/SQL Datatypes to C*

It is important to note that the `external_library_name` is case sensitive when the operating system supports case sensitivity. Even while working on Microsoft Windows, you should always treat it as case sensitive. Good PL/SQL coding habits can make your life simpler when you change work environments.

When you define the parameter lists for a PL/SQL wrapper, positional order is not important. The PL/SQL wrapper relates them by name.

Objects present a unique case with the normally implicit `SELF`. In PL/SQL, you do not have to manage an object type's `SELF` member function, because it is implicitly managed. The problem is that the `SELF` reference is a parameter in the formal parameter list. The external C program requires the PL/SQL external procedure wrapper to define a complete formal parameter list. This means that it must formally define `SELF`. You pass an object to an external procedure by using the `WITH CONTEXT` clause when you define the object type. The following example illustrates defining an external object type:

```
CREATE OR REPLACE TYPE BODY object_library_sample AS
MEMBER FUNCTION get_tea_temperature
RETURN NUMBER
AS LANGUAGE C
NAME "tea_temp"
WITH CONTEXT
PARAMETERS
( CONTEXT
, SELF
, SELF INDICATOR STRUCT
, SELF TDO
, RETURN INDICATOR);
END;
/
```

Another rule applies to passing variables by reference to an external procedure. You must append the `BY REFERENCE` phrase to all variables passed by reference.

The `AGENT IN` clause allows run-time identification of the external agent program. This is an advanced feature. It is useful when you have more than one external agent running or configured. An example that would benefit from this type of PL/SQL wrapper is an environment with multiple external applications. Making the external agent a dynamic component gives you more flexibility. You can then use stored objects to make dynamic calls to different external application libraries.

You are now ready to create your PL/SQL external procedure wrapper. The sample program to build the PL/SQL wrapper follows:

```
-- This is found in create_library1.sql on the publisher's web site.
CREATE OR REPLACE PROCEDURE write_string
   (path       VARCHAR2
   ,message    VARCHAR2) AS EXTERNAL
LIBRARY library_write_string
NAME "writestr"
PARAMETERS
   (path       STRING
   ,message    STRING);
/
```

The PL/SQL external procedure wrapper publishes the external library. It creates a data dictionary entry for a library named `library_write_string`. You should note that it qualifies the name of the external procedure without the `*.so` suffix (or on Microsoft Windows platforms, a `*.dll`). The suffix is automatically postpended. If it were included in the definition of the NAME value, the `extproc` agent would look for `writestr1.so.so` and fail.

You have learned how to define and configure a PL/SQL wrapper. Previously, you learned how to do all network plumbing, library coding, and agent configuration. It is now time to see if it was done correctly.

If you are working in Unix, use the online file. However, if you are working in Microsoft Windows, change the first argument to the `write_string` procedure. It should change from `/tmp/file.txt` to `C:\TEMP\FILE.TXT`. You can now execute the external procedure by invoking the PL/SQL wrapper, as shown in the following code:

```
-- This is found in create_library1.sql on the publsiher's web site.
BEGIN
  write_string('/tmp/file.txt','Hello World!');
END;
/
```

When the procedure completes successfully, you can then open the file in the Unix /tmp or Microsoft Windows `C:\TEMP` directory. Rerunning the program will create a new file of the same name and rewrite the same string. If the file is in the `/tmp` or `C:\TEMP` directory, only the file's date stamp will appear to change.

There are some restrictions when working with external procedures:

- You should not use global variables because they are not thread safe.

- You should not use external static variables because they are not thread safe.

- You can use this feature only on platforms that support DLLs or shared libraries.

- You can use only programming languages callable from the C programming language.

- You must use objects when you want to pass cursor or record variables to an external procedure.

- You cannot use a DB_LINK in the LIBRARY clause of a PL/SQL wrapper declaration.

- You can pass a maximum of 128 parameters. If you have float or double data types, they count for two parameters.

You have completed everything required to configure and set up a C DLL or shared library. If everything worked, please accept our congratulations. However, if something failed, you can go straight to the troubleshooting section. In that section, you will troubleshoot the most common problems.

Alternatively, it is time to look at creating Java external procedures.

Working with a Java Shared Library

As discussed when you covered the `extproc` architecture, Oracle built an extensible architecture for external procedures. It is flexible enough to support any programming language that is callable by the C programming language.

Oracle directly supports Java as part of the database (except in the Oracle Express Edition). Java libraries do not use the `extproc` agent because they are natively part of the Oracle database. This simplifies much but does restrict some activities. Those restricted activities make the case for using the `extproc` agent and external C or C callable libraries.

Java has a few advantages over C:

- Java understands SQL types. It avoids the tedious data type mapping when using C.

- Java is loaded into the Oracle database. It avoids the file management issues and listener `ENV` parameter processes because it does not use the `extproc` agent.

- Java is natively thread safe. It does not require you to deal with the threading nuances, provided you avoid static variables.

- Java does not require management of memory addresses. (Memory addresses are called pointers in C/C++.)

NOTE
Java static variables are considered class-level variables, which means they are built at compile time, not run time. There can be only one copy of a class variable in a Java Virtual Machine (JVM), provided there is only one Java class loader. Within the context of the Oracle JVM there can be more than one Java class loader. Therefore, if you plan on using a Java class for an external procedure, avoid using static variables.

Java has a few disadvantages relative to C:

- Java uses the Java pool in the SGA for processing, whereas C external procedures use their own memory space. Effectively, C external programs lower the memory consumption of the SGA, while Java increases the load on the SGA.

- Java is not as fast as C because native Java byte code needs to be interpreted by the JVM.

- Java has restricted access to files. This protects the integrity of the database. The `DBMS_JAVA` package provides a means to define read and write access for Java library programs.

- PL/SQL wrapper functions that use Java libraries impose a limit on method definitions. All Java class methods accessed by PL/SQL wrapper functions must be static. Therefore, Java libraries that support PL/SQL wrapper functions are *not* thread safe.

You will now define a simple Java library.

Defining the Java Library

Java is generally an interpreted language, as opposed to a compiled language like C. C compilation results in a file of object code, which consists of machine code or binary instructions. Java compilation results in a Java byte stream. The JVM interprets the byte stream and executes the run-time object code. JVMs are platform specific, while byte streams are generic. This is why Java class files are portable across platforms.

Compiling a Java program does several things. It preprocesses the source code by breaking it down into tokens while validating syntax. Then, it compiles the program into Java byte code and writes a Java `.class` file. Java `.class` files are dependent at run time on any included libraries.

The following program includes a standard I/O library. This will enable the database to access a physical file external to the instance. You do not define permission to Java file access in the `initSID.ora` parameter file. You must use the `DBMS_JAVA` package to grant permission from the `SYSTEM` account. The grant has already been done if you ran the online `create_user.sql` script for this chapter. The following shows the command required to grant read-only access to the `/tmp/file.txt` file:

```
-- This is found in create_user.sql on the publisher's web site.
-- Grant Java permissions to file IO against a file.
DBMS_JAVA.GRANT_PERMISSION('PLSQL'
                          ,'SYS:java.io.FilePermission'
                          ,'/tmp/file.txt'
                          ,'read');
```

NOTE
This syntax is provided only for Linux or Unix. This command fails when run in a Windows environment. If you're running Windows, change the third actual parameter to the correct local directory.

Much as when you use C external procedures, you first need to define the Java library. At a minimum, you will need to configure your Java environment. If you are using a Java IDE, it is assumed you know how to compile Java source code into class files. Only the command-line steps are covered here.

Unlike the example in Chapter 10, the Java program does not interact with the database through SQL. That means you do not need to include the class files to support SQL. Therefore, you do not need to set your `$CLASSPATH`. For reference, the Oracle SQL class files are found in `$ORACLE_HOME/jdbc/lib/ojdbc5.jar`.

Oracle 11*g* Security Alert

Java is disallowed to write to the operating system by default. This is set in the Oracle JVM properties. When you grant permissions to write files, you create a security risk. The contents of the database are much harder to hack than the server file system. When you write data to or from files, those directories pose a security risk.

The superuser account owns the privileges to open a directory for Java programs. Unfortunately, there is no equivalent mechanism for external procedures written in languages like C, C++, or C#. Any schema that can create libraries enjoys the liberty of reading content from or writing content to any directories in the DBA group. You should advise your System Administrator to take extra precautions with any directory open to database writes.

The same security rules apply to any directory configured in your `spfile<sid>.ora` to support the `UTL_FILE` package. The `spfile<sid>.ora` file contains the initialization parameters for the database. The `UTL_FILE` package also lets you read and write data between the Oracle 11*g* Database and the file system.

Assuming you have access to the Java SDK, you need to download the following program and compile it to Java byte code:

```
-- This is found in ReadFile1.java on the publisher's web site.
// Class imports.
import java.io.*;

// Class definition.
public class ReadFile1
{
  // Convert the string to a file resource and call private method.
  public static String readString(String s){
    return readFileString(new File(s)); }

  // Read an external file.
  private static String readFileString(File file) {
    // Define control variables.
    int c;
    String s = new String();
    FileReader inFile;

    try {
      inFile = new FileReader(file);

      while ((c = inFile.read()) != -1) {
        s += (char) c; }
    }
    catch (IOException e) {
      return e.getMessage(); }

    return s; }

  // Testing method.
  public static void main(String[] args) {
    String file = new String("/tmp/file.txt");
    System.out.println(ReadFile1.readString(file)); }
}
```

The program takes a canonical filename as a string and reads a file. The program can read from any directory where it has owner or group file system privileges. The static `main()` method is only provided for external testing and should be removed before deploying code in the database.

Once you have downloaded the file and compiled it, you need to load it into the database. You can do so with the Oracle `loadjava` utility, which is covered in Chapter 15. The following `loadjava` command will make the Java class available in the PLSQL schema:

```
$ loadjava -r -f -o -user plsql/plsql ReadFile1.class
```

You have now completed the library Java library definition. You will now define and call the PL/SQL library wrapper to the Java library.

Defining and Calling the PL/SQL Library Wrapper

Writing the PL/SQL library wrapper to a Java module is called *publishing* the Java library. Since you used a C external procedure, you will define a Java library function. There are a couple reasons for doing so. First, Java libraries must use static methods when they are published as PL/SQL functions. Second, it gives you an opportunity to see how arguments for Java libraries are limited.

Arrays support a pass by reference semantic in Java. A pass by reference semantic means that the memory address is passed by the PL/SQL run-time engine to the Java library. After the Java library updates the array and completes processing, it will return control to the PL/SQL run-time engine. PL/SQL knows the address and can access any changed data values. If you want to move data into and out of a Java library, you must do one of two things:

- You define a function and manage the return type of the function. The downside to a function is that it is not thread safe because you must use static method definitions.

- You define a procedure and use an array in OUT mode. The array option requires including the ojdbc5.jar file and using an oracle.sql.ARRAY[] data type. oracle.sql.ARRAY[] is a nested table collection with a numeric index value.

Java libraries and PL/SQL have a mapping relationship like C. Chapter 15 contains a table that maps PL/SQL and Java datatypes.

Most of the types are straightforward. The LONG and LONG RAW data types are limited to 32K. The oracle.sql.Datum is an abstract class. This means that it is dynamic and becomes whatever SQL type is passed to it.

You can publish your Java function by using the following wrapper:

```
-- This is found in create_javalib1.sql on the publisher's web site.
CREATE OR REPLACE FUNCTION read_string
  (file IN VARCHAR2)
  RETURN VARCHAR2 IS
  LANGUAGE JAVA
  NAME 'ReadFile.readString(java.lang.String) return String';
/
```

The PL/SQL Java library wrapper publishes the Java class. It is important to point out that you must define the formal parameter with the fully qualified package. If you attempt to use String and not java.lang.String, it will compile successfully but fail at run time. The following program can test success or failure:

```
-- This is found in call_javawrapper.sql on the publisher's web site.
SELECT   read_string('/tmp/file.txt')
FROM     dual;
```

It will return the following output from the /tmp/file.txt file if you modify the input formal parameter as described previously, that is, if you change the java.lang.String to String.

```
-- This is found in call_javawrapper.sql on the publisher's web site.
FROM     dual
           *
ERROR at line 2:
ORA-29531: no method readString in class ReadFile
```

You have now defined a Java library and published the Java class file. Next, you will take a look at troubleshooting the extproc agent and external procedures.

Troubleshooting the Shared Library

This is the section where you try to find out why something is not working. Hopefully, we have put most of the explanation in the chapter already. This section will cover some known errors and their fixes.

External procedures typically fail because of two issues. One is the configuration of the listener, shared library, or environment. That is why you went through all the components and how they fit together. Another is when the definition of the external program differs from the PL/SQL wrapper. This typically happens when data types are incorrectly mapped. Each class of problem is described in one of the two subsections that follow.

Configuration of the Listener or Environment

There are four general problems with network connectivity. They are noted here with the typical error messages and explanations.

Listener ENV Parameter Is Incorrect

As discussed in the `extproc` Oracle Net Services configuration, the following error will be raised when the `ENV` variable is incorrectly configured:

```
BEGIN
*
ERROR at line 1:
ORA-06520: PL/SQL: Error loading external library
ORA-06522: /u03/oracle/11g/11.1.0/lib/writestr1.so: cannot open shared object
file: No such file or directory
ORA-06512: at "PLSQL.WRITE_STRING", line 1
ORA-06512: at line 4
```

If you receive this error, you have experienced one of two types of failures. One is that the library is not in the directory you have designated, is named differently, or is case sensitive. Another is that you have made an error in configuring the `ENV` parameter in your `listener.ora` file.

File Path Problem

If the file path is not in the directory you have designated in the `ENV` value, correcting the file path should resolve the problem. If the file path is missing a component or is not consistent in case with the PL/SQL wrapper `NAME` parameter value or `EXTPROC_DLLS` value, synchronizing all three entries will fix it.

If the file path is in the directory and all three locations mentioned are matched in spelling and case, the problem is in the listener `ENV` parameter. Two areas can cause the problem: a bad `EXTPROC_DLLS` or a bad `$LD_LIBRARY_PATH` entry. There is a third potential error: the `$APL_ENV_FILE` value. This third error is typically a problem only when you have positioned the `extproc` agent in another Oracle home.

EXTPROC_DLLS Value Problem

You need to check the `ENV` variable in `CALLOUT_LISTENER`. The general rule is that you should have an entry for `EXTPROC_DLLS` and `LD_LIBRARY_PATH` in the `ENV` value. `EXTPROC_DLLS` should specify an equal sign, the word `ONLY`, a colon, and the shared libraries you want to use or a list of shared libraries separated by colons. Alternatively, you can choose to leave out the ONLY qualifier and provide a shared library or list of shared libraries separated by colons. If you leave the ONLY qualifier out, you have not restricted the IPC listener to only those libraries. It is recommended by Oracle that you use ONLY to narrow the privileges of the listener.

You also need to check whether the shared libraries have a fully qualified path statement, the filename, and the file extension. Likewise, the LD_LIBRARY_PATH should at a minimum specify the fully qualified path to the $ORACLE_HOME/lib directory. If your libraries require other libraries, you would use the LD_LIBRARY_PATH reference. When you have more than the one library in the LD_LIBRARY_PATH, you use a set of fully qualified path statements separated by colons.

If you would like to see this error, you can do the following:

1. Rename the shared library path in the PL/SQL wrapper. You would do this by rerunning the create_library1.sql script with an incorrect path statement.

2. Rerun the anonymous block PL/SQL call to the write_string procedure.

NOTE
If you run this test, do not forget to fix everything before you move on to the rest of the chapter.

The extproc Listener Is Incorrectly Configured or Not Running

As discussed in the extproc Oracle Net Services configuration, the following error will be raised when the extproc listener is not running or configured properly:

```
BEGIN
*
ERROR at line 1:
ORA-28576: lost RPC connection to external procedure agent
ORA-06512: at "PLSQL.WRITE_STRING", line 1
ORA-06512: at line 4
```

If you receive this error, the extproc listener is not running or the KEY parameters don't match in listener.ora and in tnsnames.ora files. You need to verify the setup of your listener.ora and tnsnames.ora files. The method is described in an earlier section of this chapter, "Defining extproc Oracle Net Services Configuration."

If you would like to see this error, you can do the following:

1. Shut down the CALLOUT_LISTENER.

2. Alter the KEY parameter value in the listener.ora file so that it no longer agrees with the tnsnames.ora file.

3. Start up the CALLOUT_LISTENER.

4. Rerun the anonymous-block PL/SQL call to the write_string procedure.

NOTE
If you run this test, do not forget to fix everything before you move on to the rest of the chapter.

There Is No Separate extproc Listener

As discussed in connection with the `extproc` Oracle Net Services configuration, the following error will be raised when three conditions are met:

- The correct environment is defined in the `extproc` listener.

- There is no separate `extproc` listener.

- The `extproc` agent is attempting to access the `DLL` or shared library in any directory other than `$ORACLE_HOME/bin` or `$ORACLE_HOME/lib`.

```
BEGIN
*
ERROR at line 1:
ORA-28595: Extproc agent : Invalid DLL Path
ORA-06522: h$n¶h$n¶
```

If you receive this error, these three conditions are met, since you have configured a perfect `ENV` variable in the standard single `LISTENER`. You now need to do one of two things. You can migrate the `extproc` agent listener to a separate listener. This is described in the section "Defining extproc Oracle Net Services Configuration." Alternatively, you can abandon the custom library directory and put the external libraries in the `$ORACLE_HOME/lib` directory.

If you would like to see this error, you can do the following:

1. Shut down the `CALLOUT_LISTENER`.
2. Using the online `listener1.ora` and `tnsnames2.ora` files, replace your `listener.ora` and `tnsnames.ora`, respectively. Do not forget to configure these files. You need to provide full path statements that match your system for them to work. Do not forget to make a copy of your modified files so that you can restore them.
3. Start up the `CALLOUT_LISTENER`.
4. Rerun the anonymous block PL/SQL call to the `write_string` procedure.

NOTE
If you run this test, do not forget to fix everything before you move on to the rest of the chapter.

PL/SQL Wrapper Defined NAME Value Is Incorrect

As discussed in the context of defining and calling the PL/SQL library wrapper, the following error will be raised when the `NAME` variable is incorrectly entered:

```
BEGIN
*
ERROR at line 1:
ORA-06521: PL/SQL: Error mapping function
ORA-06522: /u03/oracle/11g/11.1.0/lib/libagtsh.so: undefined symbol:
writestr1.so
ORA-06512: at "PLSQL.WRITE_STRING", line 1
ORA-06512: at line 3
```

If you receive this error, you need to check the NAME variable in the PL/SQL external library definition. The ORA-06522 error returns the filename of the object that cannot be found. It is unclear from the error if it was looking for the writestr1.so file in the $ORACLE_HOME/lib directory. Actually, it first looked in the designated custom library directory, then in the $ORACLE_HOME/lib directory. It could not find the writestr1.so.so file. Defining the NAME parameter of the external procedure with the filename and suffix can cause the problem. It should always be only the filename. The extproc agent implicitly appends .so or .DLL, depending on the platform.

NOTE
The extproc agent always searches the ENV defined directories first and the $ORACLE_HOME/lib last. Anytime the DLL or shared library name fails to match the value in the PL/SQL library definition, the ORA-06522 will return the $ORACLE_HOME/lib directory.

If you encounter this error and verify everything is working, shut down your extproc listener. Use the ps utility to find the running extprocPLSExtProc agent. If it is running after you shut down the listener, it should not be running. Use the kill utility to end it. Then restart your extproc listener. This eliminates the conflict with the preserved state in the extproc agent.

If you would like to see this error, you can do the following:

1. Rename the writestr.so shared library file.
2. Rerun the anonymous block PL/SQL call to the write_string procedure.

NOTE
If you run this test, do not forget to fix everything before you move on to the rest of the chapter.

The LD_LIBRARY_PATH should at a minimum specify the fully qualified path to the $ORACLE_HOME/lib directory. If you use the default location for your shared library, you can exclude it.

Configuration of the Shared Library or PL/SQL Library Wrapper

As you built the shared external library file and PL/SQL wrapper, you probably noticed that the formal parameter types mapped correctly. When they do not map correctly, you will lose the RPC connection and generate the following error message:

```
BEGIN
*
ERROR at line 1:
ORA-28576: lost RPC connection to external procedure agent
ORA-06512: at "PLSQL.WRITE_STRING", line 1
ORA-06512: at line 4
```

If you receive this error, the PL/SQL library is defining a mapping relationship that cannot be implicitly cast. This error is raised when you try to fork an external library with actual parameters that do not implicitly cast to the formal parameters of the library.

CAUTION
Implicit casting is a big nightmare. If you run into an implicit cast, you will not get an error during the call to the external procedure. You will likely get bad data from your program, and it may take a while to sort out why. Ensuring the external library types match the definition in the PL/SQL wrapper is a configuration management issue. You will save yourself countless hours of frustration and lost productivity if you create a check-in process that ensures external library definitions agree with PL/SQL library definitions.

If you would like to see this error, you can do the following:

1. Create a `writestr2.so` shared library from the online `writestr2.c` file.
2. Shut down the `CALLOUT_LISTENER`.
3. Use the online `listener3.ora` and `tnsnames3.ora` files to replace your `listener.ora` and `tnsnames.ora` files, respectively. Do not forget to configure these files. You need to provide full path statements that match your system for them to work.
4. Start up the `CALLOUT_LISTENER`.
5. Run the online `create_library2.sql` file to build the PL/SQL external procedure wrapper.
6. Rerun the anonymous block PL/SQL call to the `write_string` procedure.

NOTE
If you run this test, do not forget to fix everything before you move on to the rest of the chapter.

You have now completed the troubleshooting section. It is time to summarize what you have done in the chapter.

Summary

You have learned what external procedures do and how to configure the Oracle Net Services to support them. You have worked through defining and calling `extproc` and native Java libraries. Then, you learned how to troubleshoot the most common problems.

CHAPTER
14

Object Types

his chapter examines how you define, initialize, and use objects. It lays a foundation of what PL/SQL object types are and how object-oriented (OO) programming works by covering the following topics:

- Object basics
  - Declaring object types
  - Implementing object bodies
  - Getters and setters
  - Static member methods
  - Comparing objects
- Inheritance and polymorphism
  - Declaring subclasses
  - Implementing subclasses
  - Type evolution
- Implementing arrays of objects
  - Declaring object type collections
  - Implementing object body collections

As discussed, procedural programming functions perform well-defined tasks, and they hide the details of their operation. A collection of functions can be grouped together to perform a task that requires a set of functions. Organized groups of functions are *modules*; and the process of grouping them together is *modularization*. Modules are stored in PL/SQL packages.

Packages, like functions and procedures, hide their complexity through a predefined *application programming interface (API)*. While you can access global variables and constants that are declared in package specifications, you can't guard against their external change without implementing a Singleton pattern. The sidebar "Singleton Design Pattern" in Chapter 9 explains how you can control access with a Singleton pattern. Functions and procedures present different problems because they control all operations on their run-time variables.

Object-oriented (OO) programming solutions fix some of the shortcoming of functions, procedures, and packages because they maintain the operational state of their variables. Object types define how to store data and define API operations, also known as member functions or procedures. Operations are generally described as methods in OO programming languages, but they are implemented as class member functions or procedures in PL/SQL.

Exploring where OO programming started helps explain why maintaining object state is important. The idea for OO programming comes from the Simula language developed in Norway in the 1960s. The concept of an object evolved from the idea that simulated events pass through many small software factories, known as "finite-state" or "state" machines. State machines are miniature applications that simulate real-world events.

The object that moves through the series of state machines is like a software equivalent to a ball in a physical pinball machine. The software "ball" isn't really moving in response to mechanical devices but in response to state machines that simulate bumpers and other physical objects. The velocity, spin, and direction of the software ball are its internal state, which must be known and tracked to determine where it will strike and at what speed and spin. These factors determine how the next bumper, or state machine, will impact the software ball.

The possible characteristics and behaviors of the software ball are its attributes and operations. Since each ball starts with the same characteristics and behaviors, you can define a single piece of code to contain these attributes. The single piece of code is defined as an object type, or blueprint. Each creation of a run-time unit of this code is an instantiation, or creation of an object.

Objects are also state machines. They are defined by variables that have known and unknown values; and these variables enable or constrain the operations of real-time instances. Object type instances are objects, though realistically this formalism seems lost more often than not. Object types and objects are also known as classes in many OO programming languages. This book uses *object types to describe declarations of objects and object bodies to describe run-time instances of object types*; and interchangeably *classes to describe declarations of objects and instances of classes to describe run-time instances of object types.*

Like PL/SQL package specifications and bodies, an *object type* mirrors the behavior of a package specification. Also, an *object body* implements the object type just as a package body implements a package specification.

Inside of these object types and instances of objects you have hidden data and operations. The process of hiding data storage and operations is described by two words in OO programming. The first is *encapsulation*—the process of hiding the operational details; and the second is *abstraction*—the process of using generalization to mask task complexity. The internal aspects of object types are wrapped, as a birthday present is wrapped by colorful paper. The wrappers access the hidden components through published operations, which is similar to the package architecture described in Chapter 9.

These hidden operations and data plus their wrapper operations require OO programmers to take some time to work out what should be an object and then to define the object type. This analysis and design process is called object-oriented analysis and design (OOAD). OOAD evolved from concepts in systems engineering and business process modeling. It has gone through several variations from the 1960s, including symbolic representation models like Booch and object-modeling technique (OMT). These models were merged into the Unified Modeling Language (UML) in the 1990s.

The current method for visually representing object types is generally done in UML. Object types are represented by a rectangle divided into three rectangular sections. The topmost section contains the object type name. The middle section contains the list of attributes, which are variables used in the object type. The bottom section contains the list of methods that describes the API to the object type or object. Figure 14-1 contains a sample UML diagram describing the `MyClass` object type.

OO programming has two types of API interfaces in object types. One is known as *static,* and the other is known as *instance.* Static methods allow you to access object type variables and methods without creating an instance of a class. Static variables *aren't* available in PL/SQL. You can implement static methods like package functions and procedures.

Instance methods let you access object variables and methods of an instance of a class. They *are not static,* and they are available only after you create an instance of an object type. Then, they are capable of managing class events.

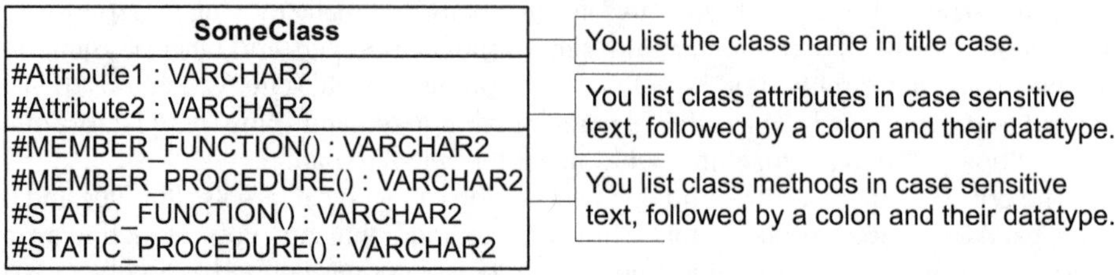

SomeClass
#Attribute1 : VARCHAR2
#Attribute2 : VARCHAR2
#MEMBER_FUNCTION() : VARCHAR2
#MEMBER_PROCEDURE() : VARCHAR2
#STATIC_FUNCTION() : VARCHAR2
#STATIC_PROCEDURE() : VARCHAR2

You list the class name in title case.

You list class attributes in case sensitive text, followed by a colon and their datatype.

You list class methods in case sensitive text, followed by a colon and their datatype.

FIGURE 14-1   *UML class diagram*

The static area of objects is generally limited to variables and functions that are common features across all class instances. PL/SQL does not support static class variables. It only supports static class functions and procedures. You can use static functions to return a copy of an instantiated class, which implements the object-oriented programming concrete builder pattern. Likewise, you can use static member functions or procedures to return what would otherwise be an instance variable. The section "Static Member Methods" later in this chapter contains an example returning an instance as a return type. That example shows you how to implement a factory design pattern in PL/SQL.

Oracle 11*g*, like predecessors since Oracle 9*i*, lets you create object types and bodies as SQL datatypes. You can use these object types as SQL datatype in four situations. You can use them as a column datatype when you define a table. They can also serve as the datatype of an object attribute when you declare an object type. You can also use them as a formal parameter datatype in the signature of a function or procedure, and you can use them as a return type for a function.

Oracle 11*g* qualifies objects as either persistent or transient objects. The qualification is made by assessing the lifetime of the objects.

Persistent objects are further qualified by dividing them into standalone and embedded objects. Standalone objects are stored in a database table and have a unique object identifier. Embedded objects *are not stored* in a database table but are embedded in another Oracle structure, like another object type. You don't have an object identifier for embedded objects, which makes using them through the OCI difficult. You can find more about persistent objects in the *Oracle Database Object-Relational Developer's Guide.*

Transient objects are instances of objects that aren't stored in the database. They have a lifetime limited to the duration of their use in a PL/SQL block. These are the primary type of objects you'll learn about in this chapter.

You will now learn how to define and implement objects in PL/SQL. While the sections are written independently, they are positioned to be read sequentially.

Objects Basics

The same naming requirements as those used with other objects in the database apply to objects. Object type names in PL/SQL must start with an alphabetical character and consist of only alphabetical characters, numbers, or underscores. *Object names share the same name space as all other objects except database triggers.*

Scope for object types is the same as for other standalone functions or procedures, and package functions and procedures. It is also limited to the defining schema. You must grant execute on an object type if you want to enable another scheme to use it.

Classes, unlike functions, cannot have return types. Class instantiation returns a copy or instance of a class. While object construction generally occurs as the source operand on the right side of an assignment operator, you can dynamically construct an object instance as an actual parameter to a function, or as a member of a collection. The existence of object instances is limited to the duration of the call, or its membership as a component of a collection.

You will find that objects are similar to those in many other languages but different enough to review the object operators. Table 3-1 provides you with a list of PL/SQL delimiters that also support example programs in this chapter.

Having met the general concepts, you will now work through the specifics of implementing *transient* object types in PL/SQL. You will begin by learning how to declare, implement, and instantiate objects. Then, you'll examine good OO programming techniques, like getters, setters, static methods, and comparative class methods.

Declaring Objects

PL/SQL object types, like package specifications, have a prototype definition. You have a couple specialized functions—CONSTRUCTOR, MAP, and ORDER. You can implement one or more CONSTRUCTOR functions, but the signatures must follow the overloading rules qualified in the sidebar "Overloading" in Chapter 9. Constructor functions determine how you build instances of object types. Constructor functions return an instance of the object type, which is known in PL/SQL as SELF, not the Java *this*. Functions can also use PRAGMA instructions to restrict their behaviors. You implement the MAP or ORDER function for comparisons. Parameter lists for member or static functions and procedures follows the same rules as standalone functions and procedures, as qualified in Chapter 6.

Attributes *(instance variables)* and methods are listed in a single parameter list that applies to the object type. You can't declare object type variables as you can package variables. All attributes are instance-only variables, which means you can only access them after you construct an object instance.

You need to list elements in the following order: attributes, constructors, functions, procedures, and the MAP or ORDER function. If you try to put an attribute at the end of the list, you'll receive a PLS-00311 error. The error tells you that the declaration of the object type is malformed because you've got elements out of sequence.

The prototype for object types is

```
CREATE [OR REPLACE] OBJECT TYPE object_name
[AUTHID {DEFINER | CURRENT_USER}] IS OBJECT
( [instance_variables {sql_datatype | plsql_datatype}]
, [CONSTRUCTOR FUNCTION constructor_name
  [( parameter_list )] RETURN RESULT AS SELF
, [{MEMBER | STATIC} FUNCTION function_name
  [( parameter_list )] RETURN { sql_data_type | plsql_data_type }
, [{MEMBER | STATIC} PROCEDURE procedure_name
  [( parameter_list)]
,{[MAP FUNCTION map_name RETURN { CHAR | DATE | NUMBER | VARCHAR2 } |
  [ORDER FUNCTION order_name RETURN { sql_data_type | plsql_data_type }}])
[NOT] INSTANTIABLE [NOT] FINAL;
/
```

NOTE
The OR REPLACE *clause is very important because without it you must drop the object type before attempting to re-declare it.*

You can build an object type with the following statement:

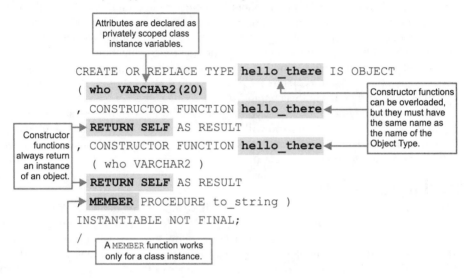

The `hello_there` basic class has two constructors and only the `to_string` instance method. Constructor function names must match the object type name, like Java classes. One constructor function creates an instance of the object without actual call parameters, while the other requires a mandatory parameter to create an instance of the object type. If you changed the mandatory parameter in the constructor function to an option parameter, you could trigger a `PLS-00307` exception at run time. This happens because the signature of a no-parameter constructor and one with a single optional parameter are equal at run time when you don't supply a value. A call made with a parameter would resolve and construct an object instance.

NOTE
The compiler raises a `PLS-00658` error when you forget to match your constructor function to the name of the object type.

The `MEMBER PROCEDURE` is only accessible once you've created an object instance. This object is instantiable *(capable of creating an object instance),* and not final *(capable of being extended or subtyped).* All object type variables are instance variables. As such, they are not available through static functions and procedures.

After you create an object type, you examine it by using the `DESCRIBE` command, like

```
SQL> describe HELLO_THERE
```

You get the following back to your console:

```
HELLO_THERE is NOT FINAL
 Name                                      Null?    Type
 ----------------------------------------- -------- -------------------
 WHO                                                VARCHAR2(20)
 METHOD
 ------
 FINAL CONSTRUCTOR FUNCTION HELLO_THERE RETURNS SELF AS RESULT
```

```
METHOD
------
FINAL CONSTRUCTOR FUNCTION HELLO_THERE RETURNS SELF AS RESULT
Argument Name                     Type                    In/Out Default?
--------------------------------- ----------------------- ------ --------
WHO                               VARCHAR2                IN
MEMBER PROCEDURE TO_STRING
```

The output is different from what you get describing a table, view, function, procedure, or package. You get a list of all instance variables, class constructor functions, and member functions and procedures.

The next section shows you how to implement this declaration. You'll also see how to construct an instance and use it in a PL/SQL block.

Implementing Object Bodies

PL/SQL object bodies, like package bodies, must implement their declarations exactly. This means you must provide an implementation for everything you have in the object type declaration. Unlike when defining package bodies, you can't add private methods known *only* to the object body. Nor can you add the equivalent of package-level variables inside an object body implementation. The only attributes, functions, and procedures in object bodies are those declared in the object type.

NOTE
Unlike some OO programming languages, Oracle 11g object types don't support inner classes.

Inside functions and procedures, you can define named functions and procedures in the declaration block, and anonymous-block programs in the execution block. You address the attributes of object types by prefacing them with SELF, a component selector *(that period again),* and the attribute name.

The following is the prototype for implementing an object body:

```
CREATE [OR REPLACE] OBJECT TYPE object_name
[AUTHID {DEFINER | CURRENT_USER}] IS
( [CONSTRUCTOR FUNCTION constructor_name
  [( parameter_list )] RETURN RESULT AS SELF IS
    BEGIN
      execution_statements;
    END [constructor_name];
  [{MEMBER | STATIC} FUNCTION function_name
  [( parameter_list )] RETURN { sql_data_type | plsql_data_type } IS
    BEGIN
      execution_statements;
    END [function_name];
  [{MEMBER | STATIC} PROCEDURE procedure_name IS
  [( parameter_list)]
    BEGIN
      execution_statements;
    END [procedure_name];
  {[MAP FUNCTION map_name RETURN { CHAR | DATE | NUMBER | VARCHAR2 } IS
    BEGIN
      execution_statements;
```

```
       END [procedure_name]; |
   [ORDER FUNCTION order_name RETURN { sql_data_type | plsql_data_type } IS
     BEGIN
       execution_statements;
     END [procedure_name];}])
 END [object_name];
 /
```

An object body is very close to a package body implementation, except it excludes local variables and components. As mentioned earlier, the MAP and ORDER functions are specialized units, and you can only implement whichever one was declared in the object type.

TIP
Exclude the object name at the end of the object body because it sometimes suppresses meaningful errors and causes compilation failure.

There are a few subtle changes between traditional functions and procedures and object bodies. The largest is the idea of an object instance. An object instance is represented inside the object body as SELF. SELF is a departure from the traditional *this* keyword from Java and other OO programming languages. Object instance attributes are elements of SELF, just as field values are elements of a record structure. The same syntax rules apply for assigning and retrieving values, as shown in the hello_there object body.

You can find the create_helloworld_object.sql script on the publisher's site. It contains the object type and body, plus the testing program units.

The following implements the hello_there object body:

```
    CREATE OR REPLACE TYPE BODY hello_there IS
      CONSTRUCTOR FUNCTION hello_there  -- Default constructor.
      RETURN SELF AS RESULT IS
        hello HELLO_THERE := hello_there('Generic Object');
      BEGIN
        self := hello;
        RETURN;
      END hello_there;
      CONSTRUCTOR FUNCTION hello_there  -- Overriding constructor.
      (who VARCHAR2) RETURN SELF AS RESULT IS
      BEGIN
        self.who := who;
        RETURN;
      END hello_there;
      MEMBER PROCEDURE to_string IS
      BEGIN
        dbms_output.put_line('Hello '||self.who||'.');
      END to_string;
    END hello_there;
    /
```

Construct a class instance by calling the overriding constructor with an actual parameter.

Assign the local class instance to the internal SELF instance.

Assign the actual parameter to the class instance variable.

Read the class instance variable.

Object types should generally provide a default constructor. Default constructors typically have no formal parameters. In objects where the formal parameters are required to make instances useful, the default constructor calls the constructor with default parameters. This is done in an object body by four steps. First, you create a local variable of the object type. Second, you instantiate the local *(internal)* class with default actual parameters. Third, you assign the transient local object to the instance itself. Fourth, you return a handle to the current object. The RETURN statement works differently in an object than a standalone function. It *never* takes an argument because it is returning a copy of the object type.

The behavior of managing a default constructor can be tricky, but they simplify the construction of object instances. The default constructor hides *(from the eyes of the consuming developer)* the details of creating an object instance. The overriding constructor provides the values to build an object instance but hides the details of how to do so.

The to_string procedure lets you see the contents of the constructed class. You can test the class by calling the default constructor, as shown

```
SET SERVEROUTPUT ON SIZE 1000000
DECLARE
  hello HELLO_THERE := hello_there;  -- hello_there() works too!
BEGIN
  hello.to_string();
END;
/
```

This anonymous block constructs an instance of the object by using the default constructor. You can construct an instance with or without empty parentheses, like function and procedure calls in PL/SQL blocks. You call the member procedure just as you would a package procedure.

The call to the instance of hello_there.to_string() prints

```
Hello Generic Object.
```

The next anonymous block calls the overriding constructor. This provides a non-default parameter to the instance. The code is

```
DECLARE
  hello HELLO_THERE := hello_there('Overriding Object');
BEGIN
  hello.to_string();
END;
/
```

It prints

```
Hello Overriding Object.
```

This section has shown you how to implement object bodies. You have also learned how to construct an object instance, and how to distinguish between a default constructor and an overriding constructor.

Getters and Setters

Getters and *setters* are common OO programming terms indicating that you get or set a class instance variable. In PL/SQL you need to write individual get_variable_name() or set_variable_name() functions for each class attribute.

The following extends the previous `hello_there` object type by adding a `get_who()` member function and `set_who()` member procedure. There's no magic in choosing a function for the *getter* because you want to take something out of the object instance. Functions return expressions, as you'll find in Chapter 6. The *setter* can be either a function or a procedure, but more often than not it's a procedure. Setter method calls don't generally return a value. In most OO programming languages, you implement setters as functions with a void return type.

The modified `hello_there` object type is

```
CREATE OR REPLACE TYPE hello_there IS OBJECT
( who VARCHAR2(20)
, CONSTRUCTOR FUNCTION hello_there
  RETURN SELF AS RESULT
, CONSTRUCTOR FUNCTION hello_there
  ( who VARCHAR2 )
  RETURN SELF AS RESULT
, MEMBER FUNCTION get_who RETURN VARCHAR2
, MEMBER PROCEDURE set_who
, MEMBER PROCEDURE to_string )
INSTANTIABLE NOT FINAL;
/
```

The implementation of these two member methods is straightforward. The *setter* passes a new value for *who,* while the *getter* retrieves the current value.

The `hello_there` object body is

```
CREATE OR REPLACE TYPE BODY hello_there IS
  CONSTRUCTOR FUNCTION hello_there RETURN SELF AS RESULT IS
    hello HELLO_THERE := hello_there('Generic Object');
  BEGIN
    self := hello;
    RETURN;
  END hello_there;
  CONSTRUCTOR FUNCTION hello_there (who VARCHAR2) RETURN SELF AS RESULT IS
  BEGIN
    self.who := who;
    RETURN;
  END hello_there;
  MEMBER FUNCTION get_who RETURN VARCHAR2 IS
  BEGIN
    RETURN self.who;
  END get_who;
  MEMBER PROCEDURE set_who (who VARCHAR2) IS
  BEGIN
    self.who := who;
  END set_who;
  MEMBER PROCEDURE to_string IS
  BEGIN
    dbms_output.put_line('Hello '||self.who||'.');
  END to_string;
```

```
END;
/
```

The *setter* assigns a new value from the actual parameter, and the *getter* grabs the current class instance value. The following anonymous block demonstrates calling these new member methods:

```
DECLARE
  hello HELLO_THERE := hello_there('Overriding Object');
BEGIN
  hello.to_string();
  hello.set_who('Newbie Object');
  dbms_output.put_line(hello.get_who);
  hello.to_string();
END;
/
```

The anonymous block successfully resets and gets the values as shown:

```
Hello Overriding Object.
Newbie Object.
Hello Newbie Object.
```

This section has shown you how to implement and use getters and setters.

Static Member Methods

The static functions and procedures let you use an object type like a standard package. Static methods can create instances of their object type, but they are limited to working with instances of the object like external PL/SQL blocks.

The nice thing about static methods is that they can provide developers with a standard look and feel of procedural programming. You can write static methods to perform standard programming tasks, or to return an instance of their class. Writing a function that returns a class instance can simplify how you use objects because you don't have to worry about long parameter lists in the constructors.

The following declares an object type that includes a static function:

```
-- This is found in create_item_object.sql on the publisher's web site.
CREATE OR REPLACE TYPE item_object IS OBJECT
( item_title    VARCHAR2(60)
, item_subtitle VARCHAR2(60)
, CONSTRUCTOR FUNCTION item_object
  RETURN SELF AS RESULT
, CONSTRUCTOR FUNCTION item_object
  (item_title VARCHAR2, item_subtitle VARCHAR2) RETURN SELF AS RESULT
, STATIC FUNCTION get_item_object (item_id NUMBER) RETURN ITEM_OBJECT
, MEMBER FUNCTION to_string RETURN VARCHAR2 )
INSTANTIABLE NOT FINAL;
/
```

The static function `get_item_object` take one parameter. The parameter doesn't map to the parameter lists in the constructors, but the static function returns an instance of the `item_object`. This means that the static function must create an instance of the object type as a local variable before it can return one to a calling program.

External programs create an instance of the object type before they can act on it. The static `get_item_object` function lets you get a initialize an object instance without calling the constructor. In fact, you can assign the result from the `get_item_object` to a variable declared as the same object type. The result is an active transient object instance.

The following implements the object body of `item_object` class:

```
-- This is found in create_item_object.sql on the publisher's web site.
CREATE OR REPLACE TYPE BODY item_object IS
  CONSTRUCTOR FUNCTION item_object RETURN SELF AS RESULT IS
    item ITEM_OBJECT := item_object('Generic Title','Generic Subtitle');
  BEGIN
    self := item;
    RETURN;
  END item_object;
  CONSTRUCTOR FUNCTION item_object
  (item_title VARCHAR2, item_subtitle VARCHAR2)
  RETURN SELF AS RESULT IS
  BEGIN
    self.item_title := item_title;
    self.item_subtitle := item_subtitle;
    RETURN;
  END item_object;
  STATIC FUNCTION get_item_object (item_id NUMBER) RETURN ITEM_OBJECT IS
    item ITEM_OBJECT;
    CURSOR c (item_id_in NUMBER) IS
      SELECT item_title, item_subtitle FROM item WHERE item_id = item_id_in;
  BEGIN
    FOR i IN c (item_id) LOOP
      item := item_object(i.item_title,i.item_subtitle);
    END LOOP;
    RETURN item;
  END get_item_object;
  MEMBER FUNCTION to_string RETURN VARCHAR2 IS
  BEGIN
    RETURN '['||self.item_title||']['||self.item_subtitle||']';
  END to_string;
END;
/
```

The `get_item_object` static function uses the actual parameter and local cursor to find a row in the `item` table. The static function uses the values from the cursor to construct an instance of the object type. It then returns the local instance variable as its actual return value.

You can test the static method by using the following anonymous-block program:

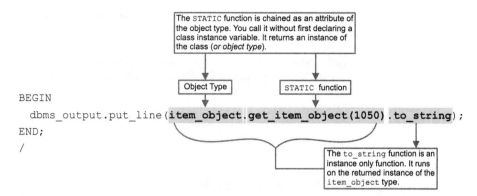

```
BEGIN
  dbms_output.put_line(item_object.get_item_object(1050).to_string);
END;
/
```

The call to the object involves a couple component selectors. Oracle refers to this process of connecting multiple pieces together with periods as attribute chaining. You call the static `get_item_object` function by referencing the schema-level `item_object` object type. The result of the static function call is a valid instance of the object type. You can then add a period and a call to the `to_string` instance function.

NOTE
The `to_string` function call works with or without parentheses, like ordinary standalone and package functions.

It prints

 `[Pirates of the Caribbean][The Curse of the Black Pearl]`

This section has shown you how to declare and implement a static function. You can use this approach to accomplish building other static methods that let you leverage object types in your database.

Comparing Objects

Comparing object instances is very important in OO programming. In the Java programming language, an *equals* method is provided for the root node of its single object hierarchy. Good programming practice dictates that you should override it when you implement your own classes that extend the behavior of the Object class.

Oracle object types don't have a root node that you extend in the same way as Java. You have a master template that you implement through SQL DDL syntax. Oracle does provide two predefined member functions—MAP and ORDER. You can implement only one MAP or ORDER function in any object type. If you attempt to define both, the object type specification raises a PLS-00154 error during compilation. The error states that "An object type may have only 1 MAP or 1 ORDER method." The MAP member function doesn't take a formal parameter and can only return a scalar type of CHAR, DATE, NUMBER, and VARCHAR2.

TIP
Subclasses can't override the MAP or ORDER functions found in a parent class.

The benefit of a MAP member function is limited. It limits you to testing for equality based on a single number that identifies a class instance. The ORDER member function is more flexible because it can take parameters of any SQL datatype. However, the ORDER member function only returns a NUMBER datatype. The parameter is the advantage, and the return type really isn't a disadvantage. You may recall that many built-in functions return a number so that you can use them in SQL and PL/SQL. If the ORDER member function returned a BOOLEAN datatype, it would only let you compare objects in PL/SQL.

The next two subsections demonstrate comparing objects with MAP and ORDER member functions. You'll have to choose what works best for you, but the ORDER member function is recommended as the better option.

Comparing with the MAP Member Function

As discussed, the MAP member function validates against a scalar type of CHAR, DATE, NUMBER, and VARCHAR2 datatype. The MAP member function works best when a single attribute value of a class instance determines whether it is equal to or greater than another object instance. When more than one attribute, or a relationship of attributes, determines ordering, the MAP member function fails to allow you to sort objects easily.

You can accomplish a barebones example by declaring only constructor and map member functions. The following declares the map_comparison object type:

```
-- This is found in the map_comparison.sql on the publisher's web site.
CREATE OR REPLACE TYPE map_comp IS OBJECT
( who VARCHAR2(20)
, CONSTRUCTOR FUNCTION map_comp (who VARCHAR2) RETURN SELF AS RESULT
, MAP MEMBER FUNCTION equals RETURN VARCHAR2 )
INSTANTIABLE NOT FINAL;
/
```

MAP is a keyword designating the function for sorting operations. The implementation of the map_comp object type is

```
-- This is found in the map_comparison.sql on the publisher's web site.
CREATE OR REPLACE TYPE BODY map_comp IS
  CONSTRUCTOR FUNCTION map_comp (who VARCHAR2) RETURN SELF AS RESULT IS
  BEGIN
    self.who := who;
    RETURN;
  END map_comp;
  MAP MEMBER FUNCTION equals RETURN VARCHAR2 IS
  BEGIN
    RETURN self.who;
  END equals;
END;
/
```

The test program creates a collection of object types in mixed alphabetical order and then runs the items through a bubble sort operation to put them in ascending order. The code follows:

```
-- This is found in the map_comparison.sql on the publisher's web site.
DECLARE
  -- Declare a collection of an object type.
  TYPE object_list IS TABLE OF MAP_COMP;
  -- Initialize four objects in mixed alphabetical order.
  object1 MAP_COMP := map_comp('Ron Weasley');
  object2 MAP_COMP := map_comp('Harry Potter');
  object3 MAP_COMP := map_comp('Luna Lovegood');
  object4 MAP_COMP := map_comp('Hermione Granger');
  -- Define a collection of the object type.
  objects OBJECT_LIST := object_list(object1, object2, object3, object4);
  -- Swaps A and B.
  PROCEDURE swap (a IN OUT MAP_COMP, b IN OUT MAP_COMP) IS
    c MAP_COMP;
  BEGIN
    c := b;
    b := a;
    a := c;
  END swap;
BEGIN
  -- A bubble sort.
  FOR i IN 1..objects.COUNT LOOP
    FOR j IN 1..objects.COUNT LOOP
      IF objects(i).equals = LEAST(objects(i).equals,objects(j).equals) THEN
        swap(objects(i),objects(j));
      END IF;
    END LOOP;
  END LOOP;
  -- Print reordered objects.
  FOR i IN 1..objects.COUNT LOOP
    dbms_output.put_line(objects(i).equals);
  END LOOP;
END;
/
```

It produces the following output:

```
Harry Potter
Hermione Granger
Luna Lovegood
Ron Weasley
```

The LEAST function determines whether the outer loop element MAP member function result is less than the inner loop element. When it is least, it swaps the values until the least of the entire set is the first element in the collection, and the rest are in ascending order. While bubble sorts are inefficient, they're nice tools for demonstrating concepts.

This section has demonstrated how you can sort by using the MAP member function. As you can see, the logic for the comparison lies largely outside of the object type. This means the sorting isn't hidden and the logic not encapsulated.

Trick or Treat'n with Persistent Object Types

While the chapter is about transient objects in the scope of your PL/SQL programs, it seems only fair to not leave you in a lurch. You could find some interesting trick or treat behavior when you try *reading objects* from the database.

The following demonstrates a quick example that helps you understand how to read your stored objects from the database. The first step is to create a `persistent_object` table and `persistent_object_s1` sequence as follows:

```
CREATE TABLE persistent_object
( persistent_object_id NUMBER
, mapping_object       MAP_COMP );
CREATE SEQUENCE persistent_object_s1;
```

Second, you'll insert the nine companions in the Fellowship of the Ring. The syntax is the same for each but you'll need to switch the names in the constructor:

```
INSERT INTO persistent_object
VALUES (persistent_object_s1.nextval,map_comp('Frodo Baggins'));
INSERT INTO persistent_object
VALUES (persistent_object_s1.nextval,map_comp('Bilbo Baggins'));
```

You can select these natively, in which case you'll see return values like

```
MAPPING_OBJECT(WHO)
-------------------------
MAP_COMP('Frodo Baggins')
MAP_COMP('Bilbo Baggins')
```

This type of query doesn't let you apply instance methods. You might start to think that these object types have little use. The *trick* is the `TREAT` function. The `TREAT` function takes a column return and *treats* it as the *object type* you designate.

The column formatting ensures it displays well for you. The following query allows you to query the column values as object instances, and it lets you sort them with their own equals function:

```
COLUMN primary_key FORMAT 9999999 HEADING "Primary|Key ID"
COLUMN fellowship  FORMAT A30      HEADING "Fellowship Member"
SELECT  persistent_object_id AS primary_key
,       TREAT(mapping_object AS map_comp).equals() AS fellowship
FROM    persistent_object
WHERE   mapping_object IS OF (map_comp)
ORDER BY 2;
```

This query sorts the object through the `MAP` function and returns:

```
Primary
  Key ID Fellowship Member
-------- -------------------
       2 Bilbo Baggins
       1 Frodo Baggins
```

The `TREAT` function works with object types or subclasses of object types, as explained in the section "Inheritance and Polymorphism" later in this chapter.

Comparing with the ORDER Member Function

The ORDER member function allows you to pass an object instance into another object and compare whether they're equal. You can also build it to judge whether one object instance is greater or smaller than another. While the MAP member function works best with single-attribute class instances, the ORDER member function supports internal validation when more than one attribute indexes an object instance.

You can accomplish a barebones example by declaring two attributes, a constructor and an ORDER member function. The MAP member function requires that you implement the matching code externally from the object type. ORDER member functions require that you resolve whether or not to sort into a single number.

You can find the order_comparison.sql script on the publisher's site. It contains the object type and body, plus the testing program units.

The following declares the order_comp object type:

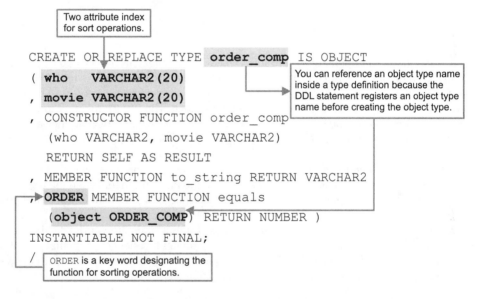

The order_comp function takes a parameter of its own object type. This mimics the equivalent behavior in Java for the *equals* method. The idea is to pass an object instance inside another of the same type because the object type should contain the validation of whether two instances are equal or not. A to_string function is also declared, which will let you examine the contents of object instances.

The following implements the object body:

```
-- This is found in order_comparison.sql on the publisher's web site.
CREATE OR REPLACE TYPE BODY order_comp IS
  CONSTRUCTOR FUNCTION order_comp
  (who VARCHAR2, movie VARCHAR2) RETURN SELF AS RESULT IS
  BEGIN
    self.who := who;
    self.movie := movie;
    RETURN;
  END order_comp;
```

```
MEMBER FUNCTION to_string RETURN VARCHAR2 IS
BEGIN
  RETURN '['||self.movie||']['||self.who||']';
END to_string;
ORDER MEMBER FUNCTION equals (object order_comp) RETURN NUMBER IS
BEGIN
  -- The primary sort.
  IF self.movie < object.movie THEN
    RETURN 1;
  -- The secondary sort.
  ELSIF self.movie = object.movie AND self.who < object.who THEN
    RETURN 1;
  ELSE
    RETURN 0;
  END IF;
END equals;
END;
/
```

The primary sort operation determines if the current object instance's `movie` attribute is less than the value of the external instance. The function returns 1 when that's true. The secondary sort operation runs only when the first attributes match. It determines if the current object instance's `who` attribute is less than the external instance. The `ORDER` member function also returns 1 when the secondary sort finds the *combination* of values less than the values of the external object instance. All other value comparisons are rejected, and the `ORDER` member function returns 0.

The `equals` function returns 1 as the true outcome, which means you should sort the instance passed as an actual parameter before the base instance. When the `equals` function returns 0 as the false outcome, the base instance should remain in its current position in a list.

The test program is a bit larger for this comparison but straightforward. Like the program that tested the `MAP` member function, this program creates a collection, initializes eight object instances, and initializes the collection. You should notice that the only change to the `swap` procedure is a change of datatype in the formal parameters.

Equals or Not Comparison

While the example does more than a standard equals method, you could implement a direct equality comparison by changing the `IF` block to

```
IF self.movie = object.movie AND self.who = object.who THEN
  RETURN 1;
ELSE
  RETURN 0;
END IF;
```

This would then return 1 when both objects are equal and 0 when they're not. It doesn't provide you with a sorting key, but you could implement another `sorting_hat` method for that.

It follows:

```
DECLARE
  -- Declare a collection of an object type.
  TYPE object_list IS TABLE OF ORDER_COMP;
  -- Initialize four objects in mixed alphabetical order.
  object1 ORDER_COMP := order_comp('Ron Weasley','Harry Potter 1');
  object2 ORDER_COMP := order_comp('Harry Potter','Harry Potter 1');
  object3 ORDER_COMP := order_comp('Luna Lovegood','Harry Potter 5');
  object4 ORDER_COMP := order_comp('Hermione Granger','Harry Potter 1');
  object5 ORDER_COMP := order_comp('Hermione Granger','Harry Potter 2');
  object6 ORDER_COMP := order_comp('Harry Potter','Harry Potter 5');
  object7 ORDER_COMP := order_comp('Cedric Diggory','Harry Potter 4');
  object8 ORDER_COMP := order_comp('Severus Snape','Harry Potter 1');
  -- Define a collection of the object type.
  objects OBJECT_LIST := object_list(object1, object2, object3, object4
                                    ,object5, object6, object7, object8);
  -- Swaps A and B.
  PROCEDURE swap (a IN OUT ORDER_COMP, b IN OUT ORDER_COMP) IS
    c ORDER_COMP;
  BEGIN
    c := b;
    b := a;
    a := c;
  END swap;
BEGIN
  -- A bubble sort.
  FOR i IN 1..objects.COUNT LOOP
    FOR j IN 1..objects.COUNT LOOP
      IF objects(i).equals(objects(j)) = 1 THEN    -- Ascending order.
        swap(objects(i),objects(j));
      END IF;
    END LOOP;
  END LOOP;
  -- Print reordered objects.
  FOR i IN 1..objects.COUNT LOOP
    dbms_output.put_line(objects(i).to_string);
  END LOOP;
END;
/
```

You should gain better use of the ORDER member function by consistently labeling it as *equals* because that mimic Java. It is a recommended solution to standardized how you deploy transient objects in your code.

The anonymous-block program simply passes a copy of one instance to the other. You *swap* them when the equals function returns 1 *(which means true)*. The function returns true when the actual parameter isn't greater than the base instance. This sorts the instances in ascending order.

You get the following output:

```
[Harry Potter 1][Harry Potter]
[Harry Potter 1][Hermione Granger]
[Harry Potter 1][Ron Weasley]
```

```
[Harry Potter 1][Severus Snape]
[Harry Potter 2][Hermione Granger]
[Harry Potter 4][Cedric Diggory]
[Harry Potter 5][Harry Potter]
[Harry Potter 5][Luna Lovegood]
```

If you change the `IF` block to check for 0 *(or false),* like this

```
IF objects(i).equals(objects(j)) = 0 THEN
  swap(objects(i),objects(j));
END IF;
```

you get a *descending* sort like

```
[Harry Potter 5][Luna Lovegood]
[Harry Potter 5][Harry Potter]
[Harry Potter 4][Cedric Diggory]
[Harry Potter 2][Hermione Granger]
[Harry Potter 1][Severus Snape]
[Harry Potter 1][Ron Weasley]
[Harry Potter 1][Hermione Granger]
[Harry Potter 1][Harry Potter]
```

This section has demonstrated how to compare objects by using the `MAP` or `ORDER` member functions. You've seen how to leverage both while working with transient object instances.

Inheritance and Polymorphism

Object-oriented (OO) programming languages demand a change in thinking, but sometimes you may find yourself asking why. The foregoing part of this chapter explains the mechanics of building object types as libraries. You can also build packages by developing a collection of functions and procedures. While building libraries of object types requires more effort and design than building packages, the return on your investment of time is their extensibility.

Objects are extensible because you can add to their capabilities by building subclasses. *Subclasses* inherit the behaviors of other class, which become known as *superclasses.* Subclasses can also override the behaviors of their superclass by creating methods to replace superclass members. The idea that subclasses extend and change behaviors of their superclasses is termed *morphing. Polymorphing* is the process of multiple subclasses inheriting the behaviors of superclasses.

The classic example is a generalized class that defines a vehicle. You can develop specializations of the vehicle class by building car, motorcycle, truck, and van subclasses. These subclasses extend the general attributes and methods provided by the vehicle class and in some cases provide overriding methods. The specialized methods manage the differences between driving a car or riding a motorcycle. When the vehicle class is subclassed, the vehicle class is promoted and called a superclass.

Objects inherit and polymorph behaviors by extending base behaviors in an organized tree called an object *hierarchy.* Object hierarchies contain libraries of object types, which are reusable programming units, or in the OO programming lexicon, reusable code artifacts.

Reusability has many facets. Using static functions and procedures to exchange information between class instances enables you to position reusable class components. These static structures have general use across all or many class instances and support sharing function and variable states.

Subclasses are created according to two patterns: single inheritance and multiple inheritance. Single-tree OO programming languages, such as Java, support the single-inheritance model. C++ supports a multiple-inheritance model. The single-inheritance model is represented in Figure 14-2.

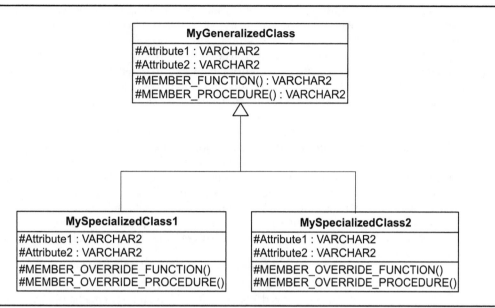

FIGURE 14-2 *Single-inheritance UML model*

The semantics of Java and PL/SQL support only the single-inheritance model, but realistically, you can use the OO principle of aggregation to overcome this limitation. Inheritance is a specialized form of aggregation, which you can implement without much effort. Ordinary aggregation requires you to define a class variable of another class, instantiate an instance of the class, and develop method wrappers that redirect action to the class instance methods. You can implement inheritance and aggregation in the same class and mimic the multiple-inheritance model.

Inheritance means that you define a class as a child of a parent class—a subclass of a class. When you create an instance of the subclass, you get an instance that has the behaviors of the parent class and subclass. If a subclass provides a method that has the same name as a parent class method, the subclass method overrides the parent class method. This means that when you call the method *(function or procedure),* it will implement the subclass method, not the parent class method.

The power of OO programming exists in extending generalized behaviors and organizing variables and functions into real-world object types. You have learned how to build and access object types and instances of objects. In the next sections, you will learn how to extend general classes into subclasses.

Declaring Subclasses

Subclasses require a bit of new and very specific Oracle vocabulary. Unlike the Java programming language where a subclass *extends* behavior, Oracle object types develop their implementation *under* the superclass. This really means the same thing—subclasses extend behavior. The UNDER keyword is consistent with the mental image you may have formed from Figure 14-2.

You must state a member method is an *overriding behavior.* While this is also a departure from how you override methods in Java, it does improve the clarity of definition. This is especially true when you inspect the declaration of an object type in the database catalog. If you started with Java, it may require an adjustment.

There are several restrictions that apply to subtypes. You can't override type attributes, which means you don't list them when you declare the subtype. If you forget the rule, the compiler reminds you with a PLS-00410 error. The PLS-00410 error is adequate but was really developed for duplication when you create a *record type.* The message is "duplicate fields in RECORD, TABLE or argument list are not permitted." The error means that an object type and all subtypes share a formal parameter list *(aka argument list).* Subtypes can implement the same attributes as other sibling subtypes but not parents. A *sibling subtype* is one that is directly subclassed from the same parent class.

The MAP and ORDER member functions are elements of the formal parameter list. They are only implemented in the object type. This limitation means that you must kludge comparative validation of subtypes by implementing another member function for comparisons. Alternatively, you can couple the parent MAP or ORDER function to all subtypes. This type of coupling requires that you maintain both when changing either. Subtypes call the MAP or ORDER member function for base object comparison, and then it performs a supplemental subtype comparison.

The compiler raises a PLS-00154 error when you attempt to put a MAP or ORDER function in a subtype where the parent already has one. This error is also triggered because of the shared formal parameter list.

The example extends the behavior of the order_comp object presented in the section "Comparing with the ORDER Member Function" earlier in this chapter. It is critical that you confirm that the parent object type is declared and valid in your schema before trying to create a subclass. You will see how to create a subclass and override a method, which in this case is a member function.

You can find the order_subcomparison.sql script on the publisher's site. It contains the object type and body, plus the testing program units.

You declare the order_subcomp object type as follows:

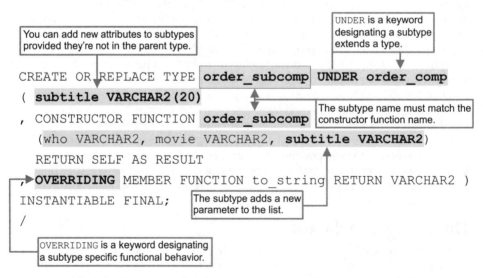

This order_subcomp subtype is deployed under the order_comp subtype. It extends the behavior of the type and inherits all behaviors that are not overridden. The subtype adds a new parameter to the list and reflects the parameter list change in the constructor function. It also overrides the to_string function of the parent subtype.

After you subtype an object type, the parent type has dependents. You can't replace the object type without invalidating the children, and then you can only do it by adding the FORCE clause to the DDL DROP TYPE statement. This means there is some significant linkage that you'll need to account for in your deployment and maintenance scripts. It is known as type evolution, and you can find a discussion of it in the section "Type Evolution" later in this chapter. The order_subcomparison.sql script it takes care of managing these dependencies for you.

Implementing Subclasses

The process of implementing subclasses is closer to the generic process for implementing a base object type. Unlike the object type declaration, the object body doesn't actually reference the object type.

You can implement this function by applying the principles covered earlier in this chapter. The implementation of the object body is

```
-- This is found in order_subcomparison.sql on the publisher's web site.
CREATE OR REPLACE TYPE BODY order_subcomp IS
  CONSTRUCTOR FUNCTION order_subcomp
  (who VARCHAR2, movie VARCHAR2, subtitle VARCHAR2)
  RETURN SELF AS RESULT IS
  BEGIN
    self.who := who;
    self.movie := movie;
    self.subtitle := subtitle;
    RETURN;
  END order_subcomp;
  OVERRIDING MEMBER FUNCTION to_string RETURN VARCHAR2 IS
  BEGIN
    RETURN (self as order_comp).to_string||'['||self.subtitle||']';
  END to_string;
END;
/
```

The implementation shows that you construct an instance of the subtype with three parameters. You should note that the constructor assigns values to the who and movie attributes, which are declared by the base object type. While you can write to those variables inside the constructor, you cannot write to or read them in other methods of the subtype object. If you want to access them, you'll need to write getters and setters to make it possible. Any attempt to directly access them in a subclass raises a PLS-00671 error.

The OVERRIDING member function presents a new syntax. The syntax lets you call to the parent class and execute any method. The overriding to_string function calls the superclass to_string function and treats the return value as an expression.

```
(self as order_comp).to_string
```

You cannot gain access to parent class attributes, because there aren't any. Your subclass initializes superclass attributes as instance attributes inside the subclass. When you call a superclass function or procedure, it operates on the instance class variables in the subtype. It doesn't matter whether they were declared in the superclass.

The anonymous block that tests this subtype is a modified version of the one in the section "Comparing with the ORDER Member Function." The only change is that one of the eight object instances is now a subtype, and the subtype works in the context of the collection of the *base* object type.

The program is

```
-- This is found in order_subcomparison.sql on the publisher's web site.
DECLARE
  -- Declare a collection of an object type.
  TYPE object_list IS TABLE OF ORDER_COMP;
  -- Initialize one subtype.
  object1 ORDER_SUBCOMP := order_subcomp('Ron Weasley','Harry Potter 1'
                                         ,'Socerer''s Stone');
  -- Initialize seven types.
  object2 ORDER_COMP := order_comp('Harry Potter','Harry Potter 1');
  object3 ORDER_COMP := order_comp('Luna Lovegood','Harry Potter 5');
  object4 ORDER_COMP := order_comp('Hermione Granger','Harry Potter 1');
  object5 ORDER_COMP := order_comp('Hermione Granger','Harry Potter 2');
  object6 ORDER_COMP := order_comp('Harry Potter','Harry Potter 5');
  object7 ORDER_COMP := order_comp('Cedric Diggory','Harry Potter 4');
  object8 ORDER_COMP := order_comp('Severus Snape','Harry Potter 1');
  -- Define a collection of the object type.
  objects OBJECT_LIST := object_list(object1, object2, object3, object4
                                     ,object5, object6, object7, object8);
  -- Swaps A and B.
  PROCEDURE swap (a IN OUT ORDER_COMP, b IN OUT ORDER_COMP) IS
    c ORDER_COMP;
  BEGIN
    c := b;
    b := a;
    a := c;
  END swap;
BEGIN
  -- A bubble sort.
  FOR i IN 1..objects.COUNT LOOP
    FOR j IN 1..objects.COUNT LOOP
      IF objects(i).equals(objects(j)) = 1 THEN
        swap(objects(i),objects(j));
      END IF;
    END LOOP;
  END LOOP;
  -- Print reordered objects.
  FOR i IN 1..objects.COUNT LOOP
    dbms_output.put_line(objects(i).to_string);
  END LOOP;
END;
/
```

The `object1` instance variable is constructed by calling the subtype. The subtype instance is then added to the collection of the base type. It is also passed as an actual argument to the base type ORDER member function and local swap procedure. In both cases the subtype masquerades as the base object type.

Subtypes are a combination of the base class and subclass code. The base object body code acts on the subclass attributes when a subclass initializes them. The subclass-specific methods act on the subclass-only components. You can also call any method from your parent class to work with attributes stored there. Together you get the attributes and behaviors of the base class and subclass.

The anonymous block implicitly *treats* all elements of the nested table as their native type. This is more or less what you accomplish by calling the TREAT function in a query. The TREAT function constructs a transient object instance from a persistent object constructor. You create the constructor when you store the object in a table. Reading the object from the table requires you to create an instance of the object at runtime as shown in the sidebar "Trick or Treat'n with Persistent Object Types" earlier in the chapter.

Subtypes are implicitly cast at runtime. This means they behave the same as transient object types. The following creates a table using the ORDER_COMP supertype:

```
CREATE TABLE harry_potter
( harry_potter_id  NUMBER
, character_role   ORDER_COMP );
```

You can then insert both a superclass and subclass into the harry_potter table, like this:

```
INSERT INTO harry_potter VALUES
( 1, order_subcomp('Ron Weasley','Harry Potter 1','Socerer''s Stone'));
INSERT INTO harry_potter VALUES
( 1, order_comp('Hermione Granger','Harry Potter 1'));
```

These insert the following raw data, which you can query with

```
COLUMN character_role FORMAT A68
SELECT character_role FROM harry_potter;
```

It shows

```
CHARACTER_ROLE(WHO, MOVIE)
--------------------------------------------------------------------
ORDER_SUBCOMP('Ron Weasley', 'Harry Potter 1', 'Socerer''s Stone')
ORDER_COMP('Hermione Granger', 'Harry Potter 1')
```

The column title for the query appends the constructor for the object superclass. One row stores a call to the subclass constructor, and the other stores a call to the superclass constructor.

You can select the object contents by using the TREAT function. The TREAT function actually constructs an instance of the object by calling recursively for each row the constructor stored in the table.

With the SQL*Plus formatting, the query returns the results of the to_string instance function:

```
COLUMN character_role FORMAT A50
SELECT TREAT(character_role AS ORDER_COMP).to_string() AS character_role
FROM   harry_potter;
```

You must include the parentheses when calling the instance method in a SQL statement. This statement returns the following:

```
CHARACTER_ROLE
-----------------------------------------------
[Harry Potter 1][Ron Weasley][Socerer's Stone]
[Harry Potter 1][Hermione Granger]
```

As you can see, the TREAT function constructs an instance of the supertype or subtype. It determines which one to call by reading the constructor call that is stored in the column. You should always declare columns with the supertype. If you forget and declare a column that uses the subtype, the database lets you insert superclass constructors, but they fail at runtime. This behavior should really raise an ORA-00932 error, which explains that inconsistent datatypes are disallowed. You receive an ORA-00932 error when you attempt to enter another unrelated object type constructor.

The rule is simple: always declare object datatypes with the top-most class in a hierarchy. Leave the subtyping to the database, unless you're querying. Queries use the TREAT function.

This section has shown you how to build subclasses, override methods, and call superclass methods.

Type Evolution

Object *type evolution* refers to changes in object types when they have dependents. This is a concern when using transient objects but is a critical issue when you actually store data in persistent objects in the database.

You can't change object types once you declare their dependents as columns in database tables. Therefore, you should be certain that you've captured one hundred percent of the requirements before you use them in database tables. Alternatively, you require a migration strategy to move the contents of older persistent object types into new ones.

If you attempt to add an attribute to the base object type order_comp when order_subcomp exists in the database, you raise an ORA-02303 error. It says that you can't "drop or replace a type with type or table dependents." The type refers to transient objects, or programming components only. Table dependents are columns that use the object type as their datatype.

When you've limited the use of object types to transient objects, you can simply drop the derived classes first. That means you drop subclasses before classes. You can find this type of logic in the order_subcomparison.sql script on the publisher's web site.

Implementing Collection Object Bodies

Collections of an object type are fairly easy because you simply declare a VARRAY or nested table of the object type. Collections are a specialized object type, as covered in Chapter 7.

Since collections don't inherit any of the behaviors from their base element datatype, you must wrap a collection type inside another object type if you want to access those behaviors. The wrapping object type can let you manage a list or array of the base-object type. Arrays limit the number of elements to a fixed size, while nested tables are open-ended lists. You should generally implement lists, not arrays, when you build collections of object types.

The next two sections show you how to declare and implement an object type collection. You should cover them in sequence because you need to understand the declaration before the implementation.

Declaring Object Type Collections

Object type collections require a base object type, and a collection of the base object type. After you create those, you can build an object type collection. This section leverages the item_object type created in the section "Static Member Methods" earlier in the chapter.

You create the collection of the item_object type with the following syntax:

```
CREATE OR REPLACE TYPE item_table IS TABLE OF item_object;
/
```

The wrapper to the collection should define at least one instance variable. The instance variable should have the `item_table` collection datatype. You should provide a default constructor that creates a collection by querying the database, and a constructor that takes a collection of the base object type.

The declaration of an object type collection of the `item_table` is

```
-- This is found in create_items_object.sql on the publisher's web site.
CREATE OR REPLACE TYPE items_object IS OBJECT
( items_table ITEM_TABLE
, CONSTRUCTOR FUNCTION items_object
  RETURN SELF AS RESULT
, CONSTRUCTOR FUNCTION items_object
  (items_table ITEM_TABLE) RETURN SELF AS RESULT
, MEMBER FUNCTION get_size RETURN NUMBER
, STATIC FUNCTION get_items_table RETURN ITEM_TABLE)
INSTANTIABLE NOT FINAL;
/
```

The object attribute is a nested table of the base `item_object` type variable. You also have a static `get_items_object` function that lets you generate and return a collection of the base object type.

Implementing Object Type Collections

This section shows you how to implement the object type collection that you have declared. It also implements another concrete factory pattern by constructing a collection through a static function call.

The object body implements the following:

```
-- This is found in create_items_object.sql on the publisher's web site.
CREATE OR REPLACE TYPE BODY items_object IS
  CONSTRUCTOR FUNCTION items_object
  RETURN SELF AS RESULT IS
    c            NUMBER := 1; -- Counter for table index.
    item         ITEM_OBJECT;
    CURSOR c1 IS
      SELECT item_title, item_subtitle FROM item;
  BEGIN
    FOR i IN c1 LOOP
      item := item_object(i.item_title,i.item_subtitle);
      items_table.EXTEND;
      self.items_table(c) := item; -- Must use something other than loop index.
      c := c + 1;
    END LOOP;
    RETURN;
  END items_object;
  CONSTRUCTOR FUNCTION items_object
  (items_table ITEM_TABLE) RETURN SELF AS RESULT IS
  BEGIN
    self.items_table := items_table;
    RETURN;
  END items_object;
```

```
  MEMBER FUNCTION get_size RETURN NUMBER IS
  BEGIN
    RETURN self.items_table.COUNT;
  END get_size;
  STATIC FUNCTION get_items_table RETURN ITEM_TABLE IS
    c              NUMBER := 1; -- Counter for table index.
    item           ITEM_OBJECT;
    items_table ITEM_TABLE := item_table();
    CURSOR c1 IS
      SELECT item_title, item_subtitle FROM item;
  BEGIN
    FOR i IN c1 LOOP
      item := item_object(i.item_title,i.item_subtitle);
      items_table.EXTEND;
      items_table(c) := item; -- Must use something other than loop index.
      c := c + 1;
    END LOOP;
    RETURN items_table;
  END get_items_table;
END;
/
```

The default constructor builds a list of all qualifying rows from the `item` table. The `get_items_table` does the same thing, but it returns a collection of base object types. You can use the static `get_items_table` function to initialize the `items_object` collection.

The following anonymous block shows you how:

```
-- This is found in create_items_object.sql on the publisher's web site.
DECLARE
  items ITEMS_OBJECT;
BEGIN
  items := items_object(items_object.get_items_table);
  dbms_output.put_line(items.get_size);
END;
/
```

The `items_object` constructor takes a call to the static function as its actual parameter. The static function returns a table of `item_object` type variables. The call to the instance get function returns the number of elements in the collection, which should be 93 if the original `create_store.sql` script wasn't changed. The instructions for the seeding script are in the introduction.

You can also use the static function to retrieve the collection of `item_object`. Once they are retrieved, you can print the contents of the individual elements by calling the base object `to_string` function.

The following demonstrates this functionality:

```
-- This is found in create_items_object.sql on the publisher's web site.
DECLARE
  items ITEM_TABLE;
BEGIN
  items := items_object.get_items_table;
  FOR i IN 1..items.COUNT LOOP
    dbms_output.put_line(items(i).to_string);
  END LOOP;
END;
/
```

Concrete Factory Pattern

A concrete factory pattern is derived from an abstract factory pattern. It provides a design approach to build object instances. There are many ways to implement this OO design pattern, as is true for most design patterns. The example in Chapter 14 uses a static member function as the factory. The static member function creates an instance of `item_object` and returns it to the calling program.

The object type declares the interface for the *factory* and *object type*. The static `get_item_object` function returns an object type. A static function is a factory when it returns an instance of an object.

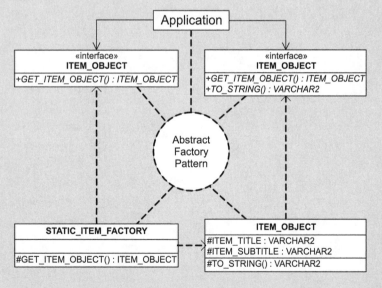

The `item_object` instance in the preceding illustration represents only the instance components. The static component has been abstracted from the instance into a separate class in the drawing. It illustrates the role of the static function as a factory.

This section has shown you how to declare an object type collection. You have also declared a static method that you can implement as a concrete factory. The static method allows you to grab an instance object type collection without explicitly constructing it in your standalone PL/SQL blocks.

Summary

This chapter has examined how you define, initialize, and use objects. You should now have a foundation of what objects are and how you can use them in your PL/SQL applications.

CHAPTER
15

Java Libraries

racle 11*g* lets you extend your applications by writing stored functions and procedures, and by creating packages for both. You also have the opportunity to write these stored programs in the Java programming language. There is one catch. While you can write the implementation in the Java programming language, the gateway between the environment and Java libraries is a PL/SQL programming specification. A specification defines a function, procedure, or package to the environment. These are much like package specifications that define package bodies. *Publishing* Java libraries is nothing more than wrapping them in PL/SQL specifications. That's why they're called PL/SQL wrappers.

This chapter covers the following:

- Oracle 11*g* JVM new features
- Java architecture in Oracle
- Oracle JDBC connection types
  - Client-side driver, or JDBC thin driver
  - Oracle call interface driver, or middle-tier thick driver
  - Oracle server-side internal driver, or server-tier thick driver
- Building Java class libraries in Oracle
  - Building internal server Java functions
  - Building internal server Java procedures
  - Building internal server Java objects
  - Troubleshooting Java class libraries
- Mapping Oracle types

This chapter builds on concepts, but if you feel you understand the basics, you should be able to jump to the section of interest, although a quick browse might save you time looking for a missing piece later in the chapter.

Oracle 11*g* JVM New Features

The Oracle 11*g* Java Virtual Machine (JVM) has matured. The following new features are in this release of the database:

- The internal Oracle JVM is now compatible with Standard Edition of Java 5 (aka as Java 1.5).
- Oracle JVM enhancements include support for `loadjava` URL, list-based operations with `dropjava`, the ability to resolve external class references by using the `ojvmmtc` utility, and increased functionality in the `ojvmjava` tool.
- The introduction of database-resident JAR files, which means when you load a JAR file, you now have the option of creating an object representing the JAR file transparently.

- The ability to share metadata between user-defined classes. This mimics the concept of a multithreaded process control block.

- A two-tier duration for Java session state is now possible. This lets you use Java as previously done in autonomous transactions within a connection, or as a persistent session with preserved state between transactions. You can use the ENDSESSION function in the DBMS_JAVA package to clear previous session state on entry. It preserves any property settings when it clears the session state. You should use the ENDSESSION_AND_RELATED_STATE function from the DBMS_JAVA package when you want to clear both the session state and property settings.

- The ability to redirect output streams externally from the database.

- The ability to set system properties that are propagated on connection to the database server.

- The delivery of a Java *just-in-time (JIT)* compiler that reduces Java byte streams directly into machine-specific code, improving performance by eliminating the interpretation phase.

Java Architecture

The Oracle 11*g* databases provide a robust architecture for developing server-side or internal Java programming components. Java components are object-oriented (OO) structures that fit naturally into Oracle's object-relational model. The component architecture is a library stack that contains

- Platform-dependent operating systems, like Unix, Linux, and Microsoft Windows

- Platform-dependent Oracle database management files and libraries

- The Oracle database instance Java Virtual Machine, which is platform independent

- Java core class libraries, which are ported to various platforms

- Oracle-supported Java Application Programming Interfaces (APIs), like SQLJ, JDBC, and JNDI

- Oracle PL/SQL stored objects, which provide an interface between SQL and PL/SQL programs, as well as server-side Java classes.

The Java Interactive Interface
The ojvmjava utility is an interactive interface to the session namespace and database instance. You can now launch executables through this tool. A new runjava option lets you run ojvmjava shell in command mode or resident class mode. The current version of ojvmjava has reduced the stack trace for thrown exceptions. You also have the ability to open a new connection without leaving the current ojvmjava session.

The Oracle and Java libraries store and manage application programs like a ubiquitous file system—ubiquitous because they are operating system independent. Oracle libraries make storing, retrieving, and recovering files a standard process across many diverse platforms. The Java Virtual Machine (JVM) provides a standard environment where you can build well-documented OO programs. Oracle PL/SQL enables the development of wrapper packages to access Java libraries from other PL/SQL stored objects and SQL. The architecture of the Oracle Java Virtual Machine is shown here.

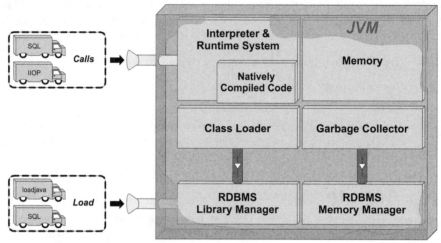

Oracle JVM uses two types of namespaces, the long name and the short name. The long name is exactly as the class is named in Java. You can call stored Java programs by their native namespace. While the chapter examples are short and not placed into packages, you'll most likely put your Java programs into packages. The namespace for Java stored code includes the entire package hierarchy. When this is larger than 30 characters, Oracle uses a hashed namespace in the data dictionary views. Use the DBMS_JAVA package and LONGNAME function to get the full namespace. You can also use the DBMS_JAVA package and SHORTNAME function to get the short name.

The JVM enjoys automated storage management, which means you do not need to allocate and free memory explicitly. Also, Java is a strongly typed programming language like PL/SQL. The combination of strong typing and a garbage collector to manage memory provides a scalable and simplified environment like the PL/SQL run-time engine.

Both Java and PL/SQL are interpreted languages and require just-in-time (JIT) compilation. Oracle 11*g* introduces just-in-time Java compilation for Java programs. Native compilation enables ahead-of-time compilation. It changes PL/SQL and Java byte code into machine-executable programming code.

Native compilation speeds execution by eliminating JIT compilation delay. Unfortunately, it takes time to compile the programs in interpreted languages into machine code. If you rarely change your code, the trade-off may be worth using native compilation.

There are three ways to put Java classes into the database instance:

- A two-step process: (a) compiling the Java source file, `<file_name>.java`, with the `javac` executable to generate a Java byte code program, and (b) using the Oracle `loadjava` utility to put the file into the database instance

- A one-step process using the `loadjava` utility to compile and put the Java class file into the database instance

■ A one-step process using Data Definition Language to build and compile the Java source file as a stored Java class

There are occasionally parser problems running DDL commands when you build Java programs. While a SQL DDL example is provided, the `loadjava` command line is recommended over SQL DDL commands. You can also call the LOADJAVA procedure from the DBMS_JAVA package to load your Java classes. The `loadjava` command both compiles and loads class files into the database.

TIP
If you opt to use the one-step `loadjava` *utility, please note you may encounter an ORA-29533 error for attempting to overwrite the file. The replace option in the* `loadjava` *utility does not work in some releases. Use* `dropjava` *with the* `-user` *option and the* `<file_name>.class` *before rerunning the* `loadjava` *utility.*

This chapter assumes you have a basic familiarity with Java. Basic familiarity means that you can compile and run Java programs. The samples include command-line instructions. There is also a Java primer in Appendix D. The Java primer also includes configuration instructions for JDBC interaction with an Oracle 11*g* database.

Java stored program units are like traditional PL/SQL program units. They are called with either definer's-rights or invoker's-rights access from a single session. There are differences between how Java works externally and internally within the Oracle database instance. Some of the differences are qualified in the following subsections.

Java Execution Control

Execution control differs from native Java. While you can now have a `main()` method inside a Java resource class, it is only accessible through the `ojvmjava` utility. Internal Java resource files have to two types of behaviors: stored program bodies and instantiable classes. Stored program bodies support functions and procedures whether schema or package level in scope. Instantiable classes support user-defined object types and provide the implementation for the object type. You instantiate the objects by using the `SQLData` interface.

Java Resource Storage

Java class resources are stored in clear text, Java byte code, and compressed Java ARchives (also known as JAR files). JAR files can be stored internally or externally in an Oracle 11*g* database instance. You can now load JAR files and concurrently define their internal object representation in the database. Oracle manages these as source, class, and resource Java objects. Schemas contain a JAVA$OPTIONS table, which can be accessed and configured by the DBMS_JAVA package, the SET_COMPILER_OPTION and RESET_COMPILER_OPTION procedures, or the GET_COMPILER_OPTION function.

Java Class Names

Internal Oracle Java class names are maintained in two forms. One is the short form that supports standard schema database objects and is limited to 30 characters. When a fully qualified package and class name exceeds the limit, Oracle automatically creates a hashed name as the class short name and stores the long name elsewhere.

Java Resolvers

The standard Java `Class.forName()` isn't supported for internal Oracle Java classes. Oracle 11*g* supports multiple resolvers, and they help you locate classes. You can get unexpected results from a search when one resolver runs another. This problem involves the way classes can be distributed among different database scheme. There are several workarounds. The workarounds all involve your qualifying the owning schema and class file. Chapter 2 in the *Oracle Database Java Developer's Guide* describes the suggested workarounds.

Java Security and Permissions

Operating resources are restricted. You can only alter these as the privileged user `SYSDBA`. Use the `DBMS_JAVA` package and the `GRANT_PERMISSION` procedure to open operating resources like file I/O.

Java Threading

Java threading works differently for Oracle internal Java classes. The Oracle JVM uses a non-preemptive threading model. This means that all threads run in a single operating system thread and the Oracle JVM merely switches contexts between threads. Switching context means that the Oracle JVM spawns one thread for a time slice and then another, in a round-robin fashion, until their execution is complete.

Oracle 11*g* now also supports class loaders, which enable you to create preemptive threading solutions. This requires you to have a master class spawn instances through different class loaders. Class loaders inside the JVM run in their own thread of execution. You should note that this changes the behavior of static variables in Java because multiple copies of static variables can discretely exist when they're not in the same class loader.

Oracle Java Connection Types

Oracle implements the Java Database Connection (JDBC) in three ways in order to meet three different needs. These are the thin, thick, and default connections. Respectively, they map to the client-side driver, the call interface driver (or middle-tier driver), and the server-side (or internal) driver. In the next sections, you'll examine all three.

The Client-Side Driver, or JDBC Thin Driver

The Oracle thin connection is probably the most used by Java applications, Java Server Pages (JSPs), and Enterprise JavaBeans (EJBs). It provides many advantages to building code without directly accessing Oracle library files.

The advantages of the Oracle JDBC thin driver are numerous for external Java applications because it requires the least setup and configuration. First, though, make sure your Java programming environment has access to the standard Java library and the Oracle JDBC library. You can set this up by configuring your `CLASSPATH` environment variable. You should include the Oracle `ojdbc5.jar` JAR file when you want the external files to match the internal JVM. You can use the `ojdbc6.jar` JAR file, but be careful with the newer features that aren't backward compatible with the Oracle JVM. You can find details about how to set these in Appendix D.

Unfortunately, you can't use the Oracle thin JDBC driver unless you've configured and started your database listener. You'll likewise need to provide the host name, listener port number, and database name, along with your user ID and password, each time you spawn a connection to the database instance.

TIP
*The Oracle client-side or thin driver returns a rather meaningless error
message if the host name, listener port number, or database name
is incorrect. In fact, it will report an* ORA-17002 *error. This error
is found in Oracle's implementation of the JDBC API. Appendix D
demonstrates a clean mechanism to audit for the error.*

The uses of the Oracle JDBC thin driver are limited to external Java applications, JSPs, and
EJBs. A multithreaded Java servlet is an example of a Java application that would implement an
Oracle JDBC thin driver file. Oracle JDBC thin connections can be optimistic or pessimistic
connections.

Optimistic connections are temporary connections transmitted using the Hypertext Transfer
Protocol (HTTP), which are limited to a 15-second pipelined TCP socket connection. TCP
connections travel through the Oracle listener for the instance. These solutions are ideal for JSPs
but resource-expensive because they must establish a connection for each communication.

Pessimistic connections are typically transmitted using a state-aware TCP socket that's open
through the duration of the connection. Again the Oracle listener supports these connections
on the server-side. Pessimistic connections are used by multithreaded Java servlets to create
and maintain database connection pools. Java servlets can be implemented in two-tier or *n*-tier
solutions.

The Oracle Call Interface Driver, or Middle-Tier Thick Driver

The Oracle call interface (OCI) driver is more tightly coupled with the Oracle C/C++ libraries
than the Oracle JDBC thin driver. If you use the Oracle JDBC call interface (or middle-tier thick)
driver, you'll need to ensure that the PATH, CLASSPATH, and LD_LIBRARY_PATH environment
variables map to Oracle libraries. The libraries need to be on the same physical platform or map
through a storage area network (SAN), like NFS in Unix.

The OCI driver can maintain persistent connection pools through Java servlets. As a rule,
you'll have an easier configuration if you use the Oracle JDBC thin driver in your servlet.

The Oracle Server-Side Internal Driver, or Server-Tier Thick Driver

The Oracle server-side internal driver is likewise tightly coupled with, and dependent on, the
Oracle C/C++ libraries. Unfortunately, there's no other choice available to build Java programs
as stored objects in the Oracle database.

The Oracle server-side internal driver uses the getConnection() method of the *DriverManager*
class to connect to the database. This poses a bit of a testing problem if you want to test the Java
program externally because the actual parameter for internal reference classes differs from the
thin client argument. It's best if you test the Java code in your development instance with the thick
connection and avoid porting it.

Unlike the OCI driver, the server-side internal driver is faster than the Oracle JDBC thin driver.
The speed comes because the libraries are all local on the server and not subject to network calls.
As you read the chapter and examine the code, you'll find that embedding Java in the Oracle
database requires a few tricks and techniques.

The next section examines how to build and troubleshoot class libraries and instantiable Java
stored objects.

Building Java Class Libraries in Oracle

When you choose to build Java class libraries, you have two deployment choices. You can build call-interface driven (middle-tier) or server-side Java class libraries.

Call-interface libraries act like server-side includes to your Apache server. They must be replicated to all nodes of your Apache server and are managed within the structure of your web server load-balancing tool. These components act like external programs that call into the Oracle server and are better treated in Enterprise Java books.

NOTE
While middle-tier Java class libraries are not directly covered, they do require a direct reference in their path to the Oracle OCI libraries. The OCI libraries are in the Oracle Application Server but not on other web servers.

Server-side Java class libraries are stored objects within the Oracle JVM, which is a subcomponent of the Oracle database. Server-side Java class libraries are the core theme of this chapter. In the next two sections, you'll learn how to build internal server Java functions and procedures.

NOTE
If you're unfamiliar with configuring and testing a Java JDBC connection, please check Appendix D for instructions.

Java programming ranges from simple to complex, but these examples should be straightforward. You have two core executables to run Java programs, which you'll use in the examples. They are

- `javac` Compiles your text file Java programs into Java byte code

- `java` Runs your compiled Java byte code programs

The file-naming convention in Java is case-sensitive, so you should ensure you name files consistent with the web-based code example files. If you attempt to compile a Java file when the filename and class name are different, you'll receive an error. Also, the file extension for Java programs is a lowercase `.java`.

You'll now build a simple `HelloWorld1.java` file to make sure the balance of the examples works. If you're working in Microsoft Windows, please open a Command Prompt window. If you're working in Unix, please use a terminal window. The following is the code for `HelloWorld1.java`:

`-- This is found in HelloWorld1.java on the publisher's web site.`

```
// Class definition.
public class HelloWorld1 {
  public static void main(String args[]) {
    System.out.println("Hello World."); }
}
```

Java text files are compiled by the following syntax:

```
javac HelloWorld1.java
```

Successful compilation does not return anything to the console. The lack of any message is a good thing. The way to verify whether or not you have a Java byte code file is to run the Microsoft Windows directory (**dir**) command or Unix list (**ls**) command for files matching `HelloWorld1.*` in the present working directory. You should see two files displayed to the console:

```
HelloWorld1.java
HelloWorld1.class
```

After building the Java byte code compiled program, you can test its execution by doing the following:

```
java HelloWorld1
```

NOTE
You do not provide the .class extension when running Java programs because it is assumed. Appending `.class` *to the filename will raise the following exception: java.lang.NoClassDefFoundError: HelloWorld1/class.*

TIP
You can also raise the java.lang.NoClassDefFoundError: HelloWorld1/ class error if you do not have your present working directory in your $CLASSPATH environment variables.

You'll receive the following results:

```
Hello World.
```

The next section covers how you build server-side or internal server Java programming units. You'll learn how to build Java class files to support stored functions and procedures and how to wrap their existence in PL/SQL packages. The following two sections are sequential, and the second section assumes you have worked through the first.

Building Internal Server Java Functions

You build an internal server Java function by building a Java class file that will use the server-side internal or JDBC Thick connection. As described earlier in the chapter, the JDBC Thick connection depends on Oracle Call Interface (OCI) libraries. All OCI libraries are directly accessible from your Java class file when you've loaded it into the Oracle JVM.

Java Database Connectivity (JDBC) lets you build connections by using the *DriverManager* class. This is a change over the `defaultConnection()` method for internal Java class files and external connections. They now both use the `getConnection()` static method from the *DriverManager* class. The only difference between a thin client and a thick one is the actual parameter provided to the method. Examples in this chapter use the internal syntax, and examples in Appendix D use the external thin client syntax.

Java internal or server-side class files are built and accessed by a three-step process. You use Java to build and compile the class file. Then, you use the Oracle `loadjava` utility to load the compiled class file into the server. Once these are built and loaded into the server, you build a PL/SQL wrapper to the Java class library.

The following assumes you have the correct CLASSPATH and PATH to use Java. If you are unable to compile or test the Java programs, it's possible your environment is configured incorrectly. As mentioned earlier, you should use Appendix D to ensure you have correctly configured your environment.

The example builds a Java class library with two methods. These methods are overloaded, which means they have different signatures or formal parameter lists. They each return a Java string. Both of the overloaded methods will map to two overloaded PL/SQL functions that return VARCHAR2 native Oracle datatypes.

```
-- This is found in HelloWorld2.java on the publisher's web site.

// Oracle class imports.
import oracle.jdbc.driver.*;

// Class definition.
public class HelloWorld2 {

  public static String hello() {
    return "Hello World."; }

  public static String hello(String name) {
    return "Hello " + name + "."; }

  public static void main(String args[]) {
    System.out.println(HelloWorld2.hello());
    System.out.println(HelloWorld2.hello("Larry")); }
}
```

The program defines two overloaded hello methods. One takes no formal parameters, and the other takes one. After you compile and run this program, the method without any formal parameters always prints

```
Hello World.
```

while the one that takes one formal parameter always prints

```
Hello Larry.
```

This happens because the static main() method always sends either no parameter or the same actual parameter to the dynamic method. As a rule, you want to remove testing components like the main() method before loading them into the database and passing actual parameters to dynamic methods.

TIP
You can leave the static main() *method in the program. It harms nothing and enables you to test the program with the* ojvmjava *interactive utility.*

If you have not built the PLSQL schema, please run the create_user.sql script now (you'll find where to download it in the introduction). When you have the PLSQL schema built, compile it with the javac utility, as covered earlier in the chapter. Once it is compiled, you'll load it into the Oracle JVM with the loadjava utility as follows:

```
loadjava -r -f -o -user plsql/plsql HelloWorld2.class
```

NOTE
On the Microsoft platform, you may get a message that states "The procedure entry point kpuhhalo could not be located in the dynamic link library OCI.dll." If you receive this error, it means you don't have %ORACLE_HOME\bin% in your PATH *environment variable.*

The loadjava utility command loads the Java HelloWorld2 class file into the Oracle JVM under the PLSQL schema. After loading the Java class file into the database, you'll need to build a PL/SQL wrapper to use it. The following HelloWorld2.sql script builds the package and package body as a wrapper to the Java class library:

-- **This is found in HelloWorld2.sql on the publisher's web site.**

```
-- Create a PL/SQL wrapper package specification to a Java class file.
CREATE OR REPLACE PACKAGE hello_world2 AS
  FUNCTION hello
  RETURN VARCHAR2;

  FUNCTION hello
  ( who  VARCHAR2 )
  RETURN VARCHAR2;
END hello_world2;
/


-- Create a PL/SQL wrapper package body to a Java class file.
CREATE OR REPLACE PACKAGE BODY hello_world2 AS

  FUNCTION hello
  RETURN VARCHAR2 IS
  LANGUAGE JAVA
  NAME 'HelloWorld2.Hello() return String';

  FUNCTION hello
  ( who  VARCHAR2 )
  RETURN VARCHAR2 IS
  LANGUAGE JAVA
  NAME 'HelloWorld2.Hello(java.lang.String) return String';
END hello_world2;
/
```

When you run this in your schema, it creates a wrapper to the HelloWorld2.class file that you previously loaded. The return type of your PL/SQL wrapper is a VARCHAR2 datatype. You map it to a java.lang.String class, and it *must be that fully qualified path.*

You can verify all components are present to test by querying the user_objects view with the following:

-- **This is found in HelloWorld2.sql on the publisher's web site.**

```
SELECT    object_name
,         object_type
,         status
FROM      user_objects
WHERE     object_name IN ('HelloWorld2','HELLO_WORLD2');
```

The script should output the following results:

```
-- This output is generated from the online HelloWorld2.sql file.

OBJECT_NAME                      OBJECT_TYPE   STATUS
------------------------------   ------------  -------
HELLO_WORLD2                     PACKAGE       VALID
HELLO_WORLD2                     PACKAGE BODY  VALID
HelloWorld2                      JAVA CLASS    VALID
```

If you did not get the same output, you'll need to see what step you may have skipped. Please do that before attempting to proceed. If you did get the same output, you can now test the Java class library in SQL and PL/SQL. You can test it in SQL with a query or in PL/SQL with the DBMS_OUTPUT.PUT_LINE statement. The following illustrates a SQL query of the wrapper, which uses the internal Java class file:

```
SELECT    hello_world2.hello('Paul McCartney')
FROM      dual;
```

The query will return the following results:

```
HELLO_WORLD2.HELLO('PAULMCCARTNEY')
-----------------------------------
Hello Paul McCartney.
```

You can also build the entire Java source, publishing specification, and implementation in a single SQL file. Then, you can run it directly from the SQL*Plus command line. This is done by using a DDL command. The prototype for the DDL command is

```
CREATE OR REPLACE AND RESOLVE JAVA SOURCE NAMED <java_class_name> AS
<java_source>
/
```

The Java class filename can serve two purposes. You can use it as a package container or ignore it to implement a procedure or function. If you implement a function or procedure, they reference only one method in your Java class. Functions and procedures unfortunately can't support overloading because they behave as normal PL/SQL functions and procedures. You can implement overloading when you publish a Java class as a package.

NOTE
You must use a forward slash to execute a DDL command that builds an internal Java class. If you substitute a semicolon, you'll raise an ORA-29536 *exception.*

You create the Java *HelloWorldSQL* class with the following DDL command:

```
-- This is found in HelloWorldSQL.sql on the publisher's web site.

CREATE OR REPLACE AND RESOLVE JAVA SOURCE NAMED HelloWorldSQL AS
// Class Definition.
public class HelloWorldSQL {
```

```
public static String hello() {
  return "Hello World."; }

public static String hello(String name) {
  return "Hello " + name + "."; }
}
/
```

The RESOLVE JAVA SOURCE NAMED targets the class filename, and it parses and compiles the Java source into the instance. You can then publish individual methods as functions or procedures, or the class as a package.

The following publishes the class as a package:

```
-- This is found in HelloWorldSQL.sql on the publisher's web site.

-- Create a PL/SQL wrapper package specification to a Java class file.
CREATE OR REPLACE PACKAGE hello_world_sql AS
  FUNCTION hello
  RETURN VARCHAR2;

  FUNCTION hello
  ( who  VARCHAR2 )
  RETURN VARCHAR2;
END hello_world_sql;
/

-- Create a PL/SQL wrapper package body to a Java class file.
CREATE OR REPLACE PACKAGE BODY hello_world_sql AS

  FUNCTION hello
  RETURN VARCHAR2 IS
  LANGUAGE JAVA
  NAME 'HelloWorldSQL.hello() return String';

  FUNCTION hello
  ( who  VARCHAR2 )
  RETURN VARCHAR2 IS
  LANGUAGE JAVA
  NAME 'HelloWorldSQL.hello(java.lang.String) return String';
END hello_world_sql;
/
```

The package provides an overloaded hello function. You can call it with or without an actual parameter. You can then publish only a single method of the class as a function, like

```
-- This is found in HelloWorldSQL.sql on the publisher's web site.

CREATE OR REPLACE FUNCTION hello
( who VARCHAR2) RETURN VARCHAR2 IS
LANGUAGE JAVA
NAME 'HelloWorldSQL.hello(java.lang.String) return String';
/
```

You can query the function by

```
SELECT hello('Nathan') AS SALUTATION
FROM dual;
```

and it returns

```
SALUTATION
-------------
Hello Nathan.
```

You have now covered how to build Oracle database instance–stored Java class files that map methods to functions. The next section will examine how you build components to deliver procedure DML behaviors.

Building Internal Server Java Procedures

Building a procedure will follow very similar rules to building functions. PL/SQL procedures have IN, IN OUT, or OUT modes. However, you cannot use an IN OUT mode in PL/SQL when wrapping a Java method. This behavior differs from that described in Chapter 13 because the restriction over formal parameters belongs to Java, not PL/SQL. All formal parameters are defined as IN mode only. When you want an output back, you should write a PL/SQL function, not a procedure.

If you attempt to define a package body with a procedure using IN OUT modes, it will raise the following exception:

```
PLS-00235: the external type is not appropriate for the parameter
```

You'll now build an IN mode procedure as a wrapper to a Java class method. When you use Java methods in the context of a procedure, you return a void type from the Java method.

Oracle 11*g* Internal Connection Instances

Over several releases the syntax for building a Java *Connection* instance has been constant. The comfortable syntax for Oracle 9*i* or 10*g* and Java 1.3 or 1.4 is

```
Connection conn = new OracleDriver().defaultConnection();
```

This syntax no longer works. You will have to *migrate the connection logic* for all your stored Java libraries. The correct syntax for Oracle 11*g* and Java 5 is

```
Connection conn = DriverManager.getConnection("jdbc:default:connection:");
```

The new syntax is used in the internal class files for this chapter.

The following Java source file supports an IN mode PL/SQL procedure:

-- **This is found in HelloWorld3.java on the publisher's web site.**

```
// Oracle class imports.
import java.sql.*;
import oracle.jdbc.driver.*;

// Class definition.
public class HelloWorld3 {

  public static void doDML(String statement
                          ,String name) throws SQLException {
    // Declare an Oracle connection.
    Connection conn = DriverManager.getConnection("jdbc:default:connection:");

    // Declare prepared statement, run query and read results.
    PreparedStatement ps = conn.prepareStatement(statement);
    ps.setString(1,name);
    ps.execute(); }

  public static String doDQL(String statement) throws SQLException {
    // Define and initialize a local return variable.
    String result = new String();

    // Declare an Oracle connection.
    Connection conn = DriverManager.getConnection("jdbc:default:connection:");

    // Declare prepared statement, run query and read results.
    PreparedStatement ps = conn.prepareStatement(statement);
    ResultSet rs = ps.executeQuery();
    while (rs.next())
      result = rs.getString(1);

    return result; }
}
```

This program creates a Java *Connection* instance using the Oracle 11*g* process. The new process calls a static getConnection() method of the *DriverManager* class. Any code from your Oracle 10*g* instance will require you to make this change.

The program implements two methods: one to insert records and another to query records. The insert statement returns a void, and the query returns a string.

TIP
While these don't use explicit cursors, statements and result sets persist across calls and their finalizers do not release database cursors. You should remember to always close explicitly opened cursors.

There is no `main()` method in the `HelloWorld3.java` class file. Including a `main()` method to test the program externally to the database would require changing the connection to a client-side or OCI driver. You can refer to Appendix D if you wish to build a test externally to the database instance.

Most likely, you have built the `PLSQL` schema, but if not, you should run the `create_user.sql` script now. When you have the `PLSQL` schema built, compile it with the `javac` utility as covered earlier in the chapter. Once it is compiled, you'll load it into the Oracle JVM with the `loadjava` utility using the following:

```
loadjava -r -f -o -user plsql/plsql HelloWorld3.class
```

The `loadjava` utility command loads the Java `HelloWorld3` class file into the OracleJVM under the `PLSQL` schema. After loading the Java class file into the database, you'll need to build a `mytable` table and PL/SQL wrapper to use it.

The `mytable` table is built by using the following command:

```
-- This is found in HelloWorld3.sql on the publisher's web site.

CREATE TABLE mytable (character VARCHAR2(100));
```

The following `HelloWorld3.sql` script builds the package and package body as a wrapper to the Java class library:

```
-- This is found in HelloWorld3.sql on the publisher's web site.

-- Create a PL/SQL wrapper package specification to a Java class file.
CREATE OR REPLACE PACKAGE hello_world3 AS
  PROCEDURE doDML
  ( dml    VARCHAR2
  , input VARCHAR2 );

  FUNCTION doDQL
  ( dql    VARCHAR2 )
  RETURN  VARCHAR2;
END hello_world3;
/

-- Create a PL/SQL wrapper package body to a Java class file.
CREATE OR REPLACE PACKAGE BODY hello_world3 AS

  PROCEDURE doDML
  ( dml    VARCHAR2
  , input VARCHAR2 ) IS
  LANGUAGE JAVA
  NAME 'HelloWorld3.doDML(java.lang.String,java.lang.String)';

  FUNCTION doDQL
  ( dql    VARCHAR2 )
  RETURN  VARCHAR2 IS
  LANGUAGE JAVA
  NAME 'HelloWorld3.doDQL(java.lang.String) return String';
END hello_world3;
/
```

This program defines two methods:

- The doDML procedure takes two formal parameters that are VARCHAR2 datatypes and returns nothing as a stored procedure.

- The doDQL function takes one formal parameter that is a VARCHAR2 and returns a VARCHAR2 datatype as a stored function.

You can verify that all components are present to test by querying the user_objects view with the following:

-- **This is found in HelloWorld3.sql on the publisher's web site.**

```
SELECT    object_name
,         object_type
,         status
FROM      user_objects
WHERE     object_name IN ('HelloWorld3','HELLO_WORLD3');
```

The script should output the following results:

-- **This output is generated from the online HelloWorld3.sql file.**

```
OBJECT_NAME                      OBJECT_TYPE    STATUS
-----------------------------    ------------   -------
HELLO_WORLD3                     PACKAGE        VALID
HELLO_WORLD3                     PACKAGE BODY   VALID
HelloWorld3                      JAVA CLASS     VALID
```

If you did not get the same output, you'll need to see what step you may have skipped. Please do this before attempting to proceed. If you did get the same output, you can now test the Java class library in SQL and PL/SQL. You can test it in SQL with a query or in PL/SQL with the DBMS_OUTPUT.PUT_LINE statement. The following illustrates a SQL query of the wrapper, which uses the internal Java class file:

```
SELECT    hello_world3.doDQL('SELECT character FROM mytable')
FROM      dual;
```

The query returns the following results:

```
HELLO_WORLD3.DODQL('SELECTCHARACTERFROMMYTABLE')
-----------------------------------
Bobby McGee
```

You've now covered how to build Oracle database instance stored Java class files that map a Java method to a PL/SQL procedure. The next section discusses how to build real Java objects wrapped by PL/SQL object types.

Building Internal Server Java Objects

The Java programming language is object-oriented (OO). In the previous examples, Java stored objects were used as static functions. The potential to use Java to accomplish significant OO computing lies in the Oracle object features introduced in Oracle 9*i* Release 2. They haven't changed much since that release because of a rumor that very few development projects use them. Beginning with that release, you can construct instances of object types and use them as objects. After you develop an understanding of implementing stored Java objects in this section, you can see how PL/SQL objects work (covered in more detail in Chapter 14).

Server-side stored Java programs support full run-time object behaviors starting with Oracle 9*i*, as noted earlier. This means you can now design, develop, and implement natural Java applications beneath PL/SQL object type wrappers. These Java classes can have instance methods, which mean non-static methods. You may also use static methods for libraries.

The balance of the differences covered earlier in the chapter still applies. You build Java object libraries by writing the Java class file and SQL object type definition. Object type bodies are not defined when the object type implementation is written in a stored Java object.

The substantial difference between external Java objects and server internal Java objects lies in the way you construct an instance of the class. You do not directly instantiate the class file and cannot use overriding constructors in the Java class file. The SQLData interface is the key to instantiating stored Java objects. It enables instantiating the Java class by passing back and forth the parameter values. This enables a class to return a reference to a copy or instance of the class.

TIP
There's no way to instantiate directly a default constructor when using a stored Java object class. You also cannot use overriding constructors. The SQLData *interface allows you to pass values to an instantiated class based on known class scope instance variables. Instance variables are not static variables. These limits are imposed by the implementation of the* SQLData *interface.*

Implementing the SQLData interface is done by providing a variable definition and three concrete methods in your Java class file. The following are the components:

- A String datatype named sql_type.

- A getSQLTypeName() method that returns a String datatype.

- A readSQL() method that takes two formal parameters and returns a void. One formal parameter is a SQLInput that contains a stream. The other is a string that contains a datatype name.

- A writeSQL() method that takes one formal parameter, which is a SQLOutput that contains a stream.

Details on implementing run-time Java classes will be illustrated in the following examples. The HelloWorld4 Java class file is designed to work as an instantiable Java stored object type body. The source code for the class follows:

-- This is found in HelloWorld4.java on the publisher's web site.

```
// Oracle class imports.
import java.sql.*;
import java.io.*;
import oracle.sql.*;
import oracle.jdbc.*;
import oracle.jdbc.oracore.*;
```

```java
// Class definition.
public class HelloWorld4 implements SQLData {
  // Define or declare SQLData components.
  private String className = new String("HelloWorld4.class");
  private String instanceName;
  private String qualifiedName;
  private String sql_type;

  public HelloWorld4() {
    String user = new String();

    try {
      user = getUserName(); }
    catch (Exception e) {}

    qualifiedName = user + "." + className; }

  // Define a method to return a qualified name.
  public String getQualifiedName() throws SQLException {
    // Declare return variable.
    return this.qualifiedName + "." + instanceName; }

  // Define a method to return the database object name.
  public String getSQLTypeName() throws SQLException {
    // Returns the UDT map value or database object name.
    return sql_type;   }

  // Define getUserName() method to query the instance.
  public String getUserName() throws SQLException {
    String userName = new String();
    String getDatabaseSQL = "SELECT user FROM dual";

    // Declare an Oracle connection.
    Connection conn = DriverManager.getConnection("jdbc:default:connection:");

    // Declare prepared statement, run query and read results.
    PreparedStatement ps = conn.prepareStatement(getDatabaseSQL);
    ResultSet rs = ps.executeQuery();
    while (rs.next())
      userName = rs.getString(1);

    return userName; }

  // Implements readSQL() method from the SQLData interface.
  public void readSQL(SQLInput stream, String typeName) throws SQLException {
    // Define sql_type to read input and signal overloading signatures.
    sql_type = typeName;

    // Pass values into the class.
    instanceName = stream.readString(); }
```

```
// Implements writeSQL() method from the SQLData interface with a placeholder.
public void writeSQL(SQLOutput stream) throws SQLException {
  // You pass a value back by using a stream function.
  /* stream.writeString('variable_name'); */ }
}
```

The Java class implements the SQLData interface. A couple of these methods provide an opportunity to discuss how internal Java classes behave. The getQualifiedName() method returns the this.qualifiedName variable, which is an *instance variable* for the class. If you were to attempt to reference a *class variable* in a Java stored class supporting a PL/SQL function and procedure wrappers, it would fail. The loadjava utility would raise an exception to prevent putting it into the database instance.

The getSQLTypeName(), readSQL(), and writeSQL() methods provide implementations or stubs for the SQLData interface. You must implement the SQLData interface to support user-defined object types. The readSQL() method manages the incoming stream, and the writeSQL() method manages the outgoing stream for the stored object type.

If you have not built the PLSQL schema, please run the create_user.sql script now. When you have the PLSQL schema built, you can compile it with the javac utility as covered earlier in the chapter. However, there is an alternative syntax that enables you to load and compile against the Oracle JVM libraries.

The HelloWorld4.java program contains import statements that require you to place the ojdbc5.jar file in your CLASSPATH environment variable. If you've not done this yet, you should do so now. The file is found in your $ORACLE_HOME/jdbc/lib directory on Linux or Unix, and %ORACLE_HOME%\jdbc\lib directory on Windows.

You can directly load *a Java source, or text, file* with the loadjava utility as follows:

```
loadjava -r -f -o -user plsql/plsql HelloWorld4.java
```

The loadjava utility command behaves slightly differently when you choose this option. It parses, stores the Java source as a text entry, and compiles the stored Java source into a Java byte stream in the Oracle JVM under the PLSQL schema.

TIP
After loading the Java class file into the database this way, you won't be able to use the dropjava *utility to remove the HelloWorld4.class file. Instead, use the* dropjava *utility to remove the HelloWorld4. java file, which also drops the HelloWorld4.class file.*

You'll need to build a SQL object type to wrap the Java stored object class. The following HelloWorld4.sql script builds the object type as a wrapper to the Java class object:

```
-- This is found in HelloWorld4.sql on the publisher's web site.
```

```
-- Create a PL/SQL wrapper object type to a Java class file.
CREATE OR REPLACE TYPE hello_world4 AS OBJECT
EXTERNAL NAME 'HelloWorld4' LANGUAGE JAVA
USING SQLData
( instanceName VARCHAR2(100) EXTERNAL NAME 'java.lang.String'
, CONSTRUCTOR FUNCTION hello_world4
  RETURN SELF AS RESULT
, MEMBER FUNCTION getQualifiedName
  RETURN VARCHAR2 AS LANGUAGE JAVA
```

```
     NAME 'HelloWorld4.getQualifiedName() return java.lang.String'
 , MEMBER FUNCTION getSQLTypeName
   RETURN VARCHAR2 AS LANGUAGE JAVA
   NAME 'HelloWorld4.getSQLTypeName() return java.lang.String' )
INSTANTIABLE FINAL;
/
```

The SQL object type wrapper defines an object type using an external name that is the case-sensitive Java class name and the `USING SQLData` clause. The `USING SQLData` clause requires at least one variable with an external name that identifies the Java datatype.

NOTE
Any attempt to use SQLData without a mapped type will raise an exception. If you want to instantiate a class and not pass any variables to it, you can designate a blank VARCHAR2(1) EXTERNAL NAME 'java.lang.String' in the wrapper. Then, you simply avoid defining the streams in the SQLData interface methods readSQL and writeSQL and pass a NULL argument when instantiating the PL/SQL wrapper in your PL/SQL programs.

After you've defined the PL/SQL object type wrapper, you can see that both the object type and the body have been registered in the Oracle instance metadata. You can see this by running the following query:

```
COL object_name FORMAT A30
COL object_type FORMAT A12
COL status      FORMAT A7

SELECT    object_name
 ,        object_type
 ,        status
FROM      user_objects
WHERE     object_name = 'HELLO_WORLD4';
```

The output, if you have run everything successfully, will be the following:

```
OBJECT_NAME                       OBJECT_TYPE  STATUS
------------------------------    ------------ -------
HELLO_WORLD4                      TYPE         VALID
HELLO_WORLD4                      TYPE BODY    VALID
```

If you use the `dropjava` utility at this point, you'll invalidate the `TYPE BODY`. Reloading the Java source file with the `loadjava` utility leaves the `TYPE BODY` in an invalid status. The first call to the object results in the following error:

`-- Available online as part of HelloWorld4.sql script described previously.`

```
DECLARE
*
ERROR at line 1:
ORA-29549: class PLSQL.HelloWorld4 has changed, Java session state cleared
ORA-06512: at "PLSQL.HELLO_WORLD4", line 0
ORA-06512: at line 10
```

A second call to the object results in success, but the Oracle instance metadata will still report that the `TYPE BODY` is invalid. The metadata report is incorrect, but you'll need to run an `ALTER` command to fix it. For example, you can use the following:

```
ALTER TYPE hello_world4 COMPILE BODY;
```

Now, you'll test this PL/SQL object type wrapper by instantiating two object instances with the following script:

```
-- This is found in HelloWorld4.sql on the publisher's web site.

DECLARE

  -- Define and instantiate an object instance.
  my_obj1 hello_world4 := hello_world4('Adam');
  my_obj2 hello_world4 := hello_world4('Eve');

BEGIN

  -- Test class instance.
  dbms_output.put_line('Item #1: ['||my_obj1.getQualifiedName||']');
  dbms_output.put_line('Item #2: ['||my_obj2.getQualifiedName||']');
  dbms_output.put_line('Item #3: ['||my_obj1.getSQLTypeName||']');
  dbms_output.put_line('Item #4: ['||my_obj1.getSQLTypeName||']');

  -- Test metadata repository with DBMS_JAVA.
  dbms_output.put_line(
    'Item #5: ['||user||'.'||dbms_java.longname('HELLO_WORLD4')||']');

END;
/
```

You should see the following output displayed:

```
Item #1: [PLSQL.HelloWorld4.class.Adam]
Item #2: [PLSQL.HelloWorld4.class.Eve]
Item #3: [PLSQL.HELLO_WORLD4]
Item #4: [PLSQL.HELLO_WORLD4]
Item #5: [PLSQL.HELLO_WORLD4]
```

The `SQLData` interface allows you to pass a user-defined type (UDT), which means you can use any defined user structure. If you debug the execution of the Java instance, you'll find that each invocation of the instance method actually reinstantiates the class instance.

The next section discusses troubleshooting the Java class library processes that build, load/ drop, and use Java server stored object classes.

Troubleshooting Java Class Libraries

This section covers how to troubleshoot Java class libraries. Some of this becomes intuitive after a while, but initially it is very tricky.

Building, Loading, and Dropping Java Class Library Objects

When you build Java class libraries, you can encounter a number of problems. Many errors occur through simple syntax rule violations, but often the PATH or CLASSPATH environment variable excludes required Java libraries. You need to ensure that your PATH environment variable includes the Java SDK released with the Oracle database you're using. It's best you research which Java class libraries you'll require and then source them into your CLASSPATH. The following illustrates the minimum for the examples used in this chapter by the operating system:

Windows

```
C:> set PATH=%PATH%;C:%ORACLE_HOME%\jdk\bin
C:> set CLASSPATH=%CLASSPATH%;C:%ORACLE_HOME%\jdbc\lib\ojdbc5.jar
```

If you want to use the JPublisher command-line tool, you need to add both of the following Java archive files:

```
%ORACLE_HOME%\sqlj\lib\translator.zip
%ORACLE_HOME%\sqlj\lib\runtime12.zip
```

Unix

```
# export PATH=$PATH:/<mount>/$ORACLE_HOME/jdk/bin
# export CLASSPATH=$CLASSPATH:/<mount>/$ORACLE_HOME/jdbc/lib/ojdbc5.jar
```

If you want to use the JPublisher command-line tool, you must add both of these Java archive files to your CLASSPATH environment variable:

```
$ORACLE_HOME/sqlj/lib/translator.zip
$ORACLE_HOME/sqlj/lib/runtime12.zip
```

Another potential problem in configuring Java archive access can be found in the LD_LIBRARY_PATH used in the listener.ora file. Check to make sure it's set as follows:

```
LD_LIBRARY_PATH=C:\oracle\ora92\lib;C:\oracle\ora92\jdbc\lib
```

You may also encounter an error like this, which says you cannot drop a Java class file directly from your database instance. The error is raised by running the dropjava utility with the following syntax:

```
C:> dropjava -u plsql/plsql HelloWorld4.class
```

The following error message should then appear:

```
Error while dropping class HelloWorld4
    ORA-29537: class or resource cannot be created or dropped directly
```

The reason for the error is that you used loadjava to compile and load a Java source file, HelloWorld4.java. Thus, you should use dropjava and the source file, which will delete the class and source file.

NOTE
The behavior is generally consistent with this preceding description, but occasionally the command will work and delete both the source and class files from the Oracle JVM.

The error signaling that you have excluded something from your CLASSPATH environment variable should appear as follows:

```
C:\>loadjava -r -f -o -user plsql/plsql HelloWorld4.class
errors    : class HelloWorld4
    ORA-29521: referenced name oracle/jdbc2/SQLData could not be found
    ORA-29521: referenced name oracle/jdbc2/SQLInput could not be found
    ORA-29521: referenced name oracle/jdbc2/SQLOutput could not be found
The following operations failed
    class HelloWorld4: resolution
exiting   : Failures occurred during processing
```

If you get an ORA-29549 error, you're missing a Java archive reference. As noted earlier in the chapter, an ORA-29549 error is also raised when the Java class is removed and replaced the first time it's called.

TIP
If you replace your Java class files, make sure you call them once from the target schema to avoid users' managing the Java session change.

Now that you've reviewed the major issues with building, loading, and dropping Java stored object class files, let's examine some errors in the SQL and PL/SQL environments.

Using Java Class Library Objects
When you use Java stored object classes, you should ensure you define only one constructor in the PL/SQL object type definition. The only constructor acted on by a PL/SQL object type wrapper is the default constructor.

TIP
Avoid overriding constructors unless you plan to call them from other Java libraries wrapped as procedures and functions.

An example of overriding constructors being ignored is found in the HelloWorld4e.sql script. The script references the HelloWorld4.class file addressed earlier in the chapter. HelloWorld4e.sql defines two constructors for the HelloWorld4.class file. One is a null argument constructor, and the other is a single formal parameter argument. Since there's no duplicate constructor defined in the targeted class file, you would expect the following object type definition to fail:

```
-- This is found in HelloWorld4.sql on the publisher's web site.

-- Create a PL/SQL wrapper package to a Java class file.
CREATE OR REPLACE TYPE hello_world4 AS OBJECT
EXTERNAL NAME 'HelloWorld4' LANGUAGE JAVA
USING SQLData
( instanceName VARCHAR2(100) EXTERNAL NAME 'java.lang.String'
, CONSTRUCTOR FUNCTION hello_world4
  RETURN SELF AS RESULT
, CONSTRUCTOR FUNCTION hello_world4
  ( instanceName VARCHAR2 )
  RETURN SELF AS RESULT
, MEMBER FUNCTION getQualifiedName
```

```
   RETURN VARCHAR2 AS LANGUAGE JAVA
   NAME 'HelloWorld4.getQualifiedName() return java.lang.String'
, MEMBER FUNCTION getSQLTypeName
   RETURN VARCHAR2 AS LANGUAGE JAVA
   NAME 'HelloWorld4.getSQLTypeName() return java.lang.String' )
INSTANTIABLE FINAL;

/
```

It does not fail, however, but instead succeeds in defining a type that misrepresents the internal Java program's capabilities. You can test this program with the `HelloWorld4e.sql` script, which demonstrates that the type fails to support the overriding constructor:

-- This is found in HelloWorld4e.sql on the publisher's web site.

```
DECLARE

   -- Define and instantiate an object instance.
   my_obj1 hello_world4 := hello_world4('Adam');
   my_obj2 hello_world4 := hello_world4('Eve');

   PROCEDURE write_debug
   ( number_in NUMBER
   , value_in  VARCHAR2 ) IS
   BEGIN
     INSERT INTO java_debug VALUES (number_in,value_in);
   END write_debug;
BEGIN
   -- Test class instance.
   dbms_output.put_line('Item #1: ['||my_obj1.getQualifiedName||']');
   write_debug(101,'Item #1 Completed');
   dbms_output.put_line('Item #2: ['||my_obj2.getQualifiedName||']');
   write_debug(102,'Item #2 Completed');
   dbms_output.put_line('Item #3: ['||my_obj1.getSQLTypeName||']');
   write_debug(103,'Item #3 Completed');
   dbms_output.put_line('Item #4: ['||my_obj1.getSQLTypeName||']');
   write_debug(104,'Item #4 Completed');

   -- Test metadata repository with DBMS_JAVA.
   dbms_output.put_line(
     'Item #5: ['||user||'.'||dbms_java.longname('HELLO_WORLD4')||']');
END;
/
```

This will send the following output to your console:

-- This output is generated from the HelloWorld4e.sql file.

```
DECLARE
*
ERROR at line 1:
ORA-06502: PL/SQL: numeric or value error
ORA-06512: at line 4
```

This would imply that the overriding constructor takes a single VARCHAR2 formal parameter that cannot support a VARCHAR2 value. The real issue is that the SQLData type is what is passed and it's managed as a SQLData type. As noted earlier, the methods used in the SQLData interface define how values are passed.

You may encounter many issues when first implementing stored Java object classes and thus may benefit from building a java_debug error management table like the following:

```
CREATE TABLE java_debug
( debug_number NUMBER
, debug_value VARCHAR2(4000) );
```

Adding the following method to your Java class files will enable you to write to the java_debug table:

```
// Define the debugLog() method.
public void debugLog(int debug_number
                    ,String debug_value) throws SQLException {
  String statement = "INSERT INTO java_debug VALUES (?,?)";

  // Declare an Oracle connection.
  Connection conn = DriverManager.getConnection("jdbc:default:connection:");

  // Declare prepared statement, run query and read results.
  PreparedStatement ps = conn.prepareStatement(statement);
  ps.setInt(1,debug_number);
  ps.setString(2,debug_value);
  ps.execute(); }
```

The two question marks in the VALUES clause of the INSERT statement let you bind positional variables from your Java program into the SQL statement. You have now covered the major issues with troubleshooting Java stored object classes. The next section summarizes the mapping of Oracle types to Java types.

Mapping Oracle Types

Oracle maps all native types and user-defined types (UDTs) to Java types. When you use SQLData, you map individual components and structures. Table 15-1 shows how Oracle types map to Java types.

Native types and UDTs can be used and managed by the SQLData conventions covered in the chapter. The Oracle JPublisher tool enables you to develop SQLData stubs and programs to use your UDTs.

SQL Datatypes	Java Class Datatypes
CHAR	oracle.sql.CHAR
LONG	java.lang.String
VARCHAR2	java.lang.Byte
	java.lang.Short
	java.lang.Integer
	java.lang.Long
	java.lang.Float
	java.lang.Double
	java.lang.BigDecimal
	java.sql.Date
	java.sql.Time
	java.sql.Timestamp
	byte
	short
	int
	long
	float
	double
DATE	oracle.sql.DATE
	java.lang.String
	java.sql.Date
	java.sql.Time
	java.sql.Timestamp
NUMBER	oracle.sql.NUMBER
	java.lang.Byte
	java.lang.Short
	java.lang.Integer
	java.lang.Long
	java.lang.Float
	java.lang.Double
	java.lang.BigDecimal
	byte
	short
	int
	long
	float
	double

TABLE 15-1 *Oracle Datatypes Mapped to Java Datatypes*

SQL Datatypes	Java Class Datatypes
OPAQUE	oracle.sql.OPAQUE
RAW LONG RAW	oracle.sql.RAW byte[]
ROWID	oracle.sql.CHAR oracle.sql.ROWID java.lang.String
BFILE	oracle.sql.BFILE
BLOB	oracle.sql.BLOB oracle.jdbc2.Blob
CLOBNCLOB	oracle.sql.CLOB oracle.jdbc2.Clob
OBJECT Object types	oracle.sql.STRUCT java.sql.Struct java.sql.SqlData oracle.sql.ORAData
REF Reference types	oracle.sql.REF java.sql.Ref oracle.sql.ORAData
TABLE VARRAY Nested table and types VARRAY types	oracle.sql.ARRAY java.sql.Array oracle.sql.ORAData
Any of the preceding SQL types	oracle.sql.CustomDatum oracle.sql.Datum

TABLE 15-1   *Oracle Datatypes Mapped to Java Datatypes* (continued)

Summary

You should now have an understanding of how to implement and troubleshoot server-side or internal Java class libraries. With these skills, you can build robust solutions in Java, providing you an alternative in lieu of PL/SQL.

CHAPTER
16

Web Application
Development

here are many opportunities for building web applications against an Oracle 11*g* database. This book contains examples of PHP web application development in Chapter 8 to illustrate LOBs, and server-side Java Libraries in Chapter 15. Appendixes C and D support these development examples. Appendix D also highlights how to use the JDBC to support Java applications.

You require a separate Apache HTTP server whether you use a scripting solution in PHP or JServlet solution in Java. This chapter explores Oracle complete solutions using PL/SQL programming solutions.

This chapter covers the following topics:

- PL/SQL web server architectures
- Configuring a standalone Oracle HTTP server
    - Describing the `mod_plsql` cartridge
    - Configuring the Oracle HTTP server
- Configuring the XML DB Server
    - Configuring static authentication
    - Configuring dynamic authentication
    - Configuring anonymous authentication
- Comparison of PL/SQL web procedures and pages
- Creating web-enabled PL/SQL procedures
    - Developing procedures without formal parameters
    - Developing procedures with formal parameters
- Creating PL/SQL Server Pages (PSPs)
    - Developing procedures without formal parameters
    - Developing procedures with formal parameters

Oracle 10*g* and 11*g* provides another alternative that relies completely on the Oracle database. It is the Oracle XML Database Server, which is more commonly referred to as the Oracle XML DB Server. The Oracle XML DB Server is a built-in Apache HTTP server. A similar solution exists for Oracle 9*i* and 10*g*, but it requires the Oracle HTTP Server (OHS).

Like Oracle 10*g*, Oracle 11*g* deploys Application Express. Application Express lets you build web applications by leveraging a framework built on the framework of the Oracle HTMLDB product. In both releases, this product uses the Oracle XML DB Server *(sometimes abbreviated as XDB)*. Unlike Oracle 10*g*, Oracle 11*g* ships without the standalone OHS.

The Database Configuration Assistant (DBCA) installs the XML DB Server as a component of the sample database instance. The XML DB Server contains a complete Apache configuration inside the database instance. It also supports its own listener, which is the XML DB Listener. You configure the XML DB through the Oracle Enterprise Manager or by using the DBMS_EPG package.

Oracle 9*i* and 10*g* shipped the Oracle HTTP Server (OHS) on the companion disk. Oracle-only web solutions required you to configure OHS to deliver standalone PL/SQL web pages. With the release of Oracle 11*g*, OHS is now considered exclusively part of the Oracle Application Server product.

PL/SQL web programs depend on the OHS or XML DB product and the PL/SQL Toolkit. The PL/SQL Toolkit is actually the *PL/SQL Web Toolkit.* The original PL/SQL Toolkit shipped with Oracle 7. It has been expanded and stabilized in subsequent releases. The PL/SQL Toolkit enables developers to render dynamic web pages based on business logic embedded in stored procedures or PL/SQL Server Pages (PSPs).

PSPs were introduced in Oracle 8*i* (version 8.1.6). These enable you to build the equivalent of Java Server Pages (JSPs) without having to master both Java and PL/SQL. PSPs follow the same pattern as scripting language, JSPs, and ASPs (Active Server Pages from Microsoft in the .NET suite). The nice thing about PSPs is that you don't have to build a JServlet because Oracle provides an alternative framework. The first production release of Oracle 11*g* ships with the PL/SQL Web Toolkit, version 10.1.2.0.8.

This chapter introduces you to the big picture of using the PL/SQL web pages. You learn how to set up OHS, and XML DB to work with PL/SQL stored procedures and PL/SQL web pages (PSPs). Setup requires that you understand the purpose of the mod_plsql cartridge and how to configure it. If you understand the architecture well, you may skip to points of interest, but each section in the chapter depends on earlier topics.

PL/SQL Web Server Architecture

The PL/SQL web server architecture depends on an implementation choice. Oracle 9*i* lets you choose to implement the Oracle Application Server or Oracle HTTP Server (OHS). Oracle 10*g* lets you choose to implement the Oracle Application Server, OHS, or XML DB Server. Oracle 11*g* lets you choose to implement the Oracle Application Server or XML DB product. The architecture of the OHS and XML DB products are discussed in the next two sections.

Discovering the PL/SQL Web Toolkit Version
You can find the PL/SQL Web Toolkit Version by running the GET_VERSION function of the OWA_UTIL package. You should connect as the SYS user and run the following query:

```
SELECT owa_util.get_version AS "PL/SQL Toolkit" FROM dual;
```

A query against the Oracle 11*g* (11.1.0.6.0) product should return the following:

```
PL/SQL Toolkit
--------------
10.1.2.0.8
```

It is very likely that subsequent releases of Oracle 11*g* update the PL/SQL Web Toolkit version.

Oracle HTTP Server Architecture

The OHS provides an HTTP listener to receive and process Uniform Resource Locator (URL) requests. It is based on the Apache HTTP server. The Apache and OHS server support the Common Gateway Interface (CGI), which enables running server-side include programs. They also support Apache modules.

CGI was the beginning of web applications, but it had a big problem. Every call to the web server launched the interpreter for a scripting language. Launching an interpreter to run a program is a form of dynamic marshaling. The process is resource intensive and fails to scale well. As the Apache HTTP Server matured, configuring and pre-spawning the programming language interpreters became an obvious solution to eliminate the dynamic marshaling load from the web servers.

Perl is one of the early scripting languages. It requires an interpreter to run programs. Perl programs are also known as server-side includes (small web server program files). Server-side includes are programs located on the web server. The web server can be a standalone machine or an application server tier in *n*-tier application computing solutions. Perl uses an Apache module known as mod_perl, which embeds a Perl interpreter inside the Apache server and reduces the overhead needed to launch requests that run Perl programs.

Oracle implements a mod_plsql module that does the same thing for PL/SQL programs. OHS defines the relationship between incoming requests based on a virtual mapping that links by a Data Access Descriptor (DAD). The DAD contains the connection information to manage an HTTP-pipelined connection to the Oracle database. Information received in the URL by the OHS listener is mapped against possible DAD values. The DAD values then map the connections to the database. The DAD is in the Apache/modplsql/conf/dads.conf physical file, which resides in the OHS home.

NOTE
The OHS home must be separate from the Oracle database home when they are on the same tiers.

There are two approaches to implementing OHS. One includes the Oracle Application Server 9*i*/10*g,* which is delivered in the standard product release. The other approach is as a smaller standalone component with the Oracle 9*i*/10*g* Database. Configuration of the Oracle Application Server 9*i*/10*g* can be found in Chapter 4 of the *Oracle Application Server 10g Administration Handbook* by by John Garmany and Donald K. Burleson (McGraw-Hill, 2004). This chapter demonstrates the configuration of the smaller solution shipped with the Oracle Database product.

The general architecture is displayed in Figure 16-1.

As you can see from the figure, the process is as follows:

1. OHS receives a PL/SQL procedure or PSP request from a client browser.

2. OHS routes the request to the mod_plsql module.

3. The request is forwarded by mod_plsql to a stored procedure on the Oracle Database. The mod_plsql module routes the request by reading the DAD mapping information, which is stored on the file system. The mod_plsql module also prepares call parameters and calls database code.

4. A stored procedure generates an HTML page by calling the PL/SQL Web Toolkit. You can create a web-enabled stored procedure or a PSP, which acts as a stored procedure.

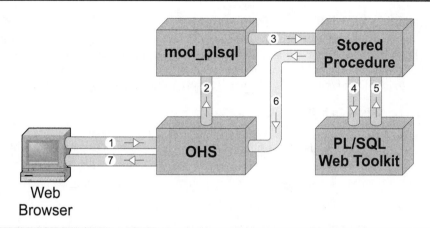

FIGURE 16-1   *Overview of the Oracle HTTP Server (OHS)*

5. The PL/SQL Web Toolkit returns HTML formatting to the calling procedure.

6. The stored procedure returns a formatted HTML page as a response to OHS.

7. OHS forwards the return HTML page back to the client browser, where it is rendered.

You have covered the general architecture for the OHS product. The next section describes the XML DB Server and its process.

Oracle XML Database Server Architecture

The XML Database Server (or XML DB Server) is an embedded service in the Oracle 11*g* database. It is an Apache HTTP Server with an embedded PL/SQL gateway. The gateway also has a Database Access Descriptor (DAD) maintained in the database. Like a standard Apache HTTP server, the XML Database Server supports CGI and Apache modules. The embedded PL/SQL gateway also has a DAD. Unlike the OHS product, the XML Database Server requires all maintenance to be done through the database.

NOTE
If you want your database server behind a firewall, you should configure it in standalone mode.

You must have the XDBA Admin role privilege to administer the XML Database Server, and you must enable the ANONYMOUS user account. By default, the ANONYMOUS user account is locked. The section "Configuring the XML DB Server" shows you how to perform these administrative tasks.

Oracle 11*g* installs the XML DB Server with the sample demonstration database when you use the DBCA tool. If you built the database instance without using the DBCA tool, you may have to install the XML DB Server separately.

The general architecture of the XML DB Server is displayed in Figure 16-2.

Installing XML DB Server from Scratch

You can install and start the XML DB Server in an Oracle 11g database if you didn't do so when you created the database. It is critical that you start the database instance in Oracle 9.2.0 compatibility or higher for the installation to work.

To install and configure the XML DB Server, follow these steps:

1. Create an XDB schema.

2. Run the `catqm.sql` creation script found in the Oracle home `rdbms/admin` directory as the `SYS` user. You need to provide the XDB password, tablespace name, and temporary tablespace name when running the script, like

   ```
   @catqm.sql xdb_password xdb_tablespace_name temporary_tablespace_name
   ```

3. Reconnect as the `SYS` user and run the `catxdbj.sql` script:

   ```
   @catxdbj.sql
   ```

4. Add the following line to your `init.ora` file:

   ```
   Dispatchers = "(PROTOCOL = TCP) (SERVICE = <sid>XDB)"
   ```

5. Restart the database and listener so that the XML DB Server can start.

6. Unlock the `ANONYMOUS` user account if you want to allow unauthenticated access to the database.

You can find the configuration sequences and discussion in the section "Configuring XML DB Server" later in the chapter. It also explains the various authentication modes for the product.

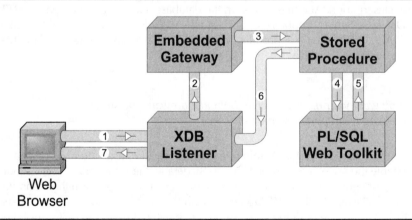

FIGURE 16-2 *Overview of the XML Database Server (XDB)*

As you can see from the figure, the process is very similar to the standalone OHS handling of requests:

1. The XML DB Listener receives a PL/SQL procedure or PSP request from a client browser.

2. XML DB Listener routes the request to the Embedded PL/SQL Gateway as specified in the virtual-path mapping defined in the DAD. The request is forwarded by the embedded PL/SQL Gateway's mod_plsql to the stored procedure in the Oracle Database. The mod_plsql module routes the request by reading the DAD mapping information, which is stored in the database. At this point, the Embedded PL/SQL Gateway authenticates access.

3. The Embedded PL/SQL Gateway's mod_plsql module prepares call parameters and calls the database stored procedure.

4. A stored procedure generates an HTML page by calling the PL/SQL Web Toolkit. You can create a web-enabled stored procedure or a PSP, which acts as a stored procedure.

5. The PL/SQL Web Toolkit returns HTML formatting to the calling procedure.

6. The stored procedure returns a formatted HTML page as a response to the XML DB Listener.

7. XML DB Listener forwards the return HTML page back to the client browser, where it is rendered.

You can configure XML DB Server to support static or dynamic authentication models. The DBMS_EPG package lets you configure the authentication model.

The XML DB Server supports XMLType tables and an XML Repository. There are Service Oriented Architecture (SOA) services that support PL/SQL and Java APIs for managing and working with XMLTypes. The PL/SQL API is defined by the DBMS_XDB package. Java is supported through Java/JNI. It also supports versioning, Access Control Lists (ACLs), and foldering technologies. You also have access to the XML Developer Kit (XDK).

The master configuration file is xdbconfig.xml. It is physically stored in the database but you can find the template xdbconfig.xml.11.0 in the /rdbms/xml subdirectory of the Oracle home. You can query the file with the following formatting:

```
SET LONG 100000
SET PAGESIZE 9999
SELECT dbms_xdb.cfg_get() FROM dual;
```

This returns the XMLType for the xdbconfig.xml file. The formatting ensures that you can see the entire XML file. You can read more about the XML DB Server in the Oracle XML DB Developer's Guide.

The following two sections describe how you configure OHS for Oracle 9*i* or 10*g*, or XML DB for Oracle 11*g*.

Configuring the Standalone Oracle HTTP Server

The OHS product changes with each release of the Oracle Database server. This section describes how it works in Oracle 9*i* and 10*g*. You also learn how to configure the mod_plsql DAD and the standalone Oracle HTTP Server shipped with the Oracle Database 9*i*/10*g*.

NOTE
The Oracle Database 10g ships the OHS product on the companion CD, so you'll need to install it. The companion disk also contains critical components for the Oracle Call Interface (OCI), which is discussed in more detail in Chapter 13.

Describing mod_plsql Cartridge

The `mod_plsql` module or cartridge is a framework that provides essential services. It was originally defined as a cartridge in the Common Object Request Broker Architecture (CORBA). You probably know it better as a module. The Oracle PL/SQL Gateway is delivered by `mod_plsql`, which provides the following services:

■ Accelerates your PL/SQL dynamic content.

■ Enables your PL/SQL programs to become part of OHS, which is an implementation of the Apache HTTP server.

■ Monitors access throughout the HTTP cycle from the URL to the HTML page return.

In Unix, the key to configuring `mod_plsql` is the DAD file. You'll find the DAD file in the `$OHS_HOME/Apache/modplsql/conf/dads.conf` file. The minimum configuration is noted next:

```
<Location /pls>
   SetHandler pls_handler
   Order deny,allow
   Allow from all
   AllowOverride None
   PlsqlDatabaseUsername          <oracle_user_name>
   PlsqlDatabasePassword          <oracle_password>
   PlsqlDatabaseConnectString     <hostname>.<domain_name>:<port>:<sid>
   PlsqlAuthenticationMode        Basic
</Location>
```

The Windows platform will require different changes. For instance, the Oracle and OHS homes in Oracle 9*i* are in the same folder on Windows. You do not modify the `dads.conf` file, but rather the `$ORACLE_HOME\Apache\modplsql\cfg\plsql.conf` file.

The syntax is very rigid, and you can explore additional parameters by referring to the Oracle HTTP Server `mod_plsql` User's Guide. You can create multiple PL/SQL DADs in this configuration file. Also, you should read and understand the following before configuring the `dads.conf` file:

■ **Location**   Defines the URL component that will point to a specific DAD. This location marker enables you to define multiple DADs for any given Oracle Database instance.

■ **PlsqlDatabaseUsername**   Defines the Oracle instance user name.

■ **PlsqlDatabasePassword**   Defines the Oracle instance user's password. It is defined in clear text but may be obfuscated by running the `dadTool.pl` program.

■ **PlsqlDatabaseConnectString**   Defines the connection string to the instance. It requires the hostname domain name separated by a dot or period. Then, there is a colon that is followed by the port number for the Oracle Database listener, which is followed by a colon and the Oracle TNS service name used by the listener.

When you have configured your `dads.conf` file, you are ready to configure OHS. In case something goes wrong and you fail to connect with a ubiquitous error like a 503 from your web browser, you should enable logging. You enable logging by editing the following line in the `$OHS_HOME/conf/plsql.conf` file:

```
PlsqlLogEnable Off
```

You should change it to:

```
PlsqlLogEnable On
```

Log files will be generated for each URL attempt to connect to the database. The log files will be found in the `$OHS_HOME/Apache/modplsql/logs/_pls` directory. The last directory name in the path statement is generated automatically according to the location value used in the `dads.conf` file.

The most often encountered problem is a failure to connect to the database. If you get an error like the following, you have a connection problem between your `dads.conf` file and the Oracle Database listener:

```
<2749636625 ms>[ReqStartTime: 3/May/2005:12:49:26]
<2749636625 ms>Request ID ReqID:3758_1115146166
<2749636625 ms>Connecting to database with connect string : "CODE"
<2749748861 ms>ORA-12154 LogOn ORA-12154: TNS:could not resolve service name
<2749748862 ms>Stale Connection due to Oracle error 12154
<2749748862 ms>Logoff: Closing connection due to stale connection
<2749748862 ms>[ReqEndtime: 3/May/2005:12:51:18]
<2749748862 ms>[ReqExecTime: 112237 ms]
```

If you receive a connection error, please check all the related values and map them to your `listener.ora` and `tnsnames.ora` files. The potential errors in your `dads.conf` file are `PlsqlDatabaseUsername`, `PlsqlDatabasePassword`, and `PlsqlDatabaseConnectString` values.

Configuring the Oracle HTTP Server

All the Oracle HTTP Server versions require you to configure an environment file. The generic environment file requirements are noted next:

Unix

```
ORACLE_HOME=/<mnt_point>/<directories>
export ORACLE_HOME
PATH=$ORACLE_HOME/Apache/modplsql/conf:$PATH
export PATH
PATH=$ORACLE_HOME/perl/bin:$PATH;export PATH
LD_LIBRARY_PATH=$ORACLE_HOME/lib
export LD_LIBRARY_PATH
```

Windows

```
set ORACLE_HOME=<logical_drive>\<directories>
set PATH=%ORACLE_HOME%\Apache\modplsql\conf;%PATH%
set PATH=%ORACLE_HOME%\perl\bin;%PATH%
set LD_LIBRARY_PATH=%ORACLE_HOME%\lib
```

The next sections cover the configuration of Oracle 9*i* and 10*g* OHS standalone environments.

Configuring the Oracle 9*i* HTTP Server

After you have a correct environment file, you should source the file into your shell environment. Then, you will be able to start, stop, and the check status for the Oracle 9*i* OHS.

NOTE
In Linux or Unix, you can use the `env` *utility to see all your environment variables.*

Linux or Unix requires that you build an environment file with the following entry in order to start the OHS Apache services:

```
PATH=$ORACLE_HOME/Apache/Apache/bin:$PATH
export PATH
```

Sourcing a File

There are different mechanisms for sourcing an environment file into a Linux or Unix shell. Sourcing means that you read a file and set environment variables. Environment variables are aliases for canonical file paths or names. You can find your shell by running the following command:

```
# echo $SHELL
```

Then, you can source your environment variables using the appropriate command:

csh or tcsh

```
# source some_environment_file.env
```

Bourne, Korn, or Bash

```
# . some_environment_file.env
```

Assume that your environment file set the `$ORACLE_HOME` environment variable. You can see the value by typing

```
# cat $ORACLE_HOME
```

Microsoft Windows also supports environment variables. The only difference is that they are sourced by executing the environment file and enclosed by % symbols. You source a file in Windows as if you were executing it. As a result of that process difference, environment files are generally batch files. Batch files have a .bat file extension.

You start and stop OHS with the `apachectl` utility. The options are start, status, and stop. When you change the DAD configuration files, you need to stop and start OHS for the changes to take effect. You may find this behavior familiar, since this is how the Oracle listener works.

NOTE
The actual environment is defined for you in Windows in the startJSV and stopJSV batch files. The `%ORACLE_HOME%\Apache\Apache\bin` *folder contains these files.*

Configuring the Oracle 10*g* HTTP Server

As with the Oracle 9*i* configuration, you need to define a correct environment file. After defining it, you source the file into your shell environment. Then, you will be able to start, stop, and check the status for the Oracle 10*g* OHS.

Linux or Unix requires that you build an environment file to start the OHS Apache services. The environment file should contain the following:

```
PATH=$ORACLE_HOME/opmn/bin:$PATH
export PATH
```

Oracle 10*g* ships with a feature called the Oracle Process Management and Notification (OPMN) utility. The OPMN utility supports a web view of your database instance. These web pages rely on the OHS server. As a result, you can no longer start OHS with the `apachectl` utility because doing so may cause unexpected behavior in the OPMN utility.

In Oracle 10*g,* you start and stop OHS with `opmnctl` utility. The options are start, status, and stop. When you change the DAD configuration files, you need to stop and start OHS for the changes to take effect. Again, you may find this behavior familiar, since this is how the Oracle listener works.

NOTE
OHS configuration in 10g Release 2 is identical to that in 10g Release 1. Release 2 adds access to the XML DB Server through the `DBMS_EPG` *package.*

You have now learned how to configure the OHS product. The balance of the chapter will illustrate building stored PL/SQL procedures or PSPs.

Configuring the XML DB Server

The XML DB Server is completely self-contained in the Oracle 11*g* database. It has two principal elements. They are the XML DB Listener and the Embedded PL/SQL Gateway. You enable the XML DB Listener by setting the `dispatchers` parameter in the Oracle `init.ora` file, and configure it through the `DBMS_XDB` package. The Embedded PL/SQL Gateway manages the Data Access Descriptor (DAD) and `mod_plsql` components. You use the `DBMS_EPG` package.

Table 16-1 shows the map between DAD attributes used in both the `mod_plsql` and Embedded PL/SQL Gateway. Table 16-2 shows how the two global attributes map between the two products. Global attributes apply to all DADs in the XML DB Server.

mod_plsql DAD Attribute Name	Embedded PL/SQL Gateway DAD Attribute Name	Legal Values
PlsqlAfterProcedure	after-procedure	String
PlsqlAlwaysDescribeProcedure	always-describe-procedure	On, Off
PlsqlAuthenticationMode	authentication-mode	Basic, SingleSignOn, GlobalOwa, CustomOwa, PerPackageOwa
PlsqlBeforeProcedure	before-procedure	String
PlsqlBindBucketLengths	bind-bucket-lengths	Unsigned integer
PlsqlBindBucketWidths	bind-bucket-widths	Unsigned integer
PlsqlCGIEnvironmentList	cgi-environment-list	String
PlsqlCompatibilityMode	compatibility-mode	Unsigned integer
PlsqlDatabaseConnectString	database-connect-string	String
PlsqlDatabasePassword	database-password	String
PlsqlDatabaseUsername	database-username	String
PlsqlDefaultPage	default-page	String
PlsqlDocumentPath	document-path	String
PlsqlDocumentProcedure	document-procedure	String
PlsqlDocumentTablename	document-table-name	String
PlsqlErrorStyle	error-style	ApacheStyle, ModplsqlStyle, DebugStyle
PlsqlExclusionList	exclusion-list	String
PlsqlFetchBufferSize	fetch-buffer-size	Unsigned integer
PlsqlInfoLogging	info-logging	InfoDebug
PlsqlInputFilterEnable	input-filter-enable	String
PlsqlMaxRequestsPerSession	max-requests-per-session	Unsigned integer
PlsqlNLSLanguage	nls-language	String
PlsqlOWADebugEnable	owa-debug-enable	On, Off
PlsqlPathAlias	path-alias	String
PlsqlPathAliasProcedure	path-alias-procedure	String
PlsqlRequestValidationFunction	request-validation-function	String
PlsqlSessionCookieName	session-cookie-name	String
PlsqlSessionStateManagement	session-state-management	StatelessWithResetPackageState, StatelessWithFastResetPackageState, StatelessWithPreservePackageState
PlsqlTransferMode	transfer-mode	Char, Raw
PlsqlUploadAsLongRaw	upload-as-long-raw	String

TABLE 16-1   *Map of mod_plsql and Embedded PL/SQL Gateway DAD Attributes*

`mod_plsql` **Global Attribute Name**	**Embedded PL/SQL Gateway** **Global Attribute Name**	**Legal Values**
PlsqlLogLevel	log-level	Unsigned integer
PlsqlMaxParameters	max-parameters	Unsigned integer

TABLE 16-2   *Map of mod_plsql and Embedded Pl/SQL Gateway Global Attributes*

Users of `mod_plsql` do not require you to set the `PlsqlDatabasePassword` or `PlsqlDatabaseConnectString` attributes. Default values are generally sufficient for most users of the Embedded PL/SQL Gateway.

There are three ways to create DADs for the Embedded PL/SQL Gateway. The first method uses static authentication. Static authentication is for those migrating `mod_plsql` applications that provide credentials inside the DAD configuration file. It relies on the schema user and password. The second mode uses dynamic authentication, which requires the user to authenticate through the browser. This is known as Basic HTTP Authentication, and it sends user credentials in clear text. This is how the XML DB Server is authenticated as a default configuration. The third method uses anonymous authentication. This is how Oracle Application Express connects to the database.

Oracle 11*g* provides you with a diagnostic script that helps you understand the current configuration of the XML DB Server. It is the `epgstat.sql` script, which is found in `/rdbms/admin` subdirectory of the Oracle home. The script checks the following:

- Configured HTTP and FTP ports of the XML DB Server (0 by default)

- DAD virtual mappings

- DAD attributes

- DAD authorizations

- `ANONYMOUS` user status (expired and locked by default)

- `ANONYMOUS` users access to XML DB repository (disabled by default)

You can run the `epgstat.sql` script anytime as the `SYS` account. Alternatively, you can grant the `XDBADMIN` role to another user you can perform most of the configuration steps.

Running Configuration Scripts from the Oracle Home

When you administer Oracle services, upgrade, or maintain the database, you learn a few tricks and techniques for running scripts from the Oracle home. One is that you can substitute a *question mark* for the environment variable `$ORACLE_HOME` (in Linux or Unix) or `%ORACLE_HOME%` (in Windows) to reference the Oracle home.

You can run the `epgstat.sql` script as follows from inside the SQL*Plus environment:

```
SQL> @?/rdbms/admin/epgstat.sql
```

In a Windows operating system, you need to replace the forward slashes with backslashes.

Before you begin the authorization sections, you should set the HTTP listening port. You do this by calling the DBMS_XDB.SETHTTPPORT procedure. In this sample, the HTTP listening port is set to 8080, but you can substitute another if you prefer.

```
EXEC DBMS_XDB.SETHTTPPORT(8080);
```

The epgstat.sql program should report the new port. Alternatively, you can run the following block to find the HTTP listening port:

```
DECLARE
  endpoint NUMBER := 1;
  host     VARCHAR2(40);
  port     NUMBER := -1;
  protocol NUMBER := -1;
BEGIN
  dbms_xdb.getlistenerendpoint(endpoint,host,port,protocol);
  dbms_output.put_line('port ['||port||']');
END;
/
```

There are three steps to creating the DAD. You create it, map a database user to it, and authorize the database user to use it. Alternatively, you can grant the EXECUTE privilege to the user on the DBMS_EPG package and the user can self-authorize. The AUTHORIZE_DAD procedure is overloaded to support these approaches. The following example uses the latter approach, given that it leaves it to the developer, not the DBA.

The next three sections guide you through these configuration types. There is duplication in the following subsections because it seemed more effective to let you read any approach without flipping pages for odds and ends in others.

Configuring Static Authentication

Static authentication is a direct corollary to a mod_plsql user who stores the username and password in the DAD. This means that the browser user doesn't have to enter any authentication to see the web page. This is fine for unsecured web pages that display dynamic but public information.

Create the DAD

You create a DAD by mapping a virtual directory to the XML DB Server. The example uses the /pls/ virtual path. You call the CREATE_DAD procedure, as shown:

```
EXEC DBMS_EPG.CREATE_DAD('PLSQL_DAD','/pls/*');
```

The asterisk (*) following the /pls/ virtual directory simply acknowledges everything in that virtual directory. After creating the DAD, you need to set the database-username attribute. You do so by calling the following procedure:

```
EXEC DBMS_EPG.SET_DAD_ATTRIBUTE('PLSQL_DAD','database-username','ANONYMOUS');
```

The DAD attribute is case-sensitive and must be lowercase. The user account should be uppercase. Leaving the DAD in uppercase works and is easier to read.

You have now created a PLSQL_DAD. The next step is authorizing the DAD.

Configure the DAD

You have two choices when you authorize the DAD. Authority can remain with only those users who hold the XDBADMIN role, or you can delegate authority to the schema that owns the PL/SQL web procedures or PSPs.

If you don't choose to authorize the user schema, you can authorize the DAD by calling this as the SYS user or another user who holds the XDBADMIN role privilege:

```
EXECUTE dbms_epg.authorize_dad('PLSQL_DAD','PLSQL');
```

NOTE
This call to AUTHORIZE_DAD requires that the user have the ALTER
ANY USER *privilege directly and not through a role.*

You can authorize the user schema by granting the EXECUTE privilege on the DBMS_EPG package, like

```
GRANT EXECUTE ON dbms_epg TO plsql;
```

Reconnect to the PLSQL user and authorize yourself with this call:

```
EXECUTE dbms_epg.authorize_dad('PLSQL_DAD','PLSQL');
```

You have now authorized the DAD. The next step is configuring the database by granting permissions and creating synonyms.

This configuration doesn't require you to grant privileges or build synonyms. It is ideal when you have dynamic content but no intent of restricting access through the DAD.

Configuring Dynamic Authentication

Dynamic authentication relies on Basic HTTP Authentication. This is a bad or good thing, depending on your perspective. It means that any time a user accesses the web pages, that user must have the database user name and password. Most security people dislike this approach and may nix it in a production system because it transmits information in clear text.

Dynamic authentication is a convenient testing mechanism when you're developing PL/SQL web applications. It lets you circumvent your ACL and test PL/SQL web procedures and PSPs directly. You can maintain one dynamic DAD while maintaining another static or anonymous DAD for end-user testing.

You create and authorize a DAD in this solution because it goes directly to the user schema for access. End-user authentication occurs in the browser.

Create the DAD

You create a DAD by mapping a virtual directory to the XML DB Server. The example uses /pls/ virtual path. You call the CREATE_DAD procedure, as shown:

```
EXEC DBMS_EPG.CREATE_DAD('DYNAMIC_DAD','/pls/*');
```

Again, the asterisk (*) following the /pls/ virtual directory simply acknowledges everything in that virtual directory. After creating the DAD, you need to set the database-username attribute. You do so by calling the following procedure:

```
EXEC DBMS_EPG.SET_DAD_ATTRIBUTE('DYNAMIC_DAD','database-username','PLSQL');
```

The DAD attribute is case-sensitive and must be lowercase. The user account should be uppercase. Leaving the DAD in uppercase works and is easier to read.

You have now created a dynamic PLSQL_DAD that uses Basic HTTP authentication. There is no next step because you don't have to authorize the DAD. You have delegated authorization to the browser and the XML DB Listener.

Configuring Anonymous Authentication

Anonymous authentication connects to a neutral schema where there isn't any data. The ANONYMOUS schema is designed to support this type of model. After enabling this schema and configuring the Embedded PL/SQL Gateway, you grant execute permissions on your procedures to the ANONYMOUS schema. Naturally, you then define synonyms in the ANONYMOUS schema to resolve directly to the schema where you've put the procedures. This process of grants and synonyms also works for PSPs.

The anonymous authentication method requires the ANONYMOUS schema. It is locked and expired by default during most installations. You will need to unlock and then open the ANONYMOUS schema before you proceed with the configuration.

Open the ANONYMOUS Schema

You open the anonymous schema by taking two administrative steps. You should be either the SYSTEM user or someone with the DBA role privilege to perform these commands.

You unlock the ANONYMOUS user with the following command:

```
ALTER USER anonymous ACCOUNT UNLOCK;
```

After you unlock the account, the epgstat.sql script will show that it is still expired. You can open the account by assigning a password to the ANONYMOUS user with the following:

```
ALTER USER anonymous IDENTIFIED BY anonymous;
```

NOTE
The dba_users view no longer contains encrypted passwords in Oracle 11g; you have to fetch them from the user$ table in the SYS schema.

While you're here, you should now grant the CREATE ANY SYNONYM privilege to the ANONYMOUS user. The user needs it to make the PL/SQL web pages available in a browser. The syntax is

```
GRANT CREATE ANY SYNONYM TO anonymous;
```

Create the DAD

You create a DAD by mapping a virtual directory to the XML DB Server. The example uses the /pls/ virtual path. You call the CREATE_DAD procedure, as shown:

```
EXEC DBMS_EPG.CREATE_DAD('PLSQL_DAD','/pls/*');
```

The asterisk (*) following the /pls/ virtual directory simply acknowledges everything in that virtual directory. After creating the DAD, you need to set the database-username attribute. You do so by calling the following procedure:

```
EXEC DBMS_EPG.SET_DAD_ATTRIBUTE('PLSQL_DAD','database-username','ANONYMOUS');
```

The DAD attribute is case-sensitive and must be lowercase. The user account should be uppercase. Leaving the DAD in uppercase works and is easier to read.

You have now created a `PLSQL_DAD`. The next step is authorizing the DAD.

Configure the DAD

You have two choices when you authorize the DAD. Authority can remain with only those users who hold the `XDBADMIN` role, or you can delegate authority to the schema that owns the PL/SQL web procedures or PSPs.

If you don't choose to authorize the user schema, you can authorize the DAD by calling this as the `SYS` user or another user who holds the `XDBADMIN` role privilege:

```
EXECUTE dbms_epg.authorize_dad('PLSQL_DAD','PLSQL');
```

As mentioned earlier in a note, a user must have the `ALTER ANY USER` privilege to indirectly authorize a DAD. You can authorize the user schema by granting the `EXECUTE` privilege on the `DBMS_EPG` package, like

```
GRANT EXECUTE ON dbms_epg TO plsql;
```

Reconnect to the `PLSQL` user and authorize yourself with this call:

```
EXECUTE dbms_epg.authorize_dad('PLSQL_DAD','PLSQL');
```

You have now authorized the DAD. The next step is configuring the database by granting permissions and creating synonyms.

Granting Permissions to and Creating Synonyms for Procedures or PSPs

This section shows you how to configure the `ANONYMOUS` user and `PLSQL` user accounts. The `PLSQL` user account holds ownership of the PL/SQL web procedures and PSPs. The `PLSQL` user must grant permissions to the `ANONYMOUS` user. The `ANONYMOUS` user then creates synonyms to the granted objects. This two-step process allows a smooth translation between the `ANONYMOUS` and `PLSQL` schemas and implements the definer rights model discussed in Chapter 9.

The easiest way to test whether you've successfully configured the Embedded PL/SQL Gateway is to run a copy of the `create_helloworld1.sql` script in the `PLSQL` schema. You can find the code in the section "Developing Procedures without Formal Parameters" later in this chapter. It creates a `helloworldprocedure1` procedure.

You should grant the `EXECUTE` privilege to the `ANONYMOUS` user, as shown:

```
GRANT EXECUTE ON helloworldprocedure1 TO anonymous;
```

Reconnect as the `ANONYMOUS` user, and create a synonym to this procedure. This requires that the `ANONYMOUS` user has the `CREATE ANY SYNONYM` privilege. You can use this syntax:

```
CREATE SYNONYM helloworldprocedure1 FOR plsql.helloworldprocedure1;
```

You can now test whether you have a PL/SQL web application. You can enter the following URL in a browser of your choice:

```
http://localhost:8080/pls/helloworldprocedure1
```

Figure 16-3 shows you what you should see. You've now learned how to configure Embedded PL/SQL Gateway anonymous authentication.

FIGURE 16-3 *Web page results from* `helloworldprocedure1` *procedure*

These sections have shown you how to configure the XML DB Server. You will use one of these configurations when you implement PL/SQL web procedures or PSPs in Oracle 11*g*, unless you also implement the Oracle 10*g* Application Server.

Comparing Web-Enabled PL/SQL Procedures and PSPs

There are two solutions to writing dynamic web pages using the PL/SQL programming language. One is writing PL/SQL procedures, and the other is writing PL/SQL Server Pages (PSPs). PSPs are similar to Java Server Pages (JSPs) because they combine PL/SQL and HTML components into a single working program.

Like PL/SQL procedures, PSPs also use the PL/SQL Web Toolkit to format HTML web pages. Table 16-3 has comparative guidelines to help you choose whether PL/SQL procedures or PSPs are best in your environment.

The remaining sections examine how you create web-enabled PL/SQL procedures and PSPs. The sections demonstrate that both approaches have much in common. PSPs syntax clearly differs from standard PL/SQL code, whereas the PL/SQL procedures are more similar.

Creating Web-Enabled PL/SQL Stored Procedures

Stored procedures work differently when they support PL/SQL web applications. They generate an HTML output stream that can't be read in the SQL*Plus environment. You can only see the stream rendered in a web page through the `mod_plsql` utility. This is accomplished by using the PL/SQL Web Toolkit.

The PL/SQL Web Toolkit provides a collection of packages that make PL/SQL stored procedures possible. Oracle 7 introduced the PL/SQL Web Toolkit. Table 16-4 lists the packages in the toolkit. The `HTP` package provides a means to render web pages, while the `HTF` package allows you to return variable-length HTML snippets that you can bundle into `HTP` package calls.

The PL/SQL Web Toolkit packages are in the *Oracle PL/SQL Packages and Type Reference*. Check them for further details on these packages.

PL/SQL Procedures	PL/SQL Server Pages
A large body of PL/SQL code that produces formatted output.	A large body of dynamic HTML to display in a single web page.
The Oracle Portal authoring tool, which uses the PL/SQL procedures.	Authoring tools effectively support PSPs.
Web pages require line-by-line formatting and control.	Web pages include JavaScript embedded tags.
Other server-side includes are used in the rendered page.	Other server-side includes are not used in the rendered page.
Migrating from static text web pages.	Migrating from Java Server Pages (JSPs) because they use the same syntax.
	Migrating Active Data Object (ADO) pages because Active Server Pages (ASPs) have a similar syntax.

TABLE 16-3   *Comparative Rationale for PL/SQL Procedures or PSPs*

Package	Description
HTP	The `HTP` procedure lets you generate HTML tags, which can be read from the `mod_plsql` module. For example, the procedure `HTP.BOLD` generates a HTML tag, like `<B>some_string</B>`

HTF	The `HTF` package lets you generate HTML tags and return them as strings to your program scope. You use the `HTF` functions when you want to nest rendered HTML tags in other `HTP` procedure calls. For example, the function `HTF.ITALIC` function creates a tag that can then be encapsulated by a call to `HTP.BOLD`, like
	`HTP.BOLD(HTF.ITALIC);`
	
	You would see a web page render:
	`<B><I>some_string</I></B>`

OWA_CACHE	The `OWA_CACHE` package helps improve performance by caching results on the application server. These functions and procedures are most suited to web architecture that uses the Oracle Application Server. You can also use this package to expire and validate caching while using the PL/SQL Gateway file system.

TABLE 16-4   *PL/SQL Toolkit Packages*

Package	Description
OWA_COOKIE	The OWA_COOKIE package lets you send, read, and remove cookies. Cookies are strings that browsers use to maintain state between HTTP calls. They limit the duration of the transaction state by setting a client session cookie expiration date. Passing cookies between the client and server is a risky business. You should minimize the data exchanged by storing state information on the server and returning only a key to the data as a cookie. The key is usually known as a session ID value. Exchanging only the session ID greatly enhance your web application security because you minimize the exchange and exposure of sensitive information to hackers.
OWA_CUSTOM	The OWA_CUSTOM contains a single AUTHORIZE function. You use the AUTHORIZE function when you are using custom or global authentication for the DAD. If enabled, the global PL/SQL agent connects to database using the DAD connection string before passing control for user validation to your application code.
OWA_IMAGE	The OWA_IMAGE package contains the GET_X and GET_Y functions. You call these procedures by using a variable of OWA_IMAGE.POINT datatype, which is a table of binary integers. The table never should contain more than two values. Index 1 returns the x-coordinate, and index 2 returns the y-coordinate. You use this package when you're managing a user-click in an image that triggers a PL/SQL Gateway event.
OWA_OPT_LOCK	The OWA_OPT_LOCK package implements an optimistic locking strategy to prevent the loss of data during updates. Lost updates can happen when a user selects, alters, and attempts to update a row whose values have already been changed. The changed values occur because another user also accessed the same data but changed it before the first user acts.
OWA_PATTERN	The OWA_PATTERN package implements a regular expression engine that allows you to match partial stings.
OWA_SEC	The OWA_SEC package provides program units to support the DAD. You use them to authenticate connections to the database from the PL/SQL Gateway.
OWA_TEXT	The OWA_TEXT package implements text manipulation functions and procedures to support the OWA_PATTERN matching features. You can also call these functions and procedures to support your code.
OWA_UTIL	The OWA_UTIL package supports dynamic SQL utilities, retrieving CGI environment variables, and date conversion from HTML strings to the Oracle DATE datatype. This package also supports your MIME content-type and header meta tags.
WPG_DOCLOAD	The WPG_DOCLOAD package provides you with the ability to download from a document repository. You must configure the DAD to support the repository before calling these subroutines. You can download or upload binary or text files in accordance with the RFC 1867 specification, "Form-Based File Upload in HTML" (IETF).

TABLE 16-4 *PL/SQL Toolkit Packages* (continued)

The next two sections show you how to implement PL/SQL procedures for web applications. The first section demonstrates how to build procedures without a formal parameter list. The next section shows you how to build procedures with formal parameter lists.

Developing Procedures Without Formal Parameters

A web application PL/SQL procedure renders an HTML web page when called by the PL/SQL gateway. You develop a web application PL/SQL procedure by using the same DDL command as you do for non-web application procedures.

The following program creates a "Hello World!" web page. It uses the HTP to create HTML tags, and the OWA_UTIL package to create an HTML metatag.

```
-- This is found in create_helloworld1.sql on the publisher's web site.
CREATE OR REPLACE PROCEDURE HelloWorldProcedure1 AS
BEGIN
  -- Set an HTML meta tag and render page.
  owa_util.mime_header('text/html');  -- <META Content-type:text/html>
  htp.htmlopen;                       -- <HTML>
  htp.headopen;                       -- <HEAD>
  htp.htitle('HelloWorldProcedure1'); -- <TITLE>HelloWorldProcedure</TITLE>
  htp.headclose;                      -- </HEAD>
  htp.bodyopen;                       -- <BODY>
  htp.line;                           -- <HR>
  htp.print('Hello world.');          -- Hello world.
  htp.line;                           -- <HR>
  htp.bodyclose;                      -- </BODY>
  htp.htmlclose;                      -- </HTML>

END HelloWorldProcedure1;
/
```

After you create the procedure, it is stored in the database. You can't access it by running it from the SQL*Plus command line. An attempt raises an ORA-06502 exception, which is a numeric or value error because the procedure expects a call from the PL/SQL gateway.

You can test the procedure by entering a URL in your web browser. The following URL assumes you've defined the DAD Location as /pls/, as done earlier in this chapter:

```
http://<hostname>.<domain_name>:<port>/pls/HelloWorldProcedure1
```

The web browser renders the image shown in Figure 16-4. The only difference between Figures 16-3 and 16-4 is that the port number changes for the OHS server. You can have both running in the same environment.

This example has shown you how to develop a static page. The next example teaches you how to build a dynamic page. The page also accepts actual parameters, which allow you to alter the returned values from the embedded query.

Developing Procedures with Formal Parameters

Web pages are dynamic when they have the ability to display different information from a data source, like a database or file system. Passing parameters to a web page enables dynamic behavior and content.

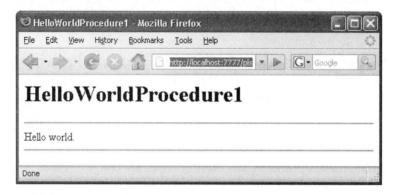

FIGURE 16-4 *Rendered HelloWorldProcedure1 web page*

There are two approaches to passing actual parameters to web pages. One is to use HTML form tags to collect input selections or data entry that are then submitted to the data source to render a new page. The other is to hard-code values in the URL statement.

PL/SQL Toolkit procedures support formal parameters just as they do in stored functions or procedures. You define the procedure with a formal parameter list, which is also known as the signature for the function or procedure. PL/SQL web pages only support the following native types as formal parameters:

- A NUMBER data type

- A VARCHAR2 data type

- A PL/SQL collection, which is limited to a table of NUMBER or VARCHAR2 data types. These are implemented by using the OWA_UTIL.IDENT_ARR type, which is an Oracle 9*i* index-by table or Oracle 10*g* associative array of NUMBER or VARCHAR2 native PL/SQL types.

You can overload procedures in PL/SQL, but mod_plsql raises an exception in some cases. For example, mod_plsql raises an exception if you use the same formal parameter name in overloaded procedures and only change the data type from NUMBER to VARCHAR2 or vice versa. However, you can use the same formal parameter name and change the data type to PL/SQL collections without raising an exception. The mod_plsql module can see the difference between a NUMBER or VARCHAR2 native type and PL/SQL collection.

You can find a basic example of this in the create_helloworld2.sql, and the script creates the following stored procedure:

```
-- This is found in create_helloworld2.sql on the publisher's web site.
CREATE OR REPLACE PROCEDURE HelloWorldProcedure2
( who VARCHAR2) AS
BEGIN
  -- Set a HTML MIME content-type before rendering a web page.
  owa_util.mime_header('text/html');      -- <META Content-type:text/html>
  htp.htmlopen;                           -- <HTML>
```

```
   htp.headopen;                                    -- <HEAD>
   htp.htitle('HelloWorldProcedure2');              -- <TITLE>HelloWorld...</TITLE>
   htp.headclose;                                   -- </HEAD>
   htp.bodyopen;                                    -- <BODY>
   htp.line;                                        -- <HR>
   htp.print('Hello '||who||'''s world.'); -- Hello world.
   htp.line;                                        -- <HR>
   htp.bodyclose;                                   -- </BODY>
   htp.htmlclose;                                   -- </HTML>
END HelloWorldProcedure2;
/
```

Like the earlier `HelloWorldProcedure1`, this is stored in the database by using a standard SQL DDL command. Once it is stored in the database, you access it by using a URL and your web browser. The following URL assumes you have defined the DAD location as `/pls/`, as done earlier in this chapter:

```
http://<hostname>.<domain_name>:<port>/pls/HelloWorldProcedure2?who=Developer
```

The URL appends a question mark and a list of variable assignments. The `who` is the defined variable name for the single formal parameter defined for the stored procedure, `HelloWorldProcedure2`. The variable name uses an equal sign to assign the next string to the value. The URL is parsed by the OHS, and the argument is managed by the `mod_plsql` module. The web browser renders the image shown in Figure 16-5.

The preceding example illustrated how you could build a dynamic PL/SQL Toolkit procedure with native types. You'll now learn how to pass a PL/SQL collection variable to the PL/SQL Toolkit procedure. The `create_store.sql` script creates an `item` table sequence and seeds the table to support the passing of a PL/SQL collection variable to a dynamic web page. As covered in the introduction, you should run the `create_store.sql` script in the `plsql` schema.

There are two approaches to managing a PL/SQL collection against the PL/SQL Toolkit. One approach is to use a single collection variable and pass it multiple times in the URL, while the other is to use flexible parameter passing.

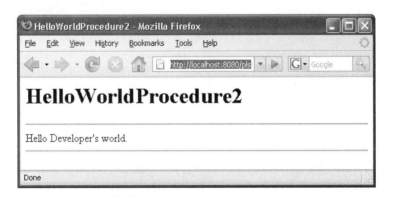

FIGURE 16-5 *Rendered HelloWorldProcedure2 web page*

The following example, found in the `create_item1.sql` script, uses a single parameter passed multiple times in the URL:

```
-- This is found in create_item1.sql on the publisher's web site.
CREATE OR REPLACE PROCEDURE item1
( items OWA_UTIL.IDENT_ARR ) AS
  CURSOR get_items
  ( begin_item_id NUMBER
  , end_item_id   NUMBER ) IS
    SELECT    item_id AS item_number
    ,         item_title||': '||item_subtitle AS item_title
    ,         item_release_date AS release_date
    FROM      item
    WHERE     item_id BETWEEN begin_item_id AND end_item_id;
BEGIN
  -- Set HTML page rendering tags.
  htp.htmlopen;
  htp.headopen;
  htp.htitle('Item List');  -- Sets the browser window and frame title.
  htp.headclose;
  htp.bodyopen;
  htp.line;
  -- Use PL/SQL Toolkit to format the page.
  htp.tableopen(cborder      => 2
              ,cattributes => 'style=background-color:feedb8');
    htp.tablerowopen;
      htp.tabledata(cvalue       => '#'
                  ,calign       => 'center'
                  ,cattributes => 'style=color:#336699
                                        background-color:#cccc99
                                        font-weight:bold
                                        width=50');
      htp.tabledata(cvalue       => 'Title'
                  ,calign       => 'center'
                  ,cattributes => 'style=color:#336699
                                        background-color:#cccc99
                                        font-weight:bold
                                        width=200');
      htp.tabledata(cvalue       => 'Release Date'
                  ,calign       => 'center'
                  ,cattributes => 'style=color:#336699
                                        background-color:#cccc99
                                        font-weight:bold
                                        width=100');
    htp.tablerowclose;
  -- Use a loop to collect the data.
  FOR i IN get_items(items(1),items(2)) LOOP
    htp.tablerowopen;
      htp.tabledata(cvalue       => i.item_number
                  ,calign       => 'center'
                  ,cattributes => 'style=background-color:#f7f7e7');
      htp.tabledata(cvalue       => i.item_title
```

```
                     ,calign       => 'left'
                     ,cattributes  => 'style=background-color:#f7f7e7');
      htp.tabledata(cvalue        => i.release_date
                     ,calign       => 'center'
                     ,cattributes  => 'style=background-color:#f7f7e7');
    htp.tablerowclose;
  END LOOP;
  -- Close the table.
  htp.tableclose;
  -- Print a line and close body and page.
  htp.line;
  htp.bodyclose;
  htp.htmlclose;
END item1;
/
```

You call this by using the following URL:

```
http://<hostname>.<domain_name>:<port>/pls/item1?items=1021&years=1031
```

The URL appends a question mark and a list of variable assignments. The first `items` parameter becomes element one in the PL/SQL collection, and the next parameter the second, and so on. This simple and easy-to-use syntax renders the following `HTP`-formatted web page shown in Figure 16-6.

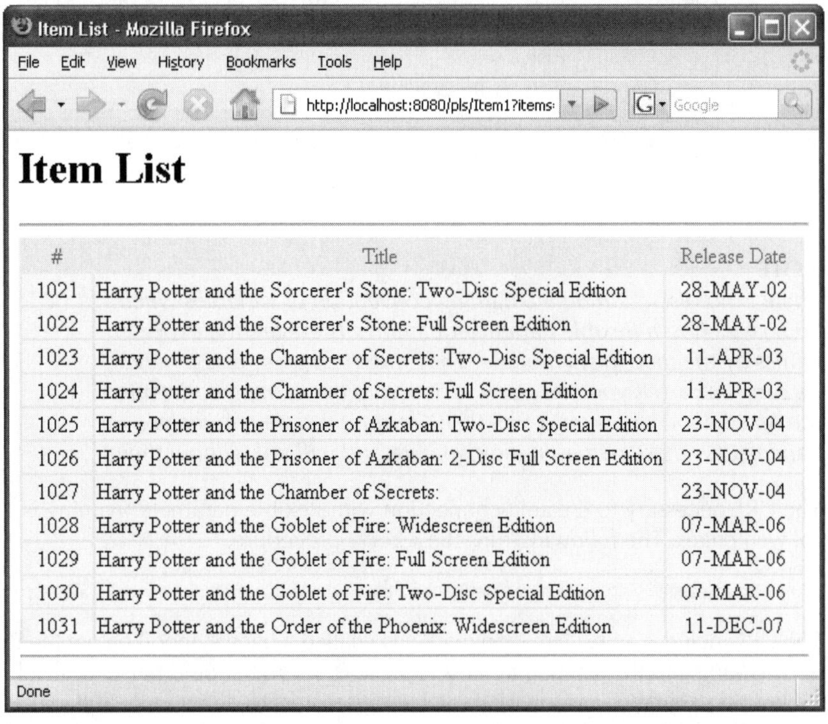

#	Title	Release Date
1021	Harry Potter and the Sorcerer's Stone: Two-Disc Special Edition	28-MAY-02
1022	Harry Potter and the Sorcerer's Stone: Full Screen Edition	28-MAY-02
1023	Harry Potter and the Chamber of Secrets: Two-Disc Special Edition	11-APR-03
1024	Harry Potter and the Chamber of Secrets: Full Screen Edition	11-APR-03
1025	Harry Potter and the Prisoner of Azkaban: Two-Disc Special Edition	23-NOV-04
1026	Harry Potter and the Prisoner of Azkaban: 2-Disc Full Screen Edition	23-NOV-04
1027	Harry Potter and the Chamber of Secrets:	23-NOV-04
1028	Harry Potter and the Goblet of Fire: Widescreen Edition	07-MAR-06
1029	Harry Potter and the Goblet of Fire: Full Screen Edition	07-MAR-06
1030	Harry Potter and the Goblet of Fire: Two-Disc Special Edition	07-MAR-06
1031	Harry Potter and the Order of the Phoenix: Widescreen Edition	11-DEC-07

FIGURE 16-6 *Rendered item1 web page*

The preceding example illustrated how you can build a dynamic PL/SQL Toolkit procedure with a PL/SQL collection type. There is also the approach using flexible parameter passing. Unfortunately, *Oracle 11g supports flexible parameter passing only when you implement the Oracle 10g Application Server.* It does work with Oracle 9*i* and 10*g,* provided you install and configure the standalone OHS product.

There are two alternatives for how you enable flexible parameter passing in standalone procedures. Oracle recommends you use two PL/SQL collection types, one as the index set and the other as the values set. While you can use use `OWA_UTIL.IDENT_ARR` or `OWA.IDENT_ARR` for variable-length strings of less than 30 characters in Oracle 9*i* or 10*g,* `OWA.IDENT_ARR` is no longer available in Oracle 11*g.* `OWA_UTIL.VC_ARR` or `OWA.VC_ARR` datatypes handle larger variable-length strings, and they are available in all releases through Oracle 11*g.*

NOTE
Flexible parameter passing works only when you use Oracle 10g Application Server or OHS, and it may be deprecated in a future release.

Flexible parameter passing is demonstrated in `create_item2.sql`, but only the signature of the procedure and actual parameters to the cursor change from the prior example. The code is unchanged except for those variable names. Flexible parameter passing requires specific variable names because they are managed by an Oracle HTTP API. The signature for the `items2` procedure follows:

```
-- This is found in create_item2.sql on the publisher's web site.
CREATE OR REPLACE PROCEDURE item2
( name_array    OWA.VC_ARR
, value_array   OWA.VC_ARR ) AS
...
  FOR i IN get_items(name_array(1),value_array(2)) LOOP
...
END item2;
/
```

NOTE
There is no discretion on the naming convention of variables when you have chosen flexible parameter naming. These are the expected names by the mod_plsql module. They must be `name_array` *and* `value_array`. *If you make any variation to the naming convention, the Apache log will show a PLS-00306 error. Flexible parameter naming uses these names in the signature and will fail without them.*

The URL necessary to create a connection with flexible parameter naming is a departure from typical web pages. The following runs the `item2` procedure:

```
http://<hostname>.<domain_name>:<port>/pls/!items2?begin=1052&end=1056
```

The URL includes an exclamation mark (also called a bang symbol) before the PL/SQL procedure name. The *bang* tells the standalone DAD that `mod_plsql` should parse for flexible parameter rules. Flexible parameter passing maps actual parameters to different PL/SQL datatypes than standard URL parameter passing without the bang. Figure 16-7 shows you the rendered web page.

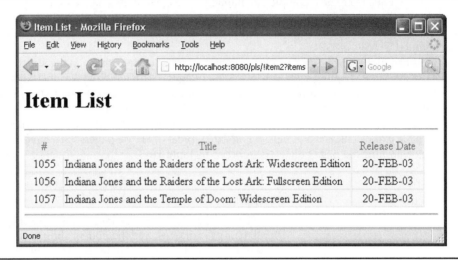

FIGURE 16-7   *Rendered item2 web page*

Ultimately, this method departs from every other web solution in the current market and is a backward-compatible legacy component. It appears that Oracle's direction moving forward may abandon flexible parameter passing. If you attempt to call this module through the XDB DB Listener, you return a file not found error (404). This occurs because the URL is parsed incorrectly.

TIP
When you want to have more than one set of PL/SQL collections passed to your PL/SQL Toolkit enabled procedure, you should avoid flexible parameter naming.

Understanding Advantages and Limitations

Advantages of PL/SQL Toolkit procedures include the ability to pass PL/SQL collections or tables of VARCHAR2 data types. Also, you can build small units called from other Java Server Pages (JSPs), from PSPs, or as links within static web pages. Calling them "static" is a misnomer, but physical files that contain links are known as static web pages.

Disadvantages are that you have a complex partial solution. PSPs offer a more flexible, intuitive, and consistent approach to dynamic page development.

Now that you have learned how to use the PL/SQL Toolkit to build dynamic web pages in this section, it's now time to explore PL/SQL Server Pages (PSPs) procedures.

Building and Accessing PL/SQL Server Pages (PSPs)

The ability to build PL/SQL Server Pages (PSPs) procedures is a powerful tool that's been available since Oracle 8*i*, Release 8.1.6. The following demonstrates how to develop and run PSP procedures with and without formal parameters, and then discusses their advantages and limitations.

You use PSPs to create a complete dynamic web page that uses native Oracle types. PSPs have an advantage because they contain a similar programming structure to JSPs. PSPs can provide a more natural solution to web programming than standard PL/SQL stored objects for those with a background in ASPs or JSPs.

PSPs can include JavaScript or other client-side script code natively in the stored procedure. PSPs use the same scripting syntax as Java Server Pages (JSPs), which makes the skills readily transferable between web development solutions. PSPs push the processing to the server and present the client browser with a plain HTML text file for rendering.

PSPs can contain text, tags, PSP directives, declarations, and scriptlets. They typically have the .psp file extension. Text and tags in PSPs are typical of HTML pages. PSPs have directives that enable controlling the page behaviors as noted in Table 16-5.

Directive	Description
PAGE	Specifies the scripting language it uses, the type of information (MIME type) it produces, and the code it should run to handle uncaught exceptions. This might be an HTML file with a friendly message, renamed to a .psp file. You must specify this same filename in the loadpsp command that compiles the main PSP file. You must specify exactly the same name in both the errorPage directive and the **loadpsp** command, including any relative path name such as ./include/.

	Syntax:
	`<%@ page [language="PL/SQL"]`
	` [contentType="content type string"]`
	` charset="encoding"`
	` [errorPage="file.psp"] %>`

PROCEDURE	Specifies the name of the stored procedure produced by the PSP file. The name is the filename without the .psp extension by default.
	Syntax: `<%@ plsql procedure="procedure_name" %>`
PARAMETER	Specifies the name, and optionally the type and default, for each parameter expected by the PSP stored procedure. The parameters are passed using name-value pairs, typically from an HTML form. To specify a default value of a character type, use single quotes around the value, inside the double quotes required by the directive.

	Syntax:
	`<%@ plsql parameter="parameter name"`
	` [type="PL/SQL type"]`
	` [default="value"] %>`

TABLE 16-5 *PL/SQL Server Page Directives*

Directive	Description
INCLUDE	Specifies the name of a file to be included at a specific point in the PSP file. The file must have an extension other than .psp. It can contain HTML, PSP script elements, or a combination of both. The name resolution and file inclusion happen when the PSP file is loaded into the database as a stored procedure, so any changes to the file after that are not reflected when the stored procedure is run. Syntax: `<%@ include file="path name" %>`

DECLARATION BLOCK	Declares a set of PL/SQL variables that are visible throughout the page, not just within the next BEGIN/END block. This element typically spans multiple lines, with individual PL/SQL variable declarations ended by semicolons.
	
	Syntax:
	`<%! PL/SQL declaration;`
	`[ PL/SQL declaration; ] ... %>`

CODE BLOCK SCRIPTLET	Executes a set of PL/SQL statements when the stored procedure is run. This element typically spans multiple lines, with individual PL/SQL statements ended by semicolons. The statements can include complete blocks, or they can be the bracketing parts of IF/THEN/ELSE or BEGIN/END blocks. When a code block is split into multiple scriptlets, you can put HTML or other directives in the middle, and those pieces are conditionally executed when the stored procedure is run.
	
	Syntax:
	`<% PL/SQL statement;`
	`[ PL/SQL statement; ] ... %>`

EXPRESSION BLOCK	Specifies a single PL/SQL expression, such as a string, arithmetic expression, function call, or combination of those things. The result is substituted as a string at that spot in the HTML page that is produced by the stored procedure. You do not need to end the PL/SQL expression with a semicolon. Syntax: `<%= PL/SQL expression %>`
COMMENT BLOCK	Specifies a comment in a PSP page. Syntax: `<%-- PL/SQL expression --%>`

TABLE 16-5   *PL/SQL Server Page Directives* (continued)

PSP procedures are loaded into the database by the `loadpsp` utility. However, there is no `droppsp` utility corresponding to `dropjava`. You drop PSP procedures by using a standard DDL DROP command from the SQL*Plus environment. The `-replace` option first removes the prior copy before attempting to load the new one. If you do not have a backup copy of your working PSP procedure, you should make one before running the `loadpsp` utility. The general syntax for the utility is

```
loadpsp [-replace] -user username/password[@connect_string]
        < [ include_file_name … ] [ error_file_name ] >
        psp_file_name.psp_file_extension
```

The next two sections show you how to develop and run PSP procedures with, and without, arguments. You will see they are very much like the PL/SQL Toolkit server-side includes that were covered earlier in the chapter.

Developing and Running No Formal Parameter PSP Procedures

You'll now build a PSP stored procedure that renders a Hello World web page. This PSP takes no formal parameters and acts much like a static web page.

The following script builds a HelloWorld1 PSP:

```
-- This is found in HelloWorld1.psp on the publisher's web site.
<%@ plsql language="PL/SQL" %>
<%@ plsql procedure="HelloWorld1" %>
<html>
<title>Expert PL/SQL - HelloWorld1</title>
<head>
</head>
<body>
<%-- Print a plain string. --%>
Hello World!<br /><br />
<%-- Print using the PL/SQL Toolkit --%>
<% htp.print('Hello World!'); %>
</td></tr></table>
</body>
</html>
```

You use the following syntax to put the PSP procedure into the database:

```
loadpsp -replace -user plsql/plsql HelloWorld1.psp
```

After the procedure is stored in the database by using the `loadpsp` utility, you can see that the `loadpsp` utility does some text conversion of the file. You can set the SQL*Plus `PAGESIZE` to 999 and see those modifications by using the following query:

```
SELECT   text
FROM     user_source
WHERE    name = 'HELLOWORLD1';
```

You can see that the procedure has been modified by running the `loadpsp` utility. The following is the stored source for the `HelloWorld1` procedure:

```
PROCEDURE HelloWorld1  AS
 BEGIN NULL;
htp.prn('
');
htp.prn('

<html>
<title>Expert PL/SQL - HelloWorld1</title>
<head>
</head>
<body>
<! Print a plain string. >
Hello World!<br /><br />
<! Print using the PL/SQL Toolkit >
');
 htp.print('Hello World!');
htp.prn('
</td></tr></table>
</body>
</html>
');
 END;
```

The `loadpsp` utility takes the PSP file and builds a standard PL/SQL procedure. It puts a `BEGIN` in front and appends an `END` to create proper block structure. It also inserts a `NULL` statement in the event you have uploaded only a shell. All HTML tags are encapsulated by using the HTP package from the PL/SQL Toolkit.

Once stored in the database, you access it by using a URL and your web browser. The following URL assumes you have defined the DAD Location as `/pls/`, as done earlier in this chapter:

```
http://<hostname>.<domain_name>:<port>/pls/HelloWorld1
```

The web browser renders the image shown in Figure 16-8. The URL is transparent to the end user whether it is a PL/SQL web procedure or PSP.

FIGURE 16-8   *Rendered HelloWorld1 PSP*

This example shows you how to build a PSP without any formal parameters. The next section explores formal parameters.

Developing Formal Parameter PSP Procedures

Dynamic content works by passing parameters that determine changing output. Developing PSPs that accept formal parameters is necessary to build real web applications. You need to know how to use formal parameters to be able to submit and process dynamic content because passing arguments determines dynamic PSPs. Obviously, you can't really write very useful programs unless you can handle formal parameters in your PSPs.

This section will review how to build a PSP to accept parameters, how to run the PSP from a URL, and also dynamically from a static web page using JavaScript components.

As covered earlier, the parameter directives are enclosed between <%@ and %> brackets. When you define parameters, they may have a PL/SQL type but not a size. Physical size will be managed in your code blocks because if you manage them in the declaration section, you can't effectively trap errors. The following `HelloWorld2.psp` script enables you to build a PSP that accepts a single parameter:

```
-- This is found in HelloWorld2.psp on the publisher's web site.
<%@ plsql language="PL/SQL" type="PL/SQL type" %>
<%@ plsql procedure="HelloWorld2" %>
<%-- Defines a parameter in a PARAMETER block. --%>
<%@ plsql parameter="who" type="VARCHAR2" default="NULL" %>
<head>
<title>Expert PL/SQL - HelloWorld2</title>
<%!
  CURSOR get_user
  ( requestor VARCHAR2) IS
    SELECT   'Hello '|| USER ||' schema, this is a '||requestor||'!' line
    FROM     dual;
%>
</head>
<body>
  <% FOR i IN get_user(who) LOOP %>
    <%= i.line %>
  <% END LOOP; %>
</body>
</html>
```

This PSP takes a parameter and uses it in a trivial cursor so that you can see how to declare a parameter, cursor, and FOR loop. This small example shows you the pieces to build larger programs.

NOTE
You must enclose all expressions in scriptlet or code blocks because they terminate the line like the semicolon in PL/SQL programs.

You use the following syntax to put the PSP procedure into the database:

```
loadpsp -replace -user plsql/plsql HelloWorld21.psp
```

After the procedure is stored in the database by using the `loadpsp` utility, you can see that the `loadpsp` utility does some text conversion of the file. You can set the SQL*Plus `PAGESIZE` to 999 and see those modifications by using the following query:

```
SELECT   text
FROM     user_source
WHERE    name = 'HELLOWORLD2';
```

Note that the procedure has been modified by running the `loadpsp` utility. The following is the stored source for the `HelloWorld2` procedure, which will append a `BEGIN` and `END` into the file (as seen previously in the chapter) as well as a single null statement. A `DECLARE` statement is unnecessary, since it's defined in the scope of a stored procedure.

After putting it in the database, you access it by using a URL and your web browser. The following URL assumes you've defined the DAD Location as `/pls/`, as done earlier in this chapter:

```
http://<hostname>.<domain_name>:<port>/pls/HelloWorld2
```

The web browser renders the image shown in Figure 16-9 was generated using the XML DB Server in Oracle 11*g*. You should note that the USER is the ANONYMOUS schema where you call the `helloworld2` procedure if you're using an anonymous authentication. This differs from both the static and dynamic methods, which could display the USER as PLSQL.

Now that you've seen a small example program, the next one is bit more like a real-world example. This program is a reimplementation of the `item1` and `item2` PL/SQL Toolkit procedures seen earlier in this chapter, except the program is now a PSP.

You should check instructions in the Introduction for running the `create_store.sql` script against your `plsql` schema.

FIGURE 16-9   *Rendered HelloWorld2 PSP*

The `create_item3.psp` script follows:

```
-- This is found in create_item3.psp on the publisher's web site.
<%@ plsql language="PL/SQL" type="PL/SQL type" %>
<%@ plsql procedure="item3" %>
<%-- Defines a parameter in a PARAMETER block. --%>
<%@ plsql parameter="begin_id" type="NUMBER" default="NULL" %>
<%@ plsql parameter="end_id" type="NUMBER" default="NULL" %>
<head>
<title>Item List PSP</title>
  <%!
    CURSOR get_items
    ( begin_item_id NUMBER
    , end_item_id   NUMBER ) IS
      SELECT    item_id AS item_number
      ,         item_title||': '||item_subtitle AS item_title
      ,         item_release_date AS release_date
      FROM      item
      WHERE     item_id BETWEEN begin_item_id AND end_item_id;   %>
</title>
<body>
<hr>
<table cborder=2 style=background-color:feedb8>
  <tr>
    <td align="center"
        style="color:#336699;background-color:#cccc99;font-eight:bold;width=50">
        #
    </td>
    <td align="center"
        style="color:#336699;background-color:#cccc99;font-weight:bold;width=200">
      NAME
    </td>
    <td align="center"
        style="color:#336699;background-color:#cccc99;font-weight:bold;width=100">
      TENURE
    </td>
  </tr>
  <% FOR i IN get_items(year1,year2) LOOP %>
  <tr>
    <td align="center"
        style="color:#336699;background-color:#f7f7e7">
      <%= i.item_number %>
    </td>
    <td align="center"
        style="color:#336699;background-color:#f7f7e7">
      <%= i.item_title %>
    </td>
    <td align="center"
      style="color:#336699;background-color:#f7f7e7">
      <%= i.release_date %>
```

```
    </td>
  </tr>
  <% END LOOP; %>
</table>
<hr />
</body>
</html>
```

This PSP shows you how to implement parameters, a cursor, and a FOR loop. It prints a dynamic set of rows in a table.

NOTE
You should note that the parameter directives use native PL/SQL types and not the package variables supported by PL/SQL procedures.

Use the following syntax to put the PSP procedure into the database:

```
loadpsp -replace -user plsql/plsql item3.psp
```

As covered earlier in the chapter, the `loadpsp` utility does some text conversion of the file. If you would like to see it, set the SQL*Plus `PAGESIZE` to 999 and use the following query:

```
SELECT    text
FROM      user_source
WHERE     name = 'HELLOWORLD2';
```

After putting it in the database, access it by using a URL and your web browser. The following URL assumes you have defined the DAD Location as `/pls/`, as done earlier in this chapter:

```
http://<hostname>.<domain_name>:<port>/pls/item3?begin_id=1067&year2=1077
```

The web browser renders the Star Wars items in the item table, as shown in Figure 16-10.

You have now learned how to build PSPs. They are powerful tools. You can develop them with the Oracle Database and the Oracle 10*g* Application Server, Oracle HTTP Server (OHS), or XML DB Server. All examples in this chapter were tested with both the Oracle 10*g* Release 2 database and standalone OHS, and the Oracle 11*g* database and XML DB Server.

Understanding Advantages and Limitations

As mentioned earlier in the chapter, PSPs are great solutions when you have a large body of HTML that includes dynamic database content. Java Server Pages (JSPs) are more complex solutions, and they generally require an IDE to support development.

The limitations of PSPs are that they work as standalone complete solutions. You cannot leverage them as modules elsewhere in your web-enabled applications.

FIGURE 16-10 *Rendered Item List PSP*

Summary

You should now have an understanding of how to implement and troubleshoot server-side PL/SQL Toolkit web pages and PL/SQL Server Pages (PSPs). With these skills, you can build robust web application solutions in native PL/SQL, and leverage the tight integration that PL/SQL enjoys with the data server in your development.

PART
IV
Appendixes

APPENDIX
A

Oracle Database
Administration Primer

his appendix introduces you to the general concepts of database architecture. It also exposes you to Oracle Database architecture and teaches you how to start and stop both the database instance and the database listener. These processes show you how to use traditional command-line processes to start and stop services, like the web-based Oracle Enterprise Manager Database Control. The appendix also will demonstrate how you can use Oracle Enterprise Manager Database Control to start, stop, or manage the database instance. These basic skills are critical to managing an Oracle database instance when you don't have a Database Administrator (DBA) handy to manage it for you, or possess some experience as an Oracle DBA.

The appendix covers material in the following sequence:

- Oracle Database architecture

- Starting and stopping the Oracle database

- Starting and stopping the Oracle listener

- Oracle roles and privileges

- Accessing and using the SQL*Plus interface

There are several books that provide general introductions to the Oracle database product stack, such as the *Oracle Database 11g DBA Handbook*. Also, you can find a summary step-by-step review in the Oracle Database 2 Day DBA or a complete review in the Oracle Administrator's Guide for the Oracle Database 11*g* release.

The appendix assumes that you will read it sequentially, and each section may reference material introduced earlier. Naturally, you can zoom forward to an area of interest when you already understand the earlier material.

Oracle Database Architecture

The Oracle Database 11*g* database will have three varieties. One is the free Express Edition (XE), which is a limited version of the premier Oracle Database 11*g* Standard Edition (SE) product. The full-featured version is the Oracle Database 11*g* Enterprise Edition (EE) product.

All versions contain all the standard relational database management system components, embedded Java, collection types, and PL/SQL run-time engine that set Oracle apart in the database industry. These components enable any of these Oracle database management systems to manage small to large data repositories, consistently accessing data concurrently by multiple users. The Oracle Database 11*g* Enterprise Edition also includes many features that empower advanced context and object management.

You can divide the components of Oracle database management systems into two groups of services:

- *Data repositories,* also known as databases. They enable a SQL interface that can access any column value in one or more rows of a table or result set. Result sets are selected values of a single table or the product of joins between multiple tables (SQL joins are described in Appendix B). Tables are persistent two-dimensional structures that are organized by rows of defined structures. You create these structures when defining and creating tables in a database instance. Databases are relational databases when they include a data catalog that tracks the definitions of structures.

- *Programs,* which enable administering and accessing the data repository, and provide the infrastructure to manage a data repository. The combination of a data repository and enabling programs is known as an *instance* of a database because the programs process and manage the data repository and catalog. A data catalog stores data about data, which is also known as metadata. The catalog also defines how the database management system programs will access and manage user-defined databases. The programs are background processes that manage the physical input and output to physical files and other required processing activities. Opening a relational database instance starts these background processes.

Integrating the data repository and administrative programs requires a relational programming language that (a) has a linear structure; (b) can be accessed interactively or within procedural programs; and (c) supports data definition, manipulation, and query activities. The Structured Query Language (SQL) is the relational programming language used by the Oracle database and most other relational database products.

Appendix B provides you with an introduction on how to work with Oracle SQL. Like any spoken or written language, SQL has many dialects. The Oracle Database 11*g* products support two dialects of SQL. One is the Oracle Proprietary SQL Syntax, and the other is the ANSI 1999 SQL. The SQL language provides users with high-level *definition, set-at-a-time, insert, update,* and *delete* operations, as well as the ability to *select* data. SQL is a high-level language because it enables you to access data without dealing with physical file access details.

Data catalogs are tables mapping data that defines other database tables, views, stored procedures, and structures. Database management systems define frameworks, which qualify what can belong in data catalogs to support database instances. They also use SQL to define, access, and maintain the data catalog. Beneath the SQL interface and background processes servicing SQL commands, the database management system contains a set of library programs that manage transaction control. These services guarantee transactions in a multiple-user database are ACID compliant.

ACID-compliant transactions are atomic, consistent, isolated, and durable. Atomic means that every part or no part of a transaction completes. Consistent means that the same results occur whether the transaction is serially or concurrently run. Isolated means that changes are invisible to any other session until made permanent by a commit action. Durable means they are written to a permanent store at the conclusion of the transaction.

The architecture of the Oracle database instance is shown in Figure A-1. The figure shows that inside a relational database instance, you have shared memory segments, active background processes, and files. The shared memory segment is known as the Shared Global Area (SGA). The SGA contains various buffered areas of memory that process queries, inserts, updates, and delete statements in databases. The active background processes support the database instance. The five required Oracle background processes are *Process Monitor (PMON), System Monitor (SMON), Database Writer (DBWn), Log Writer (LGWR),* and *Checkpoint (CKPT).* An optional background process for backup is the *Archiver (ARCn).* These six background process are found in Figure A-1. The files supporting database instances are divisible into three segments: files that contain instance variables, files that contain the physical data and data catalog, and files that contain an archive file of the data and data catalog.

The five Oracle database required instance background processes perform the following services:

- **Process Monitor (PMON)**   Cleans up the instance after failed processes by rolling back transactions, releasing database locks and resources, and restarting deceased processes.

- **System Monitor (SMON)**   Manages system recovery by opening the database, rolling forward changes from the online redo log files, and rolling back uncommitted transactions. SMON also coalesces free space and deallocates temporary segments.

- **Database Writer (DBW*n*)**   Writes data to files when any of the following occur: checkpoints are reached, dirty buffers reach their threshold or there are no free buffers, timeouts occur, Real Application Cluster (RAC) ping requests are made, tablespaces are placed in `OFFLINE` or `READ ONLY` state, tables are dropped or truncated, and tablespaces begin backup processing.

- **Log Writer (LGWR)**   Writes at user commits or three-second intervals, whichever comes first; when one-third full or there is 1MB of redo instructions; and before the *Database Writer* writes.

- **Checkpoint (CKPT)**   Signals the *Database Writer* at checkpoints and updates the file header information for database and control files at checkpoints.

The optional *Archiver (ARCn)* process is critical to recovering databases. When an Oracle database instance is in archive mode, the *Archiver* writes to the redo log file are mirrored in the archive log files as the database switches from one redo log file to another. You should have the database in archive mode unless it is a test system and the time to rebuild it is trivial or unimportant.

The other optional background processes for the Oracle 11*g* database family are Coordinator Job Queue (CJQ0), Dispatcher (Dnnn), RAC Lock Manager – Instance (LCKn), RAC DLM Monitor – Remote (LMDn), RAC DLM Monitor – Global Locks (LMON), RAC Global Cache Service (LMS), Parallel Query Slaves (Pnnn), Advanced Queuing (QMNn), Recoverer (RECO), and Shared Server (Snnn). All of these are available in the Oracle Database 11*g* products. You may only additionally configure the Coordinator Job Queue, Dispatcher, and Recoverer processes.

Understanding the *details* of how shared memory, processes, and files interact is the responsibility of the Database Administrator (DBA). You can find a fairly comprehensive guide to how to manage databases in the *Oracle Database 11g DBA Handbook* published by Oracle Press. A summary explanation can also be found in the *Oracle Database Express Edition 2 Day DBA* manual.

Beyond the database instance, the Oracle database management system provides many utilities. These utilities support database backup and recovery, Oracle database file integrity verification (via the DB Verify utility – `dbv`), data import and export (using the `imp` and `exp` utilities demonstrated in Appendix E), and a network protocol stack. The network protocol stack is a critical communication component that enables local and remote connections to the Oracle database by users other than the owner of the Oracle executables. The networking product stack is known as Net8. Net8 is a complete host layer that conforms to the Open System Interconnection (OSI) Reference Model and provides the session, presentation, and application layers. You can find more on the OSI model at http://en.wikipedia.org/wiki/OSI_model.

Oracle Net8 enables connectivity between both local and remote programs, and the database instance. Remote programs whether implemented on the same physical machine or different physical machines use Remote Procedure Calls (RPCs) to communicate to the database instance. RPCs let one computer call another computer by directing the request to a listener service.

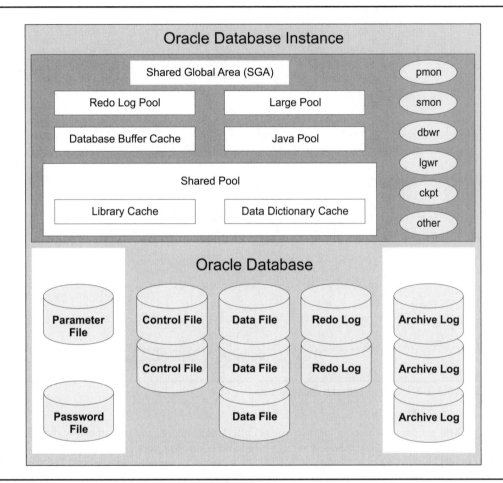

FIGURE A-1   *Oracle instance architecture diagram*

RPCs require software on both the client and the server. The remote client program environment needs to know how to get to the server programming environment, which is found by reading the `tnsnames.ora` file in the Oracle Database 11*g* Client software. The Oracle Database 11*g* Server software provides the implementation for the Oracle listener that receives and handles RPC requests. Net8 provides the packaging and de-packaging of network packets between local and remote programs and a database instance.

The Oracle listener listens for Net8 packaged transmissions on a specific port. The packaged transmissions are Oracle Net8 encoded packages. Packages are received from a network transport layer, like TCP/IP, at a designated port number. The default port number is 1521. This port is where the Oracle listener hears, receives, and connects the transactions to the local database instance.

As illustrated in Figure A-2, the package arrives at the listening port where a listener thread hears it and then hands it to the OCI thread. Then, the transaction is sent through the Net8 transport layer to remove the packaging and pass the SQL command to a transactional object in a database instance, like a table, view, or stored procedure.

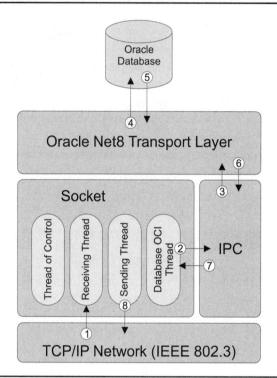

FIGURE A-2   *Oracle Listener architecture*

This process has two variations: one is called thick-client, and the other is called thin-client. Thick-client communication is the old model and supports client/server computing, which worked like `telnet` or *secure shell* (shh) across state-aware network sockets. The thick-client communication model requires you install an Oracle client software application on the client. The Oracle client software contains the necessary programs and libraries to effect bidirectional state-aware sockets between client and server computers. The newer thin-client communication model supports both state-aware and stateless transaction patterns, but it does so differently. All you need is an *Oracle Call Interface (OCI)* library that enables you to package the communication into a compatible Net8 packet. JDBC programs use an Oracle Java archive, while the C, C++, PHP, and other third-party programming languages use the OCI8 libraries to make connections to the Oracle database. The JDBC programs can work with only the Java archive file, while the others require the Oracle Database 11*g* Client installation.

Inside the database instance, user accounts are called schemas. The superuser schemas are known as `SYS` and `SYSTEM`. The `SYS` schema contains the data catalog and as a rule should never be used for routine administration. The `SYSTEM` schema has a master set of roles and privileges that enable the DBA to use it like a superuser account, and it contains administrative views to the data catalog. The SYSTEM schema views are typically easier to use than trying to kludge through the physical tables that contain the data catalog.

CAUTION
A small mistake in the data catalog can destroy your database instance and provide you with no way to recover it. Also, changing things in the SYS schema is not supported by your license agreement unless you are instructed to do so by Oracle to fix a specified problem.

Unix or Linux requires that you set an environment $ORACLE_HOME variable that maps to the physical Oracle database management home directory. Windows does not automatically create a %ORACLE_HOME% environment variable because it adds the fully qualified directory path to your %PATH% variable.

You set the correct operating environment in Unix or Linux by running the following commands in the Bash or Korn shell as the owner of the Oracle database installation:

```
# export set ORACLE_SID=oracle_sid
# export set ORACLE_ASK=no
```

You can then navigate to the default /usr/local/bin directory to find the installed oraenv file. You then source it as shown in the Bash or Korn shell:

```
# ./oraenv
```

You will find further instructions in the Oracle Database Installation Guide for your release. These are also found on the http://otn.oracle.com web site under documentation for the database.

This has provided you with a summary of the Oracle database architecture and pointed you to some additional useful references. You can also review whitepapers and administration-related database architecture notes posted on http://otn.oracle.com for additional information. In the next sections, you will learn how to start and stop the database and listener, and learn how to access SQL*Plus to run SQL statements.

Microsoft Windows Services

The design of Microsoft Windows compels Oracle to deploy services to start and stop the database and listener. This is done by the platform-specific utility ORADIM. Fortunately, the Oracle Database 11*g* installation builds these services for you when you use the Database Configuration Assistant as a post-installation step. Only change these services when you truly understand how to do so. A mistake working with the ORADIM facility can force you to refresh your operating system or manually clean up the registry.

Starting and Stopping the Oracle Database

This section demonstrates how to start and stop the Oracle Database 11*g* server. The command-line utility is `sqlplus` and works the same for the Unix, Linux, and Microsoft Windows versions. The only difference is linked to account ownership of the database. This difference exists because of how the file system and ownership models work in Microsoft Windows, Unix, and Linux. The differences evoke strong emotions from some people who prefer one over the other, but they simply present different opportunities and hurdles from varying perspectives.

The Oracle database management system can support multiple database instances. The ability to support multiple instances makes it necessary to assign each instance a unique System Identifier (SID). The generic database SID value is `orcl` when installing the Oracle Database 11*g* server. The assignment of the SID is the same regardless of platform.

While they're very similar, you will cover them separately. You can choose to read one or the other because both cover the same material from the perspective of the operating system. These subsections teach you how to start and shut down the database in the Linux and Microsoft Windows environments.

Unix or Linux Operations

Oracle Database 11*g* should install as the `oracle` user in a `dba` group on the Unix or Linux system and is set up to start at boot. When you want to shut down or start the database after the system has booted, use the *substitute user,* `su`, command. The *substitute user* command lets you become another user and inherit that user's environment variables. The following command lets you change from a less privileged user to the `oracle` owner:

```
su - oracle
```

You will assume the mantle of `oracle` by providing the correct password to the account. Then, you have two choices as to how you start or stop the database for an Oracle Database 11*g* XE installation (provided they release one). As an Oracle Database 11*g* XE user, you can use the script built during installation to *start, stop, restart, configure,* or *status* the database and all attendant services by typing the following:

```
/etc/init.d/oracle-xe {start|stop|restart|configure|status}
```

Alternatively, with an Oracle Database 11*g* SE or EE installation, you can use the `sqlplus` utility to *start, stop, restart, configure,* or *status* the database or start the Oracle listener and then the Enterprise Manager Database Control utility to *start, stop, restart,* or *status* the database.

You will need to build an environment file and source it into your environment. The following values are the minimum required values for your environment file:

```
export set ORACLE_HOME=/mount_point/11g/product/11.1.0/db_1
export set PATH=$PATH:$ORACLE_HOME/bin:.
export set ORACLE_SID=oracle_sid
export set LD_LIBRARY_PATH=/usr/lib/openwin/lib:$ORACLE_HOME/lib
```

Assuming that you are in the same directory as your environment file, you source your environment in Bash or Korn shell as follows:

```
. ./11g.env
```

Then, you can start the Enterprise Manager Database Control utility as follows:

```
# emctl start dbconsole
```

Enterprise Management Utility
If the console told you the `emctl` program was not found, it is most likely not found in your path statement. You can determine whether the executable is in your current path by using the `which` utility, shown here:

```
which -a emctl
```

The `-a` option returns a list of all `emctl` programs in order of their precedence in your `$PATH` variable. You fix the `$PATH` environment variable by adding the required directory path where the executable is found. After fixing your $PATH variable in the environment file, you should again source the environment file.

You can also issue a `sqlplus` command to connect to the Oracle Database 11*g* instance as the privileged user `SYS`, using a specialized role for starting and stopping the database. The connection command is

```
sqlplus '/ as sysdba'
```

NOTE
You can connect directly to the Oracle database only when you are the owner of the Oracle database. This type of connection is a direct connection between the shell process and the database, which means that the communication is not routed through Net8 and the Oracle listener does not need to be running.

After connecting to the `SQL>` prompt, you will need to provide the Oracle superuser password. Once authenticated, you will be the `SYS` user in a specialized role known as `SYSDBA`. The `SYSDBA` role exists for starting and stopping your database instance and performing other administrative tasks. You can see your current Oracle user name by issuing the following SQL*Plus command:

```
SQL> show user
USER is "SYS"
```

Assuming the database is already started, you can use the following command to see the current SGA (System Global Area) values:

```
SQL> show sga

Total System Global Area 1233534976 bytes
Fixed Size                  1297104 bytes
Variable Size             935765296 bytes
Database Buffers          285212672 bytes
Redo Buffers               11259904 bytes
```

You can shut down the database by choosing `abort`, `immediate`, `transactional`, and `normal`. Only the `abort` fails to secure transaction integrity, which means that database recovery is required when restarting the database. The other three *shutdown* methods do not require recovery when restarting the database. The optional arguments perform the following types of *shutdown* operations:

- **Shutdown `normal`**   Stops any new connections to the database and waits for all connected users to disconnect; then the Oracle instance writes completed database transactions from redo buffers to data files and marks them closed, terminates background processes, closes the database, and dismounts the database.

- **Shutdown `transactional`**   Stops any new connections to the database and disconnects users as soon as the current transactions complete; when all transactions complete, the Oracle instance writes database and redo buffers to data files and marks them closed, terminates background processes, closes the database, and dismounts the database.

- **Shutdown `immediate`**   Stops all current SQL statements, rolls back all active transactions, and immediately disconnects users from the database; then the Oracle instance writes database and redo buffers to data files and marks them closed, terminates background processes, closes the database, and dismounts the database.

- **Shutdown `abort`**   Stops all current SQL statements, and immediately shuts down without writing database and redo buffers to data files; the Oracle instance does not roll back uncommitted transactions but terminates running processes without closing physical files and the database, and it leaves the database in a mounted state requiring recovery when restarted.

The following illustrates the immediate *shutdown* of a database instance:

```
SQL> shutdown immediate
Database closed.
Database dismounted.
ORACLE instance shut down.
```

When you want to start the database, you have three options. You can start the database by using the `startup` command and either the `nomount`, `mount`, or `open` (default) option. The optional arguments perform the following types of `startup` operations:

- **Startup `nomount`**   Starts the instance by reading the parameter file in the $ORACLE_HOME/dbs directory. This file can be named `spfile.ora` or `pfile.ora`. The former can't be read in a text editor but is the default parameter file option beginning with Oracle 9*i*. You can create an editable `pfile.ora` using SQL as the `SYS` user in the role of `SYSDBA` *from an open database*. This *startup* starts the background processes, allocates the SGA shared memory segment, and opens the `alertSID.log` and trace files. The SID is the name of an Oracle database instance. The value is stored in the data catalog and control files. This type of *startup* is only done when creating a new database or rebuilding control files during a backup and recovery operation.

- **Startup `mount`**   Does everything the `nomount` process does, and then it continues by locating, opening, and reading the control files and parameter files to determine the status of the data files and online redo log files, but no check is made to verify the existence or state of the data files. This type of *startup* is useful when you need to rename the data files, change the online redo file archiving process, or perform full database recovery.

- **Startup open** Does everything the `mount` process does, and then it continues by locating, opening, and reading the online data files and redo log files. This is the default *startup* operation, and you use it when opening the database for user transactions.

After reconnecting to the database if you disconnected, you can issue the `startup` command. If you provide a `nomount` or `mount` argument to the startup command, only those processes qualified earlier will occur. When you provide the `startup` command with no argument, the default argument `open` is applied and the database will be immediately available for user transactions. The following demonstrates a standard startup of the database instance:

```
SQL> startup
ORACLE instance started.

Total System Global Area 1233534976 bytes
Fixed Size                   1297104 bytes
Variable Size              935765296 bytes
Database Buffers           285212672 bytes
Redo Buffers                11259904 bytes
Database mounted.
Database opened.
```

Viewing how the database moves from *shutdown* to *nomount* to *mount* to *open* is helpful. The following syntax demonstrates moving the database one step at a time from a *shutdown* instance to an open database:

```
SQL> startup nomount
ORACLE instance started.

Total System Global Area 1233534976 bytes
Fixed Size                   1297104 bytes
Variable Size              935765296 bytes
Database Buffers           285212672 bytes
Redo Buffers                11259904 bytes
SQL> ALTER DATABASE MOUNT;

Database altered.

SQL> ALTER DATABASE OPEN;

Database altered.
```

The preceding output demonstrates that the Oracle instance creates the shared memory segment before opening the database, even in a `startup nomount` operation. The memory segment is first operation because it is the container where you store the open instance. You can use an `ALTER` SQL statement against the database to `mount` and `open` the database instance.

This section has shown you how to shut down and restart your database instance. It has also provided some insights into routine database administration tasks, which you can explore further in the *Oracle Database 11g DBA Handbook* by Oracle Press.

Microsoft Windows Operations

Oracle Database 11*g* installs as a standard program on the Microsoft Windows system. You have full access from any user account that has Administrator privileges. Oracle Database 11*g* also installs several services using the platform-specific ORADIM utility. You can find these services by opening your control panel and navigating to the Services icon. The navigation path changes whether you are in the Classic or Category view. In the Classic view, click the Administrative Tools icon and then the Services icon. In the Category view, first click the Performance and Maintenance icon, second click the Administrative Tools icon, and then click the Services icon. This will bring you to the Services view displayed in Figure A-3.

As a general rule, you are best served starting, restarting, and shutting down the services from this GUI view. However, you will need the command-line utility when you want to perform data backup and recovery activities. You can access the sqlplus utility from any command prompt session to manually *start, stop, restart, configure,* or *status* the database. This is possible because the fully qualified directory path is placed in the generic %PATH% environment for all *Administrator* accounts variables during the product installation. Making changes in the database requires that you connect to the Oracle Database 11*g* instance as the privileged user SYS.

You'll use the SQL*Plus executable, sqlplus, to connect to the database. There is a specialized role for starting and stopping the database, known as SYSDBA. You connect using the following syntax:

```
sqlplus '/ as sysdba'
```

After connecting to the SQL> prompt, Oracle will prompt you for the Oracle superuser password that you set during product installation. Once authenticated, you will be the SYS user

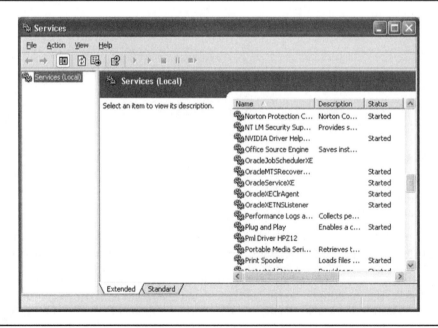

FIGURE A-3 *Microsoft Services Console*

in a specialized role known as `SYSDBA`. The `SYSDBA` role exists for starting and stopping your database instance and performing other administrative tasks. You can see your current Oracle user name by issuing the following SQL*Plus command:

```
SQL> show user
USER is "SYS"
```

Assuming the database is already started, you use the following command to see the current SGA (System Global Area) values:

```
SQL> show sga

Total System Global Area 1233534976 bytes
Fixed Size                  1297104 bytes
Variable Size             935765296 bytes
Database Buffers          285212672 bytes
Redo Buffers               11259904 bytes
```

You can shut down the database by choosing `abort`, `immediate`, `transactional`, and `normal`. Only the `abort` fails to secure transaction integrity, which means that database recovery is required when restarting the database. The other three *shutdown* methods do not require recovery when restarting the database. The optional arguments perform the following types of *shutdown* operations:

- **Shutdown `normal`**   Stops any new connections to the database and waits for all connected users to disconnect; then the Oracle instance writes completed database transactions from redo buffers to data files and marks them closed, terminates background processes, closes the database, and dismounts the database.

- **Shutdown `transactional`**   Stops any new connections to the database and disconnects users as soon as the current transactions complete; when all transactions complete, the Oracle instance writes database and redo buffers to data files and marks them closed, terminates background processes, closes the database, and dismounts the database.

- **Shutdown `immediate`**   Stops all current SQL statements, rolls back all active transactions, and immediately disconnects users from the database; then the Oracle instance writes database and redo buffers to data files and marks them closed, terminates background processes, closes the database, and dismounts the database.

- **Shutdown `abort`**   Stops all current SQL statements, and immediately shuts down without writing database and redo buffers to data files; the Oracle instance does not roll back uncommitted transactions but terminates running processes without closing physical files and the database, and it leaves the database in a mounted state requiring recovery when restarted.

The following illustrates the immediate *shutdown* of a database instance:

```
SQL> shutdown immediate
Database closed.
Database dismounted.
ORACLE instance shut down.
```

When you want to start the database, you have three options. You can start the database by using the `startup` command and either the `nomount`, `mount`, or `open` (default) option. The optional arguments perform the following types of `startup` operations:

- **Startup nomount**   Starts the instance by reading the parameter file in the `%ORACLE_HOME%\dbs` directory. This file can be named `spfile.ora` or `pfile.ora`. The former can't be read in a text editor but is the default parameter file option beginning with Oracle 9*i*. You can create an editable `pfile.ora` using SQL as the `SYS` user in the role of `SYSDBA` *from an open database.* This *startup* starts the background processes, allocates the SGA shared memory segment, and opens the `alertSID.log` and trace files. The SID is the name of an Oracle database instance. The value is stored in the data catalog and control files. This type of *startup* is only done when creating a new database or rebuilding control files during a backup and recovery operation.

- **Startup mount**   Does everything the `nomount` process does, and then it continues by locating, opening, and reading the control files and parameter files to determine the status of the data files and online redo log files, but no check is made to verify the existence or state of the data files. This type of *startup* is useful when you need to rename the data files, change the online redo file archiving process, or perform full database recovery.

- **Startup open**   Does everything the `mount` process does, and then it continues by locating, opening, and reading the online data files and redo log files. This is the default *startup* operation and used when you want to transact against the database.

As discussed earlier, all *Administrator* user accounts have the `sqlplus` executable in their working `%PATH%` environment variable. Using the `sqlplus` command, you connect to the Oracle Database 11*g* instance as the privileged user `SYS` under the `SYSDBA` role. This role lets you start, stop, and perform database administration tasks on a database instance. The command is

```
sqlplus '/ as sysdba'
```

After connecting to the database, you can issue the `startup` command. If you provide a `nomount` or `mount` argument to the `startup` command, only those processes qualified will occur. When you provide the `startup` command with no argument, the default argument `open` is applied and the database will be immediately available for transactions. The following demonstrates a standard startup of the database instance:

```
SQL> startup
ORACLE instance started.

Total System Global Area 1233534976 bytes
Fixed Size                   1297104 bytes
Variable Size              935765296 bytes
Database Buffers           285212672 bytes
Redo Buffers                11259904 bytes
Database mounted.
Database opened.
```

Viewing how the database moves from *shutdown* to *nomount* to *mount* to *open* is helpful. The following syntax demonstrates moving the database one step at a time from a *shutdown* instance to an open database:

```
SQL> startup nomount
ORACLE instance started.

Total System Global Area 1233534976 bytes
Fixed Size                  1297104 bytes
Variable Size             935765296 bytes
Database Buffers          285212672 bytes
Redo Buffers               11259904 bytes
SQL> ALTER DATABASE MOUNT;

Database altered.

SQL> ALTER DATABASE OPEN;

Database altered.
```

The preceding output demonstrates that the Oracle instance creates the shared memory segment before opening the database, even in a `startup nomount` operation. The memory segment is first operation because it is the container where you store the open instance. You can use an `ALTER` SQL statement against the database to `mount` and `open` the database instance.

This section has shown you how to shut down and restart your database instance. It has also provided some insights into routine database administration tasks, which you can explore further in the *Oracle Database 11g DBA Handbook* by Oracle Press.

Starting and Stopping the Oracle Listener

The Oracle `lsnrctl` utility lets you start the server-side Oracle listener process on a port that you set in the `listener.ora` configuration file. There are actually three files used in configuring the Oracle Net8 listener; they are the `listener.ora`, `tnsnames.ora`, and `sqlnet.ora` configuration files. The `sqlnet.ora` file is not necessary for basic operations and is not configured in the shipped version of Oracle Database 11g. You can use the `sqlnet.ora` file to set network tracing commands, which are qualified in the *Oracle Database Net Services Administrator's Guide 11g Release 1* and *Oracle Database Net Services Reference 11g Release 1* documentation. You may browse or download these from http://otn.oracle.com for supplemental information.

The network configuration files are in the `network/admin` subdirectory of the Oracle Database 11g product home directory. The following qualifies the default Oracle product home by platform:

Unix or Linux

```
/mount_point/directory_to_oracle_home/
```

Microsoft Windows

```
C:\directory_to_oracle_home
```

The Oracle product home path is typically set as an environment variable for all user accounts. Environment variables are aliases that point to something else and exist in all operating systems. You can set an Oracle product home directory as follows by platform:

Unix or Linux

`export set ORACLE_HOME=/mount_point/directory_to_oracle_home/`

Microsoft Windows

`C:\directory_to_oracle_home`

You can then navigate to the Oracle product home by using the `$ORACLE_HOME` in Unix or Linux or `%ORACLE_HOME%` in Microsoft Windows. These settings are temporary unless you put them in a configuration file that gets sourced when you connect to your system in Unix or Linux. It is a convention for you to put these in your `.bashrc` file or have your system administrator put them in the standard `.profile` account in Linux. You can also configure permanent environment variables in your *System Properties* in Microsoft Windows. You will find the instructions for setting the *Oracle Database 2 Day DBA* manual.

> **TIP**
> *You can set your environment variables by going to the Control Panel and launching the System icon, where you will choose the Advanced tab and click the Environment Variable button.*

The sample `listener.ora` file is a configuration file. A `listener.ora` file exists after you install Oracle Database 11*g*. You will find that your `listener.ora` file contains the *Oracle product home directory,* your server machine *hostname,* and a *port number.* These values are critical pieces of information that enable your listener to find your Oracle installation. These data components mirror the configuration directives that enable Apache to hand off HTTP requests to appropriate services.

The only differences between the Unix or Linux and Microsoft Windows operating system versions are different path statement for the Oracle product home and the case sensitivity or insensitivity of the host name. The *hostname* is lowercase for a Unix or Linux system and uppercase for Microsoft Windows.

```
-- This is an example of a default listener.ora file.

LISTENER =
  (DESCRIPTION_LIST =
    (DESCRIPTION =
      (ADDRESS = (PROTOCOL = IPC)(KEY = EXTPROC1))
      (ADDRESS = (PROTOCOL = TCP)(HOST = hostname)(PORT = port_number))
    )
  )


SID_LIST_LISTENER =
  (SID_LIST =
    (SID_DESC =
      (SID_NAME = PLSExtProc)
      (ORACLE_HOME = oracle_product_home_directory)
      (PROGRAM = extproc)
    )
  )
```

The `listener.ora` file has two key addressing components. The first is the actual listener name, which by default isn't too original because it is an uppercase string, `LISTENER`. The default listener name is implicitly assumed unless you provide an overriding listener name to any `lsnrctl` command. You must explicitly provide the listener name when you use anything other than the default as your actual listener name.

The listener name is also appended to the `SID_LIST_` descriptor, which registers static maps for external procedures and the Oracle Heterogeneous Server. Oracle Database 11*g* uses one external procedure configurations—`PLSExtProc`. Oracle recommends that you have discrete listeners for IPC and TCP traffic, but in the standard listener configuration file they share a listener. Unless you change the listener file, you will encounter an ORA-28595 error because user-defined shared libraries, DLLs, must communicate across an IPC channel. You will find configuration instructions to support external procedures in Chapter 13.

The `DEFAULT_SERVICE_LISTENER` is set to `orcl` in the `listener.ora` file. ORCL also is the global name of the current database instance. The `SERVICE_NAME` parameter defaults to the global database name when one is not specified in the `spfileSID.ora` or `pfileSID.ora` file. The service name for any Oracle database is the database name concatenated to the database domain. Oracle Database 11*g* defines the default database name as ORCL and assigns no database domain. You can find this information by connecting as the `SYS` user under the `SYSDBA` role, formatting the return values, and running the following query:

```
COL name FORMAT A30
COL value FORMAT A30

SELECT    name
,         value
FROM      v$parameter
WHERE     name LIKE '%name'
OR        name LIKE '%domain';
```

The query returns the following data:

```
NAME                             VALUE
-----------------------------    -----------------------------
db_domain
instance_name                    orcl
db_name                          orcl
db_unique_name                   orcl
```

Net8 is designed to support client load balancing and connect-time failover. The service_name replaces the `SID` parameter that previously enabled these features. The `tnsnames.ora` file is a mapping file that enables client requests to find the Oracle listener. The `tnsnames.ora` file contains a network alias that maps to the Oracle service_name and connection configurations to facilitate access to external procedures. The *hostname* and *port_number* enable the network alias, ORCL, to find the Oracle listener. Naturally, there is an assumption that your *hostname* maps through DNS resolution or the local host file to a physical Internet Protocol (IP) address.

TIP
You can add the hostname and IP address to your local host file when you do not resolve to a server through DNS. The `/etc/host` *file is the Linux host file, and* `C:\WINDOWS\system32\drivers\etc\ hosts` *file is the Microsoft Windows host file.*

A sample `tnsnames.ora` file is

```
-- This is an example of a default tnsnames.ora file.

ORCL =
  (DESCRIPTION =
    (ADDRESS = (PROTOCOL = TCP)(HOST = hostname)(PORT = port_number))
    (CONNECT_DATA =
      (SERVER = DEDICATED)
      (SERVICE_NAME = ORCL)
    )
  )

EXTPROC_CONNECTION_DATA =
  (DESCRIPTION =
    (ADDRESS_LIST =
      (ADDRESS = (PROTOCOL = IPC)(KEY = EXTPROC1521))
    )
    (CONNECT_DATA =
      (SID = PLSExtProc)
      (PRESENTATION = RO)
    )
  )
```

Some strings in these configuration files are case sensitive. An example is the `PROGRAM` value in the listener.ora file and the `KEY` value in the tnsnames.ora file. These values are case sensitive and must match exactly between files or you will receive an `ORA-28576` error when accessing the external procedure.

These files support the `lsnrctl` utility regardless of platform. The `lsnrctl` utility enables you to *start, stop,* and *status* the listener process. As discussed when covering how to start and stop the database instance, you will need to be the `root` user in the Linux environment and an *Administrator* user in the Microsoft Windows environment.

The default installation starts the Oracle listener when the system boots, but you should check whether it is running before attempting to shut it down. You can use the following to check the status of the Oracle listener:

```
lsnrctl status
```

As discussed, the command implicitly substitutes `LISTENER` as the default second argument. You will need to explicitly provide the listener name when *starting, stopping,* or *checking status* when you have changed the default listener name. You should see the following on a Linux system when you check the status of a running Oracle Database 11*g* listener and only slight differences on a Unix or Windows system:

```
LSNRCTL for Linux: Version 11.1.0.3.0 - Beta on 25-FEB-2007
Copyright (c) 1991, 2006, Oracle.  All rights reserved.
Listening on: (DESCRIPTION=(ADDRESS=(PROTOCOL=ipc)(KEY=EXTPROC1521)))
Listening on: (DESCRIPTION=(ADDRESS=(PROTOCOL=tcp)(HOST=host.domain)
(PORT=1521)))
```

```
Connecting to (DESCRIPTION=(ADDRESS=(PROTOCOL=IPC)(KEY=EXTPROC1521)))
STATUS of the LISTENER
------------------------
Alias                    LISTENER
Version                  TNSLSNR for Linux: Version 11.1.0.3.0 - Beta
Start Date               25-FEB-2007 19:02:01
Uptime                   0 days 0 hr. 0 min. 0 sec
Trace Level              off
Security                 ON: Local OS Authentication
SNMP                     OFF
Listener Parameter File  /mount_pt/oracle_home/network/admin/listener.ora
Listener Log File        /mount_pt/oracle_home/network/log/listener.log
Listening Endpoints Summary...
  (DESCRIPTION=(ADDRESS=(PROTOCOL=ipc)(KEY=EXTPROC1521)))
  (DESCRIPTION=(ADDRESS=(PROTOCOL=tcp)(HOST=name.domain)(PORT=1521)))
Services Summary...
Service "PLSExtProc" has 1 instance(s).
  Instance "PLSExtProc", status UNKNOWN, has 1 handler(s) for this service...
The command completed successfully
```

You can stop the service by using

```
lsnrctl stop
```

You can restart the service by using

```
lsnrctl start
```

After stopping and starting the listener, you should check if you can make a network connection from your user account to the listener. This is very similar to the idea of a network ping operation, except you are pinging the Oracle Net8 connection layer. You use the `tnsping` utility to verify an Oracle Net8 connection, as follows:

```
tnsping orcl
```

You should see the following type of return message but with a real *hostname* as opposed to the substituted `hostname` value; provided you haven't changed the default network *port number*:

```
C:\>tnsping orcl

TNS Ping Utility for 32-bit Windows: Version 11.1.0.6.0
Copyright (c) 1997, 2007, Oracle.  All rights reserved.

Used parameter files:
C:\app\11.1.0\db_1\network\admin\sqlnet.ora

Used TNSNAMES adapter to resolve the alias
Attempting to contact (DESCRIPTION = (ADDRESS = (PROTOCOL = TCP)(HOST =
hostname.domain)(PORT = 1521)) (CONNECT_DATA = (SERVER = DEDICATED)
(SERVICE_NAME = ORCL)))

OK (10 msec)
```

The `tnsping` checks the `sqlnet.ora` parameter file for any instructions that it may contain. Net8 connections first check the `sqlnet.ora` file to find any network tracing instructions before proceeding with connection attempts. The Oracle Net8 tracing layers are very powerful tools and can assist you in diagnosing complex connection problems. You will find answers to configuring `sqlnet.ora` in the *Oracle Database Net Services Reference 11*g *Release 1.*

You can use a GUI tool to *start, stop,* and *status* the Oracle listener when you are running on Microsoft Windows. You can find it by navigating to the Control Panel, then if you are using a Classic view choose Administrative Tools and Services; but if you are using a Category view choose Performance and Maintenance, Administrative Tools, and Services. Highlight OracleORCLListener in the list of services in the right panel and click Stop The Service.

This section has explained where the configuration files are and how they work to enable you to *start, stop,* and check the *status* on the Oracle listener. In the next section you will see how users connect using the Oracle listener.

Oracle Roles and Privileges

Database privileges are granted by the superuser or its designee, like `SYS` or `SYSTEM`. These privileges provide explicit permissions to perform tasks. You can group privileges into roles, which are simply a collection of privileges. When you grant roles to users, they do not always provide the same rights and permissions. Some privileges cannot be effectively granted as part of a role.

The list of privileges that require explicit grants changes with each release of the database. If you encounter a situation where your rights and privileges seem less than what you expect, then you should connect as the superuser or designee and grant that privilege explicitly. As a rule, this audit helps you find any privileges that aren't fully granted as roles. You can also check the Oracle Database 11*g* Administrator's Guide for further information.

Accessing and Using the SQL*Plus Interface

The Oracle Database 11*g* product provides you with one command-line interface to access, insert, update, or delete data, and create, alter, or drop structures in database instances. The interface enables you to interact with the database by using Structured Query Language (SQL). If you are unfamiliar with the concepts of SQL, please check Appendix B before continuing with this segment.

Oracle SQL*Plus is both an interactive environment where you can enter SQL statements and process them one by one and a batch environment where you can run scripts as batch submissions. Scripts are small SQL programs or collections of programs found in a single file. The SQL*Plus environment is also a programming shell environment and supports session-level variables, using the data types covered in Table A-1. Various ways to use these session-level variables are discussed in this book.

You have two ways to use SQL with the Oracle Database 11*g* product. One is through the iSQL*Plus web page interface, and the other is through a command-line interface. This section will cover the command-line tool. Web tools and integrated development tools are covered in Chapter 2.

The Oracle SQL and PL/SQL examples used throughout the book require a schema known as PLSQL. You will use the `create_user.sql` script available from the publisher's web site to create the user and assign privileges. You will use the default storage clause unless you modify the `create_user.sql` script with something other than the default *user* tablespace. Storage clauses enable you to designate where a user will physically store data, which is in a designated tablespace. Tablespaces are logical structures that act as portals to one to many physical files.

Data Type	Description
BINARY_DOUBLE	The BINARY_DOUBLE datatype is a 64-bit floating-point number that takes eight bytes of storage. It is defined without a formal parameter. It has the following prototype: BINARY_DOUBLE
BINARY_FLOAT	The BINARY_FLOAT datatype is a 32-bit floating-point number that takes four bytes of storage. It is defined without a formal parameter. It has the following prototype: BINARY_FLOAT
BLOB	The BLOB datatype may contain any type of unstructured binary data up to a maximum size of 4GB. It has the following prototype: BLOB
CHAR	The CHAR datatype stores fixed-length character data in bytes or characters. You can override the default by providing a formal *size* parameter. The BYTE or CHAR qualification is optional and will be applied from the NLS_LENGTH_SEMANTICS parameter by default. It has the following prototype: CHAR [(*size* [BYTE | CHAR])]
CLOB	The CLOB datatype stands for Character Large Object. They store character strings up to 4GB in size. Variables with Unicode character sets are also supported up to the same maximum size. CLOB types are defined without any formal parameter for size. It has the following prototype: CLOB
NCHAR	The NCHAR datatype stores fixed-length Unicode national character data in bytes or characters. Unicode variables require two or three bytes, depending on the character set, which is an encoding schema. The AL16UTF16 character set requires two bytes, and UTF8 requires three bytes. You can override the default by providing a formal *size* parameter. It has the following prototype: NCHAR [(*size*)]
NCLOB	The NCLOB datatype stands for Unicode national Character Large Object. They store character strings up to 4GB in size. Variables with Unicode character sets are also supported up to the same maximum size. NCLOB types are defined without any formal parameter for size. It has the following prototype: NCLOB
NUMBER	The NUMBER datatype is a 38-position numeric data type. You can declare its precision, or size, and its scale, or number of digits to the right of the decimal point. You can define it without a formal parameter, with a single *precision* parameter, or with both *precision* and *scale* parameters. It has the following prototype: NUMBER [(*precision* [, scale])]

TABLE A-1 *SQL*Plus Session-Level Variables*

Data Type	Description
NVARCHAR2	The NVARCHAR2 datatype stores variable-length strings in bytes or characters up to 4,000 characters in length. The size per character is determined by the Unicode setting for the database instance. You define a NVARCHAR2 datatype by setting its maximum *size* parameter. It has the following prototype: NVARCHAR2 (*size*)
REFCURSOR	The REFCURSOR datatype stores a cursor returned by a PL/SQL block, which can contain an array of a structure. The structure can be dynamic and may implement a structure defined in the data catalog or in a query. It has the following prototype: REFCURSOR
VARCHAR2	The VARCHAR2 datatype stores variable-length strings in bytes or characters up to 4,000 characters in length. If BYTE or CHAR is not specified, the type uses the NLS_LENGTH_SEMANTICS parameter defined for the database instance. You define a VARCHAR2 datatype by setting its maximum *size* parameter. It has the following prototype: VARCHAR2 [(*size* [BYTE | CHAR])]

TABLE A-1 *SQL*Plus Session-Level Variables* (continued)

The basic architecture of a user schema is disconnected from physical storage through a series of software abstractions. A user can access and store data in one or more tablespaces, and a tablespace can reference one or more files. This architecture enables a user to store more data than the physical file limits imposed by an operating system. You designate a default storage tablespace when you define a user/schema, but Oracle Database 11*g* plans on all users being stored in the USER tablespace. You can find the default tablespace for a user by running the following script:

```
SELECT    username
,         default_tablespace
FROM      dba_users;
```

The enclosed scripts do not attempt to override the planned intent of the product, and the script assumes you will use the default USER tablespace. If you are working in an Oracle Standard or Enterprise Edition version of the database, you should consider creating a PLSQL tablespace and modifying the scripts to place all data there.

You will work with the command-line interface first because doing so provides an opportunity to discuss the differences between the SQL*Plus and SQL environments. The discussion lays a foundation for the subsequent web page interface materials. You can further your understanding of Oracle SQL*Plus by referring to the *SQL*Plus User Guide and Reference Release 1,* or Oracle SQL by referring to the *Oracle Database SQL Reference 11g Release 1* found on http://otn.oracle.com.

SQL Command-Line Interface

The SQL*Plus command-line interface requires that you have an account on the server or that you install Oracle client software on your local machine. The command-line tool requires a thick-client connection to build a socket between a client and a server. The interactive SQL*Plus interface is provided by the Oracle client software.

You can access the SQL*Plus application directly when you are working on the same machine as the Oracle database. If you are working on a Linux machine, you will need to put the `$ORACLE_HOME/bin` directory in your environment path and set several other environment variables. You will find the instructions for setting the Oracle Database 11*g* Client environment variables in the *Oracle Database Client Installation Guide 11g*. This installation guide is platform specific.

Only Linux users will need to set the environment file. You do it by running the `oracle_env.csh` when your account uses the c or `tcsh` shell, and `oracle_env.sh` when your account uses the Bash or Korn shell.

After creating your environment variable file, you source the file into your environment, and copy the `create_user.sql` file to a working directory owned by your user account. These files build your Oracle `PLSQL` user account. Microsoft Windows users will need to open a command prompt session to access the SQL*Plus command-line tool.

In the directory *where you have copied the file,* you can now connect to the SQL*Plus environment by typing the following command:

 `sqlplus system/password@orcl`

 NOTE
You set the default password during installation. Don't misplace that password.

This assumes you own or have access to the Oracle superuser accounts, `SYS` and `SYSTEM`, and know the password. If you don't own the superuser account, you should contact your DBA to run the `create_user.sql` script from the `SYSTEM` account. The `@orcl` is an instruction to use the network alias in your `tnsnames.ora` file to find the database. When you append a TNS alias, the connection only resolves through a running Oracle listener.

You can execute scripts from the SQL*Plus environment by prefacing them with a `@` symbol. This reads the file directly into a line-by-line execution mode. Alternatively, you can use the `GET` command to read the file into the current SQL*Plus buffer, before running it. The latter method is fine when you have only a SQL statement in the file and no SQL*Plus statements. *DO NOT use the GET command with these scripts* because they contain many SQL and SQL*Plus statements.

 NOTE
*SQL commands let you interact with the database, while SQL*Plus commands let you configure your SQL*Plus environment. They also enable you to format and secure feedback from the database on the success or failure of your SQL statements.*

You create the `PLSQL` user and schema with the `create_user.sql` script. The script contains SQL*Plus, SQL, and PL/SQL components. PL/SQL, as described in the introduction, stands for Procedural Language/Structured Query Language, a language that was created by Oracle to let users write stored procedures in the database.

You have two options as to how you run the script. The first option is connecting to SQL*Plus and running the script from the command line. The second option is running the script as an actual parameter to the `sqlplus` executable. The easiest way for new Oracle users is to connect to SQL*Plus and run the script. You connect with the command

```
sqlplus system/password@orcl
```

The script will fail unless you run it as the SYSTEM user. After connecting as the SYSTEM user, you use this syntax to run the script from a local Linux directory or Microsoft Windows folder:

```
SQL> @create_user.sql
```

This script checks whether there is an existing PLSQL user in your database before creating one. It removes the PLSQL user when found. Dropping a user wipes out all objects owned by that user. This script can be rerun in case you make an error and want to wipe out your working area to start over, but remember that it wipes everything owned by the previous PLSQL user. The create_user.sql follows:

```
-- This is found in create_user.sql on the enclosed CD.

SET FEEDBACK ON
SET PAGESIZE 999
SET SERVEROUTPUT ON SIZE 1000000
SPOOL create_user.log

DECLARE
  -- Define an exception.
  wrong_schema EXCEPTION;
  PRAGMA EXCEPTION_INIT(wrong_schema,-20001);

  -- Define a return variable.
  retval VARCHAR2(1 CHAR);

  /*
  || Define a cursor to identify whether the current user is either the
  || SYSTEM user or a user with the DBA role privilege.
  */
  CURSOR privs IS
    SELECT    DISTINCT null
    FROM      user_role_privs
    WHERE     username = 'SYSTEM'
    OR        granted_role = 'DBA';
BEGIN
  -- Open cursor and read through it.
  OPEN privs;
  LOOP

    -- Read a row.
    FETCH privs INTO retval;

    -- Evaluate if cursor failed.
    IF privs%NOTFOUND THEN
      -- Raise exception.
      RAISE wrong_schema;
```

```
    ELSE
      -- Evaluate whether PLSQL user exists and drop it.
      FOR i IN (SELECT null FROM dba_users WHERE username = 'PLSQL') LOOP
        EXECUTE IMMEDIATE 'DROP USER plsql CASCADE';
      END LOOP;

      -- Create user and grant privileges.
      EXECUTE IMMEDIATE 'CREATE USER plsql IDENTIFIED BY plsql;
      EXECUTE IMMEDIATE 'GRANT connect TO plsql';
      EXECUTE IMMEDIATE 'GRANT resource TO plsql';

      -- Print successful outcome.
      DBMS_OUTPUT.PUT_LINE(CHR(10)||'Created PLSQL user.');
    END IF;

    -- Exit the loop.
    EXIT;

  END LOOP;

  -- Close cursor.
  CLOSE privs;

EXCEPTION
  -- Handle a defined exception.
  WHEN wrong_schema THEN
    DBMS_OUTPUT.PUT_LINE('The script requires the SYSTEM user and '
    ||                      'you are using the <'||user||'> schema or '
    ||                      'the script requires a user with DBA role '
    ||                      'privileges.');

  -- Handle a generic exception.
  WHEN others THEN
    DBMS_OUTPUT.PUT_LINE(SQLERRM);
    RETURN;
END;
/

-- Define SQL*Plus formatting.
COL grantee          FORMAT A8
COL granted_role     FORMAT A30
COL grantor          FORMAT A12
COL privilege        FORMAT A12
COL owner            FORMAT A6
COL table_name       FORMAT A10

-- Query user granted roles.

SELECT    grantee
,         granted_role
FROM      dba_role_privs
WHERE     grantee = 'PLSQL';
```

```
-- Query resources.
SELECT    grantor
,         owner
,         table_name
,         grantee
,         privilege
FROM      dba_tab_privs
WHERE     grantee = 'PLSQL';

COL admin_option        FORMAT A3
COL privilege           FORMAT A30
COL username            FORMAT A10

-- Query user system privileges.
SELECT    grantee
,         privilege
,         admin_option
FROM      dba_sys_privs
WHERE     grantee = 'PLSQL';

SPOOL OFF
```

Coming from a MySQL background, the script may look like the new stored procedures introduced in version 5. This file uses Oracle PL/SQL to manage the process of creating a user. The script then uses formatting commands to govern the output from two SQL queries, and the queries determine the permissions of the new user.

The COL[UMN] and SET commands belong to the SQL*Plus environment and are specific to Oracle. They let you configure the way output is rendered in the command-line SQL*Plus environment. The SPOOL command is like the tee command in MySQL and splits standard out to both the console and a file.

You should see the following output after running the script:

```
GRANTEE   GRANTED_ROLE
--------  ------------------------------
PLSQL     DBA
PLSQL     CONNECT

2 rows selected

no rows selected

GRANTEE   PRIVILEGE                        ADM
--------  ------------------------------- ---
PLSQL     UNLIMITED TABLESPACE             NO

1 rows selected.
```

These are the base permissions required for the PLSQL user. The password is set trivially as PLSQL, but you can change it to whatever you like. You have two options to change a password. The first option is to type **password** at the SQL prompt, as shown:

```
SQL> password
Changing password for PLSQL
Old password:
New password:
Retype new password:
Password changed
```

The second option for changing your password is to use the ALTER SQL command to change the PLSQL user password. The syntax is

```
SQL> ALTER USER plsql IDENTIFIED BY secret_password;
```

This has explained the standard command-line interface. There are some subtle differences when you connect through Oracle iSQL*Plus or Application Express web interfaces. In fact, if you've used the Application Express product to connect as this user, you will return different information.

After you connect through the Oracle Database 11*g* Application Express web login page, the second query against the DBA_TAB_PRIVS table in the create_user.sql script will return a different set of granted privileges. These are granted as part of your initial login through the web applications. The newly granted privileges for the PLSQL user are

```
GRANTOR       OWNER   TABLE_NAME GRANTEE  PRIVILEGE
------------- ------- ---------- -------- ------------
FLOWS_020100 SYS      DBMS_RLS   PLSQL    EXECUTE
FLOWS_020100 CTXSYS   CTX_DDL    PLSQL    EXECUTE
FLOWS_020100 CTXSYS   CTX_DOC    PLSQL    EXECUTE
```

You can now disconnect from the SQL*Plus session by typing the word **quit** and pressing ENTER:

```
SQL> quit
```

Bind Variables

As presented in Table A-1, there are session-level variables in the SQL*Plus environment. These are also called bind variables because you can bind the contents from query execution to use in another query. Likewise, you can bind values from one PL/SQL execution scope to another or a subsequent SQL statement. Bind variables is the more commonly known term for describing SQL*Plus session variables. You define a variable-length string bind variable as follows:

```
SQL> VARIABLE mybindvar VARCHAR2(30)
```

You'll notice that there is no semicolon after the definition of a bind variable and that a variable-length string must be allocated physical space, which is 30 characters in this example.

```
BEGIN
   :mybindvar := 'Demonstration';
END;
/
```

You can then query the contents of the bind variable by

```
SQL> SELECT :mybindvar AS "Bind Variable" FROM dual;
```

This prints the following to the console:

```
Bind Variable
-------------
Demonstration
```

There is a great deal more information about the SQL*Plus environment, but you will need to review it in the *SQL*Plus User Guide and Reference Release 1* manual, which is over 500 pages long.

You should check *Oracle Database Express Edition Application Express User's Guide* and the *Oracle Database Express Edition 2 Day Developer Guide* for more information on the web-based products.

Summary

This appendix has introduced you to the architecture of relational databases and demonstrated how you start and stop database instances on Unix or Linux and Microsoft Windows. It has also shown you how to start, stop, and status an Oracle listener and access the SQL*Plus environment to interact with the database.

APPENDIX
B

Oracle Database
SQL Primer

he *Structured Query Language (SQL)* is the mechanism for accessing information in relational databases. The SQL acronym has different pronunciations, but many people use the word *sequel* because IBM originally named it the *Structured English Query Language.* The SEQUEL acronym mutated to SQL when IBM discovered the original acronym was trademarked by Hawker Siddeley.

SQL is a nonprocedural programming language designed to work with data sets in relational database management systems. SQL lets you define, modify, and remove database objects, transact against data, control the flow of transactions, and query data. The SQL language commands are often grouped by function into four groups that are also called languages: Data Definition Language (DDL), Data Manipulation Language (DML), Data Control Language (DCL), and Data Query Language (DQL).

As a SQL primer, this appendix covers these languages in the order required to build database applications. The primer will refer to examples provided in Chapter 1 that support this book by creating a working model and seeding it with initial data.

- Oracle SQL*Plus datatypes

- Data Definition Language (DDL)

- Data Query Language (DQL)

- Data Manipulation Language (DML)

- Data Control Language (DCL)

DCL and DQL are not universally accepted in many published references. DCL was originally called *Transaction Control Language (TCL),* and DQL was considered part of the DML language commands. While Oracle Corporation used the TCL acronym for years to describe the *Data Control Language,* even Oracle appears to be adopting DCL to avoid confusion with the *Tool Command Language (TCL)* created at Berkeley in 1987. You will use DCL to describe transaction control commands, like SAVEPOINT, ROLLBACK, and COMMIT. DQL describes using the SELECT statement to query data without locking the rows, whereas SELECT statements that lock rows for subsequent transactions are more than a query but less than data manipulation, although they are classified as DML statements. You will use DQL to describe all SELECT statement queries.

SQL implementations differ for many reasons. They vary in their level of compliance with different ANSI standards. For example, Oracle SQL supports two semantic join models—one is the Oracle Proprietary method and the other is ANSI SQL 2003–compliant. Table B-1 covers the SQL standards.

Oracle 11*g* is ANSI SQL:2003 compliant. Window functions calculate aggregates over a window of data. You can find more about the ANSI SQL:2003–compliant features introduced in the Oracle 10*g* family products by reading the *Oracle SQL Standard Support in Oracle Database 10*g* White Paper* on the http://otn.oracle.com web site.

While these topics are arranged for the beginner from start to finish, you should be able to use individual sections as independent references. A more gradual approach to Oracle SQL is found in *Oracle Database 10*g* SQL* by Jason Price (McGraw-Hill/Osborne, 2004). The comprehensive reference is the *Oracle Database SQL Reference 11*g* Release 1* manual, which has over 1,000 printed pages and is available online at http://otn.oracle.com.

Name	Year	Description
SQL-86	1986	This is the first standardized version of SQL. It was ratified by ISO in 1987.
SQL-89	1989	This is a minor revision of SQL-86.
SQL-92	1992	This is a major revision of SQL-89 and also known as SQL2.
SQL:1999	1999	This is a major revision of SQL-92 that added recursive queries, regular expression handling, database triggers, nonscalar datatypes, and object-oriented features.
SQL:2003	2003	This is a major revision of SQL:1999 that added auto-generated columns, standardized sequences, window functions, and XML-related functions.

TABLE B-1   *ANSI SQL Standards*

Oracle SQL*Plus Datatypes

Oracle Database 11*g* supports *character, numeric, timestamp, binary,* and *row address* datatypes. These are also known as SQL datatypes or built-in types because they can be used to define columns in tables and parameter datatypes in PL/SQL. Table B-2 summarizes these SQL datatypes and qualifies two widely used data subtypes by groups. While the list is not comprehensive of all subtypes, which can be found in the *Oracle Database SQL Reference 11g Release 2* manual, it should cover the most frequently used data subtypes.

Data Type	Raw Code	Description
CHAR	96	The CHAR datatype column stores fixed-length character data in bytes or characters. You can override the default by providing a formal *size* parameter. The BYTE or CHAR qualification is optional and will be applied from the NLS_LENGTH_SEMANTICS parameter by default. It has the following prototype: CHAR [(*size* [BYTE | CHAR])]
NCHAR	96	The NCHAR datatype column stores fixed-length Unicode national character data in bytes or characters. Unicode variables require two or three bytes, depending on the character set, which is an encoding schema. The AL16UTF16 character set requires two bytes, and UTF8 requires three bytes. You can override the default by providing a formal *size* parameter. It has the following prototype: NCHAR [(*size*)]
STRING	1	The STRING datatype column is a subtype of VARCHAR2 and stores variable-length strings in bytes or characters up to 4,000 characters in length. If BYTE or CHAR is not specified, the type uses the NLS_LENGTH_SEMANTICS parameter defined for the database instance. You define a VARCHAR2 datatype by providing a required *size* parameter. It has the following prototype: STRING [(*size* [BYTE | CHAR])]

TABLE B-2   *SQL Datatypes*

Data Type	Raw Code	Description
VARCHAR2	1	The VARCHAR2 datatype column stores variable-length strings in bytes or characters up to 4,000 characters in length. If BYTE or CHAR is not specified, the type uses the NLS_LENGTH_SEMANTICS parameter defined for the database instance. This value is 2 bytes for AL16UTF16 and 3 bytes for UTF8. You define a VARCHAR2 datatype by setting its maximum *size* parameter. It has the following prototype: VARCHAR2 [(*size* [BYTE | CHAR])]
NVARCHAR2	1	The NVARCHAR2 datatype column stores variable-length strings in bytes or characters up to 4,000 characters in length. The size per character is determined by the Unicode setting for the database instance. You define a NVARCHAR2 datatype by setting its maximum *size* parameter. It has the following prototype: NVARCHAR2 (*size*)
CLOB	112	The CLOB datatype column stands for Character Large Object. They store character strings up to 4GB in size. Variables with Unicode character sets are also supported up to the same maximum size. CLOB types are defined without any formal parameter for size. It has the following prototype: CLOB
NCLOB	112	The NCLOB datatype column stands for Unicode national Character Large Object. They store character strings up to 4GB in size. Variables with Unicode character sets are also supported up to the same maximum size. NCLOB types are defined without any formal parameter for size. It has the following prototype: NCLOB
LONG	8	The LONG datatype column is provided for backward compatibility and will soon become unavailable because the CLOB and NCLOB datatypes are its future replacement types. *(NOTE: Oracle recommends you should begin migrating LONG datatypes, but no firm date for its deprecation have been announced.)* It contains a variable-length string up to 2GB of characters per row of data, which means you can have only one LONG datatype in a table definition. You define a LONG without any formal parameter. It has the following prototype: LONG
BINARY_FLOAT	100	The BINARY_FLOAT is a 32-bit floating-point number column that takes four bytes of storage. It is defined without a formal parameter. It has the following prototype: BINARY_FLOAT
BINARY_DOUBLE	101	The BINARY_DOUBLE is a 64-bit floating-point number column that takes eight bytes of storage. It is defined without a formal parameter. It has the following prototype: BINARY_DOUBLE
FLOAT	2	The FLOAT is a 126-position subtype of the NUMBER datatype column. You can define it without a formal parameter or with a formal parameter of *size*. It has the following prototype: FLOAT [(*size*)]
NUMBER	2	The NUMBER is a 38-position numeric datatype column. You can declare its precision, or size, and its scale, or number of digits to the right of the decimal point. You can define it without a formal parameter, with a single *precision* parameter, or with both *precision* and *scale* parameters. It has the following prototype: NUMBER [(*precision* [, scale])]

TABLE B-2   *SQL Datatypes* (continued)

Data Type	Raw Code	Description
DATE	12	The DATE is a seven-byte column and represents a timestamp from 1 Jan 4712 B.C.E. to 31 Dec 9999 using a Gregorian calendar representation. The default format mask, DD-MON-RR, is set as a database parameter and found as the NLS_DATE_FORMAT parameter in the V$PARAMETER table. It has the following prototype: DATE
INTERVAL YEAR	182	The INTERVAL YEAR is a five-byte column and represents a year and month, and the default display is YYYY MM. You can define it with or without a formal parameter of *year.* The *year* must be a value between 0 and 9 and defaults to 2. The default limits of the year interval are –99 and 99. It has the following prototype: INTERVAL YEAR [(*year*)] TO MONTH
INTERVAL DAY	183	The INTERVAL DAY is an 11-byte representation of *days, hours, minutes,* and *seconds* in an interval. The default display is DD HH:MI:SS, or *days, hours, minutes,* and *seconds.* The *days* and fractions of *seconds* must be values between 0 and 9. The default limits the *days* and interval is between 1 and 31, and *seconds* are returned without fractions. It has the following prototype: INTERVAL YEAR [(*years*)] TO SECOND [(*seconds*)]
TIMESTAMP	180	The TIMESTAMP is a 7 to 11–byte column and represents a date and time, and it includes fractional seconds when you override the default seconds parameter. The default *seconds* parameter returns seconds without any fractional equivalent. The fractions of *seconds* must be values between 0 and 9 and have a maximum display precision of microseconds. It has the following prototype: TIMESTAMP [(*seconds*)]
TIMESTAMP WITH TIME ZONE	231	The TIMESTAMP WITH TIME ZONE is a 13-byte column and represents a date and time including offset from UTC; it includes fractional seconds when you override the default *seconds* parameter. The default *seconds* parameter returns seconds without any fractional equivalent. The fractions of *seconds* must be values between 0 and 9 and have a maximum display precision of microseconds. It has the following prototype: TIMESTAMP [(*seconds*)] WITH TIME ZONE
BLOB	113	The BLOB datatype column may contain any type of unstructured binary data up to a maximum size of 4GB. It has the following prototype: BLOB
BFILE	114	The BFILE datatype column contains a reference to a file stored externally on a file system. The file must not exceed 4GB in size. It has the following prototype: BFILE
RAW	23	The RAW datatype column is provided for backward compatibility and will soon become unavailable because the BLOB datatype is its future replacement. *(NOTE: Oracle recommends that you begin migrating RAW datatypes, but no firm date for the type's deprecation has been announced.)* It can contain a variable-length raw binary stream up to two thousand bytes per row of data, which means you can only have one RAW datatype in a table definition. It has the following prototype: RAW (*size*)
LONG RAW	24	The LONG RAW datatype column is provided for backward compatibility and will soon become unavailable because the BLOB datatype is its future replacement. *(NOTE: Oracle recommends that you begin migrating LONG RAW datatypes, but no firm date for the type's deprecation has been announced.)* It can contain a variable-length raw binary stream up to 2GB bytes. It has the following prototype: LONG RAW

TABLE B-2 *SQL Datatypes* (continued)

Data Type	Raw Code	Description
ROWID	69	The ROWID datatype column contains a ten-byte representation of a Base 64 binary data representation retrieved as the ROWID pseudocolumn. The ROWID pseudocolumn maps to a physical block on the file system or raw partition. It has the following prototype: ROWID
UROWID	208	The UROWID datatype column contains a maximum of 4,000 bytes, and it is the Base 64 binary data representation of the logical row in an index-organized table. The optional parameter sets the size in bytes for the UROWID values. It has the following prototype: UROWID [(*size*)]

TABLE B-2   *SQL Datatypes* (continued)

You can also find examples using these Oracle SQL datatypes in the *Oracle Database Application Developer's Guide – Fundamentals* and *Oracle Database Application Developer's Guide – Large Objects.* The most frequently used datatypes are the BLOB, BFILE, CLOB, DATE, FLOAT, NUMBER, STRING, TIMESTAMP, and VARCHAR2 datatypes. International implementations also use the TIMESTAMP WITH LOCAL TIME ZONE to regionalize Virtual Private Databases available in the Oracle Database 11*g* product family.

Data Definition Language (DDL)

The DDL commands let you *create, replace, alter, drop, rename,* and *truncate* database objects, permissions, and settings. You require a database instance before you can you *create, replace, alter, drop, rename,* and *truncate* database objects. When you installed the Oracle database, the installation script created a clone of a sample database. Alternatively, the installation program could have used the CREATE command to build a database instance. After creating the database instance, you can then use the ALTER command to change settings for the instance or for given sessions. Sessions last the duration of a connection to the database instance.

The DDL section is organized into subsections and covers the following topics:

- Managing tables and constraints
- Managing views
- Managing stored programs
- Managing sequences
- Managing user-defined types

You will most frequently use DDL commands to manage tables, constraints, views, stored programs (such as functions, procedures, and packages), sequences, and user-defined types. This section works through the general form and application for these commands.

Managing Tables and Constraints

Database tables are the typically two-dimensional structures that hold the raw data that makes databases useful. The first dimension defines the column names and their datatypes, and the second dimension defines the rows of data. Rows of data are also known as records and instances of the table structure.

Tables are the backbone of the database instance. Tables are built by using the CREATE statement. You have several options when building database tables, but the basic decision is whether you are creating a structure to hold data or copying a data structure to a newly named table.

Assuming you are building a table for the first time as a structure where you will hold information, you need to determine whether the table will have database constraints. Database constraints are rules that define how you will allow users to *insert* and *update* rows or records in the table. Five database constraints are available in an Oracle database; they are: *check, foreign key, not null, primary key,* and *unique.* Constraints restrict DML commands as follows:

- *Check* constraints check whether a column value meets criteria before allowing a value to be inserted or updated into a column. They check whether a value is between two numbers, a value is greater than two numbers, or a combination of logically related compound rules is met. Also, *not null* and *unique* constraints are specialized types of *check* constraints.

- *Foreign key* constraints check whether a column value is found in a list of values in a column designated as a *primary key* column in the same or a different table. *Foreign key* constraints are typically managed in the application programs, rather than as database constraints, because of their adverse impact on throughput.

- *Not null* constraints check whether a column value contains a value other than null.

- *Primary key* constraints identify a column as the *primary key* for a table and impose both a *not null* and *unique* constraint on the column. A *foreign key* can only reference a valid *primary key* column.

- *Unique* constraints check whether a column value will be unique among all rows in a table.

Database constraints are assigned during the creation of a table or by using the ALTER command after a table is created. You can include constraints in the create statement by using *in-line* or *out-of-line* constraints. While some maintain that this is a matter of preference, it is more often a matter of finding working examples. You should consider using *out-of-line* constraints because they're organized at the end of your table creation and can be grouped for increased readability. Unfortunately, only *in-line* NOT NULL constraints are visible when you describe a table. The following demonstrates creating a table using SQL:

```
-- This is found in create_store.sql on the publisher's web site.

CREATE TABLE member
( member_id               NUMBER
, account_number          VARCHAR2(10)
, credit_card_number      VARCHAR2(19)
, credit_card_type        NUMBER
```

```
, created_by                 NUMBER
, creation_date              DATE
, last_updated_by            NUMBER
, last_update_date           DATE
, CONSTRAINT pk_member_1      PRIMARY KEY(member_id)
, CONSTRAINT nn_member_1      CHECK(account_number IS NOT NULL)
, CONSTRAINT nn_member_2     CHECK(credit_card_number IS NOT NULL)
, CONSTRAINT nn_member_3     CHECK(credit_card_type IS NOT NULL)
, CONSTRAINT nn_member_4     CHECK(created_by IS NOT NULL)
, CONSTRAINT nn_member_5     CHECK(creation_date IS NOT NULL)
, CONSTRAINT nn_member_6     CHECK(last_updated_by IS NOT NULL)
, CONSTRAINT nn_member_7     CHECK(last_update_date IS NOT NULL)
, CONSTRAINT fk_member_1      FOREIGN KEY(credit_card_type)
  REFERENCES common_lookup    (common_lookup_id)
, CONSTRAINT fk_member_2     FOREIGN KEY(created_by)
  REFERENCES system_user      (system_user_id)
, CONSTRAINT fk_member_3     FOREIGN KEY(last_updated_by)
  REFERENCES system_user      (system_user_id));
```

The CREATE statement for a table cannot include the REPLACE clause, because you must DROP a table before altering its definition. This limitation exists because of the linkages between database constraints and indexes that reference the table, both of which are implicitly dropped when you DROP a table. The preceding MEMBER table is created by using out-of-line NOT NULL constraints, which means you won't see them while describing the table in SQL*Plus. The foregoing CREATE TABLE statement demonstrates *primary key, check,* and *foreign key* constraints.

TIP
You should define NOT NULL *constraints in-line because that's the only way they'll be displayed when you describe the table from the SQL*Plus command line.*

You have the option of building constraints without names, but all of these constraints have meaningful names, which enable programmers to sort out errors much faster when they occur. The database assigns system-generated names when you fail to provide explicit names, and you will find that they are not very helpful to you when you're troubleshooting an application failure. You should always use meaningful constraint names.

You can create copies of tables by using a CREATE statement that uses a SELECT statement to implicitly derive the table structure, as follows:

```
CREATE TABLE member_clone AS SELECT * FROM member;
```

This implicit cloning of one table into another has the downside of naming all database constraints for the table using a meaningless sequence, like SYS_C0020951. However, it is convenient for building a place to store data until you can perform maintenance on the table. Using the SQL*Plus describe command,

```
SQL> describe member_clone
```

Case-Sensitive Table and Column Names

Oracle 10*g* introduced the quoted identifier delimiter. This lets you define case-sensitive table and column names in the database. The only problem with case-sensitive table and column names is that you can only query them with special handling. You must use the correct case and enclose case-sensitive table and column names inside two quoted identifiers: double quotes symbols.

You can create tables with all case-sensitive, case-insensitive, or a mix of both. The case of table and column names is found in the `USER_TAB_COLUMNS` view, or if you enjoy DBA privileges, the `ALL_TAB_COLUMNS` and `DBA_TAB_COLUMNS` views.

The following creates a table with a case-sensitive table name, and two case-sensitive and one case-insensitive column names:

```
CREATE TABLE "CaseSensitive"
( "CaseSensitiveId" NUMBER
, "CaseSensitive"   VARCHAR2(30)
,  case_insensitive VARCHAR2(30));
```

After you insert and commit the row, you can then query the record delimiting any case-sensitive column and table names inside double quotes (the quoted identifier). This query demonstrates the technique:

```
SELECT   "CaseSensitiveId"
,        "CaseSensitive"
,         case_insensitive
FROM     "CaseSensitive";
```

You can view the table definition by querying the `TABLE_NAME` and `COLUMN_NAME` columns from the `USER_TAB_COLUMNS` view. You would use the following syntax to query the database catalog view:

```
SELECT   table_name, column_name
FROM     user_tab_columns
WHERE    table_name = 'CaseSensitive';
```

You'll find that the stored definition is a mix of case-sensitive and -insensitive. Double quotes must delimit case-sensitive strings, and case-insensitive strings can be delimited by double quotes when you use uppercase text for their values.

you will see a mirror to the original table, as follows:

```
Name                                     Null?    Type
---------------------------------------- -------- ------------
MEMBER_ID                                NOT NULL NUMBER
CREDIT_CARD_NUMBER                       NOT NULL VARCHAR2(19)
CREDIT_CARD_TYPE                         NOT NULL NUMBER
CREATED_BY                               NOT NULL NUMBER
CREATION_DATE                            NOT NULL DATE
LAST_UPDATED_BY                          NOT NULL NUMBER
LAST_UPDATE_DATE                         NOT NULL DATE
```

The cloning operation redefines the out-of-line check constraints from the MEMBER table as in-line constraints in the MEMBER_CLONE table. This reinforces best development practices by demonstrating how Oracle's engine will implicitly define a clone of a table. The NOT NULL constraints are now displayed by the SQL*Plus environment DESCRIBE command.

The ALTER command provides you with the opportunity to *add, rename,* or *drop* columns while keeping the table active in the database. The ALTER command demonstrates how to *add* a column to the MEMBER table when it contains data:

```
ALTER TABLE member ADD (demo_column VARCHAR2(10));
```

You can use an *in-line* constraint when the table does not contain any data, like the following:

```
ALTER TABLE member ADD (demo_column VARCHAR2(10)
CONSTRAINT nn_member_8 NOT NULL);
```

This syntax will not work when one or more rows does not contain data in the target column. You should note that the *in-line* constraint does not identify itself as a check constraint but simply denotes the NOT NULL condition. This is typical of *in-line* constraints, whereas *out-of-line* NOT NULL constraints must be qualified as CHECK constraints. After you populate the new column in all existing rows with a value, you can add a named NOT NULL constraint by using the following ALTER command syntax:

```
ALTER TABLE member ADD CONSTRAINT nn_member_8
CHECK(demo_column IS NOT NULL);
```

You can then drop the column explicitly, which also drops the nn_member_8 NOT NULL constraint. The following ALTER command drops the column, including any values that you've added:

```
ALTER TABLE member DROP COLUMN demo_column;
```

You can also *rename* a table whether it has dependents or not. All *foreign key* constraint references are implicitly changed to point to the new table name when their respective *primary key* column exists. This happens because the ALTER command changes only a non-identifying property of a catalog table reference. Application code references in stored program units are not altered to reflect the change because they are not part of the database catalog. You can rename a table with the ALTER command, like so:

```
ALTER TABLE member RENAME TO membership;
```

Then, you can use the alternate syntax to rename it back by using

```
RENAME membership TO member;
```

The TRUNCATE command lets you remove all data from a table but keep the structure of the table. There is no rolling back the TRUNCATE command when you issue it. *Truncating a table is final!* Since we don't need the MEMBER_CLONE table's data created earlier, you can truncate the data with the following syntax:

```
TRUNCATE TABLE member_clone;
```

Database tables typically stand alone in the database, but when you add a foreign key constraint that references another table, that table has a dependent. You drop tables without dependents differently than tables with dependents. You can drop a table that has no dependents by using the following command syntax:

```
DROP TABLE member_clone;
```

You append the `CASCADE CONSTRAINTS` phrase when dropping tables with dependents, like this:

```
DROP TABLE member CASCADE CONSTRAINTS;
```

What the `CASCADE CONSTRAINTS` phrase does is tell the database to ignore the *foreign key* dependency. However, you will need to repopulate the table with the *primary key* data to support the *foreign key* values in the dependent tables, or they become orphan rows. You should identify orphan rows and discover why they've been orphaned, which is typically due to an error caused by an insertion or update anomaly. You discover orphans by using outer joins between the *foreign* and *primary key* values.

The error can be harmless or harmful. Harmless errors mean that you meant to delete the rows and forgot. Harmful errors are that the parent rows were deleted in error, which means you'll need to recover the data.

NOTE
If you dropped the MEMBER table, please rerun the database seeding scripts described in Chapter 1.

This section has covered the mechanics of the basic DDL statements. There are many other commands that you can use. Your best reference to more details about the DDL statements in the primer is the index for the `ALTER`, `CREATE`, `DROP`, `RENAME`, and `TRUNCATE` commands in the *Oracle Database SQL Reference 11g Release 1* manual.

Managing Views

Views are constructed by using `SELECT` statements to provide subsets of columns from tables, a subset of rows, a subset of columns and rows combined, or a combination of columns from two or more tables. Views are often built to display complex information in easily queried database objects. `SELECT` statements you use to build views can contain aggregation, conversion, calculation, transformation, and various types of grouping and set operations.

An example of a conversion function is using a `TO_CHAR` function to convert a `DATE` datatype column into `VARCHAR2` datatype when you want to return a known date format mask. Aggregation functions *count, average,* and *sum* are examples using the `COUNT`, `AVG`, and `SUM()` functions respectively. Grouping operators reduce the number of actual rows to summary levels by paring the repeating column values into a single row in the result set. A result set is the number of rows and columns returned from a `SELECT` statement. You can also limit the number of returned rows from a `VIEW` by using a `WHERE` clause in the `SELECT` statement to narrow selected rows based on criteria evaluation. This is often called filtering the result set.

Views are powerful structures, but they have some clearly defined limits when you want to transact against them using DML statements. The `SELECT` statement for the views cannot have any of the following in order to let you *insert, update,* and *delete* records through the view:

- ■ **Expressions**   Expressions can be conversion or aggregation functions.

- ■ **Set operators**   These can be `UNION`, `UNION ALL`, `INTERSECT`, or `MINUS`.

- ■ **Sorting operations**   These can be `DISTINCT`, `GROUP BY`, `HAVING`, or `ORDER BY` clauses.

Using Set Operators

Set operators are powerful structures when you need to build a view that contains two or more data sets filtered by different criteria. The sets may come from the same table or view or different tables or views. The restrictions on set operators are straightforward. Queries joined by set operations must have the same number of columns, and the columns must be of the same datatype. The statement parser compares columns by evaluating their position and then their type.

When data doesn't exist in one of the queries, you can fabricate it from thin air, but you must ensure that you *fabricate* a column with the same datatype. In the simplest form, you can use the pseudotable `dual` to get today's and tomorrow's date in two rows, as follows:

```
SELECT SYSDATE FROM dual
UNION ALL
SELECT SYSDATE + 1 FROM dual;
```

This returns the following if today's date is March 24, 2007:

```
SYSDATE
---------
24-MAR-07
25-MAR-07
```

The query works because adding 1 to a date increments the date by one day and leaves the datatype as a date. You can also fabricate a type by explicitly casting it as shown in the following query:

```
SELECT TO_CHAR(SYSDATE,'MON') FROM dual
UNION ALL
SELECT 'APR' FROM dual;
```

This returns two variable-length strings representing the months March and April:

```
SYSDATE
---------
MAR
APR
```

You should be judicious in how you use set operators. As a rule of thumb, the `UNION ALL` and `MINUS` are very efficient, while the `UNION` carries some overhead because of an incremental sort operation. You'll seldom use the `INTERSECT` operator because joins are typically more useful.

Eliminating these from `SELECT` statements used in views solves most problems related to `INSERT` and `UPDATE` statements. One remaining element of a `SELECT` statement can enable insertion and update anomalies, and that problem is a `WHERE` clause narrowing returned rows by some criteria evaluation. You can eliminate the potential anomalies by appending the `WITH CHECK OPTION` phrase to the end of the view creation statement.

TIP
You can check whether a view is updatable by inspecting the list of columns in the `USER_UPDATABLE_COLUMNS` *table when in doubt.*

Views are typically built by using the CREATE OR REPLACE clause because you cannot alter a view without replacing it completely. The ALTER statement can only compile a view when it has been invalidated because a referenced catalog table or view in the SELECT statement has been dropped and recreated. Sometimes you need to build views before underlying tables exist. You can do that by using the CREATE OR REPLACE FORCE syntax, but after creating the view, it will immediately become invalid because of the missing table. The benefit of using a FORCE option occurs when you want to build a VIEW when the table isn't present in the database. Underlying tables can be missing due to normal database defragmentation exercises during these maintenance windows.

The following SQL statement builds a CURRENT_RENTAL view that should only be used to query data:

```
-- This is found in seed_store.sql on the web site.
```

```
CREATE OR REPLACE VIEW current_rental AS
  SELECT    m.account_number
  ,         c.first_name
  ||        DECODE(c.middle_initial,NULL,' ',' '||c.middle_initial||' ')
  ||        c.last_name FULL_NAME
  ,         i.item_title TITLE
  ,         i.item_subtitle SUBTITLE
  ,         SUBSTR(cl.common_lookup_meaning,1,3) PRODUCT
  ,         r.check_out_date
  ,         r.return_date
  FROM      common_lookup cl
  ,         contact c
  ,         item i
  ,         member m
  ,         rental r
  ,         rental_item ri
  WHERE     r.customer_id = c.contact_id
  AND       r.rental_id = ri.rental_id
  AND       ri.item_id = i.item_id
  AND       i.item_type = cl.common_lookup_id
  AND       c.member_id = m.member_id
  ORDER BY 1,2,3;
```

NOTE
You can only build a view when the schema has been granted the CREATE ANY VIEW *privilege by a superuser account, like* SYSTEM. *This rule holds for Oracle 10gR2 forward due to a change in the scope of the* RESOURCE *role.*

This view cannot be updated because the concatenation and two functions in the SELECT statement make it ineligible for insert or update operations. However, try querying the USER_UPDATABLE_COLUMNS table with the following query:

```
SELECT    table_name
,         column_name
FROM      user_updatable_columns
WHERE     table_name = 'CURRENT_RENTAL';
```

You will see the column names appear as updatable when they're not:

```
TABLE_NAME                       COLUMN_NAME
-------------------------------  ----------------
CURRENT_RENTAL                   MEMBER_ID
CURRENT_RENTAL                   FULL_NAME
CURRENT_RENTAL                   TITLE
CURRENT_RENTAL                   SUBTITLE
CURRENT_RENTAL                   PRODUCT
CURRENT_RENTAL                   CHECK_OUT_DATE
CURRENT_RENTAL                   RETURN_DATE
```

This type of output from `USER_UPDATABLE_COLUMNS` can be misleading, but you should notice that the column names do not match actual columns in tables. The column names are aliases from the `SELECT` statement that builds the `CURRENT_RENTAL` view. If you attempt to *insert* values, you would receive an `ORA-01732` error message, and it would tell you that the data manipulation operation is not legal on this view. You provide `INSTEAD OF` triggers when you want to write to non-updatable views. These triggers translate the update to the underlying data and are discussed in Chapter 10.

The `RENAME` and `DROP` operations are the same as those for tables. You cannot use a `TRUNCATE` operation, because views contain no data of their own. They are only reflections of tables that contain data.

Managing Stored Programs

Stored programs in Oracle are written in the PL/SQL programming language or other languages with PL/SQL wrappers. You can build libraries in the C/C++, C#, or Java programming languages.

You use `CREATE OR REPLACE` syntax to build functions, procedures, and packages. Packages contain functions, procedures, and user-defined types. The `ALTER` statement works the same for stored programs as it did for views: you *alter* stored programs to compile them when they've become invalid. Stored programs become invalid when referenced tables, views, or other stored programs become invalid.

NOTE
User-defined datatypes can be dropped, but when they are, columns referencing them are dropped from tables and stored programs become invalid.

Stored programs cannot be renamed but can be dropped from the database, and re-created under a new name. The `TRUNCATE` statement does not apply because they do not contain raw data components. You will learn more about stored programs in Chapters 6 and 9.

Managing Sequences

Sequences are counting structures that maintain a persistent awareness of their current value. They are simple to create when you want them to start at 1 and increment by 1. The basic sequence also sets no *cache, minimum,* or *maximum* values and accepts both `NOCYCLE` and `NOORDER` properties. A sequence caches values by groups of 20 by default, but you can overwrite the cache size when creating the sequence or by altering it after creation, as is done in the sample code found in this book's introduction. You build a generic `SEQUENCE` with this command:

```
-- This is found in create_world_leaders.sql on the web site.

CREATE SEQUENCE president_s1;
```

Many designs simply build these generic sequences and enable rows to be inserted by the web application interface. Some tables require specialized setup rows. These rows are inserted by administrators. They often use special primary key values below the numbering sequence assigned the regular application. When you have a table requiring manual setup rows, some developers leave the first 100 values and start the sequence at 101. Other applications leave more space and start the sequence at 1001. Both approaches are designed to provide your application with the flexibility to add new setup rows after initial implementation. This lets you isolate setup row values in a range different than ordinary applications data.

The SYSTEM_USER, RENTAL_LOOKUP, and other tables in the video store example requires setup data, which is often called seeding data. The sequences for both of these tables add an initial START WITH clause that sets the starting number for the sequence values, as shown:

```
-- This is found in create_store.sql on the web site.

CREATE SEQUENCE system_user_s1 START WITH 1001;
```

Sequences are typically built to support *primary key* columns in tables. *Primary key* columns impose a combination constraint on their values—they use both UNIQUE and NOT NULL constraints. During normal Online Transaction Processing (OLTP), some insertions are rolled back because other transactional components fail. When transactions are rolled back, the captured sequence value is typically lost. This means that you may see numeric gaps in the *primary key* column sequence values.

Typically, you ignore small gaps. Larger gaps in sequence values occur during *after-hours* batch processing, where you are performing bulk inserts into tables. Failures in batch processing typically involve operation staff intervention in conjunction with programming teams to fix the failure and process the data. Part of fixing this type of failure is resetting the next sequence value. While it would be nice to simply use an ALTER statement to reset the next sequence value, *you cannot reset* the START WITH number using an ALTER statement. You can reset every other criterion of a sequence with the ALTER statement, but you must drop and recreate the sequence to change the START WITH value.

There are three steps in the process to successfully modify a sequence START WITH value. You modify a sequence START WITH value by: (a) querying the *primary key* that uses the *sequence* to find the highest current value; (b) dropping the existing sequence with the DROP SEQUENCE *sequence_name*; command; and (c) recreating the sequence with a START WITH value *one greater than the highest value in the primary key column*. Naturally, the gap doesn't hurt anything, and you can skip this step, but as a rule, it is recommended to eliminate gaps during maintenance operations.

You can alter properties of a sequence by using the ALTER statement as illustrated by the following prototype:

```
ALTER SEQUENCE sequence_name [INCREMENT BY increment_value]
        [MINVALUE minimum | NOMINVALUE]
        [MAXVALUE maximum | NOMAXVALUE]
        [CACHE | NOCACHE]
        [ORDER | NOORDER]
```

You use sequences by appending (with a *dot* notation) two *pseudocolumns* to the sequence name: .nextval and .currval. The .nextval pseudocolumn *initializes* the sequence in a session and gets the *next value,* which is initially the START WITH value. After accessing the .nextval pseudocolumn, you get the *current value* by using the .currval pseudocolumn. You receive an ORA-08002 error when attempting to access the .currval pseudocolumn before having called the .nextval pseudocolumn in a session. The error message says that you have tried to access a sequence *not defined* in the session because .nextval *initializes* or *declares* the sequence in the session.

There are several ways to access sequences with the .nextval pseudocolumn. The basic starting point is querying the pseudotable DUAL, as shown:

```
SELECT    president_s1.nextval
FROM      dual;
```

Then, you can see the value again by querying:

```
SELECT    president_s1.currval
FROM      dual;
```

Oracle 11*g* Supports Direct Assignment of Sequence Values

Historically, PL/SQL differs from SQL on how you could handle sequence values in DML statements. Oracle 11*g* fixes that difference; you can now put sequence calls directly into statements without first querying them from the dual pseudotable.

If your code must be backward compatible with Oracle 10*g* or an earlier release, you need to use a variable, a sequence, and a query to put a sequence value into a SQL statement. For example, you can build the following sequencing table and sequencing_s1 sequence:

```
CREATE TABLE sequencing (sequencing_id NUMBER);
CREATE SEQUENCE sequencing_s1;
```

In Oracle 10*g* you would use a sequence value in a PL/SQL block as follows:

```
DECLARE
  sequence_value NUMBER;
BEGIN
  SELECT sequencing_s1.nextval INTO sequence_value FROM dual;
  INSERT INTO sequencing VALUES (sequence_value);
  COMMIT;
END;
/
```

While this syntax still works in Oracle 11*g*, you can now simplify it by using:

```
BEGIN
  INSERT INTO sequencing VALUES (sequencing_s1.nextval);
  COMMIT;
END;
/
```

You can also use a sequence with a pseudocolumn to make direct assignments to numeric variables inside your PL/SQL block. This improvement makes using sequences more consistent between SQL and PL/SQL environments.

The number will be the same, provided you did not connect to another schema and/or reconnect to SQL*Plus session. You can also use the `.nextval` and `.currval` pseudocolumns in the `VALUES` clause of `INSERT` or `UPDATE` statements. The next example demonstrates their use in the *inserts* of data to related tables:

-- This is found in seed_store.sql on the web site.

```
INSERT INTO member VALUES
( member_s1.nextval
,'B293-71445'
,'1111-2222-3333-4444'
,(SELECT   common_lookup_id
  FROM     common_lookup
  WHERE    common_lookup_context = 'MEMBER'
  AND      common_lookup_type = 'DISCOVER_CARD')
, 2, SYSDATE, 2, SYSDATE);

INSERT INTO contact VALUES
( contact_s1.nextval
, member_s1.currval
,(SELECT   common_lookup_id
  FROM     common_lookup
  WHERE    common_lookup_context = 'CONTACT'
  AND      common_lookup_type = 'CUSTOMER')
,'Winn','Randi','', 2, SYSDATE, 2, SYSDATE);
```

The first `INSERT` statement accesses the `member_s1.nextval` sequence to insert a *primary key* value into the `MEMBER` table. The `.nextval` pseudocolumn *defines* the sequence in the session and returns a number. The `member_s1.currval` pseudocolumn in the second `INSERT` statement calls the *defined* sequence and returns the same number, which is used as a *foreign key* column in the `CONTACT` table. You guarantee *primary key* and *foreign key* value matches when you combine the `.nextval` and `.currval` pseudocolumns as demonstrated in the `seed_store.sql` script.

NOTE
A DQL or `SELECT` statement runs as a subquery inside both `INSERT` statements. These subqueries ensure the `INSERT` statement uses the right foreign key by querying on meaningful information the correct primary key from the `COMMON_LOOKUP` table. This type of subquery, also known as a SQL expression, returns only one column and one row. Only SQL expressions can be used inside the `VALUES` clause of an `INSERT` statement.

TIP
You need to ensure that each `SELECT` statement returns the same number of rows when running multiple `SELECT` statements as subqueries to an `INSERT` statement.

You can use the `RENAME` command to change a sequence name. Sequences have no direct dependencies at the database level but often have dependencies in stored programs and database triggers that access the sequence to mimic automatic numbering behaviors of *primary key* values.

Managing User-Defined Types

User-defined types have been available since Oracle 8*i* and were dramatically increased in scope by Oracle 9*i* Release 2. You have the ability to define two groups of user-defined types in Oracle Database 11*g* family of products: collections and object types. Object types are not *currently* supported by the Oracle Call Interface (OCI8) library and therefore cannot be used in your Java (thin client only), PHP, and other external programs. Oracle collections are supported by the OCI8 library.

There are two types of OCI8-supported collections—one is a VARRAY, and the other is a NESTED TABLE. After you create these types, you can use them as column datatypes when defining SQL objects, such as tables and stored procedures. VARRAY collections are defined as fixed-sized arrays of scalar variables, like DATE, NUMBER, and VARCHAR2 datatypes. VARRAY collections are the closest Oracle programming structure to a native *array* in most programming languages. NESTED TABLE collections are defined as variable-sized *lists* of scalar variables and naturally behave like *lists* in other programming languages. Elements in both collection types are indexed by sequential positive integers starting with the number 1.

You create a VARRAY by using the following syntax:

```
-- This is found in create_world_leaders.sql on the publisher's web site.

CREATE OR REPLACE TYPE president_name_varray
  AS VARRAY(100) OF VARCHAR2(60 CHAR);
/
```

This builds a 100-element VARRAY collection of variable-length strings that are 60 characters in length. You raise an ORA-06502 when you attempt to enter an element greater than the maximum length of the scalar variable, and an ORA-22165 when you attempt to enter a list of elements greater than the boundary size of 100 elements.

There is no boundary set when you build a NESTED TABLE because they act more like *lists* than *arrays*. You use the following syntax to create a NESTED TABLE collection for a scalar variable-length string of up to 60 characters:

```
-- This is found in create_world_leaders.sql on the publisher's web site.

CREATE OR REPLACE TYPE president_name_ntable
  AS TABLE OF VARCHAR2(60 CHAR);
/
```

The ALTER, RENAME, and TRUNCATE statements cannot be used against user-defined collections. You can use the ALTER statement to *add* and *drop* member attributes from user-defined object types, and you can *alter* those object types from *instantiable* to *final* and back again. Scalar collections are a specialized object type with a predefined implementation. You create and maintain scalar collections through SQL DDL commands. User-defined object types have a specification and body implemented in PL/SQL, like packages. Their definition and implementation follow the rules of packages. You cannot alter a user-defined object type except when you want to recompile the specification or implementation. Chapter 14 covers how you define, implement, and maintain user-defined object types.

The REPLACE command enables you to alter the definition of collection types. However, replacing and dropping user-defined types becomes complex when you have defined other objects that reference them. The problem can be demonstrated by creating a table using the president_name_ntable as a column datatype:

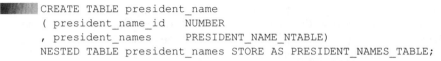

```
CREATE TABLE president_name
( president_name_id   NUMBER
, president_names      PRESIDENT_NAME_NTABLE)
NESTED TABLE president_names STORE AS PRESIDENT_NAMES_TABLE;
```

After a table is defined referencing the user-defined SQL collection datatype, attempting `CREATE OR REPLACE` or `DROP` statements raises an `ORA-02303` error. The error message explains that you cannot *drop* or *replace* a type that has type or table dependents. You can override this limitation by using the `FORCE` option for both statements, but it will remove the dependents' types from tables.

The trick to using user-defined collection types is to understand the hierarchy of sequencing dependencies, and work within the hierarchy. This means *drop* the lowest item that depends on a *type* up to the user-defined type, and replace the user-defined type before any objects that reference the *type* or the *type dependents*.

Data Query Language (DQL)

DQL commands are basically `SELECT` statements. `SELECT` statements let you *query* the database to find information in one or more tables, and return the query as a *result set*. A *result set* is an array structure, or more precisely in computerese, a result set is a two-dimensional array. The internal index for each row of data is the `rowid` pseudocolumn, which maps to the physical address for where the data is written.

NOTE
A `SELECT` *statement with a* `FOR UPDATE` *clause is a transaction and DML statement, not a DQL query. This is a fine distinction, but critical should you encounter an* `ORA-22292` *error while working with the* `DBMS_LOB` *package covered in Chapter 15.*

The first dimension of the array is a list of values indexed by *column names* from one or more tables. The elements in the list of values are sometimes called column or field values, and to the fraternity- (or sorority-) pledged database designers, they are attributes, like matrices in linear algebra. The combination of these column values is also known as a record structure. The second dimension of the array is the row, or a numerically indexed list of record structures. So, a *result set* is a collection of data values organized by column name and row number.

NOTE
Attributes and tuples are columns and rows, respectively, in linear algebraic vocabulary and suitable to hear about in college classrooms, but really they're nothing more than columns and rows.

DQL statements can be stand-alone *queries, in-line views* (or *tables*), *subqueries,* or *correlated subqueries.* They can return *scalar* or *compound* values in the Oracle database because Oracle can store *instantiable* object types as *column* datatypes. There are some restrictions governing what types of objects can be managed between PL/SQL and external third-generation programming languages.

TIP
Databases do not like zero-based numbering schemas, and queries return rows by row numbers starting with 1.

All SQL statements have the ability to join multiple tables; otherwise, database systems would be little more than complex file systems. Oracle Database 11*g* supports two join semantics. One is known as the Oracle Proprietary SQL semantic, and the other is the ANSI 2003:SQL semantic. The original join approach used by Oracle is similar to IBM SQL/DS (Structured Query Language/ Data System) and simply predates ANSI standards. You will be exposed to both and then decide which you like best.

Queries

The SQL SELECT statement has several components, known variously and interchangeably as clauses, phrases, and predicates. A *clause* is the generally accepted term, but the others work too, provided they convey the concept to your audience. The *basic* SELECT clauses and their descriptions are listed in Table B-3 for your convenience.

Clause	Description

SELECT	The SELECT clause contains a list of columns. Columns can also be defined by SQL expressions. Expressions are the result of *single-row* SQL functions. Oracle provides a set of *single-row* SQL functions, along with the ability for you to develop *user-defined single-row* SQL functions. Either type of *single-row* SQL function is supported in the SELECT clause. Columns and expressions are delimited by commas and support alias naming without whitespace and alias naming enclosed in quote marks with intervening whitespace. The Oracle SQL parser assumes an AS predicate when one is not provided in the SELECT clause. You precede duplicate column names with the table name or alias of the table name. The prototype of the SELECT clause is
	`SELECT column1 [AS alias1]`
	` [, column2 [AS alias2]`
	` [, column(n+1) [AS alias (n+1)]]]`

FROM	The FROM clause contains a list of tables when using Oracle Proprietary SQL, and a list of tables and join conditions between the listed tables when using ANSI SQL:2003. Tables can be tables, views, or *in-line views* (subqueries embedded in the FROM clause). Table names can have aliases composed of characters, numbers, and underscores. Table name aliases are a shorthand notation for table names. The prototype for Oracle Proprietary SQL is `FROM table1 [alias1]` ` [, table2 [alias2]` ` [, (in_line_view) [alias3]` ` [, table(n+1) [alias(n+1)]]]]` The prototype for ANSI SQL:2003 differs when joining on two columns that share the same name, or two columns that have different names. The SQL parser assumes an INNER JOIN when no optional join qualifier is provided. The prototype for two columns with the same name is `FROM table1 [INNER]	LEFT [OUTER] |` ` RIGHT [OUTER]	FULL [OUTER] JOIN table2` ` ON table1.column_name1 = table2.column_name2` The prototype for two columns with different names is `FROM table1 [INNER]	LEFT [OUTER] |` ` RIGHT [OUTER]	FULL [OUTER] JOIN table2` ` USING (column_name)` A NATURAL JOIN links tables using all matching columns found in both tables, and produces a *Cartesian product* or CROSS JOIN when both tables have mutually exclusive lists of column names. The prototype for a NATURAL JOIN is `FROM table1 NATURAL JOIN table2` The CROSS JOIN syntax forces a *Cartesian product* between two tables, which is a result set with row(s) of the left table matched with all the row(s) of the right table. The prototype is `FROM table1 CROSS JOIN table2`

TABLE B-3 *SELECT Statement Clauses*

Clause	Description

WHERE	The WHERE clause contains a list of column names compared against column names or string literals. Using the equal operator, the comparison operator supports joins in the Oracle Proprietary SQL syntax. You also have inequality operators, like *less than or equal to* or *greater than or equal to,* and the IS NULL or IS NOT NULL for comparison to columns containing null values. Each qualifying comparison statement is separated by an AND or OR operator. The prototype for Oracle Proprietary SQL join is
	`WHERE table1.columna = table2.columnb`
	Alternatively, you can use the WHERE clause to filter the result set from the query using ANSI SQL:1999 syntax:
	`WHERE table1.columnb = numeric_literal`
	`AND table1.columnc = 'string_literal'`
	`OR table1.columnd = subquery`

HAVING	The HAVING clause eliminates groups. The prototype uses a SUM() SQL *row-level* function to group a result set `HAVING SUM(column) > 30`
ORDER BY	The ORDER BY clause does sorting of the result set. You can use column names or numbers for the positional columns. The prototype is `ORDER BY column1 [, column2 [, column(n+1)]]`
GROUP BY	The GROUP BY clause groups ordinary columns when the query includes a row-level function in the SELECT or HAVING clause. It requires you to mirror column descriptions from the SELECT clause. The prototype is `GROUP BY column1 [, column2 [, column(n+1)]]`
FOR UPDATE	The FOR UPDATE clause lets you lock rows with a SELECT statement. It changes the query into the start of a database transaction. This clause is necessary when selecting rows for use in a PL/SQL loop, and typically present in cursor definitions. The clause is also necessary when you select Oracle BLOB, NBLOB, CLOB, and NCLOB datatypes for use in external programming languages, like Java and PHP. Beginning with the OCI8 library, you are required to use this clause to begin a transaction. You can only access BLOB, CLOB, and NCLOB datatypes within the scope of a transaction. The FOR UPDATE clause makes a SELECT statement transactional. The prototype is `FOR UPDATE`

RETURNING INTO	The RETURNING INTO clause lets you transfer SELECT clause variables into a bind variable. This clause is necessary when working with Oracle CLOB and NCLOB datatypes and external third-generation programming languages. The prototype is
	`RETURNING select_clause_variable`
	`INTO :bind_variable`

TABLE B-3   *SELECT Statement Clauses* (continued)

There are two subtypes of queries. One returns only one column and row and is known as a SQL *expression.* Expressions have wide uses in other than the SELECT statement, as seen in the subsection "Managing Sequences" earlier in this appendix. The other query subtype is the general rule for queries, and what most people think of when using the word query—a query returns zero, one, or many rows in a result set.

Join Behaviors
There are six join patterns in SQL and two join concepts: *equijoin* and *non-equijoin.* The abstract UML inheritance static class diagram illustrates how join patterns can exist as part of an object-oriented specialization tree. Figure B-1 shows the topmost node as the most general behavior and bottom nodes as the most specific. Bottom nodes are also known as leaf nodes.

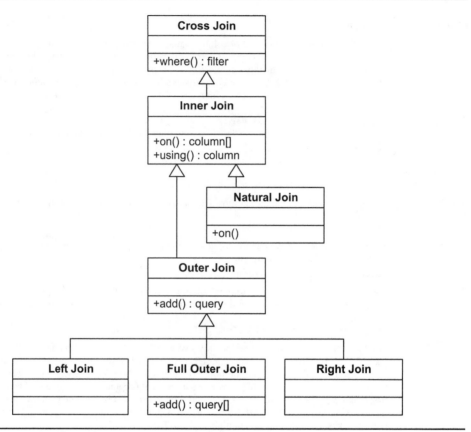

FIGURE B-1   *Join inheritance tree*

The most generalized joins are cross joins. *Cross* joins return what is known as a Cartesian product in set mathematics. It means that it returns a list of every row in one table with every row in another table. This list becomes quite long because the number of rows in the result set is the product of multiplying the rows in one table by the rows in the other. Cross joins are useful when you want to determine a relationship between one column value and a range of values found in another table. The WHERE clause filters the result set and returns only the relevant rows.

Inner joins are actually filtered cross joins. You find join statements in either the ON or USING predicate of the FROM clause or the WHERE clause of a query. A NATURAL JOIN statement works like an INNER JOIN statement. Natural joins match column names from both tables but can produce unexpected results when matching columns don't exist. When matching columns don't exist, natural joins works like cross joins. Release engineering processes can miss column name dependencies from natural joins, and you should avoid using natural joins for that reason.

Outer joins extend the behaviors of inner joins by adding the relative complement of one table to the result. Assume table A is on the left and B is on the right of the join operator. Then, the relative complement of A is the set of rows in table B not found in table A. The opposite is true for the relative complement of B.

The *left* relative complement of an outer join between table A and table B is the set of rows from table A minus any matching rows in table B. This is also known as the relative complement of table B. The *right* relative complement is the set of the rows from table B not found in table A. The right relative complement is also the relative complement of A. Figure B-2 is a Venn diagram showing the intersection and relative complements of two sets.

When A is the left operand and B is the right operand, the relative complement of set A and set B is a right join. The left join is the relative complement of set B and set A. This math rule is why Oracle's proprietary syntax puts the (+) symbol on the right to return the left complement and vice versa. The idea was to place the (+) on the side pointing to the relative complement. While the *left* and *right* joins are respectively the right and left relative complements, labeling them according to which table returns non-matching values makes better sense when writing joins.

You implement the relative complement by adding non-matching rows from one table to the matches between the tables. Figure B-1 uses an abstract class because left and right joins are mirroring behaviors. Left joins submit the table on the left as the first actual parameter and the table on the right as the second actual parameter. A right join reverses the actual parameter positions. This means that a left join of set A to set B is the same as the right join of set B to set A. When you submit both left and right joins together to get a full outer join, you return a union of the left and right joins. A union of left and right joins combines both relative complements with the intersection between the two sets.

Applying these join patterns requires you to understand two concepts. One is an *equijoin,* and the other is a *non-equijoin.* Joins behave differently, depending on which one you use.

Equijoin means you check whether the values in one column equal those in another. Joins between tables typically use equijoins. Five join patterns support *equijoin* resolution. They are the *inner, natural, left, right,* and *full* outer joins. The inner and natural joins return rows when the column values match in both tables. The others return the intersection plus one or more relative complements.

The meaning of a *non-equijoin* can also include an *equijoin* when you use a greater-than or *equal* operator. These operators look for matches and values that are less or greater than the match. It is also possible to look for only those less or greater than a column value. Using the less- and greater-than operators excludes an equality comparison.

Another type of non-equijoin performs range comparisons. Checking which month a customer rented a video compares a transaction date against the start and end dates of the month. This is a range comparison.

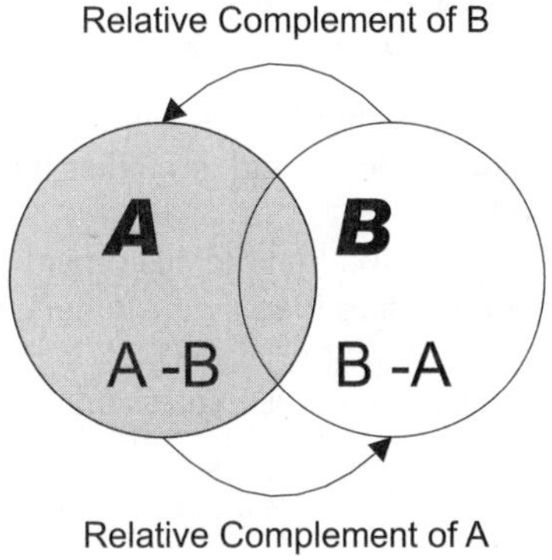

Relative Complement of B

Relative Complement of A

FIGURE B-2 *Relative complement Venn diagram*

You can also use a not-equal operator to get an anti-join. *Anti-joins* contain both relative complements minus any matching rows. Matching rows are the intersection for equijoins and relative inequality result for non-equijoins.

This sidebar has covered SQL join behaviors. The six join patterns covered were (a) cross joins, (b) inner joins, (c) natural joins, (d) left and right outer joins, (e) full outer joins, and (f) anti-joins. The *equijoin* and *non-equijoin* choices provide you with additional join possibilities. The understanding of these principles enables you to use SQL to solve problems.

The following example demonstrates a standard query from two tables using an INNER JOIN on different column names:

```
-- This is found in SelectItemRecords.php on the publisher's web site.

SELECT    i.item_id AS id
,         i.item_barcode AS barcode
,         c.common_lookup_type AS type
,         i.item_title AS title
,         i.item_rating AS rating
,         i.item_release_date AS release_date
FROM      item i INNER JOIN common_lookup c
ON        i.item_type = c.common_lookup_id
WHERE     c.common_lookup_type = 'XBOX'
ORDER BY i.item_title;
```

The query demonstrates a standard query that returns a result set of zero, one, or many rows. It uses the ANSI SQL:2003 syntax for the join between tables but really only uses features that exist in the ANSI SQL:1999 standard. The query also demonstrates both column and table aliases.

After you join two tables using a single join statement in a query, like [INNER] JOIN, LEFT [OUTER] JOIN et cetera. A third table is joined to the result set, or product, of the first join, like this:

```
COLUMN calling_name     FORMAT A30 HEADING "Calling Name"
COLUMN telephone_number FORMAT A20 HEADING "Telephone Number"

SELECT    c.last_name||', '||c.first_name||CHR(10)
||        a.city||', '||a.state_province AS calling_name
,         t.telephone_number
FROM      contact c INNER JOIN address a
ON        c.contact_id = a.contact_id LEFT JOIN telephone t
ON        c.contact_id = t.contact_id
AND       a.address_id = t.address_id;
```

The first join looks for the intersection between the primary key in the CONTACT table and the foreign key in the ADDRESS table. The second join takes the product, or result set, of the first join and performs an outer join to both the CONTACT and ADDRESS table. The outer join is necessary because it is possible in this application that the customer has only provided only an address. A missing telephone number would fail to identify customers whose telephone numbers aren't in your database with an inner join operation.

The following query demonstrates a SQL expression:

```
SELECT    COUNT(*)
FROM      ITEM
WHERE     item_type = (SELECT    common_lookup_id
                       FROM      common_lookup
```

```
WHERE      common_lookup_context = 'ITEM'
AND        common_lookup_type = 'XBOX');
```

The SQL expression determines how many XBOX items are in the video store inventory. It uses a subquery of the COMMON_LOOKUP table to find the ITEM_TYPE *foreign key* for a context of ITEM and type of XBOX. The SELECT clause contains only a SQL *row-level* function, which guarantees a single column and row in the result set.

The subquery in the foregoing example is not a correlated subquery. *Correlated subqueries* have a join to the outer query in the inner query and are prefaced by the EXISTS or NOT EXISTS operator. *In-line views* are subqueries that are found in the FROM clause. In-line views generally have an alias, and joins between them are resolved in the same way as joins between normal tables and views.

You can also reference subqueries by using equalities and nonequalities with the ALL, ANY, or SOME operators. In lieu of equalities and nonequalities, you can use IN or NOT IN for subqueries, and as noted, EXISTS or NOT EXISTS for correlated subqueries.

The CASE or Oracle-proprietary DECODE statement lets you conditionally select data. This is very useful in a number of situations. Some other developers (not you) may even write unnecessary PL/SQL program units to replace what could be done in a single query. You can use the CASE statement typically from 9*i*R2 forward without issue, but older releases rely on the DECODE statement.

The following example uses a nested CASE statement to add debits and subtract credits inside a SUM function that queries the TRANSACTION table:

```
-- This is found in seed_store.sql on the publisher's web site.

SELECT    t.transaction_account
,         SUM(CASE
              WHEN t.transaction_type =
                  (SELECT    common_lookup_id
                   FROM      common_lookup
                   WHERE     common_lookup_context = 'TRANSACTION'
                   AND       common_lookup_type = 'CREDIT')
              THEN t.transaction_amount
              ELSE 0
           END) AS cash_in
,         SUM(CASE
              WHEN t.transaction_type =
                  (SELECT    common_lookup_id
                   FROM      common_lookup
                   WHERE     common_lookup_context = 'TRANSACTION'
                   AND       common_lookup_type = 'DEBIT')
              THEN t.transaction_amount
              ELSE 0
           END) AS cash_out
FROM      transaction t
GROUP BY  t.transaction_account;
```

The preceding query uses aliases to aggregate and transform rows into aggregate columns. Some third-party Oracle material labels transforming queries like this as crosstab, matrix, or pivot queries. Unfortunately, they are not pivot queries. You could not use SQL to pivot tables prior to Oracle 11*g*; only Microsoft T-SQL possessed that feature. A PIVOT function acts with an aggregation function to pivot the columns and rows of a query.

This section has exposed you to some basics and a few tricks and techniques using queries. As you analyze business problems, always look for opportunities to optimize SQL in your PL/SQL program cursors.

Data Manipulation Language (DML)

INSERT, UPDATE, and DELETE statements define the DML commands. All of these may use joins, subqueries, correlated subqueries, and in-line views. The in-line views must be contained within a subquery or correlated subquery. DML commands can insert, update, or delete one to many rows of data.

INSERT Statements

The INSERT statement acts on rows of data. Inserting data into tables can be done row by row or by groups of rows. You have two potential ways to create *insertion anomalies* when inserting data.

One type of *insertion anomaly* happens when you insert two rows with the same information. *Primary key* constraints typically reduce the likelihood that the entire rows are duplicated, but it is possible to create repeating sets that will disable some queries from tables. You can use *unique indexes* across sets of columns to prevent this type of *insertion anomaly,* as demonstrated later in the section.

Another type of *insertion anomaly* happens when you insert incorrect data. The incorrect data can be *foreign key* columns or descriptive *nonkey* columns. The foreign key error occurs when you fail to properly leverage a sequence of .nextval and .currval attributes or fail to use SQL expressions to find the foreign keys. You should refer to the sequence coverage earlier in this appendix to understand how to use .nextval and .currval for managing *primary* and *foreign keys* in transaction sets. As demonstrated in the INSERT statements found in Chapter 1, it is important to match foreign keys by using SQL expressions.

INSERT statements differ from other DML statements in that they use the metadata definition of the table. The metadata is stored when a table is created, and acts like a function or method signature for the INSERT statement. It lists the formal parameters in the same order used by the CREATE TABLE statement, and the database appends columns to the list when they are added later by using the ALTER statement.

You can determine a table signature by querying the USER_TAB_COLUMNS view using the following query:

```
SELECT    column_id
,         column_name
,         data_type
,         nullable
FROM      user_tab_columns
WHERE     table_name = 'MEMBER';
```

The query returns the default signature of the MEMBER table, which was created earlier in the appendix. INSERT statements use the default signature unless you specify an overriding column list before the VALUES clause. Overriding the default signature is a common practice when inserting into tables that have many *null allowed* columns. The following are the results from the query against USER_TAB_COLUMNS for the MEMBER table:

```
 COLUMN_ID COLUMN_NAME          DATA_TYPE  N
---------- -------------------- ---------- -
         1 MEMBER_ID            NUMBER     N
```

```
2  ACCOUNT_NUMBER        VARCHAR2   Y
3  CREDIT_CARD_NUMBER    VARCHAR2   Y
4  CREDIT_CARD_TYPE      NUMBER     Y
5  CREATED_BY            NUMBER     Y
6  CREATION_DATE         DATE       Y
7  LAST_UPDATED_BY       NUMBER     Y
8  LAST_UPDATE_DATE      DATE       Y
```

The results from this view can be deceiving when tables are defined using *out-of-line* CHECK constraints instead of in-line NOT NULL constraints. Only *in-line* and *primary key* constraints will show an *N* in the NULLABLE column. You can check the USER_CONSTRAINTS and USER_CONS_COLUMNS views to determine whether or not there is a NOT NULL check constraint.

The following inserts a row into the MEMBER table by using the default signature just described:

```
-- This is found in seed_store.sql on the publisher's web site.
```

```
INSERT INTO member VALUES
( member_s1.nextval                                -- 1   MEMBER_ID
,'B293-71445'                                       -- 2   ACCOUNT_NUMBER
,'1111-2222-3333-4444'                              -- 3   CREDIT_CARD_NUMBER
,(SELECT   common_lookup_id                         -- 4   CREDIT_CARD_TYPE
  FROM     common_lookup
  WHERE    common_lookup_context = 'MEMBER'
  AND      common_lookup_type = 'DISCOVER_CARD')
, 2                                                 -- 5   CREATED_BY
, SYSDATE                                           -- 6   CREATION_DATE
, 2                                                 -- 7   LAST_UPDATED_BY
, SYSDATE);                                         -- 8   LAST_UPDATE_DATE
```

When you need to override the default signature, you add an overriding column list, as shown in the following prototype:

```
INSERT INTO table_name
( column1 [, column2 [, column(n+1)]])
VALUES
([column_value1 | function_call1 | fsql_statement1]
[,column_value2 | function_call2 | fsql_statement2]
[,column_value(n+1) | function_call(n+1) | fsql_statement(n+1)]])
[RETURNING column_name INTO :bind_variable];
```

You can insert a literal value, a bind variable, a locally scoped variable, a function return value, or a scalar subquery. This is true of any column value in an INSERT statement. A user-defined SQL scalar collection is also allowed when the target column is a scalar collection of the same datatype. The RETURNING INTO clause is used to shift a column value reference for an Oracle LOB datatype into a *bind* variable, as demonstrated in Chapter 8, Appendix C, and Appendix F.

The INSERT statement uses a SQL expression to find the appropriate foreign key value for the CREDIT_CARD_TYPE column. While the SELECT statement returns a single row and column, the structure of the query does not guarantee that behavior by itself. A *unique* INDEX guarantees the business rule and that the SQL expression cannot return more than one row:

```
-- This is found in create_store.sql on the web site.
```

```
CREATE UNIQUE INDEX common_lookup_u1
  ON common_lookup(common_lookup_context,common_lookup_type);
```

You can insert multiple rows with a single INSERT statement by using a SELECT statement in place of the VALUES clause, just as you created a new table by querying an old table earlier in this appendix. You can also select sequences with the .nextval pseudocolumn and nested subqueries, provided you return the same number of rows from each.

When you insert from data residing somewhere else in the database, you use the following prototype:

```
INSERT INTO table_name
AS select_statement;
```

UPDATE Statements

The UPDATE statement lets you update one or more column values in one row or a set of rows in a table. It supports different direct assignments to each column value by using bind variables, literal values, and subqueries. The WHERE clause in the UPDATE statement qualifies which rows are changed by the UPDATE statement. You can check the section "Data Query Language (DQL)" earlier in this appendix for more coverage on the WHERE clause.

NOTE
All rows in the table are updated when you run an UPDATE *statement without a* WHERE *clause.*

Update anomalies occur much like the *insertion anomalies* that happen when you insert two rows with the same information. The only difference is that the UPDATE statement alters a second row when it shouldn't. You eliminate updating multiple rows in error by using *unique indexes* across sets of columns to prevent it, as described in the preceding section, "INSERT Statements."

The UPDATE statement has the following prototype:

```
UPDATE    table_name [alias]
SET       column1 = {value | function_call | select_statement}
,         column2 = {value | function_call | select_statement}
,         column(n+1) = {value | function_call | select_statement}
WHERE     list_of_comparative_operations
[RETURNING column_name INTO :bind_variable];
```

You can use a literal value, a bind variable, a locally scoped variable, a function return value, or a scalar subquery when you set a new value in an UPDATE statement. The assigned values must match the column datatype.

You should note that *unlike when using the alias assignment in the* SELECT *clause, you must exclude the* AS *clause or you raise an* ORA-00971 error that says you are missing the SET clause. The RETURNING INTO clause is used to shift a column value reference for an Oracle LOB datatype into a *bind* variable, as demonstrated in Chapter 8, Appendix C, and Appendix F. Appendix C demonstrates uploading a large string by using the UploadBioSQL.php program. A sample UPDATE statement using a correlated subquery updates the middle initial for a single row in the CONTACT table as follows:

```
UPDATE    contact c1
SET       c1.middle_initial = 'B'
```

```
WHERE       EXISTS (SELECT    NULL
                    FROM      contact c2
                    WHERE     c1.contact_id = c2.contact_id
                    AND       c2.last_name = 'Vizquel'
                    AND       c2.first_name = 'Oscar');
```

The correlated query could have been eliminated by putting the LAST_NAME and FIRST_NAME column value comparisons in the WHERE clause. This illustrates that there are many ways to do equivalent things using SQL statements.

DELETE Statements

The DELETE statement, like the INSERT statement, works at the row level. You delete one to many rows with a DELETE statement. As when using the UPDATE statement, you generally will have a WHERE clause; otherwise, you delete all rows in the table.

Deleting data can be tricky when you have *dependent* foreign key columns in other tables. While generally most businesses do not enable foreign key referential integrity at the database level, they maintain the logic in the application interface. You should make sure the application programming logic is correct, because incorrect logic can cause *deletion anomalies.* Deletion anomalies manifest themselves in orphaned rows, join failures, and erroneous query result sets.

The prototype for a DELETE statement is

```
DELETE
FROM        table_name
WHERE       list_of_comparative_operations;
```

The following deletion statement against the video store will fail because it violates the foreign key referential integrity rules maintained by foreign key database constraints:

```
DELETE
FROM        item i
WHERE       i.item_title = 'Camelot';
```

The row in the ITEM table that contains the ITEM_TITLE value of *Camelot* cannot be deleted, because there is a dependent row in the RENTAL_ITEM table. It raises an integrity constraint violation, ORA-02292, because of a foreign key dependency.

Mixing and Matching Row Returns

Mixing and matching row returns happens when you put a SQL expression into a SELECT statement that returns multiple rows. The combination of a scalar query and a multiple-row query fails with a too many rows returned error. The imbalance of the one row returned by a SQL expression and multiple rows returned by a SQL statement triggers the error. A classic example is when you want to use a SQL expression to capture a foreign key value for each return from a containing query used to insert rows into another table.

The solution to this problem is to place the scalar subquery in the FROM clause as an in-line view. Then, you use a CROSS JOIN statement to place the same foreign key value in each row returned by the multiple-row query. This is another example of data fabrication principles in SQL.

Deleting rows is clearly simple, but the downside is that all too many rows can be deleted in error. You should use care when deleting data, to delete only the right data. It is also a great time to back up the table in case you need to recover from an error.

Data Control Language (DCL)

Data Control Language (DCL) is the ability to guarantee an all-or-nothing approach when changing data in more than one table. Table B-4 covers the key commands involved in DCL to manage transactions.

A good programming practice is to set a SAVEPOINT statement before beginning a set of DML statements to change related data. Then, if you encounter a failure in one of the DML statements, you can use the ROLLBACK statement to undo the DML statements that completed. You use the COMMIT command to make the changes permanent when all changes have been made successfully.

Summary

The appendix has reviewed the Structured Query Language (SQL) and explained how and why basic SQL statements work. The coverage should enable you to work through the Oracle Database 11*g* examples in the book.

Statement	Description
COMMIT	The COMMIT statement makes permanent all DML changes to data up to that point in the user session. Once you commit data changes, they are *permanent* unless you perform some form of point-in-time database recovery. It has the following prototype: COMMIT
ROLLBACK	The ROLLBACK statement reverses changes to data that have not yet become permanent through being committed during a user session. The ROLLBACK makes sure all changes are undone from the most recent DML statement to the oldest one in the current user session, or since the last commit action. Alternatively, when a SAVEPOINT has been set during the user session, the ROLLBACK can undo transactions only since either that SAVEPOINT or the last commit. It has the following prototype: ROLLBACK [TO *savepoint_name*]
SAVEPOINT	The SAVEPOINT statement sets a point-in-time marker in a current user session. It enables the ROLLBACK command to only roll back all transactions after the SAVEPOINT is set. It has the following prototype: SAVEPOINT *savepoint_name*

TABLE B-4   *DCL Statements*

APPENDIX
C

PHP Primer

he PHP primer introduces you to PHP programming, the Apache HTTP server, and the Oracle database web development environments. OPAL is a four-letter acronym describing a web application solution stack using the Oracle, PHP, Apache, and Linux operating systems. OPAL is an alternative to another four-letter acronym that describes a GNU solution stack—LAMP. LAMP stands for Linux, Apache, MySQL, and PHP. The P in OPAL or LAMP stacks can also represent the Perl or Python language. Both stacks can also replace Linux with the Microsoft Windows operating system.

This primer discusses the advantages you'll find when developing web applications using the PHP programming language and Oracle Database 11*g*. It also demonstrates how you use the PHP programming language; and how you work with Oracle advanced data types. It covers how you use the OCI8 library to work with collections, system reference cursors, LOBs, and external binary files. The OCI8 libraries also work with Oracle Database 8*i*, 9*i*, and 10*g* releases. In this primer, you learn how to develop PHP web applications using an Oracle database, and jump-start your productivity regardless of whether you're new to Oracle, PHP programming, or both.

This primer discusses the following topics:

- History and background

    - What is PHP?

    - What is Zend?

- Developing web programming solutions

    - What goes where and why?

    - What does Oracle contribute to PHP?

    - Why is PHP 5 important?

    - How to use PHP

    - How to use PHP and OCI8 to access the Oracle database

This primer provides examples of building PL/SQL programming units to support web-based application development. Building web-based applications using PHP is simpler to illustrate because there are fewer moving parts than Java. You can see how to build a web application without dealing with how to deploy a web container, enterprise JavaBeans, and JSP pages. My *Oracle Database 10*g *Express Edition PHP Web Programming* (McGraw-Hill, 2006) provides a complete treatment of the OPAL stack using the OCI8 libraries, which also work with other Oracle database family products.

A Java primer is also provided to demonstrate interfaces and PL/SQL development strategies using the Java programming language in Appendix D. The Java primer focuses on how to deploy server-side components, which are libraries, wrapped by PL/SQL or data abstraction layer class files supporting JavaServer Pages (JSPs). Combining Appendix D with both volumes of the *Core Servlets* and *JavaServer Pages* books provides good supplementary resources for more complex Java solutions.

History and Background

The history and background of programming languages and software products can help you find and interpret old code snippets or administrative guidelines found on the Internet. This section discusses the history and background of the PHP engine and programming model; the Oracle Database 11*g* features and opportunities; and the Zend Technologies role, tools, and support for the PHP and Oracle combination.

What Is PHP?

Today PHP is a recursive acronym for PHP: Hypertext Preprocessor. In 1995, it stood for Personal Home Page and named a bunch of utilities that evolved from some Perl scripts. It was originally developed to display the résumé of the original author, Rasmus Lerdorf. The first major release was PHP 3 in 1997, and it was based on a new engine written by Zeev Suraski and Andi Gutmans. Zeev and Andi then formed Zend Technologies Ltd., rewrote the engine again as the Zend Engine 1.0, and released PHP 4 in 2000. A second major rewrite led to Zend Engine 2.0 and the release of PHP 5 in 2004. Each change in the engine has brought enhanced scalability, greater speed, and more features.

PHP is a weakly typed language, although some prefer to label it a dynamically typed language. It has a similar syntax to Perl in many respects, including variables preceded by dollar signs—`$variable`. PHP is also a server-side-include type of programming environment, deployable
as a CGI or Apache module working with the Apache or Microsoft IIS server. It is an interpreted language, not a compiled one.

The language is flexible in two important ways: It is tightly integrated with HTML, and it has the ability to work with virtually all commercial databases. The language enables you to embed PHP in an HTML document and to embed HTML inside a PHP script. You can also use PHP as a server-side scripting language, but it has limited file I/O characteristics.

Critics assail PHP because it is weakly typed, has a single name space for functions, and is not thread safe. However, it is a flexible language that supports thousands of web applications around the world. It is also a fun-to-use programming language that is effective at solving complex problems and provides a quick prototyping solution for web applications.

What Is Zend?

Zeev Suraski and Andi Gutmans formed Zend Technologies Ltd. when they rewrote the PHP 4.0 engine as the Zend Engine 1.0. PHP 4.0 was released in 2000. Zend Corporation rewrote the PHP engine again as the Zend Engine 2.0, which was released as PHP 5 in 2004. Each change in the engine has brought greater scalability, speed, and features.

Zend Technologies is the magic behind the part of the GNU movement that brought the PHP language into the light. They provide licensing and support contracts for the Zend Engine, which contains features not found on the freely downloadable www.php.net site. The implementation of GNU software often finds resistance until a company provides support and a distribution model. Zend Technologies is doing that, and as a result the language is seeing even wider adoption by major corporations and government entities.

You must be a licensed customer using the Zend Core for Oracle and the Zend Engine 2.0 to receive support on your PHP and Oracle web applications. This also means that you are running PHP 5.1.4 or higher. This book's code was tested using this combination.

Developing Web Programming Solutions

Web programming solutions are typically composed of an Apache or IIS HTTPD server, a server-side include (CGI or Apache module), and a database. The selection of the products is often hotly contested in many IT shops. For the moment, it is assumed that you have chosen Apache 2.0.55, PHP 5.1.4, and the Oracle Database 11*g* Release 1.

What Goes Where and Why?

There are many ways to deploy these architectural components, and the choice often depends on a number of factors. These factors can include the number or frequency of web hits, the volume of data in the database, and the acceptable response time window.

In the simplest architecture, you place the Apache server, PHP engine, and Oracle database on a single platform. Assuming this simple model, the customer request goes to the Apache server, which hands off dynamic calls to the PHP engine. The PHP engine supports the scope of execution of the PHP script, which can call the Oracle database server. The call from the PHP script is made through the Oracle Call Interface 8 (OCI8), as described in later in this appendix. When the database finishes processing the request, the PHP script then writes a temporary document that is served back to the original client.

The scalable architecture of PHP is devoid of standalone processes, like the Java Virtual Machine (JVM) supporting Java Server Pages (JSPs). Each PHP program acts as a standalone process, which makes the web server tier very scalable by horizontally expanding the number of web servers. Large-volume sites use a metric server to load-balance across a series of web servers that are also known as a middle tier. This is depicted in Figure C-1.

Each web server tier machine requires an Apache or IIS server, a PHP server, and an Oracle client. You can also replace the smaller footprint of an Oracle client with the Oracle server. The deployment flexibility of this distributed architecture lets you choose where you can best put components to increase integration, distribute load, and maximize reuse of code.

The distribution of components is illustrated in Table C-1, which represents directory (dir), host name (hn), domain name (dn), and filename (fn), respectively.

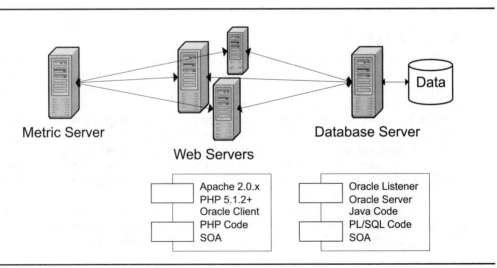

FIGURE C-1   *Oracle, PHP, and Zend architecture*

	Web Server Tier	**Database Server Tier**
HTML Pages	http://*<hn>*.*<dn>*/*<fn>*.php	
Templates	*<dir>*/*<fn>*.inc	
Business Logic	*<dir>*/*<fn>*.inc	*<dir>*/php/*<fn>*.<so | dll>
C/C++/C# Code	*<dir>*/lib/*<fn>*.<so | dll>	*<dir>*/lib/*<fn>*.<so | dll>
Java	*<dir>*/lib/java/*<fn>*.<jar | zip>	*<dir>*/lib/java/*<fn>*.<jar | zip>

TABLE C-1   *Distribution Matrix for PHP Web Application Coding Components*

The architecture also lets you share the database server–tier PL/SQL code between both PHP and JSP program units. SOA can also be exploited by deploying XMLType columns on the database tier.

What Does Oracle Contribute to PHP?

The current OCI8 version now enables PHP developers to use several advanced features, such as

- Querying and transacting with collections data types

- Querying and transacting with reference cursors from stored procedures

- Querying and transacting with BLOB, CLOB, and NCLOB data types

- Querying BFILE column values from internally referenced locators and returning externally stored files

Oracle has committed to extend the OCI8 libraries to support an increasing set of utilities and the new connection pool architecture in Oracle Database 11*g*. Oracle offers PHP a robust database that works well with PHP programs.

Why Is PHP 5 Important?

The addition of refactored OCI8 code components into PHP 5.1.4 means that PHP and Oracle now natively support the new PHP 5 reference and object models. These were introduced by the Zend Engine 2 and are a stumbling block for many PHP 4 sites adopting the newest version of PHP.

PHP 5 supports traditional and persistent connections to the database. It also supports concurrent traditional and persistent connections from the same script. This extends PHP in a similar way to how Java Server Pages leverage a JServlet that maintains a connection pool.

The object model in PHP 5 supports Oracle collection types, reference cursors, and large object types. The PHP reference and object models are natural fits because they simplify how developers gain access to composite data types. These types will also map nicely into any PHP Data Object (PDO) architecture introduced later by Oracle Corporation.

How to Use PHP

This section will introduce you to the *fundamental* semantics and structures of the PHP 5 programming language. It covers the following:

- Defining scripting tags and printing text to web pages

- Commenting code

- Defining, declaring, and naming variables

- Defining and using conditional structures

- Defining and using iterative structures

- Defining and using functions

- Defining and using objects

- Handling run-time errors and exceptions

- Reading and writing files

You should understand the basics of writing and running PHP programs after reading this section. The primer focuses on how you run PHP code from a browser, but you can also run the same code as a server-side scripting language from the command line.

NOTE
You will need to install Oracle Database 11g, the Apache Server, and then the Zend for Oracle product (available from otn.oracle.com) before testing this code.

Defining Scripting Tags

PHP is an interpreted recursive scripting language because you can embed it inside XHTML or put XHTML inside it. The interpreter requires you to enclose the PHP code inside of scripting tags. When code is not inside designated scripting tags, the web browser will treat it as ordinary text.

You have four available styles. Two are supported after the standard install and two are not. The default- and HTML-style tags are supported after installing the product stack. You need to modify the `httpd.conf` file to support the short- and ASP-style tags.

The following statements use `print` statements to render web pages as noted below:

Default-Style Tag

```
<?php
  print "Hello world.<br />";
?>
```

HTML-Style Tag

```
<script language="php">
  print "Hello world.<br />";
</script>
```

Short-Style Tag

```
<?
  print "Hello world.<br />";
?>
```

ASP-Style Tag

```
<%php
  print "Hello world.<br />";
%>
```

The print and echo statements have two different approaches that you can use: the more common form used in the preceding examples and the more formal that includes parentheses around the string. You should pick one style and stick with it to increase the readability of your code.

A standard environment test after installing the product stack runs the following `phpInfo()` function call, which returns information about your server installation:

```php
<?php
  phpInfo();
?>
```

This section has demonstrated the four scripting tag approaches, using the `print` statement. You also have an `echo` statement if you prefer. The two `print` and `echo` statements work alike, but you can only use the `echo` statement to print a string or comma-delimited set of strings to a page.

Commenting Code

You can put single-line or multiple-line comments in your PHP programs. You have the same single-line and multiple-line comments as C++, C#, or Java plus the traditional number symbol from Unix shell scripting for single-line comments, as shown:

Single-Line Comments using a C++, C#, or Java Style

```php
<?php
  // This is a single-line comment.
?>
```

Single-Line Comments using a Unix Shell Style

```php
<?php
  # This is a single-line comment.
?>
```

Multiple-Line Comments using a C++, C#, or Java Style

```php
<?php
  /* This is a first-line comment.
     This is a last-line comment.  */
?>
```

Command-Line PHP Scripting

You can also run PHP programs from the command line by calling the interpreter and passing the filename like

```
# php helloworld.php
```

Provided you modify the previous program for the command line as

```php
<?php
  print "Hello world.\n";
?>
```

it will print the following:

```
# Hello World.
```

Comments generally improve code readability. You should consider using the C++, C#, or Java comment styles because they're better known.

Defining, Declaring, and Naming Variables

Variables are defined in your PHP program namespace without a data type. You can define a variable by using any series of case-sensitive alphabetical characters, numbers, or underscores, but they must start with an alphabetical character or underscore. Variables are identified by prefacing the name with a reserved $ character. The following are valid variable name definitions:

```
$_MINE;
$myVariable;
$my_1234;
```

While these three statements define variables, you raise a notice error if you attempt to access their data type with the PHP `gettype()` function after defining them without a data type. You generally only see notice errors in your development environment, and this type of notice warns you that you haven't formally assigned a data type to a variable. The default type of unassigned variables is a null data type. This behavior is considered a benefit of weakly or dynamically typed languages, but you can also explicitly assign a valid type without assigning a value.

The reason for this behavior is not complex. The namespace keeps track of the variable name, data type, and value. When the data type is undefined, the PHP interpreter raises a notice at run time, assigns an implicit null type, and allocates memory space accordingly. The interpreter doesn't raise a run-time notice when you've assigned a data type, regardless of its value.

PHP supports three classes of variables: scalar, compound, and special. Four of the nine supported data types—`bool`, `int`, `float`, and `string`—are scalar. Scalar variables can only hold one value at any time. The compound variables are arrays and objects, while the special types are functions, resources, and nulls.

You assign type or value using the assignment operator or an operation assignment operator, as found in Table C-2. When you define and assign a value in a single statement, that is known as declaring a variable. The following script provides examples of assignments and implicit type conversions:

```php
<?php
  $myVar = 1;
  print "\$myVar [$myVar]   [".gettype($myVar)."]<br />";
  $myVar .= "2";
  print "\$myVar [$myVar]  [".gettype($myVar)."]<br />";
  $myVar++;
  print "\$myVar [$myVar]  [".gettype($myVar)."]<br />";
?>
```

Operator	Behavior Description
=	The assignment, or =, operator is a binary operator that assigns the right operand to the variable value contained in the left operand. The left operand implicitly inherits the data type from the right operand when they are not of the same type.

TABLE C-2   *Assignment and Operation Assignment Operators*

Operator	Behavior Description
+=	The increment and assign, or +=, operator is a binary operator that adds the right operand to the variable value contained in the left operand. The increment and assign operator can implicitly cast the data type of the left operand. Alternatively, you can explicitly cast the right operand to match the data type of the assignment target or left operand.
-=	The decrement and assign, or -=, operator is a binary operator that subtracts the right operand from the value contained in the left operand. The decrement and assign operator can implicitly cast the data type of the left operand. Alternatively, you can explicitly cast the right operand to match the data type of the assignment target or left operand.
*=	The multiply and assign, or *=, operator is a binary operator that multiplies the right operand by the value contained in the left operand. The multiple and assign operator can implicitly cast the data type of the left operand. Alternatively, you can explicitly cast the right operand to match the data type of the assignment target or left operand.
/=	The divide and assign, or *=, operator is a binary operator that divides the left operand by the value contained in the right operand. The divide and assign operator can implicitly cast the data type of the left operand. Alternatively, you can explicitly cast the right operand to match the data type of the assignment target or left operand.
.=	The concatenate and assign, or .=, operator is a binary operator that concatenates the right operand to the left operand. If the left operand is not a string, it is implicitly cast to a string and the right operand is concatenated to it as a string. *There is no way to avoid this string type casting behavior* with the concatenate and assign operator.
--	The decrement, or --, operator is a unary operator that decrements the contents of a variable by a value of 1. If the decrement unary operator precedes the variable name (--$var), it decrements the variable before using it. If the decrement unary operator follows the variable name (++$var), it decrements the variable after using the variable. Unary operators change the last letter of any string variable, and you should ensure that they are not applied against string variables.
++	The increment, or ++, operator is a unary operator that increments the contents of a variable by a value of 1. If the increment unary operator precedes the variable name ($var++), it increments the variable before using it. If the decrement unary operator follows the variable name (++$var), it increments the variable after using the variable. Unary operators change the last letter of any string variable, and you should ensure that they are not applied against string variables.

TABLE C-2 *Assignment and Operation Assignment Operators* (continued)

The first statement declares the $myVar variable and assigns a numeric literal value of 1 with an implicit integer data type to the variable. The next statement prints the variable name, the value, and the data type to the web page. The concatenate and assign operator then adds a string literal of 2 to the integer 1. The left operand implicitly inherits the right operand string data type and converts the $myVar variable to a string containing the value of 12. After printing the result, the unary operator increments the $myVar value by 1 and alters the variable to an integer with the value of 13. This is true whether you increment or decrement with a unary operator. The output from the script is

```
$myVar [1]    [integer]
$myVar [12]   [string]
$myVar [13]   [integer]
```

TIP
Not all outcomes of the unary operator work as nicely as the one demonstrated. A lowercase character a *string can be incremented by a unary operator from* a *to* z, *then from a single character* z *to a double character* aa, *and so forth. The same behavior exists for capital letters and strings, but a decrementing unary operator will leave the* a *string unaffected.*

Assignment for compound variables, like arrays and objects, differs from the model seen with scalar variables. Similar differences holds true for special data types—`function` and `resource`. You define the variable as a left operand, and then you assign it the result of an object constructor, like the following empty array:

```
$myArray = array();
```

It is now an empty array-type variable, which you can assign the letters of the alphabet by doing the following:

```
$myArray[0] = "a";
$myArray[1] = "b";
$myArray[] = "c";
for ($i = 0;$i < count($myArray);$i++) {
  print "\$myArray[\$i] [$myArray[$i]]  [".gettype($myArray[$i])."]<br />"; }
```

You cover the FOR loop later in this appendix. The script prints the following:

```
$myArray[0] [a] [string]
$myArray[1] [b] [string]
$myArray[2] [c] [string]
```

This demonstrates that after defining an array, you can, but do not need to, explicitly assign index values. They can be assigned implicitly with an empty set of square braces, or [ ]. Alternatively, you can also declare an array on a single line, like this:

```
$myArray = array("a","b","c");
```

Arrays are powerful structures in any programming language. There are identification, seeding, queuing, searching, traversing, sorting, merging, and splitting functions. You can check the list of functions and find examples for using them in Chapter 6 in the *Oracle Database Express Edition 10g PHP Web Programming* book. Alternatively, you can explore the documentation for them at the www.php.net site.

You will cover functions and objects later in another subsection of this section. The last types of variables you examine in this subsection are global, globally scoped, and predefined variables. *Global* variables behave like constants and work like environment variables. They are aliases to scalar variables, like numbers and strings. You declare global variables only once in a single execution scope by using the define() function. Any attempt to define the same global variable twice raises a notice error, but that will be ignored by the program's execution. Global variables also cannot be dynamically reassigned new values or change types through assignment operations, and any attempt to do so will raise a *fatal parsing* error.

The following demonstrates declaring two global variables, or environment constants:

```
define('GLOBAL_NUMBER',1);
define('GLOBAL_STRING',"One");
```

You access global variables, or environment constants, by using their name only, as in the following command to print their contents:

```
print GLOBAL_NUMBER."<br />";
print GLOBAL_STRING."<br />";
```

You can also define *globally scoped* variables by first defining them as global. The temptation is to declare a global variable, by both defining and assigning it a value. This will fail because it isn't supported. After you define a globally scoped variable, it becomes available anywhere in your program, and it can likewise be changed anywhere in your program. This becomes a risk when building libraries because a globally scoped variable can be replaced by a new definition and value altered by conflicting lines of code. Global variables are discouraged, but here's how you define and assign a value:

```
global $GLOBAL_NUMBER;
$GLOBAL_NUMBER = 14;
```

NOTE
You can define an ordinary variable by reusing the same name as a global variable. Global variables exist in a separate namespace from ordinary variables.

Predefined variables are also known as super global variables. These variables provide a powerful set of features found in Table C-3. You will use the $_FILES, $_GET, and $_POST super global variables in some examples later in this primer.

There are naturally some aspects of working with data types that were excluded due to space constraints. A significant factor is that variables can implicitly lose precision through implicit casting operations. You should be careful with how you use variables to avoid losing precision through unanticipated run-time type conversions. More on how variables behave can be found in Chapters 4 and 7 of *Oracle Database Express Edition 10g PHP Web Programming*.

This subsection has demonstrated how to define, declare, and name variables. You should be set to read and use code in the balance of the PHP primer.

Variable Name	Description
$GLOBALS	The variable contains a reference to every variable within the global scope of the script. The keys for these values are the names of the global variables.
$_COOKIE	The variable contains all HTTP cookies. It replaces the deprecated $HTTP_COOKIE_VARS array.
$_ENV	The variable contains all inherited environment variables or directly set within the script. It replaces the deprecated $HTTP_ENV_VARS array.
$_FILES	The variable contains all variables provided by HTTP post file uploads. It replaces the deprecated $HTTP_POST_FILES array.
$_GET	The variable contains all URL query string values. It replaces the $HTTP_GET_VARS array. These are always sent in plain text and a security risk.
$_POST	The variable contains all variables provided by HTTP POST. It replaces the deprecated $HTTP_POST_VARS array.
$_REQUEST	The variable contains all variables provided by GET, POST, and COOKIE inputs. The order of variable is set by the PHP variable order configuration parameter. The values in this variable are an also a security risk because it makes a man-in-the-middle attack more likely, since $_GET variables are included and vulnerable. You should use the $_POST in lieu of the $_REQUEST predefined variable.
$_SERVER	The variable contains variables set by the execution environment of the web server and current running scripts. It replaces the deprecated $HTTP_SERVER_VARS array.
$_SESSION	The variable contains variables bound to the current session. It replaces the deprecated $HTTP_SESSION_VARS array.

TABLE C-3   *Predefined Variables*

Defining and Using Conditional Structures

Conditional structures describe the if-then, if-then-else, if-then-else-if-then-else, and switch statements. These structures enable you make decisions based on single variables or collections of variables. You make conditional evaluations by comparing the contents of variables. Table C-4 contains a list of comparison operators available in PHP.

If you're coming from a purely database programming background, the identity comparison operator may be new. The idea of comparing different types of variables in PL/SQL would break the definition of a strongly typed variable, which is necessary in the scope of a database catalog. Weakly typed languages require the identity operator to ensure that some comparisons are between equally typed variables. This ensures that variable types are correct during comparison operations.

Name	Example	Description
equal	`$a == $b`	The two equal signs together returns true if the values are the same regardless of data type.
identical	`$a === $b`	The three equal signs together returns true if the values and data type are the same.
not equal	`$a != $b` or `$a <> $b`	The exclamation or bang operator and an equal sign or the less-than and greater-than symbols together return true if the values are different regardless of data type.
not identical	`$a !== $b`	The combination of an exclamation mark and two equal signs together returns true if the values and data type are not the same.
less than	`$a < $b`	The less-than sign returns true if the left operand contains a value less than the right operand.
greater than	`$a > $b`	The greater-than sign returns true if the left operand contains a value more than the right operand.
less than or equal to	`$a <= $b`	The combination of the less-than and equal signs returns true if the left operand contains a value less than or equal to the right operand.
greater than or equal to	`$a >= $b`	The greater-than sign returns true if the left operand contains a value more than or equal to the right operand.

TABLE C-4 *Comparison Operators*

If Statement   The basic if statement prototype resembles how you perform a conditional evaluation in PL/SQL, except the ELSIF is else if, as

```
if (expression)
   statement;
else if (expression)
   statement;
else
   statement;
```

Another major difference occurs because you can evaluate whether any data type is true or false in PHP but not in PL/SQL. This is also true when variables are undefined provided that you use the error suppression operator, @. The process works by evaluating a zero, empty string, or null as false and everything else as true in the context of treating the variable as an expression.

The PHP parser demands that expressions be enclosed in parentheses, which differs from how PL/SQL works. The good news is that missing parentheses will always raise a parsing error. This means the problem is very seldom encountered in programs, because they can't be unit-tested without complying with the rule.

The following demonstrates how to compare a variable against a string literal with a guarantee that the arriving variable in the expression both is a string and contains a matching value when comparing the two:

```php
<?php
  $myVar = (string) 13;
  if ($myVar === "13")
    print "Meets condition<br />";
  else
    print "Fails condition<br />";
?>
```

The script explicitly casts the numeric literal 13 when assigning it to $myVar. The expression uses the identity operation to guarantee the variable type and value is checked against the string literal.

You also have a ternary if-then-else operator, which is

```
(expression) ? true_statement; : false_statement;
```

When the expression evaluates as true, the true statement runs. When the expression evaluates as false, the false statement runs. You can also nest ternary operators in place of either the true or false statements.

Switch Statement   The switch statement has two types—one is a simple case evaluation and the other a searched case evaluation. The former requires you to use a number or string variable as the criteria variable for branching execution. Both of these use a similar prototype. The difference between the two is that the simple case switches on a variable compared against a criterion, while the searched case evaluates the truth or untruth of an expression.

Switch statements differ from multiple if-then-else-if-then evaluation because they enable fall-through. Fall-through behavior lets you enter the first successful case statement and proceed to process all subsequent case statements, including the default. Fall-through is the default behavior. You avoid fall-through by including a `break;` statement at the end of each case block. The prototype demonstrates the switch statement by preventing fall-through as shown:

```
switch ( variable | expression )
{
  case criterion:
    statement;
    break;
  default:
    statement;
    break;
}
```

The following demonstrates how you implement a *simple* switch statement that disables fall-through:

```php
<?php
  $myVar = 1;
  switch ($myVar)
  {
    case 1:
      print "\$myVar is [$myVar]<br />";
      break;
```

```
      default:
        print "Can't happen!<br />";
        break;
  }
?>
```

You implement a *searched* switch statement in a similar way. There is a subtle difference between the simple and searched switch statements. When you want to validate the truth of an expression, the switch statement does not require an actual parameter because a `bool` true is the default. You must override the default and provide a false when you want to check whether an expression is false. The following *searched* switch statement overrides the default by providing a false expression:

```
<?php
  $myVar = 1;
  switch (!$myVar) // Not true because 0 evaluates as false.
  {
    case (!$myVar == 0):
      print "\$myVar is [$myVar]<br />";
      break;
    default:
      print "Can only happen!<br />";
      break;
  }
?>
```

The first case in preceding program uses a false expression that resolves to true because of the not, or `!`, operator found in front of the expression. The combination of negation and a true expression is always false. Therefore, the program can only print the default case.

This subsection has covered comparison operators and conditional structures in PHP. You will use these techniques later in this appendix.

Defining and Using Iterative Structures

Iterative control structures include `DO-WHILE`, `FOR`, `FOREACH`, and `WHILE` loops. They provide programmers with the ability to repeat a set of instructions a specified number of times or until a condition is met.

There are different structures because you can have different purposes when you want to step through data repeatedly. Sometimes you want to do it until a condition is met, which is accomplished with the `FOR` and `DO-WHILE` loops. On occasion you want to gate entry to an iterative structure with a condition, which is what the `WHILE` loop does. In the case of a hash table or hash map, PHP provides a special iterative structure—the `FOREACH` loop.

In the following section, you will examine the purpose and use of the `DO-WHILE`, `FOR`, `FOREACH`, and `WHILE` loops. They are covered in alphabetical order because that puts the `WHILE` loop last and it behaves differently than the others by gating entry, not exit, to a loop.

DO-While Loop   The `DO-WHILE` loop does not audit conditions on entry but on exit. You will find this structure useful when you always want the logic processed at least one time before exiting the loop. The prototype for a `DO-WHILE` loop is

```
do
{
  statement;
} while (expression);
```

FOR Loop   The FOR loop does not audit conditions on entry but, like the DO-WHILE loop, on exit. You will find this structure useful when you want to put all streams of code through it and want the convenience of setting the initial value, the exit evaluation, and the incrementing pattern in one place. The pattern for a FOR loop is

```
for (expression1; expression2; expression3)
{
   statement;
}
```

The first expression declares a counter variable. The second expression sets an upward limit for an incrementing counter and downward limit for a decrementing counter. The third expression defines how the counter increments or decrements.

The FOR loop traverses numerically indexed arrays or collections. The FOR loop can cause failures while reading arrays that are sparsely populated. Sparsely populated arrays have one or more gaps in the index values that sequence them, as discussed in Chapter 7. Fresh query results from a database do not cause problems because the rows are returned sequentially. You're more likely to find the error when navigating PL/SQL index-by tables transferred in bulk with sparsely populated indexes. You should take precautions when you are unsure whether the index is sequential. Reorganizing an array with a new index solves this type of problem.

FOREACH Loop   The FOREACH loop is a useful tool to navigate hash indexes or maps. These are also known as associative arrays. Associative arrays are name and value pairs stored in structures. The names may be numeric or alphanumeric, and therefore they mimic the behavior of hash maps. There are two prototypes for this structure: one processes index values, and the other ignores them. The following prototype lets you process index values:

```
foreach ($array_name as $name => $value)
{
   statement;
}
```

The alternative prototype ignores index values:

```
foreach ($array_name as $value)
{
   statement;
}
```

WHILE Loop   The WHILE loop enables you to gate whether your program enters the loop. The evaluation check at the top of the loop provides the pre-entry check and also prevents exit until the condition is not met. The WHILE loop has the following pattern:

```
while (expression)
{
   statement;
}
```

Defining and Using Functions

All programs contain instructions to perform tasks. When sets of tasks are frequently used to perform an activity, they are grouped into a unit, which is known as a function or method in most programming languages. PHP calls these units functions.

Functions should perform well-defined tasks. They should also hide the complexity of their tasks behind a prototype. A prototype includes a function name, a list of parameters, and a return data type. The prototype should let you see how the function can be used in your programs.

Function names should be short declarative descriptions about what tasks they perform. The list of parameters, also known as a signature, is typically enclosed in parentheses; it should use descriptive variable names that signal their purpose when possible. The parameters in a function signature are considered formal at definition and actual at run time. In strongly typed languages, the parameters impose positional and data type restrictions. Weakly typed languages, like C or PHP, typically impose only positional restrictions.

There are two types of parameters—one is mandatory and the other is optional. A formal parameter becomes optional when you define a default value for it. Optional parameters should be at the end of a formal parameter list. Unlike with PL/SQL, you do not have the ability to pass parameters out of sequence by named reference. You must provide actual parameters for all formal parameters that come before an optional parameter when you want to exclude it from the list. A more effective solution is to use flexible parameter passing and avoid listing any mandatory or optional variables in the formal parameter list.

Formal parameters can also designate whether run-time values are passed by value or reference in some programming languages. The return type is a valid data type in the programming language. When there is no return type, it is represented as a void.

NOTE
Functions that fail to return a value are like stored procedures in PL/SQL, whereas functions that return values are more like stored functions. PHP functions are not exactly like PL/SQL stored functions because you can pass actual parameters by reference or by value. Functions in PL/SQL are restricted to an IN mode only, which makes them exclusively pass-by-value functions.

You can define functions with or without formal parameter lists because of flexible parameter passing. Flexible parameter passing lets you call functions by using actual parameters not defined in the function prototypes. The next three subsections describe available prototypes.

Pass-by-Value Function   A pass-by-value function receives values into new variables known as actual parameters when called. It can use those variable values anywhere inside the scope of the function. At the conclusion of the function call, the actual parameters are discarded from memory, and any variables used to pass those actual parameters are unchanged. You can also provide a default value for any defined formal parameter, as noted:

```
function myFunction($formalParameter1 [ = default_value]
                   ,$formalParameter2 [ = default_value])
{
   return $formalParameter1 + $formalParameter2;
}
```

This prototype can be called *relying on the default values* for the two formal parameters:

```
myFunction();
```

You can override the first formal parameter while ignoring the second. However, you cannot override the second parameter without first providing the first parameter. The same rule does not hold when you override the first formal parameter, ignoring the second one. The following demonstrates overriding both default parameter values:

```
myFunction(3,5);
```

You'll notice that these are actual parameters and are numeric literals. Numeric literals can only be used when providing actual parameters to formal pass-by-value parameters.

Pass-by-Reference Function   A pass-by-reference function receives a reference to an existing variable that has already been declared in the program scope. Functions of this type cannot receive a numeric or string literal because they lack a memory address where the function can update a change in the value. The ampersand, or &, designates that a formal parameter is a pass-by-reference parameter in PHP 5. Prior to the current version, you placed the ampersand on the actual parameters.

The following prototype is a pass-by-reference function that squares any declared variable:

```
function mySquare(&$formalParameter)
{
    return $formalParameter *= $formalParameter;
}
```

You can print the actual parameter variable contents before and after the function by using the following type of code:

```
$myRoot = 2;
print "Root [".$myRoot."]<br />";
mySquare($myRoot);
print "Root [".$myRoot."]<br />";
```

The code prints

```
Root [2]
Root [4]
```

Flexible Parameter Passing   Flexible parameter passing can also be described as variable-length parameter lists. Variable-length parameter lists are common patterns in programming languages. The C, C++, C#, and Java programming languages all support variable-length parameter lists, but they label them differently. A variable-length parameter list is an array or a list of values, where the values are valid PHP data types.

As discussed earlier, there are two parameter options: mandatory or optional. These options make function parameter lists more complex. A function definition or prototype that uses a single mandatory parameter requires that you call the function with at least one actual parameter but does not restrict you from passing more than one. You can actually submit any number of parameters beyond the mandatory number required by a function prototype. You can define functions without any parameters and still manage a parameter list passed to the function, which means prototypes are optional.

The absence of a parameter list frees you from sequential ordering of parameters and issues arising from whether parameters are mandatory or optional. Sending a single associative array that contains name and value pairs leaves the internals of your function to resolve when to apply or ignore formal parameter default values. The flipside of this approach to writing functions is that there is no prototype available for reuse. Functions must then include logic to manage variable-length parameter lists. Table C-5 describes three predefined functions that let you manage variable-length parameter lists.

Function	Description and Pattern
`func_get_arg()`	The function takes one formal parameter, which is the index value in the variable-length parameter list. When the actual parameter is found in the range of the parameter list indexes, the function returns that argument value. If the index value is not found in the list, the function raises a warning and returns a null value. The function has the following pattern: `mixed func_get_arg(int arg_num)`
`func_get_args()`	The function takes no formal parameters and returns a numerically indexed array of arguments. If there are no parameters passed to the function, a null array is returned. The null array has zero elements, and attempting to access element zero will raise a non-fatal error. It has the following pattern: `array func_get_args()`
`func_num_args()`	The function takes no formal parameters and returns the number of elements in the argument list. The valid range is from 0 to the maximum number of parameters. The function has the following pattern: `int func_num_args()`

TABLE C-5   *Flexible Parameter Lists*

The generic prototype for a two-element flexible parameter list is

```
function myFunction()
{
  if (func_num_args() > 0 )
  {
    foreach (func_get_args() as $index => $value)
    {
      switch $index
      {
        case argument_name1:
          statement;
          break;
        case argument_name2:
          statement;
          break;
      }
    }
  }
  statement;
}
```

This subsection has demonstrated how to implement pass-by-value, pass-by-reference, and flexible parameter lists. You should also note that PHP supports recursive programming, where a function can call another copy of itself.

Defining and Using Objects

Procedural programming functions perform well-defined tasks, and they hide the details of their operation. A collection of functions can be grouped together to perform a task that requires a set of functions. Organized groups of functions are modules; and the process of grouping them together is modularization. A PL/SQL package is a collection of related stored functions and procedures that hides their complexity through a predefined application programming interface (API). While packages can define package-level variables, they do nothing to ensure their operational state or reusability.

Object-oriented (OO) programming solutions fix some of the shortcomings of functions and modules because they maintain the operational state of variables. Object types define how to store data and define API operations, also known as functions or methods. Operations are generally described as methods in OO programming languages, but they are implemented as class functions in PHP.

The same naming requirements as that used with functions apply to objects. Object names in PHP must start with an alphabetical character or underscore and consist of only alphabetical characters, numbers, or underscores. Object names are global in scope and case insensitive, as are functions.

Scope for PHP classes, like that for functions, is global and enables you to use them anywhere in your programs. Only classes, functions, and global constants, those built by using the `define()` function, enjoy global environment scope.

Classes, unlike functions, cannot have return types. Class instantiation returns a copy or instance of a class. While object construction generally occurs as the source operand on the right side of an assignment operator, you can construct an object instance as an actual parameter to a function, or as a member of an array. The object instance existence is limited to the duration of the function or its membership as a component of an array variable.

You will find that objects are similar to many other languages but different enough to review the object operators. These are the operators that work in PHP 5. Table C-6 provides definitions that help you read the class definitions of PHP objects.

Operators	Description
`::`	The *scope resolution operator* enables you to refer to class or instance variables and functions. It is a binary operator. A class name, `parent` operator, or `self` operator must precede the scope resolution operator as its left operand. A class constant, static variable, or static function, or else the `$this` operator, can be the right operand. Using anything else as the right operand will raise a fatal exception. The prototype for using the scope resolution operator to reset a class variable is `ClassName::$ClassVariable = "new value";`

TABLE C-6 *Object Operators*

Operators	Description

`->`	The pointer operator points to a member variable or function of an object instance. The pointer operator is a binary operator. The left operand can be `$this` or a variable holding an instance of the class, while the right operand is an instance variable or function. *The `$this` operator must precede the operator inside a class definition,* as the instance of an object. Outside of a class definition, the variable holding an instance of a class must precede the member variable pointer, and the class variable or function follows its use. You can also refer to a super class by using the `parent::$this->variable` or `parent::$this->function` syntax. The pointer operator prototype outside of a class is shown by using the instance variable as the left operand of an assignment operation:
	`$ClassVariableName->InstanceVariable = "new value";`
	Alternatively, the pointer operator outside of a class can point to a function, which in this case takes an actual parameter and returns nothing:
	`$ClassVariableName->Function("parameter");`

`clone`	The `clone` operator enables you to copy an instance of a class to a new instance of the same class. The clone operator is a binary operator. It uses variable assignment as the left operand, while the right operand must contain an instance of an object type. The prototype for cloning an object instance is `$NewClassVariable = clone $OldClassVariable;`
`instanceof`	The `instanceof` operator enables you to check whether a variable is an instance of an object type. Its use mirrors that of a comparison operator, returning true when an instance is derived from an object type and false when not. The `instanceof` is a binary operator, which takes a variable holding a class instance as the left operand and the name of an object type as the right operand. It has the following prototype as a conditional expression: `if ($ClassVariable instanceof ClassName)`
`new`	The `new` operator enables you to build an instance of a class definition. The `new` operator is a binary operator. It uses variable assignment as the left operand, while the right operand must contain a constructor of an object type. The prototype for using the new operator is `$NewClassVariable = new ClassName("parameter");`

`parent`	The `parent` operator refers to a super class of an object and *you can only use it in the class definition of a subclass or in the scope of an internal class function.* You can use it in the `__constructor` and `__destructor` predefined functions. The `parent` operator uses the scope resolution operator to reference constants, static variables, or functions, and the `$this` operator, which precedes non-static variables and functions. The prototype for assigning values from superclass constants and static variables from within a subclass is
	`$NewVariable = parent::classVariable;`
	While the prototype for calling superclass static functions from within subclasses is
	`$NewVariable = parent::functionName("parameter");`
	Calling superclass instance variables and functions requires using a combination of the parent and scope resolution operators, like the following subclass function call to a superclass:
	`$NewVariable = parent::$this->function("parameter");`

TABLE C-6   *Object Operators* (continued)

Operators	Description
self	The self operator refers to a local class of an object and *you can only use it in the definition of a class or in the scope of an internal class function.* You can use it in the __constructor and __destructor predefined functions. The self operator uses the scope resolution operator to reference constants, static variables or functions, and the $this operator, which precedes non-static variables and functions. The prototype for assigning values from class constants and static variables from within a class is $NewVariable = self::classVariable; While the prototype for calling class static functions from within the same classes is $NewVariable = self::functionName("parameter");
$this	This operator refers to the local instance of a class, and you can only use it in the definition of a class. The scope limits require you to use it in an internal function, which can include the __constructor and __destructor predefined functions. The $this operator combined with the pointer operator enables you to access instance variables and functions. The following prototype represents assigning a value to an instance variable within a class: $this->classVariable = "new value"; The following prototype represents calling an instance function that returns no value: $this->classFunction("parameter");

TABLE C-6   *Object Operators* (continued)

An object prototype includes the class keyword and the body of the object type in curly braces:

```
class object_name { object_body }
```

The PHP object prototype is very similar to other OO programming languages, especially the C++ syntax. All classes are publicly accessible, which is consistent with their global scope. Table C-7 qualifies access modifiers available in PHP objects.

A sample class definition is

```
class BasicObject
{
   public $name = "BasicObject";
}
```

You can define an instance of the class by doing the following:

```
$myObject = new BasicObject();
```

After creating an instance, you can access publicly available variables or methods by using the pointer operator as shown:

```
print "[".$myObject->name."]<br />";
```

The simplistic class example relies on the default constructor and destructor functions provided implicitly for you by the PHP engine. Object constructors are like functions and have signatures that contain zero to many parameters in a list. The PHP default constructor, like the default constructor in Java, takes no formal parameter. *You cannot override the PHP default constructor signature without implementing an overriding constructor of your own.*

Access Modifier	UML Notation	Description
final	*Italicized*	*The final access modifier ensures that a class function cannot be overridden by a subclass implementation. The* final *modifier can only apply to functions.*
private	–	The private access modifier hides a variable or function from direct external class access. A public class function can also indirectly access private class variables and functions. *Both private class variables and functions are hidden from all subclasses of a class.*
protected	#	The protected access modifier hides a variable or function from direct external class access. A public function can indirectly access protected class variables and functions. *Both protected class variables and functions are available from subclasses of a class.*
public	+	The public access modifier, or default behavior, publishes class variables and functions.
static	$	The static key word designates a variable or function as accessible without creating a class instance.

TABLE C-7 *Class Access Modifiers*

The constructor and destructor functions are class operations or methods. *You can override the default constructor by using the* __construct () *function; and you can override the default destructor by using the* __destruct () *function.* The __construct () function is called when you instantiate an instance of an object type with the new operator. The __destruct () function is called when you no longer hold a reference to an object instance, which may be at the time a PHP page is rendered.

Getters and setters are common OO programming terms indicating that you get or set a class variable. In many OO programming languages, you need to write individual getVariable () or setVariable ($var) functions. You can write these custom getters and setters, or you can overload the functionality with the __get () and __set () functions in PHP. Overloaded functions can only be used with non-static variables.

The __get () and __set () functions have the following prototypes:

```
mixed __get( $var );
void  __set( $var );
```

An example of implementing a getter is

```
public function __get($var)
{
  return $this->$var;
}
```

You implement a setter typically with two formal parameters. These typically act like a name and value pair, respectively named $key and $value in the prototype example. The benefit is that a single __set() function call can now set all accessible variables, as noted:

```
public function __set($key,$value)
{
  $this->$key = $value;
}
```

This section has discussed the basics of building and accessing objects. Classes also support subclassing, inheritance, abstract classes, interfaces, cloning, and run-time reflection. You can find more about these topics at php.net or Chapter 8 in the *Oracle Database 10g Express Edition PHP Web Programming* book.

Handling Run-Time Errors and Exceptions

Run-time errors are not run-time exceptions but behave differently. Run-time errors require proactive management in your programming code. Prior to PHP 5, run-time errors were often simply suppressed by using the error control operator, or @. Beginning with PHP 5, you can manage known run-time errors by both suppressing and re-throwing them as exceptions.

Exceptions are also new to PHP 5. Exceptions use try-catch blocks, as in C++, C#, and Java. Some run-time events raise exceptions, which don't happen during the parsing phase like compile-time errors. Exception handling qualifies how you manage run-time failures in your programs.

Run-time errors thrown by many standard coding components raise three types of errors: *error, warning,* and *notice.* The first is a fatal *error,* and it will stop the running script's execution. The next two—*warning* and *notice*—are informational and will not stop running scripts. You can set error handling to prevent the display of warnings and notices in your production environment. They should generally be enabled in the testing environment to establish that developers clearly accept risks they place in their code.

The basic structure for a try-catch block used in exception handling is

```
try
{
  statement;
}
catch (Exception $e)
{
  statement;
}
```

When statements don't implicitly throw exceptions on failure, you need to throw one manually. This is a bit more involved because of the two error management systems. When a statement raises an error and not an exception, you should use the following prototype:

```
try
{
  if (@!statement)
    throw new Exception(string error_msg,int error_code);
}
```

You have the ability to define your own exceptions. User-defined exceptions are subclasses of the Exception class. They are convenient, but when you do use them, there is risk that either a standard or custom exception may be thrown. As a result of this behavior, you should define multiple catch blocks, as shown:

```
catch (MyException $e)
{
  statement;
}
catch (Exception $e)
{
  statement;
}
```

The MyException and Exception are object types, and the process of including them in your prototype is known as type hinting. You can use type hinting only when the variable can only be an object data type.

This section has covered the fundamentals of objects to define common terms necessary to understand how you manage Oracle collections and system reference cursors. These components are part of the OCI8 and implemented as objects.

Reading, Writing, and Uploading Files

This subsection covers reading and writing ordinary and comma-separated value (CSV) files. The subsection demonstrates how you upload and write to LOB data types in an Oracle database. It also supports PL/SQL examples in Chapters 8 and 12, on LOB data types and file I/O respectively.

The ins and outs of accessing files on your application server let you move data from a program variable in memory to: (a) another local program; (b) another remote program; (c) a shared memory segment; or (d) the file system. Local and remote programs that share memory segments and file systems are also known as resources. Files are a type of resource. Reading and writing files is an integral part of application design.

Reading Ordinary and CSV Files   You can read files character-by-character, chunk-by-chunk, line-by-line, comma-separated values (CSV) and as a whole unit. The examples in this section demonstrate how you read a file as a CSV data source. The following sample code *runs from the command line* and reads a text file from the local directory. It reads the file into an array of strings and then prints the array to standard out:

```php
<?php
  // Verify operating file system delimiter.
  if (ereg("/",$_SERVER["Path"]))
    $slash = "/";
  else
    $slash = "\\";

  // Check local parameters to verify and read file.
  if ((@$_SERVER["argv"]) && (@$_SERVER["argc"] == 2))
  {
    $fn = @$_SERVER["argv"][1];
    $qfn = getcwd().$slash.$fn;
```

```
    $contents = file($qfn);
    foreach ($contents as $value)
      print $value;
  }
  else
    print "No file name provided.";
?>
```

The `ereg()` function is used to determine if the file system is Microsoft Windows or Linux. Linux paths contain a forward slash for directory references, whereas backslashes are used on Microsoft Windows operating system. This ensures that the right type of delimiter is placed in front of the physical filename.

A variation to reading the contents into an array is reading a CSV into a multiple-dimension array, using lines as the first dimension and the comma-separated fields as the second. The `fgetcsv()` function reads a line and parses the delimited values into an array. The following code demonstrates reading a CSV file from the same directory as the script, and printing the contents of the file into an XHTML table. It is rendered by a browser in a web page:

```
<?php
  $fname = realpath("BookSales.txt");
  $contents = array();
  if ($fp = fopen($fname,'r'))
  {
    while (!feof($fp))
      $contents[] = fgetcsv($fp,10000,",");
    fclose($fp);
  }
  print "<table>";
  foreach ($contents as $data)
  {
    print "<tr>";
    foreach ($data as $cell)
      print "<td>".$cell."</td>";
    print "</tr>";
  }
  print "</table>";
?>
```

CAUTION
Comma-separated value files created by some versions of Microsoft Excel can leave unexpected characters that will raise warning errors.

There are several other reading functions that provide different approaches to reading files. Character-by-character reads are done by the `fgetc()` function; chunk-by-chunk and line-by-line reads are both done with the `fgets()` function.

Writing Ordinary and CSV Files Writing files differs from reading files in PHP. There is no function to write characters per se, but the `fwrite()` function is binary safe and writes strings to files. The `fwrite()` function has an alias `fputs()` function name. Alternatively, you can write arrays of strings by using the `file_put_contents()` function or as comma-separated values (CSV) files with the `fputcsv()` function.

Unlike when reading files, you are limited to writing files as strings, CSV strings, or arrays of strings. Since strings can vary from a single character to set of characters, you really have the same power as provided by the predefined reading functions.

You can run the following code from the command line to create a new file from the embedded array of strings:

```php
<?php
  // Verify operating file system delimiter.
  if (ereg("/",$_SERVER["Path"]))
    $slash = "/";
  else
    $slash = "\\";

  // Define a data stream.
  $data = array();
  $data[] = "This is line number one, and";
  $data[] = "it is followed by line number two.";

  // Check local parameters to verify.
  if ((@$_SERVER["argv"]) && (@$_SERVER["argc"] == 2))
  {
    // Build the qualified file name.
    $fn = @$_SERVER["argv"][1];
    $qfn = getcwd().$slash.$fn;

    // Delete a same name existing file.
    if (is_file($qfn))
      unlink($qfn);

    // Open to append to a file.
    if ($fp = fopen($qfn,'a'))
      for ($i = 0;$i < count($data);$i++)
        if (!fwrite($fp,$data[$i]."\n"))
          fclose($fp);
  }
  else
    print "No file name provided.";
?>
```

This generates a file with the following two lines:

```
This is line number one, and it
is followed by line number two.
```

Writing a CSV file is not much different than reading one. You should notice the similarity between writing an array of strings and writing a CSV file.

```php
<?php
  // Verify operating file system delimiter.
  if (ereg("/",$_SERVER["Path"]))
    $slash = "/";
  else
    $slash = "\\";
```

```
// Define a data stream.
$data = array(
          array("Account","Jan","Feb","Mar","Apr")
        , array("33-444-22","42","51","65","23")
        , array("33-444-23","24","15","16","17")
        , array("33-444-24","31","22","13","19")
        , array("Total:","97","88","94","59"));

// Check local parameters to verify.
if ((@$_SERVER["argv"]) && (@$_SERVER["argc"] == 2))
{
  // Build the qualified file name.
  $fn = @$_SERVER["argv"][1];
  $qfn = getcwd().$slash.$fn;

  // Delete a same name existing file.
  if (is_file($qfn))
    unlink($qfn);

  // Open to write a file.
  if ($fp = fopen($qfn,'w'))
    for ($i = 0;$i < count($data);$i++)
      if (!fputcsv($fp,$data[$i],","))
        fclose($fp);
}
else
  print "No file name provided.";
?>
```

Uploading Files to the Server   PHP supports managing file uploads with the `move_uploaded_file()` function on the server. HTML supports the means to upload files in web browsers. You can develop file uploads by using the HTML `FORM` and two `INPUT` tags.

The `FORM` tag contains an `action` attribute that specifies a URL pointing to a server-side program. The first `INPUT` tag is designated as a file type within the scope of the `FORM` tags. When an `INPUT` tag is set as a file type, a Browse button is automatically rendered to the right of the input field. Clicking the Browse button launches the operating system file chooser, which enables you to select a local file to upload to the server.

The second `INPUT` tag designates a `submit` type, which is also within the scope of the same `FORM` tags. The Submit button fires the action qualified in the `FORM` tag. The Submit button makes a call to a server-side program. Depending on the implementation details of the web browser, you should use the `POST` but not the `GET` method.

The following program demonstrates uploading a file to your server using the `POST` method:

```
<form id="uploadForm"
      action=http://sever_name/UploadFile.php
      enctype="multipart/form-data"
      method="post">
  <table border=0 cellpadding=0 cellspacing=0>
    <tr>
      <td width=100>Select File</td>
      <td>
```

```
      <input id="uploadFileName" name="userfile" type="file">
    </td>
  </tr>
  <tr>
    <td width=100>Click Button to</td>
    <td><input type="submit" value="Upload File"></td>
  </tr>
</table>
</form>
```

This renders the image shown in Figure C-2. As just discussed, when you click the Browse button the browser launches the operating system file chooser. After you select a file, the text box will display the fully qualified or canonical path and file name. You click the Upload File button to submit the HTML form contents to the server. Submitting the form sends the file to the server-side program.

The FORM tag includes three critical attributes: the action, enctype, and method attributes. As mentioned, the action tag contains a qualified URL and a server-side program that will process the uploaded file. The enctype attribute designates the file encoding type and qualifies that the HTML submission contains the regular array of form values. The method attribute designates whether it is a POST or GET method. It is recommended that you use the POST, not the GET, method.

The INPUT tag designated as a file type has two key attributes. They are the name and type attributes. The type attribute renders the Browse button and enables you to read the file system. The name attribute designates what is used as the associative array index value for the selected file in the $_FILES array variable.

The following program lets you process the file upload, move from a temporary file location, read the file, and render it in the web page:

```php
<?php
  // Define the upload file name for Windows or Linux.
  if (ereg("Win32",$_SERVER["SERVER_SOFTWARE"]))
    $uploadFile = getcwd()."\\temp\\".$_FILES['userfile']['name'];
  else
    $uploadFile = getcwd()."/temp/".$_FILES['userfile']['name'];

  // Check for and move uploaded file.
  if (is_uploaded_file($_FILES['userfile']['tmp_name']))
    move_uploaded_file($_FILES['userfile']['tmp_name'],$uploadFile);

  // Open a file handle and suppress an error for a missing file.
  if ($fp = @fopen($uploadFile,"r"))
  {
    // Read until the end-of-file marker.
    while (!feof($fp))
      $contents .= fgetc($fp);

    // Close an open file handle.
    fclose($fp);
  }

  // Display moved file in web page.
  print $contents;
?>
```

FIGURE C-2 *Upload File web page*

NOTE
This uploading script requires a temp directory to co-exist in the directory where the script resides. While it is straightforward to demonstrate how to process the uploading of a file, the permanent location should usually be in a location not accessible from the Apache server htdocs *root.*

TIP
The ereg() *function call differs from earlier examples because there are different name and value pairs when scripts are run from the Apache server than when run from the run-time command line.*

This subsection has covered how to read, write and upload files to your server. It also concludes the earlier subsection "How to Use PHP." The next subsection builds on the fundamental elements of the programming language by demonstrating how to interface with the Oracle database. You may find expanded coverage on the language at php.net or in *Oracle Database 10g Express Edition PHP Web Programming*.

How to Use PHP and OCI8 to Access the Oracle Database

This subsection discusses the three connection types delivered by the OCI8 library. It also reviews how you write SELECT, INSERT, UPDATE, and DELETE statements inside PHP programs using SQL and PL/SQL statements. This subsection helps you see the benefits and risks of dynamically building SQL statements. It shows you how to use OCI8 to bind scalar and compound variables—scalar collections, system reference cursors, and large objects. You learn how to bind pass-by-value and pass-by-reference variables in SQL and PL/SQL statements.

NOTE
While the code in prior portions of the appendix can run without configuring the complete OPAL stack, you will need to either manually configure your httpd.conf *and* php.ini *files, or run Zend for Oracle to configure them.*

OCI8 Connections

The Oracle Call Interface (OCI8) libraries provide three connection types to the Oracle database:

- **Standard Connections** Build an RPC connection that is good for the duration of a script's execution unless explicitly closed by the script. All calls to the database in these scripts use the same connection unless they open a unique connection by calling the `oci_new_connect()` function. Standard connections place overhead on the server to marshal and allocate resources that are dismissed when released by the script or after the script terminates. There is no preserved state between HTTP requests to the server for standard connections.

- **Unique Connections** Build a unique RPC connection that is good during the duration of a script's execution unless explicitly closed by the script. Unique connections allow a single script to have more than one open connection to the Oracle database, which works well when you are using them to perform autonomous transactions. Autonomous transactions run simultaneously rather than sequentially and are independent of each other. Unique connections also place overhead on the server to marshal and allocate resources that are dismissed when released by the script or after the script terminates. There is no preserved state with a unique connection between HTTP requests to the server.

- **Persistent Connections** Build an RPC connection that is good during the duration of a script's execution unless explicitly closed by the script. All calls to the database by these scripts use the same connection unless they open a unique connection by calling the `oci_new_connect()` function. Persistent connections place overhead on the server to marshal and allocate resources that are not immediately dismissed after the script terminates. There is preserved state between HTTP requests to the server for persistent connections. Persistent connections are closed after a period of inactivity between requests and require active DBA management to ensure that critical resources are not locked without useful purpose.

The following demonstrates a non-persistent connection that queries the Oracle database while avoiding the overhead of a commit action:

```php
<?php
// Connect with user, password, and TNS alias.
if ($c = @oci_connect("php","php","xe"))
{
  // Define a SQL statement.
  $stmt = "SELECT SYS_CONTEXT('USERENV','DB_NAME') AS DB FROM dual";

  // Parse SQL statement.
  $s = oci_parse($c,$stmt);

  // Execute deferring commit action on a query.
  oci_execute($s,OCI_DEFAULT);

  // Get and print column names.
  for ($i = 1;$i <= oci_num_fields($s);$i++)
    print oci_field_name($s,$i).'<br />';
```

```
  // Fetch rows, then iterate across columns.
  while (oci_fetch($s))
  {
    for ($i = 1;$i <= oci_num_fields($s);$i++)
      print oci_result($s,$i).'<br />';
  }

  // Close connection.
  oci_close($c);
  }
?>
```

You can replace the call to `oci_connect()` with calls to either `oci_pconnect()` or `oci_new_connect()` to connect and query the database. Each of these connection modes uses the constant `OCI_DEFAULT` as the default connection mode. Default connections require a call to the `oci_commit()` function to make any change permanent. You can override the default by using the `OCI_COMMIT_ON_SUCCESS` constant. Any call to `oci_execute()` using the `OCI_COMMIT_ON_SUCCESS` value is managed as an autonomous transaction. Autonomous transactions have two distinct behaviors: they commit any pending changes, and they terminate any open transaction scope. The former is most useful when you are executing standalone `INSERT`, `UPDATE` or `DELETE` statements but unnecessary overhead with ordinary queries. The latter becomes important when working with queries or statements that start transactions and work with LOB data types in an Oracle database. How you work within transaction scope and use LOB data types is covered later in this appendix.

OCI8 Bind Variables

PHP programs exchange variables with SQL and PL/SQL statements two ways. One builds statements by concatenating variables into a string like the `$stmt` variable. You expose your site to SQL injection attacks when you paste variables into command strings. The other binds a variable and data type into a parsed statement. Binding checks that you have a valid Oracle data type, eliminating SQL injection attacks.

Pseudo-Binding Using the sprintf() Function

You mimic Oracle binding by using statement preparation like the following:

```
// Define a local variable.
$host = "SERVER_HOST";

// Define a SQL statement.
$stmt = sprintf("SELECT SYS_CONTEXT('USERENV','%s') AS HOSTNAME
                FROM dual",$host);
```

This approach also works using Oracle, but it is not really equivalent to binding a variable. The `sprintf()` function lets you splice native data types into a string, but it is like grafting the root of one plant to another's trunk. The two become one after grafting.

Binding a variable lets you both assign and retrieve a value from a location in a parsed statement. Oracle's approach lets you bind scalar and compound variables. Compound variables can be scalar collections, PL/SQL index-by tables, and LOBs.

The next example demonstrates how you bind a variable into a query:

```php
<?php
// Return successful attempt to connect to the database.
if ($c = @oci_connect("plsql","plsql","orcl"))
{
  // Declare input variables.
  (isset($_GET['lname'])) ? $lname = $_GET['lname']
                          : $lname = "[a-zA-Z]";

  // Declare array mapping column to display names.
  $q_title = array("FULL_NAME"=>"Full Name"
                  ,"TITLE"=>"Title"
                  ,"CHECK_OUT_DATE"=>"Check Out"
                  ,"RETURN_DATE"=>"Return");

  // Parse a query to a resource statement.
  $s = oci_parse($c,"SELECT   cr.full_name
                    ,        cr.title
                    ,        cr.check_out_date
                    ,        cr.return_date
                    FROM     current_rental cr
                    WHERE    REGEXP_LIKE(cr.full_name,:lname)");

  // Bind a variable into the resource statement.
  oci_bind_by_name($s,":lname",$lname,-1,SQLT_CHR);

  // Execute the parsed query without a commit.
  oci_execute($s,OCI_DEFAULT);

  // Print the table header using calls to the query metadata.
  print '<table border="1" cellspacing="0" cellpadding="3">';

  // Print a open and close HTML row tags and column field names.
  print '<tr>';
  for ($i = 1;$i <= oci_num_fields($s);$i++)
    print '<td class="e">'.$q_title[oci_field_name($s,$i)].'</td>';
  print "</tr>";

  // Read and print statement row return.
  while (oci_fetch($s))
  {
    // Print open and close HTML row tags and columns data.
    print '<tr>';
    for ($i = 1;$i <= oci_num_fields($s);$i++)
      print '<td class="v">'.oci_result($s,$i).'</td>';
    print '</tr>';
  }

  // Print a close HTML table tag.
  print '</table>';
```

```
  // Disconnect from database.
  oci_close($c);
  }
  else
  {
  // Assign the OCI error and format double and single quotes.
  $errorMessage = oci_error();
  print htmlentities($errorMessage['message'])."<br />";
  }
?>
```

The script also shows a formatting trick that lets you replace uppercase column names with case-sensitive titles in an XHTML table. You do this by placing a function call inside an array subscript reference.

Table C-8 explains the prototype and rules governing the `oci_bind_by_name()` function. It lets you transfer data between your program and both SQL and PL/SQL statements. The `oci_bind_by_name()` function works with scalar variables and compound variables defined as SQL data types—these are scalar collections and LOBs. Table C-8 also covers the `oci_bind_array_by_name()` function. It lets you bind PL/SQL index-by tables. PL/SQL index-by tables are PL/SQL data types, not SQL data types. This means you have the ability to map and exchange PL/SQL index-by tables and PHP arrays. It also provides you another alternative to do bulk operations by reusing stored program units that have formal parameters defined as PL/SQL index-by table data types.

> **NOTE**
> *At present you are limited to working with PL/SQL index-by tables of scalar variables. This is like reducing functionality back to the bad old Oracle 7.3.2 days, but Chapter 7 demonstrates how to write wrappers to move PL/SQL index-by tables of structures into parallel arrays and vice versa.*

Subsequent subsections demonstrate how to use the binding functions from Table C-8. Some of the examples require defining local variables—like collections, system reference cursors, and LOB descriptors. Others require defining SQL and PL/SQL data types in the database schema.

OCI8 PL/SQL Index-By Tables

The next example shows you how to access the `GET_PRESIDENTS` stored procedure. It is an overloaded procedure found in the `WORLD_LEADERS` package. You require some PL/SQL data type definitions to make this example successful. The definitions are in the `WORLD_LEADERS` package specification, as noted:

```
-- Define an associative array (PL/SQL Table) of numbers.
TYPE president_id_table IS TABLE OF NUMBER
  INDEX BY BINARY_INTEGER;

-- Define three associative arrays (PL/SQL Table)  of VARCHAR2 by size.
TYPE president_name_table IS TABLE OF VARCHAR2(60 CHAR)
  INDEX BY BINARY_INTEGER;
TYPE tenure_table IS TABLE OF VARCHAR2(9 CHAR)
  INDEX BY BINARY_INTEGER;
TYPE party_table IS TABLE OF VARCHAR2(24 CHAR)
  INDEX BY BINARY_INTEGER;
```

These type definitions provide the package PL/SQL-only data types that can be used by package procedures. The procedures define formal parameters using the defined types. Other packages in the same schema can also refer to these package data types by prefacing them with the package name and a period. Packages in other schemas also require a grant of permissions and then the name of the owning schema before the package name.

TIP

The process of putting schema, package, and data types is known as attribute chaining in Oracle jargon.

Function	Description

oci_bind_array_by_name()	The oci_bind_array_by_name() function binds a numerically indexed PHP array with a PL/SQL associative array, also known as a PL/SQL table before Oracle Database 10*g*. The function returns a Boolean true when successful and false when unsuccessful. As of PHP 5.1.4, this function can only bind arrays of scalar Oracle data types, like VARCHAR2, NUMBER, DATE, et cetera. Oracle development plans to add support for arrays of PL/SQL record types in a future, and as yet unspecified, release. It has six parameters; four are mandatory, and two are optional. The first and second parameters are passed by value; one is a statement resource, and the second, a string name that maps to an Oracle *bind* variable in a statement parsed by the oci_parse() function. The third parameter is passed by reference, which means it can change during processing but *only when* the PL/SQL parameter is set to IN/OUT mode. The remaining arguments are passed by value. The fourth parameter is the number of items in the list, and it must be 0 or a positive number. The fifth parameter is the maximum size of the scalar values in the array. *This parameter must be the physical size of a target column when the column is defined in the data dictionary catalog, or one greater than the maximum possible field size for dynamically built columns.* You build dynamic columns by concatenating results into a single string. The sixth column is a designated data type from the following list of possible values:
	SQLT_AFC – CHAR data type.
	SQLT_AVC – CHARZ data type.
	SQLT_CHR – VARCHAR2 data type.
	SQLT_FLT – FLOAT data type.
	SQLT_INT – INTEGER data type.
	SQLT_LVC – LONG data type.
	SQLT_NUM – NUMBER data type.
	SQLT_ODT – DATE data type.
	SQLT_STR – STRING data type.
	SQLT_VCS – VARCHAR data type.
	The oci_bind_array_by_name() function has the following pattern:
	`bool oci_bind_array_by_name(`
	` resource statement`
	` ,string bind_variable_name`
	` ,array &numeric_reference_array`
	` ,int maximum_elements`
	` [,int maximum_field_length`
	` [,int mapped_type]])`

TABLE C-8   *OCI8 Library Binding Functions*

Function	Description

`oci_bind_by_name()`
ocibindbyname()
	The `oci_bind_by_name()` function binds a defined Oracle type to a PHP variable. The variable can be any scalar variable or scalar collection but cannot be used for an Oracle 10*g* associative array, also known as a PL/SQL table in previous releases. You must use the `oci_bind_array_by_name()` function when working with PL/SQL associative arrays. A scalar collection variable can have a VARRAY or *nested* TABLE data type; these types are covered in Chapter 7. The function returns a Boolean `true` when successful and `false` when unsuccessful. It has five parameters; three are mandatory, and two are optional. The first and second parameters are passed by value; one is a statement resource, and the second, a string name that maps to an Oracle *bind* variable in a statement parsed by the `oci_parse()` function. The third parameter is passed by reference, which means it can change during processing but *only when* the PL/SQL parameter is set to IN/OUT or OUT mode. The remaining arguments are passed by value. The fourth parameter is the number of items in the list, and it must be 0 or a positive number. The fifth parameter is the maximum size of the scalar values in the array. Setting the maximum field length to -1 tells the function to implicitly size the field at run time. The sixth column is a designated data type from the following list of possible values:
	SQLT_B_CURSOR – use for reference cursors, whether weakly or strongly typed.
	SQLT_BIN – use for RAW column data type.
	SQLT_BLOB – use for BLOB data type, that maps Binary Large objects.
	SQLT_CFILE – use for CFILE data type.
	SQLT_CHR – use for VARCHAR data types.
	SQLT_CLOB – use for CLOB data type, that maps Character Large objects.
	SQLT_FILE – use for BFILE data type.
	SQLT_INT – use for INTEGER and NUMBER data types.
	SQLT_LBI – use for LONG RAW data types.
	SQLT_LNG – use for LONG data types.
	SQLT_NTY – use for user-defined data types and user-defined scalar collections that are either VARRAY and *nested* TABLE types.
	SQLT_RDD – use for ROWID data type.
	You need to allocate abstract types by calling the `oci_new_descriptor()` before you bind them. Abstract types are LOB, ROWID, and BFILE data types. You also need to call the `oci_new_cursor()` function before you bind a reference cursor. The `oci_bind_by_name()` function has the following pattern:
	`bool oci_bind_by_name(`
	` resource statement`
	`,string bind_variable_name`
	`,array &numeric_reference_array`
	`[,int maximum_field_length`
	`[,int mapped_type]])`

TABLE C-8   *OCI8 Library Binding Functions* (continued)

The first GET_PRESIDENTS procedure is one of several overloaded procedures in the WORLD_LEADER package. Overloaded procedures reuse the same procedure name but have distinct formal parameter signatures. The following procedure uses PL/SQL index-by tables as data types in its signature:

```
PROCEDURE get_presidents
( term_start_in   IN     NUMBER
, term_end_in     IN     NUMBER
```

```
, country_in       IN     VARCHAR2
, president_ids    IN OUT PRESIDENT_ID_TABLE
, president_names  IN OUT PRESIDENT_NAME_TABLE
, tenures          IN OUT TENURE_TABLE
, parties          IN OUT PARTY_TABLE) AS

BEGIN

  -- Define a Bulk Collect into parallel associative arrays.
  SELECT    president_id pres_number
  ,         first_name||' '||middle_name||' '||last_name pres_name
  ,         term_start||'-'||term_end tenure
  ,         party
  BULK COLLECT
  INTO      president_ids
  ,         president_names
  ,         tenures
  ,         parties
  FROM      president
  WHERE     country = country_in
  AND       term_start BETWEEN term_start_in AND term_end_in
  OR        term_end BETWEEN term_start_in AND term_end_in;

END get_presidents;
```

This version of the GET_PRESIDENTS procedure uses four *pass-by-reference* scalar associative array types. The highlighted data types for the IN OUT mode variables are defined in the WORLD_LEADER specification as noted. They actually fit better as OUT mode–only variables, depending on what the procedure does.

The SELECT statement uses a BULK COLLECT operation. BULK COLLECT operations build implicit cursors and read all return values INTO the target variables: president_ids, president_names, tenures, and parties. The target variables are associative arrays that are densely populated and indexed by numbers starting at 1. When the SELECT statement returns null column values, they are added to the respective array and indexed. All arrays will have the same number of elements and indexes in one array identify the same row in another array. Using this approach, you create four parallel associative arrays. You can work these as compound structures by using the mirrored index values in a single iterative structure.

Parsing Differences Between SQL and PL/SQL Statements

The SQL statement string in the last example differs from the connecting example because there are actual line returns inside the string. This would fail in some languages like Java, unless you encapsulate the strings on each line and then concatenate the lines. While it is a lot of unnecessary work, you can implement that approach in your PHP code.

You *cannot* do the same thing when your statement calls a PL/SQL procedure or an anonymous-block PL/SQL program unit. This fails because the PL/SQL parser can't work with tabs and line returns in a statement string. There is also a better solution than enclosing a bunch of line-by-line strings in quotes and then concatenating them. You can use the following strip_special_characters() function to prepare your PL/SQL statements:

```
function strip_special_characters($str)
{
  $out = "";
  for ($i = 0;$i < strlen($str);$i++)
    if ((ord($str[$i]) != 9) && (ord($str[$i]) != 10) &&
        (ord($str[$i]) != 13))
      $out .= $str[$i];

  // Return character only strings.
  return $out;
}
```

This tidy function cleans up your code by making it more readable. You will find this helpful later in the appendix.

The following program uses the `strip_special_characters()` function to eliminate tabs, line returns, and carriage returns, as follows:

```
<?php
  // Return successful attempt to connect to the database.
  if ($c = @oci_connect("plsql","plsql","orcl"))
  {
    // Declare input variables.
    (isset($_GET['begin']))    ? $t_start = (int) $_GET['begin']
                               : $t_start = 1787;
    (isset($_GET['end']))      ? $t_end = (int) $_GET['end']
                               : $t_end = (int) date("Y",time());
    (isset($_GET['country']))  ? $country = $_GET['country']
                               : $country = "USA";

    // Declare a PL/SQL execution command.
    $stmt = "BEGIN
               world_leaders.get_presidents(:term_start
                                           ,:term_end
                                           ,:country
                                           ,:p_id
                                           ,:p_name
                                           ,:p_tenure
                                           ,:p_party);
             END;";

    // Strip special characters to avoid ORA-06550 and PLS-00103 errors.
    $stmt = strip_special_characters($stmt);

    // Parse a query through the connection.
    $s = oci_parse($c,$stmt);

    $r_president_id = "";
    $r_president_name = "";
    $r_tenure = "";
    $r_party = "";
```

```php
// Bind PHP variables to the OCI input or in mode variables.
oci_bind_by_name($s,':term_start',$t_start);
oci_bind_by_name($s,':term_end',$t_end);
oci_bind_by_name($s,':country',$country);

// Bind PHP variables to the OCI output or in/out mode variable.
oci_bind_array_by_name($s,':p_id',$r_president_id,100,38,SQLT_INT);
oci_bind_array_by_name($s,':p_name',$r_president_name,100,10,SQLT_STR);
oci_bind_array_by_name($s,':p_tenure',$r_tenure,100,10,SQLT_STR);
oci_bind_array_by_name($s,':p_party',$r_party,100,24,SQLT_STR);

// Execute the PL/SQL statement.
if (oci_execute($s))
{
  // Declare variable and open HTML table.
  $out = '<table border="1" cellpadding="3" cellspacing="0">';
  $out .= '<tr>';
  $out .= '<td class="e">#</td>';
  $out .= '<td class="e">President Name</td>';
  $out .= '<td class="e">Tenure</td>';
  $out .= '<td class="e">Party</td>';
  $out .= '</tr>';

  // Read parallel collections.
  for ($i = 0;$i < count($r_president_id);$i++)
  {
    $out .= '<tr>';
    $out .= '<td class="v">'.$r_president_id[$i].'</td>';
    $out .= '<td class="v">'.$r_president_name[$i].'</td>';
    $out .= '<td class="v">'.$r_tenure[$i].'</td>';
    $out .= '<td class="v">'.$r_party[$i].'</td>';
    $out .= '</tr>';
  }

  // Close HTML table.
  $out .= '</table>';
}

// Render table.
print $out;

// Disconnect from database.
oci_close($c);
}
else
{
  // Assign the OCI error and format double and single quotes.
  $errorMessage = oci_error();
  print htmlentities($errorMessage['message'])."<br />";
}

// Strip special characters, like carriage returns or line feeds and tabs.
```

```
function strip_special_characters($str)
{
  $out = "";
  for ($i = 0;$i < strlen($str);$i++)
    if ((ord($str[$i]) != 9) && (ord($str[$i]) != 10) &&
         (ord($str[$i]) != 13))
       $out .= $str[$i];
  return $out;
}
?>
```

This program demonstrates how to size a maximum return number for the PL/SQL index-by tables. It uses only one of the index-by tables to govern the exit condition of the loop structure. This can be done because all parallel index-by tables are assumed to have the same number of rows.

TIP
Errors can happen when the parallel scalar arrays return unbalanced value sets.

OCI8 Collections

SQL collections—VARRAY and *nested* tables—present another data type that you can use like PL/SQL index-by tables. They differ from index-by tables in that they are user-defined SQL data types. You must define them in a database schema, like the following for a VARRAY:

```
CREATE OR REPLACE TYPE president_name_varray
  AS VARRAY(100) OF VARCHAR2(60 CHAR);
/
```

A nested table has a similar creation process:

```
CREATE OR REPLACE TYPE president_name_ntable
  AS TABLE OF VARCHAR2(60 CHAR);
/
```

You should note *nested* tables exclude the *index-by* clause from PL/SQL index-by table definitions. Once these are defined in your schema, you use the oci_new_collection() and oci_bind_by_name() functions sequentially to define them in your PHP programs. Table C-9 contains three functions that define Oracle-specific compound data types. These functions define scalar collections, system reference cursors, and LOB descriptors. LOB descriptors support large objects stored in and out of the Oracle database.

You must define a collection in the database before you define an OCI-Collection object instance in your program. The oci_new_collection() object constructor builds an OCI-Collection instance. Defining the local OCI-Collection object is an extra step beyond working with a PL/SQL index-by table.

The following defines an OCI-Collection variable for a *nested* table:

```
$president_copy = oci_new_collection($c,'PRESIDENT_NAME_NTABLE');
```

Function	Description

`oci_new_collection()`
ocinewcollection()
	The `oci_new_collection()` function creates a PHP `OCI-Collection` object that maps to an Oracle Collection variable. It returns an `OCI-Collection` on success and `false` otherwise. At writing, these types are limited to collections of scalar variables. *Oracle may extend the collection behavior to structures and instantiated PL/SQL objects but* **has made no commitment as to when they will introduce that behavior.** The function has three parameters; two are mandatory, and one is optional. The first parameter is a resource connection, and the second is the data type name from the user/schema used to build the connection. The optional third parameter lets you specify another owning schema for the collection data type. The function has the following pattern:
	`OCI-Collection oci_new_collection(`
	  `resource connection`
	  `,string collection_type_name`
	  `[,string schema])`

`oci_new_cursor()`
ocinewcursor()
	The `oci_new_cursor()` function creates a system cursor resource when successful and returns `false` otherwise. The function has one parameter, a resource connection. The function has the following pattern:
	`resource oci_new_cursor(`
	  `resource connection)`

`oci_new_descriptor()`
ocinewdescriptor()
	The `oci_new_descriptor()` function creates a PHP `OCI-Lob` object that maps to an Oracle `LOB` variable. It returns an `OCI-Lob` on success and `false` otherwise. Table 14-1 covers the Oracle `OCI-Lob` library. The function has two parameters; one is mandatory, and one is optional. The first parameter is a resource connection and the second is the `LOB` type. `LOB` data types are treated as abstract types along with Oracle `ROWID` and `FILE` types. The following are the possible types:
	`OCI_D_FILE` – sets the descriptor to manage binary or character files, respectively `BFILE` and `CFILE` data types.
	`OCI_D_LOB` – sets the descriptor to manage binary or character large objects, respectively `BLOB` and `CLOB` data types.
	`OCI_D_ROWID` – sets the descriptor to manage Oracle `ROWID` values, which map the physical storage to file system blocks.
	The function has the following pattern:
	`OCI-Lob oci_new_descriptor(`
	  `resource connection`
	  `,int lob_type)`

TABLE C-9   *OCI8 Library SQL Object Type Creation Functions*

After you parse the statement and define the `OCI-Collection` variable, you bind local variables to parsed statements. Parsed statements can be SQL or PL/SQL statements. Bind variables can be sent as `IN` mode–only, sent and received as `IN OUT` mode, or received as `OUT` mode–only variables in PL/SQL stored procedures. You use the `oci_bind_by_name()` function because `OCI-Collections` are SQL data types, as shown:

```
oci_bind_by_name($s,':r_president_name',$r_president_name,-1,SQLT_NTY);
```

You then use the `OCI-Collection` methods to process elements in the collection. You can find the number of elements using the `size()` method, or read a specific element by using the `getElem()` method, like

```
for ($i = 0;$i < $r_president_id->size();$i++)
{
  $out .= '<tr>';
  $out .= '<td class="v">'.$r_president_id->getelem($i).'</td>';
  $out .= '<td class="v">'.$r_president_name->getElem($i).'</td>';
  $out .= '<td class="v">'.$r_tenure->getElem($i).'</td>';
  $out .= '<td class="v">'.$r_party->getElem($i).'</td>';
  $out .= '</tr>';
}
```

The same techniques for *nested* tables apply to VARRAYs. The differences between PL/SQL *index-by* tables are: (a) you must define SQL data types before attempting to bind them; (b) you use the `oci_bind_by_name()` function, not `oci_bind_array_by_name()`. More on object access methods are in the subsection "Defining and Using Objects" earlier in the appendix.

OCI8 System Reference Cursors

PL/SQL benefits from a lookalike data type that mirrors result sets from SELECT statements. Oracle developed the system reference cursor data type to meet this need. They can move result sets from one program to another. System reference cursors act as pointers to a result set in a query work area. You use them when you want to query data in one program and process it in another, especially when the two programs are in different programming languages. You also have the option of implementing a reference cursor two ways; one is *strongly typed* and the other *weakly typed* reference cursors.

You explicitly define a *strongly typed* reference cursor by assigning a %ROWTYPE attribute to the cursor. The %ROWTYPE attribute maps the structure from a catalog table or view in the database to a variable. The variable then has the reference cursor as a data type. A reference cursor is also known as a compound data type. You use *strongly typed* reference cursors when you need to control the structure of *input* parameters to stored procedures or functions. You define a *strongly typed* reference cursor inside a PL/SQL package specification by using the following syntax:

```
TYPE president_type_cursor IS REF CURSOR RETURN president%ROWTYPE;
```

You build *weakly typed* reference cursors dynamically at run time. They are more flexible generally and can be reused by multiple structures. You can also define *weakly typed* reference cursors in PL/SQL package specifications. They are useful as function return types when you require polymorphic return types. The following is the definition used in the WORLD_LEADERS package:

```
TYPE president_type_cursor IS REF CURSOR;
```

The preceding is a *weakly typed* reference cursor. You use *weakly typed* reference cursors when you (a) require more flexibility with result sets, (b) return a result set that differs from any catalog object, or (c) require polymorphic behaviors. Reusability of *weakly typed* reference cursors is also a common coding practice.

The following GET_PRESIDENTS procedure uses three scalar input variables and returns one reference cursor as an output variable:

```
PROCEDURE get_presidents
( term_start_in    IN       NUMBER
, term_end_in      IN       NUMBER
, country_in       IN       VARCHAR2
, presidents                OUT PRESIDENT_TYPE_CURSOR ) AS
BEGIN
  -- Collect data for the reference cursor.  OPEN presidents FOR
    SELECT    president_id "#"
    ,         first_name||' '||middle_name||' '||last_name "Preisdent"
    ,         term_start||' '||term_end "Tenure"
    ,         party "Party"
    FROM      president
    WHERE     country = country_in
    AND       term_start BETWEEN term_start_in AND term_end_in
    OR        term_end BETWEEN term_start_in AND term_end_in;
END get_presidents;
```

You use the suffix to distinguish the formal parameter names from valid column names in the SELECT statement. Substitution variables in SELECT statements must differ from valid column names; otherwise, the SQL parser will ignore all substitution variable names that match valid column names, using the column name values instead.

The PRESIDENTS variable is a weakly typed reference cursor defined in the WORLD_LEADERS package specification. This means the reference cursor structure is set at run time. You use the OPEN reference_cursor_name FOR syntax followed by a SELECT statement to open a reference cursor. This explicitly opens a SQL cursor and assigns the query work area pointer to the run-time instance of the GET_PRESIDENTS procedure, which is then returned to the calling program.

TIP
Oracle reference cursors must be explicitly called and cannot be referenced in implicit cursor management tools, like a PL/SQL FOR loop.

NOTE
All rows are selected and placed in a query work area in the SGA when you explicitly open a cursor. The pointer to that query work area is a reference cursor, which is returned to the calling program, as done in the ReferenceCursor.php script.

The following program takes three URL parameters, begin, end, and country. You limit the number of rows returned by providing values to the starting and ending term parameters—begin and end respectively. Absent those parameters, the program returns all former and current presidents of the U.S.A., as found in the code:

-- This is found in ReferenceCursor.php on the publisher's web site.

```php
<?php
  // Return successful attempt to connect to the database.
  if ($c = @oci_connect("php","php","xe"))
  {
    // Declare input variables.
```

```
(isset($_GET['begin']))    ? $t_start = (int) $_GET['begin']
                           : $t_start = 1787;
(isset($_GET['end']))      ? $t_end = (int) $_GET['end']
                           : $t_end = (int) date("Y",time());
(isset($_GET['country']))  ? $country = $_GET['country']
                           : $country = "USA";

// Declare a PL/SQL execution command.
$stmt = "BEGIN
           world_leaders.get_presidents(:term_start
                                       ,:term_end
                                       ,:country
                                       ,:return_cursor);
         END;";

// Strip special characters to avoid ORA-06550 and PLS-00103 errors.
$stmt = strip_special_characters($stmt);

// Parse a query through the connection.
$s = oci_parse($c,$stmt);

// Declare a return cursor for the connection.
$rc = oci_new_cursor($c);

// Bind PHP variables to the OCI input or in mode variables.
oci_bind_by_name($s,':term_start',$t_start);
oci_bind_by_name($s,':term_end',$t_end);
oci_bind_by_name($s,':c',$country);

// Bind PHP variables to the OCI output or in/out mode variable.
oci_bind_by_name($s,':return_cursor',$rc,-1,OCI_B_CURSOR);

// Execute the PL/SQL statement.
oci_execute($s);

// Access the returned cursor.
oci_execute($rc);

// Print the table header with known labels.
print '<table border="1" cellpadding="3" cellspacing="0">';

// Set dynamic labels control variable true.
$label = true;

// Read the contents of the reference cursor.
while($row = oci_fetch_assoc($rc))
{
  // Declare header and data variables.
  $header = "";
  $data = "";
```

```
      // Read the reference cursor into a table.
      foreach ($row as $name => $column)
      {
        // Capture labels for the first row.
        if ($label)
        {
          $header .= '<td class="e">'.$name.'</td>';
          $data .= '<td class="v">'.$column.'</td>';
        }
        else
          $data .= '<td class=v>'.$column.'</td>';
      }

      // Print the header row once.
      if ($label)
      {
        print '<tr>'.$header.'</tr>';
        $label = !$label;
      }

      // Print the data rows.
      print '<tr>'.$data.'</tr>';
    }

    // Print the HTML table close.
    print '</table>';

    // Disconnect from database.
    oci_close($c);
  }
  else
  {
    // Assign the OCI error and format double and single quotes.
    $errorMessage = oci_error();
    print htmlentities($errorMessage['message'])."<br />";
  }

// Strip special characters, like carriage returns or line feeds and tabs.
function strip_special_characters($str)
{
  $out = "";
  for ($i = 0;$i < strlen($str);$i++)
    if ((ord($str[$i]) != 9) && (ord($str[$i]) != 10) &&
        (ord($str[$i]) != 13))
      $out .= $str[$i];
  return $out;
}
?>
```

   This program uses oci_new_cursor() function to build a local reference cursor, against which you bind a *pass-by-reference* variable using the oci_bind_by_name() function. You also use the `oci_bind_by_name()` function to bind three input variables as pass-by-value variables. The optional fourth and fifth parameters in the `oci_bind_by_name()` function are unnecessary when passing the string and numeric literal values. These optional parameters are implicitly managed as `VARCHAR2` data types. Oracle SQL implicitly downcasts a `VARCHAR2` containing a number to a `NUMBER` data type because there is no loss of precision.

Reference cursors require the fifth parameter in the `oci_bind_by_name()` function to designate the proper Oracle data type, so you must also provide the fourth parameter too. Using a `-1` for the maximum-length fourth parameter is the simplest way to ensure that changes in the cursor do not require that you modify the *max_field_length* parameter for each call to the `oci_bind_by_name()` function. The fifth parameter should be `OCI_B_CURSOR`, which represents a system reference cursor.

OCI Large Objects

`LOB` and `BFILE` data types are highly specialized types in the Oracle database. Oracle uses the `DBMS_LOB` stored package to read from and write to `LOB` data types when working inside a session and transaction scope. The constants, functions, and procedures of the `DBMS_LOB` package service requests from the OCI-Lob object provided in the OCI8 function library.

Table C-10 covers the `oci_new_descriptor()` function. This function lets you create a link between an open large object and your PHP program code.

The contents of LOB columns are not stored in-line with other column values of a table. They are stored out-of-line. Only a pointer is stored in the column value with other scalar data types.

Function	Description
`oci_new_descriptor()`	The `oci_new_descriptor()` function creates a local PHP `OCI-Lob` object that maps to an Oracle `LOB` variable. It returns an `OCI-Lob` type variable on success and `false` when encountering an error. The function has two parameters; one is mandatory, and the other is optional. The first parameter is a resource connection, and the second is an Oracle data resource type, which is conveniently `OCI_D_LOB` by default. (Note: `LOB` data types are treated as abstract types along with Oracle `ROWID` and `FILE` types.) The function supports following resource types: `OCI_D_FILE` – sets the descriptor to manage binary or character files, respectively `BFILE` and `CFILE` data types. `OCI_D_LOB` – sets the descriptor to manage binary or character large objects, respectively `BLOB` and `CLOB` data types. `OCI_D_ROWID` – sets the descriptor to manage Oracle `ROWID` values, which map the physical storage to file system blocks. The function has the following pattern: `OCI-Lob oci_new_descriptor(` `resource connection` `[, int type])`

TABLE C-10   *OCI8 Library Large Object Descriptor Function*

The pointer is known as a descriptor because it describes the internal location of a LOB column. Some distinguish between descriptors when they apply to internally versus externally stored data—calling them respectively *descriptors* and *locators.* They use *locator* for externally stored files because the DBMS_LOB.GETFILENAME procedure returns a filename.

There are also limitations governing how you use *descriptors* and *locators* in SQL queries and transactions compared to anonymous- and named-block PL/SQL programs. The differences have to do with how they maintain references to *descriptors* or *locators* in the scope defined by the DBMS_LOB package. The DBMS_LOB package defines scope by imposing a single transaction rule, which limits both *descriptors* and *locators* to a scope that begins and ends in a single transaction.

You start a transaction against the database with an INSERT, UPDATE, or DELETE statement, or by using a SELECT statement with a FOR UPDATE or RETURNING *column_value* INTO *variable_name* clause. You end a transaction by using the COMMIT statement to make permanent any change to the data. The oci_execute() function starts and ends a transaction by default when executing a statement, which acts as an autonomous transaction. Autonomous transactions open and close a *descriptor* or *locator* reference before you can use the reference. Avoiding the default implicit COMMIT statement lets you use the oci_execute() function to interact sequentially with the database.

Oracle LOB data types are accessible through the OCI-Lob object. You must do three things to access and/or manipulate the contents of a LOB. They are: (a) you define a local descriptor variable by using the oci_new_descriptor() function; (b) you map the *descriptor* variable to a bind variable; and (c) you bind the local variable to the SQL or PL/SQL statement's *bind* variable. Then, you can use the local *descriptor* or *locator* variable name as the instance of the OCI-Lob object and use its supplied methods.

Chapter 8 covers the process for handling Oracle LOBs. The following QueryLob.php program demonstrates the easiest way to access a CLOB *descriptor,* by using the oci_fetch() function:

```php
<?php
  // Return successful attempt to connect to the database.
  if ($c = @oci_connect("php","php","xe"))
  {
    // Declare input variables.
    (isset($_GET['id'])) ? $id = (int) $_GET['id'] : $id = 1;
    (isset($_GET['name'])) ? $name = $_GET['name'] : $name = "Washington";

    // Declare a SQL SELECT statement returning a CLOB.
    $stmt = "SELECT    biography
             FROM      president
             WHERE     president_id = :id";

    // Parse a query through the connection.
    $s = oci_parse($c,$stmt);

    // Bind PHP to OCI variable(s).
    oci_bind_by_name($s,':id',$id);

    // Execute the PL/SQL statement.
    if (oci_execute($s))
    {
```

```php
      // Return a LOB descriptor, and access it with OCI methods.
      while (oci_fetch($s))
      {
        for ($i = 1;$i <= oci_num_fields($s);$i++)
          if (is_object(oci_result($s,$i)))
          {
            if ($size = oci_result($s,$i)->size())

              $data = oci_result($s,$i)->read($size);

            else

              $data = " ";
          }
          else
          {
            if (oci_field_is_null($s,$i))
              $data = " ";
            else
              $data = oci_result($s,$i);
          }
      } // End of the while(oci_fetch($s)) loop.

      // Format HTML table to display biography.
      $out = '<table border="1" cellpadding="3" cellspacing="0">';
      $out .= '<tr>';
      $out .= '<td align="center" class="e">Biography of '.$name.'</td>';
      $out .= '</tr>';
      $out .= '<tr>';
      $out .= '<td class="v">'.$data.'</td>';
      $out .= '</tr>';
      $out .= '</table>';
    }

    // Print the HTML table.
    print $out;

    // Disconnect from database.
    oci_close($c);
  }
  else
  {
    // Assign the OCI error and format double and single quotes.
    $errorMessage = oci_error();
    print htmlentities($errorMessage['message'])."<br />";
  }
?>
```

Using the `oci_fetch()` function in a WHILE loop is clearly the most consistent and easiest approach for queries returning scalar and LOB column types from SQL statements and reference cursors. The algorithm provided loops through rows and then the columns while checking for objects and null values that require special handling. The logic shown in the program manages all possibilities because CLOB variables can be *null, empty,* and *populated* CLOB column values.

TIP
Don't attempt to skip the two-step process of sizing and reading by using the single-step OCI-Lob->load() *method, because you can run out of memory with truly large objects.*

You can run this program by using the following URL when you have inserted data into the CLOB BIOGRAPHY column:

```
http://hostname.domain/QueryLob.php?id=1&name=Washington
```

A similar approach works with BLOB, NBLOB, and NCLOB data types. You would also store a MIME content-type in another column when BLOBs contain images, portable document format, or other file types. The MIME content-type would enable your web application to know how the web page should render the content.

You can use the following HTML form to upload a file containing the biography of George Washington to the PRESIDENT table in the PHP schema:

```
<form id="uploadForm"
      action=http://hostname.domain/UploadBioSQL.php
      enctype="multipart/form-data"
      method="post">
  <table border=0 cellpadding=0 cellspacing=0>
    <tr>
      <td width=125>President Number</td>
      <td><input id="id" name="id" type="text"></td>
    </tr>
    <tr>
      <td width=125>President Name</td>
      <td><input id="name" name="name" type="text"></td>
    </tr>
    <tr>
      <td width=125>Select File</td>
      <td><input id="uploadfilename" name="userfile" type="file"></td>
    </tr>
    <tr>
      <td width=125>Click Button to</td>
      <td><input type="submit" value="Upload File"></td>
    </tr>
  </table>
</form>
```

NOTE
You need to enter your hostname and domain into the action attribute of the HTML FORM tag for this to work in your environment.

You should enter data as shown in Figure C-3 when you're uploading George Washington's biography. The president's name is only used as part of the biography display, and you can enter the full name if you prefer.

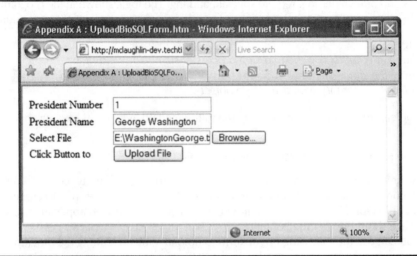

FIGURE C-3   *Upload Biography web page*

The form calls the `UploadBioSQL.php` script. This script converts the uploaded file into a string, updates the CLOB BIOGRAPHY column with the string, and then queries the CLOB column:

```
-- This is found in UploadBioSQL.php on the publisher's web site.

<?php
  // Displayed moved file in web page.
  $biography = process_uploaded_file();

  // Return successful attempt to connect to the database.
  if ($c = @oci_connect("php","php","xe"))
  {
    // Declare input variables.
    (isset($_POST['id'])) ? $id = (int) $_POST['id'] : $id = 1;
    (isset($_POST['name'])) ? $name = $_POST['name'] : $name = "Washington";

    // Declare a PL/SQL execution command.
    $stmt = "UPDATE    president
             SET       biography = empty_clob()
             WHERE     president_id = :id
             RETURNING biography
             INTO      :descriptor";

    // Strip special characters to avoid ORA-06550 and PLS-00103 errors.
    $stmt = strip_special_characters($stmt);

    // Parse a query through the connection.
    $s = oci_parse($c,$stmt);

    // Define a descriptor for a CLOB.
    $rlob = oci_new_descriptor($c,OCI_D_LOB);
```

```php
  // Define a variable name to map to CLOB descriptor.
  oci_define_by_name($s,':descriptor',$rlob,SQLT_CLOB);

  // Bind PHP variables to the OCI types.
  oci_bind_by_name($s,':id',$id);
  oci_bind_by_name($s,':descriptor',$rlob,-1,SQLT_CLOB);

  // Execute the PL/SQL statement.
  if (oci_execute($s,OCI_DEFAULT))
  {
     $rlob->save($biography);
     oci_commit($c);
     query_insert($id,$name);
  }

  // Disconnect from database.
  oci_close($c);
}
else
{
  // Assign the OCI error and format double and single quotes.
  $errorMessage = oci_error();
  print htmlentities($errorMessage['message'])."<br />";
}

// Query the updated record.
function query_insert($id,$name)
{
  // Return successful attempt to connect to the database.
  if ($c = @oci_new_connect("php","php","xe"))
  {
    // Declare a SQL SELECT statement returning a CLOB.
    $stmt = "SELECT    biography
             FROM      president
             WHERE     president_id = :id";

    // Parse a query through the connection.
    $s = oci_parse($c,$stmt);

    // Bind PHP variables to the OCI types.
    oci_bind_by_name($s,':id',$id);

    // Execute the PL/SQL statement.
    if (oci_execute($s))
    {
      // Return a LOB descriptor as the value.
      while (oci_fetch($s))
      {
        for ($i = 1;$i <= oci_num_fields($s);$i++)
          if (is_object(oci_result($s,$i)))
          {
            if ($size = oci_result($s,$i)->size())
```

```
                    $data = oci_result($s,$i)->read($size);
                  else
                    $data = " ";
              }
              else
              {
                if (oci_field_is_null($s,$i))
                  $data = " ";
                else
                  $data = oci_result($s,$i);
              }
        } // End of the while(oci_fetch($s)) loop.

        // Format HTML table to display biography.
        $out = '<table border="1" cellpadding="3" cellspacing="0">';
        $out .= '<tr>';
        $out .= '<td align="center" class="e">Biography of '.$name.'</td>';
        $out .= '</tr>';
        $out .= '<tr>';
        $out .= '<td class="v">'.$data.'</td>';
        $out .= '</tr>';
        $out .= '</table>';
      }

      // Print the HTML table.
      print $out;

      // Disconnect from database.
      oci_close($c);
    }
    else
    {
      // Assign the OCI error and format double and single quotes.
      $errorMessage = oci_error();
      print htmlentities($errorMessage['message'])."<br />";
    }
}

// Manage file upload and return file as string.
function process_uploaded_file()
{
  // Declare a variable for file contents.
  $contents = "";

  // Define the upload file name for Windows or Linux.
  if (ereg("Win32",$_SERVER["SERVER_SOFTWARE"]))
    $upload_file = getcwd()."\\temp\\".$_FILES['userfile']['name'];
  else
    $upload_file = getcwd()."/temp/".$_FILES['userfile']['name'];

  // Check for and move uploaded file.
```

```php
    if (is_uploaded_file($_FILES['userfile']['tmp_name']))
      move_uploaded_file($_FILES['userfile']['tmp_name'],$upload_file);

    // Open a file handle and suppress an error for a missing file.
    if ($fp = @fopen($upload_file,"r"))
    {
      // Read until the end-of-file marker.
      while (!feof($fp))
        $contents .= fgetc($fp);

      // Close an open file handle.
      fclose($fp);
    }

    // Return file content as string.
    return $contents;
  }

  // Strip special characters, like carriage returns or line feeds and tabs.
  function strip_special_characters($str)
  {
    $out = "";
    for ($i = 0;$i < strlen($str);$i++)
      if ((ord($str[$i]) != 9) && (ord($str[$i]) != 10) &&
          (ord($str[$i]) != 13))
        $out .= $str[$i];

    // Return pre-parsed SQL statement.
    return $out;
  }
?>
```

The `$rlob->save($biography)` call updates to the BIOGRAPHY column with the uploaded biography from an excerpt from the www.whitehouse.gov/history/presidents/ web site. Then, it closes the transaction context opened by the UPDATE statement by calling the `oci_commit()` function. After closing the transaction state, the program calls the local `query_insert()` function to display the uploaded biography. The `UploadBioSQL.php` script displays the newly upgraded biography as shown in Figure C-4.

This subsection has demonstrated how to insert and update LOBs stored in the database using SQL. You can also write PL/SQL stored procedures to read and write LOBs.

OCI8 Library Externally Stored BFILE Type

Unlike CLOB data types that can be null, empty, or populated, BFILE columns are either null or not null. They are also stored externally from the database.

The steps to configure your environment require you to (a) create an Oracle DIRECTORY reference, (b) create an Apache virtual alias and directory, (c) update a column with a BFILE locator, and (d) copy the physical file into the mapped directory. Chapter 8 has the specifics of these configuration steps. After completing these steps, you can confirm the setup with a single query using the DBMS_LOB.GETLENGTH function.

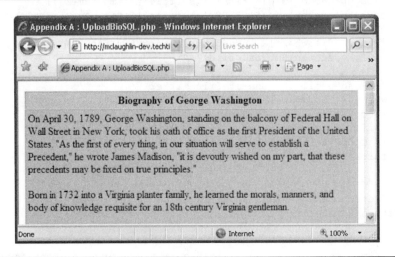

FIGURE C-4   *Uploaded Biography web page*

Configuring the Oracle and Apache Environment

You need to define a `DIRECTORY` reference in the database that points to a physical directory where you will store the binary files. You create a customized directory for these examples by creating a `DIRECTORY` reference named `MY_DIRECTORY`, as shown:

Linux or Unix

```
CREATE DIRECTORY my_directory AS
'/var/www/html/photo';
```

Windows

```
CREATE DIRECTORY my_directory AS
'C:\Program Files\Apache Group\Apache2\htdocs\photo';
```

Next, you grant `READ` privilege to your PHP schema as the `SYSTEM` user. The following command grants the `READ` privilege on a directory to the PHP user/schema:

```
GRANT READ ON DIRECTORY my_directory TO php;
```

After you modify the database, you need to configure an alias and directory in your `httpd.conf` file, as follows for your respective platform:

Linux or Unix

```
Alias /mydirectory/ "/var/www/html/photo/"

<Directory "/var/www/html/photo">
    Options None
    AllowOverride None
    Order allow,deny
```

```
      Allow from all
</Directory>
```

Windows

```
Alias /mydirectory/ "C:/Program Files/Apache Group/Apache2/htdocs/photo/"

<Directory "C:/Program Files/Apache Group/Apache2/htdocs/photo">
    Options None
    AllowOverride None
    Order allow,deny
    Allow from all
</Directory>
```

The Apache HTTP server needs to be stopped and started after you change the directives of the `httpd.conf` file. You restart Apache HTTP server using the `apachectl` utility in Linux or Unix and the Apache service in Microsoft Windows.

Querying a `BFILE` name requires calling the `FILEGETNAME` procedure of the `DBMS_LOB` package, and mapping the directory alias to a filename. This can lead some to say that you can't use SQL to navigate the `BFILE` locator. There are actually several alternative approaches to supplementing the default Oracle database environment. The easiest way is to write a wrapper function over the `DBMS_LOB.FILEGETNAME` procedure.

The `GET_BFILENAME` function in Chapter 8 creates an effective wrapper to the `DBMS_LOB.FILEGETNAME` procedure. You can use a simple query when the `GET_BFILENAME()` wrapper translates the *locator* to a filename, as shown in the following code:

-- This is found in **QueryPhotoSQL.php** on the publisher's web site.

```php
<?php
  // Return successful attempt to connect to the database.
  if ($c = @oci_connect("php","php","xe"))
  {
    // Declare input variables.
    (isset($_GET['id'])) ? $id = (int) $_GET['id'] : $id = 1;
    (isset($_GET['name'])) ? $name = $_GET['name'] : $name = "Washington";

    // Declare a PL/SQL execution command.
    $stmt = "SELECT    GET_BFILENAME(president_id) AS file_name
             FROM      president
             WHERE     president_id = :id";

    // Parse a query through the connection.
    $s = oci_parse($c,$stmt);

    // Bind PHP variables to the OCI types.
    oci_bind_by_name($s,':id',$id,-1,SQLT_INT);

    // Execute the PL/SQL statement.
    if (oci_execute($s))
    {
      // Return a LOB descriptor as the value.
```

```
      while (oci_fetch($s))
      {
        for ($i = 1;$i <= oci_num_fields($s);$i++)
          $file_name = oci_result($s,$i);
      } // End of the while(oci_fetch($s)) loop.

      // Format HTML table to display photograph.
      $out = '<table border="1" cellpadding="3" cellspacing="0">';
      $out .= '<tr>';
      $out .= '<td align="center" class="e">Photo of '.$name.'</td>';
      $out .= '</tr>';
      $out .= '<tr>';
      $out .= '<td align="center" class="v" valign="center">';
      if (!is_null($file_name))
        $out .= '<img src="/mydirectory/'.$file_name.'">';
      else
        $out .= 'No available photo';
      $out .= '</td>';
      $out .= '</tr>';
      $out .= '</table>';
    }

    // Print the HTML table.
    print $out;

    // Disconnect from database.
    oci_close($c);
  }
  else
  {
    // Assign the OCI error and format double and single quotes.
    $errorMessage = oci_error();
    print htmlentities($errorMessage['message'])."<br />";
  }
?>
```

The SQL SELECT statement calls the GET_BFILENAME function and returns the filename to a SQL statement. The DIRECTORY reference for the image is managed in the program as a relative reference to the script's current directory.

This section has demonstrated how to query a BFILE object using a SQL SELECT statement. Chapter 8 demonstrates how you write a wrapper function to this Oracle built-in procedure. The wrapper function overcomes how the DBMS_LOB.GETFILENAME procedure receives and returns actual parameters.

Summary

This primer has discussed the advantages you'll find when developing web applications using the PHP programming language and Oracle Database 11*g*. It has also demonstrated how you use the PHP programming language; and how you work with Oracle advanced data types. It covered how you use the OCI8 library to work with collections, system reference cursors, LOBs, and external binary files. More complete coverage is found in the *Oracle Database 10g Express Edition PHP Web Programming* book.

APPENDIX
D

Oracle Database
Java Primer

his appendix offers a basic primer on Java, covering how you use the Java Database Connectivity (JDBC) model to access an Oracle database. It provides PL/SQL developers supporting references to work through examples in Chapters 8, 13, and 15. This appendix covers the following:

- Java and JDBC architecture

- Configuring the Java and Oracle environment

- Java programming language primer

- Testing a client-side or thin-driver JDBC connection

- Accessing scalar variables

- Writing and accessing large objects

Java and JDBC Architecture

Java is an object-oriented (OO) programming language that is portable across platforms. This means you can write one program and then run it on Linux, Unix, or Microsoft Windows operating systems. Java accomplishes this by compiling the programs into Java byte code. Byte code, also known as byte streams, runs inside virtual machines that are known as Java Virtual Machines (JVMs).

Virtual machines create self-contained environments. JVM environments are interfaces between Java byte code and operating system services. JVMs run on all major operating systems. JVMs are written in the C/C++ programming language and compiled individually for each platform. Java programs run inside the JVM with all the rights and privileges granted to the JVM by the operating system. The `java.policy` and `java.security` files set permissions for how all Java programs run inside a JVM.

Java provides networking libraries that let you pass messages between different JVMs. Messages communicate between JVMs through sockets. A socket is built between two ephemeral ports—one where it sends the message and another where it listens for incoming messages. Java communicates with databases by using the JDBC libraries. Java also lets you build Java Servlets, known as JServlets. JServlets let you handle URL requests, as for an Apache HTTP Server. Commercial Oracle databases also allow you to write and deploy Java programs in the database. You write PL/SQL programs as interfaces to these internally stored libraries. The interfaces are known as PL/SQL wrappers.

Similar permissions to those found in the `java.policy` and `java.security` files for external programs are also found in the Oracle database. These policy files enable or restrict how Java programs work inside the Oracle database. You configure these policy files by using the functions and procedures found in the `DBMS_JAVA` package. Changes to these configuration files require you to connect using the `SYSDBA` role.

Oracle provides three JDBC drivers: the client-side or thin driver, the Oracle Call Interface (OCI8) or thick driver, and the server-side internal driver. The drivers have specific roles that govern how Java works with the database. The OCI and server-side internal drivers support Java stored inside the database. The OCI can also support external programs resident on a server with an Oracle server or client installation. The client-side or thin driver acts independent of a local Oracle database or client installation. The thin driver lets you connect remotely to the Oracle instance through the Oracle listener. The listener transfers the incoming request to the database and opens a connection to it.

Configuring and verifying your ability to use Java programs is critical to deploying the technology. You cannot connect without setting appropriate `PATH` and `CLASSPATH` environment variables. The next section discusses how to configure and test your Java installation by connecting to the Oracle database instance.

Configuring the Oracle Java Environment

The Oracle database ships with the necessary libraries to create and run Java programs. Oracle Database 11*g* ships with the Oracle JDBC libraries for Java 1.4, 5, and 6. You should note Sun changed the version naming convention with Java 1.5, making it Java 5, and so forth.

You need to set your `PATH` and `CLASSPATH` variables to work with the Java programming language. You can configure Java many ways because there are many ways to deploy your Java SDK. While you can install a separate Java SDK for external Java programs, you'll need to use the Java SDK shipped with the Oracle database for locally stored programs. The following assumes you're using the Java 6 SDK from the Oracle database, and provides syntax for the Microsoft Windows and Unix platforms, like Linux.

Windows

```
C:> set PATH=%PATH%;C:%ORACLE_HOME%\jdk\bin
C:> set CLASSPATH=%CLASSPATH%;C:%ORACLE_HOME%\jdbc\lib\ojdbc6.jar
```

Unix

```
# export PATH=$PATH:/<mount>/$ORACLE_HOME/jdk/bin
# export CLASSPATH=$CLASSPATH:/<mount>/$ORACLE_HOME/jdbc/lib/ojdbc6.jar
```

You should now be able to test basic Java programs. Source files are native Java files before compilation. They are written as plain text files and adhere to the syntax rules of the Java programming language. Class files are compiled Java source files, and they are stored in Java byte code or compressed formats such as Java archive (JAR) files.

You can find a nice Java tutorial at http://java.sun.com/docs/books/tutorial/index.html. This appendix is a short version to get you up and running with Java programs. There are two executables that you'll need to compile and run Java programs:

- **javac**   Compiles your text file Java programs into Java byte code

- **java**   Runs your compiled Java byte code programs

The file naming convention in Java is case-sensitive, and you should ensure you name files consistent with the web-based code example files. If you attempt to compile a Java file when the filename and class name are different, you'll receive an error. Also, the file extension for Java programs is always a lowercase `.java`.

Microsoft Windows Presents Challenges to Java

Microsoft Windows is a case-insensitive operating system, while Linux and Unix are case sensitive. The case matters when you create files in Windows. You can change the case of a filename by using the RENAME command.

The filename's case can differ from the case provided as an argument to the `javac` program on the Windows platform. For example, a `WriteReadCLOB.java` file can be compiled as `WriteReadCLOB.class` without raising an error. However, the case for the class filename must exactly match the name defining the class in the source code. When it doesn't, you'll get the following error when you attempt to compile the Java source code:

```
C:\JavaDev>javac WriteReadCLOB.java
WriteReadCLOB.java:32: class WriteReadCLOB is public, should be declared in a file named
WriteReadCLOB.java
public class WriteReadCLOB extends JFrame {
       ^
1 error
```

There is another nuance you need to understand. No compilation errors are raised when the filename matches the case of the internal source but the name differs as an argument to the `javac` executable. This generates a run-time error:

```
C:\JavaDev>java WriteReadCLOB
Exception in thread "main" java.lang.NoClassDefFoundError: WriteReadCLOB (wrong name:
WriteReadCLOB)
    at java.lang.ClassLoader.defineClass1(Native Method)
    at java.lang.ClassLoader.defineClass(ClassLoader.java:620)
    at java.security.SecureClassLoader.defineClass(SecureClassLoader.java:124)
    at java.net.URLClassLoader.defineClass(URLClassLoader.java:260)
    at java.net.URLClassLoader.access$000(URLClassLoader.java:56)
    at java.net.URLClassLoader$1.run(URLClassLoader.java:195)
    at java.security.AccessController.doPrivileged(Native Method)
    at java.net.URLClassLoader.findClass(URLClassLoader.java:188)
    at java.lang.ClassLoader.loadClass(ClassLoader.java:306)
    at sun.misc.Launcher$AppClassLoader.loadClass(Launcher.java:276)
    at java.lang.ClassLoader.loadClass(ClassLoader.java:251)
    at java.lang.ClassLoader.loadClassInternal(ClassLoader.java:319)
```

The solution is twofold: First, always remember to name the files the same as the source file class name. Second, always compile a class using the same case as the source file class name.

The `javac` executable compiles text files into Java byte code. Compiled code is known as Java class files. The JVM interprets Java class files at run time by using the `java` executable.

Java uses a `main()` method to start a program from the command line. The `main()` method acts as the launching pad for the program when calling it from the `java` executable. You can only use classes without a `main()` method as class instances inside other Java class files.

The smallest footprint for a Java program is a Java class with only a `main()` method definition. The following illustrates a basic program. It defines a class that contains only a `main()` method. The `main()` method calls a static method to print a string to standard output. This program lets you check whether you have correctly configured your Java environment:

```
-- This is found in HelloWorld.java on the publisher's web site.
public class HelloWorld {
  public static void main(String args[]) {
    System.out.println("Hello World."); }}
```

Assuming you're at the command line in the same directory as the Java program, use the following syntax to compile the file:

```
javac HelloWorld.java
```

You may then execute the Java program class file:

```
java HelloWorld
```

If it executes successfully, you will see the following output:

```
Hello World.
```

You have now configured and verified your Java environment. The next section provides a whirlwind tour of the Java programming language.

Java Programming Language Primer

The Java programming language was originally developed to support embedded devices. The embedded device language Oak was renamed Java in the early 1990s. Java is an object-oriented programming language. This means that the basic programming unit is known as an *object* or *class.* The programming language also shares many syntax rules with the C++ programming language.

Java Basics

The language defines a class by specifying four items. The first item is an optional access modifier, which can be *public, protected, private,* or *default.* The compiler assumes a *default* access modifier when one is not provided. The second item is a reserved word `class`. The third is a case-sensitive class name. The fourth is an implementation inside curly braces. Curly braces designate your coding blocks—class, condition if-then-else, loop, method, et cetera. The generic prototype of a class is

```
[public | protected | private] class class_name [extends parent_class] {}
```

Access modifiers determine who can execute a copy of the class. Table D-1 lists the access modifiers. You use access modifiers to qualify classes, variables, and methods. Classes can contain variable definitions, declarations, nested classes (known as inner classes), and methods. You should also organize your Java classes into packages. Packages act like database user accounts, and access modifiers act like grants to users. Packages provide libraries of related classes that work cooperatively to solve business problems.

The `extends` clause is optional in your code. You extend the base *Object* class by default. Java is a single-root node object hierarchy, and the *Object* class is the topmost class file. All classes inherit the base behaviors of the *Object* class. Classes that extend the behavior of a child node of the *Object* class inherit all behaviors of their parent class, as well as of the parent class antecedents up to and including the *Object* class.

Interfaces are also optional. *Interfaces* specify methods that classes must implement. They let you define a general set of behaviors for a set of classes.

Access Modifier	Access from Same Class	Access from Same Package	Access from Subclass	Access from Another Package
public	✓	✓	✓	✓
protected	✓	✓	✓	
(default)	✓	✓		
private	✓			

TABLE D-1 *Access Modifiers*

Packages are directories where you place your code before creating libraries. *Libraries* are known as Java archive (JAR) files. You assign directories before the class definition, using a prototype like

```
package company_name.directory_name.subdirectory_name;
```

For example, a company name of plsql and package name of fileio would look like the folder structure in Figure D-1. After you define your library of Java classes, you can use the jar executable to create a Java archive. You can then use the code in the Java archive file by referencing it in your CLASSPATH environment variable.

The package command must be the first program in your class file. It is followed by any importing commands. You import other classes that you use inside your class implementation. The following prototype imports a *Component* class from the awt package of the rt.jar Java archive:

```
import java.awt.Component;
```

There was no reference to the rt.jar file when you set the CLASSPATH earlier. None is required, because the Java compiler and run-time executables know where the file is located and it is built into the compiler configuration.

You can define attributes and methods in your class implementation. The naming rules differ from the convention. The rules are that a variable or method name (also known as an identifier) can include characters, digits, underscores, and dollar signs. Variable names cannot use any of the reserved words found in Table D-2.

You also define variables by specifying a valid type followed by a name or identifier. Java has eight primitive types that are in Table D-3. These types qualify characters, numbers, and Boolean true and false values. Any class in your CLASSPATH source may also define a variable type, such as java.lang.String.

FIGURE D-1 *Package hierarchy for FileIO.jar*

abstract	Continue	float	new	switch
assert	Default	goto	package	synchronized
boolean	Do	if	private	this
break	Double	implements	protected	throw
byte	Else	import	public	throws
case	Enum	instanceof	return	transient
catch	Extends	int	short	try
char	For	interface	static	void
class	Final	long	strictfp	volatile
const	Finally	native	super	while

TABLE D-2   *Java Reserved Word List*

Name	Range	Size
char	The char data type is a single 16-bit Unicode character. It has a minimum value of '\u0000' (or 0) and a maximum value of '\uffff' (or 65,535). 16-bit unsigned	
boolean	The boolean data type has only two possible values: true and false.	unpublished
byte	The byte data type is an 8-bit signed two's complement integer. It has a minimum value of –128 and a maximum value of 127.	8-bit signed
int	The int data type is a 32-bit signed two's complement integer. It has a minimum value of –2,147,483,648 and a maximum value of 2,147,483,647.	32-bit signed
double	The double data type is a double-precision 64-bit IEEE 754 floating point number. It has a negative range between –1.7976931348623157E+308 to –4.9E–324; and it has a positive range between 1.4E–45 to 1.7976931348623157E+308. 64-bit IEEE 754	
float	The float data type is a single-precision 32-bit IEEE 754 floating point number. It has a negative range between –3.4028235E+38 to –1.4E–45; and it has a positive range between 1.4E–45 to 3.4028235E+38.	32-bit IEEE 754
long	The long data type is a 64-bit signed two's complement integer. It has a minimum value of –9,223,372,036,854,775,808 and a maximum value of 9,223,372,036,854,775,807.	64-bit signed
short	The short data type is a 16-bit signed two's complement integer. It has a minimum value of –32,768 and a maximum value of 32,767.	16-bit signed

TABLE D-3   *Java Primitive Data Types*

After you define a variable, you assign it a value. This can be done with a string or numeric literal or with an instance of a class. Class instances are more often known as object instances, and they are run-time containers of class definitions. You create a run-time class container by "initializing" a copy of the class. You declare a variable when you both define and assign a value on the same statement line. Examples of declaring variables are

```
boolean my_boolean = true;                  // Declare a Boolean.
byte my_byte = 1;                           // Declare a byte.
float my_float = 3000F;                     // Declare a float.
String string = new String("My New String"); // Declare a class instance.
```

Two forward slashes (//) designate a single-line comment. The /* starts a multiple-line comment that is ended by the */. Single-line comments are easy but can be problematic when you have a closing curly brace that is at the end of the line. It will comment out the closing curly brace and leave your block open. You should check to make sure you don't open your code block by commenting out closing curly braces.

Variable definitions and declarations can only be made inside code block curly braces. Declaring variables also lets you call methods of the current class or referenced classes. You can designate variables as static or instance variables. A *static* variable is known as a class variable and is assigned a value at compile time. *Instance* variables are known as run-time variables and have no value until you instantiate a run-time class instance. Example of writing and using each are included in the sample code of this appendix.

Coding logic, like if-then-else statements and loops, resides in methods. Methods are functions or subroutines in class files. Two methods have special rules. The first is the main() method, which is used to run a class from the command line. It is the externally executable access to your program. The main() method from the HelloWorld.java class shows you how to implement a class file that is callable from the command line. It prints a string to the standard output device.

The second special method is the constructor method, which must have the exact case-sensitive name as the enclosing file. You don't need to provide a constructor method when you want to use the default constructor, because the compiler generates one when none is provided in the source file. Default constructors take no formal parameters. However, if you implement a class with an overriding constructor, the compiler no longer automatically creates a default constructor. After adding any constructor method, you must implement a constructor with no formal parameters when required. The following shows the default constructor built for the HelloWorld.java file:

```
public HelloWorld() {};
```

Java Assignment Operators

Assignment is straightforward when you assign the contents of one variable to another variable of the same type. You do it with the equal symbol (=). It is not straightforward when you're assigning a different type because that involves a casting operation. Casting is taking the value in one data type and moving it to another data type.

You can cast any primitive to a more precise primitive because nothing is lost. On the other hand, you must explicitly state your intent when you cast a more precise primitive to a less precise data type. This explicit acknowledgment ensures that developers know that they are intentionally sacrificing precision. An example of this is found in the following code snippet:

```
int i;
float f = 30001.4F;
i = (int) f;
```

The first line defines a variable i, and its initial value is null. The second line assigns a real number (designated by the trailing F) to the variable f. The third line takes the real number and explicitly casts it as an Integer. This is known as downcasting. You downcast when you assign a value from a more precise data type to a less precise one. The assignment tells the program to discard the right side of the decimal and assign the left side to the Integer variable.

You can also downcast Object types. Downcasting an object instance actually makes the behavior more general. An example of downcasting a *String* to an *Object* is

```
String s = new String("Hello");
Object o = (Object) s;
```

This section has covered Java basics. The next section covers how to make conditional decisions and repeat operations until conditions are met.

Java Conditional and Iterative Structures

You have if-then-else and switch statements in Java. The if statement may include curly braces that define operating scope. Curly braces are necessary when the code block is more than a single statement. You may exclude curly braces when the code block is a single statement. The following provides an example that uses curly braces with single statement code blocks:

```
if (somevariable == 0) {
   statement1; }
else if (somevariable == 1) {
   statement2; }
else {
   statement3; }
```

The if statement performs a comparison operation. Comparisons can be tricky when you forget to use two equal symbols and substitute a single equal statement. A single equal symbol performs an assignment and does not raise a compilation error. Unfortunately, these types of errors only manifest themselves during program run time. You can also compare inequalities by using the less than, less than or equal to, and other operators.

NOTE
The comparison operator is a little thing if you write more Java than PL/SQL but a big thing when the opposite is true. PL/SQL uses the equal symbol for comparisons.

TIP
You should consider using curly braces to delimit code blocks all the time. They save you time debugging when modifying code, which can add statements in conditional blocks.

Java `switch` statements work like those in C++ and C#. Unlike PL/SQL case statements, `switch` statements experience fall-through without `break` statements in each case. Fall-through is the principle of finding a match and then executing everything from that point forward until you encounter a `break` statement. You can use a `char` or `int` variable for a simple `switch` statement and any Boolean expression for a searched case. The following illustrates a simple `switch` statement using an `int` variable:

```
int someVariable = 2;
switch (someVariable) {
  case 1:
    statement1;
    break;
  case 2:
    statement2;
    break;
  default:
    statement3;
    break; }
```

Iterative statements are loops. You have the DO-WHILE, FOR, and WHILE loops in the Java programming language. The DO-WHILE loop doesn't set an entrance barrier and runs until the exit criterion is met at the bottom of the loop. Both of the others set an entrance barrier and run until the exit criterion is met at the top of the loop. Figure D-2 shows the flow charts for these loop structures.

You should note that you can use a logical and (`&&`) to make the criterion the result of two criteria. Likewise, you can use a logical or (`||`) to make the criterion the result of one of two criteria. The following example checks for real numbers not between 6 and 7:

```
if ((variableOne < 6) && (variableOne > 7))
```

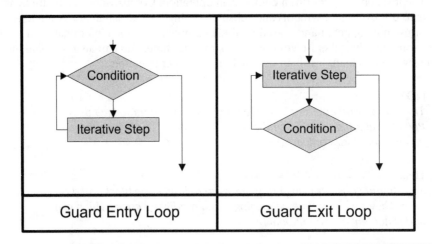

FIGURE D-2 *Iterative control flow diagrams*

The DO-WHILE Loop

The DO-WHILE loop guarantees that your loop runs *once* before checking the criterion. The criterion is generally a variable set prior to the beginning of the loop. This is known as a gate on exit loop. The while statement follows the closing curly brace and requires a semicolon because it is a statement. The general syntax is

```
do {
   repeatingStatement;
} while(someVariable == 0);
```

The WHILE Loop

The WHILE loop checks for a condition on entry. Like the DO-WHILE loop, the WHILE loop also relies on a variable set before the loop. This is known as a gate on entry loop. Unlike the DO-WHILE loop, the while statement is not followed by a semicolon because it is followed by the code block designated by curly braces. The general syntax is

```
while(someVariable == 0) {
   repeatingStatement;
}
```

The FOR Loop

The FOR loop behaves differently than the WHILE loop because the evaluation variable is set in the statement. This another variation of gate on entry loops. The criterion of a FOR loop is defined by a numeric variable, limit, and incrementing or decrementing value. The general syntax is

```
for(int i; i < someValue; i++) {
   repeatingStatement;
}
```

The i++ is a post-operation unary operator, and it adds 1 to the value of the number after performing that line's action. A pre-operation unary operator is defined by --i, and it decrements the variable before performing that line's action. The double pluses are for incrementing and the double minuses, for decrementing. They are interchangeable as pre- or post-operations.

Java Method Definitions

You define subroutines in Java as methods. They can be static or instance methods. Static methods have the ability of being called without instantiating a class, whereas you must instantiate a class for an instance method. You should assign access modifiers to method definitions. The *default* access method is assigned when you don't explicitly assign an access modifier. The downside of the *default* modifier is that the method can't be subclassed by another class.

TIP
The default method is ideal when you want to prevent subclassing a method that has tightly coupled dependencies.

The following prototype defines a private static method:

```
private static String someMethod(String someFormalParameter) {
   String someString =  new String("some string literal");
   someStatement;
   return someString; }
```

The following prototype defines a public non-static or instance method:

```
public String someMethod(String someFormalParameter) {
  String someString =  new String("some string literal");
  someStatement;
  return someString; }
```

You can execute a static method without instantiating an object instance. The excerpt from the `WriteReadCLOB.java` program demonstrates a static call:

```
clobText = FileIO.openFile(FileIO.findFile(this));
```

The static method lets you open a file chooser. It passes the `this` operator as an actual parameter. The static method returns the contents of a character file as a Java String.

Calling an instance method is always a two-step process. First, you create an instance or a copy of the other class as a variable in your current class file. Creating an instance of a class is also known as *instantiating* a class. After you create an instance of the class, you can then call an instance method by appending the class method using a period. The example from the `WriteReadCLOB.java` file creates a variable of the `DataConnectionPane` class and names it `message`:

```
private DataConnectionPane message = new DataConnectionPane();
```

Later in the same program, a call is made to an instance method of the instantiated class:

```
  host = message.getHost();
```

There are also varied means of chaining methods and return types, but they're beyond the scope of this primer. However, the basic rule is that *the object return type from a method provides a class instance, and you can then append any instance method to it.*

Java try-catch Blocks

The `try-catch` block is a mechanism to manage error handling. You place statements in the `try` block that may fail on an external resource. Then you place code to catch, report, and log errors in the `catch` block. You also have the `finally` block, and you put code in it that you want executed whether the `try` block failed or not. The following is a prototype for the `try-catch-finally` block:

```
try {
  resource_statement; }
catch (Exception e) {
  exception_handling_statement; }
finally {
  always_process_statement; }
```

You are required to use a try-catch block when calling a class method that throws an exception. If you're unaware that one is required, the Java compiler will throw an exception when you try to compile your code without the `try-catch` and one is required.

This section has reviewed the basics of using the Java programming language. Broader tutorials are found at the java.sun.com/docs/books/tutorial/ web page. The next section demonstrates how to verify a connection to an Oracle database. Subsequent sections work with various data types, like scalar variables and large objects.

Testing a Client-Side or Thin-Driver JDBC Connection

Oracle Database 11*g* introduces a significant change to how JDBC connections work. You no longer connect directly to the database, beginning with the `ojdbc6.jar` library. You connect through the new database collection pool using Java 6. This change means that every program you had working in the Java 5 must be rewritten to work in your new Oracle Database 11*g* instance. Alternatively, you may continue to use the `ojdbc5.jar` file that is also provided in the Oracle Database 11*g* instance.

Import packages for the Oracle JDBC implementation are found in Table D-4. The Oracle `ojdbc6.jar` library adds the *OracleDataSource* class and deletes the *DriverManager* class. You should consider using the new connection pool to better utilize database resources.

The examples in the appendix connect through the new connection pool. If you would like to connect directly, please see the following discussion.

The following Java program lets you test your JDBC connection. It collects input arguments to connect to an Oracle instance when you run it. The program queries a string literal from the `DUAL` table. You provide the following input parameters when you run the program:

```
-- This is output from the HelloWorldThin.java file.

---------------------------------------------------------------
Enter User [UID/PASSWD]: <userid>/<passwd>
Enter Host Name: <hostname.domain_name>
Enter Port Name: <listener_port>
Enter Database Name: <tns_alias>
```

Package Import Statements	Description
`import java.sql.*;`	Standard JDBC packages
`import java.math.*;`	The BigDecimal and BigInteger classes
`import oracle.jdbc.*;`	Oracle extensions to JDBC
`import oracle.jdbc.pool.*;`	*OracleDataSource* class used to connect through the Oracle Database 11*g* connection pool, using the `ojdbc6.jar` libraries
`import oracle.sql.*;`	Oracle type extensions

TABLE D-4   *Package JDBC Import Statements*

Comparative JDBC Syntax

You can connect directly to the Oracle 11*g* Database by using the `ojdbc14.jar` or `ojdbc5.jar` libraries. You need to put one of the older Java Archives in your `CLASSPATH` environment variable. If you have two JDBC Java archives in your `CLASSPATH` environment, the *DatabaseMetaData* class uses the driver information from the first Java Archive in the `CLASSPATH`. The following code lets you connect directly to the database:

```
// Load Oracle JDBC driver.
DriverManager.registerDriver(new oracle.jdbc.driver.OracleDriver());

// Define connection.
Connection conn = DriverManager.getConnection("jdbc:oracle:thin:@" +
                    host + ":" + port + ":" + database, user, password);
```

The new syntax connects through the Oracle 11*g* Database connection pool. It instantiates an *OracleDataSource* instance and then sets the URL, user, and password for the connections, as

```
// Set the Pooled Connection Source.
OracleDataSource ods = new OracleDataSource();
String url = "jdbc:oracle:thin:@//" + host + ":" + port + "/" + db;
ods.setURL(url);
ods.setUser(user);
ods.setPassword(passwd)

// Define connection.
Connection conn = ods.getConnection();
```

If you look closely at the difference between the connections, the old syntax uses the @ symbol to resolve through the TNS alias (found in the `tnsnames.ora` file). The new one resolves through a URL listening on the same port as the Oracle 11*g* Database listener.

You must choose which one works best for your purposes. Migrating to the new connection pool requires fixing all data abstraction layers that communicate directly with the database.

Appendix A explains what the `tns_alias` is and how it resolves connections to the database instance. The `readEntry()` method is also available in the `FileIO.java` class as a static method if you'd like to leverage a preexisting command-line interface. You would call the method like

```
String commandInput = FileIO.readEntry();
```

You can use this class file to connect to any Oracle database through the Oracle listener:

```
-- This is found in HelloWorldThin.java on the publisher's web site.
```

```
// Class imports.
import java.io.IOException;
import java.sql.Connection;
import java.sql.DatabaseMetaData;
import java.sql.ResultSet;
import java.sql.ResultSetMetaData;
import java.sql.SQLException;
import java.sql.Statement;
```

```java
// Oracle class imports.
import oracle.jdbc.driver.OracleDriver;
import oracle.jdbc.pool.OracleDataSource;
// ------------------------------------------------------------------/
public class HelloWorldThin {
  // Define a static class String variable.
  private static String user;

  // ------------------------------------------------------------------/
  private static void printLine() {
    printLine(null); }
  // ------------------------------------------------------------------/
  private static void printLine(String s) {
    if (s != null) {
      System.out.println(s); }

    // Print line.
    System.out.print  ("----------------------------------------");
    System.out.println("----------------------------------------"); }
  // ------------------------------------------------------------------/
  private static String readEntry() {
    try {

      // Define method variables.
      int c;
      StringBuffer buffer = new StringBuffer();

      // Read first character.
      c = System.in.read();

      // Read remaining characters.
      while (c != '\n' && c != -1) {
        buffer.append((char) c);
        c = System.in.read(); }

      // Return buffer.
      return buffer.toString().trim(); }
    catch (IOException e) {
      return null; }}
  // ------------------------------------------------------------------/
  public static void main(String args[]) throws SQLException, IOException {
    // Define method variables.
    boolean debug = false;
    int slashIndex;
    String userIn;
    String password;
    String host;
    String port;
    String database;
    String debugString = new String("DEBUG");

    // Print line.
```

```
    printLine();

    // Verify and print debug mode.
    if (args.length > 0) {
      if (args[0].toUpperCase().equals(debugString)) {
        debug = true;
        printLine("Debug mode is enabled."); }
      else {
        for (int i = 0;i < args.length;i++) {
          System.out.println("Incorrect argument(s): [" + args[i] + "]"); }

        // Print line and message.
        printLine();
        printLine("Valid case insensitive argument is: DEBUG."); }}

    // Prompt, read and capture credentials.
    System.out.print("Enter User [UID/PASSWD]: ");

    // Read input.
    userIn = readEntry();

    // Parse and check for token between user name and password.
    slashIndex = userIn.indexOf("/");
    if (slashIndex != -1) {
      user = userIn.substring(0, slashIndex);
      password = userIn.substring(slashIndex + 1); }
    else {
      user = userIn;
      System.out.print("Enter Password: ");
      password = readEntry(); }

    // Prompt, read and capture host name.
    System.out.print("Enter Host Name: ");
    host = readEntry();

    // Prompt, read, and capture port number.
    System.out.print("Enter Port Number: ");
    port = readEntry();

    // Prompt, read, and capture database name.
    System.out.print("Enter Database Name: ");
    database = readEntry();

    // Print line and message.
    printLine("Connecting to the database ...");
    printLine("jdbc:oracle:oci8:@" +
              host + ":" + port + ":" + database + "," +
              user + "," + password);

    // Attempt database connection.
    try {
      // Set the Pooled Connection Source
```

```java
OracleDataSource ods = new OracleDataSource();
String url = "jdbc:oracle:thin:@//" + host + ":" + port + "/" + db;
ods.setURL(url);
ods.setUser(user);
ods.setPassword(passwd);

// Define connection.
Connection conn = ods.getConnection();

// Signal connection.
printLine("Connected.");

// Define metadata object and print message.
DatabaseMetaData dmd = conn.getMetaData();
printLine("Driver Version: [" + dmd.getDriverVersion() + "]\n" +
          "Driver Name:    [" + dmd.getDriverName() + "]");

// Create and execute statement.
Statement stmt = conn.createStatement();
ResultSet rset = stmt.executeQuery("SELECT 'Hello World.' FROM dual");

// Read row returns.
while (rset.next()) {
  printLine(rset.getString(1)); }

// Close result set.
rset.close();
stmt.close();
conn.close();

// Print line and message.
printLine("The JDBC Connection worked."); }
catch (SQLException e) {
  if (debug) {
    e.printStackTrace();
    printLine(); }
  else {
    if (e.getSQLState() == null) {
      System.out.println(
        new SQLException("Oracle Thin Client Net8 Connection Error.",
                  "ORA-" + e.getErrorCode() +
                  ": Incorrect Net8 thin client arguments:\n\n" +
                  "  host name     [" + host + "]\n" +
                  "  port number   [" + port + "]\n" +
                  "  database name [" + database + "]\n",
                  e.getErrorCode())).getSQLState(); }
    else {
      // Trim the postpended "\n".
      printLine(e.getMessage().substring(0,e.getMessage().length() - 1)); }}

  // Print line and message.
  printLine("The JDBC Connection failed."); }}}
```

Before introducing the program, you saw the program output to collect arguments. The balance of the output is shown next:

```
-- This is output from the HelloWorldThin.java file.

Connecting to the database ...
-------------------------------------------------------------
jdbc:oracle:oci8:@<hostname.domain_name>:<port>:<sid>,<uid>,<passwd>
-------------------------------------------------------------
Connected.
-------------------------------------------------------------
Driver Version: [11.1.0.0.0-Alpha]
Driver Name:    [Oracle JDBC driver]
-------------------------------------------------------------
Hello World.
-------------------------------------------------------------
The JDBC Connection worked.
-------------------------------------------------------------
```

NOTE
You should check the management of the ORA-17002 error in the SQL connection catch block. It can be very useful when writing Java programs that use distributed architectures like Enterprise JavaBeans (EJBs).

Your setup is incomplete or incorrect if you encounter any error messages or console printing errors. You'll need to revisit the instructions and troubleshoot the problem.

Accessing Scalar Variables

Java Swing applications let you build nice testing tools to verify data sets returned by your J2EE or J3EE beans. The JTable works well with scalar-type variables but does not work well with Large Objects. Binary Large Objects (BLOBs) and Character Large Objects (CLOBs) are displayed in a single line. LONG data types display in JTables like BLOB and CLOB types. Character and Binary File large objects simply can't be displayed in a *JTable*.

Java Classes Stored in the Oracle Database

Internally stored Java class files require you to configure the env parameter in your listener.ora. You will need to set the LD_LIBRARY_PATH in the listener.ora file. You set it by providing the canonical path to the generic Oracle libraries in the lib and jdbc/lib directories of the Oracle home. Chapter 13 contains detailed steps to set up your listener.ora file.

FIGURE D-3 *Database Connection Input dialog*

When you run the `QueryTable.java` program, you're presented with a tabbed dialog box to enter database connection information. Figure D-3 shows how the dialog looks. You should enter your host name with a fully qualified domain name in the Host tab. Enter the listening port number for the Oracle database in the Port tab. Enter the TNS alias, discussed in Appendix A, in the Database tab. You should then enter both the user account name in the UserID tab and the password in the Password tab.

You can modify the query to work with any table using the `DataTablePane.class` library file. The class allows you to enter any valid table name. Table D-5 lists three constants that change the number of tabs displayed. An operating system prompt is provided in all cases with a Windows default value.

Constant Names	Constant Uses
TABLE_COLUMN_ALL	You use this constant to instantiate a tabbed pane with only a prompt for the table name. Use this when you want to return all columns from a table.
TABLE_AND_COLUMN	You use this constant to instantiate a tabbed pane with a prompt for table and column. Use this when you want to return all rows of a column.
TABLE_COLUMN_KEY	You use this constant to instantiate a tabbed pane with a prompt for table, column, primary key column name, and primary key column value. Use this when you want to return only a filtered set of rows of a column.

TABLE D-5 *Static Constants for the `DataTablePane.java` Class*

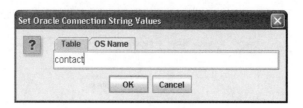

FIGURE D-4   *Database Query Input dialog*

After you are prompted for the connection string components, you will be prompted for the table name (see Figure D-4). Later in this appendix there is a variation of this interface that uses all five columns.

This program only displays dates, strings, and numbers in the *JTable.* If you want to also work with CLOB data types, you can borrow that feature from the `WriteReadCLOB.java` file later in this chapter. Other data types don't work well with the *JTable,* and you should consider alternative solutions. Figure D-5 shows the returned data after some manipulation of column widths.

CO...	ME...	CO...	LA...	FIR...	MID...	CR...	CR...	LA...	LA...
10...	10...	10...	Wi...	Ra...		2	20...	2	20...
10...	10...	10...	Wi...	Bri...		2	20...	2	20...
10...	10...	10...	Viz...	Os...		2	20...	2	20...
10...	10...	10...	Viz...	Do...		2	20...	2	20...
10...	10...	10...	Sw...	Me...		2	20...	2	20...
10...	10...	10...	Sw...	Ian	M	2	20...	2	20...

FIGURE D-5   *QueryTable.java display*

The `QueryTable.java` program shows how you retrieve, format, and display scalar types. It displays the results in a *JTable*. The program imports individual classes, so you can see all the dependencies.

-- This is found in **QueryTable.java** on the publisher's web site.

```java
// Java Application class imports.
import java.awt.Component;
import java.awt.Dimension;
import java.awt.image.BufferedImage;
import java.awt.GridLayout;
import javax.swing.JFrame;
import javax.swing.JOptionPane;
import javax.swing.JPanel;
import javax.swing.JScrollPane;
import javax.swing.JTable;
import javax.swing.table.DefaultTableModel;
import javax.swing.table.TableCellRenderer;
import javax.swing.table.TableColumn;
import javax.swing.table.TableModel;

// Generic JDBC imports.
import java.sql.Clob;
import java.sql.Connection;
import java.sql.DatabaseMetaData;
import java.sql.DriverManager;
import java.sql.ResultSet;
import java.sql.ResultSetMetaData;
import java.sql.SQLException;
import java.sql.Statement;

// Oracle class imports.
import oracle.jdbc.driver.OracleDriver;
import oracle.jdbc.pool.OracleDataSource;

// Include book libraries (available at publisher's web site).
import plsql.fileio.FileIO;
import plsql.jdbc.DataConnectionPane;
import plsql.jdbc.DataTablePane;
// ----------------------------------------------------------------/
public class QueryTable extends JFrame {
  // Define database connections.
  private String host;
```

```java
private String port;
private String dbname;
private String userid;
private String passwd;

// Define query variables.
private String tableName;

// Define data connection pane.
private DataConnectionPane message = new DataConnectionPane();
private DataTablePane table = new DataTablePane(DataTablePane.TABLE_COLUMN_ALL);

// Construct the class.
public QueryTable (String s) {
  super(s);

  // Get database connection values or exit.
  if (JOptionPane.showConfirmDialog(this,message
      ,"Set Oracle Connection String Values"
      ,JOptionPane.OK_CANCEL_OPTION) == 0) {

    // Set class connection variables.
    host = message.getHost();
    port = message.getPort();
    dbname = message.getDatabase();
    userid = message.getUserID();
    passwd = message.getPassword();

    // Print connection to console (debugging tool).
    message.getConnection();

    // Collect query parameters.
    if (JOptionPane.showConfirmDialog(this,table
        ,"Set Oracle Connection String Values"
        ,JOptionPane.OK_CANCEL_OPTION) == 0) {

      // Set class query variables.
      tableName = table.getTableName();

    // Create a JPanel for data display.
    ManageTable panel = new ManageTable();

    // Configure the JPanel.
    panel.setOpaque(true);
    setContentPane(panel);

    // Configure the JFrame.
    setDefaultCloseOperation(JFrame.EXIT_ON_CLOSE);
    setLocation(100,100);
    pack();
    setVisible(true); }
  else
    System.exit(1); }
// ----------------------------------------------------------------/
private class ManageTable extends JPanel {
```

```java
    // Define target table and query row size variable.
    private String target = tableName;
    private int querySize = 0;

    // Define containers.
    private Object[][] data = getQuery(host,port,dbname,userid,passwd,target);
    private Object[][] cells = getData();
    private Object[] columns = getColumnHeaders();

    // Define display variables.
    private JTable table = new JTable(cells,columns);
    private JScrollPane scrollPane;
    private TableModel tableModel;
    // ----------------------------------------------------------------/
    public ManageTable () {
      super(new GridLayout(1,0));
      decorate(300,100); }
    // ----------------------------------------------------------------/
    private String[] getColumnHeaders() {
      // Size container, copy column headers and return data.
      String[] headers = new String[data[0].length];
      for (int i = 0;i < data[0].length;i++)
        headers[i] = (String) data[0][i];
      return headers; }
    // ----------------------------------------------------------------/
    private Object[][] getData() {
      // Size container, copy cells, and return data.
      Object[][] cells = new Object[querySize][];
      for (int i = 0;i < querySize;i++) {
        cells[i] = new Object[data[i + 1].length];
        for (int j = 0;j < data[i + 1].length;j++)
          cells[i][j] = data[i + 1][j]; }
      return cells; }
    // ----------------------------------------------------------------/
    private void decorate (int width, int height) {
      // Configure JPanel.
      setSize(width,height);

      // Configure and initialize JTable.
      table.setPreferredScrollableViewportSize(new Dimension(width,height));
      table.setFillsViewportHeight(true);
      initColumns(table);

      // Assign JScrollPane.
      scrollPane = new JScrollPane(table);
      add(scrollPane); }
    // ----------------------------------------------------------------/
    private void initColumns(JTable table) {
      // Initialize cell width.
      int headerWidth = 0;
      int cellWidth = 0;

      // Define display variables.
      Component component = null;
      TableColumn tableColumn = null;
```

```
    TableCellRenderer headerRenderer =
      table.getTableHeader().getDefaultRenderer();

    // Initialize TableModel class.
    tableModel = table.getModel();

    // Initialize columns.
    for (int i = 0;i < table.getColumnCount();i++)
      tableColumn = table.getColumnModel().getColumn(i); }
  // ----------------------------------------------------------------/
  private Object[][] getQuery(String host,String port,String dbname
                             ,String user,String pswd,String table) {
    // Define return type container.
    Object[][] dataset = null;
    String[] datatype = null;

    try {
      // Load driver, initialize connection, metadata, and statement.
      OracleDataSource ods = new OracleDataSource();
      String url = "jdbc:oracle:thin:@//"+host+":"+port+"/"+dbname;
      ods.setURL(url);
      ods.setUser(userid);
      ods.setPassword(passwd);
      Connection conn = ods.getConnection();
      DatabaseMetaData dmd = conn.getMetaData();
      Statement stmt = conn.createStatement();

      // Declare result set, initialize dataset, and close result set.
      ResultSet rset = stmt.executeQuery("SELECT COUNT(*) FROM " + table);
      while (rset.next())
        dataset = new Object[rset.getInt(1) + 1][];
      rset.close();

      // Reusing result set and get result set metadata.
      rset = stmt.executeQuery("SELECT * FROM " + table);
      ResultSetMetaData rsmd = rset.getMetaData();

      // Declare row counter.
      int row = 0;

      // Assign array sizes.
      dataset[row] = new Object[rsmd.getColumnCount()];
      datatype = new String[rsmd.getColumnCount()];

      // Assign column labels and types.
      for (int col = 0;col < rsmd.getColumnCount();col++) {
        dataset[row][col] = rsmd.getColumnName(col + 1);
        datatype[col] = rsmd.getColumnTypeName(col + 1); }

      // Size nested arrays and assign column values for rows.
      while (rset.next()) {
        dataset[++row] = new Object[rsmd.getColumnCount()];
        for (int col = 0;col < rsmd.getColumnCount();col++) {
          if (datatype[col] == "DATE")
            dataset[row][col] = rset.getDate(col + 1);
```

```
      else if (datatype[col] == "NUMBER")
        dataset[row][col] = rset.getLong(col + 1);
      else if (datatype[col] == "VARCHAR2")
        dataset[row][col] = rset.getString(col + 1); }}

  // Set query return size.
  querySize = row;

  // Close resources.
  rset.close();
  stmt.close();
  conn.close();

  // Return data.
  return dataset; }
catch (SQLException e) {
  // Check for and return connection error or SQL error.
  if (e.getSQLState() == null) {
    System.out.println(
      new SQLException("Oracle Thin Client Net8 Connection Error.",
                  "ORA-" + e.getErrorCode() +
                  ": Incorrect Net8 thin client arguments:\n\n" +
                  "  host name      [" + host + "]\n" +
                  "  port number    [" + port + "]\n" +
                  "  database name  [" + dbname + "]\n"
                  , e.getErrorCode()).getSQLState());
    return dataset; }
  else {
    System.out.println(e.getMessage());
    return dataset; }}}}
// ------------------------------------------------------------/
public static void main(String[] args) {
// Define window.
QueryTable frame = new QueryTable("Query Table"); }}
```

The getQuery() method contains the JDBC component. The method actually processes two queries. The first query counts the number of rows, and the second selects all columns from those rows. The WHILE loop reads the rows, and the nested FOR loop reads the columns. An if statement processes DATE, VARCHAR2, and NUMBER data types. All other data types are ignored.

There are two alternatives using PL/SQL to reading scalar data types. You can read one row at a time, or a group of rows. You can use a system reference cursor or a series of scalar arrays to return a set of rows.

This section has shown you how to access scalar variables and display them in a Java application. The next section explores how to query and manage large objects.

Writing and Accessing Large Objects

Java also can access large objects. Oracle supports Binary Large Objects (BLOBs), Character Large Objects (CLOBs), National Character Large Objects (NCLOBs), and Binary Files (BFILEs). These types are generically known as LOBs or Large Objects. LOB columns are not stored inline with other data in a row. Only a reference is stored inline for LOBs. The reference points to where the LOB is stored. BLOB, CLOB, and NCLOB data columns are stored inside the database. The BFILE data type is stored externally in the file system. These columns cannot be indexed and are the principal subject of Chapter 8.

NOTE
You cannot use the DISTINCT *function with a* SELECT *clause that returns a* BFILE *column. If you attempt it, you will return an* ORA-00932 *error. This is raised because these LOB types cannot be indexed or sorted by the database.*

The inline reference is alternatively called a descriptor or locator. Both words really mean an external reference because they are stored externally from the row. The best qualification of when to use *descriptor* or *locator* is whether the LOB is internally stored in the database. Many choose to speak of a descriptor when the object is inside the database and a locator when it is external to the database.

The following two sections illustrate examples of writing and reading a CLOB to the database and reading a BFILE reference from the database.

Writing and Accessing a CLOB Column

The BLOB, CLOB, and NCLOB are internally stored structures. CLOB and NCLOB columns are frequently long character streams. BLOB columns often contain media (like PDF files) or images. This example works with reading a large character stream—the description of the items in the media store.

The WriteReadCLOB.java program depends on a CLOB column item_desc in the item table. The column can be null, empty, or populated when you run the program. Any previous data is replaced by what you load into the column. You can create and seed values by running the create_store.sql and seed_store.sql scripts found in the introduction.

NOTE
The WriteReadCLOB class can hang if you have another transaction pending against the same row. You should commit any pending changes before running the WriteReadCLOB class.

When you run the WriteReadCLOB.java program, you're presented with a tabbed dialog box to enter database connection information, as in the prior example. Figure D-3 shown in the Accessing Scalar Variables section captures the dialog's display. You should enter your host name with a fully qualified domain name in the Host tab. Enter the listening port number for the Oracle database in the Port tab, and the TNS alias, discussed in Appendix A, in the Database tab. You should then enter both the user account name in the UserID tab and the password in the Password tab.

After you enter the database connection information, the WriteReadCLOB.java program will present you with a file chooser. You should navigate to where you have stored the LOTRFellowship.txt file and choose the file. Figure D-6 shows you how the file chooser looks. The program will read the file and pass its contents as a string to the insertClob() method, where it is written to the database. After successfully writing the file contents to the CLOB column, the program calls the getQuery() method to read the column.

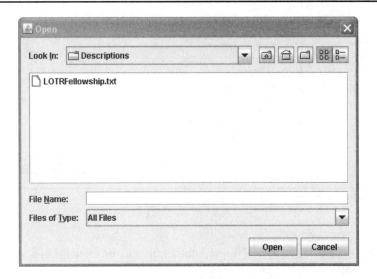

FIGURE D-6   *WriteReadCLOB.java File Chooser display*

You use the getClob() method of the *ResultSet* class to assign the column reference to your Java program. This opens a special thread to the database. Through the thread, you read the out-of-line stored CLOB using the getCharacterStream() method of the *Clob* class. The output is returned as an input stream, which can be comfortably assigned to a *Reader* class. After you have read the input stream, you need to check that the CLOB column is both not null and populated.

CLOB columns have three states—null, empty, and populated. You should only attempt to read a *Clob* instance once you know that it isn't null and contains data. Then, you read it using the read() method of the *Reader* class. The read method is a pass-by-reference subroutine (see Chapter 6 for more on types of subroutines). It reads the contents of the input stream into the buffer, returning the number of characters read or a –1. It raises an error when the stream is empty, which is why you check it first. The program also raises an error when you attempt to read beyond the length of the CLOB value.

TIP
This program manages CLOB *values that are larger than 4,000 characters but not large enough to collapse the memory of the JVM. Truly large files need to be read in chunks. You need to make sure that the total size of your buffer reads matches the length of the CLOB column. You can find the CLOB column length by using the* DBMS_LOB.GETLENGTH *function before attempting to read it.*

FIGURE D-7   *WriteReadCLOB.java display*

The `WriteReadCLOB.java` displays the `CLOB` column contents in a scrollable *JTextArea*. Figure D-7 displays the rendered results.

Leveraging Java Libraries

The `WriteReadCLOB.java` program uses a custom Java Archive file—`FileIO.jar`. You can download it from the publisher's web site as a Java Archive (JAR) file, or in its original source. The `FileIO.jar` file contains utilities for collection database connection data, and a set of libraries for reading files on Microsoft Windows, Linux, or Unix systems. You can source this in your environment by adding it to your `CLASSPATH` environment variable. It follows the same rules as the `ojdbc6.jar` file covered earlier.

You can discover the contents of any Java archive by using the following command:

```
jar -tf GenericJavaArchive.jar
```

If you want to build your own Java archive files, you should check the online tutorial at Sun Microsystems. One caveat, don't forget that each Java file must contain the

```
package path.subpath;
```

statement, which must be the first line in the file. While you can use the `jar` utility to build Java archives, any class without the correct package statement line is unrecognized by other files trying to reference it.

The following demonstrates how to read and display a CLOB column in a Java Swing application:

```
-- This is found in WriteReadCLOB.java on the publisher's web site.

// Java Application class imports.
import java.awt.Dimension;
import java.awt.Font;
import java.awt.GridLayout;
import java.io.Reader;
import javax.swing.JFrame;
import javax.swing.JLabel;
import javax.swing.JOptionPane;
import javax.swing.JPanel;
import javax.swing.JScrollPane;
import javax.swing.JTextArea;

// Generic JDBC imports.
import java.sql.CallableStatement;
import java.sql.Clob;
import java.sql.Connection;
import java.sql.DatabaseMetaData;
import java.sql.ResultSet;
import java.sql.ResultSetMetaData;
import java.sql.SQLException;
import java.sql.Statement;

// Oracle JDBC import.
import oracle.jdbc.driver.OracleDriver;
import oracle.jdbc.pool.OracleDataSource;

// Include book libraries (available at publisher's web site).
import plsql.jdbc.DataConnectionPane;
import plsql.fileio.FileIO;
// ----------------------------------------------------------------/
public class WriteReadCLOB extends JFrame {
  // Define database connections.
  private String host;
  private String port;
  private String dbname;
  private String userid;
  private String passwd;

  // Define data connection pane.
  private DataConnectionPane message = new DataConnectionPane();

  // Construct the class.
  public WriteReadCLOB (String s) {
```

```
    super(s);

    // Get database connection values or exit.
    if (JOptionPane.showConfirmDialog(this,message
          ,"Set Oracle Connection String Values"
          ,JOptionPane.OK_CANCEL_OPTION) == 0) {

      // Set class connection variables.
      host = message.getHost();
      port = message.getPort();
      dbname = message.getDatabase();
      userid = message.getUserID();
      passwd = message.getPassword();

      // Print connection to console (debugging tool).
      message.getConnection();

      // Create a JPanel for data display.
      ManageCLOB panel = new ManageCLOB();

      // Configure the JPanel.
      panel.setOpaque(true);
      setContentPane(panel);

      // Configure the JFrame.
      setDefaultCloseOperation(JFrame.EXIT_ON_CLOSE);
      setLocation(100,100);
      pack();
      setVisible(true); }
    else
      System.exit(1); }
    // ------------------------------------------------------------------/
    private class ManageCLOB extends JPanel {
      // Define display variables.
      private String clobText;
      private JScrollPane scrollPane;
      private JTextArea textArea;
      // ------------------------------------------------------------------/
      public ManageCLOB () {
        // Set layout manager.
        super(new GridLayout(1,0));

        // Assign file read to String.
        clobText = FileIO.openFile(FileIO.findFile(this));

        // Insert record before querying it.
        if (clobText.length() > 0) {
          if (insertClob(host,port,dbname,userid,passwd,clobText))
            clobText = getQuery(host,port,dbname,userid,passwd); }
        else
          System.exit(2);
```

```java
    // Construct text area and format it.
    textArea = new JTextArea(clobText);
    textArea.setEditable(false);
    textArea.setFont(new Font(Font.SANS_SERIF,Font.PLAIN,14));
    textArea.setLineWrap(true);
    textArea.setRows(10);
    textArea.setSize(400,100);
    textArea.setWrapStyleWord(true);

    // Put the image in container, and add label to panel.
    scrollPane = new JScrollPane(textArea);
    add(scrollPane); }
// ------------------------------------------------------------/
private Boolean insertClob(String host,String port,String dbname
                          ,String user,String pswd,String fileString) {
  try {
    // Set the Pooled Connection Source
    OracleDataSource ods = new OracleDataSource();
    String url = "jdbc:oracle:thin:@//"+host+":"+port+"/"+dbname;
    ods.setURL(url);
    ods.setUser(userid);
    ods.setPassword(passwd);

    // Define connection.
    Connection conn = ods.getConnection();

    // Create statement.
    CallableStatement stmt =
      conn.prepareCall("UPDATE item "+
                       "SET    item_desc = ? "+
                       "WHERE  item_title = "+
                       "'The Lord of the Rings - Fellowship of the Ring'"+
                       "AND    item_subtitle = 'Widescreen Edition'");

    // Set string into statement.
    stmt.setString(1,fileString);

    // Execute query.
    if (stmt.execute())
      conn.commit();

    // Close resources.
    stmt.close();
    conn.close();

    // Return CLOB as a String data type.
    return true; }
  catch (SQLException e) {
    if (e.getSQLState() == null) {
      System.out.println(
        new SQLException("Oracle Thin Client Net8 Connection Error.",
                         "ORA-" + e.getErrorCode() +
```

```
                              ": Incorrect Net8 thin client arguments:\n\n" +
                              "  host name     [" + host + "]\n" +
                              "  port number   [" + port + "]\n" +
                              "  database name [" + dbname + "]\n"
                              , e.getErrorCode()).getSQLState());

        // Return an empty String on error.
        return false; }
      else {
        System.out.println(e.getMessage());

        // Return an empty String on error.
        return false; }}}
  // ---------------------------------------------------------------/
  private String getQuery(String host,String port,String dbname
                         ,String user,String pswd) {
    // Define method variables.
    char[] buffer;
    int count = 0;
    int length = 0;
    String data = null;
    String[] type;
    StringBuffer sb;

    try {
      // Set the Pooled Connection Source.
      OracleDataSource ods = new OracleDataSource();
      String url = "jdbc:oracle:thin:@//"+host+":"+port+"/"+dbname;
      ods.setURL(url);
      ods.setUser(userid);
      ods.setPassword(passwd);

      // Define connection.
      Connection conn = ods.getConnection();

      // Define metadata object.
      DatabaseMetaData dmd = conn.getMetaData();

      // Create statement.
      Statement stmt = conn.createStatement();

      // Execute query.
      ResultSet rset =
        stmt.executeQuery(
          "SELECT item_desc " +
          "FROM   item " +
          "WHERE  item_title = " +
          "'The Lord of the Rings - Fellowship of the Ring'"+
          "AND    item_subtitle = 'Widescreen Edition'");

      // Get the query metadata, size array, and assign column values.
      ResultSetMetaData rsmd = rset.getMetaData();
```

```
      type = new String[rsmd.getColumnCount()];
      for (int col = 0;col < rsmd.getColumnCount();col++)
        type[col] = rsmd.getColumnTypeName(col + 1);

      // Read rows and only CLOB data type columns.
      while (rset.next()) {
        for (int col = 0;col < rsmd.getColumnCount();col++) {
          if (type[col] == "CLOB") {
            // Assign result set to CLOB variable.
            Clob clob = rset.getClob(col + 1);

            // Check that it is not null and read the character stream.
            if (clob != null) {
              Reader is = clob.getCharacterStream();

              // Initialize local variables.
              sb = new StringBuffer();
              length = (int) clob.length();

              // Check CLOB is not empty.
              if (length > 0) {
                // Initialize control structures to read stream.
                buffer = new char[length];
                count = 0;

                // Read stream and append to StringBuffer.
                try {
                  while ((count = is.read(buffer)) != -1)
                    sb.append(buffer);

                  // Assign StringBuffer to String.
                  data = new String(sb); }
                catch (Exception e) {} }
              else
                data = (String) null; }
            else
              data = (String) null; }
          else {
            data = (String) rset.getObject(col + 1); }}}

    // Close resources.
    rset.close();
    stmt.close();
    conn.close();

    // Return CLOB as a String data type.
    return data; }
  catch (SQLException e) {
    if (e.getSQLState() == null) {
      System.out.println(
        new SQLException("Oracle Thin Client Net8 Connection Error.",
                         "ORA-" + e.getErrorCode() +
```

```
                                ": Incorrect Net8 thin client arguments:\n\n" +
                                "  host name      [" + host + "]\n" +
                                "  port number    [" + port + "]\n" +
                                "  database name  [" + dbname + "]\n"
                                , e.getErrorCode()).getSQLState());

              // Return an empty String on error.
              return data; }
          else {
            System.out.println(e.getMessage());
            return data; }}
          finally {
            if (data == null) System.exit(1); }}}
    // -------------------------------------------------------------/
    public static void main(String[] args) {
      // Define window.
      WriteReadCLOB frame = new WriteReadCLOB("Write & Read CLOB Text"); }}
```

The `WriteReadCLOB.java` program has demonstrated how to write and read a `CLOB` column from the database. The next section discusses how to use database references to read externally stored files.

Accessing a BFILE Column

Accessing an image stored in a `BFILE` requires you to understand how to process graphic images in Java Swing applications. The first example demonstrates how to read an image from the file system and display the image in a Swing application. The second shows how to read and translate the references to an external files into a canonical filename. Canonical filenames are fully qualified filenames that include an explicit path statement.

Reading and Displaying an Image

Reading files from the operating system is done by using an input stream. The `ImageIO.read(new File(String file_name))` static method requires explicitly creating a *File* class and returns a *BufferedImage* instance. It hides the complexity of working with streams. You can also simplify the program by constructing an *ImageIcon* instance from a string, but this sometimes confuses maintenance programmers. The physical construction of a *File* class reference lets maintenance programmers know that the string maps to a physical filename. Figure D-8 shows how `ReadImage.java` renders the image.

FIGURE D-8 *ReadImage.java display*

File Dependency Error

The `ReadImage.java` file requires a valid `.gif`, `.jpg`, or `.png` file. You will raise the following exception when the file is not found:

```
Can't read input file!
Exception in thread "main" java.lang.NullPointerException
        at javax.swing.ImageIcon.<init>(ImageIcon.java:161)
        at ReadImage.<init>(ReadImage.java:43)
        at ReadImage.main(ReadImage.java:55)
```

The `read()` method of the *ImageIO* class also requires you to explicitly put a try-catch block in your code to handle any thrown IOException. After you read the file into a *BufferedImage,* you use it to build an instance of *ImageIcon* and then use it to build a *JLabel.* The *JLabel* is then added to the *JPanel,* and rendered when the *JPanel* is added to a *JFrame* instance. The `ReadImage.java` file demonstrates these steps as shown:

-- This is found in ReadImage.java on the publisher's web site.

```
// Required imports.
import javax.swing.ImageIcon;
import javax.swing.JFrame;
import javax.swing.JLabel;
import javax.swing.JPanel;
import java.awt.GridLayout;
import java.awt.image.BufferedImage;
import java.io.IOException;
import java.io.File;
import javax.imageio.ImageIO;

// Include book libraries (available at publisher's web site).
import plsql.fileio.FileIO;
// -----------------------------------------------------------------/
public class ReadImage extends JPanel {
  // Use to read and diaplay BFILE image file.
  private BufferedImage image;
  private JLabel label;
  // -----------------------------------------------------------------/
  public ReadImage () {
    // Set layout manager.
    super(new GridLayout(1,0));

    // Read image file.
    try {
      image = ImageIO.read(FileIO.findFile(this)); }
    catch (IOException e) {
      System.out.println(e.getMessage()); }

    // Put the image into a container and add container to JPanel.
    label = new JLabel(new ImageIcon(image));
```

```
    add(label); }
// -----------------------------------------------------------/
public static void main(String[] args) {
    // Define window.
    JFrame frame = new JFrame("Read BFILE Image");

    // Define and configure panel.
    ReadImage panel = new ReadImage();
    panel.setOpaque(true);

    // Configure window and enable default close operation.
    frame.setContentPane(panel);

    frame.setDefaultCloseOperation(JFrame.EXIT_ON_CLOSE);

    frame.setLocation(100,100);

    frame.pack();

    frame.setVisible(true); }}
```

The static `main()` method creates a *JFrame* and decorates it with an instance of the *ReadImage* class. It launches a file chooser that lets you pick an image file to display. The `FileIO.jar` file contains the file chooser code.

This section has demonstrated how to use Java to read and render an image file in a Java Swing application. The next section will demonstrate how to find the image by reading the locator reference in a `BFILE` column.

Reading and Displaying an Image by Using the Stored Reference

The inline reference for a `BFILE` column contains a virtual directory and filename. This differs from the internal reference found in `BLOB`, `CLOB`, and `NCLOB` columns. You create virtual directories before you can insert a `BFILE` column locator value. You insert the locator values by using the `BFILENAME()` functions. As qualified in Chapter 8, the `BFILE` data type is a read-only type. It is read-only because you can only insert or update these columns with a new virtual directory or filename. There is also no way to write a new external file through the database unless you provide external libraries to do it or leverage the `UTL_FILE` package. Likewise, there is also no Oracle utility that lets you read a canonical path directly. An available canonical path would let you prepend it to a filename, and create a canonical filename.

Web applications overcome this limitation by configuring an alias and a virtual directory in your HTTP server. You can use the Apache, Oracle HTTP Server, or Oracle 10*g* Application Server as the HTTP server. The alias maps to the database virtual path, and the virtual path maps to the database canonical path. Unfortunately, this type of architecture is tightly coupled, which means that when you change one, you must change the other.

Chapter 8 contains a means to overcome this limitation. It extends the database catalog by adding the `GET_DIRECTORY_PATH` function to the `SYSTEM` schema and granting access to it to the `PLSQL` schema. Then, it creates a `GET_CANONICAL_BFILENAME` function to the `PLSQL` schema. While they do not eliminate the tight coupling between the HTTP server and database, they do eliminate it for your programs interacting with the `PLSQL` schema.

Extending the Database Catalog

Virtual directories are created by the SYS or SYSTEM users and owned by the SYS user. By default SYSTEM only has read permissions to the DBA_DIRECTORIES view through the SELECT_CATALOG_ROLE. Roles limit the ability to directly access tables from PL/SQL programs, like get_directory_path.sql found in Chapter 8.

In order to grant direct permissions in this case, you must first connect without a schema as the SYSDBA user. As the superuser, you can grant SELECT privilege on the DBA_DIRECTORIES view to the SYSTEM user, as noted:

```
SQL> CONNECT / as sysdba
Connected.
SQL> GRANT SELECT ON dba_directories TO system;
Grant succeeded.
```

After granting the permission, you can connect as the SYSTEM user and run get_directory_path.sql to create the GET_DIRECTORY_PATH function. This extends the catalog behaviors, but you'll still need to grant permissions to the designated user scheme. You do this by granting the EXECUTE permission on the GET_DIRECTORY_PATH function. The following grants that privilege to the PLSQL user:

```
SQL> GRANT EXECUTE ON get_directory_path TO plsql;
```

Reconnect as the PLSQL user and create a synonym to the GET_DIRECTORY_PATH function. You can create a local copy of GET_CANONICAL_BFILE function. The following syntax builds the synonym:

```
SQL> CREATE SYNONYM get_canonical_bfilename FOR system.get_directory_path;
```

Run the get_canonical_bfilename.sql script. It builds a local copy of the GET_CANONICAL_BFILE function. The function returns a canonical filename.

The ReadBFILE.java program depends on several things. It expects that you have compiled both the GET_DIRECTORY_PATH and GET_CANONICAL_PATH functions with their appropriate grants and synonyms. If you have not run these programs, you can find full instructions to run the create_store.sql and seed_store.sql scripts in the introduction. Also, after running them, you must create a virtual directory that points to where you will physically locate the files. Chapter 8 demonstrates how to set up and grant permissions to a virtual directory.

You can test whether they're properly configured by running the following query on the respective platforms:

Windows

```
SELECT    get_canonical_bfilename('ITEM'
                                  ,'ITEM_PHOTO'
                                  ,'ITEM_TITLE'
                                  ,'Star Wars - Episode I')
FROM      dual;
```

Unix

```
SELECT    get_canonical_bfilename('ITEM'
                                  ,'ITEM_PHOTO'
                                  ,'ITEM_TITLE'
                                  ,'Star Wars - Episode I'
                                  , 'LINUX')
FROM      dual;
```

You have correctly configured your environment when this select statement returns the canonical filename. Reading the file is dependent on the correct file permissions.

The `ReadBFILE.class` uses the Database Connection Input dialog shown earlier, in Figure D-3. After entering the connection data, you are prompted to enter the query data in the database query input dialog. Figure D-9 shows you that dialog.

Clicking OK displays a *JFrame* containing the poster for Star Wars – Episode I, The Phantom Menace. Figure D-10 displays the image by resolving the path through the database and avoids using an external virtual directory.

NOTE
The `ReadBFILE.java` *class must run on the same physical machine as the database, and it must have at least* `other` *read-only file system privileges to the canonical path or directory in Linux or Unix.*

The `ReadBFILE.java` script uses a *CallableStatement,* not a *Statement.* Previous examples use a *Statement* for preparsed SQL statements. You use a *CallableStatement* when you want to submit parameters to a SQL statement. This is also known as binding values.

A *CallableStatement* also lets you work with PL/SQL stored functions or procedures. This example uses an anonymous block to capture the canonical filename. It takes one output parameter from the *CallableStatement.* You map the output parameter by using the `registerOutParameter()` method from the *CallableStatement.* You map the input parameters by using the `setString()` method, but there are other methods that support different Oracle data types.

TIP
Function and procedure calls should be made in an anonymous-block program. Incorrect calls to stored functions and procedures inside a CallableStatement instance can raise an `ORA-17033` *error. This is true using Java 5 or earlier, but Java 6 simply raises an IO error.*

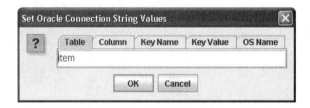

FIGURE D-9 *Database Query Input dialog*

FIGURE D-10   *ReadBFILE.java display*

You also use the `execute()` method, not the `executeQuery()` method. Out parameters can be captured by either name or positional reference. In this case, the out parameter uses positional reference. The program is

-- This is found in ReadBFILE.java on the publisher's web site.

```java
// Required imports.
import java.awt.GridLayout;
import java.awt.image.BufferedImage;
import java.io.IOException;
import java.io.File;
import javax.imageio.ImageIO;
import javax.swing.ImageIcon;
import javax.swing.JFrame;
import javax.swing.JLabel;
import javax.swing.JOptionPane;
import javax.swing.JPanel;

// Generic JDBC imports.
import java.sql.CallableStatement;
import java.sql.Connection;
import java.sql.DatabaseMetaData;
import java.sql.DriverManager;
import java.sql.ResultSet;
import java.sql.ResultSetMetaData;
import java.sql.SQLException;
import java.sql.Types;

// Oracle JDBC import.
import oracle.jdbc.driver.OracleDriver;
import oracle.jdbc.pool.OracleDataSource;
```

```java
// Include book libraries (available at publisher's web site).
import plsql.jdbc.DataConnectionPane;
import plsql.jdbc.DataTablePane;
// ----------------------------------------------------------------/
public class ReadBFILE extends JFrame {
  // Define database connections.
  private String host;
  private String port;
  private String dbname;
  private String userid;
  private String passwd;

  // Define query variables.
  private String tableName;
  private String columnName;
  private String keyColumnName;
  private String keyColumnValue;
  private String operatingSystem;

  // Define data connection and query panes.
  private DataConnectionPane message = new DataConnectionPane();
  private DataTablePane table = new DataTablePane(DataTablePane.TABLE_COLUMN_KEY);

  // Construct the class.
  public ReadBFILE (String s) {
    super(s);

    // Get database connection values or exit.
    if (JOptionPane.showConfirmDialog(this,message
          ,"Set Oracle Connection String Values"
          ,JOptionPane.OK_CANCEL_OPTION) == 0) {

      // Set class connection variables.
      host = message.getHost();
      port = message.getPort();
      dbname = message.getDatabase();
      userid = message.getUserID();
      passwd = message.getPassword();

      // Print connection to console (debugging tool).
      message.getConnection();

      // Collect query parameters.
      if (JOptionPane.showConfirmDialog(this,table
            ,"Set Oracle Connection String Values"
            ,JOptionPane.OK_CANCEL_OPTION) == 0) {

        // Set class query variables.
        tableName = table.getTableName();
        columnName = table.getColumnName();
        keyColumnName = table.getKeyColumnName();
        keyColumnValue = table.getKeyColumnValue();
        operatingSystem = table.getOperatingSystem();
```

```
        // Print table query variables.
        table.getTable(); }
      else
        System.exit(2);

      // Create a JPanel for data display.
      ManageBFILE panel = new ManageBFILE();

      // Configure the JPanel.
      panel.setOpaque(true);
      setContentPane(panel);

      // Configure the JFrame.
      setDefaultCloseOperation(JFrame.EXIT_ON_CLOSE);
      setLocation(100,100);
      pack();
      setVisible(true); }
    else
      System.exit(1); }
  // -----------------------------------------------------------------/
  private class ManageBFILE extends JPanel {
    // Use to read and diaplay BFILE image file.
    private BufferedImage image;
    private JLabel label;
    private String canonicalFileName;
  // -----------------------------------------------------------------/
  public ManageBFILE () {

    // Set layout manager.
    super(new GridLayout(1,0));

    // Query the database and read canonical filename.
    canonicalFileName = getQuery(host,port,dbname,userid,passwd);

    try {
      image = ImageIO.read(new File(canonicalFileName)); }
    catch (IOException e) {
      System.out.println(e.getMessage());
      System.exit(3); }

    // Put the image into a container and add container to JPanel.
    label = new JLabel(new ImageIcon(image));
    add(label); }
    // -----------------------------------------------------------------/
  private String getQuery(String host,String port,String dbname
                         ,String user,String pswd) {

    // Define return variable.
    String data = null;

    try {
      // Set the Pooled Connection Source
      OracleDataSource ods = new OracleDataSource();
```

```java
String url = "jdbc:oracle:thin:@//"+host+":"+port+"/"+dbname;
ods.setURL(url);
ods.setUser(userid);
ods.setPassword(passwd);

// Define connection.
Connection conn = ods.getConnection();

// Create statement.
CallableStatement stmt =
  conn.prepareCall("BEGIN " +
                   "  ? := get_canonical_bfilename(?,?,?,?,?);" +
                   "END;");

// Register the OUT mode variable.
stmt.registerOutParameter(1,Types.VARCHAR);

// Register the IN mode variables.
stmt.setString(2,tableName);
stmt.setString(3,columnName);
stmt.setString(4,keyColumnName);
stmt.setString(5,keyColumnValue);
stmt.setString(6,operatingSystem);

// Execute query.
if (stmt.execute());

// Read rows and only CLOB data type columns.
data = (String) stmt.getString(1);

// Close resources.
stmt.close();
conn.close();

// Return CLOB as a String data type.
return data; }
catch (SQLException e) {
  if (e.getSQLState() == null) {
    System.out.println(
      new SQLException("Oracle Thin Client Net8 Connection Error.",
                       "ORA-" + e.getErrorCode() +
                       ": Incorrect Net8 thin client arguments:\n\n" +
                       "  host name      [" + host + "]\n" +
                       "  port number    [" + port + "]\n" +
                       "  database name [" + dbname + "]\n"
                       , e.getErrorCode()).getSQLState());

    // Return an empty String on error.
    return data; }
  else { System.out.println("here");
    System.out.println(e.getMessage());

    // Return an empty String on error.
    return data; }}
```

```
    finally {
  if (data == null) System.exit(1); }}}
// ----------------------------------------------------------------/
public static void main(String[] args) {
  ReadBFILE frame = new ReadBFILE("Read BFILE Image"); }}
```

NOTE
*Diagnostic information for your keyed inputs is printed to the
command console when you run the* ReadBFILE.class *file.*

This section has shown you how to read and display images stored on the file system. It has
also demonstrated how you can leverage the Oracle 11*g* database to find and read canonical
filenames. The PL/SQL functions from Chapter 8 show you how to extend the data catalog to
deliver this functionality.

Summary
This appendix has reviewed the basics of working with Java and the JDBC. You have seen how to
work with scalar and large objects. This appendix has provided coding examples to support how
you'll write PL/SQL programming units to support external programming languages.

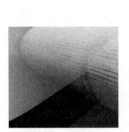

APPENDIX
E

Regular Expression Primer

egular expressions in Oracle 11*g* enable you to perform powerful context searches in variable-length strings, like the `CHAR`, `CLOB`, `NCHAR`, `NCLOB`, `NVARCHAR2`, and `VARCHAR2` character datatypes. They are strings that describe or match a set of strings. They provide a powerful set of pattern matching capabilities by combining character classes, collation classes, metacharacters, metasequences, and literals. Character classes are groups of possible characters at a point in the search. Collation classes are sets of characters and are treated like a range. Metacharacters are operators that specify search algorithms, and metasequences are operators created by two metacharacters or literals. Literals are characters, character sets, and words. Together, these let you search text by using patterns to match strings.

This appendix presents regular expressions in the following sections:

- Introduction to regular expressions

- Oracle 11*g* regular expression implementation

- Using regular expressions

These sections should explain what regular expressions are, and how you can use them in your PL/SQL application code. If you want the examples, go straight to the section "Using Regular Expressions."

Introduction to Regular Expressions

Regular expressions let you match text based on common characteristics, like case insensitive or approximate spelling searches. Some languages provide search functions to perform these operations, while others don't. Regular expressions are a major facility in scripting languages, like Perl and PHP. They provide pattern matching and flexibility when you search long strings for substrings or instances of substrings.

You build pattern matching expressions by combining character classes, collation classes, metacharacters, metasequences, and literals. These components are covered in the following subsections.

Character Classes

Character classes are groups or ranges of possible characters. They may appear at any point in your regular expression. Character classes are traditionally delimited by `[]` *(square brackets)*. You use a "–" *(dash)* inside the square brackets to designate everything between two characters. The "–" in this context is a *character-class metacharacter.*

You use the ordinal numbers from 0 to 9 and upper- or lowercase letters A through F to designate hexadecimal values. The character class `[ABCDEFabcdef0123456789]` represents the group of possible characters found in hexadecimal characters. You can represent the same letter and number range sets by using the character class `[A-Fa-f0-9]`. There is no practical limit to the number of ranges that you can put in a character class.

The POSIX specification broadens the use of character classes by introducing the concept of portable character classes (which means portable across languages). Portable character classes are nested inside the basic `[]` as `[::]` *(square brackets with colons)*. This means that the character class `[A-Za-z]` that represents all upper- and lowercase letters is equal to the `[[:alpha:]]` portable character class. Another popular character class `[A-Za-z0-9]` for all characters and numbers is equal to `[[:alpha:][:digit:]]`. This is a set of portable character classes that you can replace with the `[[:alnum:]]` portable character class for alphanumeric characters. You should note that the portable character classes are inside an additional set of square brackets. More or less, the portable character classes act like range aliases. The second set of square brackets delimits them as a character class. Unlike language-specific character classes, portable character classes map across languages and simplify globalizing search patterns. Table E-1 lists the POSIX portable character classes.

By themselves, character classes apply only to a single character or position of a string. When matched with the "+" metacharacter (which means one or more of the preceding characters or character classes), the expression may apply to more than a single character. The following example demonstrates regular expressions that use standard character classes:

```
-- This is found in character_class1.sql on the publisher's web site.
DECLARE
  counter        NUMBER := 1;
  source_string VARCHAR2(12) := 'A1';
  pattern1       VARCHAR2(12) := '[A-Z]';
  pattern2       VARCHAR2(12) := '[0-9]';
BEGIN
  -- Compare using standard character class ranges.
  FOR i IN 1..LENGTH(source_string) LOOP
    IF REGEXP_INSTR(SUBSTR(source_string,counter,i),pattern1) = i THEN
      dbms_output.put(REGEXP_SUBSTR(
                       SUBSTR(source_string,counter,i),pattern1));
    ELSE
      dbms_output.put_line(REGEXP_SUBSTR(
                       SUBSTR(source_string,counter,i),pattern2));
    END IF;
    counter := counter + 1;
  END LOOP;
END;
/
```

Character Ranges	Description
[:alnum:]	All alphanumeric characters
[:alpha:]	All alphabetic characters
[:cntrl:]	All non-printable control characters
[:digit:]	All numeric digits
[:graph:]	All [:digit:], [:lower:], [:punct:], and [:upper:] portable character classes
[:lower:]	All lowercase alphabetic characters
[:print:]	All printable characters
[:punct:]	All punctuation characters
[:space:]	All nonprinting space characters
[:upper:]	All uppercase alphabetic characters
[:xdigit:]	All hexadecimal characters

TABLE E-1 *POSIX Portable Character Classes*

This prints A1 because the first character of the `source_string` matches the `pattern1` character class, and second character matches the `pattern2` character class. The next program applies the same logic but substitutes the POSIX portable character classes for the language-specific character classes.

```
-- This is found in character_class2.sql on the publisher's web site.
DECLARE
  counter        NUMBER := 1;
  source_string  VARCHAR2(12) := 'A1';
  pattern1       VARCHAR2(12) := '[[:alpha:]]';
  pattern2       VARCHAR2(12) := '[[:alnum:]]';
BEGIN
  -- Compare using standard character class ranges.
  FOR i IN 1..LENGTH(source_string) LOOP
    IF REGEXP_INSTR(SUBSTR(source_string,counter,i),pattern1) = i THEN
      dbms_output.put(REGEXP_SUBSTR(
                         SUBSTR(source_string,counter,i),pattern1));
    ELSE
      dbms_output.put_line(REGEXP_SUBSTR(
                             SUBSTR(source_string,counter,i),pattern2));
    END IF;
    counter := counter + 1;
  END LOOP;
END;
/
```

Like the prior example, this program prints A1 because the first character of the `source_string` matches the `pattern1` portable character class, and second character matches the `pattern2` portable character class.

This section has demonstrated the basics of using character and portable character classes. You will revisit the concept later in other program samples.

Collation Classes

The *collation* class is new to regular expressions. It was introduced by the POSIX regular expression standard and is designed to allow you to collate in languages that require a collating element. Collating elements may contain more than one character, whereas traditional regular expressions limit collating elements to single characters.

You define a collation class by using [. .] *(square brackets with offsetting dots or periods)*. An example drawn from the *Oracle Database Globalization Guide* creates a collation element *inside* a character class: [a-[.ch.]]. This allows you to find whether a collating element is between an a or a ch. This is highly dependent on the NLS_SORT parameter and language implementation. The details are best left to another book, on text retrieval.

Metacharacters

A *metacharacter* provides some mechanics for performing pattern matching. Some books and documents group character classes, intervals, and scope limiting parentheses as metacharacters. This appendix takes a different tack. Character and collating classes are treated separately from other metacharacters. Both were covered earlier in the appendix. Table E-2 lists metacharacters.

Metacharacter	Name	Type	Description
( )	parentheses	Delimiter	They act as a constraint on the scope of comparison. A common use is to choose between two alternatives with the '|' (or bar), like a 't(o|oo)' regular expression that finds a *to* or *too* in a string. *You create subexpressions when you enclose evaluation criteria in parentheses.* Failure to match parentheses in subexpressions raises an ORA-12725 exception. This occurs because Oracle implements subexpressions only when they are inside parentheses. This differs from most implementations of regular expressions, and it also changes some syntax rules.
{*m*}	exact	Interval	Matches exactly *m* occurrences of the preceding subexpression or character.
{*m*,}	at least	Interval	Matches at least *m* occurrences of the preceding subexpression or character.
{*m,n*}	between	Interval	Matches at least *m* occurrences, but not more than *n* occurrences, of the preceding subexpression or character.
|	or bar	Logical	It acts as a logical OR operator; and it treats the characters to the left and right as operands in a matching operation. It returns a match when either operand is found. Alternatively, it can manage a logical OR relationship between sets of characters when they are inside ordinary parentheses. Parentheses act as scope delimiters as already noted with an *or bar* example.
.	dot	Matching	It matches any one character.
^	caret	Matching	It matches the beginning of a line in generalized regular expressions but represents the beginning of a multiple-line document unless you specify the "m" match_type_flag. Please refer to Table E-4 for more information.
$	dollar sign	Matching	It matches the end of a line in generalized regular expressions but represents the end of a multiple-line document unless you specify the "m" match_type_flag. See Table E-4 for more information.
^	caret	Negation	It acts as a negation operator only when you use it inside a character class. Then, it is technically a character-class metacharacter. The following regular expression disallows any uppercase characters between K and M: '[^K-M]'

TABLE E-2 *POSIX Metacharacters*

Metacharacter	Name	Type	Description
–	dash	Range	It acts as a range operator, but only when it is inside a character class. This limited context makes the "–" a character-class metacharacter. Please check the section "Character Classes" for more information on this metacharacter.
?	question mark	Repetition	It makes the preceding character optional in a matching solution. In other words, there may or may not be the preceding character in a string. The following regular expression checks for an American or British spelling using this metacharacter: `'colou?r'`
*	asterisk or star	Repetition	It matches any instance of zero to many characters. Thus it functions like a combination of "." and "?" for any character because it matches *any* character or *no* character.
+	plus	Repetition	It matches at least once or many times the preceding character. Returning to an early regular expression example that chooses between two alternatives, like `'t(o|oo)'`, it finds *to* or *too* in a string. You can now rewrite it as the regular expression `'t(o|o+)'`, which works for *to, too,* or *tooooo*.

TABLE E-2   *POSIX Metacharacters (continued)*

As you've seen in this section, metacharacters have many uses. Unfortunately, not all can be shown in this primer. You will find broader examples combining these metacharacters into meaningful regular expressions in the section "Using Regular Expressions" later in this appendix.

Metasequences

Metasequences are characters combined with backslashes, like those in Table E-3. The backslash strips the special nature of other metacharacters, like parentheses or a ".". They also add metacharacteristics to ordinary characters like the "<" *(less than symbol)* or ">" *(greater than symbol)* in some programming languages.

NOTE
Oracle 11g does not support the "\<" (word beginning) or "\>" (word ending) metasequences. This means you may need to leverage the LTRIM *and* RTRIM *functions.*

Oracle 11*g* doesn't support some popular regular expression metasequences. While Oracle sources have made no formal statement of how they plan to improve regular expressions, you can be certain that they will do so.

Metasequence	Name	Type	Description
\n	backreference	POSIX	It matches the nth preceding subexpression. You raise an ORA-12727 when the backreference exceeds the number of subexpressions. Oracle 11*g* requires you to enclose all subexpressions in parentheses.
\d	digit	Perl	It is a metasequence equal to the portable character class [[:digit:]] and matches any digit.
\D	nondigit	Perl	It is a metasequence equal to the portable character class [^[:digit:]] and matches any non-digit.
\w	word character	Perl	It is a metasequence equal to the portable character class [[:alnum:]] and matches any word character.
\W	nonword character	Perl	It is a metasequence equal to the portable character class [^[:alnum:]] and matches any non-word character.
\s	whitespace character	Perl	It is a metasequence equal to the portable character class [[:space:]] and matches any whitespace character.
\S	nonwhitespace character	Perl	It is a metasequence equal to the portable character class [^[:space:]] and matches any non-whitespace.
\A	beginning of string	Perl	It is a metasequence that matches the beginning of a new string. It does not find the beginnings of new lines when you enable multiple-line searches with the match_type_flag covered in the section "REGEXP_COUNT Function."
\Z	end of string	Perl	It is a metasequence that matches the end of a new string. Like the \A metasequence, it does not find the ends of lines when you enable multiple-line searches.
\z	end of string	Perl	It is a metasequence that matches the end of a new string regardless of how you've set the match_type_flag value.

TABLE E-3   *Oracle 11g Supported POSIX and Perl Metasequences*

Literals

Regular expression literal values are simply string literals as discussed in Chapter 3. They may consist of one to many characters. Regular expressions can be explicit in providing the full text of a literal string, or they can use pattern matching sequences.

Oracle 11*g* Regular Expression Implementation

PL/SQL and SQL began supporting these text search and comparison operations in the Oracle 10*g* database release. The Oracle 11*g* database supports IEEE Portable Operating System Interface (POSIX) standard draft 1003.2/D11.2, and Unicode Regular Expression Guidelines of the Unicode Consortium. Oracle 11*g* extends matching capabilities for multilingual data beyond the POSIX standard. This release also adds support for the common Perl regular expression extensions that are not covered in and don't conflict with the POSIX standard.

Oracle 11*g* introduces a restrictive subordinate expression to the REGEXP_INSTR *(regular expression in-string)* and REGEXP_SUBSTR *(regular expression substring)* functions, which were introduced in Oracle 10*g*. Oracle 11*g* also adds the REGEXP_COUNT *(regular expression count)* function.

Oracle 11*g* supports regular expressions against variable-length strings, like the CHAR, CLOB, NCHAR, NCLOB, NVARCHAR2, and VARCHAR2 character datatypes. It does not support using regular expressions with the LONG datatype. Oracle recommends that you migrate LONG datatypes to CLOB datatypes. After all, the LONG datatype is only provided as a convenience for backward compatibility.

There are five regular expression functions in Oracle 11*g*. The following subsections define them. Rather than summarize formal parameter definitions when they occur more than once, they're repeated in each function description. The exception is the match_type_flag value, which is covered once in the REGEXP_COUNT function subsection. Hopefully, this choice makes the appendix an easier spot reference for you. You can find examples by skipping to the section "Using Regular Expressions" later in this appendix.

REGEXP_COUNT Function

The REGEXP_COUNT function is new in Oracle 11*g*. It lets you count the number of times a specific pattern is found in a string. It has the prototype

```
REGEXP_COUNT(source_string, pattern [, start_position [, match_type_flag]])
```

The source_string can be any character expression, provided the datatype is a CHAR, CLOB, NCHAR, NCLOB, NVARCHAR2, or VARCHAR2. You may recall from Chapter 6 that an expression can be a string literal or a function return value that meets the datatype requirement. The character expression can also be a column value or bind variable. For example, you could use the :new.column_name as a source_string value in a database trigger. See Chapter 10 for more information on database triggers.

The pattern value can be any valid regular expression, but *the length must be less than or equal to 512 characters.* POSIX regular expressions are supported in Oracle 11*g*. You must prepend any apostrophe with a single quote because you pass the pattern value as an actual parameter into a function call. Alternatively, you can reset the quote identifier in your session. Appendix B shows you how to substitute another backquoting identifier for the default apostrophe.

The start_position value is an integer expression, whose default value is 1. It is not uncommon to find a starting point inside the string by calling the REGEXP_INSTR function as an expression for this actual parameter.

The match_type_flag value is a string literal. The string may contain either an "i" or a "c", and one or more of the following: "n", "m", or "x". Collectively, they override the default matching behavior. The default matching behavior performs as follows:

■   It uses the NLS_SORT parameter and is *generally* case-sensitive matching. It is always case sensitive matching *(by default)* when the NLS_SORT parameter is a western European character set.

■   It restricts the " . " *(dot or period)* so that it doesn't match a newline return.

■   It treats the strings as a single line, which means the *caret* (^) and *dollar sign* ($) refer to the beginning and ending of the string, respectively.

■   It matches whitespace characters against whitespace characters.

Table E-4 qualifies the override flags for the match_type_flag parameter. This table applies to all five of the regular expression functions.

You might wonder why it was so important to add the REGEXP_COUNT function in Oracle 11*g*. The answer is quite straightforward. If you want to handle the occurrences of results individually rather than collectively, counting them lets you create a dynamic range FOR loop. Conversely, it eliminates the need for you to loop through a string counting the occurrences of a pattern match. The function typically solves the latter more frequently than the former. You can find an example demonstrating this behavior in the section "Using Regular Expressions."

REGEXP_INSTR Function

The REGEXP_INSTR function is enhanced in Oracle 11*g*. You can now use a restricting subordinate expression. The REGEXP_INSTR function lets you find a position index value inside a string. You use it to find a starting point inside a string, and it is known as the regular expression in-string function.

The prototype for the function is

```
REGEXP_INSTR(source_string, pattern [, start_position [, occurrence
             [, return_option [, match_type_flag [, subexpression]]]]])
```

The new subexpression parameter lets you do priority searching on subexpressions. As qualified in the section "Introduction to Regular Expression Introductions," a subexpression matches the

Match Type Flag	Description
i	Sets the search to case-insensitive matching, overriding the NLS_SORT parameter where necessary.
c	Sets the search to case-sensitive matching, overriding the NLS_SORT parameter where necessary.
n	Enables the " . " *(dot or period)* to truly match any character, including a newline character.
m	Enables the search to recognize multiple lines inside a string. This ensures that the *caret* (^) and *dollar sign* ($) work as they normally do in scripting languages.
x	Sets the search to ignore whitespace characters.

TABLE E-4   *List of Possible Match Type Flag Values*

value on either the left or the right of the " | " metacharacter. The " | " metacharacter acts like a logical OR operator. For example, you can use a pattern of "col(o|ou)r" when you want all strings matching either *color* (American English) or *colour* (British English). The subexpression is the (o|ou). If you read the introduction, you should know that you really don't require a subexpression in this case. You can accomplish the same thing with "colou?r" because the question mark (?) treats the character that precedes it as optional.

Single-Dimension Character Array

A string is actually a single-dimensional character array. Oracle defines these character arrays by using the database character set. It also lets you override the default character set and build them to your own specifications. This means that you could have an array of elements where each element is one, two, or three bytes, depending on how you configured it.

Whether stored in one, two, or three bytes, a string is really stored like an array. If you insert the word SAMPLE into a variable or column using a fixed- or variable-length character datatype, you actually store the following:

Index Value	Character Value
1	S
2	A
3	M
4	P
5	L
6	E

This index uses a 1-based numbering system to index the characters of your string. The index lets you find and parse strings.

The source_string can be any character expression, provided the datatype is a CHAR, CLOB, NCHAR, NCLOB, NVARCHAR2, or VARCHAR2. You may recall from Chapter 6 that an expression can be a string literal or a function return value that meets the datatype requirement. The character expression can also be a column value or a bind variable. For example, you could use the :new.column_name as a source_string value in a database trigger. See Chapter 10 for more information on database triggers.

The pattern value can be any valid regular expression, but *the length must be less than or equal to 512 characters.* POSIX regular expressions are supported in Oracle 11g. You must prepend any apostrophe with a single quote because you pass the pattern value as an actual parameter into a function call. Alternatively, you can reset the quote identifier in your session or for a single assignment (as described in the "Alternative Backquoting" sidebar).

The start_position value is an integer expression, whose default value is 1. It is not uncommon to find a starting point inside the string by calling the REGEXP_INSTR function as an expression for this actual parameter.

The occurrence value is an integer expression, whose default value is 1. If you want another occurrence, you must provide a value. Override values are typically defined by business rules.

The return_option value is an integer expression. The default value is 0, which represents the position or index of *the beginning* of the first substring matched by the pattern. You can override this value by using a 1, which instructs the function to return *the character after* the substring that matches the pattern.

The `match_type_flag` value is a string literal. The string may contain either an "i" or a "c", and one or more of the following: "n", "m", or "x". Collectively, they override the default matching behavior. The subsection "REGEXP_COUNT Function" describes the default and overriding matching behaviors (refer back to Table E-3).

The `subexpression` value is zero by default. This means that it returns only those values that match the complete set of subexpressions. You can specify a value between 1 and 9 when the subexpression returns a positive integer. Then, the values matching only that subexpression are returned.

REGEXP_LIKE Function

The `REGEXP_LIKE` function lets you find a regular expression match inside a string. You use it in lieu of the old `LIKE` comparison operator.

The prototype for the function is

```
REGEXP_LIKE(source_string, pattern [, match_type_flag])
```

The `source_string` can be any character expression, provided the datatype is a CHAR, CLOB, NCHAR, NCLOB, NVARCHAR2, or VARCHAR2. You may recall from Chapter 6 that an expression can be a string literal or a function return value that meets the datatype requirement. The character expression can also be a column value or bind variable. For example, you could use the `:new.column_name` as a `source_string` value in a database trigger. See Chapter 10 for more information on database triggers.

The `pattern` value can be any valid regular expression, but *the length must be less than or equal to 512 characters.* POSIX regular expressions are supported in Oracle 11*g*. You must prepend any apostrophe with a single quote because you pass the `pattern` value as an actual parameter into a function call. Alternatively, you can reset the quote identifier in your session. Appendix B shows you how to substitute another backquoting identifier for the default apostrophe.

Alternative Backquoting

Alternative backquoting lets you substitute another character for the default string delimiting apostrophe. It is done by using a "q" as a quote substitution flag. An example of alternative backquoting follows:

```
DECLARE
  sample VARCHAR2(40);
BEGIN
  sample := q'!Q's are the quoting trick!!';
  dbms_output.put_line(sample);
END;
/
```

The "q'!" and "!'" act as delimiters. They reassign the backquoting role from an apostrophe to an exclamation mark. More or less, these form metasequences. You can assign a string with an apostrophe to a VARCHAR2 variable when the metasequences delimit it. You should also note that the exclamation mark (!) doesn't require backquoting inside the delimited string. It prints

```
Q's are the quoting trick!
```

The `match_type_flag` value is a string literal. The string may contain either an "i" or a "c", and one or more of the following: "n", "m", or "x". Collectively, they override the default matching behavior. The subsection "REGEXP_COUNT Function" contains the default and overriding matching behaviors (See Table E-3).

REGEXP_REPLACE Function

The `REGEXP_REPLACE` function lets you find and replace a substring inside of a string. The prototype for the function is

```
REGEXP_REPLACE(source_string, pattern , replace_string [, start_position
                [, occurrence [, match_type_flag]]])
```

The `source_string` can be any character expression, provided the datatype is a `CHAR`, `CLOB`, `NCHAR`, `NCLOB`, `NVARCHAR2`, or `VARCHAR2`. You may recall from Chapter 6 that an expression can be a string literal or a function return value that meets the datatype requirement. The character expression can also be a column value or bind variable. For example, you could use the `:new.column_name` as a `source_string` value in a database trigger. See Chapter 10 for more information on database triggers.

The `pattern` value can be any valid regular expression, but *the length must be less than or equal to 512 characters*. POSIX regular expressions are supported in Oracle 11*g*. You must prepend any apostrophe with a single quote because you pass the `pattern` value as an actual parameter into a function call. Alternatively, you can reset the quote identifier in your session. Appendix B shows you how to substitute another backquoting identifier for the default apostrophe.

The `replace_string` can be any character expression, provided the datatype is a `CHAR`, `CLOB`, `NCHAR`, `NCLOB`, `NVARCHAR2`, or `VARCHAR2`. If the `replace_string` is a `CLOB` or `NCLOB` datatype, then Oracle 11*g* truncates the string to 32KB.

The `start_position` value is an integer expression, whose default value is 1. It is not uncommon to find a starting point inside the string by calling the `REGEXP_INSTR` function as an expression for this actual parameter.

The `occurrence` value is an integer expression, whose default value is 1. If you want another occurrence, you must provide a value. Override values are typically defined by business rules.

The `match_type_flag` value is a string literal. The string may contain either an "i" or a "c", and one or more of the following: "n", "m", or "x". Collectively, they override the default matching behavior. The subsection "REGEXP_COUNT Function" contains the default and overriding matching behaviors (found in Table E-3).

REGEXP_SUBSTR Function

The `REGEXP_SUBSTR` function is enhanced in Oracle 11*g*. You can now use a restricting subordinate expression. The `REGEXP_SUBSTR` function lets you find a substring inside a string.

The prototype for the function is

```
REGEXP_SUBSTR(source_string, pattern [, start_position [, occurrence
                [, match_type_flag [, subexpression]]]]])
```

The new subexpression lets you do priority searching on subexpressions. A quick refresher of what this means is found in the section "REGEXP_INSTR Function".

The `source_string` can be any character expression, provided the datatype is a `CHAR`, `CLOB`, `NCHAR`, `NCLOB`, `NVARCHAR2`, or `VARCHAR2`. You may recall from Chapter 6 that an expression can be a string literal or a function return value that meets the datatype requirement. The character expression can also be a column value or bind variable. For example, you could use the `:new.column_name` as a `source_string` value in a database trigger. See Chapter 10 for more information on database triggers.

The `pattern` value can be any valid regular expression, but *the length must be less than or equal to 512 characters*. POSIX regular expressions are supported in Oracle 11*g*. You must prepend any apostrophe with a single quote because you pass the `pattern` value as an actual parameter into a function call. Alternatively, you can reset the quote identifier in your session. Appendix B shows you how to substitute another backquoting identifier for the default apostrophe.

The `start_position` value is an integer expression, whose default value is 1. It is not uncommon to find a starting point inside the string by calling the `REGEXP_INSTR` function as an expression for this actual parameter.

The `occurrence` value is an integer expression, whose default value is 1. If you want another occurrence, you must provide a value. Override values are typically defined by business rules.

The `return_option` value is an integer expression. The default value is 0, which represents the position or index of *the beginning* of the first substring matched by the pattern. You can override this value by using a 1, which instructs the function to return *the character after* the substring that matches the pattern.

The `match_type_flag` value is a string literal. The string may contain either an "i" or a "c", and one or more of the following: "n", "m", or "x". Collectively, they override the default matching behavior. The "REGEXP_COUNT Function" subsection contains the default and overriding matching behaviors (found in Table E-3).

The `subexpression` value is zero by default. This means that it returns only those values that match the complete set of subexpressions. You can specify a value between 1 and 9 when the subexpression returns a positive integer. Then, the values matching only that subexpression are returned.

Using Regular Expressions

This section provides some examples of how you can use regular expression. The prototypes for the function are not repeated from the prior section. The examples are small and rely on the paragraph found in the sidebar.

Sample Search String

The following XHTML fragment serves as a search string for these example programs:

"The prologue, spoken by Galadriel, shows the Dark Lord Sauron forging the One Ring which he can use to conquer the lands of Middle-earth through his enslavement of the bearers of the Rings of Power. The Rings of Power are powerful magical rings given to individuals from the races of Elves, Dwarves and Men. A Last Alliance of Elves and Men is formed to counter Sauron and his forces at the foot of Mount Doom, but Sauron himself appears to kill Elendil, the king of the Mannish kingdom of Gondor. Just afterward, Isildur grabs his father's broken sword Narsil, and slashes at Sauron's hand. The stroke cuts off Sauron's fingers, separating him from the Ring and vanquishing his army. However, because Sauron's life is bound in the Ring, he is not completely defeated until the Ring itself is destroyed. Isildur takes the Ring and succumbs to its temptation, refusing to destroy it, but he is later ambushed and killed by orcs and the Ring is lost in the river into which Isildur fell.<p />"

You can download the `seed_regular_expression.sql` script from the publisher's web site to build the table and seed this string.

REGEXP_COUNT Function

The new `REGEXP_COUNT` function lets you count the number of times a specific pattern is found in a string. Three examples are provided; they count the number of title-case *(where only the first letter is capitalized)*, lowercase, and case-insensitive "`the`" words in the sample string.

Title Case Count

The following query counts the number of title-case "The" words followed by a whitespace. The whitespace avoids counting any other words, like *Theory, They,* or *There,* found in the sample story.

```
SELECT REGEXP_COUNT(story_thread, 'The ') AS "Title Case"
FROM   sample_regexp;
```

It returns an integer value of 3. There is also the possibility that with a different string, you could return an incorrect count if there were a word ending in a title case "The" followed by a space. Logic tells you that it is unlikely. You see how to address that possibility in the case-insensitive search later in this section.

Lowercase Count

The next query counts number of lowercase "`the`" words preceded and followed by a whitespace. As discussed, the whitespaces avoid counting any words that begin with the pattern, like *theory, they,* or *there.* The whitespace before "`the`" rules out words that end in the pattern, like *routhe* (which means sorrow). Ironically, sorrow is what you might feel with regular expressions when you overlook a pattern-matching possibility.

```
SELECT REGEXP_COUNT(story_thread, ' the ', 1, 'c') AS "Lowercase"
FROM   sample_regexp;
```

This function call uses the optional `start_position` and `match_type_flag` values to perform a case-sensitive search. The values provided as actual parameters are actually the default values.

You can reference these formal parameters in the section "REGEXP_COUNT Function," which appears earlier in this appendix. Table E-4 qualifies the valid list of values for these parameters. The case-sensitive search also requires that you enter the regular expression pattern in lowercase characters to find lowercase "the " words. This query returns an integer value of 15 from the sidebar string.

NOTE
The regular expression functions are defined as interfaces in the `STANDARD` *package, and they did not support named or mixed notation at the time of this writing against Oracle 11g Release 1.*

Case-Insensitive Count

The first query that follows counts the number of lowercase "the" words starting a line or else preceded by or followed by a whitespace. As discussed in the prior sections, the trailing whitespace avoids counting any words that begin with the pattern but aren't the correct word, like *Theory, They,* or *There.* The leading whitespace prevents counting words that end in the pattern, like *routhe* (which means sorrow). The combination of leading and trailing line, punctuation, or whitespace avoids counting "`the`" from inside the word father. Unfortunately, the leading whitespace also eliminates the first "`The`" word because it is preceded by a double quote.

This is where patterns, subexpressions, and metacharacters solve a common searching problem. The second query that follows looks for a case-insensitive "`the`" word that may be at the beginning of a line, immediately preceded by a double quote, or preceded by a whitespace. At the same time, the pattern will look for a "`the`" word that is followed by a dash, colon, comma, semicolon, or whitespace.

There are two approaches to solving this problem. One lets you accept the default matching behavior, and the other requires you to override the default matching behavior.

This one uses the default matching properties:

```
SELECT REGEXP_COUNT(
          story_thread
          ,'((^| +)|(["'']))(T|t)he(([-:,\.;])|( +|$))') AS "Case-insensitive"
FROM    sample_regexp;
```

It accomplishes case-insensitive searches provided there are no capitals other than "T" in the "the" words. The pattern uses parentheses to create a subexpression. The subexpression checks for an uppercase or lowercase "T". This type of subexpression is sometimes labeled as an alternation. Alternation is a regular expression term that means you choose between two alternatives.

The foregoing expression also uses two character classes. One qualifies a double or single quote *(please note that it is backquoted by an apostrophe because this is Oracle)*. The other qualifies a dash, colon, comma, *(backquoted)* period, or semicolon. Both character classes are options inside subexpressions. The "`((^| +)|(["'']))`" subexpression says that either one or the other nested subexpression is true. The first nested subexpression condition is met when the first character is the beginning of a line or one or more whitespaces. The second nested subexpression checks for a single or double quote.

The next "`(([-:,\.;])|( +|$))`" subexpression examines the trailing character. The first nested subexpression condition is met when the trailing character of the "the" word is a dash, colon, period, or semicolon. Alternatively, the other nested subexpression condition is met when the trailing characters are one or more whitespaces or the end-of-line marker.

A simpler approach leverages the `match_type_flag` available as part of the function. As shown in Table E-4, the "i" string designates case-insensitive searching. It has the following implementation:

```
SELECT REGEXP_COUNT(
          story_thread
          ,'((^| +)|(["'']))the(([-:,\.;])|( +|$))', 1, 'i') AS "Case-insensitive"
FROM    sample_regexp;
```

Both of these patterns yield a count of 18 words.

This section has demonstrated several approaches that show you how to use the REGEXP_COUNT function. The caveat is always the same, whether it is PL/SQL, SQL, or regular expression programming—*know what you want, rule out what you don't want, and look for the simplest way to do it.*

REGEXP_INSTR Function

The REGEXP_INSTR function lets you find a position index value inside a string. You use it to find a starting point inside a string, or the position immediate after the pattern. You set the return_option to 0 when you want the starting point and 1 when you want the position immediately after the ending point of the pattern.

The following example finds the starting and ending positions for the first occurrence of the proper noun Sauron in the sample story:

```
SELECT REGEXP_INSTR(story_thread,'sauron',1,1,0,'i') AS "Begin"
,      REGEXP_INSTR(story_thread,'sauron',1,1,1,'i') - 1 AS "End"
FROM   sample_regexp;
```

This returns the following starting and ending values:

```
    Begin        End
---------- ----------
       57         62
```

This has demonstrated how to find starting and ending points in strings. Together these two values let you parse a substring from a string. The function becomes more useful as the complexity of your pattern search grows.

REGEXP_LIKE Function

The REGEXP_LIKE function lets you find a regular expression match inside a string. You use it in lieu of the old LIKE comparison operator. The following example searches the sample string for a line beginning "a last alliance of elves and men".

```
SELECT sample_regexp_id
FROM   sample_regexp
WHERE  REGEXP_LIKE(story_thread,' ?a last alliance of elves and men ?','i');
```

The effectiveness of this search is that you can apply it against a CHAR, CLOB, NCHAR, NCLOB, NVARCHAR2, or VARCHAR2 datatype. The search is case insensitive and actually returns the row's primary key value. You should note that it uses "?" *(question mark)* characters to make the whitespaces before and after the string optional.

REGEXP_REPLACE Function

The REGEXP_REPLACE function lets you find and replace a substring inside of a string. The following example replaces all occurrences of Sauron with Sauroman, which may disconcert some dedicated Tolkien fans. No sacrilege is intended to a great piece of fiction.

```
-- This is found in regexp_replace.sql on the publisher's web site.
DECLARE
  container VARCHAR2(4000);
  beginning NUMBER := 1;
  ending    NUMBER;
  -- Define a cursor to recover correct story thread.
  CURSOR c IS
    SELECT story_thread
    FROM   sample_regexp
    WHERE  REGEXP_LIKE(story_thread,'a last alliance of elves and men ?','i');
BEGIN
  OPEN c;
  LOOP
    FETCH c INTO container;
    EXIT WHEN c%NOTFOUND;
```

```
   -- Set the ending range.
   ending := REGEXP_COUNT(container
                  ,'((^| +)|(["''']))Sauron(([-:,\.;])|( +|$))',1,'i');
   -- Replace all instances one at a time.
   FOR i IN beginning..ending LOOP
     container := REGEXP_REPLACE(container,'Sauron','Sauroman',beginning,i);
   END LOOP;
   dbms_output.put_line(container);
  END LOOP;
END;
/
```

The search pattern counts the number of times Sauron appears in the string. It does that by looking for a starting line metacharacter, whitespace, or punctuation mark before the word literal—*Sauron*. Afterward, it looks for a punctuation mark, whitespace, or end-of-line metacharacter. The combination of subexpressions and nested subexpressions lets you check for alternatives, which means either this or that.

The anonymous block replaces all occurrences of Sauron with Sauroman by calling the REGEXP_REPLACE function. If you're familiar with Perl, this approach is cumbersome but works. You have now seen how to use the REGEXP_REPLACE function.

REGEXP_SUBSTR Function

The REGEXP_SUBSTR function lets you find a substring inside a string. The following sample finds the first 50 complete words and punctuation beginning at position 53 in the data column.

```
SELECT LTRIM(REGEXP_SUBSTR(story_thread
            ,'((^| +)|(["''']))(([[:alpha:]]+(([-:,\.'';])|( +|$))+\.?){1,5}'
            ,53,1,'i')) AS substring
FROM sample_regexp
WHERE  REGEXP_LIKE(story_thread,' ?a last alliance of elves and men ?','i');
```

It returns the following substring:

```
SUBSTRING
---------------------------
Sauron forging the One Ring
```

The starting position is in the middle of the word prior to Sauron. The interval captures the first five whole words that start at or after position 53 in the story_thread column value. If you set the start point as 1 and the maximum interval value to a number greater than the number of words in the string, this pattern returns an entire string.

Like the prior patterns, this pattern uses a compound subexpression to check for (a) either a beginning line metacharacter or whitespace, or (b) a quotation character at the beginning of the string. It then checks for an optional alphabetical string by using a POSIX portable character class. Finally, it uses another compound subexpression to check for (a) punctuation characters or (b) either a whitespace or end-of-line metacharacter.

Two search principles are demonstrated in the regular expression. First, the pattern uses a backquoted "." (period) to find the beginning of another word before using the plus metacharacter to repeat the matching behavior (check Table E-2 for more information on it). Second, the apostrophes are backquoted by other single quotes because the single quote is an identifier in an Oracle 11*g* database.

This section has presented the last regular expression function, and it has demonstrated how to capture a substring from a string using regular expressions. These features are nice for large character strings but critical for quick pattern analysis of CLOB datatypes.

Summary

This appendix has explained regular expressions and shown you how to use regular expressions to search text. You should also have learned why centralizing matching logic in the Oracle 11g database helps you avoid middle-tier string processing.

APPENDIX
F

Wrapping PL/SQL
Code Primer

racle 11*g* provides the capability to wrap or obfuscate your PL/SQL stored programs. Wrapping your code encapsulates the business logic of your applications from prying eyes by hiding the source code. It converts the clear text in the database to an unreadable stream of data. You can obfuscate the clear text by using the command line `wrap` utility or by calling the `CREATE_WRAPPED` procedure or `WRAP` function found in the `DBMS_DDL` package.

You should wrap only the implementation details. This means you should wrap only functions, procedures, package bodies, and type bodies. You enable developers to use your code by leaving the package specification and the type specification. They just won't know how it performs the task, only what actual parameters they can submit and expect back from functions or type methods. You should ensure that you comment the specification with any helpful information to take advantage of wrapped code units, especially procedures because they don't define a direct return type like functions.

This appendix is organized into the following sections:

■ Limitations of wrapping PL/SQL

■ Using the `wrap` command-line utility

■ Using `DBMS_DDL` package to wrap PL/SQL

    ■ `WRAP` function

    ■ `CREATE_WRAPPED` procedure

The limitations imposed by wrapping are qualified first, then how to wrap using the command line, and finally the built-in procedure and function of the `DBMS_DDL` package.

Limitations of Wrapping PL/SQL

There are three limits to generically wrapping PL/SQL code in the database. First, you cannot wrap the source code of a database trigger, but you can reduce the logic to a single call to a wrapped stored function or procedure. Second, wrapping does not detect syntax or semantic errors, like missing tables or views; in this respect it differs from normal compilation. Wrapped code units manifest run-time errors for missing tables or views, like Native Dynamic SQL (NDS) statements. Third, wrapped code is only forward compatible for import into the database. This means that you can import a wrapped module built by an Oracle 10*g* database into an 11*g* database but not vice versa.

While it is difficult to decipher passwords in wrapped code, it isn't impossible. Oracle recommends that you don't embed passwords in wrapped program units.

There are specific errors generated by the method that you choose to wrap your code. The limitations are explained in the next two subsections.

Limitations of the PL/SQL Wrap Utility

The `wrap` utility is parsed by the PL/SQL compiler, not by the SQL*Plus compiler. This means that you cannot include SQL*Plus `DEFINE` notation inside wrapped program units. Also, most comments are removed when wrapped.

Limitations of the DBMS_DDL.WRAP Function

When you invoke DBMS_SQL.PARSE with a datatype that is a VARCHAR2A or VARCHAR2S and the text exceeds 32,767 bytes, you must set the LFFLG parameter to false. If you fail to do so, the DBMS_SQL.PARSE adds newline characters to the wrapped unit and corrupts it.

Using the Wrap Command-Line Utility

The wrap command-line utility works with files. This is a critical point because the utility wraps everything in the file. When you use the wrap utility, package specifications and type definitions should be in different physical files from their respective package bodies and type bodies. As discussed earlier, you should wrap only the implementation details, not the published specifications.

The prototype for the wrap utility is

```
wrap iname=input_file[{.sql |.ext}] [oname=output_file[{.plb |.ext}]
```

You can qualify the input and output files as relative or canonical filenames. Canonical filenames start at the root mount point in Linux or Unix and from a logical file system reference in Microsoft Windows. The default file extensions are .sql for input files and .plb for output files. You do not need to provide either extension if you are prepared to accept the default values, but you must provide overriding values when they differ.

The example works when the wrap command runs from the same directory as the input and output files:

```
wrap iname=input_file.sql oname=output_file.plb
```

After you wrap the files, you can then run them into the database. The compilation process will not raise exceptions when there are missing table or view dependencies because there is no syntax, semantic, or dependency checking during compilation of wrapped program units. They compile because the SQL DDL commands to CREATE [OR REPLACE] functions, procedures, package specifications and bodies, and type definitions and bodies are scrambled into a form understood by the PL/SQL compiler.

The CREATE [OR REPLACE] TRIGGER statement and anonymous-block DECLARE, BEGIN, and END keywords are not obfuscated. Comments inside the header declaration and C-style multiple-line comments, delimited by /* and */, are also not obfuscated.

Using the DBMS_DDL Command-Line Utility

The DBMS_DDL package contains an overloaded WRAP function and overloaded CREATE_WRAPPED procedure. You can use either to create a wrapped stored programming unit. The subsections cover both.

The WRAP Function

The WRAP function is an overloaded function that accepts a DDL statement as a single variable-length string of 32,767 or fewer bytes, a table of strings 256 bytes in length, or a table of strings 32,767 bytes in length. You supply lower and upper bounds for the table of strings when the actual parameter is a table of strings. The lower bound is always 1, and the upper bound is the maximum number of rows in the collection of strings.

The first prototype supports using a single input parameter:

```
DBMS_DDL.WRAP(ddl VARCHAR2) RETURN VARCHAR2
DBMS_DDL.WRAP(ddl DBMS_SQL.VARCHAR2S) RETURN VARCHAR2S
DBMS_DDL.WRAP(ddl DBMS_SQL.VARCHAR2A) RETURN VARCHAR2A
```

You can use this function to wrap a stored program unit as follows:

```
DECLARE
  source VARCHAR2(32767);
  result VARCHAR2(32767);
BEGIN
  source := 'CREATE FUNCTION one RETURN NUMBER IS BEGIN RETURN 1; END;';
  result := DBMS_DDL.WRAP(ddl => source);
  EXECUTE IMMEDIATE result;
END;
/
```

The program defines a DDL string, obfuscates it into the result variable, and then uses Native Dynamic SQL (NDS) to create the obfuscated function in the database. You can see the function specification by using the SQL*Plus DESCRIBE command.

```
FUNCTION one RETURNS NUMBER
```

Any attempt to inspect its detailed operations will yield an obfuscated result. You can test this by querying the stored function implementation in the TEXT column of the USER_SOURCE table, like the following:

```
SQL> COLUMN text FORMAT A80 HEADING "Source Text"
SQL> SET PAGESIZE 49999
SQL> SELECT text FROM user_source WHERE name = 'ONE';
```

The following output is returned:

```
FUNCTION one wrapped
a000000
369
abcd
... et cetera ...
```

The function can be rewritten to use a table of strings, as follows:

```
DECLARE
  source DBMS_SQL.VARCHAR2S;
  result DBMS_SQL.VARCHAR2S;
BEGIN
  source(1) := 'CREATE FUNCTION two RETURN NUMBER IS ';
  source(2) := '  BEGIN RETURN 2;';
  source(3) := '  END;';
  result := DBMS_DDL.WRAP(ddl => source, lb => 1, ub => source.COUNT);
  FOR i IN 1..result.COUNT LOOP
    stmt := stmt || result(i);
```

```
  END LOOP;
  EXECUTE IMMEDIATE stmt;
END;
/
```

The actual table input and return value must be either the DBMS_SQL.VARCHAR2S or DBMS_SQL.VARCHAR2A datatype. The former holds strings up to 256 bytes, while the latter holds strings up to 32,767 bytes. Any other datatype raises a PLS-00306 exception because the actual parameter doesn't match the datatype of the formal parameter.

The statement is built by concatenating the strings from the table. It then calls the obfuscated SQL DDL statement and creates the two function. You can see the function specification by using the SQL*Plus DESCRIBE command.

```
SQL> DESCRIBE two
FUNCTION two RETURNS NUMBER
```

This section has demonstrated how to use the DBMS_DDL.WRAP command. The next section shows you how to use the CREATE_WRAPPED procedure.

The CREATE_WRAPPED Procedure

The CREATE_WRAPPED function is an overloaded function that accepts a DDL statement as a single variable-length string of 32,767 or fewer bytes, a table of strings 256 bytes in length, or a table of strings 32,767 bytes in length. You supply lower and upper bounds for the table of strings when the actual parameter is a table of strings. The lower bound is always 1, and the upper bound is the maximum number of rows in the collection of strings.

The prototypes support using a single input parameter or table of strings:

```
DBMS_DDL.CREATE_WRAPPED(ddl VARCHAR2) RETURN VARCHAR2
DBMS_DDL.CREATE_WRAPPED(ddl DBMS_SQL.VARCHAR2S) RETURN VARCHAR2S
DBMS_DDL.CREATE_WRAPPED(ddl DBMS_SQL.VARCHAR2A) RETURN VARCHAR2A
```

You can use this anonymous block to test the wrapping procedure:

```
BEGIN
  dbms_ddl.create_wrapped(
    'CREATE OR REPLACE FUNCTION hello_world RETURN STRING AS '
    ||'BEGIN '
    ||'  RETURN ''Hello World!''; '
    ||'END;');
END;
/
```

After creating the function, you can query it by using the following SQL*Plus column formatting and query:

```
SQL> COLUMN message FORMAT A20 HEADING "Message"
SQL> SELECT hello_world AS message FROM dual;

Message
--------------------
Hello World!
```

You can describe the function to inspect its signature and return type:

```
SQL> DESCRIBE hello_world
FUNCTION hello_world RETURNS VARCHAR2
```

Any attempt to inspect its detailed operations will yield an obfuscated result. You can test this by querying stored function implementation in the TEXT column of the USER_SOURCE table, like the following:

```
SQL> COLUMN text FORMAT A80 HEADING "Source Text"
SQL> SET PAGESIZE 49999
SQL> SELECT text FROM user_source WHERE name = 'HELLO_WORLD';
```

The following output is returned:

```
FUNCTION hello_world wrapped
a000000
369
abcd
... et cetera ...
```

The procedure can be rewritten to use a table of strings, as follows:

```
DECLARE
   source DBMS_SQL.VARCHAR2S;
   stmt        VARCHAR2(4000);
BEGIN
   source(1) := 'CREATE FUNCTION hello_world2 RETURN VARCHAR2 IS ';
   source(2) := '  BEGIN RETURN 2;';
   source(3) := '  END;';
   DBMS_DDL.CREATE_WRAPPED(ddl => source, lb => 1, ub => source.COUNT);
END;
/
```

You don't have to use Native Dynamic SQL to build the function when you call the CREATE_WRAPPED procedure. This is because the CREATE_WRAPPED procedure builds the stored program for you, unlike the WRAP function, which only returns the wrapped string or table of strings.

Summary

This appendix has shown you how to hide the implementation details of your PL/SQL stored programming units. You've seen how to use the command-line wrap utility and the built-in CREATE_WRAPPED procedure and WRAP function from the DBMS_DDL package. You should remember to only hide the implementation details, not the package specifications and object type definitions.

APPENDIX
G

PL/SQL Hierarchical
Profiler Primer

racle 11*g* introduces the PL/SQL hierarchical profiler. The profiler lets you capture the dynamic execution performance of your PL/SQL programs. It divides PL/SQL execution times into two parts: SQL statement execution times and PL/SQL program unit execution times.

A hierarchical profiler provides you with more insight than a nonhierarchical profiler. A nonhierarchical profiler only reports how much time a module consumed. A hierarchical profiler tells you which program called what subroutine, and how many times the subroutine was called. The PL/SQL hierarchical profiler stores results in a set of hierarchical profiler tables. It divides the data by subprogram units, including the relationship between calling and called subroutines, and it further subdivides execution time by the SQL statement versus PL/SQL execution segments.

This appendix describes the PL/SQL hierarchical profiler and demonstrates how to configure and use it. Coverage of the profiler is organized in the following sections:

- Configuring the schema

- Collecting profile data

- Understanding profiler output

- Using the `plshprof` command-line utility

The sections are organized sequentially, but you can jump directly to the information required provided the schema is configured.

Configuring the Schema

The first step to configure the PL/SQL hierarchical profiler is building the tables in the `SYS` schema. You do this by connecting to the database as the privileged user.

You connect from the command line:

```
# sqlplus sqlplus '/ as sysdba'
```

As the privileged user, you now build the supplemental data catalog tables required to support the PL/SQL hierarchical profiler. The following runs the `dbmshptab.sql` script:

```
SQL> @?/rdbms/admin/dbmshptab.sql
```

The script hopefully raises some exceptions for missing tables, which you can ignore. The PL/SQL hierarchical profiler uses the `DBMS_HPROF` package, which is invalid until you create the tables. Figure G-1 depicts the tables and their relationships, but you should remember that they're owned by `SYS` unless you grant `SELECT` permissions to development schemas or you rerun the `dbmshptab.sql` against the target `plsql` schema.

If you don't rerun the script against the target `plsql` schema, you won't be able to analyze your output. Therefore, you should connect to the `plsql` schema and rerun this command:

```
SQL> @?/rdbms/admin/dbmshptab.sql
```

The section "Understanding Profiler Data" has more detail on the three tables that support the profiler. It is necessary to understand this material if you want to build your own analytical modeling capability.

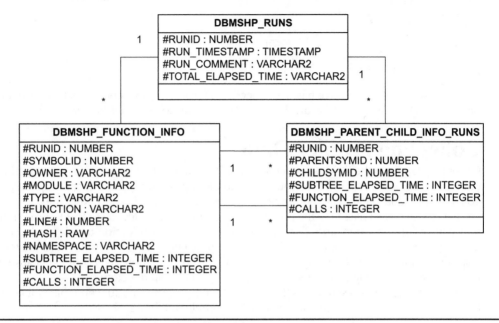

FIGURE G-1   *PL/SQL hierarchical profiler tables*

After creating the tables, you grant execute permission on the package to your target schema, create a profiler virtual directory, and grant read and write permissions on the directory to your target schema. You execute these commands as SYSDBA:

```
GRANT EXECUTE ON dbms_hprof TO plsql;
CREATE OR REPLACE DIRECTORY profiler_dir AS '/tmp/';
GRANT READ, WRITE ON DIRECTORY profiler_dir TO plsql;
```

You do not need to create a synonym because the Oracle 11*g* database seeds a public synonym for the DBMS_HPROF package. This is also true for the DBMSHP_RUNNUMBER sequence created when you build the PL/SQL hierarchical profiler repository. Verify that you can see the package by connecting as the plsql user, and describing the package:

```
SQL> DESCRIBE dbms_hprof
FUNCTION ANALYZE RETURNS NUMBER
 Argument Name                 Type                     In/Out Default?
 ----------------------------  -----------------------  ------ --------

 LOCATION                      VARCHAR2                 IN
 FILENAME                      VARCHAR2                 IN
 SUMMARY_MODE                  BOOLEAN                  IN     DEFAULT
 TRACE                         VARCHAR2                 IN     DEFAULT
 SKIP                          BINARY_INTEGER           IN     DEFAULT
 COLLECT                       BINARY_INTEGER           IN     DEFAULT
 RUN_COMMENT                   VARCHAR2                 IN     DEFAULT
PROCEDURE START_PROFILING
```

Argument Name	Type	In/Out	Default?
LOCATION	VARCHAR2	IN	DEFAULT
FILENAME	VARCHAR2	IN	DEFAULT
MAX_DEPTH	BINARY_INTEGER	IN	DEFAULT

```
PROCEDURE STOP_PROFILING
```

The DBMS_HPROF package has two procedures for starting and stopping data collection, and one function for gathering and analyzing data. The next section explains how to use these methods.

Collecting Profiler Data

Collecting data from the PL/SQL hierarchical profiler requires that you configure the database, as covered in the prior section. Then, you must start the profiler, run your test, and stop the profiler. You stop it because running it constantly consumes unnecessary database resources.

In order to collect data from the profiler, you'll need to build a test case. This test case requires that you've run the video store code scripts found in the introduction to this book. The test_profiler.sql script creates the code components, starts the profiler, runs the test, and stops the profiler. It will also verify that you got all the configuration steps correct because it'll fail if it can't call the package methods or write a file to your /tmp directory.

The first step in this test requires that you build a glue_string function that will be called for every row of a cursor statement. The function definition follows:

```
-- This is found in test_profiler.sql on the publisher's web site.
CREATE OR REPLACE FUNCTION glue_strings
(string1 VARCHAR2, string2 VARCHAR2) RETURN VARCHAR2(2000) IS
  new_string VARCHAR2(2000);
BEGIN
  IF string1 IS NOT NULL THEN
    IF string2 IS NOT NULL THEN
      new_string := string1 || ': ' || string2;
    ELSE
      new_string := string1;
    END IF;
  ELSE
    IF string2 IS NOT NULL THEN
      new_string := string2;
    END IF;
  END IF;
  RETURN new_string;
END glue_strings;
/
```

The function is designed to take two strings and concatenate them, provided one or the other isn't a null value. When one is a null value, the not-null value is returned. Naturally, a null is returned when both inputs are null because the new_string variable is declared not defined, and all declared scalar variables are initialized with a null value by default.

The next component for the test is a quantity_onhand procedure. It takes two formal parameters by value, and two by reference. Both IN OUT mode parameters are nested table collections (see Chapter 6 for details on collections).

The collections require you to define two user-defined SQL datatypes, like

```
CREATE OR REPLACE TYPE varchar2_table IS TABLE OF VARCHAR2(2000);
/
CREATE OR REPLACE TYPE number_table IS TABLE OF NUMBER;
/
```

TIP
*Oracle 11g allocates 1,999 bytes when you declare a VARCHAR2
variable of 1,999 bytes regardless of the physical size of your data.
Large variable-length strings should always be defined 2,000 bytes
or greater because their size is dynamically allocated.*

The procedure is

```
-- This is found in test_profiler.sql on the publisher's web site.
CREATE OR REPLACE PROCEDURE quantity_onhand
( item_title          IN      VARCHAR2
, item_rating_agency  IN      VARCHAR2
, item_titles         IN OUT VARCHAR2_TABLE
, quantities          IN OUT NUMBER_TABLE) IS
  -- Define counter variable.
  counter             NUMBER := 1;
  -- Define dynamic cursor.
  CURSOR c
  ( item_title_in          VARCHAR2
  , item_rating_agency_in VARCHAR2) IS
    SELECT   glue_strings(item_title,item_subtitle) AS full_title
    ,        COUNT(*) AS quantity_on_hand
    FROM     item
    WHERE    REGEXP_LIKE(item_title,item_title_in)
    AND      item_rating_agency = item_rating_agency_in
    GROUP BY glue_strings(item_title,item_subtitle)
    ,        item_rating_agency;
BEGIN
  -- Read cursor and assign column values to parallel arrays.
  FOR i IN c (item_title,item_rating_agency) LOOP
    item_titles.EXTEND;
    item_titles(counter) := i.full_title;
    quantities.EXTEND;
    quantities(counter) := i.quantity_on_hand;
    counter := counter + 1;
  END LOOP;
END;
/
```

You assign *row-by-row* values to the nested table collections, but production systems would use a BULK COLLECT (as qualified in Chapter 4). The counter variable indexes the nested table collections because the FOR loop i variable is a pointer referencing the rows returned by the cursor.

Another alternative would involve using a system reference cursor, which you'd explicitly open inside the procedure. While none is presented in the book, you can find a system reference cursor example on the publisher's web site, named `test_profiler_with_cursor.sql`.

NOTE
When a system reference cursor replaces a set of parallel collections, the IN OUT *mode* SYS_REFCURSOR *is passed back to the calling program as a pointer to the internal cursor work area.*

As mentioned, the `glue_strings` function runs for all returned rows. The anonymous-block program starts the profiler as the first action in the execution block, and it stops the profiler as the last action.

The following testing program runs the `quantity_onhand` procedure once:

```
-- This is found in test_profiler.sql on the publisher's web site.
DECLARE
   -- Input values.
   item_title          VARCHAR2(30) := 'Harry Potter';
   item_rating_agency VARCHAR2(4)   := 'MPAA';
   -- Output values.
   full_title          VARCHAR2_TABLE := varchar2_table();
   rating_agency       NUMBER_TABLE   := number_table();
BEGIN
   -- Start PL/SQL hierarchical profiler.
   dbms_hprof.start_profiling('PROFILER_DIR','harry.txt');

   -- Call reference cursor.
   quantity_onhand(item_title,item_rating_agency,full_title,rating_agency);

   -- Loop through parallel collections until all records are read.
   FOR i IN 1..full_title.COUNT LOOP
     dbms_output.put(full_title(i));
     dbms_output.put(rating_agency(i));
   END LOOP;

   -- Stop PL/SQL hierarchical profiler.
   dbms_hprof.stop_profiling;
END;
/
```

If everything is configured correctly, you will now find a harry.txt file in your `/tmp` directory. The file should have 235 lines in it.

You can simply call a stored procedure or function between the START_PROFILING and STOP_PROFILING procedures, as an alternative to testing anonymous-block programs like the example. *At this point all the data is external to the database and in the raw analyze file.*

The next section will demonstrate how you interpret the profiler's output.

Understanding Profiler Data

There are three ways to interpret the PL/SQL profiler output. You can review the raw output file, analyze the data in the analysis tables, or create hierarchical queries of the analytical data. The next three subsections explore these data analysis tools.

Reading the Raw Output

The raw output is really designed to be read by the analyzer component of the PL/SQL hierarchical profiler. However, you can derive some information before you analyze it by leveraging the indicator codes from Table G-1. A small snapshot from the raw `harry.txt` file is

```
P#X 1
P#R
P#C SQL."".""."__sql_fetch_line17" #17
P#X 27
P#R
P#C PLSQL."SYS"."DBMS_OUTPUT"::11."PUT"#5892e4d73b579470 #77
P#X 1
P#R
P#C PLSQL."SYS"."DBMS_OUTPUT"::11."PUT"#5892e4d73b579470 #77
P#X 1
P#R
P#C PLSQL."SYS"."DBMS_OUTPUT"::11."PUT_LINE"#5892e4d73b579470 #109
P#X 1
P#R
P#C SQL."".""."__sql_fetch_line17" #17
P#X 23
P#R
```

While you can discern what the lines do when you know the indicator codes, it is harder to draw the relationship and statistic information out from the raw data than from the analyzed data.

The PL/SQL hierarchical profiler tracks several operations as if they were functions with names and namespaces, as shown in Table G-2. The list of tracked operations doesn't appear comprehensive at writing. It is likely that other tracked operations may be added by Oracle later.

NOTE
This conclusion is drawn from testing that has produced gaps between parent and child keys in the DBMSHP_PARENT_CHILD_INFO_RUNS table.

The tracked operations show up as functions in your raw and filtered output, and they often bridge like a parent between a grandparent and a grandchild.

Indicator	Description
P#C	Indicates a call to a subprogram, and it is known as a call event.
P#R	Indicates a return from a subprogram to a calling program, and it is known as a return event.
P#X	Indicates the elapsed time between the preceding and following events.
P#!	Indicates a comment in the analyzed file.

TABLE G-1 *Raw PL/SQL Hierarchical Profiler Data*

Function Name	Tracked Operation	Namespace
`__anonymous_block`	Anonymous-block PL/SQL execution	PL/SQL
`__dyn_sql_exec_line`*line#*	Dynamic SQL statement call made at a specific line number in a program	SQL
`__pkg_init`	Initialization code from a package specification or body	PL/SQL
`__plsql_vm`	PL/SQL Virtual Machine (VM) call	PL/SQL
`__sql_fetch_line`*line#*	SQL `FETCH` statement occurring at a designated line number in a program	SQL
`__static_sql_exec_line`*line#*	SQL statement happening at a specific line number in a program	SQL

TABLE G-2   *Operations Tracked by the PL/SQL Hierarchical Profiler*

Defining the PL/SQL Profiler Tables

The PL/SQL hierarchical profiler tables are created when you run the `dbmshptab.sql` script, which is found in the `$ORACLE_HOME/rdbms/admin` directory. It must be run against the `SYS` schema and any user schema where you want to collect profiler data. This is required because the `DBMS_HPROF` package uses invoker rights (you can read more about invoker rights in Chapters 6 and 9).

Earlier Figure G-1 shows the UML depiction of these tables and their relationships. Tables G-3, G-4, and G-5 list the columns, datatypes, and column descriptions for the analysis tables.

The `DBMSHP_RUNS` table contains information only about the execution of the `DBMS_HPROF.ANALYZE` function. The `DBMSHP_FUNCTION_INFO` table contains information about executed functions, and the `DBMSHP_PARENT_CHILD_INFO` table has the hierarchical relationship between executed functions.

Name	Datatype	Description
`RUNID`	`NUMBER`	A surrogate primary key generated from the `DBMSHP_PROFILER` sequence
`RUN_TIMESTAMP`	`TIMESTAMP`	Timestamp set when you run the `DBMS_HPROF.ANALYZE` function
`RUN_COMMENT`	`VARCHAR2(2047)`	User comment that you provide when calling the `DBMS_HPROF.ANALYZE` function
`TOTAL_ELAPSED_TIME`	`INTEGER`	The elapsed time for the analysis process called by the `DBMS_HPROF.ANALYZE` function

TABLE G-3   *DBMSHP_RUNS Table Descriptions*

Name	Datatype	Description
RUNID	NUMBER	A foreign key from the DBMSHP_RUNS table and it is part of a composite primary key. The RUNID and SYMBOLID columns define the primary key for the table.
SYMBOLID	NUMBER	The execution sequence ID value. The SYMBOLID is unique when combined with the RUNID column value, and together they define a composite primary key for this table.
OWNER	VARCHAR2(32)	Owner of the module called.
MODULE	VARCHAR2(2047)	The module name contains a subprogram, like a package name such as DBMS_LOB, DBMS_SQL, or a user-defined package.
TYPE	VARCHAR2(32)	The module type defines the source of the module. Some examples are package, procedure, or function.
FUNCTION	VARCHAR2(4000)	A subprogram name or operation (like those in Table G-1) tracked by the PL/SQL hierarchical profiler.
LINE#	NUMBER	The line number where the function is defined in the schema owner module.
HASH	RAW(32)	Hash code for the subprogram signature, which is unique for any run of the DBMS_HPROF.ANALYZE function.
NAMESPACE	VARCHAR2(32)	Namespace of subprogram, which can be either SQL or PL/SQL.
SUBTREE_ELAPSED_TIME	INTEGER	Elapsed time, in microseconds, for subordinate tree program, excluding time spent in descendant subprograms.
FUNCTION_ELAPSED_TIME	INTEGER	Elapsed time, in microseconds, for function subprogram, excluding time spent in descendant subprograms.
CALLS	INTEGER	The number of calls to a subprogram.

TABLE G-4   *DBMSHP_FUNCTION_INFO Table Descriptions*

The RUNID maps straight across to the DBMSHP_PARENT_CHILD_INFO table as the same column name. The SYMBOLID column maps to both the PARENTSYMID and CHILDSYMID columns. When you recursively join these structures, you should ensure you join the tables on the SYMBOLID and PARENTSYMID columns. The section "Querying the Analyzed Data" contains an example of this type of join.

This section has explained the three tables that show you how to interpret the PL/SQL profiler output, review the raw output file, and analyze data. The analysis discussion has shown you how to create hierarchical queries that profile the analytical data.

Name	Datatype	Description
RUNID	NUMBER	A surrogate primary key generated from the DBMSHP_PROFILER sequence.
PARENTSYMID	NUMBER	The execution sequence ID value. The PARENTSYMID is unique when combined with the RUNID column value, and together they define a composite foreign key that maps to the DBMSHP_FUNCTION_INFO table RUNID and SYMBOLID columns.
CHILDSYMID	NUMBER	The execution sequence ID value. The CHILDSYMID is unique when combined with the RUNID column value, and together they define a composite foreign key that maps to the DBMSHP_FUNCTION_INFO table RUNID and SYMBOLID columns.
SUBTREE_ELAPSED_TIME	INTEGER	Elapsed time, in microseconds, for subordinate tree program, excluding time spent in descendant subprograms.
FUNCTION_ELAPSED_TIME	INTEGER	Elapsed time, in microseconds, for function subprogram, excluding time spent in descendant subprograms.
CALLS	INTEGER	The number of calls to a child row that is identified by a composite key of RUNID and CHILDSYMID columns.

TABLE G-5   *DBMSHP_PARENT_CHILD_INFO_RUNS Table Descriptions*

Querying the Analyzed Data

A recursive query is the best way to get meaningful results. The following query captures the nesting of method names and uses SQL*Plus column formatting to organize the output:

```
-- This is found in query_profiler.sql on the publisher's web site.
COL method_name           FORMAT A30
COL function_name         FORMAT A24
COL subtree_elapsed_time  FORMAT 99.90 HEADING "Subtree|Elapsed|Time"
COL function_elapsed_time FORMAT 99.90 HEADING "Function|Elapsed|Time"
COL calls                 FORMAT 99    HEADING "Calls"

SELECT    RPAD(' ',level*2,' ')||dfi.owner||'.'||dfi.module AS method_name
,         dfi.function AS function_name
,         (dpci.subtree_elapsed_time/1000) AS subtree_elapsed_time
,         (dpci.function_elapsed_time/1000) AS function_elapsed_time
,         dpci.calls
FROM      dbmshp_parent_child_info dpci
,         dbmshp_function_info dfi
WHERE     dpci.runid = dfi.runid
AND       dpci.parentsymid = dfi.symbolid
AND       dpci.runid = 4
CONNECT
BY PRIOR dpci.childsymid = dpci.parentsymid  -- Child always connects on left.
START
WITH      dpci.parentsymid = 1;
```

This yields the following output:

```
-- This is output from the query_profiler.sql script on the publisher's web site.
                                                Subtree  Function
                                                Elapsed  Elapsed
METHOD_NAME                    FUNCTION_NAME        Time      Time Calls
------------------------------ ------------------ ------- -------- -----
            .                  __plsql_vm             .04      .04    11
     PLSQL.GLUE_STRINGS        GLUE_STRINGS           .00      .00     0
       PLSQL.QUANTITY_ONHAND   QUANTITY_ONHAND        .29      .05     1
        PLSQL.QUANTITY_ONHAND  QUANTITY_ONHAND.C      .24      .24     1
       PLSQL.QUANTITY_ONHAND   QUANTITY_ONHAND        .12      .03    11
        SYS.DBMS_OUTPUT        PUT_LINE               .02      .02    11
        SYS.DBMS_OUTPUT        PUT_LINE               .06      .05    11
          SYS.DBMS_OUTPUT      PUT                    .02      .02     1
     PLSQL.QUANTITY_ONHAND     QUANTITY_ONHAND       3.27     3.19     1

9 rows selected.
```

This subsection has demonstrated an approach to querying the PL/SQL profiler table data. It has also introduced you the details of leveraging recursive SQL queries in Oracle 11*g*.

This section has shown you how to interpret the PL/SQL profiler output, review the raw output file, and analyze data. The analysis discussion has shown you how to create hierarchical queries that profile the analytical data.

The next section demonstrates how to generate a web page report equivalent.

Using the plshprof Command-Line Utility

The `plshprof` command-line utility lets you generate simple HTML reports. You have the option of generating a report from one or two sets of analyzed data. You'll find the `plshprof` utility in the `$ORACLE_HOME/bin/` directory.

The `plshprof` utility has several command options that let you generate different report types. Table G-6 lists the available command-line options.

You can generate an output report by using the following syntax:

```
$ plshprof -output /tmp/magic /tmp/harry.txt
```

It echoes the following to the console when generating the file:

```
PLSHPROF: Oracle Database 11g Enterprise Edition Release 11.1.0.6.0
[8 symbols processed]
[Report written to '/tmp/magic.html']
```

Option	Description	Default
-collect count	Collects the information for *count* calls. You should only use this in combination with the -trace *symbol* option.	1
-output filename	Sets the output filename. Don't include an extension, because you could end up with a strange file name, like magic.htm.html.	*filename*.html or tracefile.html
-skip count	Skips the first *count* calls. You should only use this in combination with the -trace *symbol* option.	0
-summary	Prints only the elapsed time.	None
-trace symbol	Specifies the function name of the tree root.	Not applicable

TABLE G-6 *plshprof Command-Line Options*

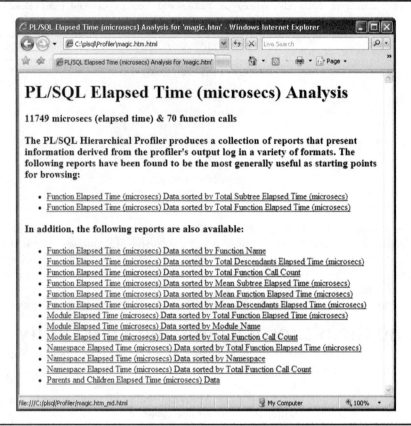

FIGURE G-2   *Sample plshprof index web page*

This generates an index web page magic.html. You use this page to navigate to the other generated web reports.

```
magic_2c.html   magic.html      magic_nsc.html   magic_tc.html
magic_2f.html   magic_md.html   magic_nsf.html   magic_td.html
magic_2n.html   magic_mf.html   magic_nsp.html   magic_tf.html
magic_fn.html   magic_ms.html   magic_pc.html    magic_ts.html
```

The magic.html in Figure G-2 demonstrates the list of reports produced by the `plshprof` utility. You can write a wrapper to read and store these into `CLOB` columns in the database or as external files accessible to your web server. Alternatively, you can simply generate them to the `/tmp` directory, browse them individually, and then remove them from the file system.

This section has demonstrated how to use the plshprof command-line utility. It generates a set of effective analysis tools that you should examine before attempting to write your own.

Summary

This appendix has explained what the PL/SQL hierarchical profiler does and shown you how to configure and use it.

APPENDIX

H

PL/Scope

ew to Oracle 11g, PL/Scope is a compiler-driven tool. It collects and organizes data about user-defined identifiers from PL/SQL source code. Identifiers can be reserved words, predefined identifiers, quoted identifiers, user-defined variables, subroutines, or user-defined types. Chapter 3 covers identifiers in PL/SQL.

The PL/Scope data is stored in static data dictionary views. These views contain declaration, definition, reference, call, and assignment of identifiers. They also provide the location of each usage in the source code.

This appendix covers:

- Configuring PL/Scope data collection

- Viewing PL/Scope collected data

You should also note that Oracle SQL*Developer can access PL/Scope data.

Configuring PL/Scope Data Collection

The default behavior of PL/Scope is disabled. You enable PL/Scope by setting the `PLSCOPE_SETTINGS` parameter to the "`IDENTIFIERS:ALL`" value. This parameter can be set at the database and session levels. Only identifiers set while this parameter is enabled are captured by PL/Scope routines.

You enable PL/Scope for a session using the following syntax:

```
ALTER SESSION SET PLSCOPE_SETTINGS = 'IDENTIFIERS:ALL'
```

Once you enable PL/Scope, it runs until the session ends or the database is altered back to the default. It is only intended for development databases, and Oracle doesn't recommend enabling it for production databases.

After you enable PL/Scope, you should monitor its impact on the SYSAUX tablespace. You can query the space consumed by using the following query:

```
SELECT space_usage_kbytes
FROM   v$sysaux_occupants
WHERE  occupant_name = 'PL/SCOPE'
```

NOTE
PL/Scope only works in an Oracle 11g database, but you can activate it during upgrade by running the `utlirplscope.sql` *script in UPGRADE mode.*

Viewing PL/Scope Collected Data

PL/Scope collected data is available by three methods. You can query static data dictionary views, use the PL/SQL Web Application demonstration tool, or write your own web-based application to profile the data.

PL/Scope only captures identifiers when the PLSCOPE_SETTINGS parameter is set to the "IDENTIFIERS:ALL" value. You can enable it from any SQL Developer session. It stores identifiers by the signature of individual stored programming units, and overloaded signatures are treated as unique identifier contexts.

NOTE
PL/Scope does not collect identifiers for wrapped program units.

You can query the ALL_IDENTIFIERS, DBA_IDENTIFIERS, or USER_IDENTIFIERS views. The definition of the ALL_* and DBA_* views include the owner, while the USER_* view doesn't. The definition of these views is

```
Name                                  Null?    Type
------------------------------------  -------- ---------------------------
OWNER                                 NOT NULL VARCHAR2(30)
NAME                                           VARCHAR2(30)
SIGNATURE                                      VARCHAR2(32)
TYPE                                           VARCHAR2(18)
OBJECT_NAME                           NOT NULL VARCHAR2(30)
OBJECT_TYPE                                    VARCHAR2(13)
USAGE                                          VARCHAR2(11)
USAGE_ID                                       NUMBER
LINE                                           NUMBER
COL                                            NUMBER
USAGE_CONTEXT_ID                               NUMBER
```

The predelivered HTML-based demonstration tool runs using the PL/SQL Web Toolkit. You'll find it as the $ORACLE_HOME/plsql/demo/plscopedemo.sql script. This script requires you to build a wrapper web page or configure the Oracle HTTP Server (OHS), which is covered in Chapter 16.

SQL*Developer lets you enable PL/Scope by right-clicking the connection name in the Connections navigator display. Then, you select Toggle PL/Scope Identifier Collection. This sets the session PLSCOPE_SETTINGS parameter to the IDENTIFIERS:ALL value. Viewing the data still requires a manual query or implementing your own web page.

PL/Scope collects the identifiers listed in Table H-1. The supported datatypes are base types defined by the STANDARD package. Labels have their unique context in PL/Scope, while iterators are only available when they are the index of a FOR loop. The ANYDATA and XMLType datatypes are examples of the OPAQUE type. PL/Scope treats object attributes, local variables, package variables (defined in the package specification), and record structures as VARIABLE datatypes. Also, PL/Scope does not resolve base object names for synonyms, which leaves you to query the *_SYNONYMS view.

ASSOCIATIVE_ARRAY	FORMAL OUT	RECORD
BFILE	FUNCTION	REFCURSOR
BLOB	INTERVAL	SUBTYPE
BOOLEAN	ITERATOR	SYNONYM
CHARACTER	LABEL	TIME
CLOB	LIBRARY	TIMESTAMP
CONSTANT	NESTED TABLE	TRIGGER
CURSOR	NUMBER	UROWID
DATE	OBJECT	VARRAY
EXCEPTION	OPAQUE	VARIABLE
FORMAL IN	PACKAGE	
FORMAL IN OUT	PROCEDURE	

TABLE H-1   *Identifiers Collected by PL/Scope*

Summary

This section has covered how PL/Scope collects and organizes data about user-defined identifiers. It has demonstrated how to collect and view PL/Scope data.

APPENDIX
I

PL/SQL Reserved Words and Keywords

ertain identifiers or words are critical to building programming languages. PL/SQL divides these critical words into two groups: reserved words and keywords. They are listed in the data dictionary with each release, and can be found in the V$RESERVED_WORDS view.

Lexical symbols are also listed as reserved words in the view. They are covered in Chapter 3 and are not part of this appendix.

It appears that some reserved words, like BEGIN and EXCEPTION, are missing the 'Y' in the RESERVED column of V$RESERVED_WORDS view. Other reserved words, like ELSIF and OUT, are missing completely from the view. Also, various editions of the *Oracle Database PL/SQL Language Reference* differ on the list elements and contents of the view.

Table I-1 lists reserved words and keywords together alphabetically for reference. Where words were missing from the view, they've been added in to the table.

Start	Reserved Words and Keywords
A	ABORT, ACCESS, ACCESSED, ACCOUNT, ACTIVATE, ADD, ADMIN, ADMINISTER, ADMINISTRATOR, ADVISE, ADVISOR, AFTER, ALIAS, ALL, ALLOCATE, ALLOW, ALL_ROWS, ALTER, ALWAYS, ANALYZE, ANCILLARY, AND, AND_EQUAL, ANTIJOIN, ANY, APPEND, APPLY, ARCHIVE, ARCHIVELOG, ARRAY, AS, ASC, ASSOCIATE, AT, ATTRIBUTE, ATTRIBUTES, AUDIT, AUTHENTICATED, AUTHENTICATION, AUTHID, AUTHORIZATION, AUTO, AUTOALLOCATE, AUTOEXTEND, AUTOMATIC, AVAILABILITY
B	BACKUP, BATCH, BECOME, BEFORE, BEGIN, BEGIN_OUTLINE_DATA, BEHALF, BETWEEN, BFILE, BIGFILE, BINARY_DOUBLE, BINARY_DOUBLE_INFINITY, BINARY_DOUBLE_NAN, BINARY_FLOAT, BINARY_FLOAT_INFINITY, BINARY_FLOAT_NAN, BINDING, BITMAP, BITMAPS, BITMAP_TREE, BITS, BLOB, BLOCK, BLOCKS, BLOCKSIZE, BLOCK_RANGE, BODY, BOTH, BOUND, BROADCAST, BUFFER, BUFFER_CACHE, BUFFER_POOL, BUILD, BULK, BY, BYPASS_RECURSIVE_CHECK, BYPASS_UJVC, BYTE
C	CACHE, CACHE_CB, CACHE_INSTANCES, CACHE_TEMP_TABLE, CALL, CANCEL, CARDINALITY, CASCADE, CASE, CAST, CATEGORY, CERTIFICATE, CFILE, CHAINED, CHANGE, CHAR, CHARACTER, CHAR_CS, CHECK, CHECKPOINT, CHILD, CHOOSE, CHUNK, CIV_GB, CLASS, CLEAR, CLOB, CLONE, CLOSE, LOSE_CACHED_OPEN_CURSORS, CLUSTER, CLUSTERING_FACTOR, COALESCE, COARSE, COLLECT, COLUMN, COLUMNS, COLUMN_STATS, COLUMN_VALUE, COMMENT, COMMIT, COMMITTED, COMPACT, COMPATIBILITY, COMPILE, COMPLETE, COMPOSITE_LIMIT, COMPRESS, COMPUTE, CONFORMING, CONNECT, CONNECT_BY_ISCYCLE, CONNECT_BY_ISLEAF, CONNECT_BY_ROOT, CONNECT_TIME, CONSIDER, CONSISTENT, CONSTRAINT, CONSTRAINTS, CONTAINER, CONTENT, CONTENTS, CONTEXT, CONTINUE, CONTROLFILE, CONVERT, CORRUPTION, COST, CPU_COSTING, CPU_PER_CALL, CPU_PER_SESSION, CREATE, CREATE_STORED_OUTLINES, CROSS, CUBE, CUBE_GB, CURRENT, CURRENT_DATE, CURRENT_SCHEMA, CURRENT_TIME, CURRENT_TIMESTAMP, CURRENT_USER, CURSOR, CURSOR_SHARING_EXACT, CURSOR_SPECIFIC_SEGMENT, CYCLE
D	DANGLING, DATA, DATABASE, DATAFILE, DATAFILES, DATAOBJNO, DATE, DATE_MODE, DAY, DBA, DBA_RECYCLEBIN, DBMS_STATS, DBTIMEZONE, DB_ROLE_CHANGE, DDL, DEALLOCATE, DEBUG, DEC, DECIMAL, DECLARE, DECREMENT, DECRYPT, DEFAULT, DEFERRABLE, DEFERRED, DEFINED, DEFINER, DEGREE, DELAY, DELETE, DEMAND, DENSE_RANK, DEQUEUE, DEREF, DEREF_NO_REWRITE, DESC, DETACHED, DETERMINES, DICTIONARY, DIMENSION, DIRECTORY, DISABLE, DISABLE_RPKE, DISASSOCIATE, DISCONNECT, DISK, DISKGROUP, DISKS, DISMOUNT, DISTINCT, DISTINGUISHED, DISTRIBUTED, DML, DML_UPDATE, DOCUMENT, DOMAIN_INDEX_NO_SORT, DOMAIN_INDEX_SORT, DOUBLE, DOWNGRADE, DRIVING_SITE, DROP, DUMP, DYNAMIC, DYNAMIC_SAMPLING, DYNAMIC_SAMPLING_EST_CDN

TABLE I-1 *Reserved Word and Keyword List*

Start	Reserved Words and Keywords
E	EACH, ELEMENT, ELIMINATE_JOIN, ELIMINATE_OBY, ELIMINATE_OUTER_JOIN, ELSE, ELSIF, EMPTY, ENABLE, ENCRYPT, ENCRYPTION, END, END_OUTLINE_DATA, ENFORCE, ENFORCED, ENQUEUE, ENTERPRISE, ENTRY, ERROR, ERRORS, ERROR_ON_OVERLAP_TIME, ESCAPE, ESTIMATE, EVALNAME, EVALUATION, EVENTS, EXCEPT, EXCEPTION, EXCHANGE, EXCLUDING, EXCLUSIVE, EXECUTE, EXEMPT, EXISTS, EXPAND_GSET_TO_UNION, EXPIRE, EXPLAIN, EXPLOSION, EXPORT, EXPR_CORR_CHECK, EXTENDS, EXTENT, EXTENTS, EXTERNAL, EXTERNALLY, EXTRACT
F	FACT, FAILED, FAILED_LOGIN_ATTEMPTS, FAILGROUP, FALSE, FAST, FBTSCAN, FIC_CIV, FIC_PIV, FILE, FILTER, FINAL, FINE, FINISH, FIRST, FIRST_ROWS, FLAGGER, FLASHBACK, FLOAT, FLOB, FLUSH, FOLLOWING, FOR, FORCE, FORCE_XML_QUERY_REWRITE, FOREIGN, FREELIST, FREELISTS, FREEPOOLS, FRESH, FROM, FULL, FUNCTION, FUNCTIONS
G	GATHER_PLAN_STATISTICS, GBY_CONC_ROLLUP, GENERATED, GLOBAL, GLOBALLY, GLOBAL_NAME, GLOBAL_TOPIC_ENABLED, GRANT, GROUP, GROUPING, GROUPS, GROUP_BY, GUARANTEE, GUARANTEED, GUARD
H	HASH, HASHKEYS, HASH_AJ, HASH_SJ, HAVING, HEADER, HEAP, HIERARCHY, HIGH, HINTSET_BEGIN, HINTSET_END, HOUR, HWM_BROKERED
I	ID, IDENTIFIED, IDENTIFIER, IDENTITY, IDGENERATORS, IDLE_TIME, IF, IGNORE, IGNORE_OPTIM_EMBEDDED_HINTS, IGNORE_WHERE_CLAUSE, IMMEDIATE, IMPORT, IN, INCLUDE_VERSION, INCLUDING, INCREMENT, INCREMENTAL, INDEX, INDEXED, INDEXES, INDEXTYPE, INDEXTYPES, INDEX_ASC, INDEX_COMBINE, INDEX_DESC, INDEX_FFS, INDEX_FILTER, INDEX_JOIN, INDEX_ROWS, INDEX_RRS, INDEX_SCAN, INDEX_SKIP_SCAN, INDEX_SS, INDEX_SS_ASC, INDEX_SS_DESC, INDEX_STATS, INDICATOR, INFINITE, INFORMATIONAL, INITIAL, INITIALIZED, INITIALLY, INITRANS, INLINE, INLINE_XMLTYPE_NT, INNER, INSERT, INSTANCE, INSTANCES, INSTANTIABLE, INSTANTLY, INSTEAD, INT, INTEGER, INTERMEDIATE, INTERNAL_CONVERT, INTERNAL_USE, INTERPRETED, INTERSECT, INTERVAL, INTO, INVALIDATE, IN_MEMORY_METADATA, IS, ISOLATION, ISOLATION_LEVEL, ITERATE, ITERATION_NUMBER
J	JAVA, JOB, JOIN
K	KEEP, KERBEROS, KEY, KEYS, KEYSIZE, KEY_LENGTH, KILL
L	LAST, LATERAL, LAYER, LDAP_REGISTRATION, LDAP_REGISTRATION_ENABLED, LDAP_REG_SYNC_INTERVAL, LEADING, LEFT, LENGTH, LESS, LEVEL, LEVELS, LIBRARY, LIKE, LIKE2, LIKE4, LIKEC, LIKE_EXPAND, LIMIT, LINK, LIST, LOB, LOCAL, LOCALTIME, LOCALTIMESTAMP, LOCAL_INDEXES, LOCATION, LOCATOR, LOCK, LOCKED, LOG, LOGFILE, LOGGING, LOGICAL, LOGICAL_READS_PER_CALL, LOGICAL_READS_PER_SESSION, LOGOFF, LOGON, LONG
M	MAIN, MANAGE, MANAGED, MANAGEMENT, MANUAL, MAPPING, MASTER, MATCHED, MATERIALIZE, MATERIALIZED, MAX, MAXARCHLOGS, MAXDATAFILES, MAXEXTENTS, MAXIMIZE, MAXINSTANCES, MAXLOGFILES, MAXLOGHISTORY, MAXLOGMEMBERS, MAXSIZE, MAXTRANS, MAXVALUE, MEASURES, MEMBER, MEMORY, MERGE, MERGE_AJ, MERGE_CONST_ON, MERGE_SJ, METHOD, MIGRATE, MIN, MINEXTENTS, MINIMIZE, MINIMUM, MINUS, MINUS_NULL, MINUTE, MINVALUE, MIRROR, MLSLABEL, MODE, MODEL, MODEL_COMPILE_SUBQUERY, MODEL_DONTVERIFY_UNIQUENESS, MODEL_DYNAMIC_SUBQUERY, MODEL_MIN_ANALYSIS, MODEL_NO_ANALYSIS, MODEL_PBY, MODEL_PUSH_REF, MODIFY, MONITORING, MONTH, MOUNT, MOVE, MOVEMENT, MULTISET, MV_MERGE

TABLE I-1   *Reserved Word and Keyword List* (continued)

Start	Reserved Words and Keywords
N	NAME, NAMED, NAN, NATIONAL, NATIVE, NATURAL, NAV, NCHAR, NCHAR_CS, NCLOB, NEEDED, NESTED, NESTED_TABLE_FAST_INSERT, NESTED_TABLE_GET_REFS, NESTED_TABLE_ID, NESTED_TABLE_SET_REFS, NESTED_TABLE_SET_SETID, NETWORK, NEVER, NEW, NEXT, NLS_CALENDAR, NLS_CHARACTERSET, NLS_COMP, NLS_CURRENCY, NLS_DATE_FORMAT, NLS_DATE_LANGUAGE, NLS_ISO_CURRENCY, NLS_LANG, NLS_LANGUAGE, NLS_LENGTH_SEMANTICS, NLS_NCHAR_CONV_EXCP, NLS_NUMERIC_CHARACTERS, NLS_SORT, NLS_SPECIAL_CHARS, NLS_TERRITORY, NL_AJ, NL_SJ, NO, NOAPPEND, NOARCHIVELOG, NOAUDIT, NOCACHE, NOCOMPRESS, NOCPU_COSTING, NOCYCLE, NODELAY, NOFORCE, NOGUARANTEE, NOLOGGING, NOMAPPING, NOMAXVALUE, NOMINIMIZE, NOMINVALUE, NOMONITORING, NONE, NOORDER, NOOVERRIDE, NOPARALLEL, NOPARALLEL_INDEX, NORELY, NOREPAIR, NORESETLOGS, NOREVERSE, NOREWRITE, NORMAL, NOROWDEPENDENCIES, NOSEGMENT, NOSORT, NOSTRICT, NOSWITCH, NOT, NOTHING, NOTIFICATION, NOVALIDATE, NOWAIT, NO_ACCESS, NO_BASETABLE_MULTIMV_REWRITE, NO_BUFFER, NO_CARTESIAN, NO_CPU_COSTING, NO_ELIMINATE_JOIN, NO_ELIMINATE_OBY, NO_ELIMINATE_OUTER_JOIN, NO_EXPAND, NO_EXPAND_GSET_TO_UNION, NO_FACT, NO_FILTERING, NO_INDEX, NO_INDEX_FFS, NO_INDEX_SS, NO_MERGE, NO_MODEL_PUSH_REF, NO_MONITORING, NO_MULTIMV_REWRITE, NO_ORDER_ROLLUPS, NO_PARALLEL, NO_PARALLEL_INDEX, NO_PARTIAL_COMMIT, NO_PRUNE_GSETS, NO_PULL_PRED, NO_PUSH_PRED, NO_PUSH_SUBQ, NO_PX_JOIN_FILTER, NO_QKN_BUFF, NO_QUERY_TRANSFORMATION, NO_REF_CASCADE, NO_REWRITE, NO_SEMIJOIN, NO_SET_TO_JOIN, NO_SQL_TUNE, NO_STAR_TRANSFORMATION, NO_STATS_GSETS, NO_SWAP_JOIN_INPUTS, NO_TEMP_TABLE, NO_UNNEST, NO_USE_HASH, NO_USE_HASH_AGGREGATION, NO_USE_MERGE, NO_USE_NL, NO_XML_QUERY_REWRITE, NULL, NULLS, NUMBER, NUMERIC, NVARCHAR2
O	OBJECT, OBJNO, OBJNO_REUSE, OF, OFF, OFFLINE, OID, OIDINDEX, OLD, OLD_PUSH_PRED, ON, ONLINE, ONLY, OPAQUE, OPAQUE_TRANSFORM, OPAQUE_XCANONICAL, OPCODE, OPEN, OPERATOR, OPTIMAL, OPTIMIZER_FEATURES_ENABLE, OPTIMIZER_GOAL, OPTION, OPT_ESTIMATE, OPT_PARAM, OR, ORA_ROWSCN, ORDER, ORDERED, ORDERED_PREDICATES, ORDINALITY, ORGANIZATION, OR_EXPAND, OUT, OUTER, OUTLINE, OUTLINE_LEAF, OUT_OF_LINE, OVER, OVERFLOW, OVERFLOW_NOMOVE, OVERLAPS, OWN
P	PACKAGE, PACKAGES, PARALLEL, PARALLEL_INDEX, PARAMETERS, PARENT, PARITY, PARTIALLY, PARTITION, PARTITIONS, PARTITION_HASH, PARTITION_LIST, PARTITION_RANGE, PASSING, PASSWORD, PASSWORD_GRACE_TIME, PASSWORD_LIFE_TIME, PASSWORD_LOCK_TIME, PASSWORD_REUSE_MAX, PASSWORD_REUSE_TIME, PASSWORD_VERIFY_FUNCTION, PATH, PATHS, PCTFREE, PCTINCREASE, PCTTHRESHOLD, PCTUSED, PCTVERSION, PERCENT, PERFORMANCE, PERMANENT, PFILE, PHYSICAL, PIV_GB, PIV_SSF, PLAN, PLSQL_CCFLAGS, PLSQL_CODE_TYPE, PLSQL_DEBUG, PLSQL_OPTIMIZE_LEVEL, PLSQL_WARNINGS, POINT, POLICY, POST_TRANSACTION, POWER, PQ_DISTRIBUTE, PQ_MAP, PQ_NOMAP, PREBUILT, PRECEDING, PRECISION, PRECOMPUTE_SUBQUERY, PREPARE, PRESENT, PRESERVE, PRESERVE_OID, PRIMARY, PRIOR, PRIVATE, PRIVATE_SGA, PRIVILEGE, PRIVILEGES, PROCEDURE, PROFILE, PROGRAM, PROJECT, PROTECTED, PROTECTION, PUBLIC, PULL_PRED, PURGE, PUSH_PRED, PUSH_SUBQ, PX_GRANULE, PX_JOIN_FILTER
Q	QB_NAME, QUERY, QUERY_BLOCK, QUEUE, QUEUE_CURR, QUEUE_ROWP, QUIESCE, QUOTA
R	RANDOM, RANGE, RAPIDLY, RAW, RBA, RBO_OUTLINE, READ, READS, REAL, REBALANCE, REBUILD, RECORDS_PER_BLOCK, RECOVER, RECOVERABLE, RECOVERY, RECYCLE, RECYCLEBIN, REDUCED, REDUNDANCY, REF, REFERENCE, REFERENCED, REFERENCES, REFERENCING, REFRESH, REF_CASCADE_CURSOR, REGEXP_LIKE, REGISTER, REJECT, REKEY, RELATIONAL, RELY, REMOTE_MAPPED, RENAME, REPAIR, REPLACE, REQUIRED, RESET, RESETLOGS, RESIZE, RESOLVE, RESOLVER, RESOURCE, RESTORE, RESTORE_AS_INTERVALS, RESTRICT, RESTRICTED, RESTRICT_ALL_REF_CONS, RESUMABLE, RESUME, RETENTION, RETURN, RETURNING, REUSE, REVERSE, REVOKE, REWRITE, REWRITE_OR_ERROR, RIGHT, ROLE, ROLES, ROLLBACK, ROLLING, ROLLUP, ROW, ROWDEPENDENCIES, ROWID, ROWNUM, ROWS, ROW_LENGTH, RULE, RULES

TABLE I-1   *Reserved Word and Keyword List* (continued)

Start	Reserved Words and Keywords
S	SALT, SAMPLE, SAVEPOINT, SAVE_AS_INTERVALS, SB4, SCALE, SCALE_ROWS, SCAN, SCAN_INSTANCES, SCHEDULER, SCHEMA, SCN, SCN_ASCENDING, SCOPE, SD_ALL, SD_INHIBIT, SD_SHOW, SECOND, SECURITY, SEED, SEGMENT, SEG_BLOCK, SEG_FILE, SELECT, SELECTIVITY, SEMIJOIN, SEMIJOIN_DRIVER, SEQUENCE, SEQUENCED, SEQUENTIAL, SERIALIZABLE, SERVERERROR, SESSION, SESSIONS_PER_USER, SESSIONTIMEZONE, SESSIONTZNAME, SESSION_CACHED_CURSORS, SET, SETS, SETTINGS, SET_TO_JOIN, SEVERE, SHARE, SHARED, SHARED_POOL, SHRINK, SHUTDOWN, SIBLINGS, SID, SIMPLE, SINGLE, SINGLETASK, SIZE, SKIP, SKIP_EXT_OPTIMIZER, SKIP_UNQ_UNUSABLE_IDX, SKIP_UNUSABLE_INDEXES, SMALLFILE, SMALLINT, SNAPSHOT, SOME, SORT, SOURCE, SPACE, SPECIFICATION, SPFILE, SPLIT, SPREADSHEET, SQL, SQLLDR, SQL_TRACE, STANDALONE, STANDBY, STAR, START, STARTUP, STAR_TRANSFORMATION, STATEMENT_ID, STATIC, STATISTICS, STOP, STORAGE, STORE, STREAMS, STRICT, STRING, STRIP, STRUCTURE, SUBMULTISET, SUBPARTITION, SUBPARTITIONS, SUBPARTITION_REL, SUBQUERIES, SUBSTITUTABLE, SUCCESSFUL, SUMMARY, SUPPLEMENTAL, SUSPEND, SWAP_JOIN_INPUTS, SWITCH, SWITCHOVER, SYNONYM, SYSAUX, SYSDATE, SYSDBA, SYSOPER, SYSTEM, SYSTIMESTAMP, SYS_DL_CURSOR, SYS_FBT_INSDEL, SYS_OP_BITVEC, SYS_OP_CAST, SYS_OP_ENFORCE_NOT_NULL$, SYS_OP_EXTRACT, SYS_OP_NOEXPAND, SYS_OP_NTCIMG$, SYS_PARALLEL_TXN, SYS_RID_ORDER
T	TABLE, TABLES, TABLESPACE, TABLESPACE_NO, TABLE_STATS, TABNO, TEMPFILE, TEMPLATE, TEMPORARY, TEMP_TABLE, TEST, THAN, THE, THEN, THREAD, THROUGH, TIME, TIMEOUT, TIMESTAMP, TIMEZONE_ABBR, TIMEZONE_HOUR, TIMEZONE_MINUTE, TIMEZONE_OFFSET, TIMEZONE_REGION, TIME_ZONE, TIV_GB, TIV_SSF, TO, TOPLEVEL, TO_CHAR, TRACE, TRACING, TRACKING, TRAILING, TRANSACTION, TRANSITIONAL, TREAT, TRIGGER, TRIGGERS, TRUE, TRUNCATE, TRUSTED, TUNING, TX, TYPE, TYPES, TZ_OFFSET
U	UB2, UBA, UID, UNARCHIVED, UNBOUND, UNBOUNDED, UNDER, UNDO, UNDROP, UNIFORM, UNION, UNIQUE, UNLIMITED, UNLOCK, UNNEST, UNPACKED, UNPROTECTED, UNQUIESCE, UNRECOVERABLE, UNTIL, UNUSABLE, UNUSED, UPDATABLE, UPDATE, UPDATED, UPD_INDEXES, UPD_JOININDEX, UPGRADE, UPSERT, UROWID, USAGE, USE, USER, USERS, USER_DEFINED, USER_RECYCLEBIN, USE_ANTI, USE_CONCAT, USE_HASH, USE_HASH_AGGREGATION, USE_MERGE, USE_NL, USE_NL_WITH_INDEX, USE_PRIVATE_OUTLINES, USE_SEMI, USE_STORED_OUTLINES, USE_TTT_FOR_GSETS, USE_WEAK_NAME_RESL, USING
V	VALIDATE, VALIDATION, VALUE, VALUES, VARCHAR, VARCHAR2, VARRAY, VARYING, VECTOR_READ, VECTOR_READ_TRACE, VERSION, VERSIONS, VIEW
W	WAIT, WALLET, WELLFORMED, WHEN, WHENEVER, WHERE, WHITESPACE, WITH, WITHIN, WITHOUT, WORK, WRAPPED, WRITE
X	XID, XMLATTRIBUTES, XMLCOLATTVAL, XMLELEMENT, XMLFOREST, XMLNAMESPACES, XMLPARSE, XMLPI, XMLQUERY, XMLROOT, XMLSCHEMA, XMLSERIALIZE, XMLTABLE, XMLTYPE, X_DYN_PRUNE
Y	YEAR, YES
Z	ZONE

TABLE I-1   *Reserved Word and Keyword List* (continued)

The following reserved_key_word.sql script lets you query and format the contents from the V$RESERVED_WORDS view:

```
DECLARE
  -- Define and declare collection.
  TYPE alpha_key IS TABLE OF CHARACTER;
  code ALPHA_KEY := alpha_key('A','B','C','D','E','F','G','H','I','J'
```

```
                                ,'K','L','M','N','O','P','Q','R','S','T'
                                ,'U','V','W','X','Y','Z');

  -- Define a single character indexed collection.
  TYPE list IS TABLE OF VARCHAR2(2000)
    INDEX BY VARCHAR2(1);

  -- Define two collections.
  reserved_word LIST;
  key_word       LIST;

  -- Define cursor.
  CURSOR c IS
    SELECT    keyword
    ,         reserved
    ,         res_type
    ,         res_attr
    ,         res_semi
    FROM      v$reserved_words
    ORDER BY keyword;

  -- Define a local function.
  FUNCTION format_list (list_in LIST) RETURN BOOLEAN IS
    -- Declare control variables.
    current VARCHAR2(1);
    element VARCHAR2(2000);
    status BOOLEAN := TRUE;
  BEGIN
    -- Read through an alphabetically indexed collection.
    FOR i IN 1..list_in.COUNT LOOP
      IF i = 1 THEN
        current := list_in.FIRST;
        element := list_in(current);
      ELSE
        IF list_in.NEXT(current) IS NOT NULL THEN
          current := list_in.NEXT(current);
          element := list_in(current);
        END IF;
      END IF;
      dbms_output.put_line('['||current||'] ['||element||']');
    END LOOP;
    RETURN status;
  END format_list;
BEGIN
  -- Initialize reserved word and keyword collections.
  FOR i IN 1..code.LAST LOOP
    FOR j IN c LOOP
      IF code(i) = UPPER(SUBSTR(j.keyword,1,1))
      AND (j.reserved = 'Y' OR j.res_type = 'Y' OR
           j.res_attr = 'Y' OR j.res_semi  'Y') THEN
        IF reserved_word.EXISTS(code(i)) THEN
```

```
          reserved_word(code(i)) := reserved_word(code(i)) || ', ' || j.keyword;
        ELSE
          reserved_word(code(i)) := j.keyword;
        END IF;
      ELSIF code(i) = UPPER(SUBSTR(j.keyword,1,1)) AND j.reserved = 'N' THEN
        IF key_word.EXISTS(code(i)) THEN
          key_word(code(i)) := key_word(code(i)) || ', ' || j.keyword;
        ELSE
          key_word(code(i)) := j.keyword;
        END IF;
      END IF;
    END LOOP;
  END LOOP;
  -- Print both lists.
  IF format_list(reserved_word) AND format_list(key_word) THEN
    NULL;
  END IF;
END;
/
```

Summary

The reserved word and keyword tables are alphabetized for you to browse them quickly. You can also recheck for changes with the `reserved_key_word.sql` script.

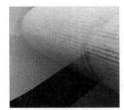

APPENDIX
J

PL/SQL Built-in
Functions

racle 11*g* provides a number of built-in functions for working with character strings, dates, and numbers. It also provides you with datatype conversion functions. This appendix covers these functions as well as functions for both object reference and error management. Last, it includes a miscellaneous section. These functions initialize large objects, perform advanced comparisons, and audit system environment variables.

Alphabetically indexed, the built-in functions are organized by type. Only a subset of all functions is listed in this appendix. These should be the more frequently used functions in your programs. Small example programs demonstrate how to use the built-in functions in PL/SQL:

- Character
- Datatype conversion
- Error reporting
- Miscellaneous
- Number

The built-in functions are a library of utilities to help you solve problems. They are often an underutilized resource for many developers.

Character Functions

Character functions actually cover characters and strings. They are extremely useful when you want to concatenate, parse, replace, or sort characters and strings. Appendix E covers the regular expression functions that are also mentioned briefly in some of these descriptions.

ASCII Function

The `ASCII` function returns an ASCII encoding number for a character. The following sample evaluates the first character of the string:

```
DECLARE
  text VARCHAR2(10) := 'Hello';
BEGIN
  IF ASCII(SUBSTR(text,1,1)) = 72 THEN
    dbms_output.put_line('The first character of the string is [H].');
  END IF;
END;
/
```

The ASCII-encoded English alphabet starts with an uppercase *A*, which has an ASCII value of 65. The lowercase letter *a* has a value of 97. Therefore, the uppercase *H* has a value of 72 as the eighth letter in the encoding sequence. The program prints

```
The first character of the string is [H].
```

This function can be used when you are searching strings for encoding matches. You'll find it useful when multiple encoding schemas have been used over time in the database.

ASCIISTR Function

The `ASCIISTR` function returns an ASCII encoding string for a character. The following sample evaluates the fourth character of the string, which is a French ê that is a Unicode character:

```
DECLARE
  text VARCHAR2(10) := 'forêt';
BEGIN
  dbms_output.put_line(ASCIISTR(SUBSTR(text,4,1)));
END;
/
```

The circumflex-annotated ê renders as a \xxxx character stream because it is a Unicode character. The quartet following the backslash represents a UTF-16 code unit. The string printed is

```
\00EA
```

This is a convenient function to convert strings into ASCII values, which lets you check if they contain Unicode characters. Enclosing the source and result strings as arguments to regular expression functions lets you compare whether the result contains more backslashes than the source string. This comparison would identify Unicode characters in strings.

CHR Function

The `CHR` function returns the binary equivalent character for an ASCII integer in the database character set or national character set. The latter behavior requires that you use `USING NCHAR_CS`, as shown in the prototype:

```
CHR(n [USING NCHAR_CS])
```

The following demonstrates sending a line break in the midst of a string through the standard out procedure, `DBMS_OUTPUT.PUT_LINE`. There is a convenient way to force a line break in the midst of an output string.

```
DECLARE
  text1 VARCHAR2(10) := 'Title';
  text2 VARCHAR2(10) := 'Content';
BEGIN
  dbms_output.put_line(text1||CHR(10)||text2);
END;
/
```

It prints

```
Title
Content
```

The `CHR` function also lets you embed extended characters into your programs. This is useful when they are constrained by ASCII encoding.

CONCAT Function

The `CONCAT` function concatenates two strings into one, and it is equivalent to using the concatenation operator (||). The prototype is

```
CONCAT(string1, string2)
```

When the datatypes of the strings differ, the function implicitly adopts the broadest one. This means that this function adheres to the traditional implicit casting model, which demands no precision be lost.

The following demonstrates the function:

```
DECLARE
   text1 VARCHAR2(10) := 'Hello ';
   text2 VARCHAR2(10) := 'There!';
BEGIN
   dbms_output.put_line(CONCAT(text1,text2));
END;
/
```

It prints

```
Hello There!
```

This function really presents an alternative syntax to the standard concatenation operator. You should use it when it makes your code more readable.

INITCAP Function

The `INITCAP` function is very handy when you want to convert a string to title case. Title case is a convention where the first letter of every word is capitalized while all other letters are in lowercase. The function takes a string and returns a converted string.

The following demonstrates the function:

```
DECLARE
   text VARCHAR2(12) := 'hello world!';
BEGIN
   dbms_output.put_line(INITCAP(text));
END;
/
```

It prints

```
Hello World!
```

This function would be handy if you were searching for Java source files in a database repository, provided they adhere to the title case convention. You could also use it if you write a parser for data entry, like customer contact notes. There is also a `NLS_INITCAP` function that works with different character sets.

INSTR Function

The `INSTR` function lets you find the position where a substring starts in a string. You also can find the starting position by using `INSTRB` when the string is encoded in bytes, `INSTRC` when the string contains Unicode complete characters, or either `INSTR2` or `INSTR4` functions for backward compatibility with UCS2 and UCS4 code points.

UCS2 provides backward compatibility like the `UTF16` character set, which is a variable-length character encoding standard. UCS2 fails, however, to use surrogate pairs and is actually a fixed-length character encoding standard that uses 16 bits to store characters. UCS4 is a fixed-length character encoding variant of UCS2; it encodes in 32-bit chunks.

The prototype for the `INSTR` family of functions is

INSTR(*target_string*, *search_string* [, *position* [, *occurrence*]])

You search the target string looking for the search string, like looking in a haystack for a pin. The position is 1 or the beginning of the string unless you specify another positive integer. You may only provide *occurrence* when you have provided a position value. The occurrence must also be a positive integer value. The regular expression REGEXP_INSTR function is a natural alternative to this function. Appendix E contains definitions of the regular expression functions.

All of the INSTR function variations work the same way: they take a string and calculate its length as a return value.

The following demonstrates the INSTR variation of the functions:

```
DECLARE
  text VARCHAR2(12) := 'Hello World!';
BEGIN
  dbms_output.put_line('Start ['||INSTR(text,'World',1)||']');
END;
/
```

It prints

```
Start [7]
```

The INSTR functions are useful when you want to parse strings into substrings in a looping structure. The INSTR and INSTRC are the safest with all character types except byte-allocated strings. Use the INSTRB for byte strings.

LENGTH Function

The LENGTH function lets you calculate the length of a string by using character units. A variant LENGTHB calculates the length of a string in bytes, and LENGTHC uses Unicode complete characters. You also have the LENGTH2 and LENGTH4 functions that count using UCS2 and UCS4 code points.

UCS2 provides backward compatibility like the UTF16 character set, which is a variable-length character encoding standard. UCS2 fails however to use surrogate pairs, and is actually a fixed-length character encoding standard that uses 16 bits to store characters. UCS4 is a fixed-length character encoding variant of UCS2; it encodes in 32-bit chunks.

All of the LENGTH function variations work the same way: they take a string and calculate its length as a return value.

The following demonstrates the LENGTH variation of the functions:

```
DECLARE
  text VARCHAR2(12) := 'Hello World!';
BEGIN
  dbms_output.put_line('Length ['||LENGTH(text)||']');
END;
/
```

It prints

```
Length [12]
```

The LENGTH functions are useful when you want to parse strings into substrings. You should probably stick to using LENGTH or LENGTHC when writing production code, and should avoid LENGTHB because it only counts the number of bytes.

LOWER Function

The LOWER function lets you demote a string to match a lowercase string literal. There is also NLS_LOWER for Unicode strings. This is convenient when you don't know the case of stored data.

The following demonstrates the function:

```
DECLARE
  text VARCHAR2(12) := 'Hello World!';
BEGIN
  dbms_output.put_line(LOWER(text));
END;
/
```

It prints

```
hello world!
```

This function and the UPPER function let you easily enter and match string literals against values of unknown case in database columns. There is no processing difference between demoting strings to lowercase and promoting strings to uppercase. You should pick one and use it consistently.

LPAD Function

The LPAD function lets you add a character one or more times at the beginning of a string. The prototype is

```
LPAD(output_string, output_length, padding_character)
```

The following demonstrates how you left-pad a string. The output length sets the new length of the string and pads with copies of the padding character until the string reaches the new length. The number of padding characters is equal to the output length minus the number of characters in the beginning output string.

```
DECLARE
  output     VARCHAR2(10) := 'Wowie';
  whitespace VARCHAR2(1)  := ' ';
BEGIN
  dbms_output.put_line('['||LPAD(output,10,whitespace)||']');
END;
/
```

It prints

```
[     Wowie]
```

The square brackets ensure that padded whitespace prints because the procedure DBMS_OUTPUT.PUT_LINE normally removes leading whitespace. Other characters are not impacted by the paring of strings before printing them.

LTRIM Function

The LTRIM function lets you remove a set of characters from the beginning of a string. The prototype is

```
LTRIM(base_string, set_of_values)
```

The `LTRIM` function imposes a limit on what is trimmed from a string. The set of values must contain all values from the beginning of the string to where you want to pare it. If any character in that stream is missing, the trimming stops at that point.

The following demonstrates the `LTRIM` function:

```
DECLARE
  comment VARCHAR2(12) := 'Wowie Howie!';
BEGIN
  dbms_output.put_line('['||LTRIM(comment,' eiwoWo')||']');
END;
/
```

The example contains all the characters to remove the first word plus an extra *o*. It cannot remove the *o* because the *H* is not found in the set. So it only removes the first word and whitespace, printing

```
[Howie!]
```

A second *o* is unnecessary because the function trims all instances of any character in the set provided there is no intervening character not found in the set. This has shown you how to trim the leading part of a string. You can also trim the right side of a string with the `RTRIM` function covered later in this appendix.

REPLACE Function

The `REPLACE` function lets you search and replace a substring in any `CHAR`, `VARCHAR2`, `NCHAR`, `NVARCHAR2`, `CLOB`, or `NCLOB` string. It returns the modified string. The prototype is

```
REPLACE(base_string, search_string, replace_string)
```

The following demonstrates how to use the function:

```
DECLARE
  base_string    VARCHAR2(40) := 'The Republican President said ...';
  search_string  VARCHAR2(40) := 'Republican';
  replace_string VARCHAR2(40) := 'Democratic';
BEGIN
  dbms_output.put_line(REPLACE(base_string,search_string,replace_string));
END;
/
```

It prints

```
The Democratic President said ...
```

The word "Democratic" has been substituted for the word "Republican." You should ensure that you're using uniform character sets for all actual parameters because the `REPLACE` function is sensitive to character set.

RPAD Function

Like the `LPAD` function, the `RPAD` function lets you add a character one or more times to a string. The difference is that `RPAD` adds the characters to the end of the string. The prototype is

```
RPAD(output_string, output_length, padding_character)
```

The following demonstrates right-padding a string:

```
DECLARE
  output      VARCHAR2(10) := 'Wowie';
  whitespace VARCHAR2(1)   := ' ';
BEGIN
  dbms_output.put_line('['||RPAD(output,10,whitespace)||']');
END;
/
```

It prints

```
[Wowie     ]
```

The square brackets highlight the padded whitespace. While the procedure DBMS_OUTPUT. PUT_LINE removes leading whitespace, it does not remove trailing whitespace.

RTRIM Function

The RTRIM function lets you remove a set of characters from the end of a string. The prototype is

```
RTRIM(base_string, set_of_values)
```

The RTRIM function imposes a limit on what is trimmed from a string. The set of values must contain all values from the end of the string to where you want to pare it. If any character in that stream is missing, the trimming stops at that point.

The following demonstrates the RTRIM function:

```
DECLARE
  comment VARCHAR2(12) := 'Wowie Howie!';
BEGIN
  dbms_output.put_line('['||RTRIM(comment,' Howie!')||']');
END;
/
```

The example contains all the characters to remove the first word, but the characters "owie" are found twice in the string. Also, there is no intervening character not found in the set. Therefore, this function pares more than what you might expect, printing:

```
[W]
```

This has shown you how to trim the trailing part of a string. It has also shown you that one character can be removed multiple times, provided there is no intervening character not found in the set of values.

You can also trim the left side of a string with the LTRIM function covered earlier in this appendix. Trimming characters more than once also applies to the LTRIM function.

UPPER Function

The UPPER function lets you demote a string to match a lowercase string literal. There is also NLS_UPPER for Unicode strings. This is convenient when you don't know the case of stored data.

The following demonstrates the function:

```
DECLARE
  text VARCHAR2(12) := 'Hello World!';
BEGIN
  dbms_output.put_line(UPPER(text));
END;
/
```

It prints

```
HELLO WORLD!
```

This function and the LOWER function let you easily enter and match string literals against values of unknown case in database columns. There is no processing difference between promoting strings to uppercase and demoting them to lowercase. You should pick one and use it consistently.

Datatype Conversion

Datatype conversion is simply casting. Casting is the process of taking a variable defined as one datatype and changing it to another datatype. Implicit casting makes the change for you automatically but only works when the rules are simple and well understood. Explicit casting lets you instruct the programming language how to assign one datatype to another when no rule applies without instructions.

Datatype conversion is often done implicitly in PL/SQL. Unlike other strongly typed programming languages, PL/SQL does implicit conversions even when there is a potential loss of precision. For example, you can assign a complex number in a NUMBER datatype to a SIMPLE_INTEGER datatype and lose any values to the right of the decimal point. Chapter 2 provides an example of this type of implicit conversion.

The datatype conversion functions are useful when you want to make a conversion that requires you to provide instructions. You have to manually convert strings to dates when strings don't adhere to default format mask conventions. Likewise, some specialized types require you to take specific actions before you can convert data.

These examples focus on demonstrating how to use these functions. You'll notice that there are no conversions between user-defined object types and standard types. You should include conversion methods in your object type definitions.

CAST Function

The CAST function is very useful because it converts built-in datatypes to another built-in datatype, or collection-typed variables to another collection-typed variable. The CAST function does have some limits; for instance, it uses only the default date conversion format mask, as discussed in Chapter 3. Unlike most functions, this function works with all but the LONG, LONG RAW, ROWID, and UROWID built-in datatypes. CAST also limits how it casts data from BLOB and CLOB types into a RAW datatype because it relies on an implicit database behavior. You raise an exception when CAST tries to convert a large object into a RAW type when it is too large to fit inside a RAW datatype.

There are two prototypes—one for scalar built-in variables and another for collections. The scalar variable built-in prototype is

```
CAST(type1_variable_name AS type2_variable_name)
```

and the collection prototype is

```
CAST(MULTISET(subquery)) AS collection_type_variable_name)
```

The following program shows how to cast a date to a string:

```
DECLARE
    source DATE := TO_DATE('30-SEP-07');
    target VARCHAR2(24);
BEGIN
    target := CAST(source AS VARCHAR2);
    dbms_output.put_line(target);
END;
/
```

This type of usage is exactly the same in both SQL and PL/SQL contexts, but the MULTISET context is restricted to SQL statements. If you attempt to use a CAST function with a MULTISET and subquery as a right operand, you raise a PLS-00405 exception. However, you can embed these in SQL statements inside your PL/SQL blocks.

The CAST operation inside a query statement requires that you cast to a SQL datatype, like a collection of scalar variables. This leaves you with a choice between varrays and nested tables. You should use nested tables because they are easier to manage and don't require incremental conversion with the TABLE function call (see Chapter 7).

This creates a nested table of strings as a SQL datatype:

```
CREATE TYPE collection IS TABLE OF VARCHAR2(5);
/
```

You should create a table or view because the MULTISET operator disallows queries that use set operators, like INTERSECT, MINUS, UNION, and UNION ALL. It raises a PLS-00605 exception when set operators are found in the subquery.

The following builds a sample table:

```
CREATE TABLE casting (num VARCHAR2(5));
```

Next, you can insert into the table the English ordinal numbers "one," "two," "three," to "nine" by using the table fabrication pattern:

```
INSERT INTO casting
(SELECT 'One'   FROM dual UNION ALL
 SELECT 'Two'   FROM dual UNION ALL
 SELECT 'Three' FROM dual UNION ALL
 SELECT 'Four'  FROM dual UNION ALL
 SELECT 'Five'  FROM dual UNION ALL
 SELECT 'Six'   FROM dual UNION ALL
 SELECT 'Seven' FROM dual UNION ALL
 SELECT 'Eight' FROM dual UNION ALL
 SELECT 'Nine'  FROM dual);
```

The sample program demonstrates how to use the CAST and MULTISET functions together:

```
DECLARE
  counter NUMBER := 1;
BEGIN
  FOR i IN (SELECT CAST(MULTISET(SELECT num FROM casting) AS COLLECTION) AS rs
            FROM    casting) LOOP
    dbms_output.put_line(i.rs(counter));
    counter := counter + 1;
  END LOOP;
END;
/
```

This prints the ordinal number words in a list. The `CAST` function returns a collection of items. Unfortunately, you also need to match a collection structure to the row structure of the query. You use this type of structure to return nested table contents from tables.

CONVERT Function

The `CONVERT` function converts a string from one character set to another. It has the following prototype:

```
CONVERT(string, destination_character_set, source_character_set)
```

Table Fabrication

Sometimes you want to create data without building a temporary table. There are two alternatives to avoid building temporary tables that can fragment your database. One is to build run-time views, which are aliased queries inside the `FROM` clause. This approach works when the data can be queried from one or more real tables. The other approach leverages the `UNION ALL` set operator to join a series of related data. This approach, known as data or table fabrication, lets you build data in a query when it doesn't exist in your database.

The following uses table fabrication to multiply the number of returned rows:

```
SELECT   alias.counter
FROM     (SELECT 1 AS counter FROM dual UNION ALL
          SELECT 2 AS counter FROM dual) alias;
```

It returns two rows because the run-time view contains two fabricated rows, and prints

```
COUNTER
-------
      1
      2
```

There are two caveats about table fabrication. You must ensure the list of `SELECT` clause columns return the same datatype, and you must provide matching aliases for any literals or expressions in any column position. These are the same rules imposed by set operators in any query.

Finding the Character Set of a Database Instance
You can log in as a privileged user, like SYSTEM, and run the following query:

```
SELECT value$ FROM sys.props$ WHERE name = 'NLS_CHARACTERSET';
```

More often than not folks are disappointed when they look in the V$PARAMETER view for the character set. The V$PARAMETER view does contain most of the configuration values for the database instance. The miscellaneous section demonstrates how you can implement a function to read the character set in the EMPTY_BLOB function section.

The following demonstrates converting the French word forêt (forest in English) from the AL32UTF8 to UTF8 character set:

```
DECLARE
  text VARCHAR2(10) := 'forêt';
BEGIN
  dbms_output.put_line(CONVERT(text,'AL32UTF8','UTF8'));
END;
/
```

This prints the same forêt, but it now takes three bytes of storage rather than two bytes. You will find this function handy when you work in multiple character sets.

TO_CHAR Function
The TO_CHAR function lets you do several types of conversion. You can convert CLOB, DATE, NCHAR, NCLOB, NUMBER, or TIMESTAMP datatypes to VARCHAR2 datatypes. This function is overloaded and has two prototypes. The prototype for string datatypes is

```
TO_CHAR({clob_type | nchar_type | nclob_type})
```

The alternative prototype for dates, numbers, and times is

```
TO_CHAR({date_type | timestamp_type | number_type} [, format_make [, nls_param ]])
```

The subsections demonstrate converting other types of strings to character strings, dates to characters strings, and numbers to character strings. The date and number subsections also have two examples each: one with the native National Language Support (NLS) character set of the instance, and one that overrides the instance default.

Converting a String to a Character String
The following demonstrates converting a CLOB datatype to a CHAR datatype:

```
DECLARE
  big_string CLOB := 'Not really that big, eh?';
BEGIN
  dbms_output.put_line(TO_CHAR(big_string));
END;
/
```

Converting a Date to a Character String

The following demonstrates converting a DATE to a CHAR:

```
DECLARE
   today DATE := SYSDATE;
BEGIN
   dbms_output.put_line(TO_CHAR(today,'Mon DD, YYYY'));
END;
/
```

While your date will reflect the current system date, this prints the day this was written:

```
Sep 27, 2007
```

When you add the National Language Support (NLS) parameter to the function, you can override the NLS setting for the database. The following resets the NLS_DATE_LANGUAGE parameter to French:

```
DECLARE
   today DATE := SYSDATE;
BEGIN
   dbms_output.put_line(TO_CHAR(today,'Mon DD, YYYY'
                                ,'NLS_DATE_LANGUAGE = FRENCH'));
END;
/
```

This then prints the date in the French style, which adds a period after the abbreviation of the month, like

```
Sept. 27, 2007
```

Converting a Number to a Character String

Converting numbers to characters works much like dates. The following illustrates converting a number to a formatted dollar amount in American English:

```
DECLARE
   amount NUMBER := 2.9;
BEGIN
   dbms_output.put_line(TO_CHAR(amount,'$9,999.90'));
END;
/
```

The format mask says print a digit if found when there's a 9 and always print a zero when there is no value. The format mask substitutes a zero, since there is no value in the hundredths placeholder, printing:

```
$2.90
```

Adding the NLS parameter, you can now format the currency return in Euros:

```
DECLARE
   amount NUMBER := 2.9;
BEGIN
   dbms_output.put_line(TO_CHAR(amount,'9,999.90L'
```

```
                                    ,'nls_currency = EUR'));
END;
/
```

This prints

```
2.90EUR
```

This section has demonstrated how to use the TO_CHAR function to convert national language and large object strings to character strings, and dates, timestamps, and numbers to character strings. The format masks only cover characters in those specific positions. You need to expand the format mask when dealing with larger numbers.

TO_CLOB Function

The TO_CLOB function lets you convert NCLOB column datatype or other character types to character large objects. You can convert CHAR, NCHAR, NVARCHAR2, and VARCHAR2 datatypes to NCLOB types.

The prototype for this is

```
TO_CLOB({char_type | nchar_type | nclob_type | nvarchar2_type | varchar2_type})
```

The following converts a string to CLOB and then uses the TO_CHAR to reconvert for printing by the DBMS_OUTPUT.PUT_LINE procedure:

```
DECLARE
   initial_string VARCHAR2(2000) := 'Not really required. :-)';
BEGIN
   dbms_output.put_line(TO_CHAR(TO_CLOB(initial_string)));
END;
/
```

This is a handy function when you're moving an array of strings into a CLOB variable. It also lets you move NLS large objects columns into a standard format for your programs.

TO_DATE Function

The TO_DATE function lets you convert strings to dates. The prototype for this is

```
TO_DATE(string_type [, format_make [, nls_param ]])
```

The following program demonstrates converting a string through implicit conversion:

```
DECLARE
   target DATE;
BEGIN
   target := '29-SEP-94';
   dbms_output.put_line('Back to a string ['||TO_CHAR(target)||']');
END;
/
```

The implicit cast works because the default format mask for a date is DD-MON-RR or DD-MON-YYYY. When the string or source is not in that format, you must provide a format mask to cast the string into a date.

The next example explicitly casts a string by providing a format mask:

```
DECLARE
  target DATE;
BEGIN
  target := TO_DATE('September 29, 1994 10:00 A.M.'
                   ,'Month DD, YYYY HH:MI A.M.');
  dbms_output.put_line('Back to a string ['||TO_CHAR(target)||']');
END;
/
```

The A.M. formatting option is a mask available in some National Language Support (NLS) languages, like American English. It is not supported in French because the appropriate format mask in that language is AM. If you apply an unsupported format mask, you raise an ORA-01855 exception.

The following example demonstrates overriding the default of language:

```
DECLARE
  target DATE;
BEGIN
  target := TO_DATE('Septembre 29, 1994 10:00 AM'
                   ,'Month DD, YYYY HH:MI AM'
                   ,'NLS_DATE_LANGUAGE = French');
  dbms_output.put_line('Back to a string ['
  ||                    TO_CHAR(target
                               ,'Month DD, YYYY HH:MI AM'
                               ,'NLS_DATE_LANGUAGE = French')||']');
END;
/
```

The nature of converting to a date from a string is a virtual mirror to reversing the process, as should be clearly seen in the example. The TO_DATE function is frequently used in PL/SQL.

TO_LOB Function

The TO_LOB function lets you convert LONG or LONG RAW column datatypes to large objects. However, there are restrictions on how you can use this function. It can only be used to convert your LONG datatypes to large objects when used in an INSERT statement as a SELECT list element of a subquery.

The prototype for this is

```
TO_LOB({long_type | long_raw_type})
```

There are several steps to build a small test case to examine this function. You need to create source and destination tables and seed the source with data.

```
CREATE TABLE source
( source_id NUMBER
, source    LONG);

INSERT INTO source
VALUES
( 1, 'A not so long string');
```

```
CREATE TABLE target
( target_id NUMBER
, target    CLOB );
```

After you've done that, you can build an anonymous block to transfer the LONG column values to a CLOB column in the new table. The following demonstrates that along with a query of the moved contents.

```
DECLARE
  CURSOR c IS SELECT target_id, target FROM target;
BEGIN
  INSERT INTO target
  SELECT source_id, TO_LOB(source) FROM source;
  FOR i IN c LOOP
    dbms_output.put_line('Clob value ['||TO_CHAR(i.target)||']');
  END LOOP;
END;
/
```

This is a handy function for data migration. If this were a real character large object value, you'd need to read chunks of the column inside a loop. The latter is best done with a combination of the LENGTH and SUBSTR (*substring*) functions.

TO_NCHAR Function

The TO_NCHAR function lets you do several types of conversion. You can convert CHAR, CLOB, DATE, NCLOB, NUMBER, or TIMESTAMP datatypes to NVARCHAR2 datatypes. This function is overloaded and has two prototypes. The prototype for string datatypes is

```
TO_NCHAR({clob_type | nchar_type | nclob_type})
```

The alternative prototype for dates, numbers, and times is

```
TO_NCHAR({date_type | timestamp_type | number_type}
         [, format_make [, nls_param ]])
```

The examples in the TO_CHAR function description also work with the TO_NCHAR function. You can modify those to qualify how the TO_NCHAR function works.

TO_NCLOB Function

The TO_NCLOB function lets you convert CLOB column datatype or other character types to character large objects. You can convert CHAR, NCHAR, NVARCHAR2, and VARCHAR2 datatypes to CLOB types.

The prototype for this is

```
TO_NCLOB({clob_type | char_type | nchar_type | nvarchar2_type | varchar2_type})
```

The examples in the TO_NCLOB function description also work with the TO_NCLOB function. You can modify those to qualify how the TO_NCLOB function works.

Alternative Migration Strategy for LONG and LONG RAW columns

While the *Oracle Database SQL Language Reference 11g Release 1* doesn't mention that you can use the TO_LOB in any other context than an INSERT statement, you can. More often than not you don't want to move a large table to a new table and then rename it as part of a single column migration.

You can solve the problem by adding a CLOB column to the table and using the TO_LOB function in an update statement. Like the INSERT statement limitation, the TO_LOB must be part of a SELECT list in a subquery. This type of movement from one column to another in the same row requires a correlated subquery. This is how you synchronize the two copies of the same table to work on the same row.

You would alter the source table with the following syntax:

```
ALTER TABLE source ADD (new_source CLOB);
```

Then, you migrate the data with the following UPDATE statement:

```
UPDATE source outer
SET    outer.new_source =
         (SELECT TO_LOB(inner.source)
          FROM   source inner
          WHERE  outer.source_id = inner.source_id);
```

Cleanup is easy; drop the old column:

```
ALTER TABLE source DROP COLUMN source;
```

Then, you can rename the new_source to source, which will map to the original column. The command is

```
ALTER TABLE source RENAME COLUMN new_source TO source;
```

This works well after you've developed the new code that expects a CLOB, not a LONG or LONG RAW column. It has the advantage of not moving the balance of columns while migrating away from the obsolete data types.

TO_NUMBER Function

The TO_NUMBER function lets you convert an expression into a numeric value. The expression can be a BINARY_DOUBLE, CHAR, NCHAR, NVARCHAR2, or VARCHAR2 datatype. You can also use the NLS_NUMERIC_CHARACTERS or NLS_CURRENCY parameters for National Language Support (NLS).

The prototype for this is

```
TO_NUMBER(expression [, format_mask [, nls_param ]])
```

The example converts a formatted string to a number by using a format mask:

```
DECLARE
  source VARCHAR2(38) := '$9,999.90';
```

```
BEGIN
  dbms_output.put_line(TO_NUMBER(source,'$9,999.99'));
END;
/
```

The program prints a number without a hundredth placeholder:

```
9999.9
```

You can also use NLS formatting like that shown in the TO_CHAR function examples, or use it this way:

```
DECLARE
  source VARCHAR2(38) := '9,999.90EUR';
BEGIN
  dbms_output.put_line(TO_NUMBER(source,'9G999D99L','nls_currency = EUR'));
END;
/
```

It also prints

```
9999.9
```

The G stands for comma, D for decimal point (or period), and L for string qualifying the currency format. There is no dollar symbol leading a currency expression when you use a ISO currency string like USA, JPY, EUR. The string provided as the value of nls_currency must also match the value in the original string.

TO_TIMESTAMP Function

The TO_TIMESTAMP function lets you convert a string expression into a timestamp. The prototype for this is

```
TO_TIMESTAMP(expression [, format_mask [, nls_param ]])
```

The example demonstrates a call to the TO_TIMESTAMP function:

```
DECLARE
  source TIMESTAMP := TO_TIMESTAMP('30-SEP-07 15:17:04','DD-MON-YYYY HH24:MI:SS');
BEGIN
  dbms_output.put_line(TO_CHAR(source,'Mon DD, YYYY HH:MI:SS AM'));
END;
/
```

This is similar to the behavior of the TO_DATE expression. It is useful to note that there is also the TO_TIMESTAMP_TZ function when you work with multiple time zones.

Error Reporting

The error reporting functions only work in the exception block of PL/SQL program units. The SQLCODE function returns the code number for the error, like ORA-01422. The SQLERRM function returns the error code and a brief message. The messages are defined by language, and you should note that in some earlier releases, some language translations have had incomplete message files.

Chapter 5 covers exception handling and contains additional examples that you may find useful. These two sections summarize the utility of the SQLCODE and SQLERRM functions.

SQLCODE Function

The SQL code error returns the Oracle error number for standard exceptions and a 1 for user-defined exceptions. You can also raise a user-defined custom error and exception message by calling the RAISE_APPLICATION_ERROR function. This section demonstrates all three approaches.

The following program generates a standard exception:

```
DECLARE
  a NUMBER;
  b CHAR := 'A';
BEGIN
  a := b;
EXCEPTION
  WHEN others THEN
    dbms_output.put_line('SQLERRM ['||SQLERRM||']');
END;
/
```

It prints to console

```
SQLERRM [ORA-06502: PL/SQL: numeric or value error: character to number ...
```

The next program generates a user-defined exception number:

```
DECLARE
  e EXCEPTION;
BEGIN
  RAISE e;
EXCEPTION
  WHEN others THEN
    dbms_output.put_line('SQLCODE ['||SQLCODE||']');
END;
/
```

It generates the following because user-defined exceptions always return 1:

```
SQLCODE [1]
```

The RAISE_APPLICATION_ERROR function lets you define a user exception number and exception. The SQLCODE value works for user-defined exceptions exactly as it does for standard exceptions.

SQLERRM Function

The SQLERRM mirrors the behaviors of the SQLCODE with the exception of the value returned. SQLERRM returns the error code and a default message. The message files are read from a generic message file in the $ORACLE_HOME/rdbms/mesg directory. The message files are found in the oraus.msg file for American English exception messages. They are language-specific files when you install Oracle in a different language. You can also evaluate error message in Linux or Unix by using the oerr utility.

You execute `oerr` utility by providing the three-character error type and five-number error message, like

```
# oerr ora 01422
```

The `oerr` utility treats the case of the three-character error type string as case insensitive. Unfortunately, it isn't available on the Windows operating system port of the database.

The `SQLERRM` function works the same for standard or user-defined exceptions. It reads the message file. The next program demonstrates raising a user-defined exception:

```
DECLARE
  e EXCEPTION;
BEGIN
  RAISE e;
EXCEPTION
  WHEN others THEN
    dbms_output.put_line('SQLERRM ['||SQLERRM||']');
END;
/
```

This program generates the following:

```
SQLERRM [User-Defined Exception]
```

You can use an `EXCEPTION_INIT PRAGMA` (a precompiler instruction) to map a user-defined exception to a standard Oracle exception. The standard exception message related to the `SQLCODE` value is printed when you map a user-defined exception:

The next program demonstrates mapping a related standard exception message to a user-defined exception:

```
DECLARE
  e EXCEPTION;
  PRAGMA EXCEPTION_INIT(e,-01422);
BEGIN
  RAISE e;
EXCEPTION
  WHEN others THEN
    dbms_output.put_line('SQLERRM ['||SQLERRM||']');
END;
/
```

It prints the following output:

```
SQLERRM [ORA-01422: exact fetch returns more than requested number of rows]
```

You can use the `RAISE_APPLICATION_ERROR` function when you require a specialized error message. Unfortunately, this function limits you to an exception range between –20,001 and –21,999. If you use any number outside that range, you'll raise an `ORA-20000` exception.

The following demonstrates the `SQLERRM` result for a user-defined exception message:

```
BEGIN
  RAISE_APPLICATION_ERROR(-20001,'An overriding user-defined error message.');
EXCEPTION
```

```
  WHEN others THEN
    dbms_output.put_line('SQLERRM ['||SQLERRM||']');
END;
/
```

Raising the following to console:

```
SQLERRM [ORA-20001: An overriding user-defined error message.]
```

This section has demonstrated how you can use standard and user-defined exception messages. You've learned that you can *only return standard messages* unless you call the RAISE_APPLICATION_ERROR function.

Miscellaneous

These miscellaneous functions initialize large objects, perform advanced comparisons, and audit system environment variables. They are very powerful features in the PL/SQL language.

The BFILENAME, EMPTY_BLOB, and EMPTY_CLOB functions initialize large objects. The BFILENAME function defines a data structure for an external file. The others initialize a large object, respectively BLOB and CLOB datatypes.

Advanced comparisons are conditional evaluations. They are performed by COALESCE, DECODE, GREATEST, LEAST, NANVL, NULLIF, and NVL. COALESCE uses short-circuit analysis to find the first not-null value in a set. If all values in a set are null, COALESCE returns null. DECODE performs if-then-else and if-then-elsif-then-else logic. GREATEST finds the highest character, string, or number in a set of like datatypes. LEAST finds the lowest value in a set. NANVL substitutes a default number when *not a number* is returned but only applies to types using native operating system math libraries. NULLIF returns a null when its two actual parameters are equal. NVL substitutes another value when the first actual parameter is null; it requires both actual parameters to be the same datatype.

The balance of the functions audit system environment variables. They are DUMP, NLS_CHARSET_DECL_LEN, NLS_CHARSET_ID, NLS_CHARSET_NAME, SYS_CONTEXT, SYS_GUID, UID, USER, USERENV, and VSIZE. DUMP and VSIZE inspect the physical size of datatypes. Oracle's National Language Support (NLS) represents how Oracle databases manage different character sets. As discussed in Chapter 3, Oracle supports two Unicode character sets: AL32UTF8 and UTF8. It also supports numerous other character sets. NLS is the umbrella term for all character sets. NLS_CHARSET_DECL_LEN, NLS_CHARSET_ID, and NLS_CHARSET_NAME let you discover the physical storage details of NLS character sets. The remaining functions audit database session information.

This section covers the large objects, comparison, and four system environment functions: DUMP, SYS_CONTEXT, USERENV, and VSIZE. Rather than create separate nesting levels, those covered are simply presented alphabetically. The descriptions qualify their purpose in the PL/SQL language.

BFILENAME Function

The BFILENAME function is used to insert or update a reference to an externally stored binary large object. It takes two parameters: a virtual directory path and a filename. Unfortunately, it makes no effort to validate whether the virtual directory or file exists. This is because you may build the reference before creating the virtual directory mapping or placing the file in the target location. It returns a binary file locator.

The following prototype demonstrates that you call the function with two strings; the first is limited to 30 characters and the second to 4,000 characters:

```
BFILENAME('virtual_directory','physical_file')
```

NOTE
Operating systems generally confine the fully qualified path to a value smaller than 4,000 characters.

You can find the mapping of virtual directories to the external file system in the `DBA_DIRECTORIES` view. The view is available when you are the privileged user `SYSTEM` or have been granted the DBA role privilege, which actually inherits the privilege through the `SELECT_CATALOG_ROLE`.

The following query lets you find the virtual directories and their physical server mapping:

```
SELECT    owner
,         directory_name
,         directory_path
FROM      dba_directories;
```

All virtual directories are owned by the `SYS` schema. You cannot access the contents from a cursor inside a stored program unit because the privilege exists through a role. Chapter 8 shows you how to query the contents of the table inside a stored procedure, which requires that the `SYS` schema grant `SYSTEM` the `SELECT` privilege on the `DBA_DIRECTORIES` view.

When you don't have the `SELECT` privilege, you are limited to using the `DBMS_LOB` package for access to the information inside a `BFILE` column. You can verify whether the file exists on the server by using the `DBMS_LOB.FILEEXISTS` function and get the physical size by using the `DBMS_LOB.GETLENGTH` function. The next program assumes you build the following table:

```
CREATE TABLE sample (sample_id NUMBER, sample_bfile BFILE);
```

Then, you insert a record like this:

```
INSERT INTO sample
VALUES (1, BFILENAME('VIRTUAL_DIRECTORY','file_name.ext'));
```

You can also use the `BFILENAME` function in the `SET` clause of an `UPDATE` statement to change either the virtual directory or the filename. These external files are read-only datatypes, and you update data as part of maintenance programs that manipulate their location or names.

This program will now read the column and return a physical size for a file, or a message that the file was not found:

```
DECLARE
  file_locator BFILE;
BEGIN
  SELECT sample_bfile INTO file_locator FROM sample WHERE sample_id = 1;
  IF dbms_lob.fileexists(file_locator) = 1 THEN
    dbms_output.put_line(dbms_lob.getlength(file_locator));
  ELSE
    dbms_output.put_line('No file found.');
  END IF;
END;
/
```

The DBMS_LOB.FILEEXISTS function was built to work in both SQL and PL/SQL. Since SQL does not support a native Boolean datatype, the function returns a 1 when it finds a file and 0 when it fails.

The next program illustrates creating a binary file locator outside of a database column, then reading the locator to find the filename with the DBMS_LOB.FILEGETNAME function:

```
DECLARE
  alias    VARCHAR2(255);
  filename VARCHAR2(255);
BEGIN
  dbms_lob.filegetname(BFILENAME('virtual_dir','file_name.gif'),alias,filename);
  dbms_output.put_line(filename);
END;
/
```

It prints

```
file_name.gif
```

This section has demonstrated how to use the BFILENAME function. You will use it when you store files externally from the database. They must be no larger than the maximum file size supported by the operating system. They are typically files like .gif, .jpg, or .png image files, sound recording files, Flash components, et cetera.

COALESCE Function

The COALESCE function uses short-circuit analysis to find the first not-null value in a set. Short-circuit evaluation means that it stops searching when a not-null value is returned. COALESCE returns null when all values evaluate as nulls.

The COALESCE prototype that works with scalar variables of the same datatype is

```
COALESCE(arg1, arg2 [, arg3 [, arg(n+1)]])
```

The following demonstrates the function using a collection of strings:

```
DECLARE
  TYPE list IS TABLE OF VARCHAR2(5);
  ord LIST := list('One','','Three','','Five');
BEGIN
  dbms_output.put_line(COALESCE(ord(1),ord(2),ord(3),ord(4),ord(5)));

END;

/
```

The function prints the first not-null element in the collection:

```
One
```

You can put a loop around the COALESCE function to perform the function repeatedly. Alternatively, you can use a FOR loop, nested IF statement, and NVL function call to print only not-null values. They consume roughly the same resources, but the latter may be clearer to most programmers.

DECODE Function

The DECODE function performs if-then-else and if-then-else-if-then-else logic in SQL statements. It is known as a pseudocolumn, and you can also use it inside your PL/SQL programs. The prototype for an if-then-else statement is

```
DECODE(evaluation_expression, comparison_expression
                       , true_expression, false_expression);
```

The alternate prototype for if-then-else-if-then-else is

```
DECODE(evaluation_expression, comparison_expression1, true_expression1
                       , comparison_expression2, true_expression2
                       , comparison_expression(n+1), true_expression(n+1)
                       , comparison false_expression);
```

The following illustrates an if-then-else DECODE function:

```
DECLARE
   a NUMBER := 94;
   b NUMBER := 96;
   c VARCHAR2(20);
BEGIN
   SELECT DECODE(a,b,'Match.','Don''t match.') INTO c FROM dual;
   dbms_output.put_line(c);
END;
/
```

It prints the following because the numbers are unequal:

```
Don't match.
```

The following program shows the case logic of a multiple if-then-else statement:

```
DECLARE
   redsox   NUMBER := 96;
   yankees  NUMBER := 94;
   division NUMBER := 96;
   headline VARCHAR2(30);
BEGIN
   SELECT DECODE(division,yankees,'Yankees clinch pennant.'
                          ,redsox,'Red Sox clinch pennant.'
                          ,'Tied Again!')
   INTO    headline
   FROM    dual;
   dbms_output.put_line(headline);
END;
/
```

While using static values, you should see the potential. Examine when you can resolve procedural questions in your SQL statements, and do it when it simplifies the program!

DUMP Function

The DUMP function examines the datatype and real length of registered datatypes. It returns a value that is independent of the database or session character set. You can only use the DUMP function inside a SQL statement.

The following block demonstrates how to find the real size of a LONG RAW variable:

```
DECLARE
  buffer LONG RAW := HEXTORAW('42'||'41'||'44');
  detail VARCHAR2(100);
BEGIN
  SELECT DUMP(buffer) INTO detail FROM dual;
  dbms_output.put_line(detail);
END;
/
```

It prints the data catalog number for a LONG RAW, the length of the data value, and the ASCII values of the original hexadecimal values:

```
Typ=23 Len=3: 66,65,68
```

You may not use this too often, but when you're trying to figure out why something is broken and the error message and web hits are limited, it may be very helpful. It certainly helps when working with the DBMS_LOB package and raw streams, as covered in the next section, on the EMPTY_BLOB function.

EMPTY_BLOB Function

The EMPTY_BLOB function lets you initialize a database column with an empty BLOB datatype. This is important because large objects have three possible states: they are null, empty, or populated. The DBMS_LOB package fails by raising an ORA-22275 exception when you attempt to work with a null BLOB column. The error is raised because there is no valid locator found in the column for null values.

The DBMS_LOB package fails by raising an ORA-01403 exception when you have an empty BLOB. This is more meaningful than the invalid LOB locator message that you'll receive when the column isn't initialized, and you can always append to an empty BLOB column. In some cases, using a default value during table creation may be a viable solution, but generally there are good reasons to leave a BLOB column null until you want to use it.

The next program assumes you build the following table:

```
CREATE TABLE sample (sample_id NUMBER, sample_blob BLOB);
```

Then, you insert a record like this:

```
INSERT INTO sample (sample_id) VALUES (1);
```

You'll need to configure your database as noted in the "Deploying a Character Set Function" sidebar. The following program demonstrates how to update a BLOB column in an existing row:

```
DECLARE
  amount BINARY_INTEGER := 100;
```

```
buffer LONG RAW := HEXTORAW('43'||'44'||'5E');
character_set VARCHAR2(12);
offset INTEGER := 1;
source BLOB;
-- Convert character length to byte length.
FUNCTION byte_length(n BINARY_INTEGER) RETURN BINARY_INTEGER IS
  al32utf8 BINARY_INTEGER := 2;
  utf8     BINARY_INTEGER := 3;
BEGIN
  -- Find database instance character set.
  SELECT value
  INTO   character_set
  FROM   nls_database_parameters
  WHERE  parameter = 'NLS_CHARACTERSET';
  -- Branch sizing for Unicode.
  IF character_set = 'AL32UTF8' THEN
    RETURN n / al32utf8;
  ELSIF character_set = 'UTF8' THEN
    RETURN n / utf8;
  END IF;
END byte_length;
BEGIN
  -- Change column value in existing row.
  UPDATE sample2
  SET    sample_blob = empty_blob()
  WHERE  sample_id = 1
  RETURNING sample_blob INTO source;
  -- Append to empty BLOB column.
  dbms_lob.writeappend(source,BYTE_LENGTH(LENGTH(buffer)),buffer);
  -- Read new content from column.
  SELECT sample_blob INTO source FROM sample2 WHERE sample_id = 1;
  dbms_lob.read(source,amount,offset,buffer);
  dbms_output.put_line(buffer);
END;
/
```

The UPDATE statement uses the RETURNING INTO clause to create a transactional opening to the BLOB column. The source variable is the opening, and it lets you change the contents of the BLOB column. The target variable of the RETURNING INTO clause acts as an implicit bind variable that you can see by peeking into the SGA. The local byte_length function divides any Unicode character set length to arrive at the byte code length. You would need to modify that function when using other multibyte character sets. If you fail to convert the byte-width of the BLOB variable, you raise an ORA-21560 error. This happens because the amount parameter is larger than the actual number of bytes in the buffer parameter of the DBMS_LOB.WRITEAPPEND function.

TIP
If you try to update a row that doesn't exist with the DBMS_LOB.
WRITEAPPEND procedure, you'll raise an ORA-22275 exception that
means an invalid LOB locator is specified in the function call. This
actually means there is no row where you can insert the LOB value.

You can also replace the `character_set` function and simplify the program by using the `VSIZE` function. `VSIZE` returns the size in bytes of expressions returned in SQL statements. The alternative local function would be

```
FUNCTION byte_length(n LONG RAW) RETURN BINARY_INTEGER IS
  realsize BINARY_INTEGER;
  BEGIN
    SELECT VSIZE(n) INTO realsize FROM dual;
    RETURN realsize;
END byte_length;
```

You also change the call, eliminating the nested call to the `LENGTH` function, in this way:

```
dbms_lob.writeappend(source,BYTE_LENGTH(buffer),buffer);
```

Clearly, this is simpler than dealing with the character sets. It also makes the case that you can leverage SQL-only built-in functions to do difficult things easily.

This has demonstrated how to use the `EMPTY_BLOB` function in an update. You can also use it the same way in the `VALUES` clause of an `INSERT` statement, or as default column value when creating a table or altering a table to include a `BLOB` column.

NOTE
The DBMS_LOB package also raises ORA-06502 errors, typically without much explanation beyond pointing to line numbers that vary between releases. These errors are most often raised by passing a null value into one of the IN or IN OUT mode parameters of the DBMS_LOB functions or procedures.

Deploying a Character Set Function

As demonstrated in the update of a `BLOB` column, the user-defined `character_set` function lets you determine the character set of the database in a restricted privilege schema. This is critical when you need the real byte count for `BLOB`, `RAW`, or `LONG RAW` datatypes.

The first step requires that you connect as the privileged user `SYS` as the `SYSDBA`. There you can grant privileges to the `SYS.PROPS$` table, like

```
GRANT SELECT ON props$ TO SYSTEM;
```

Then, you can compile the following function in the `SYSTEM` schema (*don't forget to connect as the SYSTEM user*):

```
CREATE OR REPLACE FUNCTION character_set RETURN VARCHAR2 IS
  -- Return variable.
  characterset VARCHAR2(20);
  -- Explicit cursors are always recommended.
  CURSOR c IS
    SELECT value$ FROM sys.props$ WHERE name = 'NLS_CHARACTERSET';
BEGIN
  OPEN c;
  FETCH c INTO characterset;
  CLOSE c;
  RETURN characterset;
```

```
END character_set;
/
```

You grant execute privileges on this function to schemas that require access to the database character set. The following grants that privilege to the PLSQL schema:

```
GRANT EXECUTE ON character_set TO plsql;
```

After granting the privilege to the target schema, you should connect to the PLSQL schema and create a synonym or alias that points to the SYSTEM.CHARACTER_SET function. You use the following syntax:

```
CREATE SYNONYM character_set FOR system.character_set;
```

This lets the local schema return the string representing the character set as an expression. This approach is what lets you update a BLOB column in a multibyte character set. It eliminates that nasty ORA-21560 because the LENGTH function returns the number of bytes required by the character set, not raw storage. Using it properly, this function lets you deal with the real length of binary streams. You can also use the DUMP function to find the real length for byte streams.

EMPTY_CLOB Function

The EMPTY_CLOB function works like the EMPTY_BLOB function. It lets you initialize a database column with an empty CLOB datatype. This is important because large objects have three possible states: they are null, empty, or populated. The DBMS_LOB package fails by raising an ORA-22275 exception when you attempt to work with a null CLOB column. The error is raised because there is no valid locator found in the column for null values.

The DBMS_LOB package fails by raising an ORA-01403 exception when you have an empty CLOB. This is more meaningful than the invalid LOB locator message that you'll receive when the column isn't initialized, and you can always append to an empty CLOB column. In some cases, using a default value during table creation may be a viable solution, but generally there are good reasons to leave a CLOB column null until you want to use it.

The next program assumes you build the following table:

```
CREATE TABLE sample (sample_id NUMBER, sample_clob CLOB);
```

Then, you insert a record like this:

```
INSERT INTO sample (sample_id) VALUES (1);
```

The following demonstrates how to update a CLOB column in an existing row:

```
DECLARE
  amount BINARY_INTEGER := 100;
  buffer VARCHAR2(2000) := 'Something is better than nothing.';
  offset INTEGER := 1;
  source CLOB;
BEGIN
  UPDATE sample
  SET    sample_clob = empty_clob()
```

```
    WHERE  sample_id = 1
    RETURNING sample_clob INTO source;
    -- Check that the source is empty.
    IF NVL(dbms_lob.getlength(source),0) = 0 THEN
      dbms_lob.writeappend(source,LENGTH(buffer),buffer);
    END IF;
    -- Read the first 2,000 characters of the CLOB.
    dbms_lob.read(source,amount,offset,buffer);
    dbms_output.put_line(buffer);
END;
/
```

This has demonstrated how to use the EMPTY_CLOB function in an update. You can also use it the same way in the VALUES clause of an INSERT statement, or as a default column value when creating a table or altering a table to include a CLOB column.

NOTE
An ORA-21560 *exception is raised by the* WRITEAPPEND *procedure when the second actual parameter is a null value or zero.*

GREATEST Function

The GREATEST function lets you check which of two values is the greatest. This works with scalar datatypes, like dates, numbers, and strings. The prototype is

GREATEST(*variable1*, *variable2*)

The GREATEST function requires that both actual parameters have the same data type, and it returns the least value in that datatype. Comparing the number of winning games by the Boston Red Sox and New York Yankees for the 2007 season shows 96 games wins the division pennant for the Boston Red Sox:

```
BEGIN
   dbms_output.put_line(GREATEST(96,94));
END;
/
```

Alternatively, you can compare two dates like the dates that Sammy Sosa hit 600 career homeruns against the date that Alexander Rodriguez hit 500 career homeruns. The following program uses the TO_CHAR function to demonstrate that the return type is actually a date against which you can apply a format mask:

```
DECLARE
   rodriguez DATE := '04-AUG-07';
   sosa      DATE := '20-JUN-07';
BEGIN
   dbms_output.put_line(TO_CHAR(GREATEST(rodriguez,sosa),'Mon DD, YYYY'));
END;
/
```

This prints the later date:

```
Aug 04, 2007
```

Although the earlier examples were small, the string comparison highlights using the GREATEST function as a key element implementing a traditional descending bubble sort. The local swap procedure is quite simple as a pass-by-reference procedure, which leaves the array resorted upon successful completion of the program.

The bubble sort uses a set of nested loops, which lets you compare the first element against all elements in the collection, leaving the greatest element first, or in descending order.

```
DECLARE
    TYPE namelist IS TABLE OF VARCHAR2(12);
    names NAMELIST := namelist('Bonds','Aaron','Ruth','Mayes');
    -- Local swap procedure.
    PROCEDURE swap (a IN OUT VARCHAR2, b IN OUT VARCHAR2) IS
      c VARCHAR2(12);
    BEGIN
      c := b;
      b := a;
      a := c;
    END swap;
BEGIN
    FOR i IN 1..names.COUNT LOOP
      FOR j IN 1..names.COUNT LOOP
        IF names(i) = GREATEST(names(i),names(j)) THEN
          swap(names(i),names(j));
        END IF;
      END LOOP;
    END LOOP;
    FOR i IN 1..names.COUNT LOOP
      dbms_output.put_line(names(i));
    END LOOP;
END;
/
```

The example prints the descending ordered surnames of the top four career homerun hitters:

```
Ruth
Mayes
Bonds
Aaron
```

You could also accomplish the same sorting by replacing the GREATEST comparison with the following line:

```
IF names(i) < names(j) THEN
```

You do need to watch the behavior of both Unicode and differing character sets when you do comparisons. The CONVERT function can help you ensure that comparisons are between like character sets.

These examples have demonstrated the versatility of the GREATEST function. They're revisited in the description of the LEAST function.

LEAST Function

The LEAST function lets you check which of two values is the least. This works with scalar datatypes, like dates, numbers, and strings. The prototype is

LEAST(variable1, variable2)

The LEAST function requires that both actual parameters have the same data type, and it returns the least value in that datatype. Comparing the number of winning games by the Boston Red Sox and New York Yankees for the 2007 season shows 94 games loses the division pennant for the New York Yankees:

```
BEGIN
  dbms_output.put_line(LEAST(96,94));
END;
/
```

Alternatively, you can compare two dates like the dates that Sammy Sosa hit 600 career homeruns against the date that Alexander Rodriguez hit 500 career homeruns. The following program uses the TO_CHAR function to demonstrate that the return type is actually a date against which you can apply a format mask:

```
DECLARE
  rodriguez DATE := '04-AUG-07';
  sosa      DATE := '20-JUN-07';
BEGIN
  dbms_output.put_line(TO_CHAR(LEAST(rodriguez,sosa),'Mon DD, YYYY'));
END;
/
```

This prints the earlier date:

```
Jun 20, 2007
```

Although the earlier examples were small, the string comparison highlights using the LEAST function as a key element implementing a traditional bubble sort. The local swap procedure is quite simple as a pass-by-reference procedure, which leaves the array resorted upon successful completion of the program.

The bubble sort uses a set of nested loops, which lets you compare the first element against all elements in the collection, leaving the least element first, or in an ascending alphabetical list.

```
DECLARE
  TYPE namelist IS TABLE OF VARCHAR2(12);
  names NAMELIST := namelist('Sarah','Joseph','Elise','Ian','Ariel'
                            ,'Callie','Nathan','Spencer','Christianne');
  -- Local swap procedure.
  PROCEDURE swap (a IN OUT VARCHAR2, b IN OUT VARCHAR2) IS
    c VARCHAR2(12);
  BEGIN
    c := b;
    b := a;
    a := c;
  END swap;
BEGIN
  FOR i IN 1..names.COUNT LOOP
    FOR j IN 1..names.COUNT LOOP
      IF names(i) = LEAST(names(i),names(j)) THEN
        swap(names(i),names(j));
```

```
      END IF;
    END LOOP;
  END LOOP;
  FOR i IN 1..names.COUNT LOOP
    dbms_output.put_line(names(i));
  END LOOP;
END;
/
```

This reorders the names in the collection to an ascending alphabetized list:

```
Ariel
Callie
Christianne
Elise
Ian
Joseph
Nathan
Sarah
Spencer
```

You could also accomplish the same sorting by replacing the LEAST comparison with the following line:

```
IF names(i) < names(j) THEN
```

You do need to watch the behavior of both Unicode and differing character sets when you do comparisons. The CONVERT function can help you ensure that comparisons are between like character sets.

These examples have demonstrated the versatility of the LEAST function. They're revisited in the description of the GREATEST function.

NANVL Function

The NANVL function substitutes a default value when a BINARY_DOUBLE or BINARY_FLOAT is not a number (NaN). This allows trapping an operating system math library return value of NaN.

The prototype is

```
NANVL(evaluation_parameter, substitution_parameter)
```

The primary substitution value is zero, as illustrated in the following program:

```
DECLARE
  bad_number     BINARY_DOUBLE := 'NaN';
  default_number BINARY_DOUBLE := 0;
BEGIN
  dbms_output.put_line(NANVL(bad_number,default_number));
END;
/
```

You can substitute a BINARY_FLOAT and it works the same way. This is a useful approach when performing math-intensive calculations.

NULLIF Function

The NULLIF function substitutes a null value when two actual parameters are found equal. This is equivalent to returning a null when two values match.

The prototype is

```
NULLIF(evaluation_parameter1, evaluation_parameter2)
```

The primary substitution value is zero, as illustrated in the following program:

```
DECLARE
  harry_potter   VARCHAR2(10) := 'Gryffindor';
  ron_weasley    VARCHAR2(10) := 'Gryffindor';
  cedric_diggory VARCHAR2(10) := 'Hufflepuff';
BEGIN
  IF NULLIF(harry_potter,ron_weasley) IS NULL THEN
    dbms_output.put_line('Same house!');
  END IF;
  IF NULLIF(harry_potter,cedric_diggory) IS NOT NULL THEN
    dbms_output.put_line('Different houses!');
  END IF;
END;
/
```

The first IF statement calls the NULLIF function with two members of J.K. Rowling's Harry Potter series that share the same house. It returns a null because the house values are equal. The second IF statement returns a not-null value because the houses differ, and it is checking whether the logical expression is not null. There are many opportunities to use this type of comparison, and now you know how to do it.

NVL Function

The NVL function substitutes a default value when the primary value is null. The prototype for the function is

```
NVL(evaluation_parameter, default_substitution_parameter)
```

The NVL function works well in conditional statements. It removes the possibility that comparison values are null. The following program demonstrates a NVL function:

```
DECLARE
  condition BOOLEAN;
BEGIN
  IF NOT NVL(condition,FALSE) THEN
    dbms_output.put_line('It''s False!');
  END IF;
END;
/
```

The condition variable is not initialized and therefore a null value. The conditional logic would fail if the NVL function was left out because a null value is not true or false. The NVL function converts all null values to false, making the statement true and printing the result.

SYS_CONTEXT Function

The SYS_CONTEXT function returns information about the system environment or an environment you've established by using the DBMS_SESSION.SET_CONTEXT. It replaces the USERENV legacy function and provides many more options using the USERENV context.

The prototype is

```
SYS_CONTEXT('context_namespace','parameter'[,'length'])
```

It raises an ORA-02003 when you submit an invalid parameter value, but only a null value if you submit a non-existent context namespace. Table J-1 lists the valid parameters for the USERENV context, and Table J-2 lists the deprecated parameters for the same context. All calls to the SYS_CONTEXT function return a VARCHAR2 variable that has a default maximum length of 256 bytes. You can override the size of return strings by providing a valid integer value between 1 and 4,000.

Parameter	Return Value
ACTION	The ACTION parameter identifies the position in the module. You use the DBMS_APPLICATION_INFO package to set the value.
AUDITED_CURSORID	The AUDITED_CURSORID parameter returns the cursor ID of the SQL statement that triggered an audit event. It is not a valid value when you're using fine-grain auditing, and it returns a null then.
AUTHENTICATED_IDENTITY	The AUTHENTICATED_IDENTITY parameter returns the authenticated identity in a format that differs by type of authentication, like Kerberos, SSL, password, OS, Radius, proxy, or SYSDBA/SYSOPER.
AUTHENTICATION_DATA	The AUTHENTICATION_DATA parameter contains the value used to authenticate the user, which may be a X.503 certificate.
AUTHENTICATION_METHOD	The AUTHENTICATED_METHOD parameter returns the authenticated method, like Kerberos, SSL, password, OS, Radius, proxy, or background process.
BG_JOB_ID	The BG_JOB_ID parameter returns the current session identifier when established by a background database process.
CLIENT_IDENTIFIER	The CLIENT_IDENTIFIER parameter returns an identifier set by calling the SET_IDENTIFIER procedure from the DBMS_SESSION package, the OCI_ATTR_CLIENT_IDENTIFIER attribute, or the setClientIdentifier method of the Java class Oracle.jdbc.OracleConnection.
CLIENT_INFO	The CLIENT_INFO parameter returns a 64-byte character string set by calling the SET_CLIENT_INFO procedure of the DBMS_APPLICATION_INFO package.
CURRENT_BIND	The CURRENT_BIND parameter returns bind variables or fine-grain auditing.
CURRENT_EDITION_NAME	The CURRENT_EDITION_NAME parameter returns the edition in use by the current session.
CURRENT_EDITION_ID	The CURRENT_EDITION_ID parameter returns the identifier of the edition in use by the current session.
CURRENT_SCHEMA	The CURRENT_SCHEMA parameter returns the current schema name, which you can change by calling the ALTER SESSION SET CURRENT_SCHEMA statement.
CURRENT_SCHEMAID	The CURRENT_SCHEMAID parameter returns the current schema identifier, which you can change by calling the ALTER SESSION SET CURRENT_SCHEMA statement.

TABLE J-1 *SYS_CONTEXT Predefined Parameters for the USERENV Namespace*

Parameter	Return Value
CURRENT_SQL or CURRENT_SQL*n*	The CURRENT_SQL parameter returns the first 4K bytes of the current SQL statement that triggered fine-grain auditing. You use CURRENT_SQL*n* (where *n* is an integer) to get the next 4K bytes of the current SQL statement.
CURRENT_SQL_LENGTH	The CURRENT_SQL_LENGTH parameter returns the byte length of the SQL statement that triggered a fine-grain auditing event.
DB_DOMAIN	The DB_DOMAIN parameter returns the database initialization parameter of the same name when it is set.
DB_NAME	The DB_NAME parameter returns the database initialization parameter of the same name when it is set.
DB_UNIQUE_NAME	The DB_UNIQUE_NAME parameter returns the database initialization parameter of the same name when it is set.
ENTRYID	The ENTRYID parameter returns the current audit entry number. This sequence value is shared between regular and fine-grain auditing and cannot be used in distributed scope.
ENTERPRISE_IDENTITY	The ENTERPRISE_IDENTITY parameter returns the user's enterprise-wide identity, which is an OID value set as the DN value.
FG_JOB_ID	The FG_JOB_ID parameter returns the current session identifier when established by a foreground database process.
GLOBAL_CONTEXT_MEMORY	The GLOBAL_CONTEXT_MEMORY parameter returns the number being used in the SGA by the globally accessed context.
GLOBAL_UID	The GLOBAL_UID parameter returns the current session identifier when established by a background database process.
HOST	The HOST parameter returns the machine hostname value.
IDENTIFICATION_TYPE	The IDENTIFICATION_TYPE parameter returns the method used to establish the current session, as follows: LOCAL when identified by password EXTERNAL when identified externally GLOBAL SHARED when identified globally GLOBAL PRIVATE when identified globally by *DN*
INSTANCE	The INSTANCE parameter returns the identification number of the current instance.
INSTANCE_NAME	The INSTANCE_NAME parameter returns the name of the current instance.
IP_ADDRESS	The IP_ADDRESS parameter returns the IP address for the server or virtual machine running the instance.
ISDBA	The ISDBA parameter returns true when the current user has DBA privileges and false when that user does not.
LANG	The LANG parameter returns the ISO abbreviation for the language name.
LANGUAGE	The LANGUAGE parameter returns the language and territory currently in use and the character set separated by a period.
MODULE	The MODULE parameter returns the application name set by the SET_MODULE procedure in the DBMS_APPLICATION_INFO package.
NETWORK_PROTOCOL	The NETWORK_PROTOCOL parameter returns network protocol value for a connection.

TABLE J-1 *SYS_CONTEXT Predefined Parameters for the USERENV Namespace* (continued)

Parameter	Return Value
NLS_CALENDAR	The NLS_CALENDAR parameter returns the current session's calendar.
NLS_CURRENCY	The NLS_CURRENCY parameter returns the current session's currency.
NLS_DATE_FORMAT	The NLS_DATE_FORMAT parameter returns the current session's default date format.
NLS_DATE_LANGUAGE	The NLS_DATE_LANGUAGE parameter returns the current session's language for expressing dates.
NLS_SORT	The NLS_SORT parameter returns the current session's linguistic sort basis or the default BINARY.
NLS_TERRITORY	The NLS_TERRITORY parameter returns the current session's territory.
OS_USER	The OS_USER parameter returns the operating system user account that initiated the current database session.
POLICY_INVOKER	The POLICY_INVOKER parameter returns the invoker of a row-level security (RLS) policy function.
PROXY_ENTERPRISE_IDENTITY	The PROXY_ENTERPRISE_IDENTITY parameter returns the Oracle Internet Directory *DN* when the proxy user is an enterprise user.
PROXY_GLOBAL_UID	The PROXY_GLOBAL_UID parameter returns the global user identifier from Oracle Internet Directory for Enterprise User Security (EUS) proxy users or null for all other proxy users.
PROXY_USER	The PROXY_USER parameter returns the user name of the database user who opened the current session on behalf of the SESSION_USER.
PROXY_USERID	The PROXY_USERID parameter returns the user identifier of the database user who opened the current session on behalf of the SESSION_USER.
SERVER_HOST	The SERVER_HOST parameter returns the server host name.
SERVICE_NAME	The SERVICE_NAME parameter returns the service host name.
SESSION_EDITION_NAME	The SESSION_EDITION_NAME parameter returns the edition in use by the current session.
SESSION_EDITION_ID	The SESSION_EDITION_ID parameter returns the edition identifier in use by the current session.
SESSION_USER	The SESSION_USER parameter returns the schema for Enterprise users, and the database user name by which the current session is authenticated.
SESSION_USERID	The SESSION_USERID parameter returns the database user identifier by which the current session is authenticated.
SESSIONID	The SESSIONID parameter returns the auditing session identifier.
SID	The SID parameter returns the session number, which is different than the session identifier.
STATEMENTID	The STATEMENTID parameter returns the number of the SQL statement audited in a given session. This attribute cannot be used in distributed scope.
TERMINAL	The TERMINAL parameter returns the server host name.

TABLE J-1 *SYS_CONTEXT Predefined Parameters for the USERENV Namespace* (continued)

You call the `SYS_CONTEXT` function as follows:

```
BEGIN
  dbms_output.put_line(SYS_CONTEXT('USERENV','HOST'));
END;
/
```

It returns the server's hostname value as a 256-byte string. This section has demonstrated the `SYS_CONTEXT` function, which replaces the legacy `USERENV` function.

USERENV Function

The `USERENV` function returns information about the system environment. It is a legacy function replaced by the `SYS_CONTEXT` function covered earlier in this section. Table J-3 lists the available parameters you can call by using the `USERENV` function.

While you can use the function in SQL statements, the following demonstrates using the `USERENV` function in a PL/SQL block:

```
BEGIN
  dbms_output.put_line(USERENV('TERMINAL'));
END;
/
```

It prints the hostname for the machine, like

```
MCLAUGHLIN-DEV
```

The following sets the `V$SESSION` view `CLIENT_INFO` column:

```
CALL dbms_application_info.set_client_info('Restricted');
```

You can query the contents by using the `USERENV` function, and it returns the case-sensitive word: Restricted. It is demonstrated in the following block:

```
BEGIN
  dbms_output.put_line(USERENV('CLIENT_INFO'));
END;
/
```

Parameter	Return Value
`CURRENT_USER`	Use the `SESSION_USER` parameter instead.
`CURRENT_USERID`	Use the `SESSION_USERID` parameter instead.
`EXTERNAL_NAME`	This parameter returned the name of the external user. You should use the `AUTHENTICATED_IDENTITY` or `ENTERPRISE_IDENTITY` parameter in lieu of `EXTERNAL_NAME` because they return superior information about the external user.

TABLE J-2   *SYS_CONTEXT Deprecated Parameters for the USERENV Namespace*

Return Type	Parameter	Description of Return Value
VARCHAR2	CLIENT_INFO	The CLIENT_INFO parameter returns a string up to 64 bytes long. It contains one or more values set by using the built-in DBMS_APPLICATION_INFO package. You should note that this context column is used by third-party applications.
NUMBER	ENTRYID	The ENTRYID parameter is a sequence value shared between both regular and fine-grain audit records. You cannot use this attribute in distributed queries.
VARCHAR2	ISDBA	The ISDBA parameter returns an uppercase true or false, depending on whether the current user has DBA privileges.
VARCHAR2	LANG	The LANG parameter returns an uppercase string for the ISO language abbreviation.
VARCHAR2	LANGUAGE	The LANGUAGE parameter returns an uppercase string containing the language and territory, a dot, and the character set for the database. An example of the output is: AMERICAN_AMERICA.AL32UTF8
NUMBER	SESSIONID	The SESSIONID parameter returns the auditing session identifier and cannot be used in distributed transactions.
VARCHAR2	TERMINAL	The TERMINAL parameter returns the operating system identifier for the terminal running the current session. If you use it in a distributed environment SELECT statement, it returns the identifier for the local transaction. The parameter cannot be used by distributed INSERT, UPDATE, or DELETE statements.

TABLE J-3 *USERENV Function Parameters*

This section has shown you how to use the USERENV function. It is a legacy function that appears in Oracle Applications code and other third-party applications, but you should use the new SYS_CONTEXT function in your own code. SYS_CONTEXT provides you access to more information.

VSIZE Function

The VSIZE function lets examine the real length of registered datatypes. It returns a value that is independent of the database or session character set. You can only use the VSIZE function inside a SQL statement.

The following block demonstrates how to find the real size of a LONG RAW variable:

```
DECLARE
  buffer LONG RAW := HEXTORAW('42'||'41'||'44');
  detail VARCHAR2(100);
```

```
BEGIN
  SELECT VSIZE(buffer) INTO detail FROM dual;
  dbms_output.put_line(detail);
END;
/
```

It prints the length of the data value:

```
3
```

You may not use this too often, but when you're trying to figure out why something is broken and the error message and web hits are limited, it may be very helpful. It certainly helps when working with the DBMS_LOB package and raw streams, as covered in the section on the EMPTY_BLOB function.

Number

The number built-in functions provide key typical mathematical functions. Aside from the trigonometric functions, you should find FLOOR and CEIL useful when you want to find a bottom and upper integer limit for a range of complex (fractional) numbers. Also, ROUND lets you round complex numbers to their nearest integer, and TRUNC lets you strip the values to the right of the decimal place.

You'll also find functions for modulo mathematics and exponentiation. When you understand what's available, it should increase your options while writing PL/SQL programs.

CEIL Function

The CEIL function lets you round any real number to the next higher integer. You can use it as follows:

```
DECLARE
  n NUMBER := 4.44;
BEGIN
  dbms_output.put_line('Ceiling ['||CEIL(n)||']');
END;
/
```

It prints

```
Ceiling [5]
```

This is handy when you're trying to group things into whole units.

FLOOR Function

The FLOOR function lets you truncate any remaining fraction from a number, returning the whole integer value. You can use it as follows:

```
DECLARE
  n NUMBER := 4.44;
BEGIN
  dbms_output.put_line('Flooring ['||FLOOR(n)||']');
END;
/
```

It prints

```
Flooring [4]
```

This is handy when you're trying to group things into whole units.

MOD Function

The MOD function lets you find the remainder of a division operation, like the REMAINDER function. It returns a zero when there is no remainder and the integer of any remainder when one exists.

The prototype is

```
MOD(dividend, divisor)
```

You can use it as follows:

```
DECLARE
  n NUMBER := 16;
  m NUMBER := 3;
BEGIN
  dbms_output.put_line('Mode ['||MOD(n,m)||']');
END;
/
```

It prints

```
Mode [1]
```

The MOD function uses the FLOOR function in the calculation. It is designed to work with positive integers. You will get non-classical modulo arithmetic results when either number is negative. You should use the REMAINDER function for classic modulo results when either number has a negative value or the divisor is a real number.

POWER Function

The POWER function doubles for the exponential operator, **. It is really your preference whether you use the POWER function or the exponential operator, but you should pick one and stick with it. There's *power* in writing code consistently (:-)).

The prototype of the POWER function is

```
POWER(base_number, exponent)
```

The following example demonstrates cubing a number:

```
DECLARE
  n NUMBER := 3;
  m NUMBER := 3;
BEGIN
  dbms_output.put_line('Cube of ['||n||'] is ['||POWER(n,m)||']');
END;
/
```

This prints

```
Cube of [3] is [27]
```

Modulo Arithmetic

Modulo arithmetic is a system of integer math. It is designed on the principle that numbers wrap around, like a clock. An example is how sixty seconds becomes a minute, and then the seconds reset to zero. It comes from the work of Carl Friedrich Gauss, which was first published in 1801.

The example does a bit of casting to demonstrate clock arithmetic by leveraging the system clock function—SYSDATE:

```
DECLARE
  c_time INTEGER;
  e_time INTEGER;
  n_time INTEGER;
  s_time INTEGER;
BEGIN
  LOOP
    s_time := MOD(TO_NUMBER(TO_CHAR(SYSDATE,'SS')),60); -- Use the MOD function.
    IF c_time IS NULL THEN
      c_time := s_time;
      e_time := s_time - 1;
      n_time := s_time;
      dbms_output.put_line('['||TO_CHAR(SYSDATE,'MI:SS')||']['||s_time||']');
    ELSE
      n_time := s_time;
      IF n_time <> c_time THEN
        dbms_output.put_line('['||TO_CHAR(SYSDATE,'MI:SS')||']['||s_time||']');
        c_time := n_time;
      END IF;
    END IF;
    IF c_time = e_time THEN
      EXIT;
    END IF;
  END LOOP;
END;
/
```

This prints 59 values. It starts with the current time and ends 59 seconds later with the twenty-four-hour clock value and modulo integer result. The following displays the rows immediately before and after the wrapping between minutes:

```
[53:58][58]
[53:59][59]
[54:00][0]
[54:01][1]
[54:02][2]
```

Modulo arithmetic lets you time events to the minute or hour with a divisor of 60. You can time events to the half-minute by using a divisor of 30, or to the quarter-minute by using a divisor of 15. As you explore your application needs, it is likely that you'll have several occasions to use the MOD function.

While the math libraries work well when you square or cube numbers, they do produce rounding errors when calculating cube roots, like the following:

```
DECLARE
  n NUMBER := 27;
```

```
  m NUMBER := 1/3;
BEGIN
  dbms_output.put_line('Cube of ['||n||'] is ['||POWER(n,m)||']');
END;
/
```

This prints

```
Cube root of [27] is [2.9999999999999999999999999999999999998]
```

While it should print 3, it doesn't. The math error is generally not significant because you can use the ROUND function to get the whole number cube root, like

```
ROUND(POWER(n,m),0)
```

You get three when you change the datatypes from NUMBER to BINARY_DOUBLE because the latter uses the server's local math libraries. The same program written with a BINARY_DOUBLE datatype prints

```
Cube root of [2.7E+001] is [3.0E+000]
```

You should consider using datatypes tied to the server math libraries when they're scientific in nature, like finding cube roots.

REMAINDER Function

The REMAINDER function lets you find the remainder of a division operation, like the MOD function. It returns a zero when there is no remainder and the integer of any remainder when one exists.

The prototype is

```
REMAINDER(dividend, divisor)
```

The REMAINDER function behaves differently whether the dividend and divisor are NUMBER or data types linked to the local math libraries, like BINARY_FLOAT and BINARY_DOUBLE. More or less, the results are slightly more meaningful with BINARY_FLOAT and BINARY_DOUBLE because you get a NaN (not a number) when the divisor is zero. You get a numeric or value error (PLS-06502) when the actual parameters are NUMBER datatypes.

You can use it as follows:

```
DECLARE
  n NUMBER := 16;
  m NUMBER := 3;
BEGIN
  dbms_output.put_line('Remainder ['||REMAINDER(n,m)||']');
END;
/
```

It prints

```
Remainder [1]
```

The difference between the REMAINDER and MOD functions can best be shown using a real number as the divisor. This program uses both functions:

```
DECLARE
  n NUMBER := 16;
  m NUMBER := 3.24;
BEGIN
  dbms_output.put_line('Remainder ['||REMAINDER(n,m)||']');
  dbms_output.put_line('Remainder ['||MOD(n,m)||']');
END;
/
```

There are two perspectives on this problem. One divides the dividend by the divisor and returns either a positive integer as the remainder or zero. This works when the dividend and divisor are positive integers. The MOD function uses this method; when the divisor is 3.24 and the dividend is 4, there are four whole 3.24 values, or 12.96, in 16. The divisor minus the dividend times 4 yields a remainder of 3.04.

The other perspective approximates the least remainder of the division. This means that when the remainder is greater than half the dividend, it looks for the next whole division value. The remainder in this case is the difference between what the number is and what the next higher number would be without a remainder. The REMAINDER function uses the same divisor but finds the closest possible result, or the world as it should be. From this perspective, there should be five whole 3.24 values or 16.2 in the *dividend*, which leaves a remainder of –0.2.

More likely than not, you'll use MOD more frequently than REMAINDER because application programming is dealing with reality. In the rare cases, the other fits. You now know why the REMAINDER function works the way it does.

Summary

This appendix has enumerated PL/SQL built-in functions. The examples should enable you to immediately leverage these functions in your programs.

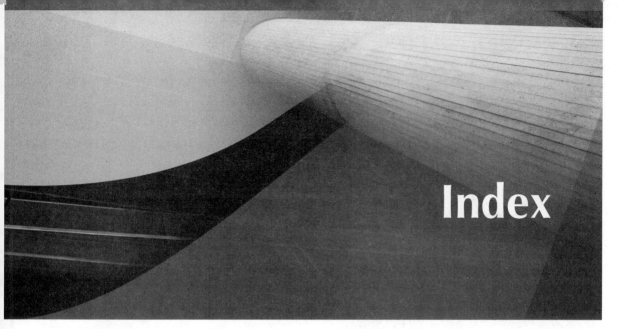

Index

GET YOUR FREE SUBSCRIPTION
TO ORACLE MAGAZINE

Oracle Magazine is essential gear for today's information technology professionals. Stay informed and increase your productivity with every issue of *Oracle Magazine*. Inside each free bimonthly issue you'll get:

IF THERE ARE OTHER ORACLE USERS AT YOUR LOCATION WHO WOULD LIKE TO RECEIVE THEIR OWN SUB-SCRIPTION TO ORACLE MAGAZINE, PLEASE PHOTOCOPY THIS FORM AND PASS IT ALONG.

- Up-to-date information on Oracle Database, Oracle Application Server, Web development, enterprise grid computing, database technology, and business trends

- Third-party vendor news and announcements

- Technical articles on Oracle and partner products, technologies, and operating environments

- Development and administration tips

- Real-world customer stories

Three easy ways to subscribe:

① Web
Visit our Web site at otn.oracle.com/oraclemagazine.
You'll find a subscription form there, plus much more!

② Fax
Complete the questionnaire on the back of this card and fax the questionnaire side only to +1.847.763.9638.

③ Mail
Complete the questionnaire on the back of this card and mail it to P.O. Box 1263, Skokie, IL 60076-8263

ORACLE

FREE SUBSCRIPTION

O **Yes, please send me a FREE subscription to** *Oracle Magazine*.   O **NO**
To receive a free subscription to *Oracle Magazine*, you must fill out the entire card, sign it, and date it
(incomplete cards cannot be processed or acknowledged). You can also fax your application to +1.847.763.9638.
Or subscribe at our Web site at otn.oracle.com/oraclemagazine

O From time to time, Oracle Publishing allows our partners exclusive access to our e-mail addresses for special promotions and announcements. To be included in this program, please check this circle.

signature (required)   date

X

O Oracle Publishing allows sharing of our mailing list with selected third parties. If you prefer your mailing address not to be included in this program, please check here. If at any time you would like to be removed from this mailing list, please contact Customer Service at +1.847.647.9630 or send an e-mail to oracle@halldata.com.

name   title

company   e-mail address

street/p.o. box

city/state/zip or postal code   telephone

country   fax

YOU MUST ANSWER ALL TEN QUESTIONS BELOW.

① WHAT IS THE PRIMARY BUSINESS ACTIVITY OF YOUR FIRM AT THIS LOCATION? (check one only)
- ☐ 01 Aerospace and Defense Manufacturing
- ☐ 02 Application Service Provider
- ☐ 03 Automotive Manufacturing
- ☐ 04 Chemicals, Oil and Gas
- ☐ 05 Communications and Media
- ☐ 06 Construction/Engineering
- ☐ 07 Consumer Sector/Consumer Packaged Goods
- ☐ 08 Education
- ☐ 09 Financial Services/Insurance
- ☐ 10 Government (civil)
- ☐ 11 Government (military)
- ☐ 12 Healthcare
- ☐ 13 High Technology Manufacturing, OEM
- ☐ 14 Integrated Software Vendor
- ☐ 15 Life Sciences (Biotech, Pharmaceuticals)
- ☐ 16 Mining
- ☐ 17 Retail/Wholesale/Distribution
- ☐ 18 Systems Integrator, VAR/VAD
- ☐ 19 Telecommunications
- ☐ 20 Travel and Transportation
- ☐ 21 Utilities (electric, gas, sanitation, water)
- ☐ 98 Other Business and Services

② WHICH OF THE FOLLOWING BEST DESCRIBES YOUR PRIMARY JOB FUNCTION? (check one only)
Corporate Management/Staff
- ☐ 01 Executive Management (President, Chair, CEO, CFO, Owner, Partner, Principal)
- ☐ 02 Finance/Administrative Management (VP/Director/ Manager/Controller, Purchasing, Administration)
- ☐ 03 Sales/Marketing Management (VP/Director/Manager)
- ☐ 04 Computer Systems/Operations Management (CIO/VP/Director/ Manager MIS, Operations)
IS/IT Staff
- ☐ 05 Systems Development/ Programming Management
- ☐ 06 Systems Development/ Programming Staff
- ☐ 07 Consulting
- ☐ 08 DBA/Systems Administrator
- ☐ 09 Education/Training
- ☐ 10 Technical Support Director/Manager
- ☐ 11 Other Technical Management/Staff
- ☐ 98 Other

③ WHAT IS YOUR CURRENT PRIMARY OPERATING PLATFORM? (select all that apply)
- ☐ 01 Digital Equipment UNIX
- ☐ 02 Digital Equipment VAX VMS
- ☐ 03 HP UNIX

- ☐ 04 IBM AIX
- ☐ 05 IBM UNIX
- ☐ 06 Java
- ☐ 07 Linux
- ☐ 08 Macintosh
- ☐ 09 MS-DOS
- ☐ 10 MVS
- ☐ 11 NetWare
- ☐ 12 Network Computing
- ☐ 13 OpenVMS
- ☐ 14 SCO UNIX
- ☐ 15 Sequent DYNIX/ptx
- ☐ 16 Sun Solaris/SunOS
- ☐ 17 SVR4
- ☐ 18 UnixWare
- ☐ 19 Windows
- ☐ 20 Windows NT
- ☐ 21 Other UNIX
- ☐ 98 Other
- 99 ☐ None of the above

④ DO YOU EVALUATE, SPECIFY, RECOMMEND, OR AUTHORIZE THE PURCHASE OF ANY OF THE FOLLOWING? (check all that apply)
- ☐ 01 Hardware
- ☐ 02 Software
- ☐ 03 Application Development Tools
- ☐ 04 Database Products
- ☐ 05 Internet or Intranet Products
- 99 ☐ None of the above

⑤ IN YOUR JOB, DO YOU USE OR PLAN TO PURCHASE ANY OF THE FOLLOWING PRODUCTS? (check all that apply)
Software
- ☐ 01 Business Graphics
- ☐ 02 CAD/CAE/CAM
- ☐ 03 CASE
- ☐ 04 Communications
- ☐ 05 Database Management
- ☐ 06 File Management
- ☐ 07 Finance
- ☐ 08 Java
- ☐ 09 Materials Resource Planning
- ☐ 10 Multimedia Authoring
- ☐ 11 Networking
- ☐ 12 Office Automation
- ☐ 13 Order Entry/Inventory Control
- ☐ 14 Programming
- ☐ 15 Project Management
- ☐ 16 Scientific and Engineering
- ☐ 17 Spreadsheets
- ☐ 18 Systems Management
- ☐ 19 Workflow

Hardware
- ☐ 20 Macintosh
- ☐ 21 Mainframe
- ☐ 22 Massively Parallel Processing
- ☐ 23 Minicomputer
- ☐ 24 PC
- ☐ 25 Network Computer
- ☐ 26 Symmetric Multiprocessing
- ☐ 27 Workstation
Peripherals
- ☐ 28 Bridges/Routers/Hubs/Gateways
- ☐ 29 CD-ROM Drives
- ☐ 30 Disk Drives/Subsystems
- ☐ 31 Modems
- ☐ 32 Tape Drives/Subsystems
- ☐ 33 Video Boards/Multimedia
Services
- ☐ 34 Application Service Provider
- ☐ 35 Consulting
- ☐ 36 Education/Training
- ☐ 37 Maintenance
- ☐ 38 Online Database Services
- ☐ 39 Support
- ☐ 40 Technology-Based Training
- ☐ 98 Other
- 99 ☐ None of the above

⑥ WHAT ORACLE PRODUCTS ARE IN USE AT YOUR SITE? (check all that apply)
Oracle E-Business Suite
- ☐ 01 Oracle Marketing
- ☐ 02 Oracle Sales
- ☐ 03 Oracle Order Fulfillment
- ☐ 04 Oracle Supply Chain Management
- ☐ 05 Oracle Procurement
- ☐ 06 Oracle Manufacturing
- ☐ 07 Oracle Maintenance Management
- ☐ 08 Oracle Service
- ☐ 09 Oracle Contracts
- ☐ 10 Oracle Projects
- ☐ 11 Oracle Financials
- ☐ 12 Oracle Human Resources
- ☐ 13 Oracle Interaction Center
- ☐ 14 Oracle Communications/Utilities (modules)
- ☐ 15 Oracle Public Sector/University (modules)
- ☐ 16 Oracle Financial Services (modules)
Server/Software
- ☐ 17 Oracle9i
- ☐ 18 Oracle9i Lite
- ☐ 19 Oracle8i
- ☐ 20 Other Oracle database
- ☐ 21 Oracle9i Application Server
- ☐ 22 Oracle9i Application Server Wireless
- ☐ 23 Oracle Small Business Suite

Tools
- ☐ 24 Oracle Developer Suite
- ☐ 25 Oracle Discoverer
- ☐ 26 Oracle JDeveloper
- ☐ 27 Oracle Migration Workbench
- ☐ 28 Oracle9i AS Portal
- ☐ 29 Oracle Warehouse Builder
Oracle Services
- ☐ 30 Oracle Outsourcing
- ☐ 31 Oracle Consulting
- ☐ 32 Oracle Education
- ☐ 33 Oracle Support
- ☐ 98 Other
- 99 ☐ None of the above

⑦ WHAT OTHER DATABASE PRODUCTS ARE IN USE AT YOUR SITE? (check all that apply)
- ☐ 01 Access
- ☐ 02 Baan
- ☐ 03 dbase
- ☐ 04 Gupta
- ☐ 05 IBM DB2
- ☐ 06 Informix
- ☐ 07 Ingres
- ☐ 08 Microsoft Access
- ☐ 09 Microsoft SQL Server
- ☐ 10 PeopleSoft
- ☐ 11 Progress
- ☐ 12 SAP
- ☐ 13 Sybase
- ☐ 14 VSAM
- ☐ 98 Other
- 99 ☐ None of the above

⑧ WHAT OTHER APPLICATION SERVER PRODUCTS ARE IN USE AT YOUR SITE? (check all that apply)
- ☐ 01 BEA
- ☐ 02 IBM
- ☐ 03 Sybase
- ☐ 04 Sun
- ☐ 05 Other

⑨ DURING THE NEXT 12 MONTHS, HOW MUCH DO YOU ANTICIPATE YOUR ORGANIZATION WILL SPEND ON COMPUTER HARDWARE, SOFTWARE, PERIPHERALS, AND SERVICES FOR YOUR LOCATION? (check only one)
- ☐ 01 Less than $10,000
- ☐ 02 $10,000 to $49,999
- ☐ 03 $50,000 to $99,999
- ☐ 04 $100,000 to $499,999
- ☐ 05 $500,000 to $999,999
- ☐ 06 $1,000,000 and over

⑩ WHAT IS YOUR COMPANY'S YEARLY SALES REVENUE? (please choose one)
- ☐ 01 $500, 000, 000 and above
- ☐ 02 $100, 000, 000 to $500, 000, 000
- ☐ 03 $50, 000, 000 to $100, 000, 000
- ☐ 04 $5, 000, 000 to $50, 000, 000
- ☐ 05 $1, 000, 000 to $5, 000, 000

100103